P9-BIX-056

Rock Lives

BY THE SAME AUTHOR

Catch a Fire: The Life of Bob Marley

Rock Stars

Rolling Stone Visits Saturday Night Live (coauthor)

HENRY HOLT AND COMPANY NEW YORK

Rock Lives

Profiles & Interviews

Timothy White

 Published by Henry Holt and Company, Inc., 115 West 18th Street, New York, New York 10011. Published in Canada by Fitzhenry & Whiteside Limited, 195 Allstate Parkway, Markham, Ontario L3R 4T8.

Library of Congress Cataloging-in-Publication Data
White, Timothy.
Rock lives : profiles and interviews / Timothy White.
— 1st ed.
p. cm.
Includes bibliographical references (p. 781).
ISBN 0-8050-1396-2 (alk. paper)
1. Rock musicians—Biography. I. Title.
ML385.W37 1990
782.42166'092'2—dc20
[B] 90-32336
CIP
MN

Henry Holt books are available at special discounts for bulk purchases for sales promotions, premiums, fund-raising, or educational use. Special editions or book excerpts can also be created to specification.
For details contact: Special Sales Director
Henry Holt and Company, Inc., 115 West 18th Street
New York, New York 10011

FIRST EDITION

Designed by Claire Naylon Vaccaro

Printed in the United States of America. Recognizing the importance of preserving the written word, Henry Holt and Company, Inc., by policy, prints all of its first editions on acid-free paper. ∞
10 9 8 7 6 5 4 3 2 1

To Mitch

Contents

PROGENY

Preface

This book is a chronicle of individuals who have devoted their lives to self-realization through popular music. It examines their ambitions and achievements, as well as their values en route. The unstated premise of each profile and interview is that a stranger is meeting a stranger, with all inquiry, vulnerability, movement, and reliance bounded by the tentative nature of the encounter. Each is a story, wedded to its era, exposing only the unfinished nature of each person. Yet each reveals the artist's unfolding links to his or her fellow musicians.

Why cover several generations of rock and roll players, composers, producers, and performers? Because, more than any other music, rock and roll is the public expression of a personal truth, offered at no small risk. Like the music itself, these stories announce that in the accomplishments of anyone there is hope for everyone.

The sometimes revised and expanded profiles and interviews collected herein also span a journalism career, from days reporting for *Crawdaddy* while still a reporter in the New York Bureau of the Associated Press, to my years as managing editor and then senior editor of *Crawdaddy* (1976–78), through my time as an associate editor and senior editor of *Rolling Stone* (1978–82). Afterward, I pursued book and broadcasting projects while serving as a contributing editor or frequent writer for *Rolling Stone, Musician, Playboy, Penthouse, Spin*, and the *New York Times Magazine*; as well as broadcasting my "Timothy White's Rock Stars" series of ninety-minute monthly national specials for the ABC Radio Network, LBS Communications, and then Westwood One Radio Networks (the show being based on my 1984 book, *Rock Stars,* portions of which appear here in revised and expanded form).

The subjects of this book are ordinary people captured in the midst of extraordinary creative outpourings. While the unbridled outbursts of a questing individual may be called primitive, similar behavior by a whole body of people can comprise a social canon and a dominion. In rock and roll, it often seems that its exponents have gained the power to act out and inhabit their ongoing visions of an ideal place. And because the rock and roll life favors reaction and gratification over reflection, such visions are generally impulsive, willful, lacking in prudence. Self-discovery is disseminated swiftly—instantly, if possible—as if it were breaking news from a secret corner of the species.

As with the lives they describe, these stories are told because each person sought out public scrutiny. They did this whenever they elected to test. Whenever they decided to trust. Whenever they saw themselves in a gesture. Whenever they forgot themselves in the moment. Whenever they hesitated. Whenever they hungered. Whenever they wanted.

Shadows & Light: An Introduction

After silence, that which comes nearest to expressing the inexpressible is music.

—ALDOUS HUXLEY

There's an old domestic travel promotion spiel: "See America First." That's precisely what rock and roll aims to do—with the top down, the radio blaring, and the gas pedal stomped to the floor. Make no mistake about it: only America, the greatest social laboratory in the history of the planet, could have produced a cultural phenomenon as singularly violent, plaintive, reckless, tender, lurid, threatening, heart-wrenching, grotesque, corruptible, and vital as rock and roll. It took a land where every soul had a fairly decent shot at the awesome state of freedom with license to hatch an art form so triumphantly incendiary.

When the Puritans landed on these shores, part of their master plan was to create a strict province of orthodox piety in the wilderness. These and other scrupulous colonists failed to comprehend that America, by its very nature, was and is a permanent wilderness, a wilderness of the spirit. For their part, the guilt-crippled Puritans saw their fiercely independent fellow settlers as necromancers and demons all. Rather, they were mortals possessed with self-realization, each consumed by the concept that, in this boundless territory, they could completely reinvent themselves.

In *Roll, Jordan, Roll: The World the Slaves Made,* Eugene D. Genovese writes, "The idea of original sin lies at the heart of the Western formulation of the problem of freedom and order. In time it tipped the ideological scales decisively toward the side of individual freedom in its perpetual struggle with the demands for social order." In other words, Americans decided that if you've got the Devil to pay simply for being *born,* you might as well have fun counting your change. While the Puritans may have agonized over why God created both good and evil, and executed "witches" in a vain attempt at purging the world of the painful paradox, the rest of America slowly learned to see the bonfire for the flames . . . and then became drawn to those flames.

Is rock and roll predicated on personal excess? Not necessarily. It depends on the practitioner. While there are those rock stars who deem rock and roll to be a declaration of war, others hunger for a quiet place, a still pool for reflection. Some need to know if they can rise above the howling tumult, feeling sure that the only way to find out is to plunge into the thick of it. One longs to unravel mysteries. Another wants to unravel psyches. But these are longings, and it is the American in all of us, whether we're from Tallahassee or Hong Kong, that fires them.

When the young heart is impossibly heavy, when the crowded mind grows ineffably lonely, when urges seem too dizzying to dare act on—and yet you do act on them because they're a part of *you*—you're *rocking.* Rock and roll is the darkness that enshrouds secret desires unfulfilled, and the appetite that shoves you forward to disrobe them. As Jerry Lee Lewis can tell you, if you want to rock, you do not go gently into that good night.

Jerry Lee Lewis has said, in no uncertain terms, that he's going to hell for playing rock and roll. And Jerry Lee—a whiskey-lapping, woman-squeezing, wild-eyed Louisiana roadhouse roustabout with no more sense of restraint, decorum, or social conscience than a shark on a July afternoon at Virginia Beach—is exactly right. Don't think for one minute that he merely stumbled onto this momentous path. Jerry Lee's parents sent their child to a fundamentalist Bible college in Waxahachie, Texas, to learn the difference between the Darkness and the Light. And he did—with a vengeance. Slipping down into each magnetic midnight on a Jacob's Ladder of knotted bedsheets, he'd dash off to downtown Dallas to seek out every forbidden pleasure the Good Book had alerted him to. And any time there was an upright piano handy to help him improvise a soundtrack to his gloriously tawdry personal saga, he'd shift his hips, bring his right boot heel down hard on high C, and start pumping out some bastardized black spiritual with all the lowdown hillbilly abandon he could muster, his quasi-Apache war whoops providing ultracoarse counterpoint.

In a country composed of more different sets of competing and conflicting rules, dogmas, prejudices, pietistic predilections, and doctrinaire obsessions than a Chinese puzzle factory, Jerry Lee Lewis declined the role of joiner. Rather, he moved to embrace the big picture. Some folks in his hometown got spitting mad at a white boy banging out black music, so he egged them on with a ringing barrage of back-alley chord play. Others raged that setting church music to the rhythms of a barroom or a bordello was sacrilege! Jerry Lee served up a dose of coal-cellar boogie-woogie just to see the furnace in their eyes. And shook his skinny ass at them for good measure.

On the lam from everything his devout forebears held dear, driven by an unbridled lust to own the moment, Jerry Lee looked at what he had wrought and saw that it was good—good rock and roll. Jerry Lee had elected, for better or worse, to explore every nook and cranny of who he hoped and feared himself to be, swallowing the gigantic promise of America in one shivering gulp and washing it down with a scalding double swig of Night Train wine.

He made his choice, crossed the line, and began devouring great balls of fire for breakfast, pushing himself to every unholy limit he could perceive in his own private universe. In so doing, Jerry Lee remade himself in the image and likeness of a rock star. And so he continues to be, through bouts with loaded pistols, overturned Rolls Royces, bags of Biphetamines and Placidyls, bottles of grain alcohol, five wrecked marriages, and seven shades of almighty mayhem swirling around eighty-eight ivories that rattle with a music bent on exorcism through possession. He dances on tombstones, bays at the moon, and pisses icewater in the faces of all who go to bed too early or remain there too long. Until, on the appointed day, at an hour known only to the Lord (or perhaps the Devil), Jerry Lee will lay down his massive, self-imposed burden and confess, probably in a wobbly whisper, "Take me now, Big Man, for I am finally *spent.*"

Lewis and others like him looked to the storied divertissements of Louisiana for their earliest inspiration. In New Orleans's Congo Square, in the early 1800s, slaves were permitted by their masters to congregate on certain days and play their native instruments. To chase their despair and alienation, to enrich their fragile sense of community, and to beguile and bewilder their captors, these displaced Ashanti, Yoruban, and Senegalese people combined their own riveting rhythms with new ones that had bombarded them during their difficult passage and in their new surroundings: hymns, sea chanteys, flamenco tempos, and brassy quadrilles.

This was a scandalous but necessary evil—in the opinion of polite society. But, in time, the torrid outdoor displays evolved into an accepted exhibition and rallying point. And when the Africans' admiration of the martial cadences of European processional rites induced them to include these rhythms in their own elaborate burial rites, the groundwork was laid for an enduring Crescent City institution: funeral marching bands. Among the youths who grew up following, and then playing in, those street parades were Joe "King" Oliver, Louis "Dippermouth" Armstrong, and one Henry Roeland Byrd—better known as Professor Longhair, the legendary "Bach of Rock," whose barrelhouse mambo-rhumba piano figures would profoundly influence Fats Domino, Huey Smith, Allen Toussaint, Mac "Dr. John" Rebennack, and by extension, every keyboard carouser from Ray Charles to Sly Stone.

A thousand miles away in Salem, Ohio, the patrons of the Golden Fleece Tavern would gather around the owner and his sons as they performed "The Arkansas Traveler," a traditional skit that tells the tale of an impressionable hayseed just returned from his first trip down to Louisiana. It is the story of a traveler who can't get this nagging New Orleans jig out of his fool head, and he takes up a fiddle in a fitful attempt to reproduce it. His efforts are accompanied by a vaudeville of give-and-take chatter with a passing stranger who repeatedly demands that the silly traveler stop jawboning and "finish the tune!"

The tipplers at the Golden Fleece would sit through every hoary straight man–buffoon exchange with gleeful anticipation, knowing full well that the stranger would ultimately take up a fiddle himself and duel the traveler to a furiously dexterous finale. It was through these workaday jam sessions and frolics—and through others of endlessly quirky variety (field hollers, chain-gang chants, bunkhouse and saddle sing-alongs, immigrant street songs, marching tunes)—that one vast, hodgepodge nation, drunk on its own adolescence, eventually gave birth to the ominously adrenalized spectacle of rock and roll.

This development occurred as the land's myriad social conventions grew more rigid, and its class, racial, religious, and sexual lines had become more dangerous, even lethal, to cross. And yet, as embodied by its major exponents—the true rock stars—rock and roll has less to do with rebellion than with an exquisite self-absorption in which there is no tug of war, only a swift, steady pull. Barriers don't exist in the minds of the most gifted rockers; their thoughts are elsewhere, locked into a feeding frenzy. At its high end, rock and roll not only eats its young, it eats everything in sight. Beyond gluttony, beyond selfishness, beyond caring, it is a banquet nonpareil, oblivious to *all* consequences. For the rapacious rocker believes that all history, whether personal history, rock history, or human history, is redeemed by eternity.

There is an enduring superstition in the rural South that every great bluesman and blueswoman had an otherworldly tutor who taught them to arrest listeners with the inky side of their souls; that they had a secret handshake with the Angel of Death, who enabled them to live so recklessly, ever flirting with dissolution while drawing others into their damning web.

It is ironic that, to an extent, rock and roll began in church, when Johnny Shines raised his voice as a child in a Memphis chapel and marveled at the sound of it, realizing there was only one John Ned Shines and he was never gonna come again. So he and Robert Johnson split from the tabernacles that had inspired them with the Lord's greatest gift—singularity—and they hit the treacherous black hobo trail to chart the parameters of their amazing onlyness. They wrote songs about sinister women, nights of nameless terror, the nearness of Satan's grip. They sang of "conjurers" who worked spells or "mojos" in boneyards after dusk, combining snakeskins, horsehair, and grave dirt into potions that might forestall the grim final reckoning. Further, one of the first times Jerry Lee Lewis played piano was at the Holiness Church Meeting of God Assembly in Waxahachie, and all he wanted the man in the pulpit to explain was: if God created pretty young virgins, fast cars, summer nights, and the fixings for bourbon, why couldn't he celebrate His handiwork?

If you want to get a healthy young man or woman plenty thirsty for something, all you've got to do is forbid it. Then stick to your guns. No liquor. No sex. No drugs. No release from fear. No accurate picture of who you really are, good or bad.

To help codify these raw rituals of denial, Carl Jung coined a term for the personality traits and smoldering drives all men refuse to acknowledge—the "shadow." Jung didn't live to hear the Beach Boys harmonize on Brian Wilson's "I Just Wasn't Made for These

Times" or witness Mick Jagger and Keith Richards whipping into "Sympathy for the Devil" or see Boy George cavorting through "Karma Chameleon" and then telling reporters, "I'm not interested in gay rights because to me gay is normal, being free to do what you want to do." But Jung would have understood the dynamic within their messages, as well as the nature of the All-American Universal Rock and Roll Ethic: what you don't see, ask for.

By 1983, the Police, a British-American band which openly craved superstar status before such temporal achievements evaporate in what they believed is the millennial onrush of a nuclear Armageddon, released *Synchronicity,* an album based on Jung's theories. The record, which became one of the biggest-selling LPs in rock history and made the Police the most popular group on the planet, was an icy assessment of the shadow side of human nature. It put forth the plea that the most significant task of any individual is to achieve harmony between the conscious and the unconscious; that is, the only antidote to evil is self-knowledge, because our dreams are the very harbingers of our potentially monstrous malevolence.

Raw self-revelations and dark admonishments are only part of the rock star's intent, however, for rock and roll craves an audience. The rock concert is a tribal rite in which an option-addicted culture is allowed to blow off its enormous stores of nervous energy. But after the show, the true rock star keeps on rocking; he or she is the potential nemesis of social order—an energy vampire eager to sate himself while there's still time—and any particular audience is merely another course in a desperate feast.

Considerable energy is expended to keep the party going; each day, the capability to invoke glorious and grotesque rock and roll visions escalates. When American popular music first became linked with electricity, a unique brand of sensory sorcery bloomed. Nobody is entirely certain how the phenomenon of electricity works, no physicist comprehends the precise chemistry of the particles of charge as they repel each other and create a propulsive new force; it's a modern sort of alchemy. Likewise, the power to fill entire arenas with the reverberating voltage of rock and roll, drums rumbling with the tumult of mountains falling, roaring guitars and synthesized keyboards keeping several thousand craniums humming, represents a quantum leap into new realms of preternatural exultation, mesmerization, and assault—the blunt death of musical limits.

When you confront your own shadow in all its incarnations,

you're inside rock and roll. And when you do it musically, onstage, in a terrible, wonderful contract with your audience, succeeding at encouraging them to stir some measure of their shadows into the spiraling maelstrom, then you're a rock star.

This is the story of rock and roll—past, present, and future—and some of its greatest stars. It is told through the fabric, texture, and dimensions of the stars' inner voracity, their art becoming their life, their life becoming their art, all of it of a piece. It explores a world apart from the normal codes of behavior, from commonplace concepts of responsibility, of loyalty, of duty, of professionalism. Unlike most other schools of musical thought, rock and roll virtually discards conservatorylike rubrics concerning study, dedication, and virtuosity. Theater traditions and showbiz ethics become blurred or trampled underfoot in the onrush of its peculiar imperatives. The show mustn't necessarily go on; rock and roll is self-absorbed almost to the point of ignoring itself.

The book is divided into three sections: the pioneers, who laid the groundwork for the rock and roll disposition; the pilgrims, who expanded the parameters of its impropriety; and the progeny, who are striving to find new applications for the uncommon conduct propagated by their role models. The choices made herein were intended not only to isolate personal styles and seminal musical contributions, but to advance the bizarre saga itself. The book is meant to be read in sequence, as a kind of story with a cumulative lesson, rather than as an exclusive encyclopedic collection. In this way, a plot emerges, one figure learning from, influencing, exciting, threatening, and spurring another. The risks become greater, and the sense of dark heritage deepens in the mind of each participant as they collide with their commingled destinies.

Any truths in the book emerge organically, whatever momentum that's achieved builds on itself, the process becomes the reward, and it is rich with the energy of living. As the torch is passed, an ethos is forged. The conscience is confronted. The truth is felt. And, in time, the soul is sold.

Rock Lives

PIONEERS

For the poor black, life on the Mississippi delta in the 1930s had an acrid flavor, and those who learned to stomach it came to exist in a curious pocket of time, set apart from the uncomprehending white world that coursed around them. The lowly sharecropper was in terminal debt to one of a vast network of corrupt white landlords whose larcenous, comically inflated fees he could barely hope to meet. The landless day laborers who worked the cotton plantations were treated like ghosts: expected to appear at sunrise, toil without complaint in the unspeakable heat, and vanish at the smoky first hint of dusk. What other sustaining labor that existed was to be found on the levees that strained to hold back the tides of the fickle Mississippi. Since the levees required constant inspection and maintenance, work camps grew up around them, often peopled by convicts from prison farms in the district. The camps were vile, squalid places that produced criminality of the most notorious sort. Violent incidents usually erupted on the weekends, when parties were held on the riverbanks; prostitutes and sporting women would be brought in by wagon or truck, and entertainment was provided by the more daring local blues musicians. Such musicians were a highly mobilized underclass of the delta caste system.

Robert Johnson

1984

These men—and a very few women—elected to drift from town to town playing a circuit of "jook joints," country picnics, and street-corners where the deputy wouldn't collar them.

Country picnics were rambunctious Saturday-night affairs (and direct rivals of Sunday-morning church services) that took place in remote fields. Invitation was by word of mouth; bottles of coal oil, with a burning rag for a wick, would be hung in trees to guide people to the sites. The highly popular jooks (probably from the West African word *joog,* meaning to "shake up") served as the mainstay of many an itinerant bluesman. Jooks were shacks, usually bootlegger-run, hidden deep in the woods, where one could find beer, bad gin, "hooch," casual sex, and dancing fed either by live music or by the "vendor," as the first crude jukeboxes were called. The musicians at picnics and jooks might be given a small fee, but usually they had to depend on the generosity of the tanked-up patrons when it came time to pass the hat.

Competition among the players to hold the floor was as keen as the spirited wooing of the available women, and fists and razors would fly over both issues. The best way to remain top dog in the "headcutting" contests that could ensue between two or more contentious bluesmen was to develop instantaneous, encyclopedic mental access to the chord patterns and lyrics of every blues record currently popular, as well as the latest output of your immediate adversaries. The trick was to concoct a well-rhymed response to an opponent's wiliest stanza, either building on or reinterpreting the man's own words, and then shifting the balance by slipping in a piping-hot verse of your own creation. Headcutting was both a way of blowing off steam and tempering your command of the craft. However, the better you were at it, the greater the odds of getting your ear torn off by a sorely enraged loser.

It was into this realm of indenture, sorrow, sin, and desperation that Robert Johnson was born. The date was May 8, 1911; the place was Hazelhurst, a little hamlet south of Jackson, Mississippi. His mother was Julia Ann Majors, and his absentee father was one Noah Johnson. Julia had married Charles Dodds, Jr., a prosperous cabinet-maker and landowner, several years before Robert was born, but Dodds was chased out of town in 1907 by a lynch mob after he'd had an altercation with two prominent white businessmen. Julia stayed behind in Hazelhurst, and Robert was the result of a liaison, during Dodd's forced exile, with sharecropper Johnson, who moved on shortly afterward. Robert wound up living in Robinsonville, Mississippi, with his mother and a man named William "Dusty" Willis. Johnson would never know his real father, and in adulthood he would vacillate between contemptuous disinterest in him and a distempered desire to locate him.

As a boy, Robert took up the Jew's harp and the harmonica as distractions and would regularly sneak off to jooks in the Robinsonville area to listen to and learn from such delta blues greats as Charley Patton, Willie Brown, and, later, Eddie "Son" House. Robert became known as something of a pest, dogging the bluesmen's heels as they made their stops, scrutinizing their solo and group playing, and asking to be shown chords and fingering techniques. Still, it seemed that music might be no more than a hobby for Robert. In 1929, he married sixteen-year-old Virginia Travis. But when Virginia died in childbirth a year later, taking their infant son with her, Robert's few fragile roots in the world were ripped out, and he adopted the ways of a determined rounder.

Moving back to the vicinity of Hazelhurst, he took up with an Alabama-born guitarist named Ike Zinnerman, an obscure figure who boasted that his mastery of his instrument stemmed from some graveyard conjury. Johnson then faded from sight. He resurfaced in Robinsonville a year later, attacking the blues with canny ferocity. This newfound flair on his hefty Gibson guitar and the flinty sophistication of his bottle-slide playing left Charley Patton, Willie Brown, and Son House stupefied. Rumors circulated that Johnson had struck a bargain with Satan. This belief would be supplemented by eerie testimony from Johnny Shines, another esteemed country stalwart out of Memphis and a frequent traveling companion of Johnson's. Shines maintained that no matter what godforsaken sleeping arrangements they would make on the road, Johnson would somehow arise from every dusty ditch or straw-strewn boxcar "looking like he's just stepped out of church! Never did nothing to himself any more than me, neither."

Some of Johnson's relatives later allowed as to how the whole Faustian deal had gone down in 1930, just after nightfall, at a certain rural crossroads: Robert had accepted his talent in exchange for his soul, payment due eight years hence. The supernatural menace of a night-engulfed crossroads looms large in folklore in the deep South; one of the few prominent landmarks in the blunt tableland of the delta, the crossroads epitomizes the vulnerability of the black in a hostile world. To find oneself at a crossroads after dark is to be stranded on open ground, an easy mark for whites who don't like the idea of a black man on the move. Hard choices are the consequences for blacks who "ain't where they supposed to be," and in blues circles, the Devil is your only friend when you need to arrive at your next destination in a hurry.

The ambition of most every bluesman was to get onto records. It was common in the late 1920s for field scouts to move through the major cities of the deep South seeking more grist for the lucrative "race records" mill. Portable recording units captured the performances of Charley Patton and Son House, and these sides were sizable hits locally; but few delta blues stylists had significant commercial impact in big markets like St. Louis, Chicago, and New York, where their sound was considered too rustic. Moreover, many of the best delta bluesmen saw themselves primarily as entertainers whose surest grubstake was their local following.

Robert Johnson, however, perceived himself as a recording artist and tailored the solo presentation of his material with such meticulousness that it scarcely varied from night to night. Rather than hold fast to the small-town hegemony that lordly tyrants like Charley Patton thrived on, Johnson was consumed with the idea of projecting his tortured perspective to the largest possible audience. This broader worldview was reflected in the mongrel qualities of his sound. His songs do possess the earthy verve of the delta; but the tense single-string guitar attack favored in Chicago and the melodic strength of the best blues emerging from the East are also apparent. Johnson's material didn't ramble on discursively or strive to evoke the harsh idioms and multihued landscape that first inspired it. On the contrary, it was tight and searing in its stark compactness, and it rocked the blues with voodoo abandon.

Most of all, his repertoire was a litany of widening mental and spiritual wounds: heaving, throbbing, scarlet patches of rent muscle and tissue, coupled with the shrieking horror that greets such sights. His recordings of "Stones in My Passway" and "Love in Vain" were you-are-there utterances of the resounding victory of despair over faith.

I got stones in my passway
An' my road seem dark as night!
I have pains in my heart
They have taken my appetite.

The appetite in question is sex, but even as he and his latest conquest rise to ravage each other, the oxygen needed to fuel it is seemingly sucked from their bedchamber, their quivering torsos near to imploding. "I got a woman that I'm lovin', boy," Johnson gasps, as the desolate two-minute confessional culminates in a harrowing carnival of psychic dismemberment, "but she don't mean a thing." Like virtually all of the existing Johnson guitar-and-voice tracks—maybe thirty titles on forty-one variant sides—"Stones in My Passway" is the sound of a doomed man thinking out loud, feeling with each cutting tug of the frets that he'll never get out of his blues alive.

One can only speculate on the cruel forces that were laying waste to Johnson, but it's clear that he ran toward rather than from them. Even as he was copping and honing exuberant rhythmic conceits, Johnson was also being influenced by one elder statesman's grotesque sense of etiquette. Charley Patton was a short, brutish son of a preacher whose motley bloodlines allowed him to pass for white, black, or Indian as circumstances dictated. He bullied his way through Mississippi while managing to avoid a single incident of manual labor. Perpetually drunk and abusive, no loggers' barbecue or cutthroats' convention was too rowdy for his tastes, and he took considerable pleasure in beating his eight common-law wives.

For Johnson's part, he never ceased his own wanton womanizing. He even concocted bizarre, misogynous ditties like "Dead Shrimp Blues" to commemorate it. After he remarried, to sweet-natured Calletta Craft, in 1931, the slender, handsome bluesman supposedly demanded that the union be kept secret, lest it cramp his lecherous style. Johnson eventually deserted Calletta. She suffered a complete nervous collapse, and, by all accounts, Johnson was unmoved. He cared as little for friendship as he did for lasting love. He was known to drop out of sight on a moment's notice—sometimes in the middle of a show—and not turn up again until weeks or months afterward. His reputation for communion with the supernatural was enhanced by his habit of frequently altering his appearance and manner and adopting a host of aliases. Contemporaries who are still living are said to wonder if they had actually met the real Robert Johnson or only an impersonator.

One thing disciples as diverse as Muddy Waters, Elmore James, John Lee "Sonny Boy" Williamson, and Junior Parker could be certain of was the veracity of Johnson's talent. Robert Johnson's first recording session was in San Antonio, Texas, on November 23, 1936. He'd been introduced to Ernie Oertle, a scout for the American Record Company and the Vocalion label, by H. C. Speir, a Jackson, Mississippi, music shop owner. The Johnson Vocalion session, which took place in a hotel room, documented some of the most formidable blues of that or any other era. "Terraplane Blues," his first 78 rpm single, was a lewd composition that compared his woman to an automobile ("When I mash down your little starter / Then your spark plug will give me fire").

While "Terraplane Blues" would rack up sizable sales in the delta and become Johnson's only real hit during his lifetime, the rest of the tunes he cut in his initial sessions did not attain status as classics until they were rediscovered by Muddy Waters et al., in the postwar heyday of electrified Chicago blues.

The most fearsome of all the inaugural tracks Johnson laid down in 1936 was "Crossroad Blues," in which he snarls through gritted teeth of the dire predicament of finally finding himself stuck on a darkened crossroads with Lucifer laughing in the wings.

In June of 1937, Johnson did a session in a Dallas warehouse and recorded more hair-raising anthems of dashed hopes, among them "Hellhound on My Trail" and "Me and the Devil Blues." The latter concludes with Johnson sternly advising, "You may bury my body down by the highway side / So my old evil spirit can catch a Greyhound bus and ride."

Robert Johnson died on August 16, 1938, in Greenwood, Mississippi, after being poisoned at a house party he'd been hired to play at. The story is told that he got himself pie-eyed—Johnson would guzzle any form of white lightning or grain alcohol—and flirted with his employer's wife. His jealous host retaliated by serving him tainted rye. Johnson is said to have lingered on in agony for several days before expiring. His remains were laid in a pine box supplied by the county; burial was in an unmarked grave. Rumors persist that the site is somewhere just off Mississippi Highway 7—where his evil spirit could indeed board a passing Greyhound and continue to haunt the turnpikes.

He had the gumption of a farmboy, running back to his roots in rural east Texas, and the flashy savvy of a cowboy, tied to an adolescence spent in the ranch country of west Texas. So it's hardly surprising that, on a dare, he took up the fiddle, that lyric frontier lathe, and went on to become one of the best players in the world.

Born in Hall County, Texas, on March 6, 1905, at ten James Robert Wills was thought to be a damn sight better at handling a horse than a bow made from its tail. But he told his cousin he was sick and tired of hearing him saw out the same sluggish old ditty on his violin. Well, could little James Robert do better? Better and *faster*, came the reply. Wills figured out the melody and a snappy technique in short order and won the dare. After dawn-to-dusk rounds of cotton picking, he would borrow the fiddle and expand his repertoire with frontier tunes like "Gone Indian."

As the stock market was

Bob Wills

1
9
8
4

crashing and gangsters were suffering wholesale slaughter in the St. Valentine's Day Massacre, Bob Wills was beginning his professional fiddling career around Fort Worth with guitarist Herman Arnspiger. They called themselves the Wills Fiddle Band. A standard barn-dance twosome, they were committed to satisfying the old folks with a mid-tempo "Cotton-Eyed Joe" and "Old Dan Tucker," but they also drew in the young folk with a saucy "La Cucaracha" and risky bits of Bessie Smith or W. C. Handy.

Texas in the late depression era was a land undergoing a dramatic transition as the ravages of the boll weevil were offset by the oil boom of the 1930s, drawing migrants from throughout the South, along with their agriculture-steeped traditions of song and story. Blacks, Chicanos, Cajuns, and white Protestants commingled in a stark new world being built on the old foundations of southern ruralism, and the music they played and shared in their free time became as pluralistic as the state's exploding population.

The cardinal rule of any touring group in the region was to have a fiddler above reproach, one who could approximate, with alacrity, songs called out from the crowd. Wills had that requirement more than fulfilled. While a collector of rhythms, styles, and songs, he was no common folklorist or slick popularizer but rather a canny enthusiast who would blossom into one of the greatest innovators in all of popular music. If country and western can be considered a valid offshoot from the country lifeline, it was Bob Wills who put the "western" into the term, and he taught it how to *swing*.

By 1930, the Wills Fiddle Band had become the larger Aladdin Laddies, and then—under the sponsorship of the Burrus Mill and Elevator Company (whence came fat sacks of Light Crust Flour)—the Light Crust Doughboys. The group performed manual labor at the mill by day and then broke at noon to play live on KFJZ or WBAP, and they prospered under the management of W. Lee "Pappy" O'Daniel. Bob himself was a star fiddler on no less than three radio stations in the area. But the Doughboys were weakened when Milton Brown, their featured singer, broke off to form the Musical Brownies. Then, in 1933, Wills was bounced from the band by Pappy O'Daniel, who disliked his immoderate drinking habits and the loutish behavior they precipitated. Wills took his banjoist brother Johnnie Lee Wills with him, and they secured a radio show in Waco, Texas.

Forming Bob Wills and His Texas Playboys (in the Doughboys mold), he settled in Tulsa, Oklahoma, and signed a contract in 1935 with Brunswick Records. The Playboys were the premier act in the Southwest; their noontime show on KVOO was the rage, 50,000 watts beaming it out to every cow town and county seat in the region. Wills earned the respect and affection of his fellow musicians for never turning an auditioning picker down. What made him a virtual folk hero, however, was the majestic band he ultimately assembled and the unprecedented dimensionality of their fiddle-based sound. Thrilled by the Big Band swing, New Orleans jazz, and bayou bluegrass of the day, and touched by the wistful sweetness of mariachi and the sprightly uplift of *nortena* polkas, Wills put horns and reeds into his thirteen-piece Playboys. What's more, he gave them a freedom to experiment as vast as the territory in which they toured.

After Prohibition was repealed in 1933, the Playboys had a helluva lot more new dancehalls and roadhouses begging to book them. The sight of their tour bus, with its Longhorn hood ornament fastened above the gleaming grillwork, quickened the pulse of many a rural farmworker, and its very arrival always drew sizable crowds. Entire families would travel as far as 200 miles to see Wills—a beefy, solidly built man with a broad face, high forehead, bushy eyebrows, and warm eyes—in his $200 suits and custom-made boots, a wide-brimmed fedora tilted raffishly on his head, puffing on a fat Corona Corona and greeting every plowhand with the affectionate good cheer of a Dutch uncle. He was one of them, a product of the red dust that mottled their knees and wrinkled their brows, the kind of man who could tell a good joke, take a stiff drink, and hook a woman with the horny twinkle in his gaze.

The band members were no slouches either, dressed in crisp, lordly western outfits and possessing some of the best musical chops in the wild new West. Leon McAuliffe was a master of the steel guitar, his speed and richness of tone unmatched; Eldon Shamblin was a crack rhythm guitarist and arranger whose duets with McAuliffe were seamless; Cecil Brower and Jesse Ashlock were formidable fiddling companions for Wills; and lead vocalist Tommy Duncan's agile country blues tack was one of the most imitated of its day. As for the horn section, it was a heart-stopping drill team, as colorful as it was controversial. When the Playboys moved their base from Tulsa back to Fort Worth, the local musicians' union initially refused to allow them to play, so flabbergasted were they by the rebellious presence of drums and brass in a country and western dance band.

Before too long, electric guitars also became part of the equation, and the Playboys' ranks swelled to eighteen. Pop music had never seen such an anomalous musical amalgam, but early rockers understood and were profoundly affected by Wills's iconoclastic tastes.

If Bob Wills was a maverick, he was also a benevolent taskmaster, his gleeful cries of "Ahhh-ha!" and "Take it away, Leon!" a genuine expression of the pride he took in the musical prowess of his team. He toured as far as California, taking what came to be dubbed "Okie jazz" to homesick servicemen training in the lengthening shadows of war, reviving their drive with renditions of "Steel Guitar Rag," "Take Me Back to Tulsa," "Sitting on Top of the World," "Mexicali Rose," "My Confession." But when Pearl Harbor was bombed on December 7, 1941, the band answered the call to avenge the infamous deed, and the Playboys were scattered.

After the war, Wills reunited the Playboys. They decided to de-emphasize the brass section somewhat, and they became better known nationally—even breaking some of Benny Goodman's attendance records as they brought their exotic western swing into major cities in the Northeast and Midwest.

In 1964, after a second heart attack, Wills broke up the Playboys, and they passed into legend as the best two-fisted cowboy tavern band that ever set "Sally Goodin" to a swinging beat. Wills had the first of several strokes in 1969, his health and mobility severely curtailed; but in 1973, he went up to Dallas to supervise the recording of a memorial Playboys album for United Artists Records. When Wills took sick again, devoted fan Merle Haggard flew in to help out. It was the last studio session for the original Texas Playboys.

A massive stroke took seventy-year-old Bob Wills on May 12, 1975, while he was being cared for at the Kent Nursing Home in Fort Worth. A true musical outlaw and beloved pioneer, he was a hero to the working poor he devoted much of his life to entertaining, and he was eulogized on country stations from the Panhandle to the Rockies. Men and women who would never forget his fond whoops and his hell-for-leather fiddle breaks wept softly as the bright strains of one of his loveliest ranch dance sonnets swirled out of their radios:

Stay all night, stay a little longer,
Dance all night, dance a little longer,
Pull off your coat, throw it in the corner,
Don't see why you don't stay a little longer.

It was one of those wild New Orleans rock and roll nights that Professor Longhair had long ago helped the town hone: a gumbo of spitfire sass, raucous good cheer, and unhinged barrelhouse rhumba-boogie. The Crescent City's reigning piano king was holding Saturday evening court at Tipitina's on the corner of Napoleon Avenue and Tchoupitoulas Street, and the music emanating from inside was, to use the somewhat prurient local parlance, "rowdy enough to knock your cock into your watch pocket." Renowned for his frenetically funky keyboard figures, which fired the imaginations of Fats Domino, Huey Smith, James Booker, Allen Toussaint, and Mac "Dr. John" Rebbenack, the spindly sixty-one-year-old "Fess," as his friends called him, was now downright frantic as his trademark yodel introduced the whimsical, self-penned party song for which the club had been named:

Tipitina, tipitina
Tipitina, tra la la
We gonna oobla walla malla
dalla
And drink some mellow wine

"He was really going at it," said his dark-haired manager, Allison Kaslow, "and he was just giving the band [the

Professor Longhair

1980

nine-piece Blues Scholars, led by Allison's saxophonist husband, Andy] about three seconds between songs. I went up to Fess on a break and said, 'Hey man, you're burning it up tonight! You've gotta give these fellas a little breather now and then.'

"But it was a joyous thing," she added with a smile. "I'd never seen him so into it, and the set was total perfection."

At the close of the show, Longhair (born Henry Roeland Byrd) erupted with a fervent blues that no one present had ever heard him play before. "I believe I'm gonna leave this town," he sang, " 'Cause it's brought me nothing but heartache and sorrow bound."

Afterward, he told a deeply moved Allison, "Tonight, I finally got it together."

That was the last time Professor Longhair, one of the most gifted and overlooked figures in American popular music, performed before the public. Four days later, at 3:00 A.M. on Wednesday, January 30, 1980, he suffered a massive coronary arrest. Trembling in his sleep, he gagged, spit out a gold front tooth, and then lay still. Alice, his wife of forty years, was at his side, begging him to wake up.

"At least I know," she confided, "he didn't suffer much in the end."

"Many years ago, my partner Ahmet Ertegun was playing a tape of Fess for a world-famous jazz piano player," said a somber Jerry Wexler, one of Longhair's former producers (at Atlantic Records), as he eulogized his friend the following Friday night at the Majestic Mortuary.

"Totally intrigued, that man sat down at the piano and tried to duplicate Fess's style. An hour and some busted knuckles later, he retired in confusion. 'I heard it,' he said, 'but it's impossible to play.'

"And it was and is—except for the select few who were the beneficiaries of his unselfish love for music and people, because this instructional part of his life didn't put penny one in his pocket or any butter on his grits."

The mourners seated on rows of wooden folding chairs before the open coffin knew it was the sad truth. Friends, neighbors, and fellow musicians had watched him struggle in impoverished obscurity for nearly a half century. In death, Longhair will be thought of as "an innovator," in Wexler's words, "who may be remembered with Louis Armstrong and Sidney Bechet and Jelly Roll Morton as yet another gift from New Orleans to American blues and jazz." But in life he was a man who had been largely ignored by the music business beyond his home state and cheated by the record-industry sharks in his native city.

He was born on December 19, 1918, in Bogalusa, Louisiana, the second son of Ella Mae and James Byrd, both musicians. (He had one brother and two sisters.) James's father, Americus Byrd, had been a slave in Alabama. Roy, as Longhair came to be called, left the Klan-dominated river town of Bogalusa with his family and moved to New Orleans when he was very young. As a boy, he worked as a street dancer under the wing of companions Streamline Isaac and Harrison Hike, who taught him such acrobatic moves as walking four feet up a wall and then somersaulting into a sidewalk split. While dancing for tips outside the Caldonia Inn and the Dew Drop Inn, Roy was exposed to the seminal barrelhouse piano styles of Kid Stormy Weather, Sullivan Rock, Robert Bertrand, Archibald, and a gentleman who would later serve as his mentor, Tuts Washington. Spurred on by his mother and Washington, he taught himself to play on an abandoned upright he found in the street. He combined a deft distillation of his own heroes' styles with a crazy jambalaya of jump blues, boogie-woogie, jazz, calypso, rhumba, samba, and his own peculiar dance rhythms.

Longhair was a collector of rhythms. From the celebrants who followed New Orleans's black marching bands, banging on bottles and pails in a strutting rhythm called "second line," he picked up his basic rhythmic orientation. From the traditional black Mardi Gras societies of New Orleans, the "Indians," who preserve a chant-like, percussive folk music that remains heavily African, he absorbed more rhythmic subtleties. He had an encyclopedic knowledge of the Latin-tinged bass patterns that New Orleans pianists had been inventing since the days of Jelly Roll Morton. He even listened to Perez Prado's mambo records. In the thirties, when he served in the Civilian Conservation Corps, he played with, in his own words, "Spanish boys, West Indians, Puerto Ricans, Jamaicans. I just copied all their changes and beats, and kept the ones I liked."

Later he earned a living as a hoofer in floor shows at local nightclubs, teaming up with Champion Jack Dupree and Redd Foxx in the early thirties. The dance trio dissolved when Foxx and Dupree departed for greener pastures. Longhair's big break as a pianist came in 1949 when he sat in for Salvador Doucette, Dave Bartholomew's keyboardist, during a set at the Caldonia Inn. Club manager Mike Tessitore subsequently dismissed Bartholomew, hiring Fess.

Tessitore dubbed the longhaired "professor" and his sidemen (drummer Big Slick, saxman Apeman Black, and guitarist Walter Nelson) the Four Hairs Combo. Before the end of 1949, Longhair had cut his biggest record, "Bald Head," for Mercury. Thereafter, backing personnel briskly came and went. The various aggregations were billed as Professor Longhair and His Shuffling Hungarians, Roy Byrd and His Blues Jumpers, and Professor Longhair and the Clippers. He also did solo work as Roy "Bald Head" Byrd and Roland Byrd. During the fifties, Fess and famed New Orleans guitarist Earl King served a stint as the featured performers with Chick Davis and the All-Night Ramblers. A lot of records resulted from these activities, among them the excellent Atlantic sides he cut with Wexler and Ertegun in 1953. Some of them, like "Big Chief," a 1964 single with King on vocals, were modest hits, but Longhair saw little or no money for his efforts.

In 1954 he suffered a stroke and was hospitalized for almost a year. For the rest of his life he would be plagued with a host of other maladies: bronchitis, pulmonary edema, cirrhosis, and arthritis.

For most of his married life, he and his family—he had seven children and eighteen grandchildren (one son is deceased)—lived in various dilapidated old dwellings on or near South Ramparts Street. It was a tough neighborhood, and Fess always carried a gun. Twice, they were left destitute by fires. Only in the last year of his life would Longhair own his own home, a bungalow on Terpsichore.

At his lowest point, in the late sixties, Longhair was reduced to sweeping out the One Stop Record Store, owned by the same man, Joe Assunto, who helped organize the recording session (for Joe Ruffino's Ron Records) for his steadiest-selling single, "Go to the Mardi Gras"—the anthem of the annual celebration. Longhair wrote the song, a remake of his earlier "Mardi Gras in New Orleans," but he did not own it, and he never received a dime for the single in either writer's or artist's royalties. (On February 7, Mayor Ernest Morial declared that 1980's Mardi Gras would be dedicated to Longhair.)

Longhair was rediscovered and rescued from poverty in 1971 by Quint Davis, a small-time promoter, road manager, and booking agent. Davis sought him out to appear at the second annual New

Orleans Jazz and Heritage Festival, an event that Davis and Allison Kaslow helped found.

"He had a bad knee and walked with great difficulty," Davis said, "but he showed up for the concert in Congo Square in a black suit, and when he started playing that upright—it sounds like a cliché—but everything else stopped dead on the other stages. There were four acts playing simultaneously, and the crowd just gathered and gaped. They had never heard anything like him. It was truly a magic moment."

In 1973 Atlantic put out an album of Longhair's late-forties, early-fifties sides, *New Orleans Piano.* And Longhair released three more LPs: *Rock and Roll Gumbo,* in 1975, on the French Barclay label; *Live on the Queen Mary* for Harvest-Capitol in 1978; and Alligator Records' new *Crawfish Fiesta,* which was being shipped to stores the day Longhair died. He also appeared on the acclaimed two-record *New Orleans Jazz and Heritage Festival 1976* LP issued by Island Records. Overall, sales were modest, but profitable tours here and abroad, playing blues and jazz clubs and music festivals (most notably, the Newport and Montreux jazz festivals in 1973, the 1978 *Grande Parade du Jazz* in Nice, and three tours of Scandinavia) helped spread his legend—and awakened him to the great affection many had for his music.

But even in the midst of an upswing in his fortunes, there was considerable sadness. "He lost one of his gold teeth while we were in Nice," Allison recalled. "It just fell out. And he told me, 'When you lose a tooth, it's a sign of death.' The day he came back from Europe, he missed his sister Johnnie Mae's funeral. Two days later, his mother-in-law died. He was heartbroken."

A year and a half later, Longhair himself was gone, and arrangements were made to inter him in the family crypt.

Lying in state at the Majestic Mortuary, he was dressed in a white tuxedo like the one he had intended to wear the next day at a scheduled taping for a National Public Television program about Tuts Washington, Allen Toussaint, and himself. Above the bier hung a bas-relief of the Last Supper, and the metal coffin was surrounded with a profusion of elaborate bouquets sent by the Neville brothers, Fats Domino, Irma Thomas, Sea-Saint Studios, Paul McCartney, and other friends and family.

Near the end of the long wake, Ernie K-Doe rose to preach and sing; Aaron Neville quietly went to the small electric organ in the corner to play and sing a heartrending "One Fine Day"; and Allen Toussaint accompanied himself in a song of tribute he had written three years earlier and then updated for the occasion, entitled "The Old Professor":

Thank you God for this very special man
And thank you for letting me be
Around to see one as great as he . . .

Now what can we say
Since you've called him on his way . . .

He's the Old Professor, the Old Professor
The Bach of Rock, the Old Professor.

"I knew every song he ever did since I was a small child," Toussaint told me. "I loved the airy, festive, Caribbean feel of his playing. It was muscular, *dynamic* playing. He had completely independent hands for working counterrhythms. And he had a blues thing in his music, but, you know, it wasn't just about suffering. It was about gettin' down any way a man possibly can.

"It would be difficult for anyone ever to play like Fess did, to get his energy and his sound, because it had so much to do with the way women would jump and wriggle when he played, and the feelings he brought to the music from the way he lived, the people he knew in the streets and alleyways of New Orleans."

Those people, approximately a thousand strong, turned out the following gray morning to pay their last respects at a traditional jazz funeral. Swarming in the streets outside the mortuary and clustered on rooftops, they patiently waited several hours in the icy chill for the slow public procession to nearby Mount Olivet Cemetery.

Inside, the parlor was packed with disconsolate mourners, and the calm voice of a local minister rose above the wails and cries.

"We ask," he implored, "that you might try to control yourselves so that we may all share in this experience together."

With that, an American flag was draped over the coffin (Longhair was an army veteran), and it was carried out to a powder-blue Cadillac hearse as the Olympia and Tuxedo brass bands struck up a series of dirges that included "The Old Rugged Cross" and "Just a Closer Walk with Thee." The crowd fell in behind the hearse and two matching limousines as they made their way down South Ramparts Street to the cemetery.

"Look at these folks," said Jerry Wexler as we walked together on the fringes of the dense throng, composed of black people of all ages and a smattering of whites in their twenties and thirties. "There are no dignitaries here from the music-industry establishment, no rock superstars, no big shots. This is just an outpouring of affection from the people here who knew Fess and his music. Down here he's *not* obscure. He means something to these people."

At graveside, Ernie K-Doe sang a hymn and then struggled to smile as he bowed his head. "Fess, hang in there. We're coming, one by one. Rest easy."

Saxophonist Earl Turbinton launched into a soaring, sorrowful jazz version of "The Lord's Prayer" that reduced almost everyone to tears. The crowd then murmured "amen," lined up to toss a bit of dirt into the crypt, and trickled away.

At Longhair's home after the funeral, there was an informal dinner of cornbread, fried chicken, ham hocks, red beans, and rice. I saw his courage mirrored in his badly shaken children and grandchildren as they inquired with tremulous voices if their guests had had enough to eat.

Allison Kaslow began talking about Longhair's hands. "I tried to spend a lot of time in the last few days looking at them, so that I'd be able to remember how they looked," she said with mounting emotion. "They were wide at the knuckles, with extremely long fingers and nails."

In 1976, I spent an evening with Longhair at Quint Davis's house, and he spoke with humility and wit about his talent and his troubles. He laughed with relief when recalling the hard times, but he also wanted to make it clear that those old realities were no less harsh for the retelling. It had indeed been a difficult existence.

Longhair recounted that at one point in his midteens he had taken up prizefighting in order to get by, and he was brutally beaten in a match with a much older man, forfeiting his two front teeth.

"I was just a boy and he took advantage," he stated. "I got my revenge with a metal pipe in an alleyway. I was laying for him, and I beat the shit out of him."

Davis wondered aloud if Longhair had broken any bones.

Fess closed his eyes and nodded with a fleeting smirk. "Yeah I did," he confessed. "But only the ones he needed to move."

Fess could be tender and he could be tough. That's how he was, and he didn't care who knew. Against all odds, he and his music endured in a harsh world where retribution was a fickle fact of life. It must have been quite a fight.

Rest easy, Fess. You've surely earned your peace.

It was 1910. The Boy Scouts were incorporated, Victor Herbert had a big hit with "Ah! Sweet Mystery of Life," and Congressman James R. Mann had a federal statute placed on the books, a statute that would later put a considerable crimp in at least one fellow's rock and roll proclivities. The White Slave Traffic Act and its amendments made it unlawful for anyone to coerce, entice, or transport females across state lines "for the purpose of prostitution or debauchery, or for any other immoral purpose." In other words—in the minds of many noxious, reprobate rockers—"There goes the weekend!"

On December 23, 1959, Charles Edward Anderson Berry of St. Louis, Missouri, was charged with running afoul of the Mann Act. The guitarist and singer, who'd had three singles on the charts in 1958 ("Sweet Little Sixteen," "Johnny B. Goode," and "Carol"), was riding out a fallow year by barnstorming the Southwest, his three-piece band and himself piled into his Cadillac. On December 1, 1959, they performed in El Paso, Texas. Here Berry had the dubious good fortune to encounter one Janice Norine Escalanti, a fourteen-year-old Apache girl with an eighth-grade education, who toiled in the town as a waitress/prostitute. Berry of-

Chuck Berry

1989

fered her a job as a hatcheck girl in his St. Louis nightspot and invited her to join the tour for the duration, selling souvenir photographs at each show. There was just enough room in the Cadillac's front seat, next to its owner-operator, to make the proposition appealing. So the five took off, scattering the tumbleweed behind them.

They reached Tucson, Arizona, under cover of darkness on December 2, and Berry procured two adjoining rooms at a motel—one for the band, the other for himself and Janice. From Tucson, the party proceeded to Phoenix, then Santa Fe, New Mexico, and Denver, Colorado, where Berry registered Janice and himself at the Drexel Hotel under the names "Mr. and Mrs. Janet Johnson." The room had one bed. Soon they were on to Pueblo, then Kansas City, Missouri. From Kansas City, Chuck flew to St. Louis; the band and the girl hit town in the Cadillac hours later.

After taking Escalanti to his house, Berry escorted her to his nightclub, where he introduced her to manager Francine Gillium, at whose home Janice was to stay. Smiles were exchanged all around. Then, on or about December 18, Chuck informed Janice that her execution of the delicate art of hatchecking was unsatisfactory, and he discharged her. Janice collected her things in a brown paper bag, and Berry drove her to the bus depot. He bought her a one-way ticket to El Paso (she'd wanted one to Yuma, Arizona), and gave her $5 before he sped off. Changing her mind about leaving town, she showed up back at the nightclub. A disapproving Berry seized the semiprecious bus ticket from her purse, leaving her to her own meager resources.

On December 22, police in Yuma got an informative phone call from Janice Escalanti. They told her to sit tight and expect the St. Louis police to pick her up. Berry and Escalanti were taken into custody and brought to a St. Louis station house. In the trial that transpired, she testified that Berry had had sexual intercourse with her in numerous locations—in the Tucson motel, twice in the back seat of the speeding Cadillac (en route to Denver), in the Drexel Hotel, in the home of Francine Gillium.

Berry entered a plea of not guilty. The jury thought otherwise. On March 11, 1960, Berry was sentenced to five years imprisonment and ordered to pay a fine of $5,000. He appealed, asserting that the evidence was insufficient to establish the intent necessary to make his admitted transportation of the girl a criminal offense. He also felt that the "hostile and prejudicial conduct and remarks of the trial court" and of Judge George H. Moore, Jr., concerning his race made the trial unfair. The appeals court concurred on the latter point and set a new trial.

At the second trial, Berry—who testified on his own behalf—was asked, "What was your purpose in bringing Janice from Texas to Missouri?" His answer: "She needed a job, and I had a job for her at the club." The jury returned a verdict of guilty, and Berry was sentenced to three years and a $5,000 fine. He spent two years in prison in Terre Haute, Indiana.

Shortly before his release in 1964, he had a Top 10 record in England with a reissue of "Let It Rock/Memphis, Tennessee." Berry's preprison recordings, including his 1950s hits—"Maybellene," "Roll Over Beethoven," "School Days," "Rock and Roll Music"—had made him a favorite and strong influence of the bands who were mounting the first British Invasion. Both the Beatles and the Rolling Stones sang his praises and covered his songs on their first few LPs. Their ebullient support helped create the environment in which Berry regained his former status as the foremost black rock and roll star, scoring with songs like "You Can Never Tell." His best material—"Round and Round," "Nadine," "Little Queenie," "You Can't Catch Me," "Sweet Little Rock and Roll," and "Living in the U.S.A."—would continue to be recorded. The leading talents of rock and roll rightfully identified with Berry's witty, slyly vulgar sendups of teenage social mores and aspirations and admired the peerless, percolating meld of country and western and blues strains.

But Berry himself would achieve his greatest commercial success with an outtake from his writing files. "My Ding-a-Ling" was a tacky fragment of bathroom humor at its most puerile, but Berry fashioned it into a festive live sing-along, and a nation with nothing better to do in 1972 bought enough copies to make it Berry's first million-selling No. 1 single. Whether his audience had sunk to his level or he'd risen to their new low-water mark is a nonburning question of the "chicken or the egg" variety; history will chronicle that Berry crossed state lines to dispense juvenile smut.

Chuck was born to Martha and Henry Berry in San Jose, a town in California's Santa Clara Valley. The date was October 18, 1926. At the height of the depression, Henry Berry took his wife and six children to St. Louis, settling in the suburb of Elleadsville. At the age of six, young Chuck began singing in the choir of the Antioch Baptist Church, but his thoughts were elsewhere. In his teens, he excelled in both hairdressing and attempted robbery. He earned a stretch in reform school (1944–47) for the latter and a Poro School of Beauty Culture degree in cosmetology and tonsorial skills for the former. While at Sumner High, he learned to play guitar on a secondhand Kay model given to him by St. Louis blues shouter Joe Sherman. St. Louis was a hotbed of rhythm and blues experimentation, and Chuck counted Billy Eckstine and Nat "King" Cole as his chief vocal influences, while Aaron "T-Bone" Walker, Charlie Christian, and Muddy Waters helped forge his cheerfully repetitive chord and riffing patterns. He supplemented his earnings from playing in the Cosmopolitan Club in East St. Louis by laboring on the assembly line of a General Motors Fisher Body plant.

In 1952, he transformed the Johnny Johnson Trio, which he'd often sat in with, into the Chuck Berry Trio, which featured Ebby Harding on drums and Johnson on piano. By 1954, Berry had a wife and two kids to support. He accepted an invitation from Muddy Waters, who'd caught him at the Cosmopolitan Club, to come to Chicago and meet Leonard Chess of Chess Records. Chuck played him two songs the trio had set down on a borrowed portable tape recorder, a blues number called "Wee Wee Hours" and "Ida Red," a traditional country tune popularized by Bob Wills. Chess took him into the studio in May of 1955, and he cut a new version of "Ida Red" which Leonard Chess renamed "Maybellene" (inspired by a hair cream of the same name). The record was sent to disk jockey Alan Freed, who accepted the payola perk of a credit as coauthor and added "Maybellene" to his playlist. The single clicked, and the rock gospel according to Chuck Berry was born; its Old Testament was fleshed out with "Roll Over Beethoven" in 1956, while the New Testament had to wait until the postprison days, with 1964's "No Particular Place to Go."

The world was presented with his impishly angular features, pencil moustache, conked curls, two-string guitar lick, and skinny-legged duck walk in a succession of rock and roll films, *Rock, Rock, Rock* (1956), *Mister Rock and Roll* (1957), and *Go, Johnny, Go* (1959). In 1966, Mercury Records lured Berry away from Chess with an advance of $150,000. But after three fruitless years, Chuck was back in the Chess stable. His greatest songs—roughly forty lightly lurid gems about the inability of modern youth to conform to parental strictures, the speed limit, and the bent arm of the law—have become so ubiquitous in Western culture that Chuck Berry is one of the few living rock and roll legends who can travel to any town on the map, carrying only his guitar, and within hours locate a young group of musicians who can back him up (on the cheap) with minimum coaching and scant rehearsal. The fat twang of his guitar and the swaggering cant of his lyrics epitomize rock and roll; they are its universal calling card . . . and then some. In 1977, when the Voyager 1 and 2 space probes were hurtled into the uncharted heavens, they carried audio equipment designed to last a billion years and a gold-plated copper record containing, among other things, the music of Chuck Berry.

Berry tours tirelessly or holes up at his house on the grounds of Berry Park (his amusement park in Wentzville, Missouri), often chasing nosy press off the property. His recording activity has been slight, but a 1972 reissue of "Reelin' and Rockin' " did well. In 1979, he had an especially momentous year, with the release of the well-received *Rockit* album (his first LP in five years), an invitation to duck walk at the White House, and a 120-day prison term after being convicted of tax evasion by the Internal Revenue Service. A few waggish disk jockeys in the Midwest, loyal to the rock and roll Pied Piper, dug out a 1956 hit. The lyrics ran, "free that *brown-eyed handsome man*!"

The 1980s saw the good-lookin' idol dodging the curious while still making most of his legion concert dates, each night cossetting the neck of his scuffed red Gibson instrument in another tank town as he sawed off chords suffused with the esprit of guitar heroes Charlie Christian and Carl Hogan. But it was in 1987 that an idol of *his* heightened Chuck's profile once more, Rolling Stone Keith Richards turning Berry's sixtieth birthday into a tortuous concert tribute that director Taylor Hackford captured on film in *Hail! Hail! Rock n' Roll.* Like Berry's autobiography of the same year, the movie was a catch-as-catch-can perspective on a crusty control freak of the most freakish caliber. Chuck's seldom-seen bride of forty-odd years, Themetta, made an on-screen interview appearance so tantalizingly brief there was barely enough time for the camera crew to test the boom mike.

"We have a wonderful marriage," she began. "We're as much in love as when we were first married."

"You'd been married five years . . ." observed director Hackford, warming to their cinema-verité chat, when the bystanding Chuck Berry shouted "That's *enough*!" shutting down that particular portion of the documentary exercise.

Berry was more coy and convoluted but just as reticent in his memoirs, although he did affirm that he served three years of a ten-year sentence at Missouri's Algoa Reformatory for auto theft, explaining that he got released on October 18, 1947—his twenty-first birthday. Precisely how he celebrated that happy evening in 1947 goes unmentioned, although the details could spill out someday in much the same fashion that the specifics of his sixtieth birthday concert jam were disclosed. Relaxing with a bottle of bourbon one evening in 1988, Keith Richards let it slip that he had to dupe the difficult old rocker in order to wrest decent audio quality out of Berry's Gibson for the film soundtrack. Seems Chuck had insisted on using his ancient tour amplifier for the shows—even though the amp's tone resembled that of a ham radio during a hailstorm—so Keith secretly wired up far-superior hardware in the basement of St. Louis's Fox Theater and ran Chuck's ax through that.

"Worked like a charm," cackled Keith, "and unless Chuck himself gets wind of this conversation, he'll never be the wiser."

It took him almost two years to lose his vision, a slow-mounting blur culminating in utter blackness. Among the sights he had to bid good-bye to were his mother Aretha's lustrous ebony hair, which ran down to her rump; the sawmill in Greenville, Florida, where honorary second mother Mary Jane Charles (his father's burly first wife) pulled water-coated planks away from the screech of the saw blade; the seasonal hog slaughter, which began with a gun muzzle jammed inside the ear, the bark of a single bullet, a slit throat, and a splash of red on the grass; wizened old Mr. Wylie Pittman approximating boogie-woogie "pie-ano" in the Red Wing general store and café. One last tableau captured in his mind's eye was that of his four-year-old brother George kicking, gasping, and ultimately drowning in the rinse water of a No. 4 washtub that his mother used for take-in laundry.

Puny five-year-old Ray had tried to pull his brother out of the water, but he couldn't and ran screaming for his mother. A few months after the funeral, his eyes began to secrete mucus and had to be pried open each morning after being daubed with a damp cloth. By the time he was seven, glaucoma had taken its ultimate toll.

Ray Charles

1989

Ray Charles Robinson was born in Albany, Georgia, on September 23, 1930, the son of Bailey Robinson, a roaming railworker he never knew. Ray's mother and Mary Jane took the child across the border into Florida in the first months of his life. The first piano he ever touched was Wylie Pittman's upright. He learned to read Braille in a segregated state boarding school for the blind ("Imagine the nonsense of segregating *blind* kids!") in St. Augustine, Florida, and delighted in *Tom Sawyer* and *Huckleberry Finn.* In 1937, near the end of his first year in school, he had to have his festering right eye removed. In 1940, word reached the family that his father had died. That same year, Ray began riding a bicycle and was able to do so freely and without need of supervision.

While in St. Augustine, he learned to compose, writing music in Braille, and to play clarinet, trumpet, saxophone, and keyboards. One of the first songs he learned to sing by heart was Lil Green's "Romance in the Dark." At the age of twelve, he lost his virginity in the restroom of a nightclub in Tallahassee, after a stint singing and playing with a combo led by a man named Lawyer Smith. Ray was fifteen and away at school when he learned that his mother had died. Leaving school, he began playing with various dance bands in the state (including an otherwise all-white hillbilly band called the Florida Playboys). He recorded his first original song, "Found My Baby There," on a wire recorder. Another similar session in Tampa produced "Walkin' and Talkin'," "Wonderin' and Wonderin'," and "Why Did You Go?"

Bored, and longing for a drastic change in his lonely life, he took his entire savings of $600 and traveled until he reached Seattle, Washington. Commandeering the piano in local cabarets like the Rocking Chair, the 908 Club, the Washington Social Club, and the Black and Tan, he'd accompany himself in imitations of Nat "King" Cole. Eventually he formed a guitar, bass, and piano act called the McSon Trio, and he adopted Charles as his last name to prevent confusion with boxer Sugar Ray Robinson. At eighteen, he smoked his first jive and shot his first smack. In 1950, he had an illegitimate daughter with a woman named Louise. A block-jawed, square-shouldered youth with a well-knit physique and a bantering zest for seduction, he had a beguiling effect on women. They liked the brash confidence of his approach and the titillating mystery of his sunglassed glare.

Charles got to know Jack Lauderdale, owner of the small Swingtime label, from bumping into him constantly in the upstairs gambling parlor of the Rocking Chair, and in 1948, they cut a song Ray had written back in Florida, "Confession Blues." A year later, they went down to Los Angeles to do "Baby, Let Me Hold Your Hand"—Ray imitating the mellow, spooky delivery of blues balladeer Charles Brown—and it reached the Top 10 on the national rhythm and blues charts in 1951. He toured with blues singer Lowell Fulsom, who was doing well with "Everyday I Have the Blues," and became the pianist in Fulsom's band.

Ahmet Ertegun, Herb Abramson, and Jerry Wexler of Atlantic Records courted Charles when they heard the enormous potential in his brusque baritone, and they bought his contract from Swingtime in 1952 for $2,000. New York sessions in 1952 and 1953 resulted in the wry boogie-woogie of "Mess Around" and the vigorous, droll novelty single "It Should've Been Me." But Ray was to discover his own special direction down in New Orleans.

Wexler and Ertegun were in the Crescent City working with Big Joe Turner at producer Cosimo Matassa's studio when they bumped into Charles, who'd just gotten divorced after being married some sixteen months to a beautician named Eileen. He was hot to do some more recording, and they eventually got two exceptional sides: a Charles original, "Don't You Know," and a cover of the Guitar Slim sobber "Feelin' Sad."

The watershed session took place in an Atlanta radio station in 1954, shortly after he'd remarried, to a woman named Della, and attended the funeral of Mary Jane Charles. It was the first studio work since his formal signing with Atlantic, and it resulted in a rollicking gospel-blues exhortation written by Charles. Gone was the polite pose of a Nat Cole impersonator. In its place was a grinning growl that shot into falsetto flights. Backed by a seven-piece band, Charles's crowing bonhomie combined the splendid degeneracy of the chitlin circuit with the whooping sanctification of a church stomp. "I Got a Woman" rose to No. 2 on the national R&B survey in 1955 and created a new market for musical sacrilege. Ray promptly bought a new Cadillac, organized his own big band, and hired the Raelettes, a call-and-response female singing trio added to keep things nicely frenzied. The gritty gospel-blues hits kept on coming ("This Little Girl of Mine," "Blackjack," "Drown in My Own Tears," "Hallelujah I Love Her So," "Lonely Avenue," "Ain't That Love"), and Ray capped the decade with "What'd I Say," an unhinged ode to saturnalia that became a million-seller.

The word in the street was that Ray Charles was a flat-out genius, able to hammer out show tunes, country and western, Latin rhythms, jazz jumps, and old standards with stunning finesse and a corrosive, soul-piercing rasp. And he was no stranger to classic rhythm and blues ostentation, riding around in a new Caddy every year, then a DeSoto Firedome, and eventually a Wiener—a customized, four-door, four-seat number made from the bodies of two Chevrolet sedans! What the bloods on the corner weren't hip to was that the brother was easing into his twelfth straight year of heroin addiction.

After a final three-song session for Atlantic, which included the wrenching "I Believe to My Soul," he jumped to ABC Records in November of 1959. Raelette Margie Hendrix took him aside to tell she was pregnant by him, and he encouraged her to have the child, a boy she named Charles Wayne. Ray conquered the pop crowd in 1960 with "Georgia on My Mind" and "Hit the Road, Jack" in 1961. In 1962, he released *Modern Sounds of Country and Western Music* and triumphed again. A single off the album, "I Can't Stop Loving You," sold a staggering three million copies. "Busted" was his biggest song of 1963, and it became a physical reality in 1964 when federal agents cornered him at Boston's Logan Field and arrested him for possession of heroin and marijuana. Prior to his trial, he resolved to kick his habit, and he checked himself into St. Francis Hospital in Lynwood, California, going cold turkey in ninety-six hours. After a one-year postponement in sentencing, he was given five years' probation.

From the mid-1960s on, Ray Charles concentrated on a slightly slicker, at times rather bland blend of commercial pop and recycled Tin Pan Alley. Exceptions included "Crying Time" and "Let's Go Get Stoned" in 1966. His versions of "Yesterday," in 1967, and "Eleanor Rigby," in 1968, were distinctive blues-accented treatments of the Beatles' hits, an affectionate homage to the group that had played an intermission during one of Charles's early 1960s concerts in Hamburg, Germany.

In the late 1970s, Charles's twenty-year marriage to Della Robinson was dissolved. He blamed the breakup on his frequent absenteeism and two ugly paternity suits that he'd lost. Charles stated he'd never denied fathership or support; "I was just denying I was the Bank of America." He acknowledges nine offspring, three by Della and six out of wedlock. Charles has pronounced himself finished with marriage and says he prefers to confine his sexual activities to all-night trysts with select groups of three or four women.

He is just as individualistic in his professional life, recording with whomever he pleases (he did a country and western album featuring Willie Nelson, *Friendship,* in 1984), taking on any extramusical assignment that intrigues (including an acting role as a homeless man in an episode of TV's "St. Elsewhere"), and playing concerts for any audience he deigns to entertain. His most controversial step in the last category was a 1980 performance in South Africa that ignored the cultural boycott of the racist government. Maintaining that the crowd was integrated, Charles asserts he'd go back there again "if the right organization invited me. . . . It can't hurt anybody." He also refuses to sign boycott pledges, drawing a philosophical analogy between the embattled African nation and an incident he experienced in Alabama when the Ku Klux Klan threatened to bomb a benefit he played in support of Dr. Martin Luther King, Jr.

"That wasn't South Africa, that was good old mother America," rages the intractable Brother Ray. "So don't tell me about no damn apartheid, don't tell me what I support. It's ignorant."

He had confronted "the ugly strain of his own damnation" back in October of 1957. "I gave up rock and roll for the rock of ages! I used to be a glaring homosexual until God changed me!" Such were the homilies of Richard Penniman in the late 1970s as he recalled his sweeping transformation from gay dissolute into—well, he's never made that entirely clear. He did become an evangelist. The Soviet launching of Sputnik had been a sign that a change had to come; this became clearer in a dream in which Richard saw "the world burning up and the sky melting with the heat." These visions occurred while he was on a tour of Australia with rockabilly stars Eddie Cochran and Gene Vincent—although, just prior to the visions, there had been the little matter of a dicey plane trip during which the fusilage caught fire. Regardless, when Little Richard reached Sydney, he cast thousands of dollars worth of jewelry into the Tasman Sea to seal his pious pact with heaven. "If you want to live with the Lord, you can't rock and roll it, too," he sermonized. "God don't like it."

Whether this fickle Supreme Being frowned on rock and roll in the 1950s but only winked at homosexuality until the 1970s goes unrecorded. This much is plain: this particular man of the cloth is a cocky ex-heathen if ever there was one.

Little Richard

1989

How many clerics, however convulsionary, can also claim to be *Little Richard,* the most monomaniacal screaming meemie to ever roll a congregation like he rocked the league of nations!

Richard Wayne Penniman was born, according to his mother, Leva Mae, on Monday afternoon, December 5, 1932. He weighed ten pounds, was named for Leva Mae's dad, and spent his childhood living at 1540 Fifth Avenue in the Pleasant Hill section of Macon, Georgia. The family was devout Seventh Day Adventist, but his bricklayer father, Bud, set an iffy example for his brood of seven boys and five girls by hatching a little "scrum" (sourmash whiskey) on the sly. The squeaky-voiced Richard attempted to amble in the footsteps of his grandfather and two uncles, who were ministers, by warbling in a gospel group and playing piano at prayer meetings, but he soon strayed. He ran away from home as a boy to tapdance and sing in Doctor Hudson's Travelling Medicine Show. Returning home attired like a "sender," sporting loud zoot suits and *lah-de-dah* lingo, he quickly earned his father's outrage. This turned to contempt when Dad found out he was gay. The diminutive Richard was disowned and took refuge in a Macon dive called the Tick Tock Club; his protectors were the white proprietors, Enotris "Johnny" Johnson and wife Ann. The couple sent him to school, encouraged his interest in race music, and permitted him to perform at the Tick Tock Club—scandalizing his family.

At the age of sixteen, Richard answered a talent call for an amateur hour, run by "Daddy" Zenas Sears of WGST radio, at the Eighty-One Theater in Atlanta. He won, and the prize was a recording contract with RCA Victor. He cut eight undistinguished jump blues sides, but his pendulous pitch and slippery phrasing were in crude evidence on "Ain't Nothing Happening," "Get Rich Quick," and "I Brought It All on Myself." In the mid-1950s, he moved to Houston and was signed to Peacock Records by owner Don Robey. Backed by two instrumental vocal groups, the Deuces of Rhythm and the Tempo Toppers, Little Richard offered some breezy rhythm and blues vamping on entertaining tracks like "Rice, Red Beans and Turnip Greens." He also cut some material with the orchestra of Johnny Otis. The label did poorly with all his records, however, so Little Richard got canned.

Bloodied but unbowed, he took a job as a dishwasher in a Greyhound bus station, moonlighted as a professional drag queen, and mailed demos to Art Rupe of Specialty Records. Rupe admired the freaky abandon in the songs, and on September 14, 1955, Rupe took Little Richard into Cosimo Matassa's J&M Studios in New Orleans with producer Bumps Blackwell and an itching-to-go rhythm section. Everybody was eager, but nothing caught fire until Richard, according to Richard, became exasperated and broke into a filthy little aria he'd howl back in the kitchen of the Greyhound station. He tapped it with the nonsense pots-and-pans curseout he'd showered the cook with when he quit—"A-wop-bop-a-lu-bop-a-wop-bam-boom! Take 'em out!"

In that vociferous outcry was the germ of a new golden era in rock and roll. New Orleans writer Dorothy La Bostrie cleaned up the whole obscene yammer, and the tape rolled on "Tutti-Frutti," a crazy-brilliant rush of piano, drums, saxophones, guitars, with Little Richard leading the way with grandiloquent glee. The words, when you could make them out over the riotous discord of "*Whoooooo*'s" and barnyard calls, concerned a gal, named Daisy, who had the singer—if not the world—crazy. One of the biggest and most sound-shaping explosions in the history of rock and roll, this song created a mayhem that was irresistible. "Tutti-Frutti" sold to black and white alike when released in 1955. And it was the first of a string of seven million-selling records of similar breakneck tempo: "Long Tall Sally," "Rip It Up," "Lucille," "Jenny, Jenny," "Keep a Knockin'," and "Good Golly, Miss Molly."

Torrents of sexual hoopla and frenzy, whipped up by an effeminate, pixilated black man with a double-dip pompadour and a $1,000-a-day drug habit, these singles were an unbridled semaphore to the straight music community that rock and roll was staging a new offensive and taking no prisoners. That Little Richard chose to quit the battlefield with "Good Golly, Miss Molly" mattered little. The scorched-earth policies he advocated continued unabated.

Settling down to life as a Bible student at Oakwood College in Huntsville, Alabama, he raged against what he had wrought, but he did it with such fervor and facility that it came off as a different side of the same coin: "I'm quittin' show business; I want to go straight. / I'm going to serve my Lord, before it's too late."

Of course, he never really packed it in. There were constant furtive comebacks under a gospel cloak, and "I Don't Know What You've Got but It's Got Me" satisfied his latent rock and roll urges. A contract with Reprise in the early 1970s produced three often-rewarding albums: *The Rill Thing, King of Rock and Roll,* and *Second*

Coming. And the Reverend Little Richard Penniman clambered in and out of the lion-infested rock and roll arena throughout the 1980s, recording and playing suspiciously secular-sounding songs like "Great Gosh A'mighty! (It's a Matter of Time)," while appearing as a piano-pummeling scamp in a string of high-spirited films like *Down and Out in Beverly Hills.* And then there have been his galloping monologues during various Grammy Awards ceremonies, each a more untamed recitation of his credentials for peerless pop trophyhood. His immortal soul may be in Limbo but Little Richard's heart is still in rock and roll.

In July of 1954, two historic, disparate, and highly controversial lines of demarcation were being drawn. One was political in nature: agreements reached in Geneva provided for a demilitarized zone between North and South Vietnam—the DMZ. The opposing sides would withdraw pending unification elections. Such elections were never held, and a monumental global trauma had taken root.

Regardless, a momentous cultural schism was in the works. The long rehearsals of two part-time Tennessee-based musicians—Scotty Moore and Bill Black—and local truckdriver/singer Elvis Presley were culminating in a trial-and-error taping session at the Memphis Recording Service studio at 706 Union Avenue. During a break, young Elvis brashly toyed with a rural blues song by Arthur "Big Boy" Crudup called "That's All Right," and his cohorts joined in. The rough-hewn syncopation of their outburst was so peculiar that the studio proprietor, Sam Phillips, interrupted the trio to ask, "What are you doing?" No one had an adequate answer for him—beyond the music itself—so they revved up again while Phillips rolled the tape. When Moore, the lead guitarist, heard the playback, he was shocked; he told bassist Bill Black that he feared the racially ambiguous sound slamming out of the loudspeak-

Elvis Presley

1984

ers would spark local outrage in the segregated city of 300,000 and possibly generate enough personal denunciation to drive the group out of town. Sam Phillips's reaction was well documented: he prevailed upon WHBQ disc jockey Dewey Phillips (no relation) to spin a pressed single of the song, backed by an agitated version of the bluegrass standard, "Blue Moon of Kentucky," on his "Red Hot and Blue" rhythm and blues program. On Wednesday, July 7, 1954, Dewey aired "That's All Right" and the WHBQ switchboard was deluged with calls demanding replays and clarification. The largely white audience was accustomed, of course, to hearing black artists on the show, and even some white performers adapting the current black fare to their own discreet idioms. But the lean, shiversome energy of "That's All Right" was unnerving in its newness, and it induced a sense of disorientation verging on vertigo. Was the singer black or white? Was his music blues? rhythm and blues? the resurrection of some sort of prehistoric country pop? The controversy stemmed solely from the deep visceral confusion gripping the listeners, the sensation that a cocky? criminal?—no, *cancerous*—hybrid had arisen to decimate their drowsy, strictly delineated existences. Their instincts derived not from any syllable of the song's lyrics but from the threatening *feeling* pouring from the singer, the sensual emotion addressing the galloping beat.

Some music critics and social observers would later see the record and its reception as the birth of rockabilly—that frenetic fusion of white hillbilly blues with country and western brio—or even of rock and roll itself. It was also considered the death knell of southern segregation and the seed of an agonized orgy of national self-hatred and cultural shame. Yes, no, maybe, perhaps. Most assuredly, it was the belated birth of Elvis Presley, the pale, shy, pimpled poor-boy crooner who had retreated to a Memphis movie house on the Wednesday night the song broke rather than face the possible embarrassment of its being mocked in the marketplace.

Legend has it that Elvis made his first record—a cover of two Ink Spots' ballads, "My Happiness" and "That's When Your Heartaches Begin"—at the Sun studio on Union Avenue in Memphis as a birthday present for his mother. That's highly unlikely; the session took place in the late summer or early autumn of 1953, long after Gladys Presley's April birth date. More probably, this four-buck recording experiment reflected a deeply rooted longing on Elvis's part. At the age of ten, he took second prize in a talent contest at the Mississippi-Alabama Fair and Dairy Show, singing the corn-pone boy-and-his-dog ditty, "Old Shep." On his next birthday, his father, Vernon, gave him an acoustic guitar. Other talent shows would follow, and with them a reputation that flowered at L. C. Hume High School in Memphis. Off-stage, his social skills were few, yet he wooed and briefly won his first (and some say his only true) love, a girl in his junior English class named Dixie Lock. His musical skills were fed not from woodshedding sessions with schoolboy chums, but from nocturnal meanderings down along Beale Street, storied main drag for the black denizens of the blues. After graduation, Elvis slipped down there to spend his $1.25-an-hour salary as a driver and warehouseman at the Crown Electric Company, the money going mostly for race records and for the peacock apparel to be had at Lansky Brothers, clothiers to Beale Street's top honkers and shouters. At night, he listened to WDIA, a flagship blues station of the South that featured such flamboyant black disk jockeys as Rufus Thomas and B. B. King (both of whom also sang live on the air).

These interests and involvements eventually led Elvis back to the Sun studios. Sam Phillips had summoned him for a formal audition as a balladeer after recalling a tape of the Ink Spots session, which an engineer had had the curious prescience to make. (In those days, such vanity recordings were usually cut directly onto an acetate disk, with no copies kept.) Phillips had run across an impressive demo by an anonymous black kid, who'd turned in a stunning performance on a love song entitled "Without You." Unable to locate the song's originator, and sensing that the material had commercial potential beyond the black audience he usually catered to, the producer was eager to find a young white singer who could duplicate the nameless performer's work.

Elvis had jumped at Phillips's invitation and arrived immediately after his phone call, boasting that he could sing anything. He couldn't. The unique vocal facility demonstrated on the nuance-laden "Without You" demo was beyond the green Elvis's grasp, and he could hardly match, much less rival, the black singer's style. In a show of vulnerability unmatched in his entire career, Elvis burst into tears after repeated, deteriorating attempts, and he began denouncing his unknown opponent. "I hate him!" he shrieked. "I hate him! I hate him!"

If Elvis hadn't had uncommon reserves still in store in the tritely tragic aftermath of the "Without You" episode, he might have remained a truckdriver. But he did, and he told a bored Phillips that he could *still* sing anything—any damned thing at all. Then *do it* fella, he was dared, and something inside the Tupelo shitkicker exploded. Stepping up to the microphone once more, he unleashed a blistering barrage composed of every sound he held in his musical memory bank, a thorny torrent of choirboy couplets, Beale Street blues snarls, rude hunks of the Hit Parade and the Grand Ole Opry. It wasn't a song, it wasn't a medley, it wasn't an audition. It was a force of nature. In that instant, a phantom leapt out of the mouth of Elvis Presley and assumed proportions that easily eclipsed conventional alter-ego status. In the decades that followed, Sam Phillips, the Grand Ole Opry, WSM's Louisiana Hayride, RCA Records, Las Vegas, Colonel Parker, Steve Allen, Tommy and Jimmy Dorsey, Ed Sullivan, Hollywood, the White House, and the uncounted multimillions who were dumbstruck by his talent all tried to wrestle some sense of self-recognition out of the gleaming ghost looming before them. For the rest of Presley's short life, the frustrated, fascinated outside world would strain to locate some trace of themselves in this wraith's eyes. They couldn't. But none would fight more expectantly, more furiously, than Elvis for a closer look. And Elvis himself was foiled, utterly, in the end.

Elvis Aaron Presley came into the world on January 8, 1935, in Tupelo, Mississippi; his twin, Jesse Garon, was born dead. His father and mother were of sharecropper stock, but they left the land behind before the twins' birth to labor as journeyman truckdriver and sewing-machine operator, respectively. They were always just a hope away from the poorhouse, drifting on and off the relief rolls, relocating when the promise of better wages beckoned. They made several more moves (usually under cover of darkness), after giving up the two-room shack Elvis had been born in, finally renting rooms above a rabbi in a house at 462 Alabama Street, Memphis.

In retrospect, the facts attending Elvis Presley's instant fame seem feeble. Elvis, Scotty, and Bill toured the South and Southwest during 1954 and 1955 on the strength of their Sun singles, among them a cover of Roy Brown's "Good Rockin' Tonight," as well as "Milkcow Blues Boogie" and "Baby, Let's Play House." In concert, well-bred southern belles ripped Elvis's clothes from his supple body; one young lady appeared on TV's "I've Got a Secret" with a pair of pants that Elvis had split in an ecstatic recording session. He purchased a pink Ford and a pink Cadillac.

In 1955, Presley met "Colonel" Tom Parker (née Andreas van Kuijk, an illegal Dutch alien), the former manager of country and western singers Eddy Arnold and Hank Snow. Parker shrewdly eased Sun-affiliated manager Bob Neal out of the picture by telling Elvis's mother that Neal was working the lad too hard. The same year, Parker orchestrated the Presley contract with RCA. Elvis went into RCA's Nashville studios on January 10, 1956, to cut "Heartbreak Hotel." Weeks later, it was at the top of the national charts. Steve Allen booked Elvis on his Sunday evening TV variety show, dressing him in tails and having him sing "Hound Dog" to a basset hound perched on a pedestal. Ed Sullivan showcased him on the tube—but from the waist up, to avoid scandalizing home viewers with Elvis's goading crotch and heaving hips.

The army drafted Elvis in December 1957. While overseas, he maintained a close relationship with a fourteen-year-old named Priscilla Beaulieu, later to become his bride; he also corralled chorus girls from a Paris nightclub for wild parties. When his mother died, he was disconsolate, crying at the funeral, "Oh God, everything I have is gone!" During his two-year stint in Europe, he enjoyed another seven chart-toppers. His subsequent hits were increasingly tied to what would be a string of thirty-one movies in which he starred, each of them doing handsomely at the box office. He and his entourage—a group dubbed the Memphis Mafia—were thrown out of some of the country's best hotels for extreme rowdiness. His cronies procured women for perverse parties in a Bel Air mansion, occasions during which the singer threw a pool cue at one woman and dragged another across a table and through several rooms by her hair. After seven years away from the concert stage, Elvis did a 1968 Christmas special for ABC-TV, an electrifying portion of which was before a live audience, with Elvis looking lean and limber in black leather.

Elvis loved karate. He gorged himself on gooey junk food. He dated Tuesday Weld and Natalie Wood. He never granted a single in-depth interview. He named his Convair 880 jet after his daughter, Lisa Marie. He got fat. He sold some 300 million records worldwide by the late 1970s. He wrote none of his songs. He had a bad temper. He once fired a gun at a television during a performance by singer Robert Goulet. He became a virtual recluse in Graceland, his mansion in Memphis. He memorized all of James Dean's dialogue in

Rebel Without a Cause and cornered the film's director to recite it. He had bouts of dependence on pharmaceutical drugs. He was appointed an honorary narcotics agent for an antidrug campaign by President Nixon. He was briefly a disciple of Yogi Paramahansa Yogananda. He got fatter.

At 2:30 P.M. on Tuesday, August 16, 1977, Elvis was found in his blue pajamas, passed out in an upstairs bathroom at Graceland. He'd been seated on the toilet, thumbing through a book entitled *The Scientific Search for the Face of Jesus.* He was rushed to Baptist Memorial Hospital in Memphis, and, an hour after he was found, Elvis was dead of heart failure. He was still wearing his blue pajamas. A hospital employee told reporters, "Elvis had the arteries of an eighty-year-old man. His body was just worn out." Most called it an accidental demise, but stepbrother David Stanley deemed it suicide. Close friends later conceded Colonel Parker's dark manipulations of Elvis could have edged the thwarted star into despair. The *Memphis Press Scimitar* hit the streets the day of his funeral with the banner headline "A Lonely Life Ends on Elvis Presley Boulevard." Air National Guardsmen formed his final honor guard. Even the Soviet Union sent a floral wreath. His fans adored him beyond the end. Sadly, because of all the smarmy, nonmusical merchandizing his own estate has authorized since his passing, Elvis Presley is everywhere in evidence but nowhere in substance.

The opinions of Elvis grow petty with time. He was a man's man. A mama's boy. A native genius of the spirit. A tentative step above white trash. A vain hick. A valiant hero. The maker of some of the finest gospel and spiritual records ever released. A sacrilegious church truant. A loyal friend. A loutish bully. An archetypal southern gentleman. A lowliving letch. A princely appreciator of his fans. A pasty-faced pillhead. The rock voice without peer. The rock enigma without equal. The King.

One thing is certain. The sudden appearance of Elvis Presley on the scene was nothing less than the full-blown arrival of modern rock and roll. By virtue of the white-hot urgency of that arrival, Elvis Presley became the "Mystery Train" he sang about in one of his early Sun sessions, an unmarked locomotive rocketing down a jet-black track, piloted by a specter, making only unscheduled stops. It was not the kind of train that brought things back.

The statement was unequivocal: "Without Elvis, none of us could have made it." Buddy Holly's words were full of characteristically open-hearted gratitude for the fellow who made rock and roll a nearly legitimate profession for a boy to try his hand at. Elvis Presley helped many a skinny high school hayseed dream big dreams and encouraged them to pick up guitars and put a hard edge on the country and western dance music that whistled out of the battered cathedral radio in the general store. In fact, the guitar had not been an especially popular instrument before Elvis transformed it into a symbol of masculine verve and power, sending sales of both acoustic and electric models up into the stratosphere.

As a boy growing up in west Texas, Holly would have had considerable exposure to the country dance rhythms so popular to the region—popular, that is, with the lower and lower-middle classes who would concede their interest in the music and who felt no shame about taking wife, girlfriend, and kin to the live "jamboree" concerts held on Saturday nights from the 1930s onward in small towns throughout the area. Unlike in Mississippi, where country music enjoyed a sit-down-and-pay-attention tradition, west Texans associated the crackling strum of a tenor banjo and the lusty skip of a fiddle

Buddy Holly

1984

with a well-waxed dance floor. Thanks to Bob Wills—who had had to bully the Grand Ole Opry into allowing his drummer onstage in 1945!—and other broad-shouldered country swing bandleaders, a Texas man who couldn't execute at least a confident two-step was something less than he oughta be, and unlike the stiff-necked custodians of the Opry, the dancer liked some assertive slapbass *and* snare drums to fill in the blanks.

What Holly would have known little of were the hoodang honky-tonks and randy rites of the black blues. Lubbock, Texas, was the very buckle of the blue-eyed Bible Belt. It was a community of innumerable churches and zero barrooms. No liquor was served or sold inside the town line. Blacks and Chicanos were seldom seen, never heard. There was plenty of hell-raising and mischief available, but it was the sort that one had to sally out through the screen door and go a-hunting for—usually along the state roads beyond the city limits.

That even in manhood a first-rate rock and roller like Buddy Holly would never go on such excursions in the service of his art says something quietly compelling about his own vision and the brief, poignant passage it prepared him for. His intensely innovative music (he was the first to use strings and vocal double-tracking, and he popularized the now-standard rock lineup of two guitars, bass, drums) was more apt to be punctuated by cheerful handclaps and tinkling cymbals than the raucous pansexual percussion of his iconoclastic, noncomposing hero. An unimposing beanpole, the soft-spoken, bespectacled Holly was thankful to Elvis for giving him the stubborn pride to keep his horn-rims on when he plunked his Stratocaster at the sock hop—Buddy was unaware that Elvis had discarded his own eyeglasses for his first amateur stage appearance. Holly thanked him for giving him the moxie to throw his towhead back and sing his untempered heart out, even though his best and boldest songs were as pristine, sweet-natured, and unjadedly childlike as Elvis's were taunting, worldly, and erotic. Holly thanked Elvis for galvanizing him with the notion that the living musical heritage of the common people was a thing of wonder, capable of being augmented by the red-blooded pulse of his own being. Buddy Holly celebrated time-honored American values, speaking with a sober honesty to the trusting, impatient heart and the risks it takes. Elvis Presley questioned time-withered American values that conspired to curb his urges and prematurely sate his wants. Only in rock and roll could a man such as Buddy Holly see a man such as Elvis Presley as his mirror image—and only through Buddy Holly's eyes.

He was born Charles Hardin Holley on September 7, 1936, the third son of Lawrence and Ella Holley. Mr. Holley was a farmboy out of northeastern Texas who had met his wife while he was working as a short-order cook. They married and moved to Lubbock in the mid-1920s, when west Texas began to experience an economic boom occasioned by the advent of cotton farming. The Holleys were a highly musical brood; Buddy's eldest brother, Larry, was proficient on violin and guitar, while his brother Travis played accordion, piano, and guitar. And sister Pat liked to sing along with her mother when the boys held forth at family get-togethers. Buddy's musical debut was something of a gentle hoax; his mother had insisted that his brothers take five-year-old Buddy along with them to a talent contest they'd entered in the nearby town of County Line. They greased the strings of his toy fiddle so he couldn't sour their sound and used him as a prop. But it was Buddy who took home a $5 prize for singing a number his mom taught him, "Down the River of Memories."

After brief passes at piano and steel guitar lessons, Buddy settled on straight acoustic guitar and began to teach himself Hank Williams songs like "Lovesick Blues." By the early 1950s, he had formed a country-oriented combo called the Western and Bop Band with school friends Bob Montgomery and Larry Welborn. The group was good enough to land a half-hour Sunday afternoon segment on local radio station KDAV. In 1956, Buddy and Bob, as the act was known on KDAV, replaced Welborn with Don Guess and the backup band became the Three Tunes. That year, Buddy was signed to Decca Records and lost the "e" in his name because of a misspelling in the contract. Holly's first release was a straight country outing, "Blue Days, Blue Nights." The Decca deal was uneventful but for another country song Buddy issued, a tune called "That'll Be the Day."

Back in Lubbock, Buddy and drummer Jerry Allison crossed over into rock and roll after opening for Elvis Presley at the Lubbock Youth Center. The next day, Holly talked Elvis into accompanying him to Lubbock High to meet some of his friends and teachers. Forming the Crickets (Joe Mauldin on bass, Jerry Allison on drums, Niki Sullivan on guitar), Buddy recut "That'll Be the

Day" with a rock edge, and it got picked up by the New York–based Coral-Brunswick label, which made it a Top 5 hit in 1957.

Buddy was unfazed by the negativity and fatalistic gaiety in the world around him, and the hit records that he would create both with the Crickets and solo in the next two years had a blushing tenderness and a rollicking brand of goodwill unlike any rock has enjoyed before or since. "Peggy Sue," "Maybe Baby," "Oh Boy!" "Rave On," "Think It Over," "Heartbeat"—each was sung with a straightforward zeal that never wavered and a bright outlook that never turned mawkish or hackneyed.

"Peggy Sue," Holly's ode to the eternal adolescent crush and the marvelous sense of belonging it provides, is an astonishing case in point. His trademark staggered-hiccup vocals alternate with a dignified expression of fondness and some remarkably uncloying baby-talk and nasal cooing, a boy wondering what it sounds like to be a man, amused he's no longer a child, happiest living in the present. The metallic vibrato rhythm guitar break, a cold shower of spunky electricity, defines in one neat downpour what it feels like to be the leader of a teenage garage band, the peek-a-boo might of your emerging personality ricocheting off concrete walls, the entire neighborhood at your feet.

Holly himself was unchanged by the acclaim that touring and recording brought him, usually appearing onstage attired like an accountant in a neat black suit or a tweed blazer, a bowtie, his horn-rims gleaming in the footlights. Holly was too sure and purposeful to ever be mistaken for a wimp, and his anachronistic appearance became so popular that fans began sporting horn-rims fitted with ordinary glass. Offstage, he rarely drank. His forays into the wild side of paradise were occasional back-of-the-bus crapshoots with roustabout Chuck Berry. But he increasingly became victimized by the depth of his trusting nature. After his marriage in the summer of 1958 to Maria Elena Santiago, a Puerto Rican girl from New York, he began to scrutinize his business agreements of the recent past. At the urging of a knowledgeable, suspicious Elena, he confronted manager Norman Petty about the presence of Petty's name in the writing credits of several songs and the purportedly slipshod way in which Petty promoted both the group and Holly, for whom he held separate contracts. Sick at heart, Holly left the Crickets, whom Petty convinced to stay behind in Texas, and moved with his wife to New York's Greenwich Village. Money was tight, so he took a new group, consisting of guitarist Tommy

Allsup, drummer Charlie Bunch, and green young bassist Waylon Jennings, on the road to raise seed money for his fledgling publishing company.

In the midst of a bus tour in the winter of 1959, twenty-two-year-old Holly chartered a private plane with costars the Big Bopper (J. P. Richardson) and Ritchie Valens in order to buy some time to get his laundry done before the next gig. The small Beechcraft Bonanza crashed shortly after 2:00 A.M. on February 3, disintegrating in a field nine miles from Iowa's Mason City Airport, killing all on board. Singer Don McLean immortalized the tragedy in his 1972 "American Pie" as "the day the music died." It was more accurately the death of innocence for rock and roll.

Nobody in Ferriday, Louisiana, had ever seen the mad dog that lingered outside the window of Elmo and Mamie Lewis's frame house on the morning Jerry Lee was born, and that cur howled like one of Satan's prize hounds at the moment the babe's first cries were heard.

Old-time Louisiana stock will tell you that it's bad business to allow children out of the state before they come of age. There's something otherworldly about Louisiana air—moist, still, so dense an infant has to swallow it like porridge to get it down. Babies get dependent on that air, come to need it like mother's milk. An unripe intellect bred on the even heavier oxygen found upwind of New Orleans, in the low-lying cotton country of Concordia County, that's an especially delicate case. Louisiana offspring can't be weaned in the thin atmosphere found in the rest of the South. The foolhardy, those rash enough to move a child, can expect beastly consequences not unlike the bends. Even a *medical* doctor will advise parents to proceed with extreme caution. Thoroughly confounded by the phenomenon, they nonetheless affirm that a sudden change of air can shrivel a child's brain stem. Still, even the wisest parents sometimes fail to take heed, and their offspring pay the price.

In order for the stricken to get proper

Jerry Lee Lewis

1990

care, they must be brought to gris-gris men out in the Cajun swamp basins. The gris-gris will tell you the baleful condition is the hex of Baron Samedi, Guardian of the Graveyards. It leaves a victim ravaged. The worst victims are those whose birth is marked by a bad sign.

By the fruits of their malady shall ye know them.

One muggy, starless night in November 1976, Robert Loyd, security guard at Graceland, Elvis Presley's mansion, was forced to confront one of the stricken. He came by automobile, a brand-new Lincoln Continental with an evil gleam. The Lincoln ripped up the gravel driveway and planted a cold chrome kiss on the iron quarter and eighth notes soldered to the webbed front gate. "I wanna see Elvis!" hollered the curly blond hooligan at the wheel. "You just tell him the Killer's here! Git on that damn house phone and call him! Who the hell does that sonofabitch think he is? Doesn't wanna be disturbed! He ain't no damn better'n anybody else!"

He was too drunk to ball, as the saying goes, but the .38 derringer in Jerry Lee Lewis's unsteady grip spoke louder than words, and Loyd felt obliged to do as he was told. Word came back from the inner sanctum to call the cops. The King would not receive the Killer. Officer B. J. Kirkpatrick of the Memphis police force led the flying wedge of patrol cars that converged on the scene. He disarmed the Killer and escorted him back to the station house as Jerry Lee vowed, "I'll have your fucking job, boy!"

But Jerry Lee's own profession was clearly keeping his hands too full for any sort of moonlighting. He was a fallen evangelist of the rock and roll persuasion, a rambling, gambling shill for the lead Horseman of the Apocalypse. Like Buddy Holly, Jerry Lee owed a debt. Elvis had paved the way at Sun Records for the rockabilly machinations of Lewis's first hit, "Whole Lot of Shakin' Going On." Their close proximity in the early days, followed by the high road handed Elvis and the dank crawlspace accorded Jerry Lee, had slowly pushed an already fevered brain into acute inflammation. Even on the fabled afternoon they'd gotten along best—December 4, 1956—when he, Elvis, Carl "Blue Suede Shoes" Perkins, and Johnny Cash crowded around the piano in the Sun studios for a little joviality on "Keeper of the Key" and "Just a Little Walk with Jesus," Jerry Lee found himself well-nigh asphyxiated, his lungs aching. Elvis seemed to draw every breath of air from the room.

Buddy Holly had willingly chosen to bask in the King's reflected glow, but Jerry Lee coveted both the throne and the light that shone down upon it. "I never considered myself the greatest," he hissed, "but I'm the best."

Jerry grew up an untamable rascal who liked to turn church hymns into saloon harangues, but the family thought he might settle down some after he got married. In his sixteenth year (he lied that he was twenty-one), Jerry Lee plighted his troth to comely seventeen-year-old Dorothy Barton, daughter of a Pentecostal preacher. For a brief spell, Jerry Lee even took to preaching himself at the Church of God on Mississippi Avenue in Ferriday. But by 1953, the whole association was history, Dorothy back home, the marriage in the wind, the Devil on the wing.

From then on, you'd find Jerry Lee down on Highway 61 outside of Natchez, Mississippi, playing piano, winking at the barmaid, and breathing the fumes of bad whiskey and worse perfume in the Dixie Club. Although some nights he was a latecomer: sometimes he got sidetracked at Nellie Jackson's cathouse on North Rankin Street.

His reputation for rocking began to grow, and Lewis wrangled a twenty-minute radio spot on WNAT radio. Jerry Lee got himself hitched again in the summer of 1953 to Jane Mitcham, another eye-catching teen queen, and the sin of bigamy besmirched his seventeen-year-old soul. In 1954, they had a fair-haired son, Jerry Lee, Jr. In 1955, Jane gave Jerry Lee a dark-haired lad, Ronnie Guy. Jerry Lee declined to call this child his own, and he issued Jane her walking papers. In December 1957, Lewis secretly married thirteen-year-old Myra Brown. Double bigamy. At this point, Jerry was a full-fledged star with a catalog of million-sellers: "Whole Lot of Shakin' Going On," "Great Balls of Fire," "Breathless," "High School Confidential." Jerry Lee made the mistake of taking Myra with him for his 1958 tour of England. The British press quickly tired of the lame line about Myra being Jerry Lee's sister, and the public outcry about his robbing the cradle pushed him into exile most foul.

Reduced to playing county fairs and the gin mill grind, he adopted Benzedrine and bourbon as his favorite repast. In 1962, his three-year-old son by Myra, Steve Allen Lewis, drowned in the family pool. In 1970, Myra left Jerry Lee after she caught him cheating on her. In their thirteen years together, she claimed she'd spent only three evenings alone with him, but they were memorable ones: "He usually arrived unannounced in the middle of the night, wanting a hot meal and hot sex." And he was not averse to cuffing and thumping his wife into submission.

In October 1971, Jerry Lee wed Jaren Elizabeth Gunn Pate, twenty-nine, of Memphis. They separated two weeks later. In November 1973, his beloved son, Jerry Lee, Jr., was killed in an auto accident. That's when Jerry Lee's rock and roll life-style really accelerated. In September 1976, he shot his bassist, Butch Owens, square in the belly with a .357 Magnum, after beckoning him to "look down the barrel of this." A few months later, Lewis's Rolls Royce somersaulted on a lonely road near Collierville, Tennessee. Hot on the heels of his pistol-packing social call to Elvis, Jerry Lee stopped into a Memphis hospital to give up his gall bladder and let doctors have a gander at his collapsed right lung and his pleurisy; the doctors also probed his lower back, which was still paining him from the tumble in the Rolls.

In 1979, an Australian tour was canceled after Jerry Lee picked a fight onstage with a fan, suffering fractured ribs in the fracas. In February of that year, the Internal Revenue Service confiscated his numerous flashy cars—for the second time—for nonpayment of taxes, busting him in the process for possession of cocaine and marijuana. A month later, Jerry Lee ran a leased white Corvette, brand-new and with plenty of horsepower, into a ditch in DeSoto County, Mississippi. To close out the year, he sued Jaren, his long-estranged spouse, for divorce. She countersued, charging him with "cruel and inhuman treatment, adultery, habitual drunkenness, and habitual use of drugs." One might ruminate as to what her allegations would have been had they stayed together for say, *three* weeks. She later drowned, not long before the final divorce settlement.

The man kept on making records, many of them pretty incendiary. And he outlasted Elvis—although he almost succumbed owing to a ruptured appendix in the early 1980s. A fifth wife, the former Shawn Stevens, was less lucky. She perished in 1983 at the age of twenty-five from what a Mississippi grand jury determined to be a self-inflicted overdose of methadone pills. While the grand jury cleared Jerry Lee of any wrongdoing—without having questioned him directly—others had misgivings. Mortician Danny Phillips, for one, was perplexed. The body was bruised; there was blood under the fingernails. In February 1984, a rather glassy-eyed Jerry Lee told

ABC News that he'd never hit a woman in his life. In April 1984, he married Kerrie Lynn McCarver.

But his new spouse had numerous rivals for her man's affections, among them the drug Demerol, an addictive painkiller that became a powerful preoccupation. He took to shooting it into his arms and legs, soon feeling nothing of any sort as he hotfooted it to every disreputable pharmacy in the deep South in search of refills. In 1986, Kerrie Lewis filed for divorce. "Finally got it through to her," Jerry Lee groused. "When you gotta go, you gotta go." And yet a tinge akin to pain had somehow delved deep enough to seize his psychic gizzard. He tumbled from a Nashville detox center to the more decorous Betty Ford Center—but he disdained the latter facility as a mere finishing school for lightweight lowlifes on the mend, and departed after a full four hours.

Jerry Lee and Kerrie reconciled in 1987, his twenty-four-year-old missus giving birth to a six-pound, three-ounce Jerry Lee Lewis III by cesarean section in a Memphis hospital. For a man who had earlier disputed the child's paternity, the papa seemed pleased.

The winter of 1988 brought fresh charges and challenges, chief among them a Chapter 7 filing by Jerry Lee for personal bankruptcy in which the Killer listed more than $3 million in debts. Testy creditors among the twenty-two listed in court papers included the Internal Revenue Service (due $2 million) and the Whiskey River Club of Spencer, Oklahoma. Lewis made it known that he had received $500,000 for rights to a film of his life—namely *Great Balls of Fire!* starring Dennis Quaid—and that he had spent the entire windfall on Demerol. The release of the movie stirred small currents of adulation from a generation too young to have either yearned for Jerry Lee's greatest hits or yielded him another bride. He coached these green recruits by joshing about his secret lecherous intentions toward nubile Lisa Marie Presley, and then counseled that "Jerry Lee Lewis is not an all-American hero story." He concluded his comments to modern youth with a "Just Say Maybe" homily on the subject of Demerol: "I wouldn't take a shot for a million dollars in cash money—and that's a damn lie."

Jerry Lee Lewis attributes his staying power to a diet of malted milk, shrimp, Scotch (he lent "It Was The Whiskey Talkin' [Not Me]" to the *Dick Tracy* soundtrack)—and "almighty rock and roll." This was once the black man's euphemism for sex, sinful magic, and moderation-scorning music; now it's a modest description of one Louisiana profligate's waking hours on this planet.

Sam Cooke 1984

He didn't like to be denied, and he took personally any attempts by anyone to do so. The son of a Baptist minister, his willful nature acquired an almost religious intensity once he achieved recognition as a singer. In June of 1964, he created a minor sensation in New York City by spending $10,000 of his own money to erect a 20-by-100-foot billboard in Times Square emblazoned with the question, "Who's the biggest Cook in Town?"

Several days later, the sign was enlarged and a 45-foot, 1,500-pound photograph added, along with a new message: "Sam's the biggest Cooke in town." And so he was, his smooth features and rakish crescent smile beaming down on the Great White Way—much to the embarrassment of his press agent, who had to explain the motives behind the insolent display when Cooke would not. "In short," the agent told the *New York Times*, "he's bothered that he hasn't been able to make it big in a New York night spot and wants people to know he's here."

Cooke was scheduled to open at the Copacabana. This splashy saloon had given him a cool reception four years earlier, despite the fact that he'd been at the top of the charts with the rhythm and blues record "Chain Gang," whose huff-and-puff male chorus and gandydancer sound effects strained the bounds of novel artificiality. The experience left the edgy, calculating former gospel singer with a permanent grudge against New York and its leading nightclub. The Times Square billboard announced the dimensions of that enmity.

Born in Chicago on January 22, 1931, he pleased his demanding father with his featured-performer status in the church choir as well as his presence in a family quartet called the Singing Children. While attending Wendell Phillips High School, he became interested in the local gospel circuit and hooked up with the house group at the Highway Baptist Church, the Highway QCs. They were managed by R. B. Robinson, baritone in the Soul Stirrers (the group generally regarded as having conceived the modern quartet sound). In 1951, Cooke replaced renowned tenor Rebert H. Harris as the lead singer of the Soul Stirrers and suddenly found himself with a sizable national following. Boasting a crisp, sonorous voice as unblemished as his complexion, and an assiduously controlled delivery, he won over diehard gospel fans accustomed to the growly vocal vaulting of his contemporaries. He also attracted a young audience, his matinee idol looks, suave demeanor, and flirtatious melismatic crooning making him a sepia Sinatra; according to gospel historian Tony Heilbut, Cooke was "the greatest sex symbol in gospel history." Signed to the Specialty label (whose name indicated their exclusive interest in black performers, especially gospel acts), the Soul Stirrers had a prosperous seven years behind Cooke's charisma. Art Rupe, Specialty's white owner, took umbrage, however, when Cooke told him that he wanted to test the waters in the R&B market; Rupe saw Cooke's interest in "worldly" music as the seeds of artistic suicide.

After a series of arguments with Cooke and his manager, J. W. Alexander, Rupe relented and took Sam into the studio with some rhythm and blues and pop material, but he resisted releasing any of it. A compromise was worked out in which the pop song "Lovable" was issued under the pseudonym of Dale Cooke. When Cooke's pop ambitions failed to abate, Rupe sold the rights to Sam's pop career to Specialty producer Bumps Blackwell, who departed to start Keen Records. Blackwell's first release was Sam Cooke's "You Send Me," a breathy pop ballad written by L. C. Cooke, Sam's brother. It sold 1.7 million copies in 1957 and reached the No. 1 spot on the R&B charts. Despite such massive sales, and even though it handily outsold Teresa Brewer's cover version, it did not appear on the mainstream pop charts; such were the tyrannies of the white-dominated pop world. Specialty responded to "You Send Me" by rush-releasing one of its shelved Cooke R&B tracks, "I'll Come Running Back to You," which made the Top 10 on the R&B charts but didn't approach the mainstream appeal of "You Send Me." Subsequent Keen hits like "Win Your Love for Me," "Only Sixteen," and "Everybody Likes to Cha Cha Cha" paved the way for Cooke's signing with RCA in 1960. His last Keen single was "Wonderful World," a lovely pledge of devotion written by Barbara Campbell, Lou Adler, and Herb Alpert.

RCA saw Cooke as the only black pop contender capable of eclipsing Columbia's Johnny Mathis, but he was much more than that. Cooke's effortless interbreed of gospel, rhythm and blues, and pop argots was the bedrock of soul music. His deft, absorbing execution of the new sound, glistening with an articulate vocal clarity unlike any of the age, gave RCA a string of huge hits between 1960 and 1964: "Sad Mood," "That's It—I Quit—I'm Movin' On," "Cupid," "Twistin' the Night Away," "Nothing Can Change This Love," "Somebody Have Mercy," "Send Me Some Lovin'," "Another Saturday Night," "Frankie and Johnny," "Good News," "Good Times," "Tennessee Waltz," "Cousin of Mine."

But Cooke would never gain the mass acceptance of Johnny Mathis—the compromises required were too great. Cooke's polish was more a matter of instinct than strategy, and he essentially avoided the vaporous, homogeneous themes Mathis favored, selecting and even writing hits that heralded the black urban experience with an emotional colloquial recipe ("That's Where It's At," "Having a Party," "Bring It on Home to Me"). Although a shrewd businessman, eventually owning his own management firm and music publishing and record companies, he did not take the racial indignities of the era lightly.

In 1963, Cooke and his wife, former high school sweetheart Barbara Campbell, were arrested in Shreveport, Louisiana, on charges of disturbing the peace; the couple and two of their friends had attempted to register at a whites-only hotel. A year later, Cooke died in a bizarre shooting incident at a Los Angeles motel. Rumors in the record industry were that Cooke had been set up for a rubout by mob figures trying to gain control of his publishing interests, but the accounts given by newspapers at the time make no mention of any such allegations.

According to the principals involved, Cooke had picked up a Eurasian girl named Elisa Boyer at a bar on the evening of December 10, 1964, and she had accepted his offer of a ride home. Instead, he drove them to a motel on South Figueroa in Los Angeles and registered as "Mr. and Mrs. Cooke." Boyer told police that she insisted he take her home, but that Cooke refused and forced her into the motel room. She testified that he "began to rip my clothes off." When Cooke went into the bathroom, she fled on foot with her clothes and most of Cooke's. Clad only in a sports jacket and his shoes, he pursued her. The manager of the motel, Mrs. Bertha Lee Franklin, told police that Cooke kicked in the door of her apartment and accused her of harboring the girl (who was actually in a nearby telephone booth, calling the police). Franklin testified that Cooke struck her twice with his fist. She responded by producing a .22 caliber pistol and firing three shots; one hit Cooke in the chest.

Mortally wounded, he continued to charge her, she said, so she bludgeoned him with a stick. When the police arrived, they found him dead on the floor.

His wife, Barbara, became hysterical when police notified her at their Hollywood home; with her were two of their children, a third child having drowned in their swimming pool that summer.

Thousands of anguished fans stormed the twin chapel at the A. R. Leak Funeral Home at 7838 Cottage Grove in Chicago during the public wake, breaking glass and splintering wood. One woman screamed, "Please let me in! I've never seen anything like this in my life!"

Shortly before Cooke's death, he had been a guest vocalist with the Soul Stirrers at an anniversary concert in Chicago. When he took the microphone to raise his pure, sweet voice in Stirrers standards like "Jesus Wash Away My Troubles" and "Nearer to Thee," the crowd fell silent and then began to castigate him. "Get that blues singer down!" they yelled angrily. "This is a Christian program! Get that no-good so-and-so down!"

Cooke walked off the stage in tears.

Sometime, you like to let the hair do the talking!" booms the massive burnt-umber visage in the gilded mirror; stubby hands briskly smooth out the sparkling surface of his highly teased bouffant with a savage styling comb the size of a shark fin. Up close, one recognizes the matte finish of his complexion as well-rendered pancake, the keen edge to his gaze as a thick application of eyeliner. This is his street face.

The puggish, broad-chested man steps back from the looking glass in the Barron Room South of New York's Waldorf-Astoria. He savors the sight of his Lustre-Silk–soaked mane and buffed countenance, as his hairdresser of some three decades scrutinizes each meticulously layered lock of conked tonsorial confection.

"Ummmmm," Henry Stallings purrs, ringed fingers weaving pinpoints of light into a cut-rate halo above his cousin's chunky head. Stallings is careful not to touch his latest James Brown 'do: No less than six hours in the making, it seemed at midpoint to be an uneasy cross between Lulu's sculpted look circa *To Sir with Love* and an expansive Jiffy Pop foil bubble. But now that the Augusta, Georgia-bred Stallings has completed his barbering, his boyhood friend's bulbous new coiffure is the spitting image of the

James Brown

1986

smart helmet of wavelets Beatrice Arthur sported during the last two seasons of the TV show "Maude."

"I look good, huh?" Brown offers to no one in particular as he contentedly strokes the lapels of his plaid twill suit. "Henry Stallings is my kin, you know. This is a man that never have said, 'I don't think that looks good on you.' He would say, 'What you want? Do you want to roll it? Do you want a bush? Or a 'fro? Right now he's only free-lancing and doing a few things 'cause he's with me on the road. But we're getting ready to build a shop around the country and we're gonna call it Groom Me. Groom Me, sir! Groom ME! GROOM ME!"

Brown repeats the name of the proposed beauty parlor chain another half-dozen times, finally adding, "We went to Silas X. Floyd Elementary School together; we was in the fifth grade." Then he drifts into a kind of stiff-limbed, glassy-eyed reverie, striking curious bent-necked poses in which he regards the four-inch cuffs of his bell-bottomed trousers as if they were roses abloom in the desert. The mammoth grin is fixed, his jug ear cocked for the comments of his sidekick.

"Met James on Spruce Street in Augusta," says Stallings, a shy fellow with close-cropped hair and an impeccable pencil moustache, as he flicks invisible lint from his three-piece caramel livery. "We used to hang in front of grocery stores in an area on the south side called the Terry, and we'd grab a shoeshine box to see if we could make a few bucks. Later on we were into boxing, trying to box. James was a loner, no brothers or sisters, and we split up for a while when I went into the service and he went to prison."

For Stallings, the service meant the army. For Brown, the slammer was Richmond County Jail on Fourth Street in Augusta, where he landed at sixteen after breaking into four cars in a single night. Following several months in the local lockup, James was sentenced to eight to sixteen years at hard labor in a state prison; he served only four in a reformatory before having his time commuted for good behavior.

"After James got out, we saw each other again and he had a big, big record with 'Please, Please, Please,' " Stallings says. "We met up on 125th Street after he came to New York for an appearance. I was working at Sugar Ray Robinson's parlor, the Golden Glove, at 123rd and Seventh Avenue, and I couldn't believe James's success, 'cause to me he had just been a shoeshine boy and an attendant at the pool hall. James Brown singing!"

It was a hobby he'd acquired in stir, where he played drums in a combo with inmate Johnny Terry. Upon Terry's release in 1952, Brown formed the Swanees, a gospel group that also included Bobbie Byrd, Sylvester Keels, and Nafloyd Scott. The act became the Famous Flames as black doo-wop took hold, and they landed a steady gig as the house band at Clint Brantley's Two Spot Club in Macon, Georgia.

"I first dug Little Richard at the Two Spot, down on the corner of Fifth and Walnut," Brown suddenly interjects. "He discovered me and I discovered him. Before I considered music, I tried sports. With Beau Jack, the *baaad* 1940s Georgia prizefighter, as my guidance, I had three fights as a professional boxer and won 'em all. But I knew a black man with a bum leg couldn't make it in sports so I had to quit that. Seeing Little Richard singing 'Tutti-Frutti' and getting over, I went on to the WIBB studios in 1954 to do a demo of 'Please, Please, Please.'

"Don Robey from Duke/Peacock Records in Houston want it, Leonard Chess of Chicago's Chess and Checker labels want it too, but Ralph Bass of Federal put his job on the front lines for that tune. We went up to Cincinnati, me and my boys, to record it right, but Mr. Syd Nathan of Federal and King Records, he didn't want no part of that record. Mr. Bass loved that record to death anyway, *lost* his job over that record, and pushed the thing hard all during 1956 in Atlanta, in Birmingham, down in Florida with the help of promo man Mr. Henry Stone. Till it was pandemonium from Federal for '56, hear me?

"Pretty soon Mr. Nathan, he saw the light, gave Ralph back his job and we git down to serious business. Because of the Lord—who I thank in a minute—everybody's been seeing that same light shine since!"

Mr. Brown, the Godhead of Get-Down, has been haunting the corridors of Gotham's grande dame of a hotel for a solid week. He joined Ray Charles, Fats Domino, the Everly Brothers, and other surviving architects of the pop pantheon in the main ballroom downstairs at the glittering January '86 inaugural induction dinner for the Rock and Roll Hall of Fame. At the ceremony he worked the summit conference of rock stars and record industry bigwigs like the dancing street pug he'd once been as he touted his scrappy hit single from the *Rocky IV* soundtrack, "Living in America." It was Brown's first ascension into the upper reaches of the pop charts since "Get on the Good Foot" lingered briefly at No. 18 in *Billboard* in the autumn of 1972, and it was an unsentimental journey of epic proportions for a man marking the thirtieth anniversary of his recording career.

This afternoon, as he hums the martial melody to "Living in America," Brown is immersed in his more mundane moment-to-moment insistence on reflex homage from the obliging retinue he's collected over the years. These include burly alto/tenor saxman Maceo Parker, who's resigned or been dismissed from the James Brown orchestra more times than anyone can count; rawboned baritone saxman/arranger St. Clair Pickney; and one Reverend Al Sharpton, Jr., portly field marshal and impromptu pitchman for the soul potentate, who announces he's secured a waiting limousine for a pressing round of errands and appointments.

"I've known Mr. Brown since I was fifteen or sixteen, hanging around the back fence of the mansion he useta have in Queens," Sharpton says brightly. "He had a castle with a moat around it on Linden Boulevard in the St. Albans section of Queens, and the kids from my neighborhood in the Hollis section of the borough would go over to look at the giant concrete gold 'Please, Please, Please' record he had imbedded in his front yard. There was a lot of big shots living on that street, but he was the only one who'd come out and tell us to stay in school. It was inspirational."

So much so, according to Sharpton, Jr.—who says his father was a preacher at Brooklyn's Washington Temple Baptist Church—that he left Rev. Jesse Jackson's Operation Breadbasket in 1971 to take up with Brown. (A spokesperson for the Washington Temple Church of God in Christ on Bedford Avenue, the only such church now in Brooklyn, says she never heard of either Al Sharpton.) When not acting as "road supervisor" or providing the halftime homily at the singer's shows, Sharpton runs a vague-sounding organization he calls the National Youth Movement. But mostly he simply keeps company with the Padishah of the Licking Stick.

Brown turns on the crisp edge of his Cuban heel and heads down the plush hallway. A phalanx of tuxedoed gentlemen pass noiselessly in the opposite direction. "Well now, look at those fellas," Brown says in a strident stage whisper. "Ain't they clean!"

"Aw, *excuse* me fellas," Sharpton brays, barely catching his cue. "But this is Mr. James Brown who you looking at, yes, indeed. Hold on now, don't hurry off. Excuse me, could somebody hold the elevator for a moment when these very fortunate business executives meet Mr. James Brown . . . ?"

In short, everything remains double fine and freakishly dandy in the uncommon world of James Brown as he nears the 1990s. Secure in his own singular element and firmly in control of his destiny, he remains the Baron of the Beat, the Feudal Lord of Funk, the Mash Potatoes Mikado, the Disco Dynast, the Marquis of the Sex Machine, the Shogun of the Cold Sweat. And that's enough, thank you—or so it has long appeared on the baroque surface of things.

As an artist, James Brown has tempered his peculiar genius in the crucible of the fickle international marketplace. In the process he's laid the musical groundwork for the best efforts by other gifted voices ranging from Sly Stone and Bob Marley to Fela Kuti and Kurtis Blow, not to mention Led Zeppelin ("Kashmir," "The Crunge") and ZZ Top.

As a socially conscious personality, Brown has assumed political stances of head-scratching polarity. He appeared live on TV from Boston Garden in April 1968 to quell race riots that erupted after the assassination of Dr. Martin Luther King, Jr. When Hubert Humphrey (noted author of James Brown liner notes) lost the Democratic nomination to George McGovern in 1972, Brown turned around and gave President Nixon a vigorous soul shake. Gerald Ford was heralded in 1974 with "Funky President (People It's Bad)."

The singer's grasp of more recent events and their underpinnings is no less shaky. In the winter of 1982 he gave former Island Records producer Paul Wexler a signed photo of himself with Ronald Reagan, along with the following piece of advice: "Paul, if you were a strong producer and had yourself a plan you'd worked hard on drawing up for your artist, would you let that artist change it all at the last minute? Of course not! Well, it's the same with Reagan and his economic and social plan for the country. So we gotta support him."

What a piece of work is James! How ignoble in reason! How finite in faculty! Yet in form and moving how express and admirable! Surely there is more to this man's man's man's overwrought frippery and fabled self-absorption than meets the overloaded eye. Or as he phrased it before the footlights of Radio City: "Can I go back? Do you *want* me to go back?! Okay, we going back to church right now, and then we gonna finish up in outer space. And bring me that lickin' stick!"

James Brown was four when his parents' marriage crumbled; six when he could buck dance to the accompaniment of a mouth organ; seven when he was living with Aunt Handsome "Honey" Washington and becoming proficient at rolling dice and picking out tunes on the household's rickety pump organ when he should have been in school.

"He would stay out of school two and three days a week, but when he came to class, he would still do more than the other children," Laura Garvin, his seventh-grade teacher, recalls. "We used to have little performances in class. We would charge ten cents to see James Brown and the children would just pile in, so we had to rule out the classroom shows. Sometimes we would move the show into the library. There was a piano there, and James Brown would play it or dance or sing. That was the real beginning."

He dropped out of the seventh grade before the end of the school year and went to live with his paternal grandmother. He earned board by pumping gas alongside his dad, dancing for tips beside the troop trains snaking out of Fort Gordon, and shoplifting. After his release from reform school he took a job as a janitor at Toccoa, Georgia, High School and married Velma Warren Brown in June 1953; the license carried the cooked data that he was born June 17, 1928, in Pulaski, Tennessee. (Joe Gardner Brown registered the birth of his son as May 3, 1933, in Barnwell, South Carolina.) After two years of evening rehearsals with the Famous Flames, Brown quit his day job and made for Macon, crediting his self-confidence to "white people in Toccoa who believed" in him.

Hitting the stage of Harlem's Apollo Theater in the early 1960s, shimmy-shuffling sideways in triple-time, balanced on one patent leather heel-and-toe propeller while the other foot was hiked up against his knee like the rudder of some runaway flamingo—*Bop!* —he'd stop, center stage, in sync with the rimshot metronome. *Bop! Bop!* He'd drop, halfway to his knees, his brutish head turned back from the fans, as he seized the mike stand by the throat and tipped it outward at arm's length. *Bop! Bop! Bop!* And he'd be back on top, slaying the crowd with "Please, Please, Please."

The band fell in behind him, splintering bass patterns and punching out horn riffs as they progressed, the rhythm guitar chopping away in twiddled time, as Mr. James Brown pleaded and bleated, giving off keening shrieks that peaked past the speedbump of human hearing, disappearing into the ultrapitched domain of a dog whistle.

The footlights would wash over his clothes. These could be citrus-colored suits with matching toreador vests and cutaway jackets, contrasting ruffle-drenched shirts with broad collars that hung down to his belt, or any number of other eye-inflaming satin or stretch-knit getups that would cling to his stumpy frame like a bad debt. On his album covers, he often included the unsurprising credit: "Clothes designed by Mr. Brown." As if these outfits, indeed *anything* about Mr. James Brown, could have been the work of anyone else.

He was ugly, uncourtly, a low piece of trumpery whose antics embarrassed everyone, but in the end even those properly repulsed would be converted, their critical appraisals short-circuited by the acrobatic might of a man so completely into himself.

At the close of "Please, Please, Please," Brown would sink to the floor, despondent, unable to regain the precious love interest whom he had driven away. Aides would take the stage to coddle and collect him, one settling a purple cape on his shoulders as they helped him up, shaking their heads as they led the pathetic, slack-jawed shell toward the wings. Halfway there, Brown would break free and shake off the cape; he would scamper, then slide back across the stage on one knee, topple the mike stand and catch the microphone as it fell, and belt "Please!" once more as the Famous Flames augmented his anguish with halting thrusts of the chorus. Again, aides would come to the sad rescue, this time draping a gold cape upon his twisted form before ushering him away. Again, he'd spin away from their grasp, rushing to the only lifeline left between him and his heart's desire. "Baaay-beeee *please!*" Finally enervated, his clothes sopping wet (he was said to sweat off seven pounds a show), he would be helped off—amid torrential cheers—in a flowing black cape.

Minutes later, Brown would appear for an up-tempo encore, impeccable in a candy-apple red traveling suit, swinging a heavily stickered suitcase, jerking his hitchhiker's thumb with a grin as brilliant as a blowtorch. And all the emcee could say was, "LADIES AND GENTLEMEN! MIS-TER JAMES BROWN! . . ."

He was near the peak of his popularity in 1967 when he purchased his first radio station, WJBE in Knoxville, Tennessee. He would purchase two more, WEBB in Baltimore and WRDW in Augusta. The summer of 1969 found Brown back in Augusta and Macon to break ground on a number of James Brown Gold Platter Pantry restaurants, whose menu was to feature "fried chicken, fried catfish, corn bread, collard greens, black-eyed peas, sweet yams, buttermilk biscuits, fried pies and 'tater puddin'." Plans called for 150 franchises in all fifty states and the Caribbean by the end of 1970.

"But no matter how big Gold Platter soul food becomes," *Newsweek* ruled, "Brown probably will resist pressures to move the headquarters of his firm outside Macon. 'Macon understood me first,' he says. 'And a man is home where he's understood.' "

It is also usually where he's sued or slapped with tax liens by the federal government. The first legal actions were divorce and paternity suits filed in 1969 by Velma Brown. Their union of sixteen years had produced four offspring and a litany of "insurmountable marital difficulties," according to court papers.

Brown temporarily retired from public appearances but re-emerged in autumn 1970 after wedding the former Deirdre Yvonne Jenkins in South Carolina. He signed a long-term contract in 1971 with Polydor Records and restructured his organization, selling off his old catalog and dismissing most of the JBs, his post-Flames tour band.

Teddy Brown, nineteen, his father's eldest son by ex-wife Velma, was killed in an upstate New York car crash in June 1973 along with two other companions from Toccoa.

The Treasury Department claimed in 1975 that Brown owed $4.5 million in back taxes for 1969 and 1970. The financial cloud deepened in 1976 when onetime manager Charles Bobbit took the stand in U.S. District Court in Newark, New Jersey, to testify that he'd given New York City disk jockey Frankie Crocker approximately $7,000 in payola payments to get Brown's records on the airwaves. Bobbit's testimony was later thrown out on a technicality.

In September 1979 a Richmond County Superior Court jury returned a $161,000 verdict against Brown and his Third World, Ltd. No. II Corporation for unpaid rent, breach of contract, and punitive damages in an Augusta property dispute. WJBE was sold in January 1978 to raise needed funds. WEBB in Baltimore was put into receivership by a judge who ordered Brown to jail for failure to appear for questioning in a suit by the station's former owner. WRDW in Augusta, second in its market until a June 1979 fire crippled its capacity to transmit, was sold at public auction by the National Bank of Georgia in April 1980.

The IRS filed tax liens of nearly $2.2 million in 1980 on twenty acres of land Brown and wife Deirdre owned in Aiken County. Cash flow improved when Brown sold his beloved D-125 Sidley Hawker jet. Deirdre drove off their sixty-two-acre Jaydee Ranch in South Carolina in 1983 with their two daughters and didn't bother to look back.

On the professional front, reluctant record companies had intimated that Brown take his own advice: Give it up or turnit a loose. "When John [Belushi] and Danny Aykroyd invited me to be a part of the Blues Brothers film, they helped me get myself going again," Brown recalled in March 1982, several days after Belushi's death. "I was going through a bad period at the time, having trouble getting my records released. Truth is truth, and I was not in demand, not wanted. Through the film and their own records, they opened the door again for me and so many other performers like me—Brother Ray [Charles], Aretha—getting us rediscovered and appreciated again. John flew in to watch me cut my stuff on the soundtrack album 'cause he knew I was nervous, and he said, 'How can I help?' He was *there* for me, unnerstand?"

Brown was again ambulatory in the public's mind, but not yet on the good foot. The success of the Tom Tom Club's James Brown–influenced. "Genius of Love" moved Paul Wexler, then producing several projects for Island Records, to explore the possibility of securing some studio time with the renascent soul pioneer. Wexler flew down to Augusta in February 1982, and a preliminary chat led quickly to contract negotiations. By April, Brown and his troops (trombonist Fred Wesley among them) were in Nassau, laying down rough tracks with resident composer Wally Badarou and the premier reggae rhythm section of bassist Robbie Shakespeare and drummer Sly Dunbar.

"Since James Brown has been the source of most modern dance music in North America, as well as a huge influence on contemporary Caribbean and African pop forms," Wexler says, "he was tense about anything that tasted of a collaboration, saying 'Nobody knows how to be James Brown but James Brown.' I tried to cool him out by explaining, 'Your musical profile is perfect as it is. I'm just suggesting an exciting new frame for it.' I couldn't see how an Afro-Carib hybrid built around James could fail."

The slim, gentle-natured Wexler, thirty-two, pushes his fingers through his thick salt-and-pepper hair and sighs heavily as he cues up a cassette of the never-released LP's rough mixes during an exclusive Manhattan listening session. "Unfortunately, it wasn't conflicting socio-musical philosophies that held the project back." Hesitating before pressing the "play" button, Wexler decides to provide some deep background to the most ballyhooed James Brown album nobody has ever heard.

"We got down to Compass Point, where the weather's always lovely," he begins, "but the climate soon turned sour. Chris Blackwell [head of Island Records] threw a big party the first night at his oceanside mansion, inviting local Bahamian dignitaries and prominent island musicians. The affair began at 7:00 P.M.

"Now this is going to sound like a minor thing, but when 9:00 P.M. rolled around, James was still at his beach house in the Compass Point complex, refusing to go until Henry Stallings had fixed his hair to where he thought it was perfect. 'Come on,' I was begging him. 'Think of your host, he's thrilled to have you as a guest.' But we ended up arriving over three hours late, with the food cold and everyone bewildered, offended, or very bummed."

Brown, Fred Wesley, and company entered into two weeks of studio brainstorming with the Sly-Robbie-Wally triumvirate still open and enthusiastic, both sides contributing original material prepared for the occasion. The mutual goodwill was destined to wilt.

"James began to get heavy with Sly and Robbie about them playing parts exactly as he dictated—and then him playing them poorly when he took over their instruments to demonstrate. Their respect was bruised but progress was being made until we got to a really excellent track Sly and Robbie had written called '(I'm a) Rhythm Machine,' which was clearly a tribute to James in its groove and mood. At the runthrough, James paid Robbie the ultimate compliment by telling him he could sustain a groove without any faltering or shifting whatsoever. 'Man!' he raved, 'you don't move an *inch!* That's discipline!'

"As we began cutting the track, James began tossing his own off-the-cuff phrases and couplets into verses, which everyone appreciated—until he called a break from the session to say he wanted the publishing on the song. Now," cautions Wexler, "I believe to this day that that was just an impulsive wrinkle of the moment which could have been eliminated with diplomacy. But some staff people overreacted and called the Island Records office to complain. Right or wrong, James is a proud and stubborn cat and the vibe evolved into unnecessary sides-taking."

But Brown's insecurities and hypersensitive suspicions boiled over into avenues quite removed from record-making. "At one point James told me he felt that he went through his dry spell in the latter half of the seventies because Gamble & Huff and the FCC were in a conspiracy to ruin him by keeping him off the radio," Wexler says. "He was also bitter about Rick James, who he feared was going out of his way to monitor and rip off James's ideas.

"Another time, I met James and the Reverend Sharpton for a business meeting over coffee in the Detroit airport. He persisted in talking about the Fedders air conditioners in the building corridors, saying, 'That's the noise they make at home, Rev! That's the noise!' Finally I asked what the hell he was talking about, and James explained that he was convinced the government was bugging him all over the country through the air conditioners. That's why he thinks he's had so many run-ins with the IRS."

As far as dissidence levels at Compass Point were concerned, all unity of purpose was irrevocably dissolved with the advent of Henry Stallings's bleeding ulcers. "James was convinced the cooks and maids had deliberately poisoned his dear friend as part of a plot," Wexler says. "That was the last straw for the Compass Point people, who have their own pride, but James had up and split Nassau anyhow."

Two months later Brown telephoned Wexler to apologize, admitting he had been woefully mistaken and wanting to resume the project. It was too late. Island had washed its hands of its phobic funk exponent; Blackwell let Brown keep both the money and the master tapes from the abortive affair.

"I must accentuate that I, for one, would do it again in an instant," Wexler maintains, "because for all the bruises on his creative psyche and fears of exploitation that stem historically from very real abuses and ripoffs, James Brown is indisputably a talent of monumental proportions. History has repeatedly shown that his finished product has always made any hassles en route seem awful paltry in retrospect."

As if to illustrate, Wexler starts the cassette. Of particular note are "ESP," a searing ballad with lightly mystical lyrics by Brown and like-minded music by Badarou; "So Tired of Standing Still (We Got to Move)," an ebullient party groovathon guided by Fred Wesley's playful trombone invention; and "U.S. (Us)," a richly contoured reggae-funk amalgam with exquisitely dusky New Orleans piano coloration in the Dr. John mode and a transcendent scat by Brown. A joy to hear, "U.S." is the Afro-Carib funk meld Wexler had hoped the experiment under the palms would yield. "What knocks me out," Wexler says with a small smile, "is that Sly and Robbie gave their heart and soul to 'U.S.' "

In 1984, Brown teamed with hip-hop honcho Afrika Bambaataa for the six-part, twelve-inch "Unity" single on the Tommy Boy label. But the record did not sell well enough to return a royalty for the Bad One Hisself.

"There was three meetings led up to me working with James," Bambaataa says. "I met him on the streets outside Yankee Stadium in 1963 when he was out just saying hello to the neighborhood. In 1973 he came up to the Bronx River Houses at East 174th to visit the mother of one of his dancing girls and he talked to us kids on the stoop. In 1983, when he caught a Zulu Nation show at the Left Bank in Mount Vernon, New York, we talked some more.

"So I told Tommy Silverman of Tommy Boy that it was my dream to record with James and he set up a meeting. We went into Unique Recording and got it down in two days, plus a video. We wanted to send a message of peace to the world, and offer a percentage to the United Negro College Fund.

"A lot of stations didn't jump on the record, though," Bambaataa continues, his tone subdued. "They didn't wanta hear the politics *or* the electro-funk. Now I hear 'Living in America' everywhere, with James Brown doing Dan Hartman instead of doing himself. But I appreciated the time he spent with me, and he taught me some smart stuff. He said, 'Keep your lyrics universal. Don't ever give anybody any more reason to attack you than they already go looking for.'

"He also told me a lot about the tax laws and how the government is always waiting to get you even if you give your damned money away. 'Be careful,' he kept saying. 'They got their eyes on you all the time. Somebody always wants to take what you got. Be wary and you won't be sorry.' "

It is no small irony that "Living in America," the first James Brown single to threaten a run at top of the charts since "I Got You (I Feel Good)" climbed to No. 3 in November 1965, employs a slightly florid reworking of the previous song's horn charts. Ray Marchica's thoroughgoing drums are engaging but lack the slight-delay fatback flair of the Melvin Parker/John "Jabo" Starks/Clyde Stubblefield combinations. Fuzztone guitar and synth keyboards mixed at midrange in the rhythm bed supplant the punishing clarity of the earlier track. But there's no question that "America" is a slick distillation of the Latin/Caribbean/New Orleans off-beat accents, stammering horns and clipped bass ostinatos (perfected by "Sweet" Charles Sherrell) of Brown's post-Famous Flames growth period (1966–73) with the JBs—while using none of the standout personnel from this fertile heyday.

"Robin Garb, who was the executive producer of the *Rocky IV* soundtrack, called me in late June of '85," says singer/producer Dan "I Can Dream About You" Hartman. "He said he and Sly Stallone were looking for a lavish James Brown–type production number for the Las Vegas scene in the film where Apollo Creed fights the Russian on Creed's home turf. Robin knew me and Charlie Midnight, my songwriting partner, from work we'd done alone or together on the *Streets of Fire* and *Krush Groove* soundtracks, and he felt we could deliver a semi-patriotic dance track that would feel like a major-contender hit record in the movie's setting.

"Charlie and I both thought it was a ridiculously tall order, because James Brown's vocals and timing have more musical depth and sophistication than most of the Top 10 these days. He has a very seasoned nonpop quality. What we went for, then, was a lyric by Charlie that described some of the classic American working man's imagery without the turnoff of overt patriotism. Meantime I wrote, engineered, and played most of the instruments for the basic track in my studio in Connecticut. I added a scratch vocal and then sent off copies to James and Stallone.

"James's only request was horns, so I contacted the Uptown Horns, a nicely gritty session unit that were on the road with Robert Plant, and they flew in from Phoenix, Arizona, for an emergency overnight session. In August James flew up from Augusta and walked into Unique Recording in Manhattan about 10:30 one night. He put on headphones, listened to the track, and said, 'You're doing James Brown music!' And when he saw the second verse on the lead sheet he called me over, telling me, 'You don't know how much of this railroad-track, hard-roll, all-night-diner stuff is about my life!' "

"God got me in on the ground floor of every kind of music," Brown exults backstage at Radio City Music Hall. "He put me into the game before Prince and Sly and Rick James and the Funkadelics. When—"

Instantly Brown cancels the thought and explodes with a torrential verbal outburst: "SEXMACHINEGOODFOOTTHINK DOINGITTODEATHICAN'TSTANDMYSELFWHENYOU TOUCHMESUPERBADCOLDSWEATFUNKYCHICKENI NEEDYOURLOVESOBADBABYBABYBABY!"

He pauses, grinning ferociously, and spews it out again. The feat of precisely merged enunciation is doubly impressive on the second pass, the humming whole too specific to be psychobabble or doggerel filler, and yet not exactly a boast either. It's more of an involuntary mantra disclosure.

"Down in D.C. they talking about the go-go but I had them kids out in the streets while they were still babies, doing the popcorn with the Original Disco Man. Funk I invented back in the fifties. The rap thing I had down on my 'Brother Rapp (Part I),' and you can check that. I enjoyed my thing with Afrika Bambaataa on 'Unity,' but I did it more for the message than for the music. Michael Jackson, he used to watch me from the wings and got his moon walk from my camel walk—he'll tell you that if you ask. Same way, I was slippin' and slidin' before Prince was out of his crib; that's why Alan Leeds, who used to work for my organization, is on his management team, tipping and hipping him. I ain't jealous, I'm zealous. I ain't teased, I'm *pleased.* Who's gonna do James Brown better'n *James Brown*? Think!"

He halts with a wheezy gasp, his nostrils flaring dangerously and the upper lip quivering on the brink of another mantra stampede. But it misfires: "SEXMACHINEGOODFOOT [*coughcoughcough*]—aheheheheh—yes suh! Show business!!" One more pair of these hotdogging larynx wipeouts and he'll be phoning in this evening's program from an oxygen tent.

"This is a family operation," Brown says, referring to his third wife as he idly unbuttons his silk burgundy shirt and unclips the waistband on his matching slacks. In late 1984 he wed Adrianne Modell Rodriguez, a TV makeup artist for the "Solid Gold" variety series and the soap operas "The Young and the Restless" and "Days of Our Lives." "Mrs. Brown, she's an artist, a beautician and a personality in her own right and that am quite a combination. She do my production coordination, sees I'm ready for the people anytime, anywhere 'cause they can want me with no notice. I can draw 50,000 people in Arkansas like *that,* or 10,000 in Chicago on a rumor I might be there. Vice President Bush sent me a letter saying thank you for not forgetting the unemployed.

"I been friends with Presidents! Johnson, Kennedy, Mr. President Habib Bourguida of Tunisia—you know where that is? I'm trying to get the dignitaries to send me over to Moscow to get the static outta the Hot Line and start everybody talking about love. Senator Strom Thurmond, he belongs to my church, and he's somebody who's been there in the background for me for years."

How's James's financial picture these days?

"Looks good, pretty good. I got me a Scotti Bros. contract since the *Rocky* movie, and Polydor and I are working on reissuing a bunch of things. Don't have all that ranch land anymore, but my wife and I still got some nice property to fall back onto. I ran into taxman troubles and had to sell my jets, had to sell my radio stations. I was the only black man in America to own three radio stations, but I traveled and left it up to accountants and they messed it every kinda way, but I'm coming back from it. I got a lotta new ideas, I wanna do a keyboard record, I wanna produce some of the young talent, find another Michael Jackson like I did before.

"And I wanna do more TV. My favorite is 'The David Letterman Show.' Them people been pretty good to me, and that band is something, in a tight groove. I dig Paul Shaffer, he's my biggest fan, and that Steve Jordan, that drummer they got, he's *furious* on the beat, jus' like a locomotion man. Both of the drummers in my band are admirers of Steve Jordan because if the beat ain't there you got to send everybody home, TV show or no TV show.

"I'm not afraid to be the boss, see? That's how James Brown music came to be. Back when everybody was listening to soap-suds songs and jingles, I emphasized the beat, not the melody, unnerstand? Heat the beat, and the rest'll turn sweet. I heard the percussion in everything—even the rhythm guitar sound like a drum to me. My guitarist, Jimmy Nolen, God rest his soul he's gone to his reward [the originator of the hugely influential signature "chickenscratch" riff died of a heart attack December 16, 1983]—Jimmy knew how to get the guitar to hit like a snare for me, 'cause I wanted a band that would punch back when I swung at 'em.

"It was a new attitude, better than the Marines, better than boot camp. I wanted the band onstage to be like soldiers, with me being the general, calling out the battle plan."

And how is troop morale?

"We gettin' on, gettin' along. Sometimes I got to lay down the law, but everybody know the rules at this point. I useta be *hard*, right," he concedes, a grin growing on his lips, "but I'm mellow now, I slowed down and lightened a little bit. I got enough veterans to take care of the vet. We funky enough to take on any takers."

Maceo Parker, an old campaigner who sparked or witnessed his share of melees and mutinies in the Brown camp, agrees. "When I came on board in 1964, it was the James Brown Orchestra, and the Famous Flames were still mostly a vocal group in the setup," remembers the impish, soft-spoken sax great. "My brother Melvin and I, we were getting tired of high school in Kinston, North Carolina, when Mr. Brown came through and promised Melvin a job as a drummer when he got older. Next time through, he hired him and took me on in Raleigh after I bought myself the alto sax he was wanting.

"In 1967 I left to go into the army and that was when Fred Wesley took over with his trombone. I came back in 1969, and then I left again in 1970, taking a lot of the band with me to do a record as Maceo and All the King's Men, which I guess didn't make Mr. Brown too pleased. But he got Bootsy Collins on bass and his brother Catfish on guitar while we were gone so it all went down okay.

"Between 1976 until November 1983 I was doing work with P-Funk, Bootsy and the Brides of Funkenstein besides some *quick* occasional sides with James, but I gotta say my favorite work as part of the JBs was on 'Papa's Got a Brand New Bag,' 'Cold Sweat,' a tune called 'Damn Right I'm Somebody, and 'Funky Good Time,' where I did a nice flute solo.

"Problem was, it used to always be kinda stressed, pretty tight quarters for all of us, in the studio and on the road. The material was worked out on the road, in the time before each night's show, with James letting us in on the grooves he'd been developing and almost giving us assignments. Everything was set up to keep you in line and sharp. Thing is there's a right way and a wrong way to do anything, and then there was James Brown's way, which always had to be considered righter than right."

Parker says he lost patience with the fifty-dollar fines and the insensitivity to *esprit de corps* they exemplified. Most grown men don't need to be told when to drink, swear, or shine their shoes, but it was Brown's fierce antidrug stance that rubbed many a sideman raw in the late sixties and early seventies.

"Everybody would be sneaking reefer and other shit on James," Bootsy Collins recalls. "He was always storming into the dressing room to ask what the funny smell was and throw a shitfit. So a lot of us headed in the other direction just to get a leg up. It was acid that eventually made things extra crazy, same as with P-Funk, which I joined after leaving James's band. One night with James, I thought the neck of my bass guitar turned into a snake. I didn't want no part of it and went back to the dressing room in the middle of the show. That pretty much cooled my deal with the Godfather."

The last straw for others on the squad was less cerebral. During a 1974 concert tour flight to Zaire that was carrying B. B. King, the Spinners, the Crusaders, and Lloyd Price, the plane almost failed to clear the runway because it was so severely overloaded with Brown's personal effects. The luggage of others had to be removed in order to make liftoff just barely possible, and several of the passengers described the stunt as potentially life-threatening. By the end of the protracted tour the following year, Parker and other key members of the troupe had tendered their resignations.

"Last really good time I had with the whole James gang was on a bus coming back from L.A. in 1975," Parker says. "We were drinking, joking, doing the dozens, and carrying on great. It was the *heck* with the fucking rules, thank God."

Did James enjoy himself as well?

"James? On that bus with us? James Brown was not on that bus, my friend. No, no, no, no."

For the time being, Parker says he's "content—print that—content" with the situation, although he feels bad he and the rest of the present lineup did not play on "Living in America."

"When the hit is on the radio, you like hearing your contribution," he muses. "If you playing with James Brown, hearing that contribution is what you definitely come to count on. I can promise you that."

Sad to say, despite the best efforts of Parker and the rest of Brown's twenty-five-piece orchestra, the first half of the Radio City show is less than an epiphany. Al Sharpton's pallid invocation gives way to excruciating treatments of the "Entertainment Tonight" theme, "There's No Business Like Show Business," and "Take Me Out to the Ball Game." The exotically pell-mell pageant doesn't catch fire until the finale, which builds from simmering versions of "Sex Machine," "Super Bad," and "Get That Feeling" to a six-minute "Living in America." A horn-screech-*cum*-rim-shot signals the start. Dead on the reverberant *bop!* Brown drops into a full split, grabbing the throat of the mike stand as he sinks and then whipping it out to cord-length as he leaps up again. With the slack wire hooked around his pinky, he executes a double spin and snaps the mike down to within four inches of the floor, catching it in his cradled palms—*this man is fifty-three years old*—as he swiftly genuflects to growl, "I live in America—say it!!"

Time alone will tell if Dan Hartman can draw out of the mideighties model the brand of visionary output that once kept Brown a decade ahead of his most savvy emulators. The secret seems to be in the degree of musical autonomy that can be provided, while steering the man away from the pointless score-setting, quirky self-parody, and paranoia that have sapped and distracted his muse in the recent past. The voice is still intact, the moves as deft as always when left to their intuitive grace, all or most critical quibblings nullified by the lasting grandeur of an American original still triumphantly immersed in his own spirit.

At the Waldorf-Astoria induction gala for the Rock and Roll Hall of Fame, Brown glad-hands with gusto all who come within touching distance to swap stories, offer congratulations, or bask in his glow. And for his part, Brown goes out of his way to laud the others being honored, his entourage nodding in congenial assent.

"Lookit Chuck Berry! Man looks good, half his age . . . Ray Charles, still have the pipes Almighty God put in his chest . . . Fats Domino got that touch . . . Everly Brothers is fine harmonies . . . Jerry Lee Lewis looking pretty well . . ."

More nods, and then nods for the nods. Heads are bobbing blissfully in Brown's corner as Reverend Al Sharpton sidles up behind him, a tightly rolled magazine in his grip, and murmurs something in the bossman's ear. The communication feeds a smirk that becomes a grin that becomes a chuckle that turns into an outright guffaw as the beneficent repartee around him escalates to where James Brown has no recourse but to chime in with the last and best word of tidings on the topic of his esteemed colleagues, his feet aflutter and his upper lip atremble as he utters with savage serenity:

"But James Brown is the only man in this here Hall of Fame who is entering the Billboard *Top 15 on the same night . . ."*

Until, reaching critical mass in the ultra-privileged realm of the mantra stampede:

"SEXMACHINEGOODFOOTTHINKDOINGITTO DEATHICAN'TSTANDMYSELFWHENYOUTOUCHME SUPERBADCOLDSWEATFUNKYCHICKENINEEDYOU SOBADBABYBABYBABYBABYLIVINGINAMERICA!!!

"And," he gulps, "I feel good."

PILGRIMS

More than anything else, William John Clifton Haley, Jr., wanted his lifelong claim to the title "Father of Rock and Roll" to be taken seriously. It never was. "The story has got pretty crowded as to who was the Father of Rock and Roll," commented Haley in a rare public statement from the late 1970s. "I haven't done much in life except that. And I'd like to get credit for it."

He was arguably the first white singer to put a high-energy edge on a black rhythm and blues hit when Bill Haley and the Saddlemen covered Jackie Brenston's "Rocket 88" in 1951, but it was Elvis Presley's plenary execution of rock and roll's forbidden pleasures that got the lion's share of the acclaim. Pubescent audiences were more eager to fantasize about a loose-limbed Lothario like Elvis. Yodeling Bill Haley (his original stage-name)—a chunky country and western singer from Highland Park, Michigan—looked like a mailman, moved like a lummox, and inspired no wet dreams. He and the Saddlemen sold 75,000 copies of "Rock This Joint," and then, after renaming the group the Comets, became the first identifiable rock and roll band to place a record on the *Billboard* pop charts with "Crazy Man Crazy." Even then, proper recognition for Haley proved elusive.

Bill Haley

1984

Swarms of amorous, tight-sweatered nymphets would hug the lip of the stage at an Elvis concert, craving the attentions of the satyr from Tupelo. So Haley tried to spread stories about how he and his band were taken to orgies in a certain small theater by their manager, who then forced them to watch from the balcony while the debauchery unfolded. Rumor had it that such a scene might have transpired in a joint in Philadelphia known as Hound Dog Hill. Haley said that while they were not permitted to participate, the view would get them sufficiently aroused to knock out another vascular rock anthem. Insiders would size up chubby-faced Bill's quaint curly forelock and the pudgy aspect of his homely sidemen, consider the gawky boosterism at the core of the music, and conclude that voyeurism was probably their *only* forte.

By 1956, Haley and the Comets had scored a number of huge hits for the Decca label, including a clamorous but sanitized version of Joe Turner's lewd "Shake, Rattle and Roll," "Dim, Dim the Lights (I Want Some Atmosphere)," and "See You Later, Alligator." The biggest was "(We're Gonna) Rock Around the Clock," a song by Jimmy De Knight that sold 22 million copies after it was selected in 1955 for the soundtrack of *Blackboard Jungle,* a Hollywood film that dramatized teen rebellion. When knife fights and bottle-throwing melees started to break out at Comets' concerts, a wave of protest against the music began to rise. This time recognition came Haley's way, all right—he got blamed. A defensive Haley stated, "The music is stimulating enough without creating additional excitement," but he soon vowed to avoid "suggestive lyrics."

Haley starred in his own film, *Rock Around the Clock,* and the nation and world were surprised at what they saw: a balding family man slipping inelegantly into middle age. Could this be the sort of fellow capable of sparking what a psychiatrist told the *New York Times* was a "cannibalistic" trend? When a second Haley film, *Don't Knock the Rock,* appeared in 1957, much of the storm surrounding Haley had passed on, along with his rowdy stateside following. An English trip in February created pandemonium, however, and British fans remained loyal long after his last Top 40 record, "Skinny Minnie," sank from view late in 1958.

Although Haley continued to tour and record with various incarnations of the Comets, the bulk of his appearances were confined to so-called Rock and Roll Revival shows. Two failed marriages and tragic family deaths clouded his later years, and he eventually became a problem drinker. In 1973, he was arrested twice in one week in Iowa for public drunkenness. Repeatedly stymied in his attempts to put down roots and establish a financially secure home base, his frequent relocations took him to various states and even down to Mexico.

Haley was south of the border in the winter of 1976 when longtime friend and gifted saxophonist Rudy Pompilli died from lung cancer. The death left an already perturbed Haley distraught and hastened his descent into alcoholism.

Haley dropped from sight, declining to perform or record for three years. Unlike Robert Johnson, he was apparently unable to locate a mojo man or necromancer to reverse his musical decline, for when, in 1979, he popped up again to cut a comeback album for Sonet Records at Fame Studios in Muscle Shoals, Alabama, few people cared. The LP *Everyone Can Rock and Roll* attracted no significant attention, but it gave Haley a chance to tour Europe once more. Queer reports trailed after him on this sorry sortie, tales of him assaulting fans and disrobing onstage.

In 1980, plans for another European tour were canceled, although he did a few poorly received dates in South Africa at the beginning of the summer. He retreated to his home in Harlingen, Texas, a small town in the Rio Grande Valley, just over the Mexican border, refusing all requests for interviews and sometimes denying his identity. Police would often find him wandering aimlessly after nightfall, lost on some remote country lane, delirious, incoherent, suffering from amnesia. He was pronounced dead of a presumed heart attack on February 9, 1981; a friend found his fully clothed body stretched out on a bed in a room in the garage behind his house. It had been lying there for approximately six hours. According to the birth date, July 6, 1925, listed on his driver's license, Haley was fifty-six, but his various press bios over the years maintained that he was as much as three years younger.

Four months before his death, Haley's eldest son, Jack, described his rock and roll father's mounting dementia in an interview for National Public Radio: "He would talk about his life in the Marine Corps, which he was never in. He was never in the service at all. He said he was a deputy sheriff down there in Texas, which he wasn't. I knew he was lying, but I never dared say it. I didn't wanna make him mad for fear that I would never hear from him again."

To the last, Bill Haley kept his story shady and his rock and roll straight. It was a sadly inverted sense of priorities.

Frankie Valli

1977

"So what's wrong with the damn TV?" he wondered.

The short, wiry man slid off the king-sized bed, scratching his compact chest in nervous irritation and then running delicate fingers through his shiny black hair. "You spend a lot of money for a good color TV, and you don't even get decent sound," he complained to himself as he approached the flickering set, his stocking feet sinking into the spongy blue pile of the wall-to-wall carpeting.

Enjoying the opulent privacy of his large, Mediterranean-style bedroom, Frank Stephen Castelluccio, thirty-three, had been absorbed in an afternoon movie when the TV's speaker began cutting out at irregular intervals. After feeling relaxed for the first time in several days, he was now on the verge of losing his Italian temper. "It's always something," muttered Castelluccio—better known to the general public as Frankie Valli, skinny lead singer of the Four Seasons—as he fiddled with the set's audio control.

Downstairs, in the kitchen of his comfortably plush home on Friedland Road in Nutley, New Jersey, his attractive wife, the former Mary Mandell, was chatting on the phone, while outdoors, young daughters Antonia and Francine, and Celia (Mary's child from a previous marriage), played noisily in the dead-end street. Frankie Valli and the Four Seasons were scheduled to open the next evening at a club in Detroit called the Rooster Tail and from there proceed to a series of Midwestern dates. The group's members, all New Jersey natives, had decided to catch a midmorning flight, after isolating a precious few free days to spend with their families.

RAP! Castelluccio struck the top of the bulky, swivel-mounted TV with an open palm. "So what's with the sound?" He adjusted the volume knob again, but still there were those curt, staggered silences. Impulsively, he vented his frustration by calling out to his wife, and that's when he heard his own voice dissolve.

Frankie froze; then he turned with a start toward the mirrored wall of closet doors on his left, regarding himself in the expansive reflection. The icy white light from the TV screen played upon his slight frame, accenting the folds in his custom-tailored slacks and sport shirt, and deepening each seam in his dour, diamond-shaped face.

The next few seconds passed in a dizzying dreamwalk. The chattering TV, his own halting speech, the children's laughter from the street, cars lumbering below the draped windows—all the sounds percolating around him were being snipped off or erased for whole moments, drifting in and out as if sputtering from an ill-tuned radio.

Frightened, bewildered, Castelluccio pressed two clammy fingertips into his hot, ringing ears, trying to prod them to attention. They would not pop.

"At first, I thought I had wax in my ears, something like that," he confides softly. "Then I figured, well, I was ill or had a cold or maybe was just run down. It was a weird feeling, because I could hear *inside* my head in a muffled kinda way; you know, my voice, my teeth tapping together, but not *outside.* It was like when you step out of the shower and your ears are still filled with water. I was off balance; I couldn't explain what was happening to me.

"The next night—this was in 1967—the Seasons and I flew up to Detroit and did the show, and it was absolutely terrifying. Half the time, really, I couldn't even hear the music being played. I could hear myself singing, but everything else was in the distance or just not there. But we were well rehearsed and so nobody in the crowd caught on to what was occurring.

"Following day, I saw a doctor. He examined me and gave me a diagnosis. Sitting in the hospital, I couldn't hear what he was saying. On a slip of paper he wrote something like, 'You're going deaf. You'll never hear again.' And then he walked away."

Frankie Valli, forty-two (he has long since legally changed his name), Mary Ann Valli, twenty-six (his beautiful second wife of two years), and myself are seated across from one another in a fancy diner in Fort Lee, New Jersey, eating a noon breakfast when a waitress carrying a tray of empty water glasses sets it down heavily at a nearby busboy's stand. My host flinches subtly at the moderate clinking. Mary Ann, noting my puzzled glance, explains.

"All these little sounds—before Frankie had his ear operation last December, he had practically stopped hearing them. I guess you could say he forgot about all the incidental sounds you hear in an average day.

"But after the operation, they all came streaming back, at least in his left ear, and it drove him crazy. For a long while we couldn't go out or even come to a place like this. It was *painful.* Just the sound of traffic, or conversation around him, or putting a glass ashtray down on a marble tabletop."

"I didn't realize how much of my hearing I'd lost until I regained it," Frankie finishes, somberly swallowing a cheekful of toast. "I hadn't noticed how great the deterioration had been until all the hearing in my left ear had been restored."

"He's going into the hospital again soon to have the right ear operated on," adds Mary Ann. "Well . . . let's talk about that at the house," counsels Frankie as he contemplates the platter of ham and eggs just placed before him.

Besides Frankie Valli, how many of the Four Seasons can you name?

It's a toughie, isn't it? Even during their Golden Era (1962–66), the backup trio was never more than three anonymous Italians with Chiclets smiles; two of 'em sorta stumpy with receding hairlines and the third a gangly, smooth-faced young fellow who should have been balancing a basketball on his hip. The group's early album covers looked like the staff portraits from a supermarket Grand Opening.

Fortunately, the times when one was on the most intimate terms with the Four Seasons were also those times when one did not have to look at them: toolin' around town with the guys on a sticky June night, or copying a girlfriend's homework in the back booth of an early-morning beanery, or grinding with a hoody teased-hair-and-chewin'-gum doll at one of the *downtown* dances. Oozing out of radios and PA systems, the Seasons' *marinara* harmonies and Frankie Valli's three-and-a-half-octave ultimatums slapped a slick veneer on all the seamy, steamy things you had to do to make teen dreams come true. And the fact that parents didn't mind the music made it even more intense.

"When you talk about some of the great American vocal groups, you've gotta talk about the Beach Boys—*and* the Four Seasons," according to Bruce "Cousin Brucie" Morrow, the legendary New York disk jockey whose Top 40 palpitations on station WABC helped define sixties AM rock for an entire metropolitan generation.

"Back in the sixties, Frankie and the guys sang my trademark, 'Go Go with Cousin Brucie' theme song," he blathers, "and the *reason* they were so right for it was because their sound epitomized how it *felt* then to be a teenager growin' up in the city. The Beach Boys were for the West Coast suburban kids with T-Birds and money to spend foolin' around in the sunshine. But the Four Seasons were urban, they were East Coast—they were New York rock! And I guess New Jersey, too. Because of that, they were not universally identifiable, but to their fans, man, they had an allergic sound.

"When I hear the Beach Boys I think of getting tanned and surfin' and summer love and all that crap, but when I hear the Four Seasons belting 'Rag Doll' or 'Dawn, go away I'm no good for you,' man, I picture smokestacks, dirty streets, tenements in the Bronx, and poor, tough kids that are *survivors.*"

After surviving fifteen years as the featured vocalist for the Four Seasons and selling some 85 million records in the process, Frankie Valli is a pop-rock baron with two star-quality homes: one a lavish retreat in Beverly Hills (while awaiting completion of a mansion in Malibu) and the other a spacious apartment in a Fort Lee, New Jersey, highrise that overlooks to the east the spectacular skyline of New York City and to the southwest the jagged brown jaws of his bleak birthplace, Newark.

It is on the husky marble coffee table in the center of the Fort Lee living room that Mary Ann sets three smoking cups of tea and a saucer of chocolate-covered donuts. Dressed in snug, tan velvet pants and loose-fitting blouse, Mrs. Valli takes a place on one of the heavily cushioned setees while her husband, in French jeans, Cuban heels, and a braced black sweater, stands gazing wistfully out the windows to the southwest. He fingers the gold record medallion his wife gave him to commemorate his solo hit, "My Eyes Adored You."

Valli says Mary Ann picked the song as a hit the first time she heard it. She must have shrewder taste than Motown Records, which sat on the track for a year and a half during the abortive period (1971–73) that the Four Seasons were signed to the primarily black label. Her husband bought back the master in 1974 for $4,000 and released it on the small Private Stock label, where it fought its way to No. 1, nationwide, a year later.

Frankie Valli says he is not bitter about the disastrous "personal" deal he made with Motown kingpin Berry Gordy, despite the fact that Gordy pledged intimate involvement in revamping the then-foundering fortunes of the Four Seasons, only to subsequently ignore them in favor of producing Diana Ross in *Lady Sings the Blues.*

"Motown never believed in 'My Eyes Adored You,' " Valli advises, just for the record. "They might have, yes, if the Jackson Five had done it. You may remember, incidentally, that the Four Seasons used to play the Apollo Theater in Harlem, and in our early days at Vee-Jay Records most people thought we were a black act. Even today, the white record market and the black record market are two totally different entities. Yet, we're probably one of the only white groups that, if it's the right record, get R&B airplay."

"My Eyes Adored You," however, was not the right record. Any song saddled with a couplet as candy-assed as "My eyes adored you/Though I never laid a hand on you" was obviously not going to catch on with the "Do It Til You're Satisfied" crowd.

Valli insists that he was not bitter when he and original Four Season Bob Gaudio were thwarted in their midsixties ambition to form their own label on Atlantic Records because the other charter members, Tommy DeVito and Nick Macicci (later changed to Massi), demanded a lot of cash up front.

"Atlantic was still an independent then," Valli instructs. "We were huge at the time, and getting in on the ground floor, it would probably have been the wisest move that we ever could have made in our entire careers." But, he says, it's all forgotten; sorry he brought it up.

Since then, the Four Seasons have undergone so many personnel changes and contractual convolutions that the name itself would be nothing more than a franchised trademark were it not for the fact that Valli still leads the group on the road. Also, the bulk of the Four Seasons' material continues to be written and produced by the wondrously prolific Bob Gaudio, the former member of the Royal Teens ("Short Shorts") who allegedly dashed off 1962's million-selling "Sherry" in fifteen minutes. He and journeyman producer Bob Crewe cowrote most (but not all) of the other hit Seasons' singles we know so well: "Big Girls Don't Cry," "Walk Like a Man," "Stay," "Candy Girl," "Dawn," "Ronnie," "Let's Hang On," "C'mon Marianne," "Bye Bye Baby (Baby Goodbye)," "Rag Doll," "Save It for Me," "Opus 17 (Don't Worry 'Bout Me)," "Big Man in Town," and they created their adenoidal novelty cover of Dylan's "Don't Think Twice," under the pseudonym Wonder Who?

Nick Massi disappeared from the group in 1964, to be replaced temporarily by sometime–Four Seasons arranger Charlie Calello, followed by Joe Long. Chunky Tommy DeVito, the one who looked like a teamster, left in 1969 after being bought out—as was Massi—by Frankie Valli and Bob Gaudio for all rights to publishing, masters, futures, pasts—the whole ball of wax. Of course, when DeVito checked out, he left Bob and Frankie holding the bag at the lowest ebb in the Four Seasons' history.

"We had a problem where some inside people overextended themselves and took more money than they should have taken," Valli says diplomatically. "By the time we made the Motown deal we were in big trouble financially. Everybody in the Four Seasons had a different job to take care of. One guy took care of business, another took care of music, another the staging of the shows, and so on. Tom handled a lot of the business end, and when he left, Gaudio and I took over a debt which came to approximately $1.4 million—and paid it off. It was *not* easy. The possibility of either Tom or Nick rejoining the group is totally remote and, as far as I'm concerned, *impossible.* But then they never got along, anyway.

"Nick, I don't know where he is now, but he's become sort of laid back and sits around and writes poetry and that kind of thing. I think he made a big mistake. The last I heard of Tom he was a dealer in Vegas and then had a pizza place."

And what of the new Four Seasons? Didn't they just have a song out about some guy getting laid for the first time? Sure, it was called "December, 1963 (Oh, What a Night)." Catchy, semi-erotic car radio fare. After an eight-year absence from the Top 10, *something* called the Four Seasons bounced back with two killer singles: the aforementioned stroke serenade and a disco dazzler entitled "Who Loves You." Both were written by a young woman named Judy Parker and a now bushy-bearded Bob Gaudio, who says he stopped touring with the group in 1970, "because I'm a lazy bum and I don't know anybody worse onstage."

Consequently, Frankie Valli embarked upon a lonely, years-long, trial-and-error talent hunt that saw the brief appearance of such plebian personalities as Paul Wilson, Bill DeLoach, Demetri Callas, and Clay Jordan, before settling on the present unit: bassist Don Ciccone, author of the classic "Mr. Dieingly Sad" while a member of the Critters ("I also sang the Cover Girl commercials and 'The Man From Nationwide' insurance song"); guitarist John Paiva, who once played on a minor hit called "Lovely Lies" while with Cal Ray and the Classaires; keyboardist/arranger Lee Shapiro, late of the Manhattan School of Music, and drummer Gerry Polci, who studied with Joe Morello of the Dave Brubeck Quartet. Of the four, only one (Don) says he was a Four Seasons fan. The others confide that they were "into *different* things."

The rest of the details add up to one of the most unique contractual configurations in the annals of the record industry. Gaudio explains: "Since the inception of the Four Seasons, Frankie and I have had a mutual agreement that whatever *he* made, *I* made and vice versa. Whatever we do creatively in this business we go 50-50 partners on, whether he's out on the road earning $20,000 a night solo *or* with the group; or whether I write 'Can't Take My Eyes Off You' and that sells x amount of records. But there's no binding paperwork between us. For fifteen years, it's all been on a handshake."

Peter Bennett, esq., the Four Seasons' attorney since 1969, fills in the blanks: "Bob Gaudio and Frankie own the name, 'The Four Seasons,' and the present members of the group are under exclusive contract to them for all personal appearances, TV, recording, everything. They are employees of The Four Seasons and do not perform without Frankie Valli. If the personnel of The Four Seasons needs to be changed for any reason, it can be done at any time by terminating the contracts of the employees.

"Also, Gaudio and Valli own the masters of all the Four Seasons' records from their biggest period with Vee-Jay and Mercury/Phillips. They are leased periodically to companies like Private Stock or the Longines Symphonette Society. This is handled very carefully. Not long ago, all the old Four Seasons product was withdrawn from the market for a period of two years as a merchandising move; we calculated that the absence of the old records would create a new demand, and we were quite correct. Perhaps we'll do that again in the future.

"When Frankie Valli signed a contract with Private Stock, and the Four Seasons signed with Warner Brothers/Mike Curb, we decided to give up the rights to future masters so that we could have two separate recording entities. Valli and Gaudio do not retain ownership of these new records but both companies can release *only* the product we designate and only when we designate it. This gives us complete control over which record follows which, and that prevents Frankie Valli's records from conflicting with Four Seasons records, especially those on which Frankie appears. One label couldn't handle it as well.

"Frankly, I don't know of any other group with an analogous contractual situation."

In other words, Valli and Gaudio at last have the independent record deal they've always wanted. The Four Seasons you used to know and love no longer exists. Even Warner Bros. realizes you wouldn't recognize the group anymore, so it didn't bother putting a photo of the present "employees" on the jacket of their latest LP. But the smart money in the industry says you'll strike up a long-term romance with these ringers, just as you embraced a reconstituted King Kong and a diet Dr Pepper. They're probably right, since "December, 1963" was the best-selling single in the group's, er, name's, er, *Four Seasons'* existence.

And what of Frankie Valli, the Flying Falsetto, the Survivor's Star, the man who holds no grudges, harbors no bitterness, and forgives all his trespasses? Well, you'd scarcely recognize him either.

"There's no real cure for my ear condition," Valli asserts solemnly as he takes a place close to his wife on the couch opposite mine. "It's a slow deterioration process, and these operations I'm having are very, very risky."

The sky beyond the high windows surrounding the three of us is overcast as we speak. Even in the muted gray light, it's plain that the ten years Valli has spent grappling with his malady have weighed upon his gaunt shoulders, hastening the aging process for the once child-faced man to where he is now best described as ruggedly handsome. Some might regard it as an improvement. The wavy, wet-look hairstyle of a decade ago has given way to a weathered, wind-blown cut, graying—although some attempt may have been made to conceal it—at the temples and sideburns. The familiar pale, fluid features are now heavily tanned and craggy, an aquiline nose flanked by ruddy cheeks and flared pores; the kind but suspicious hazel-brown eyes are framed by crow's feet and subtle yet puffy bags, and at the sides of his mouth hover two fanciful crescent creases that one could call either character or worry lines.

Allowing for the dichotomy between common dissipation and long-term distress, Frankie Valli closely resembles a youthful Dean Martin—if you can remember back that far.

"What I've got is called *otosclerosis,*" he tells me in a stiff sonorous tone that diffuses his North Jersey nasality. "To explain it simply, these calcium-type deposits build up over a period of time inside my middle ear, and the inner mechanism, that little hammer inside, can't function properly. It gets stuck, frozen, and I can only hear the very loudest of sounds. Like you, tapping your hand there; I can't hear that out of my right ear. No way.

"When I first found out, back in '67, that my hearing was going, I was *destroyed.* I wanted to throw myself out a window. If I couldn't hear anymore—could you imagine—if I couldn't *sing,* what's the point in continuing? After all the work, hardship, all the sacrifices and waiting—not being able to sing? I mean, this is my life! And, I'll tell you, I decided at the time that I did *not* want to live any longer. *Period.*"

Mary Ann Valli winces. "Can you imagine that doctor who first examined him, just handing him that note and walking away?" she asks.

"Luckily, I got a hold of myself," says Frankie, "and went to see some other doctors, the best I could find, specialists. Basically, it was my left ear in particular that was bothering me, though both were affected. I can hear fine out of my left ear now, but before undergoing the operation last year—I could have lost what I had—I went through a period of depression which was rather difficult for my wife, Mary Ann, to live with. She was super-understanding about the whole thing, which made it easier.

"The left ear is okay now, but the right ear is fading and now I have to have *that* taken care of."

It's odd that I've never heard much about his hearing troubles before, I tell Valli. How was he able to continue making records and touring?

"Well," he confesses, unsmiling, "it hasn't been easy. In the studio, for instance, the level I had to have my headphones turned up to was extremely high. Nobody could *believe* that a human could listen at this level. It was so loud it was shattering. And when we did a playback, everyone had to leave the studio because they couldn't bear it.

"The other thing that was happening on a personal front was that people must have thought that I was coming on strong and not really paying attention to any of their conversations. It got to the point before I had the ear done where I was watching lips, but I couldn't make it. And telephone calls were *impossible.*"

Valli rises and strides across the room to a telephone sitting on a lamp table. He takes the receiver from its cradle and holds it up with the underside facing me, pointing to a little black disk set into the arch of the arm. "Do you know what this is?" he wonders ruefully. "This is equipment for the deaf. When I answer the phone, say, with my right ear, I have to turn the volume up all the way with this adjustment."

He flicks the control disk until the telephone's dial tone is almost as clearly audible from across the room as a TV test pattern drone. Valli lifts the blaring phone to his right ear and speaks pensively, almost to himself: "I . . . I don't hear this so well. . . . Right now, I can't with this ear."

He replaces the receiver gingerly and then glances back at me, apparently reading the astonished expression on my face.

"So you *see* what's at stake for me here, don't you? Obviously, I can't go on like this. The operation on my right ear—I believe it will work out, but I could lose it. The other thing you have to understand is that this otosclerosis can't be cured—yet. Two or ten or twenty years from now, my left ear may be in trouble again, and each time they perform this operation it becomes more delicate, more dangerous.

"Really, when I first discovered this about myself, I've gotta admit I was not the most pleasant person to be around. But then my life, my career, has never been easy. Never. Not since the very beginning."

"We never knew my son sang," says Donna Maria Castelluccio, sixty-three, with a nod to her husband as she smooths out the lap of her blue apron. "He was a teenager with a record contract, and I never heard him sing even *once.*"

Mrs. Castelluccio, a shy, pillowy woman with a chiming laugh and a casual sense of irony, has recently returned home from the hospital after being rushed there on a heart attack scare. As she and her spindly husband reminisce in the cozy living room of their North Newark apartment, she speaks with a self-imposed impatience, as if afraid she may not get another opportunity.

"A woman who used to live across the way—what was her name?—well, she used to go, 'Mrs. Castelluccio, Frankie's gon' be singin' in the Silhouette Bar on Mount Prospect Avenue tonight. Why don' you come for once and hear your son sing!' " She pauses, pressing her hand to her breast to catch her breath. "Well, you see we always had so much sickness, my husband and I, we didn't find the time. One night Frankie come home—this was jus' after I had the last of my three sons, Bobby. An' he says, 'Mother, you have to come to New York tomorrow!'

"I says, 'New York? Tomorrow? Why, your baby brother Bobby's in the hospital!' 'Cause, see, I had recently had a hysterectomy, and a week later little Bobby caught pneumonia.

"But Frankie insisted. He said, 'Ma, you and Daddy have to come to New York to sign contracts for me.' I says, 'Contracts for what?' So we went to New York [in 1953], and Mr. Paul Kapp, who was the brother of Dave Kapp of the Kapp Records, he takes us into his office and puts a record on and it was my Frankie! Singin' so beautiful, with just a bass and guitar! And I almost cried. He never told me anything. It was, you know, a shock.

"Mr. Kapp says to me, 'You never *heard* Frankie before?' and I says, 'Never. This is the first.' An' it was so beautiful. Do you know what he was singin' on that record? He was singin' the Georgie Jessel song, 'My Mother's Eyes.' "

The Castelluccios have lived for thirty-seven years in the apartment in which we're seated, located in Stephen Crane Village, the first lower-income government housing project in the city. The two-story apartment, one in a catty-cornered complex of connected brick buildings, is so small it seems incredible that three boys could have been raised within its walls. Now the rooms are filled with friendly ghosts and fancied echoes of youthful voices. The frail couple prefers these familiar surroundings and kindred spirits to the alien rootlessness of the Los Angeles home into which their famous son would prefer they moved.

"My son wanted us outta here a long time ago," says Mrs. Castelluccio with a girlish smirk. "He told a newspaper he was gonna put a bomb under our floor, and they printed it! But I'm here all these years and my roots are here. My other son, Alex, who's a butcher in an A&P in Bloomfield, he's got four children and they're grandchildren! Frankie comes out here a lot; he can afford it. But would I see the rest of my family if I went to California? No."

"Frankie used to sing in the bathroom sometimes," recalls Valli's chain-smoking father. "He used to say to me, 'I'm gonna be a singer!' But I'd say, 'You ain't gonna be *nothing.* You're gonna go to school and get an education.' He used to sing in grammar school at Christmas and Easter plays—and then on streetcorners. But he started getting somewhere when he met this hillbilly singer named Texas Jean Valley—that's where he took his stage name from. She heard him singing in some bar and took him to her studio on Broad Street and had this 'Mother's Eyes' record made [under the name Frankie Valley and the Travellers]. I went to see Frankie a few times, like down in a bar in Harrison, New Jersey, but we were always busy working, or sick or something else. He quit high school to be a singer. He did it on his own.

"That's the way it is when you're poor," says Castelluccio. "Everything was hard for us. Nothing came easy when Frankie was growing up. We used to pass his clothes on to the other boys.

"I'm just an ordinary working man. I worked in factories, and I used to work for the Lionel Corporation—you know, the model trains? I made train layouts for department store display windows, the mountains and villages. Did it for twenty years. But I'm retired because I'm sixty-five and I've had enough. We had *nothing.*"

"When Frankie was born, my husband was very depressed," says Mrs. Castelluccio quietly. "There was no money."

"He was an obedient boy," Mr. Castelluccio continues slowly. "Even today, I could holler at him, scream at him, and he wouldn't say nothing. He's got a family of his own, and he still don't talk back. But one time I bought him a bicycle, and I told him just to ride it around here and keep outta the street. As soon as he gets home with the bike, he rides it in the street. I saw him, and I got out there with a knife and cut the tires right off the new bike. He didn't give me trouble on that, either."

"Yeah," Mrs. Castelluccio interjects timidly, "but you gave Frankie a terrible beating, Papa."

Frankie's father pauses, then averts his eyes, speaking with a quavery resoluteness. "He was a good kid. Newark was a tough place to be. Frankie was never a bad boy; I made sure. But I worried some with the singing, instead of him working regular."

Frankie Castelluccio was not a bad boy. He ran with some bad boys, true, skipping school almost daily by the time he reached Central High School to hang out all day at the Branford Lanes, or Puggy Ross's pool hall in Belleville, or just to loll around some corner off Franklin Avenue, tackling some buddies' impromptu *a cappella* arrangement of the Spaniels' "Baby It's You."

Frankie was too small to be a really bad boy, which is why he hung out with some of the *big* bad boys who liked to throw hands at the weekend dances down at the Whiteway Ballroom and shoot craps against the curbstones.

Still, he was hardly a reprobate; his father made certain he always had a legitimate job, whether it was stocking shelves and labeling bottles of linseed oil in the Pepper Bros. paint store on Broadway, or caddying, delivering milk, or spotting pins in the bowling alleys on Bloomfield Avenue. Yet the allure of the streets was irresistible.

"You have to realize that most European parents were geared to push the children to get at least a minimum amount of education," counsels Frankie Valli. "Then they had to go to work. It was just something I could never see myself doing. I was singing under streetlights and getting my education in pool rooms, cutting school to hustle nine ball for a dollar a man, or pill [rotation] pool for a dollar a ball. And I was winning $60, $70, $100 some nights. I was about fourteen and pool, you know, it's like golf—it's something you have to do all the time to get good. So I did it all the time.

"I came out of that whole *doo-wop,* streetcorner environment," he admits, "and I'm not ashamed to tell anybody. I didn't know a kid in my life who didn't steal an apple from a peddler. When I was older there were always fights at football and basketball games; a riot every time, started by whoever lost, with pipes and feet flying. There were fights at dances constantly, from somebody making a pass at somebody else's girl or a girl from outta the neighborhood. I saw a lot of my friends fall by the wayside and get wasted; found in a car with their heads blown off or in the city dump in the trunk of a car. I'm not bullshitting you. It was *West Side Story* time. I actually had a problem with a gang because I was going with a girl from *their* neighborhood. I mean, me fighting six guys?! I took a good beating.

"There was an incident in my first year in high school where I had some difficulty with a much bigger kid. Being the oldest of three brothers, I had to fight my own battles. This kid, he was shaking me down in school—up against the wall, pockets out—and he was like *four* of me. I was never any bigger than I am now [5′ 7″], and at that time I couldn't have weighed more than 110; I could never make 114 to be eligible for the football team. There was no chance in the world of fighting the guy, but I said to myself, 'This is going to be a four-year problem unless I straighten it out right away.'

"I went home one day, got a bat, came to school and got up behind the guy and smashed him with all my might in the head with it. Thinking about it now, I could have killed him, but it was something I couldn't live with; he was really leaning on me.

"Next day, there's this guy back in school with his head totally bandaged! He must have had sixteen or eighteen stitches—and he's doing exactly what he was doing to me to some other kids who were a little weaker. The same shakedown bullshit! I looked him straight in the face and walked into school. He never bothered me again. Tried to become one of my best friends, but I wouldn't have anything to do with it. It was better to take a beating than be scared. That was *survival.*"

And it was nowhere. Frankie knew he was merely auditioning for a spot in one of those car trunks in the city dump, but he didn't know how to break free—until Texas Jean Valley pointed the way. She got him a job singing and faking the upright bass with her brother Jody's country and western combo. From there he jumped to a local lounge act called the Variety Trio, which became the Variatones, the Four Lovers, and finally—the Four Seasons. Working under the guidance of veteran producer Bob Crewe (coauthor of the Rays' 1957 hit "Silhouettes"), the Seasons issued their initial release, a cover of "Bermuda," on Gone Records. The second was a silly thing called "Sherry."

"Frankie was on the verge of giving up at that stage," his father remembers. "He was twenty-eight by then, a man with a family and no future. He had a maintenance job for the city of Newark, and he went to a hairdresser's school [The American College of Cosmetology]. He was gonna cut hair, like my father wanted me to do!"

Mrs. Castelluccio nods in agreement. "He struggled, and I knew my Frankie would get a hit record someday. He never had a lesson, but he could sing you church music, cowboy, rock and roll. I was surprised though, when it happened. We were over his house one day, and the boys from the group was there and they were rehearsin' their new song. I says, 'Sherry, won't you come out tonight? What kind of a song is that?' "

There has long been an often heated controversy both inside and outside the Four Seasons organization concerning who deserves the majority of credit for the "genius," as Frankie Valli puts it, behind the group's sound. Apart from the glaring presence of Valli's technically amazing voice, some say their considerable commercial success should be attributed in the main to the compositional flair of Bob Gaudio. Others feel the kudos should go to Bob Crewe, who was cranking out hits with Frank Slay and other collaborators before, during, and after the Seasons' halcyon days. The matter isn't close to being settled, having recently contributed to a rift between Crewe and Valli. (The other reason, according to Valli, is that Crewe stuck him with "$30,000 to $40,000 worth of unfinished tracks" for a forthcoming solo album, and ran off to produce Disco-Tex and his Sex-o-lettes.)

"I don't mean to discredit anybody," says Valli, "but Bob Gaudio in my opinion had produced *everything* in those early Four Seasons records. He also sat and worked out every arrangement on everything the Four Seasons or Frankie Valli ever did—including 'Can't Take My Eyes Off You'—and never was credited."

Why is that?

"Because he was not the assigned producer, and he was an intricate part of the Four Seasons. Bob Crewe was the official producer, and he wasn't about to split his production credits with *anybody.* Bob Gaudio has had ten or twelve years of classical music under his belt; besides the fact that he also writes lyrics. Bob Gaudio is, was, and always will be a melody chord writer, a true music writer.

"Bob Crewe is a music writer in this sense: Without anybody to play chords and melodies, how are you gonna write music?! Bob Crewe has not had any writing success unless it's been with somebody else—which tells you something immediately."

Bob Crewe, taking an opposite view, has something to tell Frankie Valli.

"I don't know what kind of credit [Gaudio] wanted," he says evenly. "I think Bob *got* his credit as a writer. If you're gonna start that, you have to start giving more credit to the assigned arranger, who was usually Charlie Calello. There are no bad memories in my head. If somebody feels something was done improperly, I don't. If you want to go around throwing bitter pills, saying 'Hey, I put that music together, I should have been called the producer,' well, that problem is your own to digest. That was one of the reasons why we split."

Getting down to specifics, Bob Gaudio maintains that he wrote "Sherry" literally in fifteen minutes before leaving for one of the Seasons' rehearsals: "I sat down at the piano, and the melody came instantly. I had no tape recorder, so in order to remember the melody—I didn't write music then—I had to put a quick lyric on it. That's what I did, and those became the lyrics! Also, Frankie used to do a popular jazz improvisation in clubs of 'I'm in the Mood for Love' called 'Moody's Mood for Love,' using his falsetto extensively, and I wrote 'Sherry' specifically with that number in mind. We rehearsed the song and sang it over the phone to Bob Crewe, and he thought it was a smash."

Crewe's memories are slightly different. "I saw Frankie in a place in Point Pleasant, New Jersey, one night, and he did an imitation of Rose Murphy with castanets and a scarf around his head, singing a jazzy 'I'm in the Mood for Love.' I said to Bob Gaudio, 'If you could incorporate that high falsetto into your material, we'd have something!' Two or three weeks later Bob came up with 'Sherry.' At first it was called 'Jackie,' in reference to Jackie Kennedy. It seemed like a positive way to go, but then we changed it.

"After 'Sherry' hit, we didn't know what the hell to follow it up with," Crewe continues. "I was up late one night in my apartment, worrying and watching a dreadful movie, I think it was with John Payne and some blonde bombshell. I had been drinking out of desperation, and I was drifting in and out of sleep. I woke up at one point, and Payne was smacking the blonde across the face and knocked her on her bottom. He said something like, 'Well, whadda ya think of that, baby?' She gets up, straightens her dress, pushes her hair back, stares at him, and says, 'Big girls don't cry!' and storms out the door. I ran and jotted down the line. The next day Bob and I knocked out the song in no time, and, of course, it was a hit."

Egos aside, one of the most fascinating stories behind the origin of a Four Seasons' standard is the poignant impetus for "Rag Doll":

"Back around 1964," Bob Gaudio begins, "there was one particular place on Tenth Avenue, I think, in New York City where there's a long traffic light; it must have been forty-five seconds long. I'd go by there a lot, and there were little kids around it that would come up and offer to clean your car windows while you were waiting. You'd pay them a quarter or fifty cents. One particular time this little girl came over to me, and I had no change at all; the smallest thing I had was a five-dollar bill, so I gave it to her because it would have broken my heart to not give her anything.

"The look on her face—she didn't say *anything*—stayed with me for weeks. The description of the rag doll in the song was a description of that little girl. I guess you could say the five dollars was an investment."

Crewe and Gaudio are both willing to admit to their mistakes, the former conceding that "you battle over your share of the hits and conveniently forget the flops." Gaudio, for instance, is extremely repentant on the subject of *Genuine Imitation Life Gazette*, a Four Seasons' "concept" LP released in December 1968 whose clever gatefold newspaper format predated similar album packaging for Jethro Tull's *Thick as a Brick* and John Lennon's *Sometime in New York City*.

It was a dry period for the Four Seasons: no Top 20 singles in two years. Gaudio got the idea for the concept after hearing Jake Holmes sing the title song one night at the Bitter End. The two became friends and cowrote the entire record, whose dulcet, pneumatic music closely paralleled, interestingly enough, portions of the Beach Boys' *Surf's Up* and *Sunflower*.

Unfortunately, from a thematic standpoint the songs were abominable, with a lot of leaden, finger-wagging lyrics about social ills and gossipy old women. Encountering the *Gazette* in the nation's record racks that year, most hip Christmas shoppers shrugged and bought the Beatles' White Album instead.

"The *Gazette* was the mark of the Four Seasons' downfall," says Gaudio. "I know it was right for me but wrong for us. I saw the market changing, and we had a terrible internal problem. I was alone in my feeling that we could do other things besides 'I Love You, You Love Me' songs, and I forced the issue. The group relied on me for material, and I said it was this or nothing; either this or you're gonna have to find somebody else.

"The record did badly, and a deep confusion set in. After that we regressed, and even the records we tried to make in our old Four Seasons sound were bad imitations. As an alternative, we tried Motown, but that was the worst, mentally *and* creatively; the wrong place at the wrong time.

"I remember a week or so when Motown had Frankie in a studio every night with a different producer, desperately trying to get *anything* going. We put out an album called *Chameleon* on the label, but you couldn't get arrested with the thing."

Taking time out from the production chores on the Four Seasons' forthcoming *Helicon* album (for which he and Judy Parker wrote all the songs), the thirty-five-year-old Gaudio thanks Mike Curb and Warner Bros. for helping to restore his disintegrating self-confidence. He says he hit his stride again while working on the *Who Loves You* LP; even so, Gaudio discloses that "December, 1963," the Seasons' first No. 1 single since "Rag Doll," came perilously close to being a clunker.

"The song was originally called 'December 5, 1933,'" he explains. "It was about the repeal of Prohibition. Judy was never completely happy with the first lyrics. She felt they were too cute, probably bordering on some of the things on the *Gazette* album. Finally we wrote new words, and I reworked the melody. There's no question it was an improvement."

To illustrate his point, he reads aloud one of the old verses:

Mushin' mash beneath their feet
Doin' the Charleston in the street
Ain't no way to be discreet
Rollin' 'round in a rumble seat

Oh, what a night! December 5th in 1933. . . .

With Frankie's mother's health failing and Frankie himself due to be hospitalized soon, the holiday mood around the Castelluccio household is somewhat subdued. I am rising to go when a petite girl of about eighteen descends from upstairs. Antonia Valli, Frankie's eldest daughter, has been living with her grandparents since a recent falling out with her mother, who presently resides in nearby Bloomfield with Antonia's younger sister Francine and stepsister, Celia.

Antonia is waiting for her boyfriend to pick her up, and so we chat. She possesses an inordinate amount of poise for a girl her age, and admits she grew up "too fast."

"My father couldn't always be home when I was growing up, but I think it was more upsetting to him than us," she offers timorously. "He hardly has any time to himself, but he never forgot to call me on a birthday or a holiday—never. I was out in California with my father last year before his last ear operation, and he said, 'I have some time off. We'll spend some time together, do some fun things, and just have a good time!'

"I said, 'Great!' But most of the time it was spent going to meet this writer or eat dinner with that one. The little time he does have to himself, I don't know how he does it 'cause he's always gotta be ten-in-one all the time. But still it's incredible how he remembers everything."

Antonia has nothing to say about her mother; her parents' parting was a painful one for all concerned. She has glowing praise, however, for her father's second spouse.

"Mary Ann is tops with me," she says. "She's all for my father and stuck by him through his troubles. She told me that after the last operation he had to be in quiet seclusion for at least a month. I didn't realize, myself, how bad it was for him until I was over his apartment in Fort Lee one afternoon when the phone rang. My father asked me to answer it, and I said, 'Hello—*Aaah!*' The receiver was so loud I couldn't talk into it because it hurt my ear!

"I was so afraid my father would be left without hearing, that he could never talk to me or hear my voice again. I wanted to tell him all the things I feel now so that he could hear me say them."

"COME ON," roars Frankie Valli, "LET ME HEAR THE LOVE!!"

And they respond, leaping to their feet, thousands strong, predominately teenaged—and female. He has barely enough time for a graceless retreat from the tip of the stage when they rush with arms outstretched, some pleading, others crying, and a few screaming as if in open anguish of being, to borrow a phrase, "so close and yet so far away."

It is the last show of the Four Seasons' sold-out 1976 tour, and as the SRO throng in the Lansing, Michigan, Civic Center demand—and get—a fourth encore, hundreds of young girls shower the diminutive man in the cream-colored Nudie outfit with flowers, jewelry, shameless shouted promises, and dozens of tightly folded notes containing God-only-knows-what impatient scribbles of the heart. It's a red-letter evening for the little lady killer, right up there with the night several cities ago when that woman threw her panties onstage, complete with address, phone number, and a pass key.

In an era of Peter Frampton and Boz Scaggs, where did all these pubescent girls find the time to discover Frankie Valli?

The group has run through their recent hits and exhausted their solid-gold repertoire, yet as they erupt for the second time in Valli's new single, "Boomerang," the lunging young ladies on the front lines reply with the ultimate accolade: "OHHHH, FRANKEEE!"

Ten minutes later, the house lights are up and the auditorium almost empty when a comely blonde coed, looking anxiously over her shoulder from a side exit, suddenly returns to the stage to rescue a doubled bit of paper from the path of a push broom.

"What have you got there?" asks a roadie standing nearby. "Did you toss *him* that note?"

Stuffing the unopened scrap into the pocket of her blue suede jacket, she turns without answering and then back again with a question of her own.

"What's Frankie Valli, thirty-five?" she inquires. "He's about the same as Mick Jagger 'n Neil Diamond, right?"

"He's forty-two," the roadie says flatly.

"But he's *good*-looking," she retorts archly.

Changing planes in Cleveland's Hopkins Airport the following morning to catch the 9:50 into Newark, Valli and I stroll together to the gate, him doing most of the talking.

"Did you get everything you need?" he challenges. "The Four Seasons have been together over fourteen years."

Rather than contest the viability of that remark, I let him ramble on about an article ("Who's Afraid of Growing Old?") he'd read in the United Airlines magazine during the connecting flight.

"They say if you don't think about growing old when you're young, you'll feel young when you get there," he announces, brandishing his rolled-up copy of the magazine.

"I once read another article where they said that heroin slows down aging," he relates, fascinated. "People in the Orient have been smoking opium for centuries, and they live to be 100 or more. If they could separate the pure essence from the drug's addictive properties, they say it could suspend you at the age you were when you began taking it!

"I don't think about the future anymore," he continues gravely. "That kind of tense thinking kills you. And when I'm on the road I tear up itineraries. Even elderly people will tell you that *activity* is the key to happiness. My only vacation will be after the ear operation, when I'll rest and do nothing only because I'll have to . . ."

He has been rubbing the back of his right hand all morning; I ask if he's worried about something.

"No," he says, holding out his hand to show me two nasty gouges above his knuckles.

"Last night at the show this crazy blonde girl in the audience reached up and grabbed my hand, digging her nails right into the skin. Didn't she realize she was hurting me? I mean, shit, what did she want?"

He shrugs in passive disgust. "Anyhow, have you considered that in all these years we've never learned how to treat our elders? These people work all their lives in order to make a simple statement, and we show our appreciation by discarding or mistreating them . . ."

The young sometimes fear the old, I tell him.

"There's nothing to be afraid of," he assures solemnly, and walks down the ramp into the waiting plane.

Brian Wilson

1988

Brian Wilson is alone.

The reclusive leader and most famous member of the Beach Boys has just completed his daily six-mile morning jog along Pacific Coast Highway. His bodyguard was to have waited with him at the gatehouse of Southern California's Malibu Colony until my arrival; from there they were to guide me to Wilson's secluded house several miles up the coastline.

No one, however, has converged on schedule, owing to Wilson's placid pace, and the bodyguard's having been called away on another errand. The heavily shielded Wilson, who is normally as inaccessible to the press and public as Michael Jackson, is left unattended for perhaps the first time in years.

When I pull up in my rental car, Wilson—in expensive sneakers, powder blue T-shirt, and a snug pair of yellow athletic trunks emblazoned with surfboards and tropical flowers—is dawdling uncertainly at the stucco gatehouse. He is plainly unnerved by his unaccustomed freedom.

"Gosh! This has been strange—er, funny," he says with a tremulous gulp as he folds his six-foot-plus frame into the passenger seat. "I'm not used to being in a lonesome situation. It's a different feeling."

Anyone who remembers the rock

musician of the 1970s and early 1980s would be astonished by the Brian Wilson of today. Then, disdaining all moderation in food and alcohol, and careless of the amount of drugs he consumed, the man who was the Beach Boys' creative genius was an unkempt, 320-pound dissolute.

Brian Wilson today is lean and fit. In repose, the forty-six-year-old singer-songwriter looks like someone's handsome but rather somber dad. And when he smiles, there are glimmerings of the fresh-faced innocent he was twenty-seven years ago, when he and four other teenagers introduced the exuberant "California sound"—one that was to create the fable of a carefree life of sun, surf, and sand. But to spend any time with Wilson is to be in the company of a man who retains the painful shyness of his youth, still trying desperately to cope with the demands of success and fame.

Wilson's happy myth of an untrammeled life of endless summers struck a chord in American suburbia in a way no other popular musicians had done. The essence of the American dream is the belief that anyone can escape the limits and sorrows of his background by reinventing himself. A musical group that started out in a garage with three brothers, a cousin, and a neighborhood chum, the Beach Boys themselves embodied and celebrated that dream. Stuck in a characterless corner of the greater Los Angeles suburban sprawl, the band imbued the neighboring tract townships, tangled highway cloverleafs, and municipal beach parks with storied sparkle. And by doing so became the most successful musical group in American history.

When James Watt, who then was Interior Secretary, attempted in April 1983 to ban the Beach Boys from the annual Fourth of July celebration in the Washington Mall—because rock groups, he said, attracted the "wrong element"—the ensuing uproar only reinforced the group's standing in the popular imagination. President Reagan subsequently had the band play at the White House.

The uncomplicated, joyous sound of the Beach Boys, however, long masked not only growing friction among the group members but Brian Wilson's own rapidly disintegrating world. Wilson's journey back from the abyss began in early 1983, when he placed himself under the twenty-four-hour-a-day supervision of Eugene Landy, a Los Angeles psychologist whose patients must have the financial resources—he charges $200 an hour—and be willing to submit to his draconian method of treatment. In 1976, Landy had briefly had the songwriter under his care; the psychologist's more recent treatment of Wilson, however, is under investigation by the California Attorney General's office, which, among other complaints, accuses Landy of acting improperly as Wilson's business manager while he was his therapist.

"See, I had a helluva time getting through some of the frustrations that go along with being a successful record artist," Wilson recalls quietly as we speed along the road parallel to the sloping Santa Monica Mountains. "When I got out there with the Beach Boys, at first I was OK, because I was riding a wave, riding a crest." The obvious surfing analogy is delivered without irony. "But then, later on, ten years later, I got scared, and I got *lost,* and I was eating caramel sundaes for breakfast. I was all out of whack!

"Now I try to stay in shape so that I'm able to handle the stress that comes up in my career," he explains, blinking into the blazing sun. "Living close to the sea is good for your head. You're living at the foot of eternity, and it gives you perspective when you're overly fixated on survival. I know that if I wasn't in good shape physically today, I'd be in bad shape mentally."

A measure of how far Wilson has come, both personally and as a songwriter, is his first solo album, *Brian Wilson,* which was released in July 1988. "I had decided to do a solo album back around 1985," says Wilson, "because I was pretty disappointed with the lack of success of the last Beach Boys album" (*The Beach Boys,* released that year), "and I thought I could do better on my own. Dr. Landy thought so, too."

The composer of such unfettered Beach Boys classics as "Fun, Fun, Fun" and "Good Vibrations" has written eleven new songs that retain the pure, pealing harmonies and heart-tugging vulnerability of his best Beach Boys songs, while displaying a deft ability to bend modern studio technology—synthesizers, computerized sound mixing—to his own poignant themes.

"Rio Grande," an extended song Wilson wrote with a fellow songwriter, Andy Paley, is about a grueling pilgrimage across forbidding terrain. For Wilson, it is considerably more: "The storyline is stating the impossible, with lyrics like 'Rio Grande, Rio Grande / I'd swim you but I can't.' It spells out the scary mental challenge of this whole album."

"I tend to want to 'shell up' and not relate," Wilson admits as he points the way to the back door of his house overlooking Santa

Monica Bay. "And there are times when I just want to quit." In a departure from previous encounters, when he would glance furtively at his interviewer, he makes confident eye contact as he continues talking, his blue-green gaze as piercing as his tone is placid. "I feel like somehow if I shell up and don't relate to people, somehow I'm getting back at somebody for crippling me."

Who might that somebody be?

"That's hard to say. It was probably . . ." He hesitates, trembling slightly, either from the chill ocean gusts or from the hard words he is stammering. "M-my father . . . I don't think about him consciously too much anymore, but I think maybe my father was a little bit too rough on me, and he kinda did a *boom! boom! boom!* thing on my head."

He gets out of the car and ambles to the back door of the expensive rental, a cantilevered bungalow whose three floors of bedrooms, mini-atriums, and deck patios would nicely serve a couple with several children. Wilson has two teenaged daughters, Carnie and Wendy, but they live with his former wife, Marilyn. By mutual agreement, Brian has little contact with them; Marilyn Wilson once told an interviewer that the songwriter had suffered so much from an abusive parent that he, afraid of repeating what his father had done, abrogated his duties as a father.

As Wilson hurries in through the kitchen, he apologizes to the resident security-chief-*cum*-bodyguard, Kevin Leslie, for being slightly late. (Wilson's recording associates refer to the taciturn, blond, and brawny security man as "The Surf Nazi.") He then goes to the gym opposite the master bedroom for a thrice-weekly workout with his exercise coach.

As he does his leg lifts, Wilson soberly summarizes his childhood: "All our lives, from the time we were born, my brothers and I raced to be what my father used to say we were: winners. 'So go out there and be winners!' he'd yell. I mean, really scream. And he'd turn and tell me, 'Write this song and make it a No. 1 record!' When your father tells you to do something, you do it, because all you've ever known since you were a little baby was that he was boss. It was very difficult."

The son of a Hawthorne, California, heavy-machinery salesman, Brian Douglas Wilson was born on June 20, 1942, and grew up deaf in one ear—possibly the result of a childhood blow administered by his father. When Murry Wilson, a frustrated songsmith and failed businessman, wasn't berating his wife, Audree, or badgering his

sons Dennis and Carl, he was beating up the eldest boy, Brian, for not living up to his hazy expectations. Murry Wilson's punishments ranged from a tongue-lashing to the bizarre practice of taking out his glass eye and forcing Brian to peer into the open socket.

The early sense of alienation that Brian's hearing impediment produced was heightened by the tough lower-middle-class environment of his community, a semi-industrialized tract on the fringes of Southern California's postwar manufacturing boom.

"It was the damned boondocks," Brian Wilson recalls. "I walked around paranoid that somebody was going to pound the hell out of me every second. The kids were bullies, angry and insecure about living in this ugly place instead of Malibu or Beverly Hills or Santa Monica. I tried to escape with sports like football, and I was a quarterback on the second-string team, but the punishment and competition were too much and I quit the squad. Then I tried baseball, which I loved, because I used to stand out there in center field and kinda sing to myself in between pitches."

Murry Wilson's flip-flopping role as freakish bully and overbearing booster ultimately found focus in the singing abilities that his brood demonstrated at holiday family musicales. The three boys had grown up listening to their parents' improvisations on the piano and organ. Brian, who had a beautiful boy soprano voice, sang at school functions and with the church choir.

Seeing the effect Brian's crisply angelic voice had on relatives and friends, Murry Wilson soon permitted his eldest son to pound freely at the parlor piano. In 1960, he provided instruments for a casual combo that included all three boys, plus a first cousin, Mike Love, and a buddy, Al Jardine.

The material the eighteen-year-old Brian devised with his companions was essentially a revamping of the prudish campus chorales of the Four Freshmen (a 1950s pop vocal act) grafted onto a Chuck Berry–inspired rock beat. In 1961, when Brian—who freely admits to a terror of the water—penned a song called "Surfin'," based on his brother Dennis's exploits, the group found its focus. "Surfin' " led to a contract with one of the nation's chief pop labels, Capitol Records.

Before the sudden ascension of Brian's Beach Boys in the pop hegemony of the early 1960s, Philles Records owner/producer Phil Spector had been the undisputed soothsayer of rock and roll, his towering "Wall of Sound" studio craft with such girl groups as the Ronettes and the Crystals appearing impervious. In their first three

years with Capitol, the Beach Boys placed eight singles in the national Top 20. Among their sunny, lightly buffed hits were "Surfin' Safari," "Fun, Fun, Fun," "I Get Around," and their quintessential smash, "Surfin' U.S.A." (which also sounded so much like Chuck Berry's "Sweet Little Sixteen" that lawyers stepped in and Berry was given cowriting credit with Brian).

The music that toppled Spector wasn't pushy and street-smart like Philles' widely imitated urban jangle. It was more idyllic and companionable, and the centerpiece of Brian's arranging style was a tabernacle of untutored, unabashedly nasal male voices.

The lyrics and music of the young, gifted songwriter reflected his own fantasies of a happier adolescence. Odes to beach-blanket puppy love, the novelty of surfing and borrowing your dad's car on date night touched a generation for whom suburbia had until then meant blandness and stagnation.

In 1963, Brian scored a Top 10 success with "Surfer Girl," a simple but astute interweaving of instruments and vocal harmonies that signaled the advent of the suburban rock *auteur.* For the first time, a pop artist had served as writer, arranger, producer, and featured performer of his band's own hit output. But the unrelenting pressure to produce hits, to top himself again and again, soon overwhelmed the ultrasensitive superstar. In late 1964, while on a plane bound for Texas, Wilson came undone.

The plane was five minutes out of Los Angeles, en route to Houston, when the screaming started. The tall, dough-faced young man sitting in the forward section, whose manic stares before takeoff had since given way to white-knuckled catatonia, had suddenly begun crying and then making jagged, high-pitched yowls as he grabbed for his pillow. His traveling companions leaped to his side, trying to pry the pillow from his swollen face.

"Cool it, Brian!" barked Al Jardine.

"My God, what's wrong, Brian?" asked pudgy Carl Wilson. "Brian, please tell me what's wrong!"

By now Brian Wilson had spun out of his seat and was on the cabin floor, sobbing convulsively.

"I can't take it!" hollered Brian, as he rolled and lurched about the plane. "I just can't take it! Don't you understand? I'm not getting off this plane!"

Wilson went on to perform that night, but he woke up at the

hotel the next morning with a crippling knot in his stomach. Throughout the day, he burst into tears at half-hour intervals. The group's road manager put Brian on the late plane back to Los Angeles, where he was met by his mother, Audree. She drove her son to his boyhood home at West 119 Street in Hawthorne, California. (The Wilsons had moved to a new house in Whittier, but they'd held on to their previous home.) Once inside his old bedroom, the emotional floodgates burst. Over the next seventeen months, Brian would have two more serious breakdowns. His doctors advised him that continued touring could prove disastrous not only to his psyche but also to his hearing. Since childhood, Brian had been deaf in his right ear, and his left ear was being overtaxed by the escalating decibels at live rock and roll concerts. It was a low blow. The Beach Boys had been his creation, his window to the world. Through them he had been able to break out of his childhood shell, overcome his paralyzing reticence. He loved performing—stepping up to the microphone and singing his lyrics, in his harmonies, set to his music.

Now that outlet was done, and he shunned all personal appearances, making recording rooms his preferred lair. Holed up in his Bel Air mansion for months on end, he fed his depression with a diet of milkshakes, hashish brownies, and random psychedelic drugs.

Employing the *Billboard* sales surveys as a yardstick for his own isolation, Brian's vicarious infatuation with the seaside faded as he lost interest in virtually everything but bettering the flourishing Beatles. Anguished at how they continued to batter the Beach Boys in the record charts, and awed by the artistic cohesion of *Rubber Soul,* Brian brought his group's output to an abrupt halt. He wanted to make a concept album, one that, like *Rubber Soul,* would have a unity of mood, but one that would have a cumulative emotional impact as well. *Pet Sounds* was to be Brian Wilson's bid for acceptance as an "artiste." It was to be an analysis of romance, centering on the theme of a young man growing into manhood, falling in love and out again, all the while probing himself for the reasons behind his restless yearnings. An intricate thirteen-song exploration of the emotional trials of adolescence, *Pet Sounds* has often been cited by Paul McCartney as an inspiration for the Beatles' own masterpiece, *Sgt. Pepper's Lonely Hearts Club Band.*

Much of the pessimism and dejection that pervaded the album was tied to the problems Brian and his wife, Marilyn, were experiencing at the time. The record produced two hit singles, "Sloop John B" and "God Only Knows / Wouldn't It Be Nice," but the album itself sold poorly. Brian was devastated but still determined. He rebounded in October 1966 with "Good Vibrations," an ingenious synthesis of the sounds and imagery of the current psychedelic wave, plus close harmonies sung to the hilt. While he included enough exotic instruments (sleigh bells, Jew's harp, wind chimes, harpsichord, flutes, organ, and theremin) to send Phil Spector packing, the song retained the Beach Boys' ingratiating airiness. It was the complete statement Brian had been aiming for, and "Good Vibrations" became the group's best-selling single.

Having outdone himself on every level, earning the accolade of "studio genius," Brian Wilson next set about doing himself in. Much of the next year was set aside for the recording of another epic album, at first called *Dumb Angel,* then renamed *Smile.* Collaborating with impressionistic songwriter/composer Van Dyke Parks, Brian (who was now heavily into LSD) locked himself in the studio for days at a stretch, recording, erasing, creating, and then destroying days and weeks of work. In September 1967, a revamped album, *Smiley Smile,* was issued. Acid mania, creative depression, and sinister acquaintances scarred the next two years, during which the Beach Boys released *Wild Honey,* which had been recorded in the reclusive Brian's Bel Air living room, and *20/20,* an album featuring a song—cowritten by Charles Manson and Dennis Wilson—originally entitled "Cease to Exist," but released as "Never Learn Not to Love."

Late in 1969, the Beach Boys jumped to Reprise, which gave them a custom label, Brother Records. Working largely in Brian's house or out of their own studio in Santa Monica, the Beach Boys tried to downplay the fact that Brian was no longer a fully functioning group member, not even in the control booth, as they worked on the charming but poorly selling 1970 album, *Sunflower.* Van Dyke Parks and Brian produced some material for the follow-up, *Surf's Up,* but it also failed to find favor in the marketplace.

In 1972, the group lured the retired Brian, who had opened a North Hollywood health-food shop called the Radiant Radish, to the Netherlands. He refused to work on anything but a twelve-minute children's fantasy called "Mount Vernon and Fairway." When Warner Bros. heard the finished product, *Holland,* they rejected it. It was accepted only after Van Dyke Parks forced an admittedly deranged Brian to sit down at a piano and write a decent single for the spacy album. ("Hypnotize me into thinking that I'm not insane! Convince me I'm not insane!" Brian pleaded in the taped demo session. "Cut the shit, Brian!" Van Dyke answered.)

It was four years before Brian was pulled back into service again. Producer-singer Terry Melcher (Doris Day's son) had signed Brian to a production deal, but it proved a bust. ("He wouldn't touch anything in the control booth," said Melcher. "He acted like he was afraid to.") In 1976, Warner Bros. released *15 Big Ones,* an anniversary compilation of covers of rhythm and blues oldies like "Blueberry Hill" and new songs from Brian and company. Brian got production credit on the LP and was touted as having undergone dramatic drug rehabilitation through the psychiatric care of Dr. Eugene Landy. But it wasn't long before he was back in the shadows again.

Internal struggles plagued the Beach Boys throughout the late 1970s and early 1980s. They fought openly, sometimes even onstage. A mutual restraining order prohibited Mike and Dennis from physically provoking each other. Undistinguished albums came and went. The band has never fully recovered (although it scored a fluke No. 1 hit in 1989 with "Kokomo" and remains a popular touring group).

"I always gave the Beach Boys a good song to sing—and now I find myself totally disillusioned with the Beach Boys," Wilson volunteered in a talk that spring during a break from the final remixing of his solo album. "The Beach Boys left me to figure out all there was to figure out with records and with people. They left me with this feeling inside of 'You better get another album out or we'll kill ya!' Although we stay together as a group, as people we're a far cry from friends.

"One time we were doing an interview together, and the interviewer asked Carl what it was between him and me. He goes, 'Well, Brian and I don't have to talk to each other. We're just Beach Boys, but we don't need to be friends.' And that's true. Although, whenever I think about him, I feel rotten."

The remaining members of the Beach Boys—Carl Wilson, Mike Love, Al Jardine, and Bruce Johnston, who joined the band in 1965 (Dennis Wilson drowned in 1983, while intoxicated)—have not recorded with Brian Wilson in any substantive way since 1985. Contractually, the band has long been permitted to tour and record without its leader, although until recently his participation had been actively sought.

"Brian hates to tour," says the Beach Boys manager, Tom Hulett. "That's the problem, 'cause the band tours constantly. Brian hits and misses these days, sometimes doing as many as forty dates with us, sometimes less. If one of the band gets sick, sometimes he'll substitute, which we appreciate."

Over the last few years, the distance between Wilson and the other members of the Beach Boys has widened, aggravated by his solo project and by the band's collective dislike of Eugene Landy. (The estrangement is such that none of the Beach Boys would comment for this article.)

There is no disagreement that Eugene Landy has played a large role in the rehabilitation of Brian Wilson. What has become controversial is the psychologist's continuing dominant role in the musician's daily and creative life.

Andy Paley, who was brought in as a day-to-day coordinator during the production of Wilson's solo album, recalls a recent incident that indicated the extent of Landy's control over the songwriter's life.

"I was on the phone in the studio one day as we were completing a song called 'Love and Mercy,' and Brian strolled in and asked who I was talking to," says Paley. "When I told him it was my mother, his face instantly took on this sober, reflective cast. He went to the other phone in the control room, punched up a number, and said, 'Mom? This is Brian. I know it's been a long time, and I feel bad, but I think that every son should stay in touch with his mother.' He told me that call was the first time in over three years that he had spoken to her."

When asked about this during the drive to his house, Wilson answers: "Dr. Landy doesn't like me to be in touch with my family too much. He think's it's unhealthy." Others in Wilson's limited sphere, who watched as Landy had the production staff change studios every few weeks, venture stronger criticisms. A member of the production staff contends that "Landy doesn't want Brian to form any lasting new professional relationships."

"I had a good time with Brian when he was focused and working," says Russ Titelman, a coproducer with Wilson on the solo album. "What bowled me over also was how fast Brian was in the studio. He plays and sings virtually every part, but for a few accent touches supplied by synthesizer specialists. . . . For tracks like 'Love and Mercy' and 'There's So Many,' which have complex overdubbed harmony vocals, Brian would rush out to the microphone, put on his headphones, and shout, 'I need eight tracks!' He laid down all these interlocking vocal parts in fifteen minutes. I said, 'Brian, you're doing amazing work!' He just blushed."

"His problem," Titelman continues, "is that he's always got to call Dr. Landy to check in"—Wilson wears a phone beeper on his belt at all times—"or Landy is calling him with studio directives."

Indeed, Landy's unorthodox treatment of his famous patient may result in the loss of his license to practice as a psychologist. In February, the California Attorney General's office, acting as attorneys for the executive officer of the state Psychology Examining Committee, filed a formal charge of "gross negligence" in his treatment of Brian Wilson. (The Attorney General's office will not disclose the name or names of those who instigate such investigations.) The committee accused Landy of illegally dispensing prescription drugs and of violating his professional integrity by acting as Wilson's business manager, business adviser, cosongwriter, and executive producer while serving as his therapist. (Dr. Landy ultimately admitted he unlawfully administered drugs to Wilson and surrendered his license.)

I meet with the short, swarthy psychologist one afternoon at Mason's, an elegant new L.A. restaurant in which he is an investor. "With Brian, I didn't perhaps do what a normal doctor would have done," he responds, with a fixed smile, to the allegations. "But this is an abnormal situation. I used my talents as a doctor, and then I used my instincts as a friend."

Several members of Wilson's solo album production staff also maintain that the fifty-three-year-old psychologist is moving in on the lucrative song-publishing end of his patient's business. Staffers were outraged when, after Wilson had composed songs in the studio by himself or with others, Landy would arrive with his companion, Alexandra Morgan, also a cowriter on the album, and quickly supply new lyrics to the songs.

"Most people feel a doctor can't write songs or write at all—or manage or produce," says Landy in response. "But look at [film director] Blake Edwards's psychotherapist. He's written screenplays with his patient, who's also his friend."

Landy ran afoul of record-company executives during the final production stages of Wilson's solo album. While fighting to remove the production and authorship credits of others, he demanded—and got—additional cowriting credits on the album.

Recapping his history with Brian Wilson, the psychologist says that the only major success the Beach Boys have had in recent years was the album *15 Big Ones,* which "Brian did when I was with him during 1976. Brian and I did that together. Right after that, I had to leave the situation."

Although Wilson's wife, Marilyn, had hired Landy in the first place, she was persuaded to dismiss him by Steve Love, then the Beach Boys' manager. Says Landy, "I was interested in making Brian a whole human being; they were interested in getting another album done in time for 1977."

By 1983, with Brian Wilson a complete physical and mental wreck, the psychologist was rehired by an ad hoc committee of Wilson's advisers at the time, who included his brother Carl and the Beach Boys' manager, Tom Hulett. Ironically, Landy's prescription for the songwriter did not include further contacts with the band: "He had to stop dealing with the Beach Boys because you can't deal with people who only want to use you." Two years later, Wilson was free of his excessive weight and his dependence on stimulants.

As to the charge that he has almost total control over the songwriter's life, Landy says: "He's got a car phone in his car. If he wants to call somebody, he calls somebody. . . . He can go anywhere, on his own, anytime he wants."

According to the psychologist, Wilson's twenty-four-hour-a-day treatment stopped more than a year ago. "Instead, we started writing together," he says. "Since he and I started working together on music, he sees another doctor, a therapist, Dr. Sol Samuels. . . . He's an old-timer, and he represents to Brian the 'good father.' . . . The people who are with him now are a part of his family. They're not the old family that were very negative. They're the new family."

They are also mainly on salary, paid to help Wilson to cope, while sharing in his comfortable life-style. At the time he was getting a divorce from his wife, in 1980, court documents showed that the value of the songwriter's assets was $1.5 million. The amount would have been far more considerable if, back in 1963, the Beach Boys had not signed with Murry Wilson's brand-new song-publishing company, Sea of Tunes.

It was this company's catalog—which includes all the songs written during Brian's most productive period, 1961–67—that the elder Wilson sold, over his son's protests, for $700,000 in August 1969. Four years later, Murry Wilson was dead from heart disease, and Brian Wilson's former music copyrights have gone on to be among the most lucrative and commercially exploited in the annals of American popular song. The melody to "Good Vibrations," for instance—used by the Sunkist company for its ads—has generated a fortune in royalties and revenues for everyone but the person who created it. (In September 1989, Wilson filed a $100 million suit in Los Angeles to recover copyrights to songs his father sold to A&M Records and Irving Music, charging the parent company and its publishing affiliate with fraud and Wilson's former attorneys—Mitchell, Silverberg & Knupp of Los Angeles—with legal malpractice in connection with the sale.)

Asked about Wilson's life beyond business/psychiatric bounds, Landy says, "He's his own man, just bought his own car, and has female friends he takes sailing and to the race track." Brian, however, says, "I'm not dating a soul," and no one outside of Landy's employ can recall seeing him drive a car in years without supervision.

Wilson himself seems to be of two minds regarding the care he has gotten from his psychologist. When asked in Landy's presence what he thought of the treatment he was receiving, Wilson's quick response was: "I owe everything to Dr. Landy. I don't know what I would have possibly done without him; I might be dead if it wasn't for Dr. Landy."

But during our drive to his house, the moment of relative privacy appeared to bring out a different perspective. "I have to stand on my own two feet," he said vehemently, "especially when it comes to my music or the Beach Boys' music."

Meanwhile, Brian Wilson seems content to substitute for the rest of the band. When the Mattel Toy Company, based in Wilson's hometown of Hawthorne, approached the Beach Boys' representatives to record a miniature bonus single to include with the new "California Dream Barbie," the band turned it down. Wilson decided to record the song himself.

Why is such a modest project important to him?

He sits back from the mixing console in the recording studio and directs a burning gaze at me. "Because it involved little children and, maybe, the quality in a few minutes of somebody's childhood," he says softly. "The song's called 'Living Doll,' but I didn't want to treat it like a toy. If it's got my name or the Beach Boys' name on it, I've got to be sure it has a crucial ingredient."

What's that?

"Just a bit of love," he says, sounding forlorn. "Ordinary love. Either do it with that caring . . . or wait 'til you feel you can."

As a boy, he was fond of risk. His childhood hero was Just William, the untamed scamp in a popular series of youth novels by Richmal Crompton. A favorite game involved hanging by a rope knotted to a lofty tree limb overlooking Menlove Avenue in the Liverpool suburb of Woolton, pushing off into the path of approaching double-decker buses, and swinging out of the way at the last minute. He also enjoyed "slapping leather" (as he called shoplifting) and taunting nuns. His Uncle George taught him one of his first songs, an alternate version of a popular favorite that began, "In the shade of the old apple tree / Two beautiful legs I can see . . ."

A choirboy at St. Peter's Church, he was eleven years old when he was permanently barred from Sunday services after repeatedly improvising obscene and impious lyrics to the hymns. He was caned for squirting his schoolmasters with a bicycle pump filled with ink. Fond of circle jerks in which he and his classmates called out the names of starlets as they "tossed off," he was infamous for once yelling out "Winston Churchill!"

His first exposure to American rock and roll was through "The Jack Jackson Show," a late-night program on Radio Luxembourg. The first song to make a

John Lennon

1983

marked impression on him was Bill Haley's "Rock Around the Clock," and Gene Vincent's "Be-Bop-a-Lula" cemented his fascination with the form; but it was the ascension of Elvis Presley that captivated him.

In his late teens, John Lennon began to make a name for himself as a musician, appearing with his combo in dives in the notoriously tawdry Reeperbahn section of Hamburg, Germany. Holding forth on the tiny stages of strip joints like the Indra Club, the Beatles played from 7:00 P.M. to 3:00 A.M. six or seven nights a week. Like the other band members, Lennon dressed in a white T-shirt, leather pants, cowboy boots, and a denim or leather jacket, and he had his greasy D.A. haircut transformed into a bowl-shaped, banged "French cut." Imitating the gimpy strut of rockabilly star Gene Vincent, whose withered left leg was the result of a motorcycle injury, Lennon would sometimes stalk the stage in his jockey shorts, a toilet seat around his neck, shouting, "*Sieg Heil!* Wake up all you bloody Nazis!" A jealous lover, he attacked a hulk who was flirting with girlfriend Cynthia Powell, cracking a bottle on the chap's skull. John himself, however, eschewed fidelity and was a frequent habitué of the Herbertstrasse red-light district.

By day, John and the boys were lonely bantlings, hungry for remnants of home. By night, they were drunk, loutish bullshit artists, riding high on speed and looking forward to some predawn whoring with a penicillin chaser. On the Sabbath, they rested—all but John. His lodgings abutted a Catholic church, and he liked to urinate on the clergy from on high, or to rattle parishioners by dangling a crude dummy of the Son of God out his window, a ballooned condom between its legs.

One of rock and roll's greatest roustabouts, social mavericks, and sharp-tongued philosophers, John Lennon was born on October 9, 1940, at an Oxford Street maternity home in the midst of a blitzkreig attack. His father, Freddy, was a ship's waiter aboard a passenger liner; his mother, the former Julia Stanley, was a cinema usherette. Freddy disappeared in 1940, and his son would see him only twice more in the next two decades.

When Julia took up with Bobby Dykins, an alcoholic hotel waiter with his own children, her sister Mimi volunteered to raise the boy. During his late adolescence, John came to know the errant Julia as someone more akin to a carefree older sister than a parent;

her house, a short bus ride from Aunt Mimi's, was always a haven for truancy.

John cloaked his feelings in an unending sardonicism, reinforced with an off-putting sartorial display that approximated the turnout of the foppish "Teddy Boy" toughs of the era. Dressed in black drainpipe jeans, a colored shirt, and a raincoat with padded shoulders, his light brown hair swept up into a "Tony Curtis" roostertail pompadour accented by "lice ladder" sideburns, he was a menacing presence in his quiet country village.

In 1956, Julia bought John his first guitar, a secondhand model from Hessy's Music Store. John formed a group with best friend Pete Shotton and other local boys, which Pete christened the Quarry Men. Their first significant public appearance was at an outdoor summer fete in some fields beside St. Peter's Church on July 6, 1957. After the set, John met Paul McCartney, an accomplished guitarist (he could *tune* one!) who soon after joined the group. Then George Harrison began to tag along. Shotton, who was afflicted with stage fright, got the idea he was no longer appreciated when John broke his tin washboard over his head. Paul and John began to write songs together, sometimes performing as the Nurk Twins.

After breaking up for a time following the death of Julia Lennon in 1958 (she was killed instantly after being hit by a car), the group re-formed in 1959 as the Silver Beatles (in waggish emulation of Buddy Holly's Crickets), with John, Paul, and George on guitars; art student Stu Sutcliffe on bass; forklift driver Tommy Moore as a sometime drummer, to be replaced in time by Pete Best. In 1961, while in Germany, the (no longer "Silver") Beatles recorded "My Bonnie Lies Over the Ocean." Sutcliffe was replaced on bass by Paul, and Best was dropped to make way for Richard Starkey, a.k.a. Ringo Starr. The transformation of the Beatles was complete.

In short order, the Beatles became the scruffy royalty of the "glad-all-over" Merseybeat sound, with its bright, chiming rhythms and heavy bass-drum sound. A national tour fomented Beatlemania, stoked by "She Loves You," the best-selling single of all time in the United Kingdom. In 1963, they gave a Royal Command Variety Performance for Princess Margaret and the Queen Mother. Lennon introduced the finale, "Twist and Shout," by nodding to the royal box and announcing, "Would the people in the cheaper seats clap your hands? And the rest of you—if you'd just rattle your jewelry . . ."

While John and company were celebrated enough to kid the Queen Mother, they carried no weight in America, where surf music was the order of the day. Manager Brian Epstein flew to America with an acetate copy of "I Want to Hold Your Hand" and met with the producers of the "Ed Sullivan Show." Having been at Heathrow Airport the previous year as the Beatles returned from Sweden, Sullivan knew firsthand how rabid their British following was, and he gambled, booking them to headline for two consecutive Sundays, February 9 and 16, 1964. During the numerous press conferences held during their fifteen-day visit to the States, John jousted with reporters, who thought the Beatles an easy mark. Asked if the group could sing a song for the press, he said, "No, sorry. No, we need money first." How did they account for their fantastic success? "Good press agent." Why did millions of Beatles fans buy millions of Beatles records? "If we knew, we'd form another group and be managers."

In April 1964, "Can't Buy Me Love" was No. 1 on both sides of the Atlantic, with "Twist and Shout" and three other singles fleshing out the remainder of the American Top 5. That summer, the film *A Hard Day's Night* opened in America. The planet was charmed. Tens of thousands flocked to the venues on the Beatles' first and only world tour. Next came another movie, *Help!*, a soundtrack LP, and a mature new collection of work, *Rubber Soul.* On October 26, 1965, the foursome received Member of the Order of the British Empire medals from Queen Elizabeth II. By this time, Lennon and McCartney had ceased their active songwriting collaboration. Yet John insisted that all future Beatles songs by either would be credited to "Lennon-McCartney," a manifestation of the irrational private insecurities that pestered John all of his career.

Summer, 1966. The world gets a consummate taste of Lennon's acerbic iconoclasm. An earlier interview he'd given the *Evening Standard* (after reading the book *The Passover Plot*) attracted recirculation and outrage: "Christianity will go. It will vanish and shrink. I needn't argue about that. I'm right and will be proved right. Jesus was all right, but his disciples were thick and ordinary. It's them twisting it that ruins it for me. We're more popular than Jesus Christ right now."

Drained and daunted by the rigors of travel and mindless audience clangor, the Beatles relinquished touring after an August 29, 1966, concert at San Francisco's Candlestick Park and retreated to the studio, where they began work on *Revolver* (originally titled *Abracadabra*). This often chilling record reflected their growing, albeit random, interest in drugs and mysticism. "Dr. Robert," for example (released in the United States on *Yesterday and Today*), was coy praise by John for Charles Roberts, a New York physician greatly appreciated by the Beatles and Andy Warhol's crowd.

In June 1967, *Sgt. Pepper's Lonely Hearts Club Band* was released. A remarkably aggressive and prepossessing exploration of state-of-the-art four-track control-room technology and abstract conceptual density, it featured John's "Lucy in the Sky with Diamonds," a shimmering pastiche of childlike imagery and dreamy, celeste-laden chant vocals that many charged to be an evocation (if not endorsement) of LSD. John bristled, insisting that the title and lyrics were prompted by his son Julian's description of a painting he'd done at school. Lennon was bitterly amused that an earlier hit of his, "Day Tripper"—which *was* about LSD and included the line "She's a prick teaser"—seemed to bother no one. He took an increasingly rueful interest in slipping vulgarisms and maddening non sequiturs into his songs to mock and befuddle nitpickers and message mongers. After the death of Brian Epstein by sleeping-pill overdose in 1967, there was no one to screen out such pranks.

Magical Mystery Tour appeared in 1967, released as a double EP in England and an album in the States. The film that accompanied it was roundly panned—even the Queen made a negative public criticism of it. Still, critics had marveled at the surreal power of Lennon's "Strawberry Fields Forever" and "I Am the Walrus."

After the Beatles appeared worldwide via satellite to sing "All You Need Is Love" for the "Our World" international TV special, they retreated to Wales to spend what would be a half-year of absorption in the teachings of Maharishi Mahesh Yogi. The Beatles' part in a nine-week 1968 celebrity sabbatical with Mia Farrow, Donovan, and Mike Love at the Maharishi's ashram beside the Ganges ended abruptly when John got fed up with the guru's niggardly rationing of the secrets of the universe. Lennon also resented the advances the Maharishi allegedly made toward Mia Farrow and other female guests; and while in India, John wrote "Sexy Sadie" to ridicule his guru. When John informed him that the Beatles would soon depart, the Maharishi blanched and asked, "Why?" "You're the cosmic one," John answered. "You ought to know."

In May 1968, shortly after a particularly potent tab of acid had momentarily convinced John Lennon he was Jesus Christ, he rang up one of his quirkiest groupies, Yoko Ono. Their affair translated into the *Unfinished Music No. 1: Two Virgins* album, released the same month as the Beatles' so-called *White Album.* John's six-year marriage to Cynthia dissolved shortly after.

From then on, the lines in Lennon's life were sharply drawn; everything was seen in either pro-Yoko or anti-Yoko terms, the Beatles increasingly relegated to the latter category. John and Yoko were married in the Crown Colony of Gibraltar on March 20, 1969, and they spent their honeymoon staging a week-long antiwar "Bed-In" at the Amsterdam Hilton. During the next two months, John changed his hated middle name from Winston to Ono, and the couple released "Give Peace a Chance."

Abbey Road, the Beatles' best-selling album, was released in 1969. John's songs for the record included "Because" and "I Want You (She's So Heavy)," both written about him and Yoko. Thirteen days prior to the LP's release, Lennon further asserted his independence from the group by flying Ono, guitarist Eric Clapton, bassist Klaus Voorman, drummer Alan White, and himself to a rock and roll revival show in Toronto; he billed the group as the Plastic Ono Band. A few weeks later, John told Paul he wanted a "divorce" from the Beatles; he was dissuaded from any action until legal disputes between the group's company and short-lived manager Allen Klein could be settled. In November 1969, Lennon returned his MBE (Member of the British Empire) Medal to the Queen, giving England's involvement in war-torn Biafra and its support of U.S. troops in Vietnam (plus, wryly, the poor sales of his "Cold Turkey" single) as reasons. He and Yoko mounted an abortive "WAR IS OVER! IF YOU WANT IT!" peace campaign and issued another single, "Instant Karma," produced by Phil Spector.

By the spring of 1970, the Beatles were in tatters. *Let It Be,* the last album, was resurrected from a stack of session tapes. Then, in April 1970, Paul issued a solo album and the surprise statement that the Beatles were over with—to John's ire and chagrin. Even as he strayed from it, John saw himself as the prime mover in the quartet. Moreover, Paul had been the one to talk John out of an earlier decision to announce the split. John felt Paul had robbed him of his much-needed chance to show the world he'd been the one who was confident enough to ring down the curtain on the Beatles *and* Lennon-McCartney.

In the decade that followed, John and Yoko released various solo and collaborative albums under the Plastic Ono Band umbrella. Their initial efforts were brutal refutations of his counterculture-costumed contemporaries' lofty ambitions and of their greed, contrasted with a brutal owning up to Lennon's own delusions and dybbuks. The songs were gripping in their vulnerability and eloquent in their spare settings. Later work, though, often comprised obnoxious scoldings and overproduced drivel.

In the mid-1970s, John and Yoko were badgered by the FBI and at odds with the Nixon White House, which wanted to deport Lennon, seeing him as an undesirable drug felon and leftish rabble-rouser. The couple separated for a year and a half, during which John dated aide May Pang (at Yoko's suggestion), drank heavily, and partied with Harry Nilsson, at one point causing a ruckus in a Los Angeles club while wearing a Kotex napkin on his head. He returned to his wife in March 1975 and began life as a "househusband" after Yoko gave birth to a son, Sean, on John's thirty-fifth birthday. John and Yoko released *Double Fantasy* in November 1980, and it yielded a No. 1 hit, "(Just Like) Starting Over." Then, on December 8, 1980, a pudgy twenty-five-year-old drifter pumped seven bullets into John Lennon as he strode through the arched entryway of the Dakota, his apartment residence on New York's Upper West Side. Earlier in the day the singer had given his assailant an autograph. When police arrived, they found the murderer standing on the sidewalk, calmly reading *The Catcher in the Rye.* Yoko was bent over John's blood-soaked body.

In January 1984, John Lennon's last songs, plus additional compositions by Yoko Ono, were released as *Milk and Honey—A Heart Play.* The album included the bouncy, outspoken "I'm Stepping

Out" and a haunting ballad John wrote for Yoko, "Grow Old With Me."

After his death, there was a tendency to view Lennon as a saintly figure for an idealistic generation. More accurately, he was a ceaseless, ravenous experimenter whose natural disdain for any sort of constraints led him into every sort of clearing and cul-de-sac. He was both in awe and in terror of the power he had over his own life, but he never lacked the courage to exercise it in new ways.

Paul McCartney 1987

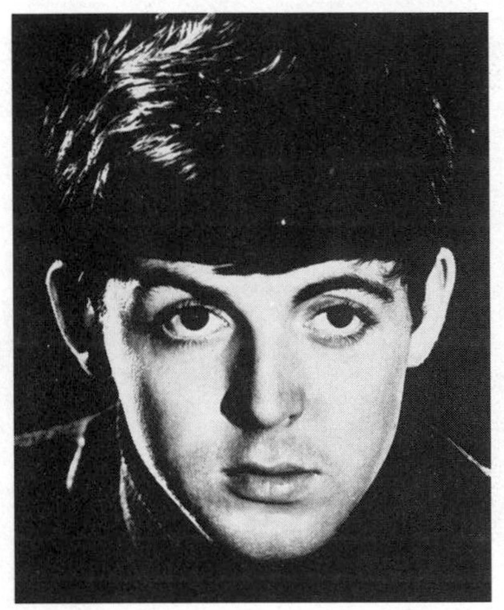

His seems an existence played out in an English music hall, evoking that sentimental mid-nineteenth-century tradition—featuring pantomime, sketch comedy, and the song-and-dance man—that developed from entertainment in inns and taverns. In his music, misfortune is a pratfall, tragedy is dirgeful melodrama, happiness is a comic fluke, and fulfillment is an illustrated postcard captioned "Ardor." In his personal life, the same perspective holds true.

He is a man of minor mysteries, a casual creator of miniature shadows and quaint secrets, one who gently epitomizes another age, perhaps Victorian, in which styles and manners were needlessly flowery, excessively genteel. But Paul McCartney's role is more working-class in its textures, evoking a time when low-born fellows of intelligence and ambition reached for such effects, yet leavened their deeply felt attempts with a playful self-deprecation.

Self-taught, partially deaf pianist James McCartney led a dance band in the 1920s, the Jim Mac Jazz Band, that provided amusement for Liverpool flappers and, on at least one occasion, musical accompaniment for the silent cinema at the local run of *The Queen of Sheba.* By day, Jim was a bachelor salesman for a cotton-brokerage firm, and the arrangement of his time and personal commitments was sufficiently cozy that he did not marry until he was due to turn forty. Mary Mohin, a visiting nurse in her early thirties, was the lucky girl. She was Irish Catholic, he was Irish Protestant, but there were no quarrels between them. They had two boys: James Paul, born June 18, 1942, and Michael, born two years later. Though money was tight in the postwar years, the McCartneys lived comfortably, even blissfully, in the Liverpool suburb of Allerton until Mary, a working mother, suddenly took sick and died of breast cancer.

Jim was crushed, the boys astonished that their world could be shattered on such short notice. "What are we going to do," lamented the forlorn, ever-practical Paul, "without her money?"

Paul was fourteen years old, an excellent student, a considerate son, worthy of the trust invested in him by his loving but sometimes careworn father. Galvanized by the rise of skiffle star Lonnie Donnegan, Paul requested a guitar, and his parent happily obliged. Jim McCartney recognized that a mutual interest in music was a way of keeping his boy close to the hearth. In the evenings after work, Jim would man the piano in the parlor and call out chords for his son to try. Paul's efforts were problematic until he realized that, although right-handed, he played better with his left. Skiffle quickly took a back seat to rock and roll. At first, Paul fell hard for the lunatic warbling of Little Richard, but ultimately he preferred the less raucous approach of the Everly Brothers, their interlocking harmonies and lilting chordings demonstrating the melodic beauty possible in a music best known for its bombast.

When Paul was invited to join the Quarry Men, neighbor John Lennon's skiffle group, he and John immediately turned what had been a chance encounter into a two-man guitar clinic, passing entire afternoons and evenings in Paul's living room mastering their instruments. Paul was the more accomplished of the two, and John peered through his accursed horn-rims at every fingering in his new mate's repertoire. An outsider might have presumed that pushy, high-strung John was the prime mover in the group, but it was Paul who suggested they adopt formal uniforms, counseled (and was overruled) against giving its manager equal pay, and stressed the importance of long rehearsals and esprit de corps. Under their tutelage, the Quarry Men began to attract a broader range of bookings; audiences were either amused or agitated by John's biting bandstand banter, but they were consistent in requesting Paul's Little Richard imitation. Then one night, in the midst of a date at the Broadway Conservative Club, Paul unveiled "I Lost My Little Girl," a song he'd written himself. Intimidated, John intensified his own compositional explorations, and the two began to pace each other.

Jim McCartney got a kick out of his son's involvement in the Quarry Men, but his initial approval turned to consternation and then dismay when the boys began to hold court at the Cavern and then to plan a trip to Hamburg. Paul had just passed his final exams at Liverpool Institute, and Jim was keen to see him go on to teacher-training college. Paul and his brother had to gang up on their father. They minimized the summer stint in Germany as a lark before settling down to more weighty matters. Jim was naïve enough to believe them, practical enough to envy the itinerary, and harried enough to recognize he had no choice.

Considering the sheltered life he'd led in Allerton, Paul was totally unprepared for the tawdry glories of the Reeperbahn. The first lodgings the Beatles were given were next to the public toilets in a porno theater called the Bambi Kino. When he wound up being deported after supposedly trying to burn the place down (actually, he set fire to a prophylactic as a joke—the kind of stunt John Lennon had acquainted him with), neither he nor his father could decide if things had turned out for the best. One thing was certain: the experience left Paul with a permanent grin on his suddenly worldly looking babyface.

The breakthrough in the Lennon-McCartney songwriting alliance occurred in the autumn of 1963, when the two of them dreamed up a tune called "I Want to Hold Your Hand." As their output grew, it became obvious that McCartney and Lennon, while supportive of each other's writing, had divergent styles. Paul preferred story songs of a whimsical or heartfelt nature. Both concerns dovetailed in an offhanded melody called "Scrambled Eggs," which grew plaintive in tone when lyrics were added, becoming "Yesterday." "Penny Lane" was a childlike recollection of everyday commerce and the social niceties in the villages of Allerton and Woolton, focusing on activities at the traffic circle between the two. "She's Leaving Home," the doleful narrative from *Sgt. Pepper's Lonely Hearts Club Band,* stemmed from an account Paul read in the *Daily Mail.*

By the time of *The Beatles* (the so-called *White Album*) in 1968, Lennon was producing tracks like "Happiness Is a Warm Gun" while McCartney penned "Martha My Dear" about his dog of the same name. John favored raw, shrill, confessional music with an often belligerent feel to it, and he considered Paul's dulcet ballads "granny music." The dichotomy was never more obvious than in the infamous single from the *White Album,* Paul's wistful "Hey Jude" paired with John's "Revolution."

Contrasting family backgrounds had forever colored the sensibilities that grew from them, John working through the grudge he had against the Fates, Paul simply wanting to create the kind of music that his father could have played for his own sweetheart. That the Lennon-McCartney partnership would end was inevitable.

The parting with John emerged from the faltering fellowship of the Beatles as a whole, but, in the end, it was a personal falling out. *McCartney,* Paul's first solo LP, appeared in the stores on April 17, 1970, about a month before *Let It Be,* the last Beatles studio album, saw the light of day.

McCartney took a lot of heat from critics for the distinctly homemade qualities of *McCartney.* Beatles' albums weren't noted for nubbly textures, and any product that failed to include (that is, excluded) the others was bound to draw fire. The critical derision was redoubled in 1971 when *Ram,* the LP credited to Paul and Linda McCartney (whom he'd wed in 1969), was issued: it was charged that Linda couldn't sing, that her presence as an artist made a mockery of Paul's previous standards, that Paul was casting sloppy seconds and table scraps into the marketplace. No one could fathom the man's reasoning. For all the barbs—the most cutting being a venomous song by Lennon, "How Do You Sleep?"—*Ram* had a No. 1 single in the U.S. with "Uncle Albert/Admiral Halsey." When the song publishing on the album was attributed to Mr. and Mrs. Paul McCartney, thus giving Linda 50 percent of the royalties, Lew Grade, overseer of the Beatles' publishing arm, Northern Songs, cried foul, disputing Linda's competence. A lawsuit resulted—which Paul and Linda won. As a conciliatory gesture, Lew Grade was asked to produce a TV special, "James Paul McCartney," which saw worldwide distribution a year later and helped cement the new team of Paul and Linda in the minds of the public.

In an unusually bold move, McCartney next took steps to begin all over again, auditioning musicians in New York City and London for a band he would call Wings. *Wild Life,* their debut album, bombed, as did Paul's 1972 single, "Give Ireland Back to the Irish," which hit the stores shortly after the "Bloody Sunday" incident in Londonderry, Ireland, in which British paratroopers killed thirteen civilians during a demonstration. Furious that the BBC banned the record, McCartney retaliated with a single version of a children's nursery rhyme. Surprisingly, "Mary Had a Little Lamb" did well.

Throughout the mid-1970s, Wings prospered; personnel shifted periodically, and albums appeared with Beatles-like regularity. Complaints, often justified, of insipid songwriting continued to be leveled at McCartney, but his popular success easily eclipsed that of the other solo Beatles, and his sales sometimes achieved Beatles-sized dimensions. Two more Wings albums rounded out the decade. One, *Back to the Egg,* was an annoying series of song snippets that prompted the following overview in *Rolling Stone:* "This ex-Beatle has been lending his truly prodigious talents as a singer, songwriter, musician, and producer to some of the laziest records in the history of rock and roll."

One pursuit to which McCartney had applied himself with considerable vigor was indiscreet ganja-smoking, and his record of arrests is formidable. But the Eastman family (Paul's in-laws) and their law firm have served McCartney well, repeatedly helping him beat the marijuana raps. Also through their efforts, Paul gained control of the entire Buddy Holly catalog, as well as the music to *A Chorus Line, Grease,* and *Annie,* making him the richest rocker (estimated to be worth $900 million) ever.

In the early 1980s, after the breakup of Wings, McCartney released three albums. The mature, sophisticated *Tug of War* earned the greatest praise accorded a McCartney project since *Band on the Run,* primarily for the record's thoughtful reflections on Paul's tempestuous relationship with the late John Lennon. McCartney seemed to be turning a new corner as a talent. Yet with the release of *Pipes of Peace* late in 1983, he was back creating syrupy melodies intertwined with mawkish lyrics, exasperating critics and confounding even his loyal fans. His heavy-handed film, *Give My Regards to Broad Street,* also fit the bathetic mold. These were projects that would never have passed muster in the Reeperbahn, but they surely would have made Jim McCartney [who passed away in March 1976] very proud.

"I recently took my kids Halloween trick or treating in America," says Paul McCartney, as he reclines in the darkwood-and-artwork-lined den of his London townhouse headquarters. "We went door-to-door to perfect strangers in a residential area around Los Angeles. I had on a black top hat and a big rubber mask that made me look like a ghoulish goofy."

No one guessed that the dad behind the false face was a rock legend, although a few gave him quizzical glances. "I did start off with me own brown bag, but the look I was getting off some people was, '*Here,* buddy, wait a minute. This *is* for kids!' "

It is November 1987. The holiday season always makes McCartney feel wistful and vulnerable. It spells change, transition, the onrush of winter, the cold requisites of growth. He copes best by plunging into the next cycle, even if he must travel incognito. What bothered him most about the Halloween jaunt was the fact that he needed to be present at all.

"These days, I'm *not* sending the kids out there alone," he assures. "Because of the safety and security thing, a lot of people won't play trick or treat. Instead, a lot of doors just close, residents being very unwelcoming, Dobermans growling in the yards."

The world has changed since James Paul McCartney awoke to its vagaries in 1942.

For the first decade and a half of his post-Beatles career, everything Paul McCartney touched turned to gold. His critics said that such effortless success kept McCartney from pushing himself as hard as he should, but the public clearly loved the man *and* his music. Lately, though, the hits have not come so easily. His last several albums, *Pipes of Peace, Give My Regards to Broad Street* (the final CBS LPs), and *Press to Play* (the first under a hefty new Capitol pact) met with a quiet commercial reception. The inner and outer pressure to demonstrate his viability in the rock landscape of the dawning 1990s is clearly mounting. "Paul's out there searching," says Capitol president Joe Smith, "and I told him to please don't be in a rush, because he's right where Paul Simon was before he came out with *Graceland.*"

McCartney's already made his own African trek, returning in the early 1970s with the splendid *Band on the Run.* This time, he's seeking songwriting renewal through a grassroots generational alliance with another son of a Liverpudlian, Declan Patrick McManus, a.k.a. Elvis Costello. The immortal Lennon-McCartney epoch, as well as the McCartney-McCartney era of collaboration with wife Linda, could soon make way for McCartney-McManus.

"A fair bit of thought went into Paul's decision to approach Elvis

Costello," says Richard Ogden, McCartney's personal manager. "Paul felt it was helpful that they had both an Irish heritage and Liverpool family roots in common. But one of the things Paul liked best about Elvis's songwriting was his strength as a lyricist. Paul sensed his own melodies and ideas could be excitingly compatible with Costello's literate style."

The possibilities inherent in this Anglo-Irish pairing of pop checks and petulant balances are provocative. The man who once had the good sense to recast a song called "Daisy Hawkins" as "Eleanor Rigby" now suspects he can learn something from the chap who retitled an album *This Year's Model* instead of *Girls! Girls! Girls!.* But come what may, the Paul McCartney anthologized on *All the Best!* will never be quite the same again.

At forty-five, McCartney retains the features of a bantling, but a trace of soft wrinkles accents his sad eyes and frames his smile-bent lips. His character is like his complexion: supple but staunch, ruddy but unblemished. There is solidity in his natural air of openness, but a subtle fatigue from its cumulative toll.

What Paul has excelled at all his life is the ability to adapt, to match inexorable change with creative resolve. When something as sure as winter is approaching, he counters the seasonal shift with a chipper measure of control.

But the matter most on Paul's mind this bracing afternoon in London town is what the New Year will bring. After months of diplomacy, Paul McCartney finally agreed to confront the calendar of his later career, giving himself over—on the eve of an uncertain new chapter—to an unprecedented discussion of all that was and can never be. Listen to what the man said.

This feels like a pivotal time in your career. And because it's never been done before, I'd love to examine your entire solo pilgrimage. The British version of your All the Best! *retrospective has material not on the American collection. "Once Upon a Long Ago" is a track you did with producer Phil Ramone.*

The English market, or so they tell me anyway, likes compilation things and "Hits" albums; they're very popular. Whereas in the States, even if it's something like Springsteen's live compilation, apparently they reckon the market isn't as keen on stuff like that. So over here people put your hits together and then put a new song on it for a bit of interest and added enjoyment. In America the record company was more concerned with just having the hits. I like the extra song, "Once Upon a Long Ago," but America for some reason didn't want it. Who am I to argue?

The flip side of "Long Ago" is a track you wrote with Elvis Costello, "Back on My Feet."

I started doing some writing with Elvis—[*breaking into a brogue*] or Declan McManus, as 'is real name is; 'tis a real Irish name for a Liverpool lad. We originally said, "Well, look, let's not *tell* anyone we're working together, because if it doesn't work, we're gonna look like idiots." You do that; you get excited about a collaboration, and then nothing really comes of it. But we've now written quite a number of songs together, and this was the first.

How we started off writing together was that, rather than just jump in the deep end, he played me a couple of songs he'd been having trouble finishing, and said, "Tell me what's wrong with these." And then "Back on My Feet" was one where in *my* case, I wasn't totally happy with my lyrics, though I'd pretty much written it. So I fixed up his two songs, he fixed up this one of mine, and we were off and running. The next song we wrote from scratch, which was better yet!

There's now about nine of them that we've written together, and some will show up on the next album [*Flowers in the Dirt*]. I'm not worried now about saying I'm writing with him because we're both quite happy with the standard of the work.

Was there any contrast between the way you and Costello write? Does he write with a piano? A guitar?

I think he normally writes with guitar, but he's a bit like me and will do either. We wrote on guitar, mainly, with two where he played a bit of piano. You just ring the changes, really. The minute you get into a formula, you're *goosed*—it's the truth! So when we found one way of working, we'd say let's do another thing. We tried to keep each song different, because you fall into ruts easily. You think you've got the hang of something and you say to yourself, "Ah, we write upbeat numbers." So we'd say, "Okay, on the *next* one, let's try to write a soully ballad, or a rocker."

Using All the Best! *as a guide to your post-Beatles body of work, let's talk about "Maybe I'm Amazed" and the rest of the 1970* McCartney *album. Rod Stewart and the Faces immediately made that song a feature of their live concerts and then formally covered it.*

Oh yeah! It's *always* a compliment that somebody does your songs or likes them enough to put one in their act. The Faces liked that album, and I remember a couple of the lads telling me later on that they'd been on tour when it came out and they'd got into what they called the "freshness" of it a lot. It was a great album to make, because I just made it in me living room with a four-track machine, and plugged into the back of it directly, without a mixing desk. I just got the noise right in front of the microphone like this—[*he repeatedly snaps his fingers*]—hearing then that, "no, that level's not too good," so I'd move off the mike a bit more. I'd physically adjust myself in the room rather than through a mixer.

It was a very *free* album for me to do, because I'd get up and think about breakfast and then wander into the living room to do a track. It's got that feel on it, and there's a lot of stuff that you, the listener, might have thought twice about, but I didn't. Like crazy little instrumentals like "Momma Miss America"; I like them when I hear them now, thinking, "Did I do that? Boy, that was cheeky!" Generally you wouldn't think I'd do an instrumental; McCartney things tend to always have a vocal.

It all was probably occasioned by Linda saying to idle me, "Come on, you know you play good guitar. *Play* it!" She always likes to hear me playing guitar, 'cause I don't really play much guitar, though I started off on rhythm guitar like everyone who came from that Beatles era. I've always admired people like Hendrix, and I like playing nice *loud* electric guitar. It's one of my top thrills in life. So she encouraged that on that album. That's probably why certain instrumentals crept in that I might have saved otherwise for B-sides or throwaway things.

Was "Maybe I'm Amazed" expressly for that record?

Yeah, that was very much a song of the period. When you're in love with someone—I mean, God it sounds soppy—but when you are in love and it's *new* like that, as it was for me and Linda with the Beatles breaking up, that was my feeling. Maybe I'm amazed at what's going on—maybe I'm not—but *maybe* I am. "Maybe I'm amazed at the way you pulled me out of time, hung me on the line." There were things that were happening at the time, and these phrases were my symbols for them. And other people seemed to understand.

Another song on the album I liked was "Teddy Boy," which you had started writing back in the Beatles days. It took an image of adolescent street toughness and turned it into a lullaby.

That was the intention! And it *was* from the Beatles period. There was always a song that'd lie around for a coupla years with one good part and you'd mean to finish it one day. The words "teddy boy" to English people had always meant what you might have called a "hood" in America, a motorcycle-type guy. To us, it was these fellas in Edwardian long coats, a big fashion when I was growing up. I also have a cousin Ted, so he was the other meaning.

Tell me about "Another Day," your first solo single in February of 1971.

Anyone who was around back then was bored with stories of the Beatles breakup, the business disputes, and all these negative things that were going on. It was really difficult to know what to do, 'cause you were either going to say, "Okay, I've been a Beatle, and now I'll go back to the sweet shoppe or do something else with my life." Or, "I'll try to continue in music!" But then the thought came, "Yeah, but you're gonna have to try and *top* the Beatles," and that's not an easy act to follow.

It was intimidating to even think of staying in the music business. But I had a talk with Linda. If she's a singer, she's very much a Shangri-Las type singer; I don't think any of them could get into opera, but I *prefer* them to opera. Linda wouldn't put herself up as a great vocalist, but she's got a great style—I think anyway.

So she just said, "If it's gonna be kinda casual and we're not gonna sweat it, we could maybe do something together." So we started it on that basis. [*pause, sly grin*] Of course the critics didn't see it like that. They said, "*What's 'e got 'er onstage for?*" Between ourselves, it was, why not? What's the big deal? She's just singing with me, for Chrissake. She's not exactly taking over the lead in *La Traviata* or anything. It's just a bit of background harmonies here.

That was the kind of spirit we approached it all in, and it was the only way we *could* have done it, I say. If we'd have gotten too paranoid about it, we wouldn't have even dared stay in the business! So we ended up in New York, and "Another Day" was one of the first tracks we released with that attitude.

There was a hurtful controversy at first with Northern Songs Publishing about your material together . . .

Because nobody believed we'd written them! See, I had a contract with Northern Songs for me and John as writers. As I wasn't collaborating with John anymore, I looked for someone else to collaborate with.

I assumed that there wouldn't be any sweat, and I would say to Linda, "How do you like the words?" She'd say to change that little bit, only minor changes, but they were denying she was a cowriter when she had actually changed a few lines. But you can see what they thought: "*Hallo! He's pulling a fast one 'ere!*" And, in fact, they were so wonderful to me after all the success I'd brought them with me and John—more than they ever dreamed of earning anyway—they immediately slapped a million-dollar lawsuit on us here and in New York! So they were charming pals who shall be remembered ever thus.

Listen, people do have a strong proprietary instinct toward the Beatles.

Well, I suppose it's like, what would you say if Mick [Jagger] brought Jerry Hall onstage? Now, I wouldn't mind—particularly if she could sing a bit. She looks all right to me. I think whatever artists wanna do is fine. Art is sufficiently broad that if you want to lie on the floor and wriggle like a snake, that's art. Merce Cunningham's made a career out of it! But you wouldn't have passed any Royal Ballet School exams with that stuff.

It is ironic that people had such a rigid perspective on Lennon-McCartney. They fail to realize that creativity is a very organic thing. You work with what's going on in your world.

Exactly. I said, "Well, look! If my wife is actually saying 'change that' or 'I like that better than that' then I'm using her as a collaborator." I mean, John never had any input on "The Long and Winding Road," and Yoko still collects royalties on it. You've gotta flow with these things.

The joke at that time was that Linda was the only one getting paid in our household, 'cause we were all held up with Apple being subject to litigation! I wasn't seeing *any* money. I was literally having to say to all the Wings members, "Don't worry, lads. One of these days we'll see some money." It was ridiculous! Every businessman who had ever known me was suing me. I felt, I'm damned if *she's* not gonna get paid for it; I'll put in a bill for her services! The money still came through. They weren't major checks, but they were the only checks we were seeing because she was the only one free of all contracts in our house.

The main thing about it all was that we managed to stay positive and keep the old Beatle philosophy when our heads were on the ground. 'Cause in early days with the Beatle music, no one wanted to know. We were up in Liverpool meeting the train every day, and when Brian Epstein would come we'd say, "Have they signed us yet, Bri?" He said, "I'm sorry chaps, they don't want you." Between saying "bloody hell!" we had this little thing we always used to come out with, which was "Well, *something* will happen." It was real *dumb*—but it always worked! And me and Linda, we got over those lawsuits, because all things must pass, as the man said.

You did the 1971 sessions for Ram *in New York City, with the New York Philharmonic helping out.*

Right, and then in L.A., too. We worked at the CBS studio and at Phil Ramone's old A&R Studios. We did "Uncle Albert/Admiral Halsey" there with the Philharmonic. I didn't realize they were so wonderful and revered. I thought they were just a bunch of guys. At one point Phil said, "Why don't you conduct them?" I hadn't actually written the score, but George Martin and I had talked about it, so I ended up doing it. One of the Philharmonic guys walked out during a moment when we all had to work a little later one evening. Phil managed to persuade everybody but this one guy who got humpy and took the hoof.

The Philharmonic types were always pulling that on the Beatles. We had the orchestra who played on "Hey Jude" in England in 1968 all together and said, "We've got this bit at the end of the song that goes, 'Na-na-na . . .' and we'd like you to chant and clap along." A couple of them said [*haughtily*], "We're not clappers, we're fiddlers." "OOOOOO!" we said, "Off you go then, dearies!" [*laughter*] There's just some people who aren't up to that stuff.

Was there an Uncle Albert who inspired that song?

I *had* an Uncle Albert; I was sort of thinking of him. He was an uncle who died when I was a kid, a good bloke who used to get drunk and stand on the table and read passages from the Bible, at which point people used to laugh. *A lot.* It was just one of those things—"Ohh, Albert, don't get up and read the Bible again! Shuttup! Sit down!!" But he's someone I recalled fondly, and when the song was coming it was like a nostalgic thing. "I think I'm gonna rain" was the wistful line, really, and I thought of him.

I say, I never can explain why I think of a particular person when I write. "We're so sorry, *Auntie Edna*"—you know, it could have been her. As for Admiral Halsey, he's one of yours, an American admiral. I could have gone, "Gen-e-ral Ei-sen-how-er," but it doesn't work as well. And then people say, "Ah-hah! I know why he used Halsey! In the Battle of Salaami in Nineteen-Forty-Hee-Hee he was instrumental in—" *None* of that sort of bit is hardly ever true. I use these things like a painter uses colors. I don't know where I got Halsey's name, but you read it in magazines and sometimes they just fall into your songs because they scan so well.

"Girls School," the loopy, memorable rock track on the flip side of your huge "Mull of Kintyre" single, also came from some intriguing newspaper scanning, right?

True. It was from the porn ads, which I always *have* to check out—just to see what's going on. [*smirk*] I don't approve, of course. I just love all those titles of the girlie movies, they're so mad. There's a girl in the song called Roxanne, which came out of a porn movie, and because all the titles were very bizarre I jumbled them all together and made this idea of a kinky girls' school where all these people like Roxanne and Yuki the schoolmistress, would be characters, one of them being the teacher, another the head girl, and so on. There's a metal group called Girlschool, isn't there? I always wondered if they took it off that song!

What was the origin of the name Wings, when you formed the band in 1971?

Linda and I were having our second baby. She was doing most of the work on that, I must admit, but I was there in attendance. It was a difficult pregnancy, and I had to be with her a lot. I used to get a camp bed and kip in the hospital. When one of the matrons told me no, I couldn't sleep there, I said, "We're gonna use another hospital!" and we did, until we found one that'd have us.

So finally we were in Kings College Hospital, and our baby was in intensive care. She's now a sixteen-year-old girl named Stella, so everything worked out great, but it was dodgy at the time. So rather than just sitting around twiddling my thumbs, I was thinking of hopeful names for a new group, and somehow this uplifting idea of Wings came to me exactly at that time. It just sounded right.

Wild Life, *the debut Wings album of '71, was done in a pretty compressed span of time. The track that still stands out is "Dear Friend."*

That was written for John—*to* John. It was like a letter. With the business pressures of the Beatles breaking up, it's like a marriage. One minute you're in love, next minute you hate each other's guts. I don't think any of us really ever got to the point where we *actually* hated each other's guts, but the business people involved were pitting us against each other, saying, "Paul's not much good, is he?" or "John's not all that good, heh, heh, heh."

It's a pity because it's very difficult to cut through all that, and what can you do? You can't write a letter saying, "Dear pal of mine, I love you"—it's all a bit too much. So you do what we all seemed to do, which was write it in songs. I wrote "Dear Friend" as a kind of peace gesture.

No matter how much all the business was, whenever we did have a good phone conversation or anything, maybe one or two of those things, those gestures, got through. And luckily before John died we had got it back to that, thank the Lord, because otherwise it would have just been terrible. I would have brooded on the fact that we were always bitching with each other forever. We ended up with a good relationship, which was something. Some consolation.

I think many were shocked, certainly over here, when the first Wings single in the U.K. was "Give Ireland Back to the Irish." It was written about the Bloody Sunday Irish massacre of January 1972, and I'm sure you sensed there would be a strong reaction to it.

Up till that point, whenever anyone said, "Are you into protest songs?" I'd say I liked Bob Dylan but I'm not. I didn't like political songs; such songs can be boring. Particularly if the thing being written about didn't happen in your country. I always vowed that I'll be the one who doesn't do political songs, but what happened over here was they had this massacre when some people had been doing a peaceful demonstration. Our soldiers, my country's army paratroopers, had gone in and had killed some people. So we were against the Irish; it was like being at war with them. And I'd grown up with this thing that the Irish are great, they're our mates, our *brothers.* We used to joke that Liverpool was the capital of Ireland, there's so many Irish living and working there. And if you didn't have that image, you certainly had the one of John Wayne as a "fair broth of a boy" in all those films where he goes back to the Auld Sod as the American cousin.

Suddenly we were killing our buddies, and I thought, "Wait a minute, this is *not* clever, and I wish to protest on behalf of us people." This action of our government was over the top! And in nobody's language could it be seen to be a good move, I don't think. I'm still shocked. And now we've reached the point where the IRA is just "terrorists." "We're the Goodies, they're the Terrorists!" No one seems to remember we nicked Ireland off 'em. That seems to have gone by the bar. Hey, fellas, we *robbed* their country! Is no one gonna remember that?!

I did that song and was rung up by a lot of people who said, "Please don't release this, we don't need this right now." And I said [*firmly*], "Yes we do. *Gotta* have it." It was No. 1 in Ireland and, funnily enough, Spain! I can't quite work that out, unless it was the Basque separatists. Then I went to Austria, and this sincere fellow comes up to me and says, "I've written a cover version, 'Give

Bavaria Back to the Bavarians.' " [*chuckles*] You've gotta laugh. But seriously, it was something I had to do, and I'm glad I did it.

"C Moon," a more light-hearted Wings song that same year, was sparked by Sam the Sham & the Pharoahs.

It was from "Woolly Bully," which we always loved; it was a great crazy record, like "Louie, Louie." We used to sing "Woolly Bully," and where Sam said, "Let's not be L7," we never really knew what it meant. I somewhere read an explanation of the lyrics, and apparently it meant that the "L" was one half of a square, and the "7" formed the other bit, so L7 meant "square."

I was messing around with that idea and I thought, what's the opposite of L7? Well, it's gotta be two things that make up a circle, so it's the letter C and a half-moon. C Moon became "cool," "chilly," or whatever. I wrote it all into a Daddy-doesn't-understand-the-kids song.

"Hi, Hi, Hi" was a single from the same year. I liked the energy in it.

I think "Hi, Hi" now is kinda dated. It's got words and phrases in it like "bootleg" and "we're gonna get high in the midday sun," and it's very much a song of the times when there were festivals and everyone had long hair, flared trousers and macramé jackets: very sixties. To me, that was my parting shot at those days.

It got banned over here—a sex and drugs song; can't have it! There was the controversy over a supposed phrase in the song, "body gun." But in actual fact I had used a really mad word from a surrealist play by a man called Alfred Jarry, a French playwright who wrote around 1900. He was a real nutter who used to cycle around Paris on his bike, and he used to have this thing called the Pataphysical Society. It was nothing but a drinking club, but to be a Professor of Pataphysics sounds great. I used that term in "Maxwell's Silver Hammer"—"he studied Pataphysical."

At any rate, Jarry wrote this theater sketch called *Ubu-Roi*, which has this character Ubu, who's always going around worried about his "polyhedron." Which I think is actually a geometrical figure. So I put a line in "Hi, Hi, Hi" where I said, "Lie on the bed and get ready for my—" I wondered what should I put here, so I said "polygon," which was another daft geometrical figure, all of this being influenced by Jarry. The people taking down the lyrics for us thought I said "body gun," which I thought was *better.* And that's the basis the song got banned on!

In Beatles days we used to throw saucy little things in, but most of it was stuff the critics made up, although when you read it, it seemed very feasible. That's how the times were anyway, all colored by acid and pot. Mainly those songs were very straightforward, but our image was so bizarre.

Giving rise to things like the "Paul is dead" theories.

[*Nodding*] Like me walking across the crossing on Abbey Road [on the album cover] with no shoes on. The truth was, it was a hot day and I had sandals on, and I slipped 'em off for the photo session. That got blown up out of all proportion. I mean, there was a Volkswagen that happened to be parked in the street which had 28 IF [on the license plate, purportedly inferring Paul would have been twenty-eight if he'd lived to see *Abbey Road*'s release]. That Volkswagen has just recently been sold for a fortune. But it meant *nothing*, you know.

So much of our music has been taken to mean *deep stuff.* We did throw one or two things in. When we were filming *Magical Mystery Tour* the Walrus head didn't fit John, who obviously wrote "I Am the Walrus," so I wore it. In "Glass Onion" on the *White Album*, John put in the line about "the Walrus was Paul," knowing that people were gonna search our lyrics for clues. What do you want from young lads, purity? You're not gonna get it. That's just the way we are, having a laugh that flowed into our lyrics. Your reputation walks ahead of you, and legends are created.

"Live and Let Die" in 1973 was the most commercially successful James Bond theme up to that time. Interestingly, even before the McCartney *LP, you did music in 1967 for a film called* The Family Way. *Do you like writing for movies?*

The Family Way was quite a nice little British film, with Haley Mills and her dad, John. I like films and film music. Before rock and roll you thought of your heroes as Cole Porter and Rodgers and Hammerstein, people from that generation. I've always thought of myself with the idea of a songwriter being someone who could turn his hand to this or that as a craftsman, rather than be stuck in one rock and roll mode or ballad mode.

When I was asked to do a Bond film, I thought, "Why not?" I said, "Look, give me a week. If I can't do it, I'll back out of it." I don't normally write to titles, for instance. But I read the Bond book the next day, on a Saturday, because they hadn't finished the film, and I wrote the song on a Sunday. I was ready to go with George Martin the next week. I found it came easily.

But when George took it to one of the producers, he said,

"That's fine for the demo. When are you gonna record the real thing?" George said, "That's *it,* boys!" It was one of the best demos we ever made. But it was hard to do, the trick being how to combine my writing with the "Bondiness" of the soundtrack orchestration riffs. I'll tell you who liked that song, and I was always surprised: Neil Young! He told me, and I said I wouldn't have thought it'd be to his taste [*laughter*].

Well, it's true that in most creative areas in order to succeed you've got to completely invent your job.

You've got to. And you do tend to listen to other people, but every time, honest, man, you think, "Why the hell did I?" When I made [the film *Give My Regards to*] *Broad Street* in 1984, I listened to *them.* About everything. See, I thought "they" knew.

There are no infallible rocket scientists out there.

But you think there are, don't you? Particularly in movies. As a kid growing up you think there's a big man up at Twentieth Century Fox with white hair, and he's gonna sort of bless you, my child, saying, "This is a good movie, and we're gonna put all our people on this one." It's not like that. And so, with humbling experience, you learn.

I wanted to ask about 1973's Red Rose Speedway *LP, an interesting mix of ethereal love ballads and coarse rock, rosy fantasies and harsh realities.*

Yes, and it wasn't named after Rose, my housekeeper, to debunk another myth. I remember the evening we did the album cover, Linda took that photo of me as I sat next to a motorbike with a rose in me mouth all evening, listening to *Innervisions,* Stevie's album. At one point while I had some of the tunes going, we were up in Scotland at my sheep farm—which all seems very lovely on the postcards, until you get to lambing. Of course a few of them die; it's life and death, and a lot of farmers just don't want to get involved. They say, "Right," and just chuck them over the wall.

But you can't help it if you're a bit sensitive—particularly in a household full of children—and there was one lamb we were trying to save. The young ones get out into the weather and collapse from exposure; you find them and bring them in. We stayed up all night and had him in front of the stove, but it was too late and he just died. I wrote a song about it, "Little Lamb Dragonfly," and the line was "I can help you out, but I can't help you in." It was very sad, so I wrote my little tribute to him.

For Band on the Run, *how did you come to record in Lagos, Nigeria, in the autumn of 1973?*

I'd written "Band on the Run," "Jet," and enough other songs to go into the recording phase, and I got this feeling that it would be boring to record in England. If you record in the same place all the time, music can become work, and you want it always to be play. I think you get the best results that way. We didn't all get into music for a job! We got into it to *avoid* a job, in truth—and get lots of girls.

I rang up EMI, my record company, and asked where else they'd got studios. The list included Rio de Janeiro, China, and Lagos. I thought Lagos sounded *great:* Africa, rhythms, percussionists! On that basis, without knowing anything more about it, we went off.

They were building up the studio in this place called Apapa when we got there. They didn't use booths or separation barriers, so they were constructing booths just for us, and the guy was saying, "Do you want glass in them?" They were just gonna make big wooden things with holes in them! [*laughter*] We did a little work in Ginger Baker's ARC Studio as well, because there was a little political thing which we hadn't realized, in that Ginger was slightly in competition with EMI. I thought, we can't let old Ginger down, so we went and worked there too just to show no favoritism.

We got mugged out in Lagos. Linda and I were on foot, in the middle of darkest Africa, and we got mugged one night and they took all this stuff—a lot of tapes, the demos of the songs! We got to the studio the next day, and the head guy there said, "You're lucky you didn't get killed! It's only 'cause you're white you didn't. They figure you won't recognize them."

You know, there were public executions in Lagos back then, before their oil boom. They had an execution one day on the beach! They just take this guy out, tie him to an oil drum, and go, "pop." And then they sell wooden souvenirs of the dead guy, little carvings. We said, "Er, we're not used to *this,* lads." The next day it was a beach again—"Hoorray! Come and swim!" *Weird.* It was pretty different from all we expected. I anticipated great weather, and it was monsoon season, the sky peeing down all the time. [*laughs*] Great recording weather, though, great weather for being *in*doors. When we got back to England, we got a letter from the managing director of EMI, saying, "Dear Paul: Would not advise you going to Lagos, as there has just been an outbreak of cholera." *Ahhhh!!!!*

Still, out of the adversity came one of our better albums.

Band on the Run *was such a smash both sales-wise and critically, yet you were down to a trio at that point—only you, Linda, and Denny Laine.*

The night before we were due to go on the trip, two of the guys in Wings, the guitar player [Henry McCullough] and the drummer [Denny Seiwell], rang up and said they're not going. I said, "Thanks for letting us know . . ." Your jaw just hits the ground, and you go, "Ohhh dear me."

They didn't want to come to Africa, got cold feet. Reduced to a trio, we went and did it like that. Actually it was good because it meant I could play drums—or that we were *stuck* with me as the drummer, depending on your outlook. I've just gotta be simple in my playing, because I can't *be* complicated. Fleetwood Mac style is my kind of drumming: dead straight, right down the stropping!

You've done some respectable drumming from McCartney *onward.*

The best compliment I got from that was when I was out in L.A. in 1974 visiting John when he was doing his *Pussy Cats* album with Nilsson, and they were having *one* wild time out there. It was boys on the rampage, that was. John and Nilsson, and Keith Moon was staying with them. What a crowd! But I remember Keith saying, "Say, who was that drummer on *Band on the Run*?" [*grinning*] That was the biggest accolade I could get. I mean, my favorite drummers are Ringo, Bonham, and Keith. Moony had more flash, and Bonham was a *bit* more flash, but Ringo is right down the center, never overplays. We could never persuade Ringo to do a solo. The only thing we ever persuaded him to do was that rumble in "The End" on *Abbey Road.* He said [*sourly*], "I hate solos."

I agree with him. Those moments in a concert where everyone goes off for a drink and you're left with this drummer going *dabadubba dabadubba,* with lights flashing, are a total yawn. A quarter of an hour later, the band return, out of their skulls [*laughter*] to play the last number, with the poor drummer left sober as a judge.

Where'd you get the Band on the Run *LP's prison break theme?*

There were a lot of musicians at the time who'd come out of ordinary suburbs in the sixties and seventies and were getting busted. Bands like the Byrds, the Eagles—the mood amongst them was one of desperados. We were being outlawed for pot. It put us on the wrong side of the law. And our argument on the title song was, "Don't put us on the wrong side, you'll make us into criminals. We're *not* criminals, we don't want to be." We just would rather do this than hit the booze—which had been the traditional way to do it. We felt that this was a better move; we had all our theories.

So I just made up a story about people breaking out of prison. Structurally, that very tight little intro on "Band on the Run"—"Stuck inside these four walls"—led to a hole being blasted in the wall, and we get the big orchestra and then we're off. We escape into the sun.

"Helen Wheels" was written before Lagos.

"Helen Wheels" was my Land Rover. That song described a trip down the M6, which is the big motorway to get from Scotland down south to England. So that song was my attempt to try and put England on the map. All the Chuck Berry songs you ever heard always had things like "Birmingham, Alabama!" shouted out, these American places like "Tallahassee!" But you couldn't put the English ones in. It always sounded daft to us. "Scunthorpe!" "Warrington!" It doesn't sound as funky.

One of the great things about the success of *Band on the Run* was the interest of Al Coury, then a hot promotion man at Capitol. Normally you didn't talk to them much, but he rang me up from America and said, "You gotta let me work on this record, I've got a real feeling about it!" It'd been No. 1, but it was slipping down the charts and he said he felt there was still stuff left on it. He released "Jet," which I wasn't even thinking of releasing as a single, and then "Band on the Run" too. He was objective about it, 'cause if you've been working on it for months, you can't even see the label, it's such a blur. He single-handedly turned that album around.

Band on the Run *documents a helluva lot of traveling. "Picasso's Last Words (Drink to Me)" came from a Jamaica holiday you took.*

Dustin Hoffman and Steve McQueen were in Jamaica to make the picture *Papillon.* We went to nose around on the film set.

One evening Dustin invited us to dinner, and he said, "How do you write songs?" I said, "They just come out of the air, I dunno." He said, "Can you write them about anything?" I said, "If you're inspired, yeah." He said, "I've got a great thing, you've gotta try this," so he ran and got this *Time* magazine reporting the death of Picasso. It explained that the night before he died he was having dinner with his friends and he said, "Drink to me, drink to my health, you know I can't drink anymore," then went upstairs and died. I said, "Well, you could probably write a song about that." I think that in my mind I sorta switched to Dylan, 'cause having someone in your head who could sing it is a good way to write a song, so I switched to Dylan, singing [*nasal Dylan drawl*] "*Dreenk to me . . .*" Dustin leapt up, trying to find his missus, hollering, "Look, he's doing it. Goddamn it! Holy shit!" I took it out to Lagos, and we put backwards drum on it and percussion with Ginger Baker.

You went down to Nashville in the summer of 1974 and did the "Junior's Farm" hit, "Sally G," and other things.

We went there mainly to get out of town and rehearse the new band lineup with a new guitarist [Jimmy McCulloch] and drummer [Geoff Britton]. We spent the days practicing in the garage of this pal Curly Putnam's house, and met up with quite a few local people: Johnny Cash, Chet Atkins. I sorta look up to Chet and certain people like that who're gents; not snobs but true gentlemen, or what I call toffs. One day, I was talking to Chet about a song my dad had written—the only song he ever wrote.

You mean, "Walking in the Park with Eloise"?

Yes! Chet said, "It'd be really nice to make a record of that, Paul, for your dad." Chet got Floyd Cramer to come along to play piano, Chet played guitar, I played bass—and then washboard, which had them in hysterics. And I named the band the Country Hams.

The record came out in '74 with "Bridge Over the River Suite" on the other side. "Bridge" came about in '73 while I was on another song called "Country Dreamer," a countryish song [on the B-side of "Helen Wheels"], while working with Alan Parsons, who at that time was our engineer. He had just engineered *The Dark Side of the Moon,* and then he became the Alan Parsons Project.

On the intro to "Country Dreamer," while we were getting the feel, I did a five-minute guitar thing, picking it, and then went into the song and did the take. Alan liked this long guitar jam on the front and spliced it all together, editing it down and presenting it to me a few days later. I took it to Nashville, overdubbed a little horns, and that became this strange B-side. I rather liked that Hams single; it's like film music.

New Orleans was the next stop for Wings' recording jaunts, in the winter and spring of 1975. You did Venus and Mars *at Allen Toussaint's studio. Do you have a favorite track from those sessions?*

I would say "Listen to What the Man Said." I really liked what Tom Scott did on there with sax. We just went for it live. I also liked "Letting Go." And then there was "Medicine Jar," written by the late Wings guitarist Jimmy McCulloch and his friend Colin Allen from Stone the Crows. Jimmy wanted to write an antidrug song. As to *why* he wanted to, I'm not sure, but I'd say he'd seen the personal warning signs. That song, I think, was Jimmy talking to himself. Listening to it now and knowing the circumstances of how he died, I'm sure that's what it is. He's really saying to himself, "Get your hand out of the medicine jar." I don't think he managed to. He was a great guitar player, but he was into a little too much heavy stuff. But if I'm reading too much into it, then let's just say I'm just as bad as the fucking critics, okay?

I recall a portion of the '75–'76 Wings world tour when the stage lit up like an English music hall marquee, and you performed "You Gave Me the Answer." There is that strong song-and-dance music-hall tradition in your material.

You're right, and I think it's from when I was growing up. See, what you've got to remember is that when people of my generation—who would have been born in the 1940s and obviously be around forty now—were growing up, rock and roll hadn't been invented yet! Blues had started, but that was nowhere near as popular; you had to be a real folkie to be into blues. Anything up to the 1950s was the old traditions, and in Britain that was music hall, or vaudeville as you call it.

My dad, sitting around the house tapping out things like "Chicago" on the ivories, he used to get told off by *his* dad for playing what his dad called "tin can music." To me it's the great old standards now. It's silly to realize, but the waltz was once a scandalous dance, and "Chicago" was once considered raucous pop. If anyone wanted to go into show business before the mid-1950s, you were looking at a Sinatra-type person as the most rocking you were gonna get. Then suddenly Elvis arrived, and Chuck Berry, Fats Domino, Little Richard, Jerry Lee, and all the guys. From then on, that was the whole direction.

Anyway, as a result my father was very sympathetic when I was getting into music, and consequently there was a lot of that music-hall music around our house on the radio and the telly. Later, occasionally, you began to hear little pieces of that influence in songs I had begun writing. "When I'm Sixty-Four" was one of mine in that vein. I was about sixteen when I wrote that [*smiles*] and my dad would have been fifty-six or fifty-eight. Retirement age over here is sixty-five, so maybe I thought sixty-four was a good prelude. But probably sixty-four just worked good as a number; I don't always think these things out.

So that's where I get all my music-hall stuff from. And when I used to introduce "You Gave Me the Answer" in that show you're talking about, I always used to dedicate it to Fred Astaire. He's one of my favorite dancers *and* singers. I love his voice on things like "Cheek to Cheek." His style and delivery were real neat, and he was a great athlete. A combination of all that has led me in that slightly fruity direction, [*chuckles, shrugs*] but I like it.

Come clean, what was the intention behind that oddball Thrillington *album, that lush instrumental version of* Ram, *that you issued in April 1977?*

Well, you always see these albums like *James Last Does Tchaikovsky* or *Nelson Riddle Plays Mantovani.* I thought it'd be amusing to have your own tunes from an album and take them to the middle of the road as a mischievous way to infiltrate the light TV programs and things that use such fluff. It was another silly idea along the way, but we scoured the world for orchestra leader Percy "Thrills" Thrillington. [*winks*] Finally found him in Ireland! He and a friend of his did some arrangements and laid this album. Now, I think it should all have been done up *louder!*

"Mull of Kintyre" in 1977 was your biggest British hit ever, and it doesn't sound like anything else you've done. Isn't that named after a Scottish peninsula?

Yeah, in an area in Scotland where I've got my farm. Well, you heard these Scottish folk songs in films, and nearly always they're *old* songs. I got the theory that there isn't such a thing as a modern Scottish song, unless they tend to be Americanish or British. I decided to see if I could write a Scottish folk song. I've got a lot of feeling for Scotland, which has got the ancient Celtic thing before England was taken over by all the Romans. We were barbarians, you see, and it's that connection I like.

It was a throwaway at first, and the next thing was to get the local Campbeltown pipers into a big barn I had, turning it into a studio by getting a mobile unit there. The leader of the band came up to show me what notes a bagpipe could play; I suddenly realized they can't play just anything, since they've got a certain scale and they can't modulate and change key. When he came up he wouldn't play in the kitchen. He reckoned it would deafen us all, so he took me out in the garden in his full gear. Afterward, I wrote a song that included these insights. Then they all came into the barn to cut it, and it was quite a night—and quite a noise. We had a few beers and we had a hit!

The 1979 Concerts for the People of Kampuchea that you sponsored with the U.N. were a pre–Live Aid initiative to help refugees.

That was an early one, yeah, but it was a much smaller event. It was conceived as a week of concerts at an urban venue [London's Hammersmith Odeon], and it wasn't internationally satellite-ed. Musically, the album turned out all right, but I hated the show itself. I think that show was the last thing we did with Wings, and a lot of it was the fault of the monitors onstage, because if you can't hear yourself you think you've done a terrible show. My bass sounded like a *squeak.* It gave me the cold sweats.

But historically, George's Bangla Desh show was the real forerunner of ideas like Live Aid—which was great too, fabulous. It was nice to see the music guys that you thought were just wallys being so concerned. It's become quite a thing now, with the Amnesty International concerts centering attention. Often you find your musicians do more good than your bloody government does. Certainly on Live Aid, they did.

How did you come to build the Abbey Road "replica studio" in the basement of MPL headquarters in 1978–79?

There'd been a room in EMI's Abbey Road Studios that we'd always used to mix in as the Beatles. And so you knew the room. We'd recorded "Hey Jude" at a studio called Trident that had marvelous playback facilities. You dropped a pin, coughed, anything you did sounded fantastic. So it was very deceptive. You could make a bunch of rubbish, and it sounded fabulous. It was like being drunk! So we took "Hey Jude" to EMI, where they had very unglamorous speakers, and it sounded really bad. We had to pump full bass and full treble into the recording before we got it right.

That illustrated the idea that you can get confused in a studio you don't know the sound of. Much later on, in '78, I had to get into that studio and couldn't; Cliff Richard had it booked forever. I asked what would be involved in making a replica of it in the basement of MPL. It wasn't that much: certain walls, finishes on walls, etc. We recorded "Goodnight Tonight" there—and "Daytime Nighttime Suffering," that record's great undiscovered B-side—and a lot of the *Back to the Egg* LP. Then we dissassembled the studio, and now the downstairs is just a basement again.

Had you gone into "Goodnight Tonight" intending to create a contemporary dance track?

That's what it was. I like dance tracks, and if I got to a club there's no point in hearing ballads all night. You need something to get you up on the floor, and I'm into a lot of that stuff. We recorded it in a long version, as opposed to stretching it like they do now. I think I got fed up with the remix mechanizing, the dub stuff; I think it'll date very quickly.

It's not that I'm following the crowd, but if there's a lot of people into a thing I generally check it out to see why they all like it. When reggae came out and all the skinheads in England bought the great early *Tighten Up* albums in the late 1960s, early 1970s, that was the first time I'd heard of it, but I learned of it *through* the skinheads' interest. It's like rap now. There's some people that I really like: Eric B and Rakim, and B Fats.

You did McCartney II, *your second completely solo LP, in the summer of 1979. How different do you see that from the first* McCartney*?*

The second one seemed less sophisticated in my mind. I don't know whether it is or not. The second one was done not with all the home comforts of the first, but in a derelict farmhouse in the countryside in southern England that was about to be knocked down. I recorded in what had been the front parlor, with a tape machine, a couple of sequencers, and some amps, bass, guitar, and drums.

The overriding memory of making that album was that I did some songs in their original versions in about ten minutes. Then I'd have to go back and add, say, the maraca part for ten minutes, too. Bloody hell! I'm alone in the middle of the country and it took, like, *self-hypnosis* to keep going shaking the maracas like a baby after about eight fucking minutes!

For "Coming Up," I believe I heard something on the radio by Sly Stone or Sister Sledge; it was pre-Prince, for certain, and the song I heard might even have been "We Are Family." But I went into the tape machine with that vibe and began to make something up around my own groove. The sax sounds on it are Mellotrons sped up like tight little munchkins. "Temporary Secretary" I also liked. The story behind it was sex, I suppose, [*chuckle*] but that's always the story.

Which albums did you spend the most time making?

I think *Tug of War,* from 1980 to '82, and then *Pipes of Peace.* I was working with George Martin at the AIR London and Montserrat studios. We took a *lot* of time on those two albums. In fact, we took so much time, when I saw the bill for it all I thought, "I could have made an entire studio for this!" And that's in fact why

I've since made my own new studio. As for the songs on those two albums, I favor the title tracks. "Pipes of Peace" has a solid mood to it, an undercurrent that grabs you, and "Tug of War" worked as a commentary on my career thus far, an accurate summing up.

Press to Play *in '86 was your last new studio album, arriving three years after* Pipes of Peace. *The standout tune was its title single, "Press."*

That was what Jerry Marotta used to call the "Massage Song." [*sly smile*] That *was* the inspiration. Everybody loves a massage, touching each other. I like the groove, but the lyrics leave a little to be desired. And the line, "Oklahoma was never like this!"—no one ever understood that line. It meant a lot to me, either referring to the boonies, the sticks, or to the old movie itself, where the "corn is as high as an elephant's eye" was never like *this* song.

You're as well known for your bass-playing as you are for songwriting. Even avid fans tend to forget that you took up the bass out of a sense of duty rather than desire. As I recall, you originally changed from guitar to bass way back in June 1961, during the Beatles' third three-month stint at the Top Ten Club in Hamburg. Stuart Sutcliffe, the bass player at that stage, had just elected to quit the Beatles and move in with German fiancée Astrid Kirchherr rather than return to Liverpool with the rest of the band.

[*nodding*] So with Stuart staying in Hamburg, I became the bass player—I kinda drew the short straw and got lumbered with bass. It was not really the instrument people liked to play in those days; you wanted to be a big guitarist.

I got myself the little Hofner violin bass because it was symmetrical for left-handed playing, meaning if you turned it upside down it still looked all right. I worked with that and in the beginning I was doing what everyone else in bands did, which was basically rooting the songs with bass. Then 'round about the year before *Sgt. Pepper*, Rickenbacker gave me a new bass and I started to record with that. On the *Pepper* stuff I got into the more melodic basslines. In fact, some of the best-paced bass-playing I ever did was at that time, but more recently I can say that "Goodnight Tonight" has got quite a good bassline, and the bass underpins "Silly Love Songs" quite nicely.

Really, my stuff is the "old" style of bass-playing, because I didn't make the leap into thwacking with the thumb. I do a little bit of the thumb trip, but it's not really what I'm into. A lot of the young guys now, that is where they *start* with bass. It's something

I tend to leave to others—having worked with Stanley Clarke, for example, who's done that for me.

A lot of guitar players and singers like the old style of bass because it *anchors* the song. I was talking to Jeff Beck, who likes my style for that kind of thing, and he said, "Don't undervalue it, man, just because these other people are into their percussive stuff." Whereas when you've got all that percussion-style bass within the rhythm, it can be everything but the kitchen sink and yet there's still no bottom. There's no *ass* down there!

I prefer bass that's impressive not percussively but *musically,* where it's more a melody thing than the actual style of playing. I'm not really into a million notes a minute. It's more important to me what notes are played, and what they do to the song.

Bassists tend to use the root note, so if you're in "A" they're playing "A." But my inspirations are people like Brian Wilson on *Pet Sounds,* because he always puts an odd note against the chord. For instance, if he's in "A," he'll often play an "E" as the bass, which sort of stands the song on its head, and for certain sections that's great. I did stuff like that as early as "Michelle."

I went through a period where I let other people play bass on my records, but I prefer playing it for the studio work I'm currently doing. I'm using a Fender Jazz of medium age at the moment, 'cause it just records great. But, listen, I'm not one of those fellows who talks on and on about certain amps and things. I went into some shop in America recently, and this guy at the counter said, "Hey, I'm a bass player! What kind of strings do you use?" I said [*confidingly*], "Oh, I prefer those shiny ones!"

Michael Jackson's recent surprise purchase of the ATV Music company that controls your song catalog remains rather shocking. As our talk here makes plain, you've been incredibly prolific, but this shrewd incident sealed the only chance you might have ever had to own your own musical offspring.

[*Grim*] Here's what I really think. When John and I came down from Liverpool, we didn't know anything about songs, didn't know what a copyright was—and no one was about to explain it to us, either. They *saw* us coming. There were big, big grins on their faces when these guys who were good writers turned up and said, "I don't know, doesn't everyone own songs?" They said, "Yes, step this way. Come into my parlor," as the spider to the fly.

We were very naïve, and I think it was fair enough to take advantage of that, since young writers will do anything to get published. But after you've made millions, and after, let's say, a decent period of three years, I think it would be nice if you could go back to them and say, "This is a slave deal. Let's change it."

John and I ended up with the first deal that we had in the beginning, which was that the publisher automatically took the copyright. So we never saw anything. I think that was the unfairness. These days, kids see half of the copyrights if they're lucky and they've got tough lawyers.

They came to us originally and said, "We're gonna make you your *own* company." Me and John went, "Wow!" In actual fact, it was *their* company within a company, and they kept 51 percent for themselves and gave us 49 with no control anyway. It was all a fake. Then when we went to India with the Maharishi, Dick James, who held the publishing, sold it behind our backs. So we were well and truly screwed. And the guy who bought it next was Lew Grade.

But it's not so much the financial thing. "Yesterday," for example, I wrote on my own; here's this Liverpool kid falling out of bed and writing "Yesterday." I took it to the guys in the band, and they said, "There's no point in drumming or playing anything on that. You just be on the record on your own." Then I take it to my publishers. They say, "Great, that's a Lennon-McCartney." I said, "Wait a minute. Couldn't it be a McCartney and Lennon?" "No, no, no."

The Beatles catalog was thereafter bought from Lew Grade by an Australian, Robert Holmes à Court. And *then* Michael came along. Michael rang me up way back in the late 1970s, and I said, "What do you want?" He said, "I want to make some hits!" I said, "Great, come on over."

He did, and he was keen to do stuff, so I wrote "Girlfriend" for him, which I did later on *London Town.* Then we wrote "Say Say Say" and "The Man" together, and then he wrote "The Girl is Mine." It was fun, and he was a nice guy to work with and everything. But it always used to keep coming up that he'd say, "Paul, I *need* some advice." I'd give him that advice and say, "Look, get good financial people, people you can trust." I took him under my wing, and we'd always be in little corridors discussing this stuff. I thought it was just fine, but he used to do this little joke; he'd say, [*mimicking Jackson's meek tone*] "I'm gonna buy your publishing, ya know."

I'd go, "Ha! Good one, kid!" Then one day I get phoned up, and they said, "He's just bought your stuff!" I thought, "Oh, you *are* kidding." But that was it, really. He had the money to buy it; he was rolling in it after *Thriller* and had it to burn.

As you say, I could have bought it, but in actual fact there were complications with Yoko which prevented me from getting it. That's a whole other story. Anyway, Michael's got it, and all's fair in love, war, and business, I suppose. But it's a little galling *now* to find that I own less of "Yesterday" than Michael Jackson! It's a thorn in my side, and I keep thinking I should phone him up.

[*Grinning fiercely*] I don't hold a grudge, but if you're listening, Michael, I'll have "Yesterday" and "Here, There and Everywhere" back—just for a laugh—and a couple of others.

So the legal and aesthetic disputes over the commercial exploitation of the Beatles catalogs continue to grow hotter. But you're the custodian of Buddy Holly's songs.

It's very difficult, because I do feel differently in both cases. As far as the Beatles' stuff is concerned, in actual fact what has happened is some people have used it without the *right* to use it. People who haven't got the right have been giving away the right. So it's a different affair than with the Buddy Holly stuff, where I do have the right to let people use it because we're the publishers of that.

But the most difficult question is whether you *should* use songs for commercials. I haven't made up my mind. The other day I saw "Something," George's song, in a car ad, and I thought, "Ewww, yuck! That's in bad taste." Earlier I saw "Twist and Shout" in *Ferris Bueller's Day Off,* which I liked as a film, but they'd overdubbed some lousy brass on the stuff! If it had needed brass, we'd have stuck it on it ourselves.

Generally, I don't like it, particularly with the Beatles stuff. When twenty more years have passed, maybe we'll move into the realm where it's okay to do it. That's a little bit why I feel it's not so bad with Buddy. There may be people out there who say you shouldn't do it with Buddy. I've done it once or twice with him, but I don't really like doing it, I must admit.

One thing I can't do with Buddy is ask him. One thing they can do with us, since there're still three of us alive, is ask *us.* That'd be a good move, to say, "Do you fancy being a car ad?" And we'd say, "No."

Yet you get your advisers saying, "So you're gonna turn down all that money, are you?" If I was being a purist, I'd say no one should give the songs to ads. My *heart* says that. [*pause, eyes downcast*] But, you know, you're not always as pure as you think.

He came as soon as he heard. It's 10:37 A.M. on Tuesday, August 25, 1987, in Burbank, California, and although he's been missing for five years, nobody minds. Because today he swore he'd deliver.

George Harrison arrives alone at the headquarters of Warner Bros. Records, carrying the master reference disc of his new album direct from Bernie Grundman Mastering, where he's spent the last twenty-four hours facing the music and deciding it was finally time to share it. No one at the company has listened to the finished version of *Cloud Nine.* And no one was invited to—until this moment.

He strides through the morning haze, his pale fingers gripping the plain white cardboard sleeve that holds the end product. Dressed in a raven tweed jacket, white silk shirt, charcoal slacks, black bucks, and red-and-gray argyle socks, he takes the tiled front steps with a tread as heavy as his attire.

Lenny Waronker, bashful

George Harrison 1987

and boyish president of Warner Bros., meets him at the threshold of his office with a warm smile and a wary electricity in his gaze. Two literally trembling hands present the perspiration-pocked dust jacket, *George Harrison* inscribed across it in careless script from a felt marker. Waronker cups the prize at its lower corners, holding it against the front of his short leather driving jacket as if it were a citation.

"George!" calls a voice over Waronker's shoulder, and from an adjoining office suite appears Mo Ostin, chairman of the board of the Warners record group. Balding, beaming, his white sport clothes and bronze skin telegraphing an easy zeal for the unfolding ceremony, Ostin beckons the two principals and a guest inside. Two chairs are angled before Waronker's deskside turntable for the private listening session. Mo reclines on a couch behind them.

In the instant before the stylus finds the pressing, there is no sound in the room but that of George Harrison, forty-four, sipping sharply from a cup of tea. Lenny leans forward, his eyes now closed. Mo contemplates the ceiling.

The first track, "Cloud Nine," descends upon the paneled room with absolute authority, an unmistakably reverberant vocal suffusing its space with biting, angular grace. The arrangement is rich but focused, pretty but austere, and when it surprises at the bridge with an exquisite upward spiral of harmonies, the composer makes his opening comment. "I put," he states above the surging music, "some 'Beach Boys' at the bridge." Mo manages a horizontal nod. Lenny places his palms over his sealed eyelids.

"That's What It Takes" bursts forth, attacking the ears as if from a windswept dashboard radio. "Fish on the Sand" is next, heightening the sense of breeze-tossed forward dispatch. The singer is biting the words, snapping them off with an aggressive drive. "Just for Today," a ballad of bottomless sadness, takes hold. Then "This Is Love" builds a case for new promise, the vocals full of yearning. Quickly, a fresh aural landscape approaches with "When We Was Fab," the tantalizingly familiar filigrees acting as magnets for the arrangement's sly twists.

As the song fades, Waronker looks up from his cradled hands. "That was," he says, "a *killer* sequence of tracks."

"I can't wait," Ostin giggles, "to catch the second side." And "Devil's Radio" is worth the anticipation. The ferocious rocker is an unearthly delight. Harrison permits himself the merest smile of impish satisfaction, which widens as whoops erupt from his audience.

"I had to rescue this song, redo it to give it a better chance," he volunteers, his dense Liverpool diction slicing through the speaker's throb, as the ethereal "Someplace Else" begins. "This was wasted on a soundtrack to an unsuccessful Madonna–Sean Penn film I produced."

The tough, tart "Wreck of the Hesperus" is the third track on the second side, its witty vocal parries a neat counterpoint to the stabbing guitar. The lush "Breath Away from Heaven" provides an atmospheric slice of intrigue. Then, as the finale, "Got My Mind Set on You," kicks in with a primitive rock and roll wallop, George Harrison reveals his glee with the wry ode to checkbook romance. "This'll teach the yuppies!" he crows.

"This album'll teach a *lot* of people something," Mo Ostin rejoins, on his feet and radiant with relief. "We'll give them 'Got My Mind Set on You' as the first single!" "And then for the second single," adds a jubilant Waronker, "we can choose from 'That's What It Takes,' 'This Is Love,' or 'When We Was Fab.' The 'Fab' track is like a movie, it's so vivid, and it's a graceful and riveting acknowledgment of the past. This whole album's got the good rock roots and new excitement radio has been needing."

Harrison's jaw drops: "Then you mean that I passed the final examination? Well, hoorray for that much!" A hearty round of backslapping and guffaws erupts as the former Beatle (born February 25, 1943) is reminded of an incident way back in his Liverpool origins, when sixteen-year-old George burned his report card—he'd failed every subject but art—in 1959 and quit school. By that time George, John Lennon, and Paul McCartney had already played together in the Casbah Coffee Club, a cellar café owned by future drummer Pete Best's mum, Mona.

You likely know the rest: The Beatles fire Pete Best in August 1962 and hire Rory Storm & the Hurricanes' drummer, Ringo Starr. Whereupon irate Pete Best fans enter the Cavern Club and blacken George's eye in a fracas. That September the Beatles cut their first single, "Love Me Do," in EMI's Studio 2 in St. John's Wood. Producer George Martin asks the lads, "Anything you're not happy about with us?" "Yes," George quips, "I don't like your tie."

Several hundred million records later, on November 1, 1968, the first outside LP project by a Beatle, George Harrison's *Wonderwall*

Music, is issued on Apple Records. In 1969, shortly after the Beatles notch a No. 1 U.S. hit with Harrison's "Something" from *Abbey Road,* dissension in the group grows grievous. In early 1970 the Beatles disassemble. George Harrison, after releasing the experimental *Electronic Sound* on the Zapple subsidiary, makes a massive individual impression in 1970 with the three-record set, *All Things Must Pass,* and thereafter plots a new path for himself.

Cloud Nine, produced with Electric Light Orchestra maestro Jeff Lynne, is George Harrison's thirteenth solo album (if you count *The Concert for Bangla Desh* and a Capitol greatest hits collection). It's the fifth of his Warner Bros. albums in the States, and his only LP since the unjustly ignored *Gone Troppo,* a genial 1982 gem. Moreover, in Lenny Waronker's estimation, "*Cloud Nine* is the finest album George has made since *All Things Must Pass,* and probably his best ever."

Harrison's core band for the record consists of George on guitars and sitar; Jeff Lynne on bass and guitar; Ringo, Jim Keltner, and Ray Cooper on drums and percussion; Elton John and Gary Wright on keyboards; and Jim Horn on horns. Also featured is Eric Clapton, still George's best friend after fabled misadventures, principally luring away wife Patti Harrison in the midseventies—"but I also pulled a chick on him once," George has noted. Indeed, Harrison was such a forgiving soul that he, Paul, and Ringo performed "Sgt. Pepper's Lonely Hearts Club Band" at Eric and Patti's wedding reception.

"You've come a long way from Liverpool Technical Institute," I observe, after Harrison and I bid good-bye to the Warners brass and press on to our appointed lunch-interview. "Well, yes and no," George assures with a mischievous blink of his brown eyes, "because the Gretsch guitar I got several months after splitting from Liverpool Tech is the very same one I'm holding on the cover of *Cloud Nine*!"

How did you hook up with Jeff Lynne?

I'd been trying to imagine, for a few years, somebody who could co-produce my albums. I'm sure there's plenty of talented people out there, but I haven't really worked with many people on the production line. In the old days we just had George Martin working with us. And after that, well, I worked a little while with Phil

Spector. That became more trouble than it was worth, and I ended up doing most of the work myself.

People sometimes forget Spector was involved in All Things Must Pass *and* The Concert for Bangla Desh.

Well, on *All Things Must Pass* Phil came in and we did half the backing tracks. Then, because of the condition he was in, he had to leave, and I completed the rest of the backing without him. And did maybe 50 percent of the overdubbing, all the backing vocals and all the guitar parts. Then he came back when I was mixing it. All of this was over a four, five-month period. But he still had to keep going to the hospital, seeing a doctor. He was going through a bad time with drinking, and it made him ill.

What was his role in recording Bangla Desh*?*

Phil was at the concert dancing in the front when it was being recorded! There was a guy, Gary Kellgren, who did the key work in the live recording. Then when Phil came to the remix, again Phil was in and out of the hospital.

Phil worked on the second solo album, *Living in the Material World,* but by that I mean he was around. Again, he kept falling over and breaking his ankles, wrists. The guy who was his helper was having heart attacks.

Phil was never there. I literally used to have to go and break into the hotel to get him. I'd go along the roof at the Inn On The Park in London and climb in his window yelling, "Come on! We're supposed to be making a record!" He'd say, "Oh. Okay." And then he used to have eighteen cherry brandies before he could get himself down to the studio. I got so tired of that because I needed somebody to *help.* I was ending up with more work than if I'd just been doing it on my own.

Wasn't "Try Some Buy Some" from Living in the Material World *supposed to be on a Ronnie Spector album?*

That's right. It didn't come out, because Phil couldn't last in the studio for more than a few hours. We did about four very rough backing tracks. A couple of the songs Phil had written. One of them was very good in his pop vein.

He liked my "Try Some Buy Some," so we orchestrated it and knocked off a B-side for a Ronnie single on Apple in '71. The B-side's a killer, "Tandoori Chicken." It's a twelve-bar thing done on the spot with Mal our roadie and Joe the chauffeur—"I told Mal / my old pal / to go with Joe / and they should go / and get some tandoori chicken." And a great big bottle of wine! [*laughter*] We did it one-take, with a lot of improvised scat singing in the middle. It's hysterical.

We also did a song which I later used on *Extra Texture* called "You." It was high for me, singing it, because I wrote it in Ronnie Spector's key and put my vocals on the instrumental track we'd completed.

I loved those Ronettes records and those Phil Spector records. I still do. And I love Phil. He's brilliant. There's nobody who's come close to some of his productions for excitement. Tina Turner's "River Deep Mountain High" probably was one of the only Cinemascope-sized records ever. But Phil didn't have enough energy with me to sustain an album for Ronnie. Still, he had a sense of humor, and if you're reading, Phil, I still think you're one of the *greatest.* He is, you know, and he should be out there doing stuff right now—but not with me!

After that I just worked on my own, although during 1978 I did one album, *George Harrison,* with Russ Titelman, who was a great help. At that time I felt I didn't really know what was going on out there in music, and I felt Russ, who was in music day by day, would give me a bit of direction. I didn't do an album until *Somewhere in England* in 1980–81 and then *Gone Troppo* the next year. The problem is that when you write, perform, *and* produce, there's a good chance of getting lost.

So recently I thought, "Who could I possibly work with?" I don't really know many people who would understand me and my past, and have respect for that, who I also have great respect for. And then I hit on Jeff Lynne, thinking he'd be good—*if* we got on well.

I'd never met him, but I was talking to Dave Edmunds and he said he knew and had just worked with Jeff. "Well," I mentioned, "if you talk with him, tell him I'd like to meet him." Dave called me back and said Jeff was going to be down in London, and I said to ask him if he wants to come over the house. So I met him like that, and we had a nice dinner and a couple of bottles of wine and I got his phone number.

We hung out a bit. It's been two years now since I met him, and the more we got to know each other it just evolved into this thing. Jeff was fantastic, the perfect choice. I couldn't have worked with a better person.

You and Jeff cooked up "When We Was Fab" as a homage to your formative years.

I got this idea for a few chords, and I started the tune while Jeff and I were messing around in Australia last November at the Australian Grand Prix. I began the song on a little guitar someone loaned me, and I got three or four chords into it when the string broke. We had to go to dinner but luckily there was a piano at the person's house where we went, so with people frying stuff in the background, we got on the piano and pursued three chords. They turned into the verse part of "When We Was Fab."

The first thing I constructed was a tempo announcement, with Ringo going, "One, two, *da-da-dum, da-da-dum!*" Next we laid the guitar, piano, and drum framework, and I wasn't too sure what it was gonna turn into. But the idea was that it would evoke a Fabs song. It was always intended to be lots of fun.

Maybe it's this California setting, but the first bygone Beatles track it made me think of was one you wrote for Magical Mystery Tour *based on your temporary 1967 L.A. address between Beverly Hills and Laurel Canyon.*

"Blue Jay Way." It's in there. And also this funny chord, an E and an F at the same time, like one I had on the old Beatle record, "I Want to Tell You." It also has that chord in John's "She's So Heavy."

Anyway, every so often we took the tape of "Fab" out and overdubbed more, and it developed and took shape to where we wrote words. This was an odd experience for me; I've normally finished all of the songs I've done—with the exception of maybe a few words here and there—before I *ever* recorded them. But Jeff doesn't do that at all. He's making them up as he goes along.

That to me is a bit like, "*Ohh nooo,* that's too mystical. I wanna know where we're heading." But in another way it's good because you don't have to finalize your idea till the last minute. We put wacky lyrics in the last line of each chorus like, "Back when income tax was all we had." Another one says, "But it's all over now, Baby Blue." It's tongue-in-cheek and shows how Jeff could assist my muse. To do it live, we'd need the Electric Light Orchestra for all those cellos!

The Beatles were a huge influence on ELO, but a nice thing about Cloud Nine *is that it doesn't sound like Jeff Lynne, but rather like George Harrison saying, "I'm back!"*

That's the great thing about Jeff. He wanted to help me make *my* record. But there's so much in there Jeff contributed to. "Fab" was a 50–50 contribution, but "This Is Love" was a song where I said, "Why don't you write me a tune?" So he came down with lots of bits and pieces on cassette, and almost let me choose. I routined that song with him, and we wrote the words together. In fact, he had so many permutations of how that song is, he can still write another three songs out of the bits left.

I think he's one of the best pop songwriters around. He's a craftsman, and he's got endless patience. I tend to feel, "Okay, that'll do," and go on, and Jeff'll still be thinking about how to tidy what's just been done.

Are you a Jeff Lynne–like saver of tracks and ideas?

Not consciously, but I think all experiences go in here [*taps his head*] and our nervous systems compute them. If something's good, you tend to remember it, [*smiles*] and sometimes if it's bad, too. I don't think you can get away from your past, if you want to put it like that.

Tell me the story behind "Got My Mind Set on You."

That's something that I've just had in the back of my head for twenty-five years. It's a very obscure song, and I had it off an old album by this guy James Ray. In the very early sixties our manager, Brian Epstein, had his two NEMS—North End Music Stores—shops at Charlotte and Whitechapel streets in Liverpool, and he made it his policy to have at least one copy of every record that came out in England. We used to go through all the records in the two shops, and that's why the Beatles records in those very early days were made up of both all the obvious things we liked, like Chuck Berry and Little Richard, but also things which were obscure. Most of them were American records, but a lot were not even known there!

We did a James Ray song, "If You Gotta Make a Fool of Somebody," in our show for years. When we started making records, we did a lot of covers but we never covered that one—although we might have done it live in some BBC recordings. But all these North of England bands started doing a lot of the tunes we used to do, and actually had hits with some of the tracks. The Swinging Blue Jeans took Chan Romero's "The Hippy Hippy Shake" from what we used to do.

So I came here to America in 1963—*before* the Beatles came here—and I bought that James Ray album that had "If You Gotta Make a Fool of Somebody." The album itself was really terrible, but the best three songs were written by this guy who discovered James

Ray, a former mailman named Rudy Clark. Clark wrote "It's Been a Drag," and "Got My Mind Set on You Part One/Part Two"—although it didn't have any break in between. If you listen to the song now, it's very different from how I've done it. I've updated it and changed the chords, because I preferred it the way I heard it in my head. Clark and Ray's version of it was coming out of the old jazz/swing era, and it has these horrible screechy women's voices singing those backup parts.

I did that song because Jim Keltner got this drum pattern going one day that was a cross between swing and rock. Gary Wright turned around and said, "Hey! Doesn't that remind you of that song, 'Got My Mind Set on You'?" [*laughter*] I was so surprised that anybody else had *ever* heard that tune!

You've covered some rare chestnuts on your own. On Gone Troppo, *you cut "I Really Love You," a bouncy R&B number that was a hit for the Stereos in 1961.*

Yes! And if you remember that song then I'll tell you that the Beatles wrote a song that I think was actually a nick, a bit of a pinch off that one. It was a song that John wrote and I sang on the very first Beatle album called "Do You Want to Know a Secret." If you check that against the song you're referring to on *Troppo,* that's round two of where "Secret" came from [*laughter*]. It's a fun track.

What was it like working with John on Imagine *in 1971? You contributed slide guitar or dobro to "Crippled Inside," "How Do You Sleep?" "I Don't Want to Be a Soldier Momma," "Gimme Some Truth," and "Oh My Love."*

It was nerve-wracking, as usual. Previously I'd worked on "Instant Karma." At that time very strange, intense feelings were going on. Sometimes people don't talk to each other, thinking they're not going to be the one to phone you up and risk rejection. With John, I knew Klaus Voorman, the bass player, so I could at least *ask* what was going on over at his little eight-track studio in his house at Tittenhurst Park, and how Klaus was doing. John said, "Oh, you know, you *should* come over," so I just put me guitar and amplifier in the car.

I turned up, and he was openly pleased I came. I enjoyed "How Do You Sleep?"; I liked being on *that* side of it with Paul [*chuckles*] rather than on the receiving end. Moreover, I was earnestly trying to be a slide guitar player at that time, but I always blacked out at solos, especially live ones. I seemed to have no control over what was happening, and my mind'd go blank. That was one of them where I hit a few good notes and it happened to sound like a solo. We did all that work in one day.

Just as "How Do You Sleep?" and "Crippled Inside" were John's snipes at McCartney, your song "Wah-Wah" on All Things Must Pass *was aimed at Paul during* Let It Be.

[*Nods*] I'd left the band at that period. Everybody's seen that film [*Let It Be*] now, and what was supposed to be us rehearsing new material. They were going to film us recording it live, but the rehearsal became the movie. After we got over all the rows we had, us recording it live just ended up in Apple Studio and on the roof.

I just got so fed up with the bad vibes—and that arguments with Paul were being put on film. I didn't care if it was the Beatles, I was getting out. Getting home in that pissed-off mood, I wrote that song. "Wah-Wah" was saying, "You've given me a bloody headache."

Further on, the song worked well live at the Bangla Desh concert, considering there was no rehearsal. *That* whole show was a stroke of luck. I'd rehearsed *some* with Ringo, the horn players, and the guys from Badfinger, but it was all happening so fast it's amazing we managed to get anything on tape.

"Not Guilty," on George Harrison, *written during the sessions for the Beatles'* White Album, *was a pointed barb at your old bandmates.*

It was me getting pissed off at Lennon and McCartney for the grief I was catching during the making of the *White Album.* I said I wasn't guilty of getting in the way of their careers. I said I wasn't guilty of leading them astray in our all going to Rishikesh to see the Maharishi. I was sticking up for myself, and the song came off strong enough to be saved and utilized.

You've drawn some strong statements from sorrow. "Deep Blue" was very affecting, and since it was on the flip side of the "Bangla Desh" single, it became a jukebox favorite in bars in the States.

I'm glad you noticed that one. You're sure they weren't just punching up the wrong side of the record? I got the impression people never heard a lot of these songs.

When I was making *All Things Must Pass* in 1970, not only did I have Phil Spector going in the hospital and all this trouble, besides organizing the Trident Studios schedule in London with Derek & the Dominos—who many forget got their *start* on that record—but also my mother got really ill. I was going all the way up and down England to Liverpool trying to see her in the hospital. Bad time.

She'd got a tumor on the brain, but the doctor was an idiot and he was saying, "There's nothing wrong with her, she's having some psychological trouble." When I went up to see her, she didn't even know who I was. [*voice stiffening with anger*] I had to punch the doctor out, 'cause in England the family doctor has to be the one to get the specialist. So he got the guy to look at her, and she ended up in the neurological hospital. The specialist said, "She could end up being a vegetable, but if it was my wife or my mother I'd do the operation"—which was a horrendous thing where they had to drill a hole in her skull.

She recovered a little bit for about seven months. And during that period my father, who'd taken care of her, had suddenly exploded with ulcers and he was in the same hospital. So I was pretending to both of them that the other one was okay. Then, running back and forth to do this record, I wrote that song. I made it up at home one exhausted morning with those major and minor chords. It's filled with that frustration and gloom of going in these hospitals, and the feeling of *dis*-ease—as the word's meaning truly is—that permeated the atmosphere. Not being able to do anything for suffering family or loved ones is an awful experience.

Let's talk about "Devil's Radio," a raging track!

That was a tune I hit on accidentally. I passed a little church in England near where my boy Dhani, who's now nine, goes to school. There was a poster on the side of this church saying, "GOSSIP! THE DEVIL'S RADIO! DON'T BE A BROADCASTER!" I just thought it was a dead ringer for a rock tune. At that point I'd just been to see Eurythmics a couple of times, and I'd forgotten about that kind of straightforward rock and roll song that they go for so effectively. Somewhere down the line I'd gotten into all these thick chord songs, and I forgot, until I was watching Eurythmics, how great that straight-from-the-gate force in rock rhythm is. I thought, "God, I can do this!" So the song was the result of seeing that poster and then the Eurythmics. The only thing missing is that it should be Bob Dylan singing it. [*laughter*]

That song starts out like a voice from on high: "I heard it in the night / words the thoughtless speak / like vultures swooping down below / on the Devil's Radio / I hear through the day / airwaves getting filled with gossip broadcast to and fro / on the Devil's Radio."

There's a line that seems to refer to your reclusive profile of late: "You wonder why I don't hang out much."

Yeah, it's something about [*haunted-house voice*]: "It's wide and black / like industrial waste / pollution of the highest degree / you wonder why I don't hang out much / I wonder why you can't see / it's in the films and song / and on your magazines / it's everywhere that you may go / the Devil's Radio!" Boo!! [*laughter*]

But really, gossip is a terrible thing. We all do it, and all our minds are polluted by it. You know what I mean? Somebody said, "The next time you gossip, gossip about yourself and see how you like it." It just creates a mud of negativity, false information, and puts bad atmosphere out. Like the church poster said: "Don't be a broadcaster." I like to remind myself of this, because I'm just as bad as everyone else.

Recently in Rolling Stone, *they had a rock trivia quiz in which John Lennon's* Two Virgins *was said to be the first Beatle solo album. But that's wrong. You stuck your neck out four weeks before the November 29, 1968, release of* Two Virgins *with* Wonderwall Music.

[*Grinning*] And it's not trivia, it's history! I remember doing it in London at the end of 1967, and then went to Bombay and recorded part of it in a studio there. There was this guy who directed the movie, *Wonderwall,* called Joe Massot. I don't know where I met him, but he said he wanted me to do the music to this movie—which didn't come out until 1969. I said, "I don't know; I haven't got a guess of how to write music for a movie." He said, "Aw, we've got no budget for the music anyway, so whatever you give me, I'll have it!"

I was real nervous with the idea, because he wanted music running through the whole film, but he kept on with me. What I'd do was go into the film studio with a stopwatch—it was really high-tech stuff, eh?—and I'd just be what they call "spotting" the scene to see where the music was going to go, doing click-click with the watch. I'd go back into my studio and make thirty-five seconds, say, of something, mix it and line it up with the scene.

It gave me a great opportunity. I was getting so into Indian music then that I decided to use the assignment partly as an excuse for a musical anthology to help spread it. I used all these instruments that at that time weren't as familiar to Western people as they are now, like shanhais, santoor, sarod, surbahars, tablatarangs. I also used tambura drones and had Eric Clapton playing blues guitar backward over them. And loads of horrible mellotron stuff also.

I got a kick that there was a snatch of "Crying" from Wonderwall

Music *spliced in, thirteen years later, at the close of* Somewhere in England's *"Save the World."*

You spotted that? Three points for you! The whole "Save the World" song blows up in the middle, where we all get nuked, with babies crying. That latter song is very serious, but at the same time is hysterical. The lyrics have got a lot of funny things about "dog-food salesmen" and "making your own H-bomb in the kitchen with your mom." At the end, I just wanted to let the whole song go out with something sad, to touch that nerve and maybe make you think, "Ohhh shit."

I thought of that instrument I used on *Wonderwall Music* called the thar-shanhai, which means "string" shanhai. It's like a one-string fiddle, a bowed instrument with the sympathetic strings resting over a stretched skin, so it has that hollow, echoey resonance, a wailing, crying sound.

Electronic Sound, *released on the Zapple label in May 1969, was your second solo album. How'd you go from touting these esoteric acoustic Indian instruments to creating that dense mass of synthesizer gizmo effects?*

All I did was get that very first Moog synthesizer, with the big patch unit and the keyboards that you could never tune, and I put a microphone into a tape machine. I recorded whatever came out. The word *avant-garde,* as my friend Alvin Lee likes to say, really means, " *'Aven't-got* a clue!" So whatever came out when I fiddled with the knobs went on tape—but some amazing sounds did happen.

Only two albums appeared on Zapple, Electronic Sound *and John Lennon's* Life with the Lions: Unfinished Music No. 2. *The third scheduled release,* Listening to Richard Brautigan, *was never issued.*

See, we conceived of an offshoot of Apple Records that would be arty music that wouldn't normally gain an outlet, a series where people could talk or read their work, as with the Brautigan thing. The intention was to get Lenny Bruce and all these kinds of people. But as with so many other things at Apple, it seized up before it really got going. Both of the albums that *did* come out are a load of rubbish, yet they're interesting from a collector's point of view. The theory was, we wanted to let serendipity take hold.

You told Mitch Glazer in Crawdaddy *in 1977 about the entirely happenstantial origins of Cream's "Badge" in 1968: Eric Clapton mistook your scribbled note about the song's "bridge" for the title "Badge," and the lyric "I told you 'bout the swans, that they live in the park" was just a drunken mumble from Ringo.*

Uh-huh. Nobody'd asked me about "Badge" before. That whole song was quite silly. Ringo was sitting around drinking, out of his brain, saying anything. The part about "Our kid, now he's married to Mabel," well, "our kid" is a common Liverpool expression that usually means your younger brother. We were amusing ourselves. And my "L'Angelo Misterioso" credit must have been thought up by Eric. I just saw it on the back of the album when it came! In those days, of course, if you played on anybody else's album or even one track, EMI used to get funny about it, thinking, "Oh, the fabulous Beatles publishing catalog," and try claiming royalties on it. So if we did that, we always had to make up names. Ravi Shankar used to put on "Hari Georgson" or "Jai Raj Harisein." John preferred "George Harrisong."

What were the influences on your slide guitar-playing over the years? It's an incredibly distinctive signature.

I'm not sure of the influences. The first time I ever played slide was in 1969. I suppose I stuck one of those things on my finger somewhere before that, but in 1969 Eric Clapton got his manager to bring Delaney and Bonnie over to England, and Eric was in the band. I went to see the first show in December. It was such a good rocking crew; I figured it'd be nice to be in it. They said, "Okay, we're coming to your house in the morning." And they pulled up the bus outside my house and said, "Come on!" I just grabbed a guitar and an amp and went on the road with them.

They had a song out called "Comin' Home," which Dave Mason had actually played slide on. Delaney gave me this slide bottleneck and said, "You do the Dave Mason part." I'd never attempted anything before that, and I think my slide guitar-playing originated from that.

I started writing some slide songs on that tour, one of which later came out on *33⅓*, called "Woman Don't You Cry for Me." Then I started playing that way at home, and I suppose I was always trying to pretend to be a blues player in my style. Another thing that influenced me was, during the sixties, I played the sitar and got heavy into Indian music. That may account for some quality that you can't quite put your finger on; it's in there somewhere and comes out. For two or three years I was only playing the sitar.

After I decided I'd better get back to playing the guitar and writing pop tunes in the late sixties, I found I couldn't really play these solos or get a good sound, because I hadn't touched the guitar other than the Beatles sessions for records; I started playing slide, thinking maybe this is how I can come up with something that's half-decent. I got into doing corresponding guitar harmonies to the bedrock slide parts, double-tracking them, like on "My Sweet Lord" and other portions of the *All Things Must Pass* album.

Is there a certain guitar you use for slide-playing?

I used to use anything; I didn't understand how to do it properly. Eventually I found the best way: Ry Cooder, who is my favorite guitar player in that vein, has his bridge cranked up high, with heavy-gauge strings. That's what you really need, otherwise you get all that rattling on the frets. Ry's got a good touch and a good ear for melody. It's one thing to be able to play slide efficiently, but if you can't get a tune out of it, too, it's not very likeable.

I set up this Strat, an early-sixties model that was originally pale blue, for slide play before we did "Nowhere Man." In the late sixties I painted it psychedelic—it was the one I used for the '67 satellite thing for "All You Need Is Love" and also on "I Am the Walrus" on *Magical Mystery Tour.*

But I've never had the technique that Ry Cooder has with finger-style picking. I've tried to get this without a flat pick, using your right hand so that you can dampen down all the notes. But if you were to isolate my slide tracks on some of the old records, there's all this *racket* going on behind. Whereas, I'm sure if you were to do the same thing with Cooder, you could hear just what he's playing—it's really clean.

I've got two slides, and the main one I've used is actually a piece off the old Vox AC-30 amplifier stand. I asked the roadie we used to have in the Beatles, Mal Evans, if he could get me one, and he just got a hacksaw out and sawed through a piece of the amp stand. I used that a lot, and I had some glass slides made also. I find the glass slide tends to be a warmer sound, whereas the metal one is more slippy and is brighter. But I couldn't tell you which one I've used where [*chuckles*], because I don't make notes on it.

Do you have any hobbies besides film-producing and being a Grand Prix buff? On Somewhere in England *you were shown on the cover in front of a Mark Boyle painting. Do you collect art?*

That painting was wonderful. He'd done a cast of the pavement and the gutter and a piece of the road. It's quite an amazing process, like a sculpting of the street. I like certain artists, but by the time I *got* to like them they were too expensive to collect, like Dalí and

Magritte. Paul's got a bunch of Magrittes. He bought them for, like fifty dollars each. Then the guy died in 1967, and now they're worth millions.

Whatever happened to the four songs—"Lay His Head," "Tears of the World," "Sat Singing," and "Flying Hour"—that Warners dropped from Somewhere in England*?*

Funny you should ask that, with us discussing art. I'm doing another book with Genesis Publications, who did my 1980 book, *I, Me, Mine.* For some reason, and I don't remember why, *I, Me, Mine* later came out in a cheap version, but it was only really made as a limited edition, because how it's made was almost more important than what's inside.

But there's this new book I've been working on with an artist, Keith West, for about two years now. He's illustrating the lyrics to my songs. It could only be done in a limited edition because if you printed it cheap, you'd lose the value of it. We're making it two volumes.

To answer your question, we decided to put a free record inside the books of some songs that have gotten left out over the years. I finished the record for the first book just before I came here, and it's of those four songs you just mentioned—and a live version of "For You Blue." It all comes in a big leather box with a little drawer for the record. It's called *Songs by George Harrison,* and it should be out by Christmas, but there's only 2,000 copies being done, and it does cost £200. It's expensive, yes, but in a world of crass, disposable junk, it's meant to be a lovely thing.

That anticipates my next question. Now that the surviving Beatles are suing Nike for the "Revolution" sneaker ad, what's your view of the commercial-abuse controversies regarding the Beatles' recorded legacy?

Well, from our point of view, if it's allowed to happen, every Beatles song ever recorded is going to be advertising women's underwear and sausages. We've got to put a stop to it in order to set a precedent. Otherwise it's going to be a free-for-all. It's just one of those things, like the play *Beatlemania.* We have to do certain things in order to try to safeguard the past. The other thing is, even while Nike might have paid Capitol Records for the rights, Capitol Records certainly don't give us the money.

It's one thing if you're dead, but we're still around! They don't have any respect for the fact that we wrote and recorded those songs, and it was our lives. The way I feel, I don't care who thinks they own the copyright to the songs, or who thinks they own the masters of the records. It was our lives, we said it, and they should have a little respect for that.

Dark Horse, *the album and the single, made for a powerful but pessimistic image of desperate competition with your former bandmates and with yourself.*

That album had some good material, but the pressure I got under that year was ridiculous. I went through so many things: produced two other albums, *Shankar Family and Friends,* and *The Place I Love* by Splinter. And I produced an Indian music festival, which had taken me years to get together, with fifteen or sixteen classical Indian musicians all playing ensemble, like an orchestra—which they never do. In India you see solo players or two performers with a tabla player. In 1974 I went to India, got them all together, they came to Europe, Ravi wrote all the material. It *rocked.* Then came my own album and this tour I had lined up. And I also met my wife, Olivia Arias, around then.

I wrote the song "Dark Horse" in the studio with Ringo and Keltner, and I never got to finish it. I took this half-finished album with me to tour rehearsals in Los Angeles and got my voice blown out by singing all day long. I decided, because I had to teach the band the songs anyway for the tour, that we'd mike up the soundstage in one of the studios at A&M and record it live. If you listen now, it's *sort of* okay. It was all done in a rush, with rehearsals by day and mixing at night.

For the artwork on the inner sleeve, I was so behind that moments before we went on the road I got a blank dust cover and wrote out all the credits by hand, put a few thumb prints on it, and gave it to the record company for the printers. The cover shot was my high school class photo from Liverpool Institute, with lots of gray students who all look the same, and this big gray building in the background. I positioned the blown-up photo so that I'd be in the middle, put an album cover over the length of it, and cropped it off. I moved the headmaster, who never liked me anyway, from where he was in the photo, and I put him in the middle with a bull's-eye Capitol logo on his chest. I got the art guy to paint the Himalayas in the background with a few yogis in the sky, and put exotic T-shirts on everybody.

Is that Peter Sellers you're with on the inside shot?

Sure, that's us strolling 'round Friar Park. I was quite close with Peter. Long before I met him I was a fan of *The Goon Show,* and then I used to see him at parties. I got to spend a lot of time with him in the sixties when I was with Ravi Shankar, because Peter liked Ravi a lot.

Once Peter Sellers, Ravi, and I all went to Disneyland in 1971. Can you imagine all of us going on the Pirate and the Haunted Mansion rides together? Peter was a devoted hippie, a free soul. He came on tour with me in 1974, flew on the plane with us. When Peter was up, he was the funniest person you could ever imagine; so many voices and characters. But that was his problem: When he wasn't up, he didn't know who he was supposed to be.

He was a considerable influence on my getting into the film world. Peter used to come to my Henley house with all these 16-millimeter films, and we'd sit 'round and have dinner and watch. His favorite picture—which has been mine ever since Peter showed it to me—was Mel Brooks's *The Producers.* He kept saying, "You've got to see this movie!" Eventually we put it on, and I've never taken it off.

The bubble caption in the photo of Peter and me on the *Dark Horse* jacket is from *The Producers,* from Max Bialystock's line to his partner Bloom: "Well Leo! What say we promenade through the park?"

People always say you're so serious and broody, but I'd say you have a ready sense of humor.

Me too! I've *always* had a sense of humor—and I think it's absolutely necessary. I think what happened is, I was tagged as somber because I did some spiritual things during a sizable phase of my own career, and sang a lot of songs about God or the Lord or whatever you want to call Him. You can't be singing that material laughingly, but if you're not smiling people draw that conclusion of *seriousness.*

I don't think anybody's all serious or all comical, and I've seen comedians who are deadly serious when they're offstage. Frankly, I always thought it was very funny when people thought I was very serious! Maybe it's also because the last time I did interviews back in the 1970s it was all that heavy hangover from the hippie sixties, when everybody was into this discipline, that doctrine, and the other. I've got a very serious side of me, but even within that, I always see the joke too. That's why I always liked Monty Python.

Which brings up The Life of Brian *and your other film production. It's a great body of work—from* Time Bandits, *on through* Mona Lisa *and* Withnail and I*—that you've done with partner Denis O'Brien for your HandMade Films.*

It's my hobby! It's taken time, but we've gained a little respect from film people. We try to be nice to people—it's not always easy—and most of the things we've done were films nobody else wanted to do; they were rejects. The only film that was *not* enjoyable making was the only one on which we've ever been involved with anybody from Hollywood: *Shanghai Surprise.* We were a day away from scrapping that when suddenly Sean Penn and Madonna got involved. But that was such a pain in the ass!

We've got good relationships with other people we've worked with, however, like Michael Caine, Maggie Smith, and Bob Hoskins. *Withnail and I,* the first film Bruce Robinson's directed, was a chance to support a project everybody else turned down. It's the same right now with a movie we're shooting about a band of gypsies in Czechoslovakia that Bob Hoskins has written, directed, and is acting in himself. It's called *Raggedy Rawny.*

I'd like to think we help people achieve some of their ambitions. At the same time, when we took on *The Life of Brian,* I was so into Monty Python I didn't care what anybody thought. In those days we had to put up all the money, didn't get any advances from studios—nothing.

When you produced Life of Brian, *many people questioned why the man behind "My Sweet Lord" would produce a supposedly sacrilegious biblical farce.*

Ah-hah! Actually all it made fun of was the *people's* stupidity in the story. Christ came out of it looking good! Myself and all of Monty Python have great respect for Christ. It's only the ignorant people—who didn't care to check it out—who thought that it was knocking Christ. Actually it was upholding Him and knocking all the idiotic stuff that goes on around religion, like the fact that many folks often misread things and will follow anybody. Brian's saying, "Don't follow me. You're all individuals."

It's like Christ said, "You'll all do greater work than I will." He wasn't trying to say, "I'm the groove, man, and you should follow me." He was out there trying to, as Lord Buckley would have said, "Knock the crows off the squares," trying to hip everybody to the fact that they have the Christ within.

You're a fan of hipster comedian Lord Buckley, which is where your 1977 hit "Crackerbox Palace" came from.

I was down at that MIDEM music publishing convention in France in 1975, and I was stuck at some boring dinner when I saw Dylan's manager, Albert Grossman. I went over to him, and he was with this fella George Greif, who was himself a manager. We got talking, and I said to Greif, "I don't know if this is a compliment or an insult, but you remind me of Lord Buckley." He said, "I managed him for eighteen years!"

I couldn't believe it, so we spent a few hours talking, and he said that Buckley lived in this little shack he called Crackerbox Palace. I wrote that down on my cigarette packet, and, again, like Devil's Radio, it was a good phrase for a song. Near the end of the single there's a line in it in direct relation to Lord Buckley: "I met a Mr. Greif / and he said / I welcome you to Crackerbox Palace / was not expecting you / let's rap and tap at Crackerbox Palace / know that the Lord is well and inside of you." I made the raw input into a story about getting born and living in the world, but again, everybody thought I was talking about the *other* Lord.

You mention knowing Albert Grossman. I always wondered how the Band came to invite you up to Woodstock in November 1968. You wrote "I'd Have You Anytime" with Dylan during that visit.

I wrote "All Things Must Pass" there as well. To this day you can play *Stage Fright* and *Big Pink,* and although the technology's changed, those records come off as beautifully conceived and uniquely sophisticated. They had great tunes, played in a great spirit, and with humor and versatility.

I knew those guys during that period, and I think it was Robbie Robertson who invited me down. He said, "You can stay at Albert's. He's got the *big* house." I hung out with them and Bob. It was strange because at the time Bob and Grossman were going through this fight, this crisis about managing him. I would spend the day with Bob and the night with Grossman and hear both sides of the battle.

Artistically, I respected the Band enormously. All the different guys in the group sang, and Robbie Robertson used to say he was lucky, because he could write songs for a voice like Levon's. What a wise and generous attitude. The hard thing is to write a song for yourself, knowing you've got to sing it. Sometimes I have a hard time singing my own stuff.

You once remarked that you were trying to write a Robbie Robertson kind of song with "All Things Must Pass."

"The Weight" was the one I admired, it had a religious *and* a country feeling to it, and I wanted that. You absorb, then you interpret, and it comes out nothing like the thing you're imagining, but it gives you a starting point. We used to take that approach with the Beatles, saying, "Who are we going to be today? Let's pretend to be Fleetwood Mac!" There's a song on *Abbey Road*, "The Sun King," that tried that. At the time, "Albatross" was out, with all the reverb on guitar. So we said, "Let's be Fleetwood Mac doing 'Albatross,' " just to get going. It never really sounded like Fleetwood Mac, just like "All Things" never sounded like the Band, but they were the point of origin.

What was it like writing with Dylan? He was still a hermit from his motorcycle accident of July 1966. Was he shy?

We were *both* shy. He'd been out of commission socially since his accident. I was nervous in his house, and he was nervous as well. We fidgeted about for two days and only relaxed when we started playing some guitars. The song "I'd Have You Anytime" was an accident. I was just saying, "Hey, man, how do you write all these words?!" Which people probably said to him all the time.

I kept thinking he would come pouring out with all these lyrics! He wrote the middle—"All I have is yours / all you see is mine / I'm glad to hold you in my arms / I'd have you anytime"—and it was *simplicity* itself. [*smiles*] Meantime he was saying, "How do *you* get all them chords?" I showed him some weird ones and happened to hit those two major sevenths, one after another. They turned into that melody. Understand, I sang that opening lyric off the top of my head to try to communicate with *him:* "Let me in here / I know I've been here . . ."

The man who built your Henley Castle, Sir Francis Crisp, was both a prominent lawyer in the 1800s and an architect. I've heard that inscriptions and artwork he added to the interior inspired such songs as "The Ballad of Sir Frankie Crisp (Let It Roll)," "The Answer's at the End," and "Ding Dong."

It's a Victorian house, and when I bought it, it was about to be demolished, so I got it in its roughest state. Over the years I've fixed it up, and it's a fabulous place, a treasure of Victorian artifacts, even though a lot of things originally made for the house had been sold before I bought it. But there are inscriptions all over the place: some in Latin, some in Old English, many of them poetry of obscure authorship.

"Ding Dong," which I wrote in five minutes, came from some Tennyson carved over either side of the fireplace with little bells: "Ring out the old / ring in the new / ring out the false / ring in the true." Outside in the building where the gardener's sheds are, carved over one window is: "Yesterday—today—was tomorrow." The adjacent window has: "Tomorrow—today—will be yesterday." And those parts became the middle eight of "Ding Dong."

The quote above the entrance hall says: "Scan not a friend with a microscopic glass / you know his faults, now let his foibles pass." Opposite, it reads: "Life is one long enigma true my friend / read on, read on, the answer's at the end." *Extra Texture,* where that was used, was a grubby album in a way. The production left a lot to be desired, as did my performance. I was in a real down place. Some songs I like, but in retrospect I wasn't very happy about it. "Grey Cloudy Lies" described clouds of gloom that used to come down on me. A difficulty I had. I've found over the years that I'm more able to keep them away, and am quite a happy person now.

The flip of "Ding Dong" displays the cloudy side of you. "I Don't Care Anymore" never appeared anywhere else.

I had to come up with a B-side, and I did it in one take. The story was in the attitude: I-don't-give-a-shit!

Yet you often seem to care a great deal about the care and feeding of many of your songs, to where you've done sequels to several. Extra Texture's *"This Guitar (Can't Keep from Crying)," and "Here Comes the Moon" on* George Harrison, *are dramatic examples.*

Concerning my "Guitars" songs, if you're a guitar player, guitars have a genuine fascination and it's nice to have songs about them. I recently saw a guitar program on TV in England, and it got into how it's phallic and sexual. Maybe that's so. I don't know in my case, but ever since I was a kid I've loved guitars *and* songs about them, like B. B. King's "Lucille." But the sequels in this case had to do in large part with me not enjoying "Guitar Gently Weeps." I love what Eric did on guitar for the original, but versions I did live are better in some respects. See, in the Beatles days, I never liked my singing. I *couldn't* sing very good. I was always very paranoid, very nervous, and that inhibited my singing.

"This Guitar (Can't Keep from Crying)" came about because the press and critics tried to nail me on that 1974–75 tour, got nasty. I had no voice on the road, and I was shagged-out, knackered. I had a choice of cancelling the tour and forgetting it, or going out and singing hoarse. I always think people will give others more credit than they do, so I assumed they'd know I'm in bad voice but still feel the music's plentiful and good. I wrote that song about being stuck on a limb, and being down, but not out.

For "Here Comes the Moon," I think I was on LSD or mushrooms at the time and was out sunning in Maui. The sun was setting over the ocean, and it gets pretty stunning even when you're not on mushrooms. I was blissed out, and then I turned 'round and saw a big, full moon rising. I laughed and thought it was about time someone, and it may as well be me, gave the moon its due.

Did "This Song," the single about the "My Sweet Lord" / "He's So Fine" suit, provide you with any catharsis?

It did get it all off my chest; it was a laugh and release. Saying "This song's got nothing Bright about it" after Bright Tunes Publishing sued me, was amusing, at least to me. I also cracked, "This song could be 'You,' " meaning the Ronnie Spector song, and then had Eric Idle of Monty Python dub in two arguing voices saying, "Sounds like 'Sugar Pie Honey Bunch' "; "Naw! Sounds more like 'Rescue Me'!" I see now where everybody's doing videos with courts and judges like I did for that single—not to mention Madonna helping herself to "Living in the Material World" for "Material Girl." I was ahead of my time. [*chuckle*]

Living in the Material World, *the album after* All Things, *was a smash hit in America. It was number one for five weeks in the summer of 1973, with the "Give Me Love" single on top simultaneously, and it's sold over three million copies.*

Yes, but they [Capitol-EMI] still never gave me the royalties, did they? No! Ugh!*

Cloud Nine *rescues two worthy songs, "Someplace Else" and "Breath Away from Heaven," that you wrote for that Madonna/Sean Penn movie,* Shanghai Surprise.

I never did a soundtrack album, because the film got slagged off so bad and we had such a rotten time with them while making it. I didn't want to lose the songs, especially "Breath Away from Heaven," which has nice words—although I haven't included the lyrics to any songs on this album. I always did before, but I thought that the practice is getting passé. Maybe I'm looking for a few new leaves to turn over.

Could they include a return to touring?

It's a possibility. Ringo can't wait to go out, and Eric Clapton keeps telling me he's gonna be in the band. Eric's such a sweet cat. I caught one of his own shows in the Los Angeles Forum just

*According to a Capitol-EMI spokeswoman, "All recording royalties due him since 1973 have been paid to date."

before Easter of this year. I stood at the side of the stage, holding up my cigarette lighter for the encore. [*laughter*] Really! I love him that much!

Through the thick and the thin, Eric and I have always preserved and protected our friendship. One of the only things that Eric's ever held against me is that I met Bob Marley while I was out here on the West Coast in the late seventies, and Eric's never forgiven me for not taking him along to meet Bob Marley.

[*Sighs*] It's hard to see the greats go, and I'm a big fan of so many kinds of rock and popular music, from Bob Marley to Cole Porter to Smokey Robinson to Hoagy Carmichael. I mean, I wrote "Pure Smokey" on *33⅓* as my little tribute to his brilliant songwriting and his effortless butterfly of a voice. The Beatles did Smokey's "You Really Got a Hold on Me," and there was a song John did that was very much influenced by Smokey—"This Boy." If you listen to the middle eight of "This Boy," it was John trying to *do* Smokey. It suddenly occurs to me that there's even a line in "When We Was Fab" where I sing, "And you really got a hold on me"!

As for Hoagy Carmichael, I've been nuts for him since I was a kid. I cut his "Hong Kong Blues" on *Somewhere in England*, and there's still a few more of his I wouldn't mind doing, like "Rockin' Chair." Maybe one day—not just yet, but one day when I get a bit older—me and Eric can sing "Old rocking chair has got me . . ."

There seems to be a running thread here about music and its powerful hold, eh? And it's that way, too. We who love music, we love the people who make it, we love the sound of it, and we love what it does to us, how it makes us feel, how it helps *us* love.

When I was writing "Cloud Nine" I had these ideas in mind. I'd read once in some spiritual context that the bad part of you is your human limitations, and the good part of you is God. I think people who *truly* can live a life in music are telling the world, "You can have my love, you can have my smiles. Forget the bad parts, you don't need them. Just take the music, the goodness, because it's the very best, and it's the part I give most willingly."

He was crying, tears spilling in thin streaks down his pimpled face. She was shocked that London's leading bad boy could be broken so bloody easily. "You ought to use the experience," she chided through the prison bars. "You should write a song about it or something."

It was June 29, 1967, and Michael Phillip Jagger was spending his third night in jail, having just been fined £100 and sentenced to three months confinement for illegal possession of several Benzedrine tablets of Italian manufacture. The bust had occurred several days earlier at Redlands, the country home of guitarist Keith Richards, where police had discovered eight men and one woman (she attired only in a fur rug) lounging about.

The lady swaddled in the rug was Marianne Faithfull, actual owner of the pep pills, girlfriend of Mr. Jagger, and visitor this very day at Brixton Jail. She assured her blubbering beau that he'd be out of stir within the next twenty-four hours; the overpaid lawyers were working tirelessly to countermand the trumped-up verdict. And sure enough, the High Court sprung both Jagger and Richards the next day. At month's end, an appeals court gave Jagger a conditional discharge and overturned Richards's conviction.

The established order that the Stones

Mick Jagger

1989

held in such smirking disdain had come through in a pinch. Mick was on the street again, hitting the pubs, his fleshy lips set in his best bratty sneer. But his main squeeze and other insiders would never forget how easy it had been to wipe that cocky wrinkle off his sallow face.

Mick Jagger—born July 26, 1943, in Dartford, England—grew up on the same block as Keith Richards. The son of a physical-education instructor, Mick was five years old when he met Richards (also born in 1943) at Wentworth Primary School. They lost track of each other when the beleaguered Richards family moved to a housing project at the other end of town. Then, in 1960, Mick and Keith met again by chance and realized that they both had an advanced interest in American rhythm and blues. They also discovered they had a mutual friend in Dick Taylor, a classmate of Keith's, who played guitar with Mick in a combo called Little Boy Blue and the Blue Boys. Keith joined the band and became tight with Jagger. At a gig of Alexis Korner's Blues Incorporated, they met Brian Jones, a blond-haired lady's man whose rousing slide-guitar solos quickened the crowd. Brian thought they should form their own group, and they invited Dick Taylor, pianist Ian Stewart, and traveling salesman–drummer Tony Chapman on board. Brian named the pack the Rolling Stones in homage to a Muddy Waters standard. A pat appellation; a sapient lot.

Brian, Mick, and Keith began sharing a flat in Edith Grove, Chelsea. They lived on boiled potatoes and pipe dreams, pestering entrepreneur Giorgio Gomelsky for a Sunday-afternoon spot on the bill at the Crawdaddy Club, the epicenter of the emerging blues craze. Advertising designer Charlie Watts replaced Chapman, and Bill Wyman took over the bass slot from Taylor. Gomelski finally acceded to their pleas. The Rolling Stones drew sixty-six people the first time out at the Crawdaddy and made £24.

Two weeks later, a nineteen-year-old hustler named Andrew Loog Oldham signed the Stones to a management contract. The Stones scored a deal with the Decca label, and straitlaced Ian Stewart was demoted to session-pianist status as Oldham moved to freeze the group's image as loutish snots, thus putting them at odds with the well-scrubbed Beatles. In the space of seven more days, the Stones cut "Come On," an obscure Chuck Berry song, and Willie Dixon's "I Want to Be Loved." Both sounded terrible, and Decca insisted they be redone. A reworked single of the two songs, with "Come On" as the A-side, was released on June 7, 1963. Oldham secured airtime on the "Thank Your Lucky Stars" television show, and the Stones' first release rose to No. 22 on the British charts. The pushy young manager ignored the producer of "Lucky Stars," who urged him to dump the mangy lead singer with the "tire tread" lips, and instead put Jagger and his ruffians onstage at the National Jazz and Blues Festival.

The *Daily Mail* was succinct in interpreting the Stones' escalating appeal: "They look like boys whom any self-respecting mum would lock in the bathroom! But the Rolling Stones—five tough young London-based music makers with doorstep mouths, pallid cheeks, and unkempt hair—are not worried what mums think!"

By April 1964, the Rolling Stones had an album out in the United States and in the United Kingdom, had sparked riots in Chicago, and had seen their chart-topping British single "Little Red Rooster" banned in the States as obscene. The pandemonium that attended their appearance on the "Ed Sullivan Show" moved the host to bark, "I promise you they'll never be back on our show."

Renegades of the well-groomed British Invasion, the Stones were denied the mainstream acceptance of the Beatles. They did, however, win over a loyal fringe that steadily expanded. "The Last Time" was their first big international success, kicking off the banner year of 1965. Jagger's spastic élan and puckered pout invested white rhythm and blues with a snippy vainglory typified by "(I Can't Get No) Satisfaction."

The Stones were asked back to the Sullivan show in 1967. But, behind the scenes, the cocky group was in dire disarray. The drug raids that plagued Jagger, Richards, and Jones from 1967 on had been precipitated by dabblings in black magic, hard drugs, and innovative debauchery that had strained all bonds in the group's cosmology. Jagger had taken to mocking the adulation of the uncomprehending audience; rabblement became commonplace at concerts on the Continent, giving the Stones a reputation as a bad risk in a social climate already characterized by civil unrest and youthful calls for revolution.

As the Stones withdrew from live performances, Jagger—who had adopted a healthful regimen of exercise and nutrition that was downright bizarre for a rock star—became in all ways the leader of the group. Richards, meanwhile, established himself as the sublimely parlous soul of the outfit, the waggish wastrel and indefatigable party shark who single-handedly defined the lethal grandeur of rock excess. Jones, the Stones' finest musician, was usually too wasted or unbalanced to play. He withdrew into himself, undergoing a severe personality disintegration further aggravated by barbiturates, LSD, and drink.

Jagger assumed the cachet of a lanky Lucifer after the Stones tried in 1967 to better the Beatles' *Sgt. Pepper* LP with their dourly psychedelic *Their Satanic Majesties Request.* The record bombed with Christmas shoppers, but Jagger and Richards rebounded with the demonic "Jumping Jack Flash," an invocation of the patron fiend of hoochie-coochie men and soul-cursed sorcerers. Jagger starred in the film *Performance*, an "amorality play" intertwining bisexuality, drugs, and rock; Mick described it as "the perverted love affair between *Homo sapiens* and Lady Violence." On and off the set, he took to wearing pancake makeup, eye shadow, and lipstick.

Nineteen sixty-eight closed with the appearance of *Beggar's Banquet,* which featured the chilling "Sympathy for the Devil" and the incendiary "Street Fighting Man." "Anarchy is the only slight glimmer of hope," citizen Jagger told critics who quaked at the album's air of indiscriminate provocation. "Anybody should be able to go where he likes and do what he likes."

In June 1969, Brian Jones was drummed out of the Stones. It was after midnight on July 3 when friends found his body at the bottom of the swimming pool at Cotchford Farm, the Sussex estate where A. A. Milne had written *Winnie-the-Pooh.* The coroner ruled his death at twenty-six as "due to immersion in fresh water under the influence of drugs and alcohol." Others suspected foul play.

On July 11, the day following Brian Jones's burial in his hometown of Cheltenham, the Stones released "Honky Tonk Women," followed in six months by *Let It Bleed* (a callous rejoinder to the Beatles' *Let It Be*). Jagger and Richards cowrote the two tracks on the LP that received the most radio exposure: "Gimme Shelter," notable for its hellish chorus—"Rape! Murder! It's just a shot away!"—and "Midnight Rambler," a reptilian nocturne to Albert deSalvo, the Boston Strangler.

Jagger was determined to mount a concert that would outdraw the Woodstock Festival. He vowed that the event would be "the last and greatest concert of the sixties." Altamont Speedway in Livermore, California, was a last-minute choice for a venue on December 6, 1969.

As Jagger stepped out of the helicopter that had dropped him at the site, a man broke through the crowd and struck him in the face, screaming, "I hate you!" All around the grounds, the scene was ugly. A drunken contingent of Hells Angels had been hired to police the crowd and had spent the hours previous to the Stones' arrival beating members of the audience with pool cues and clubs, breaking jaws, shattering teeth, smashing heads. Then, during "Sympathy for the Devil," a black man in a green suit popped up from a sea of contorted faces and seemed to point a pistol at Jagger.

Bystanders watched as the Angels killed the gun-wielding figure, an eighteen-year-old named Meredith Hunter. Hunter had pulled the gun out to defend himself after he had been slashed in the back by a biker who'd singled him out because of Hunter's white, blonde girlfriend. Hunter was maniacally stabbed in the face and the back as he tried to run. Once down, he was kicked until his nose and jaw were shattered. A steel bucket was twisted into his eyes until his piercing cries of agony crested and ceased.

Mick Jagger left Altamont with a bulging suitcase of cash and flew straight to Switzerland. In his wake were a slew of lawsuits and condemnations, few more virulent than that from American promoter Bill Graham: "I ask you what right you had, Mr. Jagger . . . to leave the way you did, thanking everybody for a wonderful time, and the Angels for helping out? . . . What right does this god have to descend on this country this way? . . . Mick Jagger is not God Junior. . . . But you know what is the greatest tragedy? That [man] is a great entertainer."

In May 1971, Jagger wed Bianca Perez Moreno de Macias, the fine-boned daughter of Nicaraguan shopkeepers. The wedding took place in St. Tropez, and no one missed the obvious: she was a ringer for Mick. Friends snickered that the popinjay preener could now make love to himself. As a harbinger of the new jet-set life-style he and his bride lusted after, Mick was named one of the Hot Hundred Best Dressed Men by the natty *The Tailor and Cutter.* He later had an emerald implanted in his front tooth, replaced it with a ruby, then settled on a diamond.

The Stones secured their own label, Rolling Stones Records, which would be distributed by Atlantic. Andy Warhol designed an official logo—a caricature of Jagger's full lips and wagging tongue. *Sticky Fingers,* the debut release, and the scandalously sexist single

"Brown Sugar" (in which a white slave master trades cunnilingus for fellatio with a black dancer while comparing her to unrefined heroin) made them a darkly chic international sensation. *Exile on Main Street* completed the masterful trilogy of macabre urban reconnoiters that had begun with *Beggar's Banquet* and continued with *Sticky Fingers.* Music that lionized the underbelly of human existence, it was not the sort of aural ambiance one would wish in an empty room after sundown, but it was true to the pernicious spirit of the tar-hearted delta blues denizens of yore.

Mick Taylor left the Stones in December 1974, and runty, bird-haired Ron Wood, lead guitarist for the Faces, signed up in April 1975. Stones albums continued to tumble out of a quarry where the sun rarely shined, some of them awful *(Goat's Head Soup, Black and Blue, Love You Live, Sucking in the Seventies, Still Life),* some mediocre *(It's Only Rock and Roll, Tattoo You, Undercover),* and one of them excellent *(Some Girls)* for all the right—that is, effectively irksome—reasons.

Jagger shed Bianca in a hotly contested 1979 divorce, sharing custody of their daughter, Jade. In 1983, he turned forty as an effete multimillionaire whose official residence became the Caribbean Island of Mustique, and a family man who'd fathered three girls (the second, Karis, by actress Marsha Hunt, the third, Elizabeth, by model Jerry Hall, who also gave him a son, James). He was the most famous rocker on earth, a survivor of the star wars, but most young comers considered him to be either a fading hero or an irrelevant old fart.

This estimation gained credence when, in the wake of the Stones' unsteady *Undercover* album, Mick had issued *She's the Boss* in February 1985. The effort was earnest, but the concept of a Mick Jagger solo career seemed vaguely absurd, since his strength had always been as a cunning catalyst for a clutch of staunchly peevish mates. Sales of *Boss* proved piddling, but after the Stones put out the dreary *Dirty Work* in 1986, he decided to skip the obligatory band tour in favor of another solo project that became the improved but still unappetizing *Primitive Cool.* Mick had really applied himself to the *Cool* album, yet Stones fans caught a whiff of Jagger hauteur in the gesture, a cavalier sense of commercial entitlement akin to his $3 million 1983 book deal for an autobiography he refused to share enough of himself within to render publishable.

Long after Mick had alienated and then reconciled with the Stones, embarking on the gala road trip for their engaging 1989 *Steel*

Wheels reunion album, the faithful reembraced the group but cast a jaundiced eye on its front man. Jagger's effete activities during those twelve telling months in 1983 still rankled: his jealousy toward the rejuvenated, post-heroin Keith Richards; his fussy restoration of his eighteenth-century "La Fourchette" chateau in the Loire Valley; his taste for Napoleon brandy and '64 Chateau Beychevelle. And then there was Om, the East Indian chauffeur for his bronze 6.3 Mercedes. What was right with this enduring picture?

Two days after Christmas 1983, Mick had showed up on the backstage celebrity list for an electric blues concert. Tired of watching from the wings, Jagger slipped out into the hall to catch the spirited show from the orchestra section. After dancing among the audience for some ten minutes, he attempted to return backstage. Beefy security guards barred the way. He tried to barge past them. They threw him back. Told him to beat it.

Abruptly, it dawned on him that absolutely no one recognized who he was. He cursed. Squinted at his tormentors. Reasoned with them. Cursed. Paced. It was not until he flashed his American Express card that anyone believed him.

This was indeed Mick Jagger.

Black is his favorite color.

His mother claimed he had perfect pitch since age two.

As a boy, his idol was Roy Rogers.

When he was ten, his aunt sent him a map of California, a treasure he guarded for years afterward.

The first record he purchased was a Woolworth single on the Embassy label. On it, a singer imitated Ricky Nelson.

His mother bought him his first guitar for £7.

He won his first fight by swinging a bicycle chain at his opponent.

He was a regular at the one snooker hall in his hometown.

He was expelled on his last day of school for leaving half an hour early.

He considers his most admirable virtue to be compassion.

While in art school, he liked to pop Benzedrine and Midol tablets. Sometimes, he shared his pills with a cockatoo in the zoo.

He was strongly against releasing "(I Can't Get No) Satisfaction," feeling the song he'd largely written was "album filler" . . . "terrible" . . . "It could just as well have been called 'Aunt Millie's Caught Her Tit in the Mangle.' "

After being fined for driving without a license, he arranged for an aide to im-

Keith Richards

1989

personate him for his driving test. The aide passed, forged Keith's signature on the necessary documents, and the Ministry of Transport granted a license.

"What I'm doing is a sexual thing," he told a journalist in 1966. "I dance, and all dancing is a replacement for sex. What really upsets people is that I'm a man and not a woman."

During his trial in June 1967, following the police raid on Redlands, his country home, Richards told the judge, "We are not old men. We are not worried about petty morals."

Girlfriend Anita Pallenberg talked him into purchasing a Nazi staff car in the late 1960s. He had the huge Mercedes refitted at a cost of $5,000. The day it was delivered, he wrecked it. The car went back to the auto shop. A year later, it was roadworthy once more. The day it was delivered, he wrecked it again.

The character from fiction he would most like to have been is Smiley from John LeCarré's *Tinker, Tailor, Soldier, Spy.*

In 1970, he moved with his family to Nellcote, a Roman-style villa above Villefranche-sur-Mer on the Côte d'Azur, as a tax dodge, and he had heroin shipped to him on a regular basis, concealed inside his son's toys.

While in France, he graduated from snorting smack to shooting smack.

In April 1972, Anita Pallenberg gave birth to Dandelion, her second child with Keith. As with Marlon in August 1969, Dandelion was delivered while Anita was addicted to heroin.

On December 14, 1972, police descended on Nellcote, discovering quantities of heroin, cocaine, and hashish.

When Anita was arrested in Jamaica in December 1972 for possession of marijuana—and repeatedly beaten and raped in her jail cell—Keith privately offered $12,000 to anyone willing to kill the man who had set up the bust. He had no takers.

His favorite bourbon is Rebel Yell.

His idols are the Great Train Robbers.

His definition of the height of misery is being caught with a cold and no handkerchief.

He and Anita Pallenberg acquired a reputation around London for corrupting the servants supplied by a Chelsea employment agency with heroin, thereafter taking the money they needed for requisite fixes out of their wages. Eventually, the agency refused to send any more prospects to the couple.

Following the shooting of George Wallace at a political rally in

May 1972, Keith began to carry a .38 police revolver for his personal protection.

On July 4, 1972, Keith introduced Rolling Stone Records chief Marshall Chess to heroin in Washington, D.C.

He once told a London reporter that he believed Redlands was a site for UFO landings.

On June 26, 1973, London bobbies uncovered guns, Chinese heroin, and Mandrax tablets during a raid on Keith's home on fashionable Cheyne Walk.

A desperate Marshall Chess reportedly phoned Keith from a Knightsbridge hotel late one evening in the early 1970s, informing him that he believed he was dying from an overdose of the $1,000 worth of bad heroin they'd split earlier that evening. Keith is said to have hung up on him—repeatedly—later telling an aide to buy back whatever smack Chess had left over.

Needing to clean up for the Rolling Stones' 1973 European tour in support of *Goat's Head Soup,* Keith and Marshall traveled to Switzerland to get a forty-eight-hour blood transfusion—a supposed cure for heroin addiction. A Florida doctor named Denber officiated. The cure appeared to work. Shortly afterward, both men took up the drug again.

On March 26, 1976, Anita Pallenberg gave birth to a second son, Tara Richard, in a Swiss clinic. Ten weeks later, the infant died. No public explanation was ever given for his death.

On May 19, 1976, Keith fell asleep at the wheel of his Bentley and ran it off an English highway into a field. No one in the car was hurt, but an investigating officer found an unidentified substance in the car. After arriving two hours late for the trial, Keith told the judge he was waiting for his trousers to come out of the dryer. "I find it extraordinary," replied His Honor, "that a man of your stature has only one pair of pants."

While Richards was being sentenced in Canada for heroin possession and trafficking, Sid Vicious slit his wrists. "He's trying to steal my headlines!" said Richards.

After he and Anita Pallenberg allegedly kicked heroin through neuroelectric acupuncture treatment in New York, a Canadian judge gave Richards a suspended sentence for the heroin rap and ordered him to perform a benefit concert for the blind.

"The last thing I could bear," he says, "is to feel guilty about smack."

He would like to die "humbly."

In December 1983, he married Patti Hansen outside Cabo San Lucas, Mexico. She was nine years old when "Satisfaction" was an international hit.

After sixteen months of wedlock, Patti gave birth to a seven-pound, fifteen-ounce daughter named Theodora Dupree Richards. A photo of toddler-age Keith riding a tricycle was hung over the infant's crib. A year later, the couple had another daughter, Alexandra Nicole.

In 1988, Keith Richards teamed with noted New York drummer/guitarist/songwriter Steve Jordan to write and produce Keith's first solo album, *Talk Is Cheap.* The acclaimed LP was followed by a brief but triumphant American tour with a band he dubbed the X-Pensive Winos.

"I'm a Sagittarius," he told his approving public, "half-man, half-horse with a license to shit in the street."

The day after his tour ended, he turned up at a New York fete sporting a T-shirt stenciled with the motto Loose Fun and greeted his wife by falling to his knees and kissing her toes. "On top of the fact that I love the bitch to death," he confided, "she keeps up with me, she keeps me going."

On his guitar picks are stamped the words: "I'm innocent."

The following interview took place in Manhattan in the late autumn of 1988, shortly before Keith and the X-Pensive Winos embarked on their U.S. concert trek. Keith arrived in a midtown recording studio dressed in black, with a wine-colored head-tie, and sporting a weary pair of suede ankle boots that looked like they'd been ripped off from Rip Van Winkle. (He went on to feature the same spent footwear on the entire Rolling Stones' *Steel Wheels* tour.)

Keith sat down, cracked open a bottle of Rebel Yell, and showed himself to be the most affable figure in all rock. As the talk concluded, he produced a crayon, picked up the half-empty bottle of Rebel Yell, and noted the precise level of its contents with a fat little line, saying with a wink, "I'm marking this sucker for the next time we get together."

After twenty-five years with the Rolling Stones, you've begun a new career with the solo Talk Is Cheap *album and tour. What I'm wondering is why you hadn't done a solo album earlier?*

Good question. To me, the idea of planning and making a solo album while you're actively working with a band like the Stones is impossible. I couldn't imagine any reason on earth to put myself in such a situation. If I wrote a song with that in the back of my mind, I would have to be like Solomon with the baby and cut it in half, wondering if I should put one piece in the Stones' pocket and keep the other for myself. Why rip yourself apart?

Even when the Stones decided not to work after *Dirty Work,* I still had no plans to make a solo record until around the time I was doing the *Hail! Hail! Rock and Roll* movie with Chuck Berry.

Steve Jordan and I'd been working for about a year together by then, and we realized that we had something going. Also, I was finding other musicians, most of whom I had known for years, who wanted to do it with us. I was finding the nucleus of a band again, *another* band. And to me that's essential. The whole joy of making rock and roll music is the interaction between guys playing, and trying to capture that on tape.

Steve Jordan had been the drummer on the 1986 "Jumping Jack Flash" session that you produced for Aretha's single version of the tune. Was that the first time you and Steve played together?

Yeah, on a pro gig, although I'd known Steve since he was working on "Saturday Night Live" ten years ago. Slowly over those years we kept bumping into each other, and it was one of those things you don't realize is going down at the time. Ronnie Wood, when he used to live in New York, had a little studio, and Ronnie is what I call the holy host—you know, "Come on over and play!" So a lot of times there'd be jam sessions down in Ronnie's little studio, and that's where Steve and I started to really play together.

Why do you think you work so well with Steve? What do you think the chemistry is between you?

[*Smiling*] Well, chemistry was one of those subjects in school that I was never good at. But I think it's the *unknown* bit—the mysterious spark—that does it. It's the same with the Stones. I mean, line 'em up against a wall, and they're the most unlikely *good* rock and roll band that you could find!

Tell me what you were listening to for fun at the time you and Steve began writing for Talk Is Cheap.

I find that that the older I get and the longer I do this gig, the more tolerant I've become about other kinds of music. I still listen to a lot of blues of the Chicago electric variety—Muddy Waters, especially—and you'll also catch me listening to a lot of Bach and Mozart, and Beethoven, too.

At the time of the album, I happened to be listening to a lot of South African Soweto street music—which was intriguing me a lot, because it seems to me that Africa, which produced the rhythms and heartbeats of American music and especially rock and roll, was now throwing it back to us again with electric instruments! That's where the Soweto sound is at! And *somehow* this is where I got the idea for the accordion and fiddle on "Locked Away." [*shrugs, chuckles*]

Actually, on "Locked Away," there're three generations of rock roots represented. You've got Ivan Neville, son of one of the Neville Brothers. You've got Buckwheat Dural, zydeco accordian great, and violinist Michael Doucet from Beausoleil, the fine Cajun band.

[*Nodding*] I knew that "Locked Away" needed some more color on it. Sometimes you almost *dream* an idea. I guess the fact that I had been listening to Buckwheat's latest record and the South African music was critical, and suddenly it just clicked in my mind. I'd say, "Why didn't I think of this months ago?"

If there was an overall concept to this album, it was to keep it musical. The public, they're so sick of the slick, push-button, drum-machine records. There's nothing wrong with any of this high-tech stuff, the toy department stuff. It's just a matter of what you do with it. Steve and I were trying to get things up to the hardware department.

On the radio favorite from your album, "You Don't Move Me," you sing, "You made the wrong motion / You drank the wrong potion / It's no longer funny / It's bigger than money." I wanted to discuss the origin of that song. I think it came about because you were asking Steve for writing suggestions?

Yeah, true. I'd written about thirty to forty songs, and one day I just looked to him for advice, saying, "I can't find how to continue, I can't find more to hook onto, or additional subject matter to write about." Steve looked at me with this big grin and said, "When in doubt, write about Mick," because he knows it'll make the juices flow in me. [*laughter, winks*] Which means the track's not *exactly* about Mick, but it's a kickoff point. It's about anybody in that position where you have a friend you feel you can't get through to, and you're trying to let them know.

Let's go back to the early sixties, when you were the lead guitarist for the top club band in London. If someone had called the Rolling Stones a rock and roll group at that point, it would have offended you guys, because you were working in the rhythm and blues idiom and that was the route you wanted to travel.

That's true! At the time the Rolling Stones started off in England, rock and roll had degenerated to where it meant, like, Fabian and Frankie Avalon. 'Cause by '59, who did you have left? Elvis was in the army. Buddy Holly had taken the dive. Jerry Lee Lewis was disgraced. Little Richard had thrown his bracelets and jewelry into the sea and gone back to the church.

Hence we stressed the rhythm and blues end of it, and we went in through the jazz club approach to playing. The places were a lot smaller, but at least you had more choices of what you could do.

The record business is always *behind* the public. With the Beatles and the Stones, they couldn't understand how some little club groups could suddenly grab the imagination of the world. Foxed them entirely.

The jazz club scene then included the Round House, the Rhythm & Blues Club in Ealing, the Marquee Club on Oxford Street, and lastly the Crawdaddy Club, where you guys played on Sunday nights. What was the Crawdaddy Club like, say, at the point when it moved from the Station Hotel to the Richmond Athletic Club?

God, you know a lot about West London, man! [*laughter*] It started off as a fairly small thing. We just took it over because we managed to convince the guy that owned the pub that we could bring in more people—and hence he would sell more drinks—than the local Dixieland band that he had playing there. He tried us out for a bit, and within two or three weeks there was a huge line going across the railroad tracks, until it became a huge event.

I believe an average early Stones set at the Crawdaddy would consist of "Route 66," Bo Diddley's "Do the Crawdad" . . .

. . . And then some Jimmy Reed stuff, a lot of Muddy Waters stuff, and some Howlin' Wolf. We were kids of eighteen or nineteen then, and we were like *missionaries.* We weren't out to promote the Rolling Stones. We were out to promote this music that never got heard very much.

Your own band's name came from Muddy Waters's 1950–51 hit, "Rollin' Stone," which in turn came from the still-older "Catfish Blues" by Tommy McClennan and Robert Pickwick.

[*Laughter*] Yeah, and I wonder where *they* got it from?! There's really only one song in the whole world, and probably Adam and

Eve hummed it to each other, and everything else is a variation on it in one form or another, you know?

As far as historical backtracking goes, the Stones had their blues-oriented dreams come true when you got the chance to record at Chicago's Chess Studios in 1964.

Yeah! In fact, Muddy Waters was actually painting the studio when we walked in! There's this guy on top of a ladder wearing a white suit—anybody who wasn't selling records at Chess, they'd have to make themselves useful, it seems. So somebody says, "Well, meet Muddy Waters," and we look up and he's standing on a stepladder painting the ceiling. And we're all toppling over ourselves, bewildered, thinking, "What is this? Is this a hobby of his?"

Can you imagine? And we're recording in the same studio where he made his records! After that, you start to realize how tough the business can be. Here's one of your gods painting the ceiling, and you're making a record of some of *his* songs.

That raises another point. Did the Stones have any problems touring the deep South in the midsixties while essentially playing black music?

No, not from black people, at least. The first tour we did of the South, no one was hung up about how genuine it was for us to be playing black music. Mainly, we offended white Southerners in those days because of the *hair.*

You know, we were arrested once for topless bathing. This was outside of Savannah, Georgia. Some people were driving by and swore that there was a load of chicks leaping in and out of the pool with just a pair of drawers on. So the cops came zooming up to bust these chicks, and of course the closer they got the more stupid they must have felt. Especially when they heard these South London accents, saying, "Aye, whattaya mean, mate?!"

Your very first solo release, "Run Rudolph Run," backed by "The Harder They Come," was a 1978 holiday single. You cut it with Ronnie Wood, Charlie Watts, and who else?

Ian Stewart. What a beauty, that song. It's a real rough version, just for fun. It's really just an outtake on a Stones session, and I thought it was written by Chuck Berry but actually someone sent it in to him.

If I'm not mistaken, on the original '78 label, rather than the '79 re-release, the credit just reads "Richards."

'Cause I couldn't find who wrote it. We couldn't find anyone that claimed it. So the management go, "We can't find the sucker, claim it for yourself. If he crops up out of the woods, we'll transfer it." The lyrics were just my best recollection anyhow.

I want to ask you a very personal question. At thirteen, you joined the Boy Scouts, but you didn't keep on with them. What changed your mind about Scouting?

[*Grinning*] Well, I joined the Boy Scouts 'cause I thought me dad would be proud of me. And within three months I was a patrol leader! Believe it or not, it was the Beaver Patrol. [*hoarse laughter*] That was a commando unit, that patrol, compared to what the Boy Scouts were supposed to be about!

I was in the Scouts for about two years, and I learned an awful lot about how to live out there in the woods. Certainly, that's what I wanted to learn. But every year they had these huge gatherings of us Scouts from all over the country, like summer camp—a jamboree. And at one of them I smuggled in a coupla bottles of whiskey. Soon afterward there were a couple of fights that went down between us and some Yorkshire guys, and so I was under suspicion. All the fighting was found out after I went to slug one guy—but hit the tent pole instead—and broke a bone in my hand! A few weeks later I had some dummo recruit come in, a kid just offensive to me in every way, and I punched him out, so I got thrown out.

I couldn't imagine going on and on with it anyway, but I learned certain aspects of leadership from that, and I also learned that if you dump me on top of a mountaintop with just the bare necessities, I'll survive.

I believe the first record you ever bought was a Woolworth single on the Embassy label. It was a Ricky Nelson impersonator. But what was the tune?

"Never Be Anyone Else But You." I couldn't afford the real version, and the Woolworth version was cheap. It was just something for me so that I could get the guitar chords down, and all we had anyway was a wind-up Gramophone.

Gus Dupree, your grandfather on your mom's side, first encouraged you to play guitar.

He encouraged me by never pushing it on me. He was an amazing guy. He used to play sax for a dance band in the thirties. Played fiddle too and was one of the loosest, most outrageous guys I've ever met in my life. When I'd go to visit him, he had a piano and on top of it used to be this guitar. But it would only just sit there. He would never make any reference to it.

It was only a few years ago, in talking to one of my aunts, that

I found out the guitar was only there when he knew I was gonna come and visit, and the minute I left it was back in its case. But I used to think it was just a fixture, part of the house—you know, some people had a piano with the guitar on top. But now you can see what a canny character he was.

Wasn't one of your earliest heroes Roy Rogers?

Oh yeah, because I liked the kind of cowboy who carried a guitar instead of a rifle slung along the side of his horse. I'd meet Mick in the playground—we were only about four or five years old then and lived very close together—and I'd tell him, "OOOH boy, that Roy Rogers! And that palomino, Trigger! Wow, man, they're something else!!

Did you have any exposure to Roy Rogers's music with the Sons of the Pioneers?

It never interested me at all, the music he played. And the release of American records in England when I was growing up was the bare minimum.

It was just the image, the guitar. When you're a kid, cowboys are very intriguing.

The first paying job you ever had was a couple of days' work at the post office. Didn't you give your mom your wages so she could get a Billy Eckstine/Ella Fitzgerald record?

Yeah! I thought I was loaded, man; I'd never seen so much money in my life. But, understand, if I bought her the record, she'd have to buy a record player that was apart from the old wind-up thing we had. So it was not so much of "What a wonderful son!" but rather a little bit of devious thought going on there.

One more thought about your boyhood. You were a choirboy, and actually sang for the Queen one Christmas.

In '56 or '57. I was a soprano. To me, it was a way of getting out of Physics and Chemistry, because if you gave me a bunsen burner back then I'd set the school on fire.

I was a very good soprano, although you wouldn't believe it now to listen to me. [*growling chuckle*] And the weird thing is, for a kid of twelve, thirteen to get a gig at Westminster Abbey for the Queen—I couldn't get that gig now! This career is going downhill.

There was a certain part of the "Hallelujah Chorus," a section for three sopranos, and it was me, a guy called Spike, and another named Terry. We were the reprobates of the school, definitely, but at the time we sang like angels.

Tell me about "Happy," probably one of your best-known vocals with the Stones. It was 1972, from Exile on Main Street, *you recorded it in France, but there weren't too many Stones actually playing in the track. What are your recollections?*

The basic track was Bobby Keys on baritone sax, myself on guitar, and Jimmy Miller on drums. "Happy" was cut one afternoon because the whole record was cut in the basement of my villa with the Stones mobile truck parked in the driveway. So sometimes I'd be ready to play, and some of the guys would come over early. It was really like a warm-up; but I had this idea for a song.

We were basically doing the sound check, making sure that everything was being set up for the session, and the track just popped out. It was just because, for a change, people weren't down lying on the beach or at a local bar in Nice.

Keith, let's move along through the Stones catalog and your solo work in that catalog. Musically, "Sleep Tonight" on Dirty Work *seems to have been the forerunner of this new solo career. Why do you think it sounds that way?*

Mainly because Mick was already involved with his solo thing and wasn't there very much. Charlie was going through a weird period, which he does from time to time. Very rarely do all of these things coincide—they *never* coincided before. So Ronnie played drums on that track, and I wrote it on piano. I love the changes on it. I realized that I was getting into another area that I hadn't expected for myself, and to me it was, in a way, an indication of what could be done on *Talk Is Cheap.*

Did you have any vocal qualms when you began your solo album?

I personally didn't have any doubts about doing the vocals when I went into this record. I figured that if I got to sing all of these songs, which I intended to do, that the more I practiced the better I would get at it. Practice doesn't make *perfect*, but it does make *better.*

I got a lot of push, also, from the guys I was working with. Nobody was there saying, "Oh God, this guy's paying us, we gotta say, 'Yes, Keith, yes Keith.' " To me that's important.

Do you have a favorite vocal on Talk Is Cheap?

I keep coming back to "Make No Mistake," because I realize there that I'd started to feel comfortable with singing. It was bold of me to take it down an octave and come out with [*he drops his tone to a raspy rumble*] *maake naw mis-take.* Rather than always trying to pitch the vocals to the outer limits of my top range.

How do you feel about the guitar aspect of your music these days? Are you coming up with any new edges and angles?

Right now I'm pretty happy with the way I'm playing. I'm coming up with more variations, and I've expanded a little bit on things that I do. All of that has to do with working constantly in the last two years, from Aretha to the Chuck Berry movie to *Talk Is Cheap.*

You know, the Stones got so big after "Satisfaction" that we would work frantically for several months recording, and then have eighteen months sometimes in which we'd do absolutely nothing. You wouldn't even see the guys!

The bigger you get, the less you can work—which is never a good thing for a musician. So I've been playing constantly, and I've noticed that it helps me. I mean, I play guitar at home, but it's not the same thing as playing with a band.

The other thing I have to say about guitar is that no guitar player can go wrong if they play acoustic guitar steadily, if they keep their hand in on the acoustic. If you don't, you can get too into the electronics, the sustain and feedback, and you can lose a lot of touch and feel.

Acoustic guitar is *the* instrument because it can't fool you, you can't make trick with the acoustic. If you keep the acoustic up, it'll help the electric guitar-playing. Otherwise you can get into that Fastest Guitar in the West syndrome, which is, for rock and roll, absolutely a dead-end street. That's rock music, but it ain't rock and roll.

Take the *Talk Is Cheap* record: I have more exact, more perfect or skillful takes of each of these songs, but the more you try to literally perfect them, the more you lose the *instinctive* thing. Instinct is what I want.

The truth is, I'm more interested in the roll than I am in the rock.

What began in the sunny glow of a daytime phone call almost ended in a backwater brawl in the fathomless predawn. Atlantic Records vice-president Jerry Wexler had received a hot tip: Aretha Franklin had just gotten out of her contract with Columbia Records. Wexler rang Aretha immediately. He chatted sweetly with the shy singer and her husband, Ted White, and within days they had a deal.

For Wexler it was a godsend. He'd been emerald with envy ever since Columbia's John Hammond had picked up on the eighteen-year-old spiritual singer. Aretha had been the centerpiece of the pew-pounding services at her father's New Bethel Baptist Church, and Hammond hired her shortly after she'd wriggled loose from her father's wayfaring evangelist caravan. "She was the best natural singer I'd heard since Billie Holiday," said Hammond. Columbia tried to steer her away from the narrow gospel category in which James Cleveland and

Aretha Franklin

1989

Aretha's aunt Clara Ward had excelled and toward the fully orchestrated show tunes and bleached jazz-pop that were leading the Hit Parade. She started out in 1960 with "Today I Sing the Blues," got detoured to "If Ever I Should Leave You" from *Camelot,* and, after ten albums, had seen only one feeble pop hit, "Rock-a-Bye Your Baby with a Dixie Melody." Nothing could have been less "natural."

Wexler booked a week at Rick Hall's Fame Studios in Muscle Shoals—plenty of time to cut an entire LP—and requested a certain integrated roster of musicians that would include a leading black horn section. It didn't go down that way, and when Aretha and her testy spouse found themselves in the deep South, with a sea of white faces peering over their music stands, it was bad ethnic arithmetic. Aretha remained game, quietly going to the piano to explain the parts she'd worked out, but Ted White clenched his teeth. Sure enough, one of the trumpet players started trading thinly veiled racial repartee with White as they got drunk from the same bottle. Curt winks gave way to cold stares and cutting retorts. The sun sank like a sick joke, taking all civility with it, leaving too much liquor behind and the wrong men intent on consuming it. As the witching hour approached, Wexler took to his bed in the motel where everyone was staying and prayed for the storm to pass.

He awoke to the sounds of heavy footsteps in the night. Doors slammed. He thought he heard shots going off. The phone rang. It was Aretha, calling from a diner. A boiling brouhaha of no small scope had developed between Ted and the trumpet player and had spilled over in all directions. She and Ted had an ugly fight, and she'd run away.

At 7:00 A.M., Wexler found himself in Aretha's room, Ted White laying him out, cursing a blue streak, and calling down dreadful oaths. "Man," he fumed, as Aretha wept, "why did you bring her down here with these rednecks!" Husband and wife split on the next flight North, vowing never to return.

Wexler was left with only one completed track, "I Never Loved a Man," and "Do Right Woman—Do Right Man," a work-in-progress. He knocked off some master tapes, mailing them out to prominent rhythm and blues DJs for feedback. He got a tremendously positive reaction. Problem was, Wexler couldn't put the single out because he had no completed B-side, and he was unable to locate Aretha. Catching up with her a couple of weeks later, Wexler suggested that they try to make amends in neutral territory—New York City. She gave her cautious assent. The basic band from Muscle Shoals was brought up, plus the Memphis horns buttressed by saxophone great King Curtis, a favorite of Aretha's.

"I Never Loved a Man (The Way I Love You)" became a Top 10 hit in 1967, and it was the prelude to Aretha Franklin's five-year reign as the preeminent black artist in the world: Lady Soul, the Spirit in the Dark.

She also gained repute as a remote, woe-laden woman of precarious fortune but irreducible dignity. For all her hard luck and travail, she would never circulate complaints, never broadcast bitter asides, never so much as acknowledge a single reversal. But the pain was in her singing, a pliant, plangent wail that childhood houseguest Sam Cooke had believed would never be palatable outside of a witness-bearing holiness shout in church. As Wexler put it, she became "the mysterious lady of sorrow."

She came out of Detroit's east side, humble home turf to the Supremes and Smokey Robinson, but her house was a large one on a tree-lined street. Her father, Reverend Clarence L. Franklin, was one of the best-known preachers in the country, making thousands of dollars per homily on his barnstorming runs, and boasting a brisk-selling catalog of over seventy albums of sermons on the Chess label.

Aretha was born on March 25, 1942, in Memphis, Tennessee, one of five children by the former Barbara Siggers. Her father brought the family North when Aretha was two, first to Buffalo and then to Detroit, where he became pastor of the New Bethel Baptist congregation. Aretha was six when her mother abandoned the family. In 1952, word came that she had died. The children often found themselves in the care of hired help when her father traveled with his troupe. At twelve, Aretha soloed in church to a joyous reaction and cut some sides with JVP Records; then Clarence Franklin took her to see his people at Chess. Two singles resulted.

Inspired by Sam Cooke's bold break with the church in the mid-1950s, eschewing Sundays at New Bethel for Saturday nights at the Flame Show Bar, Aretha moved to New York City and auditioned for theatrical agent Jo King. A Columbia contract was offered and snatched up, but Aretha wasn't ready. Outside of a church, without the uplifting press of pious spectators, she lost her bearings. Under Wexler, however, the environment was funky, relaxed, even cloistered. There was no excess, and plenty of rehearsal time in which to gestate and experiment. Aretha relaxed and began writing more songs; her innate approach—with its piercing heights and supple melisma—flowered and steadied. "I Never Loved a Man" sold a million copies; four more gold singles were cut that year, including the peerless "Respect"—a wonder, written by Otis Redding, that was captured live in the studio. Aretha's first albums on Atlantic, *I Never Loved a Man the Way I Love You* and *Aretha Arrives,* were cohesive works, free of filler, and their honesty and directness made them standards by which listeners measured themselves.

The Southern Christian Leadership Conference gave her a special citation for her contributions to black culture, and she was a bona fide heroine, devoid of the gloss and cynical self-aggrandizement of a Diana Ross or the rhinestone-studded vapidity of a Nancy Wilson.

Riding the acclaim of her superb *Lady Soul* LP and "Chain of Fools" single, Aretha opened the 1968 Democratic Convention with a truly soul-stirring version of "The Star-Spangled Banner" that said more about rightful citizenship in the land of the free than any speech delivered at that accursed convocation. She placed four more singles in the Top 10 before Christmas: "Since You've Been Gone," "Think," "The House That Jack Built"/"I Say a Little Prayer," and "See Saw."

Her homelife was less transcendent. She gave birth to three children during her teen years, products of an unhappy union. Fans were outraged when Ted White roughed her up in public in 1967. Their divorce some two years later was as unpleasant as their time together, lightened only by the birth of a son in 1970.

In 1970, she brought out *Spirit in the Dark.* It boasted "Don't Play That Song," a brilliant performance that connected with the peaks of *Lady Soul.* By the end of 1971, Aretha had had more million-sellers than any female singer, thanks to "Don't Play That Song," "Bridge Over Troubled Water," "Spanish Harlem," and "Rock Steady." But her mood swings increased in the 1970s. Then, during a session down in Miami, she contracted pancreatitis. It was Wexler who looked after the singer, wheeling her to the X-ray room, monitoring her care. Oddly, her entourage had deserted her. "There was nobody but me," said Wexler. "I couldn't understand it."

Live at the Fillmore West in 1971 brought her together with Ray Charles and King Curtis and primed the pump for *Young, Gifted and Black,* the 1972 LP that would be her last soul-baring effort, a wrenching look back on her tormented marriage. She found solace and renewal in gospel on *Amazing Grace.* But further epiphanies failed to occur. Aretha's stage shows and television appearances defied interpretation in their gross ignorance of her intrinsic charm. She would hurry through scores of costume changes in an unintentional sendup of *Gentlemen Prefer Blondes* or waddle onstage attired as a black Emmett Kelly.

In 1978, Aretha married actor Glynn Turman; the Rev. C. L. Franklin performed the ceremony as the Four Tops sang Stevie Wonder's "Isn't She Lovely." In 1979, her father was shot by burglars and left in a coma. She left Atlantic amid financial difficulties augmented by her father's medical bills and signed with Arista, and once again was given simpler settings in which to work out her vocal insecurities, let her heart be heard, and permit some magic to take hold. Rising singer-producer Luther Vandross gave her a hit with the title track of *Jump to It* in 1982 and won her new fans with *Get It Right* in 1983, both exceptional records. She was due to make her Broadway stage debut in 1984 with *Sing, Mahalia, Sing,* a musical based on the life of gospel great Mahalia Jackson. She didn't appear for rehearsals owing to her fear of flying, and the show never opened. Producer Ashton Springer, who dropped a bundle on the pre-production, sued the Queen of Soul for breach of contract; a New York federal judge ruled that Aretha was liable for damages of $234,364.07. In the interim, she divorced Turman, buried her father, and found renewal with the hit single "Freeway of Love." She also joined with Keith Richards and Steve Jordan to cut a new rendition of the Rolling Stones' "Jumping Jack Flash" and dueted with George Michaels on "I Knew You Were Waiting." But her finest singing in a decade arrived with the 1987 release of a self-produced double album of spirit-rousing gospel music, *One Lord, One Faith, One Baptism.*

Her career restabilized, Aretha concentrated again on her private life, dating Detroit cab fleet owner Willie Wilkerson, working out on Nautilus equipment—while still smoking a pack of Kool Lights a day—and keeping up with professional boxing, the soaps, and her fear-of-flying classes.

As the future continued to brighten, Aretha kept her own counsel. A rare soliloquy from the start of her boom years with Atlantic serves as the best summation of her trials and of her deep dark spirit: "Trying to grow up is hurting, you know. You make mistakes. You try to learn from them, and when you don't it hurts even more."

Bob Dylan 1989

During an interview in the fall of 1983, singer/songwriter Paul Simon was asked: *Who besides John Lennon do you believe has been a positive inspirational figure in rock?*

"Dylan. He made us feel at a certain time that it was good to be smart, to be observant, that it was good to have a social conscience. These are all things that are out of fashion now. Real art remains when the fashion changes, but art can run conjunctively with fashion. Both can occasionally be quite intelligent at the same time."

Blessed with the hindsights of adulthood, what's the smartest thing you ever heard anybody in rock and roll say?

[*Long pause, small smile*] "Be-bop-a-lula, she's my baby."

Paul Simon, then forty-three, couldn't help but chuckle after confessing that the opening line of rockabilly star Gene Vincent's palpitating 1956 pop yodel about puppy love was the most luminous he could recall. But he wouldn't retract the statement.

Paul Simon's career took shape in Bob Dylan's shadow, and he held the man in the same awe as the rest of his contemporaries. He envied Dylan's intuitive ear, was charged by his trenchant wit and his understanding, admired his temerity, was humbled by his talent, arrested by his mystique.

Dylan's sketchy background was deliciously intriguing Americana. He was born Robert Allen Zimmerman in Duluth, Minnesota, on May 24, 1941, son of a hardware store owner, formed a high-school group called the Golden Chords, took Dylan Thomas's first name as his last when he began playing at cafés while at the University of Minnesota. He came to New York City in 1961, sought out a dying Woody Guthrie in an East Orange, New Jersey, hospital, and begged him for his blessing. John Hammond, A&R sleuth at Columbia Records, discovered Dylan at Gerdes's Folk City.

Ahh, but that was 1962, when his debut *Bob Dylan* LP on Columbia set smug Greenwich Village talking about a gangly broccoli-haired stick of a kid who could lend fresh import to traditional ballads, a street poet who could get people thinking about something other than current pop pap like Ray Stevens's "Ahab the Arab" with such originals as "Song to Woody" and "Talking New York." By 1963, he'd become *The FreeWheelin' Bob Dylan,* pictured on the album cover heading down West 4th Street with a honey blonde on his arm, not dressed against the cold, making you feel just how cold it was going to get with such songs as "A Hard Rain's a-Gonna Fall," "Blowin' in the Wind," and "Masters of War." In 1964, *The Times They Are a-Changin'* made him a protest singer without peer—lauded and loathed—but he showed the world that he was one leftist troubadour who could come down off the barricades and write exceptional love songs when he closed out the year with *Another Side of Bob Dylan.* Come 1965, his *Bringing It All Back Home* continued in the folk-rock direction he'd started when he'd given his "Mr. Tambourine Man" to the Byrds. Dylan endured boos at the Newport Folk Festival for the electric guitar around his neck, then got a No. 2 record with the savage "Like a Rolling Stone." Nineteen sixty-six saw the beginning of Dylan's incarnation as the star-crossed satirist-savant, his public pleading with him for clues to the cerebral songs on *Highway 61 Revisited* and *Blonde on Blonde,* Dylan racking up another No. 2 hit with the unruly wobble-rhythms of "Rainy Day Women # 12 & 35," Dylan getting a broken neck and amnesia after a motorcycle crash in Woodstock, New York . . .

Then came 1968 and Dylan's comeback with the mordant *John Wesley Harding,* his marriage to twenty-five-year-old model Sarah (Shirley Noznisky) Lowndes, his interest in Zionism and his Jewishness. His further movement toward country music came in 1969, with *Nashville Skyline* and "Lay Lady Lay." There was a tepid return to Greenwich Village in the early 1970s with *Self-Portrait* and *New Morning*; a tentative redux of social consciousness with the Concert for Bangla Desh, and his "George Jackson" single. And then the cagey dismantlement of the myth, testing, tearing, pushing it to the limits with the soundtrack and cameo role (his character's name was "Alias") in Sam Peckinpah's *Pat Garrett and Billy the Kid*; the *Planet Waves* LP; the 1974 tour documented in *Before the Flood*; the unexpectedly poignant, contemplative, and prismatic *Blood on the Tracks* (1974) and *Desire* (1975); *The Basement Tapes* (1975), cut with the Band during Dylan's recuperation from the cycle spill; the ragtag Rolling Thunder Revue caravan that enlisted Allen Ginsberg, Ronee Blakley, Joni Mitchell, Roger McGuinn, Arlo Guthrie, Mick Ronson; his divorce from his wife in 1977; the release in 1978 of his disastrous four-hour parable of rock ennui, *Renaldo and Clara.*

By 1979, after two uneven live albums *(Hard Rain, Live at Budokan)* and a moribund studio LP *(Street Legal),* Dylan showed himself to be an arrogant, uncharitable, born-again Christian, but his music had regained snap and bite, especially on his *Slow Train Coming* and *Saved* albums. He was certain of its strangeness, excited by its obscurity. *Infidels,* released in 1983, was intended to be a setting aside of his ever-shifting religious obsessions, and it suffered from a transparent self-consciousness. The broad irony, evident in such famous remarks as, "Oh, I think of myself more as a song-and-dance man, y'know," was long gone.

Dylan spent the second half of the 1980s doling out footlight artifacts *(Real Live)* and assemblages of half-drafted writing *(Empire Burlesque),* as if to demonstrate that activity alone could corroborate his posture of superability. Reluctant commercial reintrenchment resulted in 1986 in a long-overdue historical compilation album, the five-record *Biograph.* Dylan attempted to minimize his involvement in the undertaking, as if it had been done without his endorsement, but the intricate interview-derived liner notes (the best Dylan self-explanation extant, via journalist Cameron Crowe) made it clear the project was a feast of self-reflection.

Gripped by the humility of the moment, Dylan was generous in acknowledging compositional debts to specific Irish and Scottish folk songs, citing his borrowing from Brecht's "The Ship, The Black Freighter" for "The Lonesome Death of Hattie Carroll," and the presence of Chuck Berry's "Too Much Monkey Business" in the melody of "Subterranean Homesick Blues." And in his decision to share previously unreleased versions of "Visions of Johanna," "Lay

Down Your Weary Tune," "You're a Big Girl Now," "I Don't Believe You," "Up To Me," and "Heart of Mine," Dylan rewarded loyalists even as he certified the depth of his tenderness during his first two decades of love balladry.

Knocked Out Loaded (1986) was the closest Dylan ever came to releasing a worthless piece of dross, the album so shoddy and outlandishly trite that it insulted even random curiosity. Although *Loaded* was justly ignored by buyers, Dylan had begun drawing sizable crowds for package tours with Tom Petty and the Heartbreakers and, in 1987, the Grateful Dead. The joint concerts were much more confused and fitful than observers were willing to acknowledge, Dylan's perplexity with his public too palpable for comfort.

Seemingly at his wits' end in 1988, Dylan tossed out a grab bag of session gambols under the meaningless title of *Down in the Groove* and actually struck a well-deserved chord with young ears. As he jammed and joked with guitarist Danny Kortchmar and drummer Steve Jordan on Wilbert Harrison's "Let's Stick Together," and "The Ugliest Girl in the World" (coauthored, as was the shining "Silvio," with Grateful Dead lyricist Robert Hunter), the grizzled Aladdin of folk-rock had finally allowed himself an infectious good time. He next permitted himself to be pulled into the whimsical Traveling Wilburys studio troupe along with Tom Petty, George Harrison, Roy Orbison, and Jeff Lynne, but Bob remained the most retiring of its membership.

In September 1989, Dylan's *Oh Mercy* was given a grand welcome as "the Dylan record of the kind that made you a fan in the first place." The heavily orchestrated praise proved a gross injustice because it robbed too many listeners of the chance to discover the LP's best songs ("Ring Them Bells," "Man in the Long Black Coat," "Everything Is Broken") for themselves. What made *Oh Mercy* worthwhile was the terror in the tracks, Dylan nearly forgetting his outmoded image of aloofness as he quaked at all he beheld: casual violence becoming epidemic, nature nearing a standstill, society grown too vulgar to apply even the brakes of vanity and self-interest. In "What Good Am I" he dared to coyly question decisions made en route to adulthood, especially the moral issues he only toyed with in pursuit of an expedient spirituality.

Bob Dylan was scared, plain and simple, and as both an artist and a man he made the right choice on *Oh Mercy* by confessing that inconvenient fact. Although the record redeemed his reputation as a commentator, its accomplishment stopped there, because its anxious music revealed a singer who still could not name his own vulnerable role in either the future's grave prospects or the past's grim toll. After hesitating, Bob Dylan had again shrouded himself in his hymns. When *Oh Mercy* came to commercial grief, it tipped the consequent LP project toward a grasping series of supersessions with such pop genies as Elton John. Rock and roll was always intended to be one of the best ways a musician can stand naked. It was never meant to serve as either a safe pulpit or a hiding place.

Bob Dylan's songs, so fierce in their enduring vitality, are ultimately of the "time-and-place" stripe. They are welded to signposts, highway ramps, overpasses; places his contemporaries have done time in, raced through, moved away from. They run wide and deep, but they somehow do not exist on their own terms. "Be-Bop-a-Lula" does. It is an emotion preserved in song, unconditional, wholly without boundaries. It is too guileless to be quaint. Too forthright to be trivialized. Impervious to age. As universal as a planted kiss.

Paul Simon is rich now, famous, his distinguished place in the rock annals is secure. He can sit quietly in his offices in New York's Brill Building, the onetime headquarters of Tin Pan Alley and teen pop, and recall songs that bring back the challenges of his youth, the various phases of his career, the aura of coffeehouses, SNCC, the Mobilization, Kent State, the fall of Saigon, the Hearst kidnapping, the gradual embracing of adulthood, the accomplishments of his rock and roll colleagues. Dylan songs remind him of these things, and vice versa. They have rich meaning; they challenged conventional wisdom and helped get things done. They depict a time when a young man in a hurry could locate himself in and measure himself against his heroes, change his name and identity to gain proximity to their legends—maybe even eclipse them—and then win applause for the nerve these deeds require. Such songs are too shrewd to be pure, too clever to be instinctive, too studied for practical reasons to be the smartest of the smart.

Once Bob Dylan had been like no one else. Now he was like all of us. A still-restless dabbler, the tale of his reinvention too often retold, an ordinary man whose eyes stared inward, branded with his generation's now-familiar expression of perplexity. He was a common victim of the American Curse: too many choices.

It had been described as a "Day in the Key of Life" on the engraved invitations. Some 200 journalists, celebrities, and music-business executives were cordially requested to spend twelve hours with Stevie Wonder, Motown's resident soul visionary, for the unveiling of his magnum opus, *Songs in the Key of Life.* It was autumn 1976.

Guests were welcomed at a groaning-board breakfast buffet at a midtown Manhattan hotel, escorted to a conga line of chartered buses, and carried to the airport. A private jet redeposited them on an airfield in the woods of Massachusetts. The tarmac landing strip was a trifle too short for the large plane, and only the judiciously violent braking of the pilot kept the craft from veering too close to the heart-halting drop at the end of the strip. Those unfazed passengers who'd held onto their eggs Benedict and sauteed zucchini swiftly deplaned and were met by more buses that hauled all comers to the end of the line: Long View Farms.

Stevie Wonder

1989

A billowy white banquet tent had been pitched between the house and the barn; and while the guests milled about sloping acres of woods, lawns, and meadows, a chef and his staff readied lunch. On the second floor of the farmhouse, a slim, broad-shouldered black man was being dressed by two middle-aged valets.

The man was twenty-six years old, blind from birth. He hummed a melody, sporadic and low. His cream-colored western shirt was being buttoned by one valet and a matching Stetson hat set upon his head by the other. He said little, playing with the drawstring on his hat, tightening it under his chin so that it pulled the brim near to his eyebrows.

"You don't be wanting the hat to be on your head all that hard, it's too far down," said one attendant. Stevie Wonder sat expressionless, saying nothing, scratching his moustache, humming, rubbing his goatee, ceasing to hum. His feet were guided into a cream-colored pair of boots, and he was asked to stand. Around his waist was put a leather holster belt. Its pistol sheaths had been replaced with two cardboard mock-ups of his album jacket; flat wooden handles, painted to resemble the butts of cocked sixguns, protruded from them. Sunglasses were put in place, and Stevie pressed these against his brow. Downstairs, an awkward announcement was made by a well-dressed black woman, then repeated verbatim by an equally elegant black man; they were going to play the first side of Wonder's new record.

The studio monitors began to hiss as guests crammed themselves into the dark, circular room, and multitracked "oohs" burst forth, followed by Wonder's sung introduction to "Love's in Need of Love Today."

The song was a mournful plea for brotherhood, Wonder's almost viscose tenor sinking from a wistful falsetto to an emphatic growl, a harmonized gospel descant drifting in and out, while drums, bass, tinkling rhythm guitar, and synthesized blurps nudged the doleful lyric onward. The next song, "Have a Talk With God," was equally somber and keyed to the ominous striking of a bell. "Village Ghetto Land" was a pastoral on poverty and neglect, complete with a synthesizer parroting both a preachy pipe organ and strings that whined a dirgeful minuet. "Contusion" was a herky-jerky jazz-rock fusion instrumental. The side ended with "Sir Duke," a peppy tribute to Duke Ellington that punctured the dolorous mood with a kooky horn fanfare.

As the cerebral sermonizing faded from the monitors, the tall, trusting Wonder was led downstairs by the elbow to meet the assembled. His unwieldy holsters repeatedly got caught in the bars of the railings; the crown of his hat dented slightly as he strained to keep his head down during the cramped descent. At the sight of this unconsciously ostentatious space cowboy, the crowd fell silent, perplexed. Wonder looked miscast, fleeced of his innate dignity, his incongruous costume communicating an unintentional whimsy, much like that of a guileless trick-or-treat toddler who is paraded before the oldsters before his Halloween rounds. A break for lunch was called, and Wonder was taken outside and eased into a crooked swing hung from a great tree to pose for photos. A copy of the album jacket was held up ceremoniously, and many guests were taken aback at its ugliness, raggy concentric rings of burnt orange enclosing a blurred sketch of Stevie that was at best a clumsy likeness.

"Is that the finished cover?" one writer asked with trepidation. "This is it!" replied a Motown rep in an expansive tone. Asked to comment on the graphics, Wonder said he guessed they symbolized "universal love." Fifteen minutes later, Wonder was taken back upstairs. He made no further appearances.

For the remainder of the afternoon, installments of *Songs in the Key of Life* were unveiled at half-hour intervals. For almost two hours of music, it was low on padding and well produced. Relieved that the fete had offered more than sumptuous hype, the guests settled into a sunny alfresco afternoon of eating, drinking, and casual conversation. But there was something distinctly off-center about the affair, an absence of naturalness and grace, supplanted by a feeling of having been offered a haphazard peek at an unfortunate, even unnecessary puzzle. Eyes kept straying to the second-floor window. What was it like to be Stevie Wonder? To be the centerpiece of splendid parties in which he did not participate, a musical wunderkind who lived in his head, dependent on the ministrations of others, a victim of their visual, sartorial, and who knows what other tastes? On the plane back to New York, one writer for a newsweekly turned to another reporter and insisted that, as far as it was known, Wonder was extremely well cared for by his devoted family, freed from petty concerns to focus totally on his music, but made all important decisions himself. The results of the arrangement spoke for themselves.

"All I know," murmured one black journalist, "is that if somebody ever tried to get Ray Charles into some weird getup and put him on display like a doll, Ray would have personally kicked their ass."

He was born blind on May 13, 1950, in Saginaw, Michigan, Steveland Morris according to his birth certificate. Adept at playing piano, drums, and harmonica by his eleventh year, he was signed to the Hitsville U.S.A. label (later renamed Motown) through the good graces of singer Ronnie White of the Miracles. White had auditioned the boy, introduced him to staff songwriter Brian Holland, and got owner Berry Gordy, Jr., to take on the twelve-year-old prodigy. Little Stevie Wonder, Gordy called him. In concert, Wonder was presented as a pint-sized musical jack-of-all-trades, jumping from drums to organ to piano and then pulling out his silver mouth organ to bring his mighty feat to a furious close. He was seen by many as an inspirational novelty attraction who'd conquered a handicap with astounding style, but white acceptance was always much on Motown's mind, so, in 1964, Wonder was a featured performer in two surf movies, *Muscle Beach Party* and *Bikini Party.*

In 1966, he deepened his crossover appeal with an affecting cover of Bob Dylan's "Blowin' in the Wind." By 1968, he was having hits with such superior rhythm-and-blues ballads as "I Was Made to Love Her" and "For Once in My Life." By the time he'd turned nineteen, his balladry, though sugar-coated, had the trappings of sophistication, as in the well-received "My Cherie Amour" and "Yester-Me, Yester-You, Yesterday."

As the history of Motown shows, Wonder's renegotiated 1976 Motown pact, a reported $13 million deal whose terms filled 120 pages, was an epoch-disintegrating document. Formed in the late 1950s after retired Detroit boxer Berry Gordy lost his record store to bankruptcy, Motown Records was an autocratic organization. Every facet of its artists' careers and finances—of their entire lives—was controlled by "the Corporation" with Gordy acting as Big Daddy. Each act was selected by Gordy and groomed under his patronage, sent to charm schools, given voice and diction lessons, grilled in choreography. Then they were placed in the hands of a battery of staff writers and producers like the trio of Lamont Dozier and Brian and Eddie Holland, who specialized in gospel/blues-rooted grit primed to fit a lustrous pop grid. When royalties rolled in, the cash was consigned to banks and paid out to the performers in weekly allowances.

Wonder was the pioneer in eroding this chafing hierarchy, but, as was characteristic of others who were similarly assertive, he reflexively spun an opaque and secretive new human cocoon around himself, one that was the scaled-down equal of the immediate Motown "family" from which he'd distanced himself. Moreover, he set the oft-repeated precedent of peopling his new world with personnel from the parent organization. Besides introducing the fortressed factory tradition into the black arm of the modern record industry, Gordy had implanted in his people a paranoid "Motown mentality," a "them-or-us" bunker sensibility that spread to other black-owned or black-dominated record labels. Stevie ignored the fear-mongering but adhered to the familial code of camouflage and covert action.

The albums that Wonder did for Motown in the 1970s were no baker's dozen of hit-bound confections. Wonder produced highly integrated statements, the socially conscious (if mystically detached) songs overlapping to impart a complex overall impression. *Where I'm Coming From* (1971) was a rickety bridge into this new terrain, but *Music of My Mind* (1972) got the sensibility across confidently. *Talking Book* was issued several months later and, aided by an opening berth on the Rolling Stones' continental caravan in 1972, it became Wonder's mainstream calling card and spawned two chart-toppers, "Superstition" and "You Are the Sunshine of My Life." *Innervisions* (1973) and *Fulfillingness' First Finale* (1974) continued in a similar vein.

On August 6, 1973, while riding along a North Carolina highway, a log from a flatbed truck slid through a windshield and pinned Wonder by the head, robbing him of his sense of smell and nearly ending his life. That he rebounded from such additional cognitive loss with a statement as lush as *Songs in the Key of Life* is perhaps indicative of his peculiar strengths.

He next set aside three cloistered years for *Journey Through the Secret Life of Plants,* a gossamer grab bag of euphony meant to be the soundtrack of an unreleased nature film. But just what sort? Walt Disney's *The Living Landfill? National Geographic Visits the South Bronx?* And to what end? The two-record set (a pale-green package that when opened gave out a Shalimar-inspired scent) was a puerile tangent long in the making. Only a recluse with bankable mystique could have finessed such a skewered chorale of botanical babytalk. No one bought it, but no one was too piqued by the florid sidetrip. Nineteen eighty's *Hotter than July* was a bucket brigade of scrupulous Motown tunecraft that put a glossy finish on newly arrived pop forms—for instance, his ratification of reggae (inspired by Bob Marley) in "Master Blaster (Jammin')"—and erased all memory of Stevie's bald indiscretion. He then pressed on contritely in sanguine hits like "That Girl," "Do I Do," and "Ebony and Ivory," the last a duet with Paul McCartney.

His *Woman in Red* film soundtrack won sentimental hearts on the strength of his drum machine–driven serenade, "I Just Called to Say I Love You"—a No. 1 single in September 1984. "Part-Time Lover" from 1985's *In Square Circle* also topped the charts, but the cerebral leaps of his work in the 1970s were now undergoing linear reenactment. With the 1987 *Characters* album, his songs began stalling on *Billboard*'s black charts, his across-the-board impact waning as artists like Prince, Living Colour, De La Soul, A Tribe Called Quest, and Bobby Brown eclipsed him in terms of energy and invention.

By the sundown of the decade, the limits of Wonder's intuitive prowess were manifest: his signature songs are a voracious accumulation of contemporary instrumental leitmotifs, wedded to addled but affecting lyrics that are transporting when experienced, embarrassing when written out. Aptly—too aptly—there is scant emotion in his work save wonderment, few instincts beyond a sublime disavowal, no outlook firmer than anticipation—the blind bedazzling the blind. For the record, no singer has ever offered such uniform, unearthly escape to integrity.

Ingrid Thompson's* husband was in Portugal on account of business. Jim Morrison's wife was in France on account of her husband—he was unendurable. On November 19, 1970, Jim took a room at the Chateau Marmont Hotel, located just off the Sunset Strip in Los Angeles, and he and Ingrid began spending nights there.

November nights passed in the Chateau Marmont with Ingrid were largely devoid of moderation. One moonless evening, he brought home champagne and a film canister filled with cocaine; Jim and Ingrid devoured both in the space of three hours. Ingrid, tipsy, hoping the evening had not yet peaked for herself and the bloated, bearded singer of the Doors, began to ruminate about her layabout friends in Scandinavia. These friends, she said, occasionally drank blood. Jim perked up. He pressed Ingrid into finding a razor blade. She stabbed herself in the fleshy mound between her thumb and forefinger. He caught the blood in a champagne glass. They sipped at their plasma cocktail, had intercourse, and smeared the gore on their bodies.

The next morning, they awoke far too

*A pseudonym, granted by authors Jerry Hopkins and Danny Sugerman in their 1980 book, *No One Here Gets Out Alive,* to shield the woman's identity.

Jim Morrison

1984

sober to smirk at the sight: the sheets blotchy and musty-sour, the rust of death upon their pale skin.

In October 1970, the body of singer Janis Joplin had been found in a room at the Landmark Hotel in Hollywood, the red pinpoints on her arm fresh evidence of an accidental heroin overdose. Two months earlier, Jimi Hendrix had been asphyxiated by his own barbiturate-soaked spew. Morose and inebriated, Morrison had recently informed friends, "You're drinking with number three."

Jim Morrison was, a few days after a memorable Miami concert in March 1969, arrested and charged with committing a felony (lewd and lascivious behavior) and three misdemeanors (indecent exposure, open profanity, and drunkenness) while onstage. The court claimed that he "did lewdly and lasciviously expose his penis, place his hands upon his penis and shake it, and further the said defendant did simulate the acts of masturbation upon himself and oral copulation upon another." If there had been an encore or a curtain call, the bill of particulars failed to note them. It also lacked such footnotes as the twenty-odd paternity suits that were pending against Morrison.

In September 1970, a Miami jury acquitted Morrison of lewd behavior—the felony charge—and public drunkenness. However, they did convict him of profanity and public exposure. On October 30, Judge Murray Goodman sentenced Morrison to a total of eight months at hard labor, to be followed by twenty-eight months of probation, plus a $500 fine.

The case was in appeal when he met Ingrid. The case was pending when he joined wife Pamela Curson Morrison in Paris in 1971. The case was still undecided when he was found dead in a bathtub on July 3, 1971, from a heart seizure, at the age of twenty-seven. He was buried in secret by Pamela and some associates at Père Lachaise, the oldest cemetery in Paris, site of interment for Oscar Wilde, Frederic Chopin, and Edith Piaf. Pamela herself perished in Hollywood in April 1974 owing to a heroin overdose.

The Doors were formed in 1965 by keyboardist Ray Manzarek and Jim Morrison, both of whom had attended the UCLA Graduate School of Film. They got the idea of starting a band while on the beach in Venice, California; Jim would write the songs, Ray would set them to music. Manzarek's brothers pitched in on guitars until drummer John Densmore and guitarist Robby Krieger, formerly with the Psychedelic Rangers, joined the group. Morrison christened them the Doors, courtesy Aldous Huxley's William Blake–derived book on mescaline, *The Doors of Perception.* Their intentions were quasi-profound, but their music was fairly pedestrian, and the bulk of Morrison's opaquely platitudinous lyrics was chuckleheaded word spinning.

During Jim's life, the Doors made eight LPs for Elektra Records, a company that had capitalized on the folk-pop boom of the early 1960s. The best albums were the first, *The Doors*—which was released in 1967 and which contained the No. 1 hit "Light My Fire"—*Strange Days*—which yielded "People Are Strange," a Top 20 success—and the last, *L.A. Woman*—which contained the Top 20 songs "Love Her Madly" and "Riders on the Storm."

James Douglas Morrison, son of Clara Clarke Morrison and her husband, Steve, a career naval pilot, was born on December 8, 1943, in Melbourne, Florida. The family moved often. After graduating from George Washington High School in Alexandria, Virginia, and spending a year at St. Petersburg College in Florida, Jim slipped off into his own discrete trajectory. By 1965, he was a listless maunderer who had read enough reasonably cerebral literature to describe his depressions, written enough halfhearted suicide notes to call himself a poet, and grown tired enough of his poems to want a rock band to put them to rest. Saturnalia, incestuous rape, and other debauched sensualisms were the working themes, but they were the narcissistic fantasies of an imaginary sybarite. Morrison himself was not overly particular about his pleasures, his pastimes, his surroundings.

Why the bathtub? Because it was there.

Something in him longed for the new romantics, for their fashion sense, their renegade style, their club lust, their dance fever, their natty nonvalues, their *outré* experiments in scene making, their shedding of conscience—and then of consciousness. He'd been around the bend at least twice before, leading a group called the High Numbers in the Shepherd's Bush section of London during the heyday of the mods; dressing up in mohair, madras, stovepipe slacks, two-tone chisel-toed shoes; popping amphetamines; and becoming, in famed manager Peter Meaden's vision, "the lean, trig, and untamed vanguard of the Mod movement."

In 1965, the Who (the former High Numbers) released "My Generation," whose stuttering narrator was the apotheosis of the dapper mod brat, braying, "Hope I die before I get old." The singer was Roger Daltrey, he with the blond bouffant and circus-stripe trousers, but the writer was Pete Townshend.

The Who went on to reap the sunny, acid-stoked spoils of being hard rockers in the harried days of the late 1960s and early 1970s, when it was de rigueur to thrust guitars into amplifiers, reduce drum kits to pearly splinters, back limousines into swimming pools, heave color TVs out of hotel windows, and then in-

Pete Townshend

1989

vite underage groupies up to the executive suite to watch you scrawl bad verse on the walls.

At thirty-six, Townshend was getting a bit too stiff in the knees and long in the tooth to be dallying with Steve Strange and other New Romantic movers at the Club for Heroes. But then the central message of "My Generation" had been a deeply held philosophy of his, a plea for justice, actually, and in the two decades since, he'd never admitted to himself that he hadn't given up on the "live fast, die young, leave a good-looking, mohair-swaddled corpse" ethic. It was as dear to him as rock and roll itself.

Born Peter Dennis Blandford Townshend on May 19, 1945, to Cliff Townshend and his wife, the former Betty Dennis, he grew up, along with younger brothers Paul and Simon, in a Shepherd's Bush household where frying pans were always airborne and crockery forever being smashed. His parents had never been able to get along, and their rows were outlandishly destructive. Peter's grotesque homelife was in synch with his own self-image. A long-faced boy with a trowel-sized nose and small, deep-set eyes, he thought he looked like a carnival freak. At the age of twelve, his grandmother gave him an inexpensive Spanish guitar. The guitar gave way to a banjo, and Peter was quickly drawn into the traditional jazz fad of the late 1950s. He joined a Dixieland band with trumpeter/schoolmate John Entwistle. Entwistle quit in 1960, taking up the bass guitar he'd been toying with since his early teens, and joined the Detours, a group led by guitarist-singer Roger Daltrey, also a Shepherd's Bush mate. When they lost their rhythm guitarist, Townshend was invited to fill the gap. They changed their name to the Who after seeing a band called the Detours on TV.

Publicist Peter Meaden and doorknob manufacturer Helmut Gorden began to manage the group, Meaden cajoling them (with much initial resistance from Townshend and Entwistle) into adopting the mod look and thus acquiring a guaranteed following. Meaden renamed them the High Numbers, drummer Doug Sandom was excused, and seventeen-year-old Keith Moon, an apprentice electrician formerly with a surf band called the Beach Combers, auditioned. More or less. What Moon did was talk himself onto the bandstand during a gig at the Royal Oldfield Hotel, bragging he could do better than the guy onstage. He sat down, demolished the drum set, and got the job.

A mods-angled single written by Meaden, "I'm the Face," was released by Fontana Records in 1964 with a sizable publicity campaign, but it was a miserable failure; hip mod listeners were aware that the melody was a direct rip-off of Slim Harpo's "Got Love If You Want It." The band took up with new managers, filmmakers Chris Stamp and Kit Lambert, and became the Who again. When Townshend inadvertently snapped the neck of his guitar one night while wielding it in a low-ceilinged club, he lost his temper and smashed it. Moon, always happy to play Betty Townshend to Peter's Cliff, leveled another drum set. Lambert noted the frenzied response from the audience and made the destruction sequence the standard sign-off at all Who concerts.

The Who were signed to Decca and cut a Townshend song, "I Can't Explain," in 1965, the group taking off after Peter pulverized his guitar with sledgehammer grace. Their cocky, cacophonous sound, peppered with Moon's reverberant drumming, Townshend's loud, slashing, chord-based lead guitar (a technique originally devised to conceal his technical limitations), and Daltrey's scrappy vocals—Entwistle stood stone-still—made them a top act in the United Kingdom. "Happy Jack," from their 1966 *A Quick One* LP, broke into the Top 30; but it wasn't until an appearance at the Monterey Pop Festival in 1967 and a spot on the Smothers Brothers' television program that they had any lasting impact in America.

The Who Sell Out, a concept album built around an antic radio broadcast, did well in the United States in 1967, and the single "I Can See for Miles" went Top 10. *Magic Bus,* a sampling of singles and obscure sides, was released in 1968 to a tepid reception, but 1969 brought *Tommy,* the ninety-minute rock opera about a dictatorial deaf, dumb, and blind "pinball wizard" that became one of the most acclaimed records since the Beatles' *Sgt. Pepper's Lonely Hearts Club Band.* Various stage productions of the album were mounted, and director Ken Russell directed an atrocious film version in 1975. Daltrey, Moon, Tina Turner, Elton John, and Eric Clapton all took part.

Live at Leeds, one of the finest arena-sized live albums ever recorded, appeared in 1970. *Who's Next,* a sagacious synthesizer-woven studio experiment, ruled FM for the entirety of 1971. Prodigious tracks such as "Won't Get Fooled Again" and "Baba O'Reilly" received enormous airplay and helped to make the record a multimillion-seller. Townshend had become a disciple of Indian spiritual master Meher Baba, temporarily renouncing drugs and alcohol and dedicating a solo LP, *Who Came First,* to his guru in 1972.

Nineteen seventy-three's *Quadrophenia,* Townshend's second rock opera, explored the bleak underside of the adolescent mod ethos, its creator looking back in anger and bewilderment. After its release, the Who began to lose the thread of its battered mission. Members turned out spotty solo albums; group projects in the late 1970s and early 1980s on the MCA and Warner Bros. labels *(The Who by Numbers, Who Are You, Face Dances, It's Hard)* largely lacked fire, and the band's leader and chief songwriter was in shaky shape. Only *Rough Mix,* a 1977 collaboration with Ronnie Lane, and *Empty Glass,* a searing 1980 solo album that scrutinized Townshend's tendency toward personal excess as well as the collapsed punk movement, satisfied.

Fans first got wind of the fact that Townshend was bent on getting terminally blotto when, in the spring of 1981, the guitarist fell asleep onstage while performing solo during the first night of the Secret Policeman's Ball, a series of concerts to benefit Amnesty International. After roaring through "Pinball Wizard" and "Drowned," spraying the crowd with a magnificent barrage of fat riffs as he attacked his ax with his trademark windmill motion, he went to his dressing room to await the finale. A bottle of brandy was sent up to keep him company. By the time the call came to return, he was a bit bleary, sallied onstage, and nodded out with his Gibson acoustic cradled in his arms. It was a very short snooze, but people had come to expect a bit more than a public nap from rock's most athletically agitated guitarist.

What the faithful weren't aware of was that Townshend was well into what had been a more than year-long binge, having all but abandoned his family (wife Karen, daughters Emma, thirteen, and Minta, eleven) for the bottle, the nightlife, cocaine, and freebase laced with heroin.

Townshend had reason to want to draw the curtain on himself. Over $1 million in debt with no clear-cut route out, he'd found it almost impossible to write and compose. His band was falling apart and was soon to do a farewell tour. In terms of aging gracefully, the Who family had not been faring very well as of late. In August 1978, old standard bearer Pete Meaden committed suicide by drug overdose. On September 7, 1978 (Buddy Holly's birthday), Keith Moon expired from an overdose of Heminevrin. In April 1981, Kit Lambert died from a fall down the stairs at his mother's house.

In the clutches of a canyon-sized depression but desperate to pull out of it, Townshend took himself to an alcoholism clinic for help. Ativan was perscribed. Ativan is a tranquilizer. Combined with alcohol and coke, its punch is devastating, and Townshend, an alcoholic, became hooked on it. Those knowledgeable about such things maintain that Ativan is more ensnaring than smack. Shortly afterward, he was rushed to the hospital after overdosing on freebase and heroin with Ativan thrown in for good measure.

Early in 1982, Townshend flew to San Diego, California, to get the same electro-acupuncture treatment that had delivered Eric Clapton from heroin addiction. As he cleaned up, he resolved to save his marriage, decided to fold the Who (with Kenney Jones replacing Moon) after one fine-edged last hurrah, and discovered, to his astonishment, that he no longer wanted to die.

The day he was released from the San Diego clinic, he went for a walk on the beach and found a little bottle of white powder washed up on the shore. He uncapped it, licked a fingertip, poked it inside, and took a taste. It was cocaine of the highest quality—a lot of it—likely tossed overboard during some shore-patrol drug bust. He hesitated, his hand shaking, and then smashed it on the rocks at the water's edge. If the Devil can, he will fool with the best-laid plans of mice . . . and rock musicians.

The following thoughtful discussion took place in Chicago one July evening during a stopover on the Who's 1989 reunion tour. The lavish road show also coincided with the release of Townshend's *The Iron Man* solo LP, a musical parable about a mysterious metal giant. The album's story line was adapted from the 1968 children's book by British poet laureate Ted Hughes. (Children would be much on Townshend's mind throughout '89, his wife giving birth to their first son in November.) At one point Townshend pointed out that the book was published the same year he began work on another children's allegory set to rock and roll, *Tommy.*

Pete Townshend, bearded, disheveled, and nursing a nagging cold virus, sipped Perrier, listened intently to each question, often hesitated before answering, and then cut loose with a candor he later said had startled even him.

As a songwriter or a singer, even when you've engaged in storytelling, there's always been a directness to your songs and vocals that tran-

scended mere performance. They seemed more visceral than that. Would you agree?

Well, we can argue about what we think the modern song is *for.* I can just tell you what I've used it for: I've certainly used it to pursue innovation and originality. I've tried to use songs to seduce, to make people long for me, to keep people away, to threaten people, to define my territory, to talk about my fears. But also to turn people toward God, and to give people hope who haven't got any hope, especially people who might feel inadequate because of the way they look—because they're too fat or too thin or whatever. So some of the things I've used songs for are very, very good, and some of them are very selfish.

In the sixties, the purpose of songs changed. The kinds of songs that my parents used to listen to were about relationships, true love, conviction, romance, nostalgia, sentimentality, good wholesome sex, kissing full on the lips. What our generation doesn't seem to be able to put up with are singers singing others' songs. We want the *writers* to sing the songs. A song is a message, a song is a letter, nothing more, nothing less.

I think I've also tried to raise people's consciousness about what's really happening in the world, and what's *been* happening in the world since the last world war, which has been my preoccupation. And a lot of the anger which is currently in rock is *my* anger.

It's a very crude thing, music. Look at the two crappy little things that most of us have in our hi-fi systems to make it work: two bits of black cardboard connected to a magnet with a couple bits of wire. It may be crude, but look at the emotions it can produce!

The story of The Iron Man *is essentially one of living creatures at odds with each other out of fear and miscomprehension.*

What I liked about *The Iron Man* story and what fired me up is it reminded me of my life, and I'd been writing about my life for years with great success [*laughs*], and obviously touching the spot with a lot of people who feel the same way as I do about their lives. So I thought I'd take that pathway again.

I'd wondered if, from your own experience, there was a post-World War II sensibility woven through The Iron Man *and* Tommy, *since you were born ten days after the Nazis surrendered in 1945.*

Yeah, definitely. The war didn't stop for me because my father was in a Royal Air Force orchestra called the Squadronaires, and my mother was a singer in an R.A.F. orchestra called the Sydney Torch Orchestra. They met and got married, and the war went on as far as they were concerned. They stayed in uniform until I was five years old. And music to me was about the Air Force, and about men in uniform. There was definitely a function to my father's musical life, which was to pretend that there was no tragedy—to play romantic music for people who were separated from their loved ones, or who had actually lost loved ones in battle. So music for me has always been a lot more than just entertainment.

In my family I remember the day that my father handed over to me the function that he felt he had been carrying out up until the sixties. He said, "Things have changed, Pete, and now it's your turn."

What were the circumstances?

Those circumstances were that I was just into art school at sixteen years old, and I was making about £30 a week with the band, playing American officers men's clubs in London. We used to play one in particular called Douglas House, which was a U.S.A.F. club, and they would have country music bands come to visit. But because of my parents' connections we got this date, and eventually the band we replaced was my father's band!

It's interesting to me because I loved the music that my parents played. I loved that Big Band stuff, and the writing of Cole Porter and Gershwin, and the lyrics of Johnny Mercer. And I still love the craftsmanship. It's just that it was inadequate.

Some people believe rock and roll was caused by World War II, that it was a reaction to Hiroshima, the Holocaust, and a host of other previously unthinkable nightmares. There had to be a lively art form that could answer back, saying people are still a force more powerful than the bomb.

That's a very real possibility. Certainly I ascribe to that directly. As a form of communication, music *had* to change because of that war.

The interesting thing is that Europe had a machinery for dealing with cranky people that worked well up until Hitler: it used to ignore them, and the lunatics would usually go away.

I said something to a friend the other day, quite unwittingly, and I think it may be one of the most controversial things I've said. I said I think Adolf Hitler discovered rock and roll. I mean he was the guy who started with the kids in the street. He went straight past the parents; he went straight past the people who had imagined grievances about Jewish traders and Jewish bankers and Jewish moneylenders.

How would a fifteen- or sixteen-year-old have a feeling about a Jewish family? He probably doesn't give a shit; he doesn't hate Jewish people. He probably wants to fuck all their daughters. It's his father and grandfather who were wondering why the Jewish people weren't suffering as they were through the German depression. And that was because the Jewish people were gypsies originally, they were travelers, because they'd never had a country of their own, and so they carried their wealth in collateral—in gold or diamonds. They didn't use money. So they weren't affected by currency being devalued.

Hitler knew how disillusioned the kids in the streets were with their parents. The kids were looking at their parents and seeing befuddled defeat. So Hitler tricked them with a monstrous scenario, and backed it up with rock and roll–style rallies.

Right! And it all happened on the streets.

People are often sent on rampages because of thwarted emotions, the public being diverted from its pure motives by a perverted leader. An argument could be made that most of the evil in the world comes out of thwarted emotion.

I think that's absolutely true. We even see it now with the ecology, people being told they can't live without food that isn't wrapped in sixteen layers of manufactured plastic. People look to the people at the top, and the people at the top universally are assholes.

We're all thwarted—we're thwarted by the fact that we don't want to not have something that somebody else has got. Live Aid makes us feel a bit more comfortable to slightly relieve the discomfort of a nation in famine. But really the only way we can make them much more comfortable is by enduring a much higher level of discomfort ourselves. And we're not willing to do that. *I'm* not willing to do that. And I think that is evil.

Gestures are important, but it takes a dynamic group goal of a much larger order to change things—meaning government—which, by the way, should exist only to serve people. But people need to present an agenda. In the song "Dig" on The Iron Man, *scared farmers are saying "We old ones have seen two wars"—meaning they've lived through horror and don't want to live through it again. These people are very frightened of the Iron Man. They want to dig a hole, trap this big guy, and end what they think is a reign of terror. The little boy, Hogarth, he expresses his emotion about the situation in a much more direct and original way.*

What you actually have from Hogarth is probably the only true response—which is curiosity.

What sort of philosophical mood were you trying to convey with "Dig"?

The idea that working hard will save us. That we can dig our way out of this, that we can dig trenches, we can dig down, we can find treasure; there's more oil down there, more coal; we just have to dig! [*chuckles*] And it's *futile!* But there's a "Bless-their-little-cotton-socks" kind of feeling about it. These are the old folks, this is the way they do things.

But digging a hole in the ground is actually not going to solve their problems.

You've got a song on The Iron Man *called "A Friend Is a Friend." Speaking through the eyes of the young boy Hogarth, how would you describe friendship to someone who's never experienced it?*

Your ideas about friendship are formed when you're very young, and I don't think you make friends when you're very young. Because when you're between the age of three—when you first become conscious of other children—and eleven or twelve, I don't think you have friends then. You don't have friends 'cause you don't need friends; you're just . . . cool. At that age you just stay away from people you don't like. If you're suspicious of anybody, you ostracize them. And if you can, you hang them on a hook.

So as a child you spend time with similar people, you don't pretend to be anything you're not, you don't try to change the world, you just groove along. But nonetheless, despicable creatures that we are when we're children—absolutely hateful, spiteful, nasty and bloody-minded—we *still* think that the friendships we make when we were children are the kinds of friendships that we must have when we become adults! We think we've got to come from the same street, or live next door to one another, and whenever you knock on my door and ask for a dollar I give you one and vice versa.

I don't think that's what friendship is about. I think friendship is something which is proved. It's proved by what you do. It's proved by what other people do to you.

It's a crucible, a test.

Yeah! It's a process.

What is Hogarth learning about friendship, perhaps for the first time, after the farmers have dug this pit and this big but harmless metal man has fallen in?

Well, I wrote the song from the point of view of a boy who has suddenly realized that he's making his own world, that he's writing his own future. He looks into the eyes of the Iron Man in the pit as they start to throw earth over him, and Hogarth realizes that *he* wasn't afraid of the Iron Man, but he has helped trap him and he has to share the responsibility. This moment leads him to a questioning of the most important of all human ideas, which is the responsibility of a friend to a friend. And he also realizes at that moment that he is the Iron Man's friend, and probably his only friend.

Let's focus on a juncture of personal self-realization, the point you began to make records solely for yourself, beginning in 1972 with Who Came First. *That album you did with various guest musicians was a big stylistic departure from the Who. The songs were more intimate and offhanded.*

I think of one song in particular called "Sheraton Gibson." On it, you sang about a Cleveland afternoon during a Who tour much like this current one. In fact, you just arrived here from Cleveland. Do you recall anything about that bygone hotel setting?

The only thing I still know about it was that the hotel was called the Sheraton Gibson. I took as the song's model the *Self-Portrait* album that Bob Dylan had just done, on which he had recorded about twenty songs. I found that album very inspiring because a lot of that music wasn't very good, it was just Dylan's ramblings. Some of it was really quite *bad.* And I thought, "I wonder what would happen if I did that?" So I turned on the tape machine, and I sang about twenty songs, with my Gibson acoustic guitar, off the top of my head, making the words up as I went along.

And I can remember some of them now. One was called "Mister Tie-Dye," and it was about John Sebastian and the idea that dressing up in bright-colored clothes makes you [*smiling slyly*] *a nice person.* Another song was called "Classified," about the classified papers, and another was "Sheraton Gibson." I just made them up as I was going along. I never corrected the lyrics or anything. And then I played them back and they were all great! [*laughter*] They were all weird songs, but they were all really good.

Your next solo move was Rough Mix, *an album you did in 1977 with ex-Faces bassist Ronnie Lane.*

When I worked with Ronnie what was actually happening was that, I suppose, I was filling in time. I didn't feel that the record was going to be that significant. Ronnie nagged me to do it. He was very hard up, he was my best friend at the time, and I really respected him for leaving the Faces. Although there was a bit of a guilt trip going on, because when Ronnie Wood had asked me whether he should stay in the Faces or go on and join the Stones, I said, "Are you kidding? Join the Stones!" So I think I may have been worried about what might happen to Ronnie Lane as a result of that.

I didn't go into that album all that willingly, and I didn't really enjoy making it very much, and I'm always amazed at what a nice record it turned out to be. What Ronnie was hoping was that we would write together. I'd always said that I couldn't write with anybody. I still find it very, very difficult even to contemplate. And it was in that session that I realized Ronnie wasn't well. He could sing okay, but he couldn't play the bass.

I got angry with him about halfway through the session because I just thought he was a drunk, just a drunken pig. I mean, I don't know why I was being such a hypocrite—I used to drink far more than he did. But he was falling all over the place, and I got angry with him in the hallway and I pushed him—I punched his right shoulder to emphasize a point—and he went flying down the hall.

It was then that I realized he was sick. And it was only a couple years later that it emerged that he had multiple sclerosis.

Yet with this record, and bullying me into doing it on the basis of, "Pete, if you don't help me I'll starve to death," he very, very cleverly got me to really start my solo career. [*laughter*]

Some of the strongest songs on Rough Mix *are the most informal. "Keep Me Turning" seems to be this nice carefree love ballad about backstage passes, but there's a catch there.*

I suppose I was going through an early midlife crisis. I was married and I was happy, but I was writing lots of songs about girls! And "Keep Me Turning" was about this idea of: keep me young, don't tell me this is all there is, don't tell me I've got to stop now, don't tell me I can't ever be infatuated with somebody; just allow me to go on doing what I'm doing 'cause I like it.

There's a line in the song where I say, "I want to hand in my backstage pass." I wanted the ritual to end but the real thing to continue.

Empty Glass *in 1980 was your first official solo record. It represented a new development because fans of the Who hadn't yet heard many lead vocals from you. Were you self-conscious at all about stepping out of your image as bandleader for the Who and becoming Pete Townshend solo singer?*

I still find it very difficult. I still find that the song is so connected to the face. That's sad, because I think the voice is so much better than the face. [*laughter*] But, you know, I don't think I've ever written a love song. No, I don't think I have. I wouldn't know quite how to go about it. I've written cynical songs about love. [*pauses, thinking*] But no, I've never written a proper love song. I mean, this is much to the regret of all the women in my life.

Sometimes when I've written songs and I've dedicated them to my wife or to some other woman that I hold in high regard, they're always very disappointed: "What's *this?*"

It really comes down to how you feel about love. Maybe friendship is more important to me than love. Love is like a longing, an energy. It's like magnetism, it's like gravity. And at its highest it's about spiritual salvation.

Do you see "Let My Love Open the Door" as a love song?

No [*laughter*], it's about spiritual redemption, really. I think "Let My Love Open the Door" is a song that would fit very well in some decent, wholesome Christian programming. I said to a born-again Christian the other day, "You know, I wanna hear my stuff on Christian radio." Most of my songs are about Jesus. Most of my songs are about the idea that there *is* salvation, and that there is a Savior. But I won't mention his name in a song just to get a cheap play.

Incidentally, what made you decide, from Empty Glass *onward, to make solo albums a priority?*

What I decided to do after the 1979 *Who Are You* album—since Keith Moon had died the previous year—was perhaps take the opportunity to leave the Who completely. Most people thought I shouldn't do that, that the Who was more my property than anyone else's, with a lot of my heritage there; and although John and Roger were very important, it was really my decision and they would have to abide by that. At the same time, people were also saying that this was my opportunity to develop as a solo artist: "*Pete, you can have it all.*"

Basically, I think I made the wrong decision—I decided to make Who records and solo records alternatively. What I was gonna do was take whatever songs were available after Who albums and use them. "Empty Glass" was a song that we did with the Who for *Who Are You,* and which didn't work with them.

Was "Rough Boys" written for the Who?

No, no. How could "Rough Boys" be written for the Who? It's about homosexuality.

The party line has been that the song was triggered by Jimmy Pursey of Sham '69, the punk band, after he'd put the Who down in public.

No. What, in a sense, "Rough Boys" was about was almost a coming-out, an acknowledgment of the fact that I'd had a gay life, and that I understood what gay sex was about: it was not about faggery at all. It was about violence in a lot of senses. It leans very heavily into the kind of violence that men carry in them.

If men have a violence which cannot be shared with women, then it can't be shared with them sexually. And so there's only one place for that violence and that's with other men. A lot of adolescent displays are not for other girls, they're for other men. You wear leather jackets, you wear tight jeans, you learn how to stand on the street, you get involved in fights, you hit somebody over the head with a bottle. You know that women aren't going to be impressed with that stuff, so who are you doing it for? And why are you doing it? [*voice rising*] And why are they such *sexual* things? Why are they such sexual messages?

So in a way it was like me saying, "Listen, one of the first things I'm gonna do, in the first track that you're gonna hear from Pete Townshend as a solo artist, is say, 'I *know* what's happening, and I am not that kind of macho rock star.' " It was really important to me because 80 percent of the Who's audience was men.

I wrote another song about homosexuality for that album called "And I Moved." Which I wrote for Bette Midler to sing. She said, "Somebody's gotta write me a song for a real woman," and I said something like, "The way to write a song for a real woman is to write a song for a real man [*laughter*], and you can sing it!"

One of the things that stunned me when *Empty Glass* came out was that I realized I'd found a female audience, just by being honest. Not necessarily by saying, "I am gay, I am gay, I am gay." But just by being honest about the fact that I understand how gay people feel, and I identify. And I know how it feels to be a woman. I know how it feels to be a woman because I *am* a woman. And I won't be classified as just a man.

To an extent the gay lobby infuriates me sometimes. With *Empty Glass* I got lots of letters from gays who said, "Good on you, Pete, for coming out." And I would write back and say, "No, I *haven't* come out."

And then I realized maybe that was just pride. That in a way it was a coming-out. That it was a real acknowledgment of the fact that I'd been surrounded by people that I really adored—and was actually sexually attracted to—who were men. And that the side of me that responded to those people was a passive side, a subordinate side.

I think to be a complete artist that you've got to have that. So I think that anybody who's a complete artist has got it, and if they say they haven't they're denying it.

You've done so many concept albums and theme projects, like Tommy, Quadrophenia, *and now* The Iron Man, *which you hope to eventually make a stage musical. Songs like "Behind Blue Eyes," which appeared on* Who's Next *and then your own* Scoop *album, were originally part of an unfulfilled project circa 1971 called* Lifehouse. *Basically, the story line of* Lifehouse *concerned a deeply troubled future world in which rock and roll was forbidden. Where did* Lifehouse *go wrong?*

Where *Lifehouse* went wrong was that it was a theatrical work. We were supposed to be doing it in workshop with the Young Vic, which was an experimental theater attached to the Old Vic in London. What we did was we took over the theater, and I wrote a number of songs and a rough story. And the idea was to perform the songs over a period of weeks. We were gonna have an open-door policy for two weeks. The band was gonna do this long, long concert with the doors open all the time. And in fact we did a three-day concert there, and we kept the doors open for three days. The only people that came [*chuckling*] were a load of little runts who just heckled throughout the show, and asked us to play whatever was at the top of the charts at the time.

But the *Lifehouse* story line was actually very simple. It was about the misuse of entertainment power, and that the only art that tells the truth is music. There're some good songs that came out of that idea.

"Behind Blue Eyes" is not a song about me. It was written to try to show how lonely it is for the powerful. Sometimes I write very effectively when I write about things *other* people feel. I mean, I've got blue eyes and so has Roger Daltrey, but I've never felt that [*quoting from the song*] "love was vengeance." It's remarkable how many people just identify with that song from a personal point of view: how everybody feels that they're driven to deceit in order to feel love, so that love will always be like vengeance, will always be painful for the recipient. Quite interesting.

In 1985, you put out the White City *album, whose title referred to a racially integrated housing development in England. The Who had broken up, and your new creative life was reflected in the record's theme.*

[*Nodding*] *White City* was about what had actually happened. I had left the band and I'd left show business, so I was dealing with another life, and I was looking at the rock and roll venues of my adolescent roots with completely different eyes. Some of those venues were in White City, Shepherd's Bush, Goldhawk Road, that whole area.

The main message of *White City* was that wherever you stand, and wherever you look, you can always see evil somewhere. Practically all of the young black social workers I met at White City were obsessed with apartheid and South Africa.

There's a track on White City *called "Hiding Out" that has an Afro-pop feel to it.*

At one time I was pursuing that quite positively. I was going to do the whole album that way.

How did you come to write that particular song?

I read this account in a South African newspaper about a "necklace burning." They'd put a rubber tire around your neck and set light to it. It was something that blacks tended to do with blacks.

Obviously a horrible torture of some kind.

Yes. And the song was about trying to find some kind of beauty in hiding, some kind of peace in being imprisoned. Because the South African community is really in prison, and they really do believe they've got no hope. You look at somebody like Nelson Mandela—he's still in jail and has been for a long, long time. That's his life.

So he's obviously one of those people who's had to try to find something good in what is essentially an awful set of circumstances. I think that, in a way, that's what I felt when I personally went back to White City. I suddenly felt, "Well, life isn't that bad." And *they'd* actually found that. They'd found a way to live. I remember the anger and frustration in that kind of housing estate when I was a young man.

By the way, when you listen to that song, see if you can guess what song I used as a model for the lyric. "The Sounds of Silence" was the model!

Speaking of those old days as well as enduring music influences from the period, you've got a song on The Iron Man *called "Fire," which was a 1968 hit by The Crazy World of Arthur Brown. And it's interesting because you were the executive producer of Brown's original song.*

Right! I worked it up with Arthur. I've got a couple of versions on tape in which I played the guitar! Our managers and the band put a record label together in Britain called Track. I suppose our most famous artist was Jimi Hendrix. We signed him before he even came to America.

At the point the label was first created, I immediately started to work with Arthur Brown, and I was going for a No. 1 hit [*it reached No. 2*]. It felt appropriate to use "Fire" again because I felt so close to the old song.

My last question concerns "All Shall Be Well," the finale of The Iron Man. *It sounds so uplifting. But is this song a case of Pete Townshend being spiritual, loving, cynical, or none of the above?*

[*Smiling*] What's interesting about "All Shall Be Well" is that it bridges the last five or six years of my life. It's based on a phrase from Mother Julian of Norwich—an English nun who was canonized—in which she said: "All shall be well, and all shall be well, and all manner of things shall be well." I was just deeply struck by that, and felt it was a great dictum for living.

What's important about doing good in life is *detail.* God looks after the big stuff—or Nature does, if you're not religious. Nature can look after Niagara Falls, the Antarctic, and Space. What we can look after are tiny details.

It *is* important to call your mom—it *is* important. It *is* important to tidy your room. It is important to make sure you don't have too many drinks and kill somebody on the way home, or even scrape somebody's car. It's those little details that we have control of.

So the song is about *that* kind of fire because, in life, the right thing leads to the right results, and the wrong thing leads to the wrong results.

Steve Winwood

1982/89

It is a sentimental journey under a shifting midsummer sky, the gray and yellow quilts of clouds that hover above the English countryside showing neither approval nor disapproval; properly they evince a benign, atmospheric British frown. Driving expectantly through Berkshire, briefly cruising along parallel with the bright red pleasure barges slipping down the narrow upper reaches of the ancient Thames, the car is throttled past the riverside hideaway in Pangbourne where a certain Jimmy Page once lived (three doors down from the local pub) during the early seventies. Swinging onto the winding two-lane thoroughfare leading into the village of Wallingford, the roadside attractions along the route evolve in a gentle blur from unassuming dry good stores and vegetable stalls to genteel shops selling fine riding apparel and outfittings for the hunt. Not too distant from here, of course, is Lambourne, home of the Queen's stables and paddocks, where her mounts are trained.

Bursting out of the town square, one finds oneself poised upon a sloping rise overlooking the breathstealing Berkshire downs, acre after prime acre of flowing farming, riding, and hunting lands stretched out in all directions. It's a sight to tranquilize the peasant's soul and to fire the poet's imagination. And the grand, sweeping patchwork with its undulating emerald and gold waves of thriving wheat, potatoes, asparagus, and barleycorn—especially barleycorn—heralds the proximity of a humble repository of rock and roll mythology, the quaint cottage to which Jim Capaldi, Dave Mason, Chris Wood, and Steve Winwood retreated in 1967 to sow and harvest the first seeds of Traffic's musical legacy.

This is the land of "Berkshire Poppies" and "Coloured Rain," where heaven was ever in the lads' sometimes hash- and acid-addled minds, as they tripped down to a pub in tiny Aston-Tirrold called the Boot to shoot the breeze about Mr. Fantasy, the Pearly Queen, 40,000 headmen, and fellows with no face, no name, and no number.

"It was some house, some era," Capaldi recalls fondly. "The rented cottage was our permanent address for two years, and then it became a jam center for us and all our heavyweight space cadet companions, like Denny Laine and Ginger Baker. We always had a running battle going with the gameskeeper. He looked after the property for the laird, William Pigott Brown, a friend of Chris Blackwell, the head of our label, Island bloody Records! The gameskeeper used to put big sticks with nails stuck in them across the roads to foil our jeeps and keep us off the damned property!

"Some heavy numbers went down there, for sure; a friend on acid flying off the roof of a minivan as it headed down the driveway into the path of William Pigott Brown, the poor tripper waking up the next day in the hospital with a broken collarbone; the band recording hundreds of tapes outdoors, many of them filled with birds tweeting wildly in the background so you could scarcely hear what the devil we'd been aiming for; tough Teddy Boy gangs coming 'round occasionally to break in; Joe Cocker & the Grease Band taking over the cottage down by the last bend, joining in the festivities as only they could. Indeed, quite an era."

It's not much farther now, just past the fork that leads either to Aston-Tirrold, or to the small bustling grainery beyond which sequats the gameskeeper's house, a scarecrow with a white tin pail for a head swaying in his garden. Up the tire-rutted chalk road, and there, in the center of a copse of hazelnut and pine trees, is a two-story wisteria-draped white brick dwelling with a slate roof and squat red chimney, the song-immortalized "House for Everyone."

"Listen, I'm not claiming everything we wrote and recorded

back in that time was fabulous," says Capaldi. "Many things backfired or we were off the mark. But I sometimes look back and feel that we were an experimental group that went out into the natural wilds just to sort of hammer it all out. Back then, all the rock music was anchored to the city life. The fact that the four of us—all country boys from the Midlands to begin with—went back out to the country to abandon the urban distractions and get into the music set a definite trend."

Two decades onward, Steve Winwood is once more the stalking horse for a stylistic tendency in rock, one that likewise entails geographic as well as musical shifts. Before his head was turned by Berkshire poppies, his roots had been in the hearty pragmatism of American rhythm and blues. And although he and cohort Jim Capaldi still revisit an outpost in Gloucestershire to renew artistic ties with the British countryside, Steve's heart, mind, and music have all recently succumbed to an Atlantic crossing.

"I really love Americans and American musical roots," Steve Winwood offers. "It could be my British need for discipline that makes me admire the American appetite for freedom and passion. I've always been fascinated with the possibilities of drawing all these Southern, Detroit, Caribbean, and African grooves together, along with what some people hear as a 'Church of England' thing in my keyboards. I don't argue that it isn't spiritual-sounding. I'm a former choirboy, after all, and I've played Sunday organ at this church in Gloucestershire. I think my music remains more individual than my influences, but I have to confess"—he pauses for another swallow of sandwich in a London café—"that, in fact, I based the original Traffic on Jr. Walker's All-Stars!"

In light of the homage Winwood pays Walker on the title track of *Roll with It,* his latest LP, the admission surely seems apt, but perhaps a tad exaggerated?

"No! No! Think about it: The original lineup of the All-Stars was sax, organ, guitar, and drums, with no bass—and that was the Traffic concept, although it did get modified over time. Vocally, I've definitely been influenced by the great saxophonists, and Jr. Walker is certainly one of those. I'm a huge fan, and I'll go anywhere to catch a performance. I'll never forget the last time I saw him at the Lone Star Cafe in New York City."

He was ripping it up, eh?

"Jr.? Of course—but so was I. This was the night I met my wife, Eugenia! She was there with some friends, and me, with mine, and

I started chatting with her at a table! Yes, it's a wonderful little bar, and Jr. serenaded us!"

His marriage on January 17, 1987, to Tennessee-bred Eugenia Crafton has clearly furthered Winwood's Americanization. These days Steve and Jeannie divide their time between a farm south of Nashville and a manor house in Gloucestershire, England. *Back in the High Life* (1986), the greatest hits album *Chronicles* (1987), and the new *Roll with It* all reflect the growing contentment of Steve Winwood. Coming to America seems to have been a wise move. "Oh, absolutely," he says. "Though I'll always keep our house in England. But there's something about the mix of everything in the States that really grabs me. And, of course, Genia grabbed me, too."

So Jr. Walker practically introduced him to his wife. Who introduced Jr. Walker to Winwood?

"The first person who ever played me any Jr. Walker was Brian Jones of the Rolling Stones. When the Spencer Davis Group toured with the Stones in the beginning, I stayed 'round Brian's place in London and we got on great, playing records and talking music for hours. We'd also listen to Otis Redding, the Mar-Keys, all that great Memphis Stax-Volt stuff."

Did he consider settling in Memphis rather than the Nashville area? "Good question. My wife's family is from around Nashville, so that seemed most natural, but I wouldn't have minded being in Memphis at all. They're all just a stone's throw from each other, anyhow. Nashville sounds like light-years away from Muscle Shoals, but it's just a hundred miles down the road. And of course all the people from Muscle Shoals are still in and out of Nashville constantly, while a lot of the Memphis musicians are likewise regulars in Nashville.

"Sessions are the nicest way to make friends among Nashville musicians. I did one with Mike Lawler, a keyboard and synthesizer whiz who's worked with James Brown and the Allman Brothers, and another with Jo-El Sonnier, the great Cajun zydeco accordionist. I just loved how sociable these people are in the control room."

Has he ever considered hanging out a shingle in Music City, U.S.A.? "Oh, I have already! I rent a little office right on Music Row in Nashville, and I go in there with some keyboards, a drum machine, and a little four-track cassette recorder. I got quite a few ideas for the new album down there. The new album seems a definite continuation of the band sound of *Back in the High Life,* and it's also got that cross of Motown and Stax qualities, but I would argue that this combination, merged with my own Irish, Scottish, and Anglican church borrowings, dates well back to Traffic. Remember that on the 1973 *Shoot Out at the Fantasy Factory* album we had Roger Hawkins and David Hood in the band, and they're Southern fellows who are associated more with Muscle Shoals and the Memphis sound than anything else.

"But every time I say things about Southern music, people recoil and say, 'He's not gonna make Steve Winwood country and western albums!' " He shrugs his rail shoulders. "Fact is, wherever I do an album, it ends up sounding for better or worse like me, whether it's in Gloucestershire, New York, Jamaica, or—maybe someday—Nashville."

To spend five minutes with today's Steve Winwood is to see precisely where the boyish glee of vintage rock stardom has been preserved. Stephen Lawrence Winwood was born on May 12, 1948, in the sooty Handsworth sector of Birmingham, England, and grew up in the suburb of Kingstanding. While his father, Lawrence, toiled at Hall's Iron Foundry, young Stevie studied Elgar and Vaughan Williams in music classes at Great Barr Comprehensive School. During summers he hiked and camped in Cornwall and Devon with the 236th Perry Barr Boy Scout Troop and then performed with combos he and older brother Mervyn "Muff" Winwood organized in town. Victimized for his forbidden musical leanings, the classically trained Steve was first expelled from Great Barr Comprehensive (by headmaster Oswald Beynon), and then from the Birmingham and Midland Institute, for the sin of playing rock and roll.

Not only did his sax-playing father not punish him for these failings, but Mr. Winwood imparted a few worldly tips from his own experience as a moonlighting bandleader, telling his boy how he advertised his own combo as if it was two different outfits, one very expensive and snobbish, the other working-class and cheap. "One way or another," his son says, "they always got work. Pretty shrewd, I thought." Soon Stevie was off gigging in Midlands cabarets from Birmingham to Manchester, keen to absorb the entire musical gamut, from Garnet Mimms and the Enchanters to the fugues of modern German composer Paul Hindemith.

At forty, Winwood retains the same humility, zestfulness, and convoluted conversational zeal that charmed bandleader/Birmingham University instructor Spencer Davis back in 1963. Davis first spied the fourteen-year-old Ray Charles soundalike during an evening gig of the Muff Woody Jazz Band (headed by Steve's bassist brother) at Birmingham's Digbeth Civic Hall.

"He was playing piano, an Oscar Peterson–type thing," says Davis. "Then Steve got hold of a melodica like Ray Charles used to play and did a version of 'One Mint Julep.' You know when you hear something that gets down to the bottom of your spine, and you realize you're in the presence of something different? And I didn't hear him sing—he was just playing."

Steve and Muff promptly signed on with the Spencer Davis Rhythm and Blues Quartet, Steve at first restricting himself to guitar. It was an impromptu acquaintance with the house-owned Hammond B-3 at a Stoke-on-Trent club called the Place that moved Winwood to merge his clarion vocals with the rich attack of electronic keyboards. By 1964 the (newly abbreviated) Spencer Davis Group and its soul-belting teenage keyboardist had a No. 1 hit in the United Kingdom with Jamaican reggae songwriter Jackie Edwards's "Keep on Running," while the next two years saw the release of a pair of global Top 10 smashes, "Gimme Some Lovin' " and "I'm a Man."

"Lyrically, 'I'm a Man' was the brainchild of New York producer Jimmy Miller, who had a feeling for the American market," says Spencer Davis, "and Jimi Hendrix showed me the E-7th guitar chord on the track. Steve provided the rest of the American R&B edge with his marvelous vocals and keyboards, and it's funny, because the song had originally been intended for a 'Swinging London' film.

" 'Gimme Some Lovin' ' was also written with an American perspective. We used to rehearse at the Marquee Club in London, and Muff had a bass riff from an old record by Homer Banks [the prolific Stax songwriter] called 'Whole Lotta Lovin'.' I hadn't heard that song, but I thought the riff Muff was playing was fantastic. I added a G, A, and a C Minor to it, Steve played a Ravel's 'Bolero' kind of thing, and Steve said to me, 'Don't play major, play minors.'

"The English version was a stark, haunting thing, but the American version, which everybody knows best, had backing vocals. It was No. 2 in England and the only thing that kept it from No. 1 was 'Good Vibrations' by the Beach Boys. Steve and us had just the sound America craved! Pity the Spencer Davis Group never toured the States."

Steve Winwood was not yet eighteen when the Spencer Davis Group disbanded—a result of Steve's musical restlessness—and it would be another decade of splashy ensemble work with the Powerhouse, Traffic, Blind Faith, Ginger Baker's Airforce, and Go before Winwood got around to distinguishing himself on his own. Clues to Steve's current stateside allure as a solo performer seem woven into his band-to-band search for a cohesive career identity.

Winwood earned the accolade of "a mate's mate" from friends like Jim Capaldi, who admired his personal loyalty. Capaldi and Winwood's coauthorship of "Hearts on Fire" on *Roll with It* marks twenty-two unbroken years of fraternity.

Watching Capaldi and Winwood interact one Gloucestershire morning in 1982 while on a break from coproducing Jim's *Fierce Heart* LP, Steve reveled in his chum's lavishly deprecating Traffic anecdotes. Most centered on the group's pot-stoked folk-rock flights.

For all the good humor, however, Winwood firmly maintains that Traffic's bucolic merger of English folk idioms and American blues-rock was "a very conscious thing; we had a ball as people, but musically we were *not* merely mucking about."

"Steve has a gleam in his eye for anything he decides to participate in," says producer Russ Titelman, who shared a Record of the Year Grammy for *High Life*'s "Higher Love," "and he can communicate strength even when he's fearful, because he doesn't indulge his weak side."

If there is one qualm observers have with the New Steve Winwood, it's his controversial decision to license certain songs to sell Michelob beer. Winwood's outlook, akin to his "kill only what you'll consume" philosophy as a devotee of game sports: "I'm not offended by people endorsing a product they actually use in their daily lives." While many take issue with this dangerously simplistic perspective, crass commercialism being at least one American influence all compromised rockers will likely regret, Winwood has indeed been a regular imbiber of the suds he helps hawk. Excuse him or don't, but there is nothing half-baked about Steve Winwood, whose acute curiosity for life is leavened with a collegial composure worthy of Mr. Chips. "I'm a believer in natural law, in the sense of any strong religious outlook," he says, referring to the theory that ethical precepts are fundamental to human nature and discoverable by simple reason. "I was brought up with the belief that you take nothing for granted, that all good fortune is a gift. Sounds austere, eh? And perhaps it is a bit, but I respected my father for his will to balance the hard times with the happy ones. When things go badly, I try to bear up and go on, but it does affect me greatly. And I guess it shows up most in my music. In recent years I've written a lot of songs about death and loss.

"Let's take a track like 'Vacant Chair,' " a ghostly ballad from 1977's *Steve Winwood.* "That song always needed explaining. It's a song about death, and I wrote it with Viv Stanshall [of the Bonzo Dog Band], and it was a reaction to a wave of deaths of great British and West Indian jazz musicians that had gone on, like Graham Bond and Harold McNair. Graham had drug problems, and his body was found under a train. I was very affected by these deaths, and this was a way of coping with them. The African lyric in the chorus is a Yoruban chant which means, 'Only the dead weep for the dead.' "

At the time Winwood cut the song, many in the press had pegged him as another imminent music-biz casualty, never guessing that the gaunt, withdrawn pop star had actually been a long-suffering victim of peritonitis, an acute inflammation of the tissue covering the abdominal cavity. "I spent absolute *years* recovering, during which touring and the like were unthinkable."

Accustomed to spending considerable time on his own, Winwood installed a sophisticated home studio in the Gloucestershire house he shared with his first wife, Nicole (they were divorced in December 1986). His deft solitary composing resulted in both *Arc of a Diver* (1979) and *Talking Back to the Night* (1982), which contained a good deal of intensely reflective material.

" 'While You See a Chance' was the first song I wrote with Will Jennings, who's since been my chief lyricist. I met him through my publisher at the time, Island Music. I'd said I desperately wanted somebody to write songs with, and they said, 'Oh, there's this bloke. . . ." Jennings, a former English professor from east Texas, who's also penned sizable hits for Randy Crawford and the Crusaders ("Street Life") and Whitney Houston ("Didn't We Almost Have It All"), recalls that "when Steve played me the music that became the song 'While You See a Chance,' it was like looking right into his soul."

It was a soul so scarred by infirmity, career disappointments, and financial woes that he was seriously contemplating quitting rock and roll. "I thought, 'I'm just going to make a record, and then I shall settle up financially, and move, if necessary, to a small flat or join a gypsy caravan. I figured I'd continue doing some things that

I like doing and enjoy life as best I could in diminished circumstances."

That sad reckoning never arrived, however. Soon after the finished tape for "While You See a Chance" was delivered to his record company, the single shot into the Top 10 worldwide and transformed *Arc of a Diver* into a stunning fiscal windfall.

While freed from any further threats to his bank account, Winwood was still not immune to assaults on his spirit. Sick at heart as former Traffic mates Chris Wood and Reebop Kwaku Baah descended into narcotics-related demises, Steve retreated again to his home studio with a mind to create an entire album decrying the rock-and-drugs symbiosis.

"*Talking Back to the Night* was really an antidrug album, the whole thing, but not in a very obvious way," he now explains. "The title track started with a poem Will Jennings wrote on the subject, and it spread from there. 'Valerie,' for instance, isn't a song remembering this girl I was madly in love with. It's not that at all. It's a plea to a certain girl singer—someone I don't know personally but who Will Jennings had drawn my attention to—not to destroy herself with drugs. The narrator in the song is saying, 'I'm back, and I'm the same person I used to be—so why isn't she?' "

The irony of *Talking Back to the Night* was that fans felt that Winwood was indeed the same man he'd been on *Diver,* and they found his homemade sound distinctly stagnant.

"I'm sure you're right," Winwood concedes. "I believe there was a production failing on the record; it was *under*-produced. But I was lucky enough to go back and remix certain of those tracks with Tom Lord Alge for *Chronicles.* We put certain tweaks of production on 'Valerie' so it'd sound better on the radio."

Winwood spells out the obvious, cyclical challenge that was *Roll with It:* to craft a follow-up record consistent with his last high point. To this end, Will Jennings and Steve spent weeks in September 1987 sightseeing, pubhopping, and brainstorming over Steve's latest crop of Gloucestershire demo tapes. The album was recorded at McClear Place Studios in Toronto and U2's Windmill Lane in Dublin. Veteran Titelman was succeeded by notoriously efficient (though far less innovative) upstart Tom Lord Alge, the engineer on *High Life.* "He's a superb engineer," says Steve of Lord Alge, "not a slide-rule man, and he has a straightforward New Jersey attitude that kicks me in the pants."

Billy Joel, one of Winwood's best American buddies, has a

funny story about the kick *he* got meeting Steve. Not in 1985, when Winwood played on Joel's *The Bridge,* not in '83, when he visited sessions for *An Innocent Man*—but way back in 1967—when a very nervous Joel knocked on the door of Traffic's New York hotel room. Young Billy was anxiously combing his frizzled hair when Winwood opened the door. "Well, hello then!" said Winwood, throwing the door wide, disclosing the presence within of Traffic's Jim Capaldi and Chris Wood. "It is *Billy,* isn't it? So now, what would you like to interview us about?" "Oh no!" Joel corrected, "I'm not a journalist! I'm a keyboard player in a band, the Hassles. Here in America, we're on the United Artists label, same as you guys!"

"Steve remained the perfect gentleman, hardly concerned either way," says Joel with an affectionate grin, "and he was just content to talk music. He was amazed that the Hassles played 'Mr. Fantasy' in concert, and that we had also recorded 'Coloured Rain.'

"He just sat there, looking sorta thrilled and sorta shocked. '*STEVE, MAN,*' I said, 'we love you over here. Honest! You just gotta spend more time in the U.S.A.!"

Billy Joel wonders to this day if Winwood noticed how nervous he was at their initial meeting. "Actually," Winwood confesses sheepishly, "there is one small thing that comes back to me from that hotel get-together. Billy didn't expect me to answer the door, and Billy was combing his hair when I suddenly appeared. It startled him, and he says he left the comb in his hair for the whole time he was in our room talking!"

"Since he's one of my role models, it's been a thrill to see how much he's grown," says Joel. "I guess you might say Steve has returned and is having a larger effect than ever, but for me he was never gone. Like Keith Emerson with the Nice and Felix Cavaliere with the Rascals, Steve's style has been an immense influence on any kid who ever sat down at a keyboard. But especially Steve—who was as good at piano as he was at organ, and always featured both instruments on record. For my generation, it was considered sorta wimpy to have taken keyboard lessons until the Spencer Davis Group caught fire, and Traffic just confirmed the idea of the guy at the keys being a leader.

"After twenty-five years as a professional," Joel concludes, "any compliment floors Steve, any trace of recognition surprises him, and any little thing he can learn or discover is a source of delight. From him, you get a man's wisdom as well as a boy's love of fun."

Joel's words of affection and praise are conveyed to Winwood and Steve turns a deep crimson, literally hiding behind his lapel.

"Stop!" he pleads, "You're embarrassing me! Billy was even kind enough to invite me to go to Russia with him on his special trip, which I would have loved, but with my marriage and the new album and setting up home here and in the States, we've been tied up for quite a bit." Hesitant pause. "I've also managed a few non-musical accomplishments, you know."

Such as?

"Well, please don't make too much of this, but I've recently learned to swim while in America. I was born in Birmingham, in the core of the Midlands, which are totally landlocked, but that's no excuse, because Britain *is* an island. As a kid, my dad had wanted me to follow him into the foundry, and you don't get 'round to too many water sports in those places. But anyhow, I got some breast-stroke and side-stroke lessons while I was in New York last, from this fellow who once swam for the British Honduras Olympic team.

"I know—you'd think somebody who did a record called *Arc of a Diver* could swim, but I was scared *stiff.* Those who learn all this as a child can never understand the *fear* that you face as an adult, but I conquered it, and I consider it one of my proudest recent accomplishments. I suppose I always need the spark and inspiration of another person or two to urge me on."

So what's next for rock's country gentleman?

"Next? You mean I have to do *more*?" He exuberantly stretches his slim frame. "*Weeeelll,* after the tour for the new album, I'm going to settle in with my new family [which includes Steve and Genia's two infant daughters, Mary Clare and Elizabeth Dawn], and maybe even pay a long-due visit to my relatives back in Birmingham. Then at some point I'll write songs for yet another album."

Is there material left over from all his 1980s studio activity?

"I've got a few unused things in the can, but I don't have a whole store of them like some people. One song I wrote with Viv Stanshall for *High Life* is titled 'If That Gun's for Real.' It's very funny, a real Percy Sledge–flavored track that you wouldn't believe! I suppose it describes my relationship to a lot of things: how I can be taken completely off-guard by good luck, and how I often reveal myself at odd and—even for me—very unexpected little moments. It's marvelous and confounding, this life," he chuckles, "but I'm learning to adapt."

Of a half-dozen interviews this writer did with Winwood over a decade, the following talk at his Gloucestershire house in the summer of 1982 was the first. Steve sat in his garden eating a lunch of egg sandwiches and orange juice while Jim Capaldi tinkered indoors in the studio.

You've been at the rock and roll game for a remarkably long time, since before your teens if I'm not mistaken, yet I've never read anything about your home environment as a boy; how you were raised, and what your parents were like.

That's 'cause nobody's asked me. I grew up at 70 Atlantic Road, a pleasant tree-lined street [in Kingstanding]. It was a small house, with a piano in the parlor. The whole family was musical on both sides, with my mother's father being a church organist who could also play flute, fiddle, tin whistle. Same with my dad's people. We'd have musical parties at Christmas, playing folk songs. My father's a very sensible man, a very hardworking man—and strict. Neither he nor my mother nor even my grandparents ever drank or smoked. As a result I think I was much better brought up than most of my friends.

Frankly, a big part of my development was the Boy Scouts; I was both a Cub and a Boy Scout. The Scouts are a fantastic movement. I was reading in the paper the other day where some idiots are trying to get rid of the Boy Scouts, saying that a brilliant man like Baden Powell, the founder, had created nothing more than a sort of fascist youth movement. I was absolutely incensed! I loved the time I spent in the Scouts, camping and hiking; and doing bob-a-job; working at odd jobs in the community for a shilling. Got a lot out of it; I went straight from the Boy Scouts into rock and roll. [*laughter*] Fancy that!

As for parental guidance, my father was not the sort of fellow to sit me down and give me a lot of heavy advice, but both he and my mother were very helpful in terms of overall support and encouragement. My dad was the manager of Hall's Foundry in Birmingham, laboring in the same profession as his father, and he would have liked me to carry that on, but exerted no pressures.

So he endorsed your musical ambitions?

Very much so. But you must be aware that rock and roll is not now nor ever has been considered real music in Britain. Please don't take this lightly; this is a crucial point for anyone trying to understand the outlook and perspective of an aspiring popular musician in this country. Ours is a very stratified, disdainful social structure in which anything produced after the days of Elgar and Vaughan Williams is not considered to be of any value whatsoever. It isn't *considered*, period. And I'm not exaggerating. I was kicked out of Great Barr Comprehensive School at age sixteen because of my "unsavory activities" with the Spencer Davis Group. A warning came at a school assembly, where it was announced publicly that "certain students" in the school were known to be connected with untoward musical companions.

Soon afterward the headmaster summoned me to his office for a one-sided discussion. I stood before him in my uniform of gray slacks, black blazer with the school crest on the pocket, and green, white, and black striped tie, and he sacked me on the spot for playing rock and roll. Being sixteen, my attitude was, "Well, screw you too, geezer!" But what was most important was that my father and mother backed me up and were not upset that I'd been kicked out. They regarded the whole matter as being thoroughly ridiculous, which I've always deeply appreciated.

Well, you've taken some hard knocks and been handed some raw deals in your post–Great Barr Comprehensive School experiences. It's not generally known, but you nearly died from a bout with peritonitis during the period (1972–73) that you were touring and recording Shootout in the Fantasy Factory.

True. That was when I was writing songs like "Sometimes I Feel So Uninspired." That song reflected a lot of things: the state of the rock and roll world at that point, my own frame of mind, struggle with my health. It was just an honest thing; the song was talking about a definite sometime-feeling I get. We can't be inspired all the time, can we? And those of us who are made to feel that we have to be, grow weary and even ill from the stress of the crazy, unfair responsibility put on us.

My peritonitis started as appendicitis, and what happens is that these poisons spread throughout your entire body and you virtually fill up with toxins. I was desperately ill, trying to keep touring and functioning, and my condition was such that it wasn't until I'd gone through several doctors, various trips to the hospital, and exploratory surgery that they figured out I was in a most delicate and serious state. Peritonitis, by the way, is what killed Houdini. One of the toughest times of my life—but by no means the only one.

Hmmmm. Makes me reluctant to ask what the others might have been.

Well, disbanding Traffic in 1974 was difficult, of course. But the period between the completion of the long-promised—or threatened—Steve Winwood solo LP in the spring of 1977 and the release of *Arc of a Diver* in 1981 was quite hard for me professionally. The music industry went through such a strange stretch in 1977, especially in this country, with the whole punk rock thing coming about. Punk was rebellious—and justified in that response—but it had very little to do with music, and so it created a highly charged but frighteningly floundering atmosphere that I found very, very disheartening. Musical quality for me has always been an important part of rock and roll—and winning recognition for that has long been an uphill battle all the way. Punk seemed like rock and roll utterly *without* the music.

Did you also suddenly feel as if there was no audience receptive to your reemergence? That your music had suddenly become anachronistic in the marketplace?

Not really; I was concentrating less on the marketplace than on myself. I realized that if I was going to carry on in this business, then 1977 was the beginning of my ultimate trial, but rather than let that burden lay too heavily on me, I decided that the creation of the sequel to the first solo record was the key objective. My career needed new continuity. Also, at that time I was going through writing problems as well. Capaldi, who was the only person I'd ever written with, in terms of a true ongoing partnership, had moved away to Brazil for tax reasons. I had no lyricist I could rely on, and no band. In the days of Traffic and the Spencer Davis Group, there was always a group requiring new things to play, so I'd somehow dig in with a collaborator like Jimmy Miller or Capaldi and get it done.

It's funny, though, because in this case as well as others, the really bad periods for me have tended to be rather good periods after a while. It's the bad periods that were the times of realization and gestation which made possible the resurgences.

If you were so hard up for collaborators, why didn't you simply follow Capaldi to Brazil?

Well, because I couldn't put a price on not living where I wanted to live; I was too selfish. I was willing to pay the disastrously dear price of giving 95 percent of what I earned to the British government in order to stay where I was. It was pretty decadent of me, when you think about it, and pretty stupid too. Thank God, things aren't so bad now with the Thatcher government.

I'll tell you straight: the pressures on me were huge. I was quite literally running out of money. Following the Steve Winwood record, which I cowrote with Capaldi and Viv Stanshall, I knew I was looking at my last shot to stay in the business. If the next album wasn't at least mildly successful, I would have had to leave the record industry because I simply couldn't afford to be in it any longer. I would have had to undergo some drastic professional and personal life-style changes.

Are you saying that, with the lack of significant sales of the first solo album and the second looming before you, Steve Winwood was considering quitting as a performer?

Quite possibly, yes. I knew I was going to run out of cash and resources soon, and I was thinking about exploring other areas, perhaps getting a job with a record company as a producer. My brother Muff was head of A&R at CBS in England. I'd considered and tried sheep farming, cattle farming, all kinds of alternate ways of making a living. But I quickly realized that all the mistakes I'd made in the record business over the years were very valuable, that I'd paid my dues and, for better or worse, staked out my territory in terms of competence.

So you literally approached Arc of a Diver *as a make-or-break project?*

[*Nodding grimly*] But I suppose I still refused to believe that the strain from such a situation is what maybe makes a successful album. I expected absolutely nothing from *Arc of a Diver. Nothing.*

Must have been pretty scary.

See, now this is the thing: when it gets right down to it, it's *not* scary at all. I would have managed to have a gentle, peaceful life, somehow. You don't have to have a big house and a lot of land to have a peaceful life. You can create it in other ways.

But, as I say, although that was such a low point, it was a good juncture too because I came to a lot of realizations about myself and about materialism. It was just material things that I was really worried about. I figured that I could do without them, and so I was able to take a lot of the load off myself. If I'd have been making a record feeling, "This has *got* to be a hit," there would have been no hope at all. These were the kinds of things that were on my mind, I can tell you, when I wrote "While You See a Chance."

You also seemed to be attempting to minimize the heat you were feeling artistically by billing Arc of a Diver, *on the inner sleeve, as "an album of songs by Will Jennings, George Fleming, and Viv Stanshall." How did you come to take your perilous last plunge in that company?*

Just from needing to find lyricists. I was working with a lot of different ones, and that proved to be good because it taught me a lot about songwriting. *Talking Back to the Night* is the first time that I've actually sat down calmly and written songs. Right now, I'm in the position where I truly want to write so much, but I don't seem to have the time, basically due to the fact that I'm now making records in this solitary and very time-consuming fashion.

On the new record, Will Jennings basically wrote the lyrics and I wrote the music, but there was a bit of a dynamic collaborative overlap too. I have not written a lot of songs by myself, mind you. The first song I ever wrote, at the age of twelve, was "It Hurts Me So," which the Spencer Davis Group recorded several years later. I wrote "Empty Pages" by myself for Traffic, with a bit of help from Capaldi; I wrote "Had to Cry Today," "Sea of Joy," and "Can't Find My Way Home" for Blind Faith, and I wrote "Two-way Stretch," the B-side of "There's a River," which is on the new album but which came out first as a Christmas single in 1981.

You've worked in the studio with a lot of very different people: Stomu Yamashta and Michael Shrieve, the Fania All-Stars, Marianne Faithfull, Sandy Denny, Toots & the Maytals, George Harrison, Mike Oldfield, even Hendrix, playing the organ on "Voodoo Child." But there must have been some unheralded live backup work in the early days, when the Spencer Davis Group and the early Yardbirds were doing gigs at haunts like the legendary Crawdaddy Club in Richmond, Surrey.

Sure! I did backups for Sonny Boy Williamson—as everybody did—but also for T-Bone Walker, Charlie Foxx, John Lee Hooker, Memphis Slim. John Hammond, too. I met John on a train, while going down from Birmingham to London; this would have been about 1963, and I was fifteen. He told me he had a gig in Birmingham the next week at the College of Advanced Technology, and I showed up and played piano behind him. Those kinds of spontaneous musical meetings were special back then, and definitely helped shape my growth. I also played with Jimmy Page for a solo album of his after he'd left the Yardbirds. The music wasn't heavy like Led Zeppelin, as I recall. It was quite nice.

Who would you say were your biggest influences vocally, apart from Ray Charles?

Just about every blues and R&B singer I heard on the radio as a lad had an effect on me, but particularly people like Garnet Mimms and Jackie Wilson. I used to hang out a lot in a Birmingham record store called the Diskery—which is where Capaldi claims I first met him in 1966—and I loved to listen to all the great black American singers. I also listened to a lot of skiffle too; Lonnie Donnegan and the rest. Oddly enough, I was not a big record buyer. Back in the fifties, my uncle Alfred, who was a marvelous inventor and electronic wizard who had worked on the design of the Norton motorcycle, constructed a tape recorder from scratch and then gave it to Muff and me. For a homemade model it was fairly good-looking, and we used to keep it up in the bedroom we shared. At night we'd stay up and tape everything off the radio. It was much better than a record player, really, and owning a tape recorder at that time was quite a novelty. Before long, we had a wonderful collection of tapes of Fats Domino, Louis Jordan, Ray Charles, you name it.

I can hear all of those people threaded through your own work, but one thing I've always been curious about was the integration of the Hammond organ into your sound. How did that come about?

Frankly, I'm not that good a piano player. Elton John is much more accomplished on the piano; it's a percussion instrument, and he knows how to get the most of it in terms of figures, chording, and live performing. But I don't think he's as good an electric piano, organ, or synthesizer player as I am.

The difference between piano and the other three is vast. You can get expression from organs and synthesizers through pedals but generally not through touch. The feel, the dexterity, and the dynamics are arrived at from different directions, but I would argue that the musical possibilities are the same, qualitatively, for percussive keyboards and electronic ones. Yet it is peculiar how the truly fine piano player is frustrated by the technology and lack of immediate subtlety in organs and synths. Actually, the "touch" *is* there for the latter, lying beyond the basic key-contact tonality, but you must learn how to find it.

Now, people think I play difficult things on piano and organ. My part on "Glad" sounds difficult, but it really isn't. I shouldn't say this, but it's true. When I was very young, I received about two years formal training at the Birmingham Midland Institute, studying theory, technique, a bit of the classics, so that gave me a foundation. But I'm not a virtuoso. What I got from the experience was the knowledge that I was *never* going to be much of a piano player—and that was very valuable. At least I knew then that the way for me was organs and synths. My old teacher's name was John Rust. As Neil Young says [*laughs*], "It's better to burn out than to rust!"

How do you overdub your vocals on these solo albums?

I generally put a vocal down fairly early on, and then I do a second one when the track is nearing completion. Usually I end up using the original. I find that in my original there are a lot of deft lines that I patch into the master. I don't keep going until I sing one track that is right all the way through. I've found out at great cost that that's not the intelligent way to use recording equipment.

How do you mean, "at great cost"?

By erasing great performances that contained flaws while working to get one that was absolutely correct! My God! I can't think of any instances where that *hasn't* happened! I was talking on the phone the other day with Peter Townshend, and he was saying how he always does all these damned demos for himself. I said that I had recently vowed that I was *never* going to make another demo! You've got to resolve to capture the original spirit. In the old days, you wrote the song, went in and cut it, and that's how it should be. Forget these demos, because when you make them you decide in the first place that it's not going to be any good, that it's just to play for so-and-so who might want to use the song or give you a deal. Why limit the possibilities? It makes no sense! I say, cut every track as if it might be a worldwide smash and then utilize it from there! Chop it up any way you please but use what's good. I've decided to value everything I do—but I must say that the tape gets very expensive.

I did a lot of trial tapes for *Talking Back to the Night,* recording them at slower speeds to save tape space. I tried to recut them later but said, "Sod it!" and went back to the originals. You've got to forget all preconceptions when you sit down to record and let things happen. Especially when you're working alone. That way surprising things can be allowed to occur.

Give me an example of an unexpected moment that was saved for the record.

The ethereal beginning of "While You See a Chance." What happened there was that in the studio, I had record switches for each track that were mounted flush with the board desk, on top of which was habitually piled reams of notes and paperwork.

At one point, I inadvertently knocked a record button on as I went down into the studio to do a vocal. Twenty bars into the song, I suddenly said to Nobby Clarke, my engineering assistant, "I can't hear the bloody drums!" He stopped the tape immediately, and we found that we'd accidentally wiped the drums off the first part of the track—originally they'd come in at the top of the tune. I spent months trying to patch in the drums again, and never got it right. We were getting close to delivery day for the tapes to be mastered, so I just left the drums and vocal out, and reshifted all the verses. It actually *made* the song. That's how bizarre the recording process is.

"While You See a Chance," "There's a River"—they all sound like they'd practically be acceptable in an Anglican cathedral.

[*Grinning*] "There's a River" is downright hymn-like, isn't it? As a boy, I sang in choir at St. John's, Perry Barr. Used to get into a bit of mischief back then, as well, mucking around behind the altar screen during services, making nasty cracks or horsing around afterward in the vestry and stealing the communion wine. They were good days; not overly reverent.

In terms of my singing, I have always loved to hear the sound of the big voice resonating in my head. It's so thrilling, and never fails to keep me happy. I loved the vibrations and the auras that choral singing brought out in my voice, so I must have gravitated toward that music a bit for that reason alone. The churchlike overtones are definitely there in my music, and I would say that that dimension came on naturally and not deliberately. I like that people hear it in there. They're not just imagining it.

There is a sense of longing there, perhaps, but I don't analyze it. To touch a listener is great, though. Those moods and emotional shadings are there, but I like to think that I'm down-to-earth with them, particularly as of late. As time goes on I feel more rooted, more grounded. In the early seventies, I was like a lost soul, wondering what the hell I was going to do with my life. And from 1974 to 1977, I did almost nothing except to kick back and get to know people I'd never known before, like farmers, simple tradesmen, and country folk who had no idea who the hell I was.

Interestingly enough, the fact that I wasn't doing much music during those years didn't bother me because, Lord knows, I'd been at it for twelve years by the time Traffic broke up in 1974, just shortly after we'd released *When the Eagle Flies.* [*laughing*] I couldn't feel guilty about it when I'd been playing professionally literally since I was in short pants!

Are the royalties from your early work substantial?

Well, the royalties from "Gimme Some Lovin'," and from most of the various Traffic records are. As I said before, I've been pressed for money in the recent past, but I don't want to make it sound as if I was almost completely down-and-out.

What was the best-selling Traffic record, to the best of your knowledge?

I think it was *The Low Spark of High-heeled Boys.* Not *John Barleycorn Must Die,* as some believe. *Barleycorn* came after the breakup of Blind Faith in the early seventies. I'd knocked around a bit with Ginger Baker's Air Force, and then I was supposed to do my solo album; I was going to call it *Mad Shadows.* But Capaldi and Chris Wood joined in, and it turned into a Traffic album.

"John Barleycorn" is an ancient British folk song with hundreds of versions. How did you come to record it as the title track of a Traffic album?

That goes back to the basis upon which Traffic was formed. The reason I left the Spencer Davis Group in 1967 was because I didn't want to continue playing and singing songs that were derivative of American R&B. I'm sure it's no accident that "I'm a Man" was one of the last things I ever cut with the group. It was a fine record, which we did on the first or second take. It was intended for some sort of Swinging London–type film called *The Ghost Goes Gear,* or whatever; one of those silly films we were involved with back then. I just believed I had more to offer than that. Also, I wanted to play with younger people, fellows my own age. I was fifteen when I joined up with Spencer, Muff, and Peter York. They were all a bit older than me, with different musical orientations.

I'd begun to make younger friends like Dave Mason, who was working for Spencer Davis as a roadie, and Capaldi, who was the lead singer in a group I'd jammed with called Deep Feeling. And I sang some blues stuff briefly with Eric [Clapton], Jack Bruce on bass, Paul Jones played harp, and so on; we were called the Powerhouse. When Jim, Dave, Chris Wood, and I went up to the Berkshire cottage in 1967 to start Traffic, it was the result of a lot of enthusiastic planning and time spent playing together informally. What came out of those talks and things was a desire on the part of the four of us to make a uniquely British form of rock and roll that incorporated or evoked traditional music like "John Barleycorn"—the Berkshire cottage was in the center of acres of wheat and barley—while breaking new ground artistically.

Are you saying that there was no determination collectively to turn out a variation on the psychedelic rock then gaining ground commercially?

No, no! Absolutely not. We would smoke our share of pot and hash and so forth, but that was never on our minds in any specific way when we wrote songs. We were trying to keep the images in the music clear and simple, not complex and cerebral. We were hippies of a sort, I guess, and those were heady times; a whole era—sitting with a colorful, nervous, lovely bloke like Hendrix in a Greenwich Village studio, or brainstorming in the Berkshire cottage with Traffic—that was filled with a vast, unfounded kind of pleasure at tearing down any and all barriers. I'm not sure why, now, because if you destroy too much you're just left with a gigantic mush, which is kind of what happened a bit, isn't it?

And then again, Traffic can't take credit for removing barriers as much as others because we were so keen to work in established areas of folk and folk-rock music.

Did you believe at the time that you were getting anything concrete out of your hash-smoking reveries in the cottage?

I thought I was getting something from it, yes, but I've since realized that I got nothing whatever from it. I see myself as having been misled. The whole notion of reaching another consciousness through the smoke was a lot of crap. But I've few regrets. There're probably little batches of songs here and there during the period which, with hindsight, I should not have released or put out in their now permanent form, but to be very honest, I figured, "What the hell! Put it out, sod it." It's not all great, but, I mean, how often is anything great?

The way you record now, so meticulously, at your own pace and on your own terms, the temptation to go back and tinker with your old material must be enormous.

Oh, you don't know! You can't imagine! Especially in light of all I've learned about the studio. But I don't want to drive myself batty over it. The answer is, "Yes, certainly. But I'd have to be crazy."

The cover of When the Eagle Flies, *Traffic's swan song, was as bleak and funereal as the music within. Was that a reflection of a collective state of mind?*

Yes. It just kind of turned out that way; it doesn't seem like a Traffic record so much, does it? The whole record is very doomy, and I suppose it's the way we saw both Traffic and the music of the era going. It was an extension of "Sometimes I Feel So Uninspired." The kind of depression that comes from endings and ultimatums, and the title of the album reflects that as well.

What occasioned the demise of the band? On precisely what day did it fold?

If there was a single, final moment I can't recall it now. We'd broken up so many times previously, with Dave [Mason] leaving and coming back, the Blind Faith sideline after the first three Traffic albums, and us constantly adding new players like Rich Grech, Rebop, Roger Hawkins. But I shed no tears. On the contrary, I felt a great relief. Same with my Spencer Davis exit. As I left I felt very cold and callous about the action and much excitement about the future.

You've been quoted as saying you "walked out" on them.

I can't deny that. But what I was trying to convey was that it was time for all of us to disperse. I don't know of any hard feelings between any of us.

Is it true that in the summer of 1976, just before you began the first solo album, you'd seen graffiti around London that read: "Steve Winwood Lives!" And that it rattled you considerably, as if the public actually had given you up for dead?

It was weird, except that I knew who was responsible. It was this bloke who was trying to become my manager. That was his idea of creating new excitement about me. I had friends who'd seen it in Kensington and 'round the side of Harrods and told me about it. So this bloke eventually came to me and said, "You see what I can do for you?" I said, "That's what you can do for me? Remind me I'm still breathing?! Thank you very much and move on, you bloody fool!!"

Do you have any hobbies or interests that give you a little release from all these musical chores you're locked into?

Well, I do have an absorbing interest in field sports, game birds, hunting, falconing, and coursing—which is hunting with hounds. But I don't like to talk about it much because I fear people might not understand how and why I can enjoy such things.

In 1970, I thought that I would become a vegetarian, and I kept on with it for about six months, but I had such a craving for meat. So I decided that if I was to go back to eating meat, I must learn how to kill my own, doing it efficiently, humanely, respectfully.

Also, I resolved that I would not hunt for the mere sport of it, or kill more than I could or would definitely eat, to keep the bargain honorable, and I've stuck to it, I'm happy to say. It seems to have more integrity to me than going to the market to buy a fowl, like most people, yet not facing up to the reality of the situation. Also, things like falconing and the hunt are commonplace in these parts.

Do you ever ride to the hunt?

I used to have horses, which I gave up. A very good friend of mine works for the hunt, but he doesn't ride. He's more of an organizer of it. I like coursing better, I think. I love the outdoors, hurrying about in the fields, if only for the scenery.

The biggest tour you've ever been on was the one that had the least to do with your career—the 1969 U.K.-U.S.A. Blind Faith cavalcade. While I'm not one to belittle the album critically—actually, I've always liked it a lot—the Blind Faith tour was one of the tackiest rock circuses of all time. You opened to a horde of 100,000 in Hyde Park in London in June and proceeded to bend every ear in America near the breaking point for two months cross-country. Though it didn't last long, it was a fairly vulgar spectacle, and turned off a lot of people who, understandably, took Clapton, Baker, Grech, and yourself seriously. Could that have lastingly soured you on your own personal in-concert presence?

The album stands up very well on its own merits. But the show *was* vulgar, crude, disgusting. It lacked integrity. There were huge crowds everywhere, full of mindless adulation, mostly due to Eric and Ginger's success with Cream and, to a more modest extent, my own impact. The combination led to a situation where we could have gone on and farted and gotten a massive reaction. *That* was one of the times I got so uninspired.

The attitude backstage was, "These people think we're great, and we better damned well *give* them something great," but it didn't help. And it wasn't the audiences' fault. The blame all rightfully belonged in our laps. We did not sound good live, due to the simple lack of experience being a band. We'd had no natural growth, and it was very evident onstage.

Whose idea was Blind Faith?

Eric and I had known each other for ages and had been saying we must get together sometime and play in a real, stable band. Since I'd just left Traffic and Eric had canned Cream, we decided that was the time, and we rehearsed for two weeks at Eric's house in Surrey. We went in and cut the record, and then toured.

I still say, however, that it's better to have a good record and a bad tour than vice versa. Memories always mellow, but the record lingers on intact. At least the album indicates that we could get on a bit musically. But we had to break up because that was the only way we could get out of the whole mess. And it was a complicated deal, because Eric and Ginger were held by Atlantic, and the deals for each member were struck individually, with Chris [Blackwell] working a thing out with Ahmet Ertegun for me. Not the best way to form a group. Live and learn.

Are there any lingering miscomprehensions that you think the public has about Steve Winwood that you'd like to set straight?

Yeah! I've read in a number of places, both books and articles, about Steve Winwood being "a victim of the drugs he ushered in," or "a casualty of the drug scene." When Will Jennings, my writing collaborator, first met me, he thought from all this rubbish in print that I was a junkie, or at any rate had been! Because that's what the writers seemed to be implying.

Over the years, my blood has really gotten up about this crap. I'd be all set to take legal action, but then I'd calm down again—only to see me described in yet another rock anthology, by someone who's never met me, as a "burned-out relic." Just when I was ready to boil over again for the last damned time, I saw that *Arc of a Diver* was at the top of the charts around the world. I said to myself, "That's satisfaction enough for me."

Any other vintage axes to grind?

One more. People think—and this happens much more in England—that I'm some kind of a recluse, which I strongly object to. I've spent a lot of time on farms in the recent past, granted, and these new records require me to do the work of eight people, so I often seem to be living in the studio. But I work on these things for my enjoyment and, hopefully, the enjoyment of others, and when people turn around and call me an antisocial freak I resent it!

I do concede that I was out of the mainstream from 1974 to 1977, but ever since, I've still been labeled a hermit. It's understandable, I suppose, because I don't tour, but I want people to know that I do get out of my cave and see a lot of friends and lead a fairly full social life.

Not to pry, but who would some of those people be?

Actually, besides old and dear friends, there are people I've known vaguely over the years that I seem to be drawn closer to these days, like Pete Townshend and Van Morrison, whom I see a lot of. We seem to have gone through similar experiences and have much to talk about. It's bringing us very close together.

Do you feel like you're part of a fraternity of elder rock statesmen?

[*Shy grin*] Yeah. Definitely. We can sit together and observe younger musicians doing things brilliantly or badly and identify with them, or criticize them, or cheer them on. This is really why I want to get on to producing, because I want to pass on a certain amount of knowledge to others. More and more, I find that I can instantly pinpoint what's wrong with certain records, although I rarely dare to offer it at all.

Are there any more things you've cut that haven't made it onto vinyl yet?

I did a song called "Waiting for Orders" that didn't get used on any album, for the simple reason that it wasn't as good as the other tracks.

Considering the title of the tune, perhaps that's a symbolic irony.

[*Smiling*] You may have hit on something there. For myself, I'd say that most of the waiting is over.

In 1968, Jimi Hendrix said, "It's funny the way most people love the dead. . . . Once you are dead you are made for life." It was not an opinion borne of low wit so much as a knowing judgment concerning a certain chilly kind of journey, a spirited jog along the River Styx. Some say it started for Hendrix in his fourth year, when his father renamed him, legally transforming Johnny Allen Hendrix into James Marshall Hendrix. There's an old superstition among certain native American tribes that it's unwise to name a child twice because it splits his eternal spirit in two, half of it ascending into Heaven and half of it going straight to Hell. Jimi Hendrix's great-grandmother was a full-blooded Cherokee.

Lucille, Al Hendrix's tubercular, hard-partying jitterbugger of a war bride had given birth to Johnny at 10:15 A.M. on November 27, 1942, in damp, gloomy Seattle General Hospital. Another son, Leon, arrived in 1948, but by then the family unit was a bust; and the

Jimi Hendrix

1984

overdue divorce came down in 1950. Since the Marshall part of Jimmy's new appellation had been bestowed in honor of Al's brother (who'd been a professional dancer), Al Hendrix tried to develop the showboating capabilities of his favorite son, teaching him a bit of buck-and-wing, demonstrating how to play the spoons or to quick-strum a ukulele, and tucking a five spot into Jimmy's shirt pocket so he could buy his little buddy's old hollow-body guitar. Jimmy began skipping school to cruise the blues joints in the misty and mean Seattle ghetto, getting high on codeine cough syrup and Benzedrine, stealing sharkskin threads through the gratings of shop windows. He was jailed after getting nabbed joyriding in two stolen cars inside of a week. A lenient judge suggested he cool his heels in the armed forces, and Jimmy was assigned to the 101st Airborne outfit in Fort Campbell, Kentucky.

In January 1962, he wrote his dad, requesting that he ship down Jimmy's Stratocaster guitar, which the left-handed grunt had a habit of playing upside down. When the Strat arrived, Jimmy painted "Betty Jean" on the side in memory of an old inamorata and spent his evenings alone with it in the barracks. Sometimes he'd thrum it hard and pump the vibrato bar until the taut strings produced an oscillating whine resembling the drone of an air transport at 10,000 feet—or he would cuff the humming strings with the heel of his palm and hit a sequence of tarantular chords, the skinny, pointy fingers of his right hand crowding the strings to one side of the neck, invoking a rude, whistling bark.

Word spread around the base that Hendrix slept with his ax and conversed with it after mess hall as if it were a comely young doxy. He was shunned by most of the men, but a boisterous black bassist named Billy Cox sought him out. Once they were discharged, Jimmy and Billy headed for Nashville to get tight with other black musicians playing non–country and western dives like the Club Del Morocco. Jimmy then moved on to Vancouver, Canada, to join a lounge group. Little Richard blew through town in 1963, in need of support men who were willing to endure his egotistical psychoprattle, and he pulled Hendrix onto the road with him for long, long nights of "Keep a Knockin' " with "Tutti-Frutti" encores.

Hendrix made his first known appearance on record for the Los Angeles Revis label. The song, "My Diary," was a minor local hit. More recording ensued, all of it unimpressive, but onstage he was stepping out more and more from the rigid soul review ensemble rubric of the day, doling out controlled bursts of daft virtuosity and histrionic sound. He picked up T-Bone Walker's old trick of soloing with the guitar held behind his head, and it seemed to other performers like vaudevillian gimmickry—until Hendrix brought forth sardonic hosannas and atavistic chaos from the instrument.

In 1965, Hendrix settled in New York City. Gangly, imposing, bushy-haired, he was tiring of the spit-and-polish regimentation of the soul groups and gravitating toward the bohemian life of Greenwich Village. It was in the Café Wha? that twenty-eight-year-old Brian "Chas" Chandler, bassist for the leading British group the Animals, discovered Hendrix. Chandler was knocked out by Hendrix's wild, atmospheric approach to rock guitar, knew it was time to pounce, and induced Jimmy to come back with him to England.

Hendrix obliged and fell headlong into the Swinging London upheaval and its roguish undercurrents. French rock star Johnny Halliday was astonished by Hendrix's solos and entreated him to appear on a bill in Paris two weeks later. With that deadline before them, Chandler and Hendrix created an instant group comprising novice bassist Noel Redding and former British TV child star John "Mitch" Mitchell on drums. The Jimi Hendrix Experience was born.

When *Are You Experienced?*—the inaugural album—appeared in 1967, it was a London sensation, heralding, in both its streamlined fuzz-tone guitar monologues and the hip-gypsy garb of its members, the advent of psychedelic rock. And the exhortations of the chortling lead singer were a Rabelaisian invitation to a coitus-and-controlled-substances bender of the first rank. At Paul McCartney's urging, the Jimi Hendrix Experience got themselves added to the bill at the Monterey Pop Festival in the summer of 1967. Hendrix whipped the outdoor concert audience into a mighty lather with a barrage of electronic guitar distortion that soared, missile-like in its sonic arc, over their dazed heads. At the finale of the set, he doused his Stratocaster with lighter fluid and set it aflame, bowing out to an ecstatic roar as the unearthly drone of the burning instrument streamed out of the speaker towers.

In 1968, the Experience released the highly experimental *Axis: Bold as Love* LP, and critics marveled at the waterfall feedback and dazzling fluidity of this guitar avatar, not to mention the impenetrable quasi-Hindu acid hodge-podge that made up the lyrics. Later that year, *Electric Ladyland,* a blues-rooted two-record electronic soundscape, appeared. The record became a best-seller in the United

States and the United Kingdom and a staple on FM radio, but it was increasingly obvious that Jimi was growing faster than his audience—and that his Dionysian concerns were keeping pace with his musical ones. Throughout the album there is a feeling of floating, spiraling sexual contentment that is then despoiled by crude violence or rent apart by anonymous agents of rage. All of *Electric Ladyland*'s songs alternately deify and defame womankind, the bitch goddess pulled through the wringer over four sides of supernatural seduction, menace, and mayhem. Hendrix's guitar solos on the record are in a dozen different styles, and his singing is equally kaleidoscopic. He can sound like a rollicking blues shouter, his crackling good humor hugely engaging, and then his spirit turns saturnine, bitter, and ultimately maniacal.

Rolling Stone pegged him: "Hendrix is the Robert Johnson of the sixties." *Electric Ladyland* became the album of choice among pot-smoking American troops fighting in the rice paddies and rain forests of Vietnam—just in time for the band to break up. Redding and Mitchell were put off by Hendrix's expanding ego and his habit of leaving the stage in the middle of sets if the audience didn't seem sufficiently adoring. His excessive drinking and his round-the-clock drug-taking were making him difficult to communicate with. The only people to get his full attention were the phalanxes of groupies who attended him. The groupie underground pronounced Jimi "Best Score" because he never denied any of their swollen ranks. Things got ugly, however, when it was rumored Hendrix had thrown one girl down a flight of stairs. During the same period, he wrecked two new Corvette Stingrays on two successive nights. His drug intake was also on the rise. In the early days he kept it down to several acid trips a week; lots of good reefer, beer, and whiskey to keep the edge off; and party favors like a plastic baby bottle filled with Methedrine-spiked water. Now he was interested in anything and everything, around the clock, and the rest of the Experience could not keep up. On July 1, 1969, the group was spontaneously dissolved in Denver.

Hendrix played the Woodstock festival with a loose aggregation called the Electric Sky Church. Afterward, he bowed to pressure from Black Power groups and formed an all-black outfit called the Band of Gypsies. Their debut concert at New York's Fillmore East was taped and turned into a live album, but the band existed for only one more show. Hendrix, who was reeling from a tab of bad acid in Madison Square Garden, took his guitar off in the middle of a song and told the 19,000 people gathered in the arena, "I'm sorry, we just can't get it together."

In 1970, Hendrix cut an uneven album entitled *The Cry of Love.* During the fall, he was immersed in composing the music for an occult film heavily influenced by the Tarot, which was to be called *Rainbow Bridge.* With a straight face he had begun informing close friends that he was from "an asteroid belt off the coast of Mars."

Jimi Hendrix died at 11:25 A.M. on September 18, 1970, at St. Mary's Abbot Hospital in London. He had been sleeping at a friend's flat; vomit had been discovered coming from his mouth and nose, and Jimi could not be awakened. In an ambulance en route to the hospital, he was placed in a sitting position; this contributed to his suffocating on his own puke. An autopsy showed that Hendrix had consumed nine tablets of a prescription drug called Vesparax, normally taken in one-half-tablet doses. Also in his system at the time of death were tranquilizers, amphetamines, depressants, and alcohol. The coroner ruled the cause of death to have been "inhalation of vomit due to barbiturate intoxication." There was an "open verdict" on the question of suicide.

The Dead don't take a vacation in this land.

Thus, fresh from completion of their *Built to Last* album, the band has assembled at Le Clube Front, their whimsically named warehouse, recording studio, and rehearsal hall in San Rafael, California, to spend the morning practicing for another in their endless itinerary of concert appearances.

Lead guitarist Jerry Garcia, a gray-bearded buddha in purple T-shirt, jeans, and sandals, leads the more youthful but similarly attired Bob Weir into the center chamber of the cavernous facility. Groping around in the dark, they locate just enough switches to bring basic power and light to a shadowy chaparral of amplifiers, percussion platforms, recording consoles, and customized electronic gadgetry. Weir plugs in his own guitar, tunes up in tandem with Garcia, and launches without comment into "Death Don't Have No Mercy," a classic blues by the late Reverend Gary Davis that

Grateful Dead

1989

the Dead have recently revived from their own late-seventies road-show repertoire. Dead drummer Bill Kreutzmann surfaces from behind the stacks to provide a crisp downbeat, and soon the rest of the group (drummer-percussionist Mickey Hart, bassist Phil Lesh, keyboardist Brent Mydland*) have arrived to augment and anchor the stately blues-rock groove. Garcia moves to a boom mike and raises his inimitably nasal voice to sing:

Death don't have no mercy in this land,
Death don't take a vacation in this land . . .

As the song's casual run-through ripens into a lusty jam, lights spring on in other precincts of the two-storied Le Clube Front, and members of the Dead staff hurry around corners, dwarfed by the massive full-color stage scrims (like that of the fiddle-playing skeleton first glimpsed on the cover of the *Blues for Allah* album) which cloak the high walls. The entire building seems upholstered with several layers of Dead memorabilia, rusty San Francisco street signs for Haight and Ashbury overlapping with European tour posters and promotional placards for bygone tours with the Who, Dylan, and Tom Petty and the Heartbreakers. Prominent among the band mementos are graffiti and knickknacks that celebrate the songwriters (Robert Hunter, John Barlow, Gerritt Graham, etc.) and sound, production, and technical crew (Ramrod, Steve Parish, Dan Healy, John Cutler, Harry Popick, John Bralove, Eileen Law, and so on), whose names are as familiar to Deadheads as the players in the band.

June 7, 1990, marked the twenty-fifth anniversary of the Grateful Dead and, in that quarter-century, the band, its organization—and its crazy-loyal fans—have comprised an extended family unique in the heritage of American rock and roll. Musicially, the ancestry of the Dead encompasses a host of preliminary combos. Bob Weir (born Robert Hall on October 16, 1947) was with a high school band called the Uncalled Four the night he met Jerry Garcia (who began as Jerome John Garcia on August 1, 1942) while backstage at the Tangent in Palo Alto, California. Jerry was playing banjo with the Black Mountain Boys at the time, but in 1964 Jerry and Bob joined with a blues harmonica player named Ron "Pigpen" McKernan to form Mother McCree's Uptown Jug Champions.

A year onward, Bill Kreutzmann and Phil Lesh helped usher the

*Mydland, thirty-eight, was found dead in his Lafayette, California, home on July 26, 1990.

Jug Champions into electric blues-rock notoriety in the Bay Area as the Warlocks. Believing there was another Warlocks currently recording, they decided in mid-1965 to change their name. In a hefty dictionary Garcia found the phrase "Grateful Dead," itself derived from both an Egyptian prayer and a folk song identified by British ethnomusicologist Francis Childs. The band saw the phrase as emblematic of cyclical change rather than macabre surrender, and they embraced it.

Late in 1967, the members took up residence at 710 Ashbury Street and became regulars at Bill Graham's Fillmore Auditorium and the Family Dog's Avalon Ballroom—when they weren't spearheading a steady series of free shows in Golden Gate Park. The Bay Area during 1966–67 was the hub of a radical cultural transformation, and the Dead were key figures in its colorful convulsions as they experimented with LSD, played the Trips Festival, and partied with Ken Kesey and the Merry Pranksters. Percussion virtuoso Mickey Hart joined the Dead in 1967 and accompanied the band in its relocation to Marin County early in 1968 to concentrate on recording their singular meld of folk, country, rock, blues, Afro-Asian forms, and experimental composition à la Stockhausen.

Signed by Warner Bros. executive Joe Smith in 1967, the band released two LPs (*The Grateful Dead,* 1967; *Anthem of the Sun,* 1968) before becoming the first musicians in the world to utilize sixteen-track recording hardware, on which they produced *Aoxomoxoa* (1969) and a 1970 live album. By 1971, this quintessential live band proposed another live LP it planned to title *Skullfuck.*

As Joe Smith recalls, the artwork the band submitted to Warner Bros. for the two-record live set was "a skull with *Skullfuck* on a scroll across it. I looked at it and muttered, 'Is this another prank?' See, they hated Warners, and I was the only one they would talk to—and they hated *me*—but they hated me less.

"So I called a meeting. I prepared by phoning district attorneys around the country, plus major stores with record departments, like Sears and J.C. Penney, asking all of them, 'What would you do if you were confronted with an album called *Skullfuck*?' "

The response was grim, but the band was adamant. So the Dead and its support crew came down from San Francisco for a formal confrontation with the Warners brass at L.A.'s Continental Hyatt. "Why are you all here?" Smith asked when confronted with the crowd of concerned parties. "Because it's a family decision!" they roared back.

After hours of debate, Smith said, "Look, you're deep in debt. If we call it *Skullfuck,* it will get into a handful of headshops—which you can't collect money from anyhow—and you'll sell eight thousand copies, tops. Moreover, no radio station will touch an album with this title. In other words, out there, it will never exist. *And* you'll owe us one hundred thousand plus." The band huddled, and then said they had tired of the wrangle. As far as they were concerned, Warners could call the album anything it liked, including *Grateful Dead*—which it became, selling a million and a half units.

Also, in 1970, came *Workingman's Dead* and *American Beauty,* two superb albums whose unique, country-tinged songs ("Uncle John's Band," "Truckin'," "Ripple," "Box of Rain") spotlighted Garcia's melodies, Weir's harmonies, and Robert Hunter's lyrics. Jerry's innovative work on the pedal-steel guitar afforded still-broader creative avenues for the Dead, and old chums from the band's folk and country origins were enlisted to create a countrified spinoff band, the New Riders. Both bands toured during 1970 as a family bill: "An Evening with the Grateful Dead, Featuring the New Riders of the Purple Sage."

Constantly striving to preserve the live, improvisational sparks that were their hallmark, the Dead recorded a third successful live album, the hugely extravagant *Europe '72.* During this period, Pigpen's poor health had led to the addition of pianist Keith Godchaux in 1971 and vocalist-wife Donna Jean Godchaux in 1972. On March 6, 1973, Pigpen died of liver disease.

Jerry Garcia put out his first solo album (*Garcia,* the cover showing his right hand with its missing third finger—the result of a childhood accident) on the Warners label in 1972, as did Bob Weir *(Ace).* Jerry released another outside project with organist Howard Wales on Douglas Records called *Hooteroll,* as well as *Live at the Keystone,* an ensemble turn with keyboardist Merle Saunders and chums that the Fantasy label put out in 1973. After the Dead's Warners contract expired in 1973, they issued albums on their own Grateful Dead Records label or its Round Records subsidiary. The Dead releases were *Wake of the Flood* (1973), *From the Mars Hotel* (1974), and *Blues for Allah* (1975), and among the largely Round-relegated LPs generated by the family circle were two from Robert Hunter (*Tales of the Great Rum Runners,* 1974; *Tiger Rose,* 1975), two solo albums by Jerry (*Compliments of Garcia,* 1974; *Reflections,* 1976), a live string band session with guitarist/vocalist Peter Rowan and others (*Old and in the Way,* 1975), plus a record of electronic music by Phil Lesh and Ned Lagin called *Seastones* (1975). And Kingfish, a side band Weir had formed with ex–New Rider Dave Torbert, released a debut album in 1976.

After a short stretch with United Artists Records, which helped *Blues for Allah* and 1976's *Steal Your Face* get distributed, the Dead folded their own labels and signed with Arista Records. Mickey Hart, who had drifted into a solo orbit for several years—playing with the Diga Rhythm Band and issuing the 1972 *Rolling Thunder* solo album—was back in the fold, and the Dead allowed outside producers to pilot their studio output for the first time. Keith Olsen produced *Terrapin Station* in 1977, and Little Feat leader Lowell George guided *Shakedown Street* in 1978. The same year, Jerry created the solo album *Cats Under the Stars,* and Bob Weir cut *Heaven Help the Fool.* Also in 1978, the Dead performed for three evenings at the Great Pyramid in Egypt, the final night culminating in a total eclipse of the moon, plus, twelve hours later, the signing of the Camp David peace accords between Egypt and Israel.

As the Rhythm Devils, Hart, Kreutzmann, and Lesh composed the percussion soundtrack for the Francis Ford Coppola film *Apocalypse Now* in 1979, releasing it in 1980 under the title *Play River Music.* The Godchauxes left the Dead at this juncture and were replaced by Brent Mydland, who contributed much to 1980's *Go to Heaven,* which was produced by Gary Lyons. Next were two double live albums for 1981, the acoustic *Dead Set* and the electric *Dead Reckoning,* plus Weir's solo *Bobby and the Midnights.* In 1982, Garcia issued *Run for the Roses.*

For five years, the Dead toured extensively while undertaking numerous offbeat projects, including recording music for the CBS TV series "The Twilight Zone." The long hiatus for Dead albums was ended in 1987 with the appearance of *In the Dark,* the record yielding the band's first Top 10 hit, "Touch of Grey." (And Robert Hunter issued his *Liberty* collection.) The Dead spent much of the next two years engrossed in a public awareness campaign to save the world's rain forests. In 1989, as their twenty-fifth anniversary neared, they assayed their unprecedented commercial outreach with *Built to Last,* scoring a respectable chart success with the single "Foolish Heart."

Emerging during the heyday of the hippie biker and the streetwise flower child, the Dead's hopeful music offered an alternative to modern cynicism in the face of urban society's mounting failings.

The band's perspective broadened as its eclectic sound blossomed, until its communal approach to its own work became a vigorous universal metaphor for the virtues of interdependence.

As the following interview with Garcia and Weir—conducted at Le Clube Front in October 1989—makes plain, the Dead have managed to survive (and thrive) with both their sense of humor and their sense of purpose intact.

The Dead have always said that they exist primarily as a concert rather than a recording band. Built to Last *contains a lot of material that had been played during the Dead's last year of live shows. How do performances influence recorded versions? Did "Foolish Heart" have that chiming, filagreed guitar sound from the start?*

GARCIA: No, not really. Like all Grateful Dead material, this material has all been through an evolutionary process. Normally, that process is one where we learn a tune, then evolve an arrangement. Everybody evolves their parts onstage over many performances. A lot of times, when we write a song for a record, it really doesn't turn into what it's gonna become until we've been performing it a few years. So normally our records are usually failures on that level; they're not representative.

Let's use "Foolish Heart" to explain how the Dead compose. How were the melody lines worked out?

GARCIA: Actually what you're mostly hearing on that song as far as the melodic support of the tune's structure is Bob and Brent's musical conversation, and the way Phil . . .

WEIR: . . . Accentuates and punctuates the conversation.

GARCIA: Absolutely. Now, normally this process takes many performances—like two or three years—before it starts to get that kind of a personality. But the way we did it this time, it gave everybody a chance to evolve their part in more of a hurry. Originally, conceptually, I was thinking of something like an open, Pete Townshend acoustic guitar, full-chord style. Something between U2 and the Who. But everything sounded better than that. Finally, I play an occasional chord or the fundamental notes, but mostly . . .

WEIR: . . . It's all lines and arpeggios. Everybody's playing at once.

GARCIA: Right, it's like Dixieland. Everybody's playing something. Nobody's just padding.

WEIR: Everybody's out of their head, all of the time!

GARCIA: Then I got together with Mickey [Hart] for the rhythm overdubs and thought that what would be nice would be—instead of the typical, sustained add-to-the-groove elements, like shakers or maracas, or stuff that is there for every bar—it'd be nice to have events that happen on particular accents but only appear every four bars. So those percussion things are like salt and pepper over the whole thing. The nice thing about that tune is that it's basically the Grateful Dead. There's not a lot of overdubs on it, no extra keyboards.

WEIR: It's basically the way it's gonna come off on stage as well. [*smirking*] Except it's gonna be different because no one's gonna remember the lines they played! But it will be in the same ballpark.

The pensive theme of "Foolish Heart," echoed throughout the album, makes it seem that this is a record about values.

GARCIA: See, [*laughs*] I had a problem with that, since I didn't write the lyrics to the tune. When [Robert] Hunter and I were working on this tune, I said, "This is an advice song!" I mean, the lyrics are, "Never give your love, my friend/to a foolish heart." Is that really good advice? Is that what we want to say? Shouldn't we tell them, "Hey, brush your teeth twice a day!"

WEIR: It was Jerry at his avuncular best! This is our Dutch uncle tune.

GARCIA: But I don't know whether I feel good giving that kind of advice, but a lot of people have informed me that, hey, that's good advice.

WEIR: All it really is is a story. Here's this guy, telling the story, and implicit in it is the notion that he's probably been through this himself. He's speaking from the depths of experience.

GARCIA: Yeah! "Do every crazy thing that you could imagine that you can do, but one thing that you might wanna *not* do . . ."

But is it just accidental that you're touching on values throughout Built to Last, *particularly in the title track?*

GARCIA: That's another one of Hunter's songs that's a successful song if it brings something to mind but doesn't tie you down to any one idea. But the kicker in there for me is the "Built to last" line. It's a great slogan, GMC [General Motors Corporation] loved it.

How often will you discuss it when Robert or someone else comes in with a lyric? Will you come right out and say, "I don't know about this."

WEIR: [*Smiling*] We went through that with "Victim or the Crime." It took me a while to endear the rest of the band to the gist of that song.

GARCIA: It was just about like pulling teeth.

WEIR: From the first line, where we used the hideous J-word [junkie].

GARCIA: "Patience runs out on the *bunny*" was what we wanted him to sing, but he wouldn't do it. [*laughter*]

Bob, your lyricist friend Gerritt Graham did the better part of those lyrics.

WEIR: What happened was, one night the chorus came to me; I don't know where from. I think it might have been a full moon night, for that matter. I kicked that chorus around for a little bit; the music came at the same time. I showed it to Gerritt, who said, "Hey, listen, can I take that home?" I said sure, but we hadn't worked together up until then.

He came back the next day with the song pretty well fleshed out, including all the tough-to-take lines. [*laughter*] We thought, "Patience runs out on the *monkey*"? It just doesn't do it. We came up with whole other lines aplenty, and nothing really did it, so I told Gerritt we were stuck with this because it has plenty of punch. Maybe a little too much.

GARCIA: It turned out to be a really wonderful composition.

WEIR: Post-adolescent mental angst.

The song also has—if the word can still be used—a "psychedelic" feel to it.

GARCIA: It's a song that's very difficult tonally, harmonically. It's not a song that you can play freely. It's complex as can be; very dense. But the lyric and the gesture of the song are also its strong points. It's angular and strange, so it seems like a good idea to capitalize on the strangeness.

I talked to Weir about having a beam solo on it too—this is an instrument that Mickey plays. It's something you love and hate at the same time, a big metal I-beam that's got fifteen–twenty piano strings on it that are all tuned in unison. He plays it with bars and rocks and pieces of metal, banging and sliding on it and creating all these industrial shrieks. It's electrified to boot. We went and sampled it, put 'em on keyboards, and added it in places where it seemed appropriate. Mickey had gone and recorded these things. We also have a virtual machine shop in there of stamper and presser sounds; they're part of the rhythm section.

WEIR: And breaking light bulbs and great big metal punches. One huge stamper that goes *ca-chunga,* we tossed that in on top of the snare drum.

Bob, there's also an intricate chord progression that you said was influenced by . . .

WEIR: . . . a Bartok piece.

GARCIA: He's always doing that kind of stuff! A lot of times you don't get it until the last minute, and then you go, "Ohhh! Far out!" [*mutual laughter*] "Picasso Moon" was another weird one like that, but it turned out terrific. I'm simple melody–oriented. I want to hear how the melody goes. Usually that's the last thing that Bob writes, or at least it's way down the road from the rest of it.

WEIR: I try to leave room for it, and let it emerge. I got the idea for "Picasso Moon" during a long bike ride, but that almost always happens to me. At that particular point I think I was on my road bike, my Spectrum Titanium, headed for the studio here. I had a piece of music that I had written for another lyric, but Brent had written something for that lyric. Seeing as I was gonna have to fight with [John] Barlow [Mydland's frequent collaborator] over it, I decided to withdraw this piece of music and put it with something else.

We were sitting around here bullshitting in the front room of the studio like we do, and when the conversation quieted Phil said, "Picasso Moon. I don't know why I said that." I was listening and something went *ding! click!* and then on my bike ride back home that evening I flashed on it and decided it was what I wanted for the chorus and could build a whole song around it.

Barlow worked on the lyrics with me, and while I was working on the music [John] Bralove [the Dead's electronics whiz] was busy sitting back saying, "No, that's not it, go with this." He came up with a few lyric suggestions, while keeping Barlow and me away from each other's throats.

GARCIA: [*Laughing*] They had an adversarial relationship.

The song is a science fiction landscape.

WEIR: You got it. That's basically what it is.

GARCIA: It's techno-punk.

Did you guys feel any pressure after In the Dark *became such a big hit, along with the single, "Touch of Grey"?*

WEIR: [*Wryly*] I couldn't sleep nights.

GARCIA: We're pretty inured to that sort of pressure anymore.

WEIR: "You gotta repeat! You gotta repeat! You guys have the chance, but you gotta repeat!"

GARCIA: But we can't do it. We're constitutionally incapable of doing it, anyway, so we don't fight it anymore.

WEIR: We're constitutionally incapable of taking much seriously.

Yet it must seem a novelty at this point to have that commercial corridor open up for your music. Because you guys have flourished for decades without ever needing to think about a hit single.

GARCIA: That's been very lucky for us, yeah. It's hard to tell whether it matters or not. Our audience has been growing logarithmically anyway. And whether the album did it or the audience did it is hard to tell. When you don't release a record for seven years, and the audience is still growing, it's hard to tell at that juncture if there's *this* many people who will buy a Grateful Dead record, or . . .

WEIR: . . . The record *itself* is so strong that it commands a following.

GARCIA: It's not clear to us that one has added to the other, or where they stop influencing each other. It's not as though the record has given us a big boot, but it's been a novelty, certainly.

WEIR: As far as having a commercial corridor for our records, if you take us and put us in the corridor and give us a little push, we'll walk right into whatever wall we can find. [*laughter*] We won't be able to find our way down that corridor! We can't do that; it doesn't work for us. We don't go straight in any direction. So that's not a viable option for us. What we've gotta do is take each record individually.

GARCIA: I think *In the Dark*, though, made us feel some confidence about making our own records again, instead of letting producers do it. And this record has made it so it can almost be fun.

WEIR: I had a ball making this record. But we had a coupla previous stints trying to make this record.

You mean you had a false start?

GARCIA: We had at least a couple of them!

WEIR: We got hopelessly hung up on the croquet tournament out in front of the Marin Civic Center [*laughter*], and so we fled the Civic Center and went up to Lucasfilm [the Skywalker Ranch] . . .

GARCIA: Where we got hopelessly hung up by the beauty of the scenery and the surroundings.

WEIR: And barbecueing and all that sort of stuff. Then we came back down here and made the record, and *that* didn't happen. So we started more or less fresh down here at Front Street in April [1989] and sort of idled through April. While it took us about two years to figure how we were gonna go about doing it—and how we weren't—it only took about a month and half to finally do it.

Brent's "Just a Little Light" has a unique sound. How do you see Brent's influence on the band?

GARCIA: He's obviously come into his own. He's getting comfortable, is what it is, and he's starting to trust everybody. There's a thing that you have to go through in the Grateful Dead where if you really love your own music, you have to go, "Well, it's not gonna be the way I *want* it, but it's gonna be good."

His "I Will Take You Home" is beautiful, an authentic emotion—especially if you have daughters—and it works perfectly well with just him and a piano. Brent has always been really talented, but this record is a chance to show him off, and he's comfortable being the guy in that position.

WEIR: He has a certain prosaic earthiness that the rest of us lack. It's not really my strong suit, nor Jerry's.

GARCIA: And on "Just a Little Light" I thought it would be a good chance for me to imitate the guy in the New Bohemians who imitates me. [*laughter*] Since all I heard in this last year was, "Have you heard that guy that sounds like you?"

Bob, do you see yourself primarily as a songwriter or musician?

WEIR: As a conjurer. Joseph Campbell labeled me a conjurer one night. He was watching us play and said, "What you are is a conjurer." I thought about it for a coupla months and decided, "Yeah, you're right." [*smiling*]

So I see myself in that role these days. If something occurs to me, if I get a well-integrated flash of something that I want to portray, I'll go with that, regardless of *what* it is.

GARCIA: Magic is what we do. Music is the way we do it.

WEIR: The better I get at it, the more trouble I'm often inviting. With "Victim or the Crime," I went through heartaches trying to get that past the band. And past the fans—at concerts they stop dancing and everything!

GARCIA: [*Laughing*] This is an audience-freeze song. This is where all the smiles dissolve. There's ten thousand people with big question marks over their heads.

Sounds like some spells are easier to cast than others.

GARCIA: You gotta go for the weirdness, you have to take a stab at it!

When you do touch the Zeitgeist, is it usually from an intuitive standpoint?

GARCIA: Yes. That's what art does. From my point of view I don't see a song like "Built to Last" as a very worldview-oriented song.

I find it to be personal and universal rather than topical and local. There's also an emotional content that doesn't exactly come out of the lyrics; it comes from somewhere else, but it's the way the thing falls together.

WEIR: It's tough to find something to write about these days, something you can dive into, after you've written a few songs.

How do you guys regard the Arista era, looking back at that body of work?

GARCIA: We've actually had some pretty good music, but in working with other producers, it was the thing of us being crowded into their methodology. *Shakedown Street* was a little looser than the others because Lowell [George] was a looser guy.

WEIR: It's really a pity with *Shakedown Street* that Lowell had to go out on tour pretty much in the middle of it, leaving us. Then we went to Egypt and then came back and finished it rather hurriedly. That could have been a much better record than it ended up being—if Lowell had stuck around and there had been some overview all the way through. Or, if Lowell had not been involved at all.

Yet I could single out tracks from Shakedown Street *that will always be included in the canon of great Grateful Dead songs, like "I Need a Miracle," "Fire on the Mountain," and the title track. How did Lowell George get drawn into the project in the first place?*

GARCIA: At the time we were going with the Arista suggestion that we work with producers; we were being cooperative. We liked Little Feat's music, and we figured, "Here's a guy who has to deal with the dynamics of a band. He understands a band's work and what it's like." And he did, he was perfect. He was a good ol' boy, sympatico.

WEIR: I interviewed him for the gig. We went to dinner at the Golden Dragon Café the night after there had been a horrendous Chinatown gangland shoot-out there. They were still sweeping up the glass, and there wasn't much blood around, but there were plenty of bulletholes and lots of new silverware.

As for the interview, I just said to Lowell, "Hey, sounds like fun to me, how's it sound to you?" He said, "When do we get started?" That was pretty much it.

But it was kinda silly of us choosing him as a producer. Little Feat's studio records had never done very well for the same reason as ours—because they never lived up to their live sound; they were always thin by comparison.

GARCIA: But still, the songs you mention are great ones.

How about Terrapin Station*? It had excellent songs like Bob's "Estimated Prophet."*

WEIR: That song was in 7/4 time. Not many people realized that.

GARCIA: A reggae song in 7/4 time! Don't try this at home, kids! Meanwhile, we still do "Terrapin" too.

WEIR: And "Sampson and Delilah" often gets pretty ripping when we play it live.

How about the Go to Heaven *LP?*

GARCIA: We still do "Alabama Getaway" sometimes. Also "Althea" and "Feel Like a Stranger"—a good tune. And we do "Don't Ease Me In," that's one of our chestnuts. But we don't relate to these records, we relate to the *tunes.*

WEIR: And we do "Saint of Circumstance" often enough. So, yes, we do plenty of stuff from that album. I just wish that back then we had the MIDI technology and Dolby SR technology we have now. This hardware makes it possible to do various generations of recording without losing any sound quality. We can put in more time with the records because I can work at home, Mickey can work at his place, and Jerry can work here, and we can bring our parts together and throw them into the soup to see if they work.

Was there pressure during these Arista years to just get the records out?

GARCIA: [*Chuckling*] We don't put 'em out unless we get pressure. We'll work on them 'til Hell freezes over unless someone says, "You *must* release this record."

WEIR: Our standard way of doing it is, we create a deadline somewhere in the impossible, hazy future but it's a real firm deadline. And then we just ignore it. [*laughter*] When the real world's-gonna-end deadline comes, we keep ignoring it until panic sufficiently motivates us to get to work. Then we make most of our records in about a month and a half. The last two weeks are particularly hellish.

How were things during the midseventies existence of the Grateful Dead Records label, the era of Wake of the Flood, From the Mars Hotel, Blues for Allah, *and so forth?*

GARCIA: Those were six-week projects. *Blues for Allah* was the exception in that we worked on it until it was done. We had a formula for that one. We were not gonna develop anything outside of the studio. We were gonna get together every day up at Weir's place, and anything that came out of that we were gonna use. We weren't gonna go home and write songs and bring them in. It all got written there at Bob's, but a lot of songs went through tremendous convolutions.

"Crazy Fingers" started off as a power-rock raver, and turned into something completely different by the end of it.

Have you guys ever made an album you wouldn't dare release for some stylistic reason?

GARCIA: There are certains cuts, like "Barbed-Wire Whipping Party," which is out anyway among the fans. I don't know where they got it from, but it's on the streets. It's not exactly a song, it's more a lunatic babble riff. In fact, it's not music at all.

WEIR: Boy, that's bad news. People are actually listening to *that*? Don't play that for your children! It's more of a performance poetry piece of some kind. But I don't know *what* kind.

GARCIA: Mickey has done a lot of things of the kind you mean. He's done a telephone album. He's done a bug album that's hilarious; it's got all these songs about insects, the war on insects.

WEIR: He had big plans for that one! [*convulsive mutual laughter*]

GARCIA: Mostly, we're always out on the road working, because we earn our living by playing. So we haven't had much of the luxury where you just go into the studio for no particular reason to screw around.

WEIR: There's tape somewhere of Mickey playing someone's head! And between rehearsal takes we have fifteen or twenty versions on tape of "The Mexican Hat Dance" and "The Frozen Logger."

Speaking of playfulness, Jerry, what were you like as a little kid?

GARCIA: I was a wiseguy, I talked too much, I spoke out of turn. And I was a notorious unachiever.

You once described yourself as being "a hoodlum at the age of thirteen."

GARCIA: Yeah, I had a certain attitude. I was born in San Francisco and I went to Denman Junior High and Balboa High in San Francisco, both of which were razor-toting schools. It was a matter of self-preservation. Either you were a hoodlum or you were a puddle on the sidewalk. I was part of a big gang, a nonaffiliated gang.

At that time in the 1950s San Francisco was broken up into two loose groups, called the Barts and the Shoes. The Shoes were the white shoe, Pat Boone–looking types, out on the avenues among the upscale people. The working-class neighborhoods were where the Barts were—"Black Bart Greasers" would be another expression for them.

The city was divided bilaterally like that, and there would be incursions into other neighborhoods where you'd beat everybody up, or everybody would beat you up. It was a state of war, and I didn't last long in that. I spent a lot of time in the Mission Emergency Hospital on weekends, holding my lip together, or my eye, because some guy had hit me with a board.

But I also got three merit badges in Boy Scouts, for Knot-Tying, Compass-Reading, and Lifesaving. The last one was useful. In the late sixties I was involved in lifesaving in a swimming pool when my stepdaughter, Sunshine, fell in and we found her floating face-down, all blue. The ultimate horror trip. I pulled her out and mouth-to-mouth resuscitated her. It would have been awful if it didn't work.

Jerry, didn't your dad's people come from Spain?

GARCIA: They came from Corunna, which is on a peninsula on the western coast of Spain. I don't really know much about my family. My father, José—or Joe—Garcia, died when I was five. My father was a musician in San Francisco. I don't know why they came to the States. I imagine it was because of some economic problem, or possibly the First World War. They came around 1914. There was a malaise in Europe at the time.

The whole family came directly to the West Coast. They were upper-middle-class Spaniards. There's a whole slew of Garcias still here and back there in Spain, but they don't have any truck with me. I'm a black sheep; in fact, I'm a black sheep of black sheep—I understand my father was a black sheep too. They're very straight, and I don't see them. They're the kind of people who'd change their name to *Grayson*, and they're not Hispanic-looking. They're sallow, brown-haired, red-haired kind of people.

All my cousins were very bright, and fun to hang out with, but real straight.

Bob, how about growing up in Atherton, California?

WEIR: It was considerably more bucolic. Atherton is like the Bel Air of Northern California. My dad was an engineer—mechanical engineering. He designed heating and cooling systems for big buildings, hotels, factories.

I played ball; I was a jock. I wasn't much into baseball, except I really liked Willie Mays. Mainly, I was into football. I liked John

Brody, Gene Washington, and Y. A. Tittle, the Bald Eagle. And I ran track.

The Weir family tree is Scottish and German, I think. I was adopted, but it was a great family to be adopted into. My dad's name is Frederick, and the Weir side of the family goes back to the third ship after the *Mayflower*, believe it or not. My mom, Eleanor, was born in Switzerland. And I'm related to a guy named Benedict Arnold—not *the* Benedict Arnold but a guy who was governor of Rhode Island.

How about your early childhoods?

GARCIA: I was asthmatic as a kid, so it kept me off the streets a lot. And so I was in bed, reading. It probably was a boon for me. Ray Bradbury was my favorite writer: *The Martian Chronicles,* that kind of stuff. I also collected EC comic books, which were the comic books every parent was afraid of during the fifties, ultra-horrible comic books: *Tales from the Crypt, Vault of Horror.* EC also did *Mad Comics,* which later became *Mad Magazine.* They had the most intelligent writing, and the best artwork by far. They'd scare the hell out of you. So that was early literacy for me.

WEIR: That was about the only kind of reading I could handle. I'm dyslexic in the extreme, and pretty nearly functionally illiterate, except I can read the sports section. But they had never really heard of dyslexia when I was young, so they just figured I was lazy—which I was. But this was the kind of stuff you really can't get over.

Still, I got decent grades. In fact, toward the end of my school career I started getting good grades. I developed a good memory. I also developed an ability to bullshit teachers. I managed to stay awake for at least half my classes, and got A's.

I got to be fairly roundly hated for it, because I didn't take books home or anything. I was good at English Literature and History, which I found fascinating.

GARCIA: Art, English, and Spelling were my good subjects. I've always been good at that kind of stuff—anything that had to do with reading. But Mathematics was the pits, forget it. I stopped doing homework in the seventh grade because I thought it was a waste of time.

WEIR: My main hobby and pastime was girls. I went to seven—count 'em—seven schools, and I was kicked out of every one I attended. And you know, I even ran away to be a cowboy once. I had gone to school—Fountain Valley School in Colorado Springs,

Colorado—with a guy whose parents owned a ranch, and they offered me a job on their ranch in Wyoming. So I skipped out of Colorado Springs with a buddy and went there.

GARCIA: The buddy is John Barlow. I thought I'd bring that up.

WEIR: So we lived in the bunkhouse, got up way too early, and did work that was unpleasant and hard. We did the unpleasant stuff that the cowboys wouldn't do—shoveled lots of stalls. Miserable work, but I was almost happy doing that, since it was way different from anything else I'd been doing. I was just getting into it when my parents found me, but they became fast friends with my buddy's folks.

GARCIA: Incidentally, Barlow's spread is one of the last of the American land and cattle baronies, the pre-oil and steel wealth, so he was a remnant of the Old West.

Jerry, speaking of remnants of the past, what were your days in the army like during the pre-Vietnam-draft era?

GARCIA: Well, when you're seventeen, you can handle the army, you don't mind. At least for as long as I was in, which was for about nine–ten months. Then I got kicked out. I had pathological antiauthoritarianism. But I joined the army to avoid going to jail. It was just one of those situations where I had used up everything, every option. My mother moved me up to Cazadero on the Russian River, and I went to Analy High School in Sebastopol, because things were just getting too intense for me in San Francisco. Then I started cutting school up there at Analy, and I'd steal my mother's car and I'd go down to the Peninsula—I had a girlfriend down there. So things were catching up with me.

To me, at the time, I thought, "Well, I'll show 'em, I'll join the army!" My mother thought, "Great, fine." She signed the papers for me, and I went in. The ironic thing is that I didn't get out of California, and consequently I cut school from the army, too, which is one of the reasons I got kicked out.

I did my basic training in Fort Ord, and then they stationed me in the Presidio, which is where I lived—San Francisco!—which was really stupid.

Once you're out of basic training, being in the army is like having a bad job. I didn't take it seriously. They're very tough about things like showing up for the morning roll-call trip—reveille. And if you're not there, that's called AWOL. You pile up about nine or ten of those, and it doesn't look good on the record. I was assigned to a headquarters company, which is the ultimate padded work.

Nobody does anything, there's no work involved; it's a showpiece company. The guys there had jockeyed for years to be stationed permanently in the Presidio, *and they don't want any trouble of any kind.*

I was there for about three or four months, and the commanding officer just said to me, "Garcia, how would you like to get out of the army?" I said, "Okay. I've seen enough."

But you did bring your guitar into the army with you.

GARCIA: Yes I did. I brought an electric Sears Silvertone, the Harmony model. I was just a three-chorder then. I was self-taught, and I had never met another guitar player, actually, until I got into the army. Then I met this recruit who played a little bit of finger style, and I was totally fascinated by it.

Of course, this was a guy who was trouble incarnate. I hung out with him and got into ten times more trouble. He was a liquor store holdup man; one of those kinds of guys. [*laughter*] I started hanging with him, and things got so deep! One time just after I got out of the army, I was staying with a friend in East Palo Alto, and this army pal turns up with a stolen car. He's got a fella with him, both of 'em dressed in suits and packing irons, and they had just done a series of bank robberies up and down the coast!! I thought, "Hmmm, maybe I'd like to not see so much of this guy and his crime scene any longer."

Bob, what was the first song you ever wrote?

WEIR: I rewrote "New Minglewood Blues," and then I was involved in the writing of "New Potato Caboose," and then I wrote "Born Cross-eyed." I got my first guitar at fourteen as a gift for graduating junior high school. It was a $17 Japanese guitar. It was a pretty miserable guitar, but I learned to play it a little bit. The first song I learned to play on it was "Sloop John B."

GARCIA: The first music I ever probably wrote, back when I was a five-string banjo player, was a tune that I called "Garcia's Breakdown."

Jerry, as an adolescent, you were also interested in art, correct?

GARCIA: [*Nodding*] Fine art. When I was still in school in the city, I went on evenings and Saturdays to what's now the Art Institute in North Beach, but used to be the California School of Fine Art. This was during the heyday of the beatnik era. I was a painter, and I *still* paint, draw, and do lots of graphics stuff on computers. I do a lot of it, but I have no interest in showing it.

Paul Klee, Van Gogh, Picasso, those were my real fireballs. I just loved everything I saw of theirs. Paul Klee, especially, for the sense of humor and the wonderful textural qualities. Van Gogh for the incredible vibrance and the madness.

Who would your fireball guitar inspirations have been?

GARCIA: Chuck Berry, from a very early age, was *it* for me. I liked the classics: Little Richard—not for guitar but for the music—and I loved Gene Vincent and the Blue Cats, and the guitar player in that band [Cliff Gallup]. That was a great, nasty little band. I loved Eddie Cochran, and I loved James Burton's playing on Rickie Nelson records—those little four-bar and eight-bar interjections James would stick in there were cool as hell. Those guys were gods for me.

And yet, Jerry, you seemed to be into string bands when you first began to perform.

GARCIA: When I was first loving rock and roll and I was fumbling around with my first electric guitar, my old Danelectro, my teacher at art school used to play records while we were painting. He played a Big Bill Broonzy record that I was in awe of; it was the first time I heard anybody play acoustic blues. I ran out as quickly as I could save up enough money and bought that Big Bill album. I listened to it, but it never occurred to me to try and play like it. [*laughter*] I absorbed it unconsciously, and it started to turn up years later.

After I got out of the army, I fell in with [Robert] Hunter, and we were influenced by the folk scare—the Kingston Trio and that kind of stuff. I didn't know how to find my way into that music 'til I met some people who were more involved with it, like Marshall Lester, who was a friend of mine from when I was ten to thirteen. By now he was a college guy, and he turned me on to bluegrass music and to old-time string band music. He played a little frailing banjo and introduced me to the Reverend Gary Davis. I heard that sound, and I just had to be able to make it.

That's when I started to tighten up and have a direction. Before that, I loved music but I wasn't *learning*. A guy showed me a finger-picking pattern, and I sat down and worked and worked until I could do a coupla respectable quick-picking rolls on the guitar.

WEIR: Joanie Baez influenced me a whole lot. Around my sophomore year of high school she made it big, and she caught my ear. She was way different from the Kingston Trio and seemed to have a whole lot more integrity. Then when I got back from Colorado and Wyoming to California, I started hanging out in the folk scene in Palo Alto. Whatever was hot around there—including Jerry, here—was what caught my attention. I tried to pick up on any or all of what came through town. There was a guy named Michael Cooney who showed me a lot of stuff. And Jerry too—but we very quickly got involved with a jug band right after meeting.

Then guys like Lightnin' Hopkins and Mance Lipscomb and Doc Watson would come though, and I'd be all over them, trying to pick up anything I could.

GARCIA: Those were great days, 'cause of lot of those old-timers like Mississippi John Hurt were still alive, and you could hear them. That was fabulous, the exposure to those players.

How do you feel, listening back now to Workingman's Dead *and* American Beauty*?*

GARCIA: They're flawed masterpieces. It's another case of underachieving. They could have been a *little* bit better, but they hold up.

WEIR: The country and rock thing was happening at that time, but we had our own synthesis. We brought *more* to it than that, because Phil brought a lot of classical baggage and twentieth-century avant-garde stuff like Stockhausen and Varese with him, and Mickey was bringing North Indian classical. Plus, Billy [Kreutzmann] was good at fatback R&B, and Pigpen was packing the mail as well.

GARCIA: At that point we were trying to get out of that bag of spending a year in the studio and feeling so weird. It was like, "Let's try to do something *simple.* Let's make it as painless as possible." We were playing the *Live Dead* album's music when we were recording *Workingman's Dead,* so there was a big difference between what we were recording and performing.

WEIR: *Workingman's Dead* happened so fast, but it was like a light went on, and everybody sorta flashed on, "Hey, form follows function. Let's simplify." In other words, let's make every *component* as strong as it can possibly be and see what that renders. That changed things for me, and since then I've lived my life by that idea as best I can. If that hadn't happened, what I do would have become incredibly complex and I'd still be working on my next piece!

GARCIA: Those records were Grateful Dead neoclassicism.

What comes next for you two, individually and with the band?

GARCIA: I don't have a whole lot individually on the back burner. I'm shopping around for something to do that no one will like.

WEIR: You want to irritate some folks?

GARCIA: [*Smiling*] Yeah, yeah! But the Grateful Dead is happening for me right now.

WEIR: I'm working with [bassist] Rob Wasserman in my spare

time. It doesn't take much time to work with Rob because the whole band is just this other guy. And he has such a lot to offer that, in just a coupla hours, we can rehearse a bunch of stuff in a lot of different directions, and scare ourselves. We're talking about an album.

GARCIA: My solo band is like that too. It's not very work-intensive. It doesn't require a whole lot of rehearsal. That's helpful.

Recently Paul McCartney was asked why he wanted to get back out on the road again, doing concerts. People wondered if it was the Who that spurred him on, or the Stones. He said, "No, it was Jerry Garcia and the Dead."

GARCIA: I've heard that. But he inspired *us!* The Beatles are at least as responsible for us being here as anybody else is.

WEIR: The Beatles were why we turned from a jug band into a rock and roll band. We turned the corner when, after a year as a jug band, we went and saw the film *A Hard Day's Night.* What we saw them doing was impossibly attractive. I couldn't think of anything else more worth doing.

GARCIA: All of our songs are kinda Beatlesque, I think, and "Here Comes Sunshine" was a direct take on Beatles tunes.

One last question: Do you fellas ever regret not insisting on calling that [1971] *live album* Skullfuck*?*

GARCIA: [*Slyly*] Every day of my life. It would have been perfect.

WEIR: We weren't so serious about it as we were about fucking with them. [*giggles*] We just wanted to see them squirm. And they did! It was wonderful fun.

GARCIA: [*Nodding, grinning*] It was most gratifying.

The first rule of rock and roll is to show up. There is no second rule; the rest is entirely up to you, including *when* and *how* you choose to show up. Sly Stone is the man who somehow stretched the lone precept of this profession far beyond its almost limitlessly elastic limits, until, incredible as it may seem, he ultimately broke it.

Back in his hometown of Dallas, Texas, he had been a punctual churchgoer and a child prodigy who launched a recording career with a sacred single, "On the Battlefield for My Lord," released at age five. Born Sylvester Stewart on March 15, 1944, Stewart sang the song with a family group, the Stewart Four, as well as playing drums and guitar with several doo-wop groups. At sixteen, he cut "Long Time Away," a solo record that did well in the region. At Vallejo Junior College, he majored in music for three semesters, with an emphasis on theory and composition, and sang in the college choir. He used his edu-

Sly Stone

1
9
8
9

cation to put various bar bands together for weekend dates at go-go joints in North Beach and rock and roll dances at American Legion halls. He met Tom "Big Daddy" Donahue, the renowned Bay Area disc jockey, at just such a Legion hall, and Donahue told him he'd left radio to concentrate on a record company he'd formed with another ex-DJ, Bob Mitchell. Stewart joined Autumn Records, a zealous enterprise that aimed to harness the uncategorized local rock upheaval, and sharpened his arranging skills. He made two undistinguished records of his own, "I Just Learned to Swim" and "Buttermilk, Parts 1 & 2," before turning his attention to a band called the Beau Brummels. He also put Grace Slick's first group, the Great Society, through over 200 takes of "Free Advice," a song that landed on the flip side of the original release of "Somebody to Love."

In early 1966, he departed Autumn Records, using his royalties to buy his folks a home in Daly City, and took a job as a jock with KSOL in San Francisco. Smarts acquired in a three-month course at the Chris Borden School of Modern Broadcasting helped keep the airwaves wriggling with the sounds of "Super Soul." Employing request lines and such stunts as flushing-toilet sound effects after Ex-Lax commercials and live piano renditions of "Happy Birthday" for listeners, he built a solid following. Later, at KDIA in Oakland, he became a star attraction from 6:00 to 9:00 P.M. But his main interest remained in his band, the Stoners. When it dissolved in 1966, he and trumpeter Cynthia Robinson formed the Family Stone band, a clutch of "soul hippies" that included sister Rose on piano and brother Freddie on guitar.

Everybody in Haight-Ashbury was preaching togetherness in 1967, and Sly wanted to merge white rock and black soul into a musical archetype of everybody's stoned-out musings. After a trip to Vegas with the Family Stone, he left the safety of the radio booth for the great indoors of the Bay Area's rock palaces.

Sly and the Family Stone's first single, "I Ain't Got Nobody"/"I Can't Turn You Loose," led to a signing with Epic Records; but their first LP, *A Whole New Thing,* lacked the fizzy familial feel of their live shows. *Dance to the Music* was a raging rebound. *Life* gave the group a No. 1 single, "Everyday People," whose call for racial harmony floated on rippling waves of march-tempo glee. The primeval funk of James Brown had been broadened, blended, turned more pliant on this brilliant track and then embroidered with all the soot and smiles of a superior street fair. *Stand!,* released in the summer of 1969, was the album-length masterwork that "Everyday

People" had presaged; in one fell stroke it gave black music a new inner complexion while revolutionizing every other rock rhythm section extant.

The hits kept coming—"Hot Fun in the Summertime," "Thank You Falettinme Be Mice Elf Agin," "Everybody Is a Star"—but where was Sly? Concert promoters across the nation were promised he'd arrive any minute . . . or thereabouts. He canceled twenty-six of the eighty dates he'd committed to in 1970 and roughly half of the next year's shows. When he did put in an appearance, he was often as much as five hours overdue.

A *Greatest Hits* package was hurried out, selling 3 million copies, but an all-new LP was two years late when his manager sued Sly for $250,000 in loans and back commissions. The idea of having a lien put on every shaky show moved Sly to refuse to tour. The suit was dropped in exchange for promises of productivity and reorganization. Yet even when Sly began living in a van parked out in front of the recording studio, he proved tardy—if not missing in action. Epic put him on suspension and froze his royalties. He was evicted from his $250,000 house because he couldn't make the mortgage payments. He took refuge in a Beverly Hills apartment house, where he blared sound equipment from sunset to sunrise; his landlord filed a $3 million lawsuit, charging him with conspiracy to drive off the other tenants.

Complaining of Sly's cocaine use and dual personality, his manager read Sly the riot act. Sly answered with *There's a Riot Going On,* a broody, militant, savage indictment of all the decayed determinism of the 1960s—Sly's, the country's, the world's. *Riot* codified his fury at having to produce, his rage at needing to retreat and then hide, his self-loathing about the drugs he could not let go of when the street fair dispersed, his bitter disappointment that his wildly sequined sense of style had not transmogrified into an acceptable excuse for content.

Out of morbid fascination, his audience bought enough copies of this symphony of detritus that it made No. 1. It was a fortuitous accident that could not be sustained, and members of the Family Stone were reshuffled or replaced in the confusion and mayhem that followed.

In the meantime, police across the country had grown hostile toward Sly and his seeming endorsement of the Black Panthers; the Panthers seemed to grow equally angry with the singer's fickle fence-straddling. The cops took the initiative. Sly had no less than five confrontations with the law in the latter part of 1972. July found him in custody after the Family Stone's mobile home was stopped on Santa Monica Boulevard in Los Angeles. Two vials of narcotics and two pounds of marijuana were found in the vehicle, but charges were later dismissed; a judge decided there was insufficient evidence to prosecute. Then, while sitting in a car in a friend's driveway, he was busted for disturbing the peace. As he was leaving a sickle cell anemia telethon in Los Angeles, he was stopped and searched. Before a concert at Madison Square Garden, Sly was arrested on West 45th Street for supposedly threatening an old lady with a Colt .44 cap pistol he was wearing in a holster. In December, police invaded his Bel Air home, saying they'd had an anonymous report of a robbery and dead bodies on the premises. Finding nothing, they handcuffed Sly for having no identification and led him away.

Early in 1973, he canceled an East Coast concert swing, without explanation, after two shows. Later in the winter, Sly was arrested in another raid on his L.A. home and charged with possession of cocaine, cannabis, and dangerous drugs, and possession of the last for sale. He got a year's probation.

Come spring 1973, the word was that Sly was moving to New York and getting married to his nineteen-year-old Asian girlfriend, Kathy Silva, who was expecting their child in August. He also announced that a new LP was in the works and told the *New York Times* why he had missed so many concerts and how he planned to save his band: "Sometimes you don't feel your soul at 7:30. But we've been recording, rescheduling, regrouping and recoping [*sic*] on everything we like to do, what we have to do, and things we wish we could do."

Fresh was released before the year was out, with "If You Want Me to Stay" becoming a hit as much for its sad-sack irony as for its own modest merits. In June 1974, Sly and Kathy Silva were wed in a televised ceremony prior to a sold-out concert at Madison Square Garden. By October, Silva had sued for divorce, asking custody of their one-year-old son, Sylvester Bubb Ali Stewart, Jr., plus alimony and child support. The *Small Talk* LP came and went.

There were more missed concerts, among the most decried no-shows being a benefit for muscular dystrophy in Washington, D.C., in December 1974, which nearly sparked a full-scale melee—until the crowd was let in free. A spokesman from Sly's record company said the star bowed out, insulted, when he'd discovered that he'd been paid for what was supposed to be a free appearance. Sly would have nothing to do with the money or the event. "I think it was a failure of communication," said the Epic source.

The *High on You* set and a *High Energy* collection both appeared in 1975, their equivocal titles happenstantial. Sly made three albums in the next eight years, all of which had sheepish names *(Heard You Missed Me, Back on the Right Track, Ain't But the One Way).* None attracted much attention. He also worked with Funkadelic on a 1981 album called *Electric Spanking of War Babies* and continued to book, cancel, and sometimes actually give concerts of suitably erratic quality.

In August 1981, Sly was arrested on charges of cocaine possession. July 1982 brought new misadventures: he was nabbed after a brawl at a hotel in the Westwood suburb of Los Angeles. Sly identified himself as his brother Fred, but a fingerprint analysis established his true identity; police said they had found a freebasing kit in his room and a small handgun and cocaine in his briefcase, and they charged him accordingly.

Nineteen eighty-three. Another bumper year for busts. In February, Sly and four other men were detained in Paxton, Illinois, because the registration for their van had expired. During a search of the vehicle, authorities found a sawed-off shotgun and a quantity of "white powder." In June, Sly was found passed out in a motel room in Fort Myers, Florida, with a woman companion; he was arraigned on charges of possession of cocaine and drug paraphernalia. In August, he was charged with grand theft in Fort Lauderdale. He was collared at a gay nightclub where he was appearing, police offering a detailed explanation of the deeds that preceded the arrest. While at the King Neptune Hotel, where he and his manager were staying, Sly had allegedly admired a $5,000 gold ring belonging to Maryanne Magness, part owner of the hotel. He tried it on and then, as Magness became "distracted" by her duties, "forgot" about it, moving on to play a Pac Man video game. Leaving town for a quick trip back to his home in San Francisco, he noticed he was still wearing what police described as the "huge" ring and gave it to Novi, his one-year-old daughter by new wife Olinka. When he returned to Florida, Sly found himself confronted by an irate Magness, who demanded he cough up her absent jewelry. She told police the ring was particularly valuable because she had received it from her father just before his murder three years ago.

At Sly's September arraignment in Broward County Jail on the theft charge, Judge Howard Ford was in the midst of releasing him on $10,000 bail when he paused to yell, "Are we keeping you awake?" at the slumped, dozing star. It later came to light that Robert Eaton, the arresting officer, couldn't resist the temptation to get an autograph from the accused while he had him in custody, so he impulsively made the singer sign the back of his Miranda Rights Waiver Form. "It was the only thing I had," said Eaton.

In May 1984, Stone made a statement from the Lee Mental Clinic in Fort Myers, Florida, where he was undergoing a six-month program to kick freebase: "Drugs can take you up, but they can also take you out. . . . I want to do music and have that express itself." But his self-redemption would be postponed. In December 1989, he was sentenced to fifty-five days in prison in Los Angeles after pleading guilty to a misdemeanor charge of driving under the influence of cocaine. The forty-five-year-old Sly had been arrested by FBI agents in Connecticut and returned to LA after fleeing California following a 1987 narcotics charge. He still faced trial on other drug felonies. Agin.

From the viewpoint of a practitioner of magick, there is no happenstance in this world or any other. The planet does not revolve, the rain does not cease, the woman does not conceive, the illness does not set in, the sparrow does not drop from the sky—unless some animate force wills it to occur. The maker of magick does not believe in the existence of accidents.

Aleister Crowley was a magickian, purportedly one of the most formidable who ever lived. He was also a painter, poet, world traveler, mountain climber, bisexual satyriac, and heroin addict. He was a member since 1898 of a secret fraternal organization called the Order of the Golden Dawn. Founded by several Rosicrucians for the purposes of practicing magick, its objective was that mankind "may ultimately regain union with the Divine Man latent in himself." Crowley's aim was to gain the know-how to invoke his Holy Guardian Angel; his philosophy was distilled in his customary greeting: "Do what thou wilt shall be the whole of the law."

William Burroughs, for one, feels Crowley was on to something, and that rock and roll is a modern force with a kindred perspective. "Rock," he wrote in 1975, "can be seen as one attempt to break out of this dead and soulless universe and reassert the universe of magic[k]."

Jimmy Page

1990

Crowley's home was at Boleskine, near Loch Ness in Scotland. The building was erected on the site of a church that had burned to the ground with all of its unfortunate congregation trapped inside. Prior to Crowley's taking occupancy, a beheading and a host of suicides had taken place within its walls. After Crowley's passing, several tenants went straight from the house to insane asylums.

Thus acquiring something of a sinister reputation, the address became difficult to rent or sell, but, in the midseventies, a realtor negotiated its purchase for Jimmy Page, avid devotee of mysticism and magick, lead guitarist of the Yardbirds and of Led Zeppelin, the latter one of the most popular rock bands in the world. Asked why he picked the remote place as a hideaway, Page said, "I'm attracted by the unknown."

James Patrick Page was born on January 9, 1944, in Heston, Middlesex, England, and spent his early years in Felton, a community in the shadow of Heathrow Airport. An only child, he enjoyed the isolation his status afforded him, and the gift of a secondhand acoustic guitar when he was twelve further enhanced his sense of apartness. After hearing Elvis Presley's "Baby, Let's Play House," he made up his mind to be a professional musician.

Yardbirds bass player Paul Samwell-Smith left the group in 1966, and Page took his place. When physically ravaged lead guitarist Jeff Beck dropped out of the band five months later, after suffering a nervous breakdown (according to Beck: "Inflamed brain, inflamed tonsils, and an inflamed cock and everything else"), Page took over the reins, asking studio bassist John Paul Jones and drummer John Bonham, with whom he'd worked on Donovan's *Hurdy Gurdy Man* LP, to join him. Robert Plant, vocalist with a group called the Band of Joy, completed the revamped act, and they fulfilled the previous lineup's lingering commitments in Scandinavia as the New Yardbirds. Various other names for the band were proposed, but Led Zeppelin was agreed to after Keith Moon of the Who predicted the band would go over like a "lead balloon."

Led Zeppelin, released in 1968, was unlike any other album of its era. Its hollow, thudding percussion, stupored melodies, and strangled, clarion vocals suggested a somnambulistic Goliath in the throes of an opium trance. The playing was blues-based but coated with fuzzy overtones and splenetic distortion. This was "heavy metal," fully realized in all its precise, ponderous, pealing pomp.

The term "heavy metal" first appeared in the opening lines of chapter fourteen of *The Soft Machine,* novelist/ex-heroin addict William Seward Burroughs's psycho-sexual science fiction masterpiece, published in 1961. The phrase was coined to depict a young thug—Uranian Willy the Heavy Metal Kid—but by chapter fifteen it also described a tempest in a mythical, war-torn world: " 'Citizens of Gravity we are converting all out to Heavy Metal! . . . Do not believe the calumny that our metal fallout will turn our planet into a slag heap . . . Heavy Metal is our program and we are prepared to sink through it . . .' " Critic Lester Bangs later salted a *CREEM* Magazine review of the Yardbirds with a reference to "Heavy Metal Kids," providing the music with a fitting handle it could proudly hammer home.

Meanwhile, the lazy afternoon of psychedelic idylls and flower power was over, and *Led Zeppelin* heralded the approach of the great storm. Zeppelin was destined to be an FM radio taste, their albums selling millions, their tours gigantic affairs, their image one of gloom and mystery. *Led Zeppelin II* yielded a Top 10 hit in 1969 with "Whole Lotta Love," but the group disdained singles.

The spell they cast was a potent one. Few groups could control a vast crowd with the broody confidence of Led Zeppelin, the gawky, bedraggled Page lording over the worshipful with a flourish of the violin bow he used for various ear-hemorrhaging solos. Stooped at his Les Paul electric guitar or a gleaming acoustic, dispensing songs rife with Celtic mythology and Druidic symbolism, he resembled a man-sized praying mantis in a gothic sci-fi novel.

1970's *Led Zeppelin III* (featuring the popular radio track "Immigrant Song"), the band's untitled fourth LP (1971), and *Houses of the Holy* (1973) saw Led Zeppelin perfecting its members' images as electric blues modernists whose music flirted with the supernatural. It was Page's idea to leave the fourth album nameless, substituting four separate runes for the musicians' names, and he took to calling the record *The Four Symbols.* The album's best known track, "Stairway to Heaven," typified the pensive theurgical themes of its packaging. The record jacket opened to reveal "The Hermit," a melancholy illustration by artist Barrington Colby, a friend of Page's. Jimmy has confided that the idea for the drawing—depicting a hooded, lantern-toting figure atop a snowy peak, an awed follower seen climbing far below—"actually comes from the Tarot card, The Hermit, and the ascension to the beacon, The Light of Truth. He's on top of the mountain, and there's this person who is aspiring towards him, but it's a long ascent. A general philosophy, I suppose, of 'Ever onward.' "

Even as Page led Led Zeppelin to the pinnacle of rock preeminence, its fellowship was decimated by bizarre misadventures and tragedies, hotel trashings and groupie fests giving way to full-scale riots and other, weirder twists of fate. Robert Plant and his wife and two children narrowly escaped death in the summer of 1975, when their car rolled off a narrow highway on the Greek island of Rhodes. Plant later said that all he could hear in his head during the incident was the obsessive chant ("Oh my Jesus! Oh my *Jee-sus!*") he sings in "In My Time of Dying" (from the *Physical Graffiti* LP). The band's activities were curtailed by the crash and a series of other coincidental setbacks that some believers attributed to Page's occult involvements. In 1976, the semidocumentary *The Song Remains the Same* and a soundtrack album were released, the film filled with the iconology of the black arts. In 1977, Plant's young son Karac died of a rare viral infection, sending the singer into a tailspin of grief that lasted two years. The group's last studio album, *In Through the Out Door,* appeared in 1979. In 1980, drummer John Bonham died at Page's Windsor home, asphyxiated on his own vomit, after falling asleep in a state of acute intoxication. In December, a press release was circulated, indicating that the group would not continue; *Coda* sealed the crypt in 1982.

After consenting to provide the film score to *Deathwish II,* the brutish 1982 Charles Bronson vigilante fable, Page went on to form a new act, the Firm, with former Bad Company lead vocalist Paul Rodgers, which resulted in a pair of impermeable LPs, *The Firm* (1985) and *Mean Business* (1986). Page also joined Plant for his rhythm and blues sojourn on *The Honeydrippers, Volume One* (1984) and united with British folk stalwart Roy Harper on *Whatever Happened to 1214 A.D.* in 1985. Robert Plant (born August 20,1948, in Bromwich, Staffodshire, England) launched a solo career that spawned five sparkling albums between 1982 and 1990: *Pictures at Eleven, The Principle of Moments, Shaken 'n' Stirred, Now and Zen,* which heralded a full-scale Led Zeppelin revival with its sampled segments of signature Zep material, and *Manic Nirvana,* plus a 1985 collectors' edition "mini-album,"*Little By Little.* Page should have also reaped dividends from this popular resurgence by virtue of his first true solo outing, *Outrider* (1988). However, he made the mistake of cluttering what might have been an instrumental star-turn by asking two undistinguished British vocalists (John Miles, Chris Farlowe), as well as Plant, to front his compositions. The magnetism of Page's playing was neutralized by the audition-quality singing, leaving the insecure guitarist with an only figmentary first step toward artistic independence.

Married, with one son, James Patrick, Page continues to enthrall as a studio guest star and live performer. But he remains a gloomy, arcane figure, seldom granting interviews, his personal and artistic goals unclear. He may have offered a clue in a Crowleyesque statement he made in 1975: "Just say that I'm still searching for an angel with a broken wing. It's not very easy to find them these days."

In his hands was the passkey to heaven and hell, the instrument of damnation and exultation; his touch gave it life, triggered its power, and—as he wielded it—it turned his fingers a translucent white or a charred black. When he played a barbarous blues lick, it transformed the people clustered before him into demons bathed in red. When he played a brace of sweet chords, the onlookers became angels, basking in an incorporeal glow. It was San Francisco. It was 1971. Eric Clapton was out of his skull on LSD, but the apparitions he was provoking with his guitar had a gravity to them that superseded the deceptions of any drug.

"I am and always will be a blues guitarist," said Eric Clapton at the start of his career, and he has repeated the oath with regularity ever since. He prefers playing to angels, he says, but admits that devils claim the bulk of his concentration.

An only child, Eric Patrick Clapton was born on March 30, 1945, and raised by grandparents in Ripley, Surrey, England. He was the sole offspring of Patricia Molly Clapton and Edward Fryer, a Canadian soldier stationed in England, who refused to wed Patricia and returned to Canada. In anguish, she moved to Germany and married Frank MacDonald, an-

Eric Clapton

1989

other Canadian soldier, by whom she had two daughters and a son. Having left little Eric in her grandparents' care, all parties sought to pass Patricia off to neighbors as Eric's sister when she rejoined the grandfolk's household in 1957. Stung by the hurtful ruse, Eric declined to serve as an emotional accomplice for the sake of appearances. Scrawny, belligerent, with small, sad eyes and a downturned mouth, he had few friends beyond a group of schoolmates in Ripley who were labeled "the loonies" for their well-deserved outcast status. He became curious about American blues after reading that "rock and roll has its roots in the blues" on the sleeves of import albums by artists like Chuck Berry and Buddy Holly. At seventeen, he took up the guitar, wanting to find an outlet more visceral than the stained-glass design he was studying at Kingston Art School. Like most British working-class kids, he loathed the rigidity of the country's social order and was titillated by the freewheeling essence of American culture, preserved and expanded by generations of hot-footed rounders and musical vagabonds who maximized the pleasures of a land without a heritage of proprieties. Like himself, a bluesman had few lasting ties, few forebears to shame, no background worthy of acknowledgment, no obstacles to wantonness.

He adopted the blues creed almost immediately, finding a polestar in the orthodoxy of Big Bill Broonzy, Sonny Boy Williamson, and Buddy Guy. But, like a dedicated seeker, he settled at last on Mephistopheles's bandmaster, Robert Johnson. Clapton spent his novitiate period as a street musician around Kingston and Richmond, then, for the better part of 1963, worked with a rhythm and blues group called the Roosters. Meeting most of the best young blues-focused musicians of the day in the usual London haunts, he preached his doctrine of grueling purity with all who would listen and, with any luck, elect to jam on the issue with him. Hard up for funds, he briefly compromised his mission in a seven-date flirtation with a commercial cover band, Casey Jones and the Engineers. But late in 1963, he settled into the Most Blueswailing Yardbirds, a five-man band that played electrified Chicago blues. Chummy with the Rolling Stones, the Yardbirds gained a standing invitation to headline the Crawdaddy Club in their absence. It was a compliment attributable to the bewitching wiles of their immoderate and at times lacerating vamps on the blues, aggravated by the stinging outbursts of Eric "Slowhand" Clapton, their lead guitarist. Amplified to the threshold of pain and pegged to storm-trooper percussion, the Yardbirds' sound was the precursor of a new form of rock, later labeled "heavy metal." *Five Live Yardbirds,* their first album, was released in England in 1964. *For Your Love,* their American debut, came out a year later and won numerous fans with its scruffy verve, the archetypal single "For Your Love" doing well on the charts.

Sonny Boy Williamson and the Yardbirds and *Having a Raveup with the Yardbirds* both appeared in 1966, but Clapton was present on only four tracks on the second record, having quit the group in 1965 (right after the "For Your Love" session) rather than comply with the pop direction they were veering toward. He held body and (blues) soul together as a day laborer on construction sites for several weeks before finding a kindred spirit in Manchester guitarist John Mayall. He took the top guitar post in Mayall's Bluesbreakers and recorded with the group, as well as doing studio sessions with bassist Jack Bruce, keyboardist-singer Stevie Winwood, and guitarist Jimmy Page. He became preoccupied with speed and articulation in an extended-solo style that attracted idolizing fans for whom the electric guitar was a symbol of masculine heroism and potency. "Eric Clapton is God" was scrawled in the tunnels of the London Underground and became a graffiti staple of the late 1960s.

Gloomy, troubled, and greatly dissatisfied with his playing, Clapton dropped out of the club and recording scene for a year, reportedly locking himself away with his guitar and receiving no callers—communing, like his musical forebears, with the infernal muse, coming to grips with the sepulchral depths of his blues calling. His next band was Cream, a saga-sized 1966 merger of ashcan power drumming and bare-knuckles British blues, also featuring Jack Bruce and wiry Ginger Baker, a flailer of no small repute. Whenever the three combined to construct their self-described "neocontrapuntal" numbers, the total effect was that of a Concorde backfiring in a wind tunnel. Clapton himself had tapped into some obscure source of voltage and assumed a uniquely elegant appetency for fluid, unerring phrasing. For two years, Cream was at the pinnacle of the rock pile, Clapton the premier guitarist, his back to the crowd and his face in shadow as he played an extended version of Robert Johnson's "Crossroads" that was supernatural in its virtuosity. Cream's onslaught created audience reactions that nearly drowned out the pandemonium onstage, and the four albums they cut during their short existence sold hugely. In 1968, *Wheels of Fire* became the first album to be certified as a platinum (million-units-sold) record.

Clapton, who insisted that the band "was originally meant to be a blues trio," began to grouse publicly that it had become "a jazz-rock group" and therefore distasteful to him, although he was pleased that "Crossroads" had been one of the group's hits. The farewell concert came on November 26, 1968, at the Royal Albert Hall, and *Goodbye* capped the breakup in 1969.

Confused about his future, Clapton was induced in a moment of weakness into becoming part of Blind Faith, a "supergroup" that counted Ginger Baker, Stevie Winwood, and bassist Rik Grech as its other stars. The decision pulled him further from the blues than before and made him susceptible to other, less wicked influences. While backstage during the group's first and only U.S. tour, he chanced to meet two devout Christians who entered his dressing room and said, "Can we pray with you?" He nodded, knelt, and supplicated himself, amazed to find that he suddenly felt better than he had in years.

Strolling around the room, overwhelmed by a feeling of elation and well-being, he told his pious acquaintances that he wanted to show them a poster of Jimi Hendrix he treasured. Unfurling it, he found another poster rolled up inside it, a poster that he'd never seen before. It was a portrait of Christ. He reacted to the image like St. Paul on the road to Damascus and embraced the faith on the spot. Earlier, he had written "Presence of the Lord" for the *Blind Faith* album in order to celebrate his relocation from London to Surrey, a move that enabled him to escape the clutches of Officer Pilcher, a cop who'd made a career of busting rockers; this action was now seen by him as having been a portent of his conversion.

After the Blind Faith tour—more a high-decibel circus of excess than a string of concerts—Clapton knocked around with Bonnie and Delaney Bramlett, whose country-fried blues and blue-eyed gospel-rock had made them an esteemed opening act on the supergroup's bill. He recorded with the Mississippi guitarist and his singing wife, and they with him. Delaney produced the *Eric Clapton* solo LP in 1970; the album hit with J. J. Cale's "After Midnight."

Clapton's career was acquiring a semblance of stability, but his personal life was a ticking bomb because of a love triangle in which he'd become enmeshed. The other guy was best friend George Harrison, and the woman was Harrison's wife, Patti Boyd. Rattled by the strain of the situation, Clapton upped his already flourishing intake of cocaine. His drug dealer would only score quantities of Colombian marching powder for him if he agreed to buy smack as well, and Clapton kept stashing the unwanted heroin in a drawer at his home in Sussex. When Patti threw him over and went back to Harrison, the anguish of unrequited love drove him to despondency and then to the drawer. Clapton became a junkie.

Sinking into a measureless netherworld, he gave himself over to his misery and the monkey that rode his back, writing languid tunes steeped in the clouded tunnel vision of heroin hunger, living death, and the disintegration of the heart. These found their way onto *Layla and Other Love Songs,* a sardonically titled album made in 1970 with a collection of intemperate associates from the Delaney and Bonnie days, the most flagrant being fellow junkie guitar wizard Duane Allman. Eric named the band Derek and the Dominos. With the exception of Neil Young's 1975 *Tonight's the Night* (an LP about the drug deaths of two friends), no record has ever come closer to making distilled emotional horror physically tangible. In the 1730s, London gin shops used to advertise "drunk for a penny, dead drunk for tuppence, and straw for nothing." *Layla* offered cold alienation on side one, acceptance of humiliation by side two, forlorn freefall by side three, and a screaming fast fade with "Layla," a seven-minute, ten-second onrush of harrowing guitar virtuosity that conveyed the perverting power of ruined love and defined despair itself. It was aimed at the soul of Eric Clapton, with direct quotes from Robert Johnson's "Love in Vain," by way of Patti Boyd Harrison, and it found its mark with devastating accuracy.

Clapton expected to die before he reached thirty. He wasn't alone in this presumption. He told friends that ever since he'd begun singing, he wanted to have a voice as tortured as the chords he wrenched from his guitar, a voice like Ray Charles's at the height of his addiction. In order to truly sing the blues, your soul must be as empty as your stomach, and only smack can take you all the way to a perfect vacuum, to a place where you learn how it feels to feel nothing at all and come to love the sensation. The last scrap of caring he still possessed was incinerated when Clapton learned on September 18, 1970, of the death of his own guitar god, Jimi Hendrix.

"I went out in the garden and cried all day because he'd left me behind," said Clapton in 1974. "Not because he'd gone, but because he hadn't taken me with him. It just made me so fucking angry. I wasn't sad, I was just pissed off."

For nearly three years—the better part of 1971, 1972, and 1973—

Clapton did not play in public. He'd left the Dominos after some touring, showed up for the Concert for Bangla Desh in August 1971, and that was it. In Surrey, heroin was his housekeeper, his lover, his refuge. Then Pete Townshend of the Who, genuinely believing the end might be near for Clapton, coaxed Eric out of his lethal lair to prepare for a comeback concert at the Rainbow Theater in London in September 1973. His performance was unsteady, jagged, but he found the courage to turn it into a live record just to convince himself he could still function at an accountable level. He kicked heroin through electro-acupuncture treatment, convalesced on a farm in Wales, and then flew to Miami in 1974 to record *461 Ocean Boulevard,* an insouciant, humbly spiritual album that had a No. 1 hit with his cover of Bob Marley's "I Shot the Sheriff."

"I've got this death wish; I don't like life," the twenty-nine-year-old guitarist confessed after *461* was released. He said he knew he could never get out of the hardcore blues alive, so they were now relegated to the drawer in which the smack had once been stowed. He preserved the blues textures in his music, but merely as catchy coloration, and looked to other rustic, but more upbeat, idioms to carry his now-becalmed singing, which was sometimes shaded by female vocals. His guitar solos, when they appeared at all, were compact and muted. *Slowhand* and *Backless* gained Clapton a new, younger audience that admired his laidback romanticism. The rosy "Lay Down Sally" floated to No. 3 in 1978, and "Promises" went Top 10 the following year, when a slim, fit, but still sad-eyed Clapton won back the love of his life, marrying Patti Harrison. He put out four soothing albums in the early 1980s and did well in 1981 with the lively "I Can't Stand It."

In 1983, he released *Money and Cigarettes* and, when stricken buddy Ronnie Lane (formerly with the Faces) approached Clapton to raise money for the cause, appeared on a benefit tour for Action Research into Multiple Sclerosis (ARMS) that started in London and traveled to America.

Clapton, dressed in a sleek silver-blue suit, led the band in an offhanded set that included "Layla" and blues like Lightnin' Hopkins's "Have You Ever Loved a Woman?" As a rule, it started out subdued and built steadily to a stately climax. On occasion, though, the guitarist's studied reserve would rupture, and he would spin away from the audience, bowing his head, shutting his eyes, unleashing a fusillade of punishing runs, jarring fans too young to be aware that this benign balladeer had once beseiged the blues like a man possessed . . . and showing that the fiendish spirit behind his past offensives had not yet been exorcised.

In 1984, Phil Collins supervised *Behind the Sun*, an album so staid that Warner Bros. insisted livelier songs be added, among them "Forever Man," his biggest hit in five years. *August* (1987) brought a red-blooded return to the concert stage, this time with a superb young band that could also reinterpret the Cream catalog with jazz-edged abandon. The *Crossroads* compilation that came in 1988 would have been an immaculate trophy to his genius, had it not been tainted with a version of "After Midnight" done expressly for a beer commercial. It was a lamentable move, made all the more unfortunate by the fact that Clapton was a recovering alcoholic. He had been in treatment in a Minnesota clinic in December 1987 when the original beer ad came on the TV in the facility's recreation room. As Eric later recalled the incident, all his fellow problem drinkers turned to him and asked incredulously, "Is that *you*?" "Yep," he said skittishly.

With sobriety came a desire for a more settled life-style. He now had a son to raise: two-year-old Conor, from a relationship with Italian TV personality Lory Del Santo. So he concentrated on renovating his home of nearly twenty years, located in the countryside south of London, and cultivated an interest in both Thoroughbred horses and fly fishing.

With the appearance in 1989 of the rompish, blues and R&B-pinioned *Journeyman*, Clapton had jumped to a new peak. Reveling in the mileu that had never failed him, joined by old friends like George Harrison, yet guided to new hands Daryl Hall and Chaka Khan by canny producer Russ Titelman, Eric the musician was loosed from the torments of yore. As for his personal life, he said it remained in near-constant "chaos," shyly conceding that "my dedication to my music has driven everyone away. I've had girlfriends, but I always end up on my own. I don't particularly like it, but I don't see a way 'round it."

The following talk took place in a suite at the Mayfair Regent Hotel on Park Avenue in autumn 1989, just prior to Clapton's most extensive world tour in a decade. Eric, dressed in a smartly tailored gray worsted suit and suede wingtips, had just returned to the States from England after a rest following the completion of *Journeyman*. He looked strikingly fit and seemed in fine fettle.

You've got a long concert road ahead of you. How are you feeling at the starting gate?

Well, this year hasn't been great for my health. I bashed in my finger playing cricket. And I trapped a nerve in my neck on a flight back from Africa. Have you ever had that? You trap a nerve in your vertebrae, and it keeps hitting your funny bone for twenty-four hours. So I actually had to stop playing guitar for a while; it got quite painful. But it's cleared up now, so I'm ready to go again.

How did the cricket accident come about?

I'm just too old for that stuff. I don't know why I play this game, because although it looks like a very safe, slow game, it's quite dangerous. You don't use any protective gear on your hands, and if you're gonna catch a ball you've really gotta be quick. There's a lot of injuries to the hands, so it's one of the last things I should be doing, really.

I just didn't open my hands, I didn't *cut* them properly, and the ball hit the end of my middle finger on my right hand and almost tore the nail off.

What position do you play in cricket?

[*Laughter*] Sweeper! I hide behind the wicket-keeper, basically. This was one of those rare occasions when I wanted to be a hero and tried to catch this guy out. The ball came at a hundred miles an hour, and my reflexes were just not there.

Trying to be Willie Mays—as we would put it.

[*Smiling*] Exactly.

Well, let's talk about Journeyman, *your new album. There's such a variety in the tracks, and even a sense of you playing to all your stengths and doing them one better.*

I had a subconscious feeling that we didn't want it to be too much of a samey album. We could have made a pure R&B album, or a pure blues album, or just a straight rock album because we had enough material to make it that way. I'm like that—I will choose deliberately a lot of opposites, if I'm given complete control. Which Russ Titelman gave to me. He was my guide, but basically he let me have total freedom when I came to choose the material. And that's the way I wanted to go, I wanted to touch lots of different bases.

A song like "Bad Love," which you wrote with Mick Jones of Foreigner fame, the song really swings. I was thinking that this was as good as many of the songs from the Derek and the Dominos days.

Well, that was a conscious effort to go back to that sort of atmosphere. We had, in fact, almost wrapped the album up and we got a little feedback from Warner Bros., and it's usually the same thing, like, "Where's 'Layla'? We need a 'Layla'!" I thought, well, if you sit down and write a song in a formulated way, it's not so hard. You think, "What was 'Layla' comprised of? A fiery intro modulated into the first verse, and a chorus with a riff around it."

I had this stuff in my head, so I just juggled it around, and Mick came in to help tidy up. He was the one who said, "You should put a 'Badge' middle in there." So we did that. Although it sounds like a cold way of doing it, it actually took on its own life.

That's something I've always shied away from doing. I've always been inclined to look outside myself for new directions. It's a big failing of mine, and something I'm trying to resolve. But this was one occasion where I went *back* to what I know how to do.

People have a tendency to look at this album as a new stage in your career, since the Crossroads *retrospective got so much attention. In listening to* Journeyman *I felt that you were drawing from your own background, your solo career from 1970's* Eric Clapton *onward, going back to all those experiences over almost twenty years.*

It's good that you mention that *Crossroads* collection, because the fact that it was so well received was a great source of encouragement to make a record like *Journeyman.* Because I knew that it was safe, in a way, to play around with all my different influences, and not worry about that. I felt that I could actually do *anything* that I wanted, and it would please somebody, somewhere.

"Pretending" and "Anything for Your Love" are two new songs that songwriter Jerry Williams did with you. One of the things that I like about both those tracks is that there's such a nice vocal sound on them. It seems throughout this record that you put new care into your singing.

Well, working with Russ—and I have to give him credit again here—you know very well that whatever you do, he's going to be able to make it sound good. And on top of that, with the fact that Russ has been a musician, he understands the problems. You know you're with a peer.

That was also true working with Phil [Collins], but with Phil I felt that he was an established singer and one of great dimension, so I sometimes found that a little intimidating. I knew that if he was singing this, it would be better than *I'm* doing it. So if you're looking at Phil behind the glass and singing, it inhibited you a tiny bit. But with Russ I had more freedom; I felt more confident.

"Running on Faith" has some lovely dobro-playing, which has al-

ways been a strong side of your guitar work. Who would you consider a major dobro influence?

The only one I can safely say is Duane Allman. He could play dobro any way, and in fact he played it *his* way. The first dobro playing I heard that seemed to have a freedom of expression was definitely Duane's. I wasn't aware of that until we were doing the *Layla* sessions, and there were a couple of quiet ballads where he decided to play straight dobro. It was the only time I heard dobro that wasn't strictly confined to being country dobro—meaning lap-style dobro, very regimented. He's the only guy who played dobro free of any catalog style. That really was a big influence for me, and that's what I wanted to do.

You use the dobro on "Running on Faith" as another voice, like a duet. It's not coloration.

I don't have a developed style. If I was to play dobro unaccompanied, I'd revert to playing like Bukka White, that kind of stuff where you're hitting the bass strings with your thumb. That's how I'd do it if I were playing a piece like "Jitterbug Swing," one of those songs Bukka would do that had a set guitar pattern.

But if I'm playing the thing with a band, with all the accompaniment provided, my style has to change. I normally revert to playing a melody line, and the obvious one to play on that song is the *vocal* line.

When was the first time you ever stepped out as a vocalist?

My first gigs when I was fifteen, sixteen were just me and a guitar, and a drummer friend whose name I can't honestly remember. I used to borrow Mick [Jagger]'s microphone, 'cause he used to carry this Reslow mike in his pocket everywhere in case there was an opportunity to use it, and I used to borrow that some days. I'd put the mike on top of a couple of boxes, and stand behind the boxes and sing into this along with a guy with a snare drum and brushes. This would be in a club, or what you'd call a high school gym, for a Saturday night hop. We'd get paid for it, and dish out Chuck Berry, Bo Diddley, and the odd blues like Jimmy Reed's stuff.

Speaking of those early days, you've got a completely recast version of "Hound Dog" on the new album. Rather than a blues or barrelhouse style, you gave it an unusual New Orleans second-line rhythm.

It was our intention to do it the way it was originally done on the Big Mama Thornton version. But when we listened to that we realized it was really sloppy—in the nicest possible way—but it was just *loose.* On our sessions we had Robert Cray and Jim Keltner, and this was an obvious track to do with Jim because he writes his own part as he plays it; you don't tell him what to play. So we just listened to Mama's Thornton's version once and then went out and cut it our way in two or three takes. We let Jim provide the groove and then played along with it.

"Run so Far" on Journeyman *is a George Harrison song, and it also has his unmistakable slide guitar. George's slide attack is interesting because he's told me in the past that he didn't even get into slide until he joined you as a player with Bonnie and Delaney.*

Yeah, I suppose that's true! He got into Robert Johnson and the other blues slide players through collaboration with me and Delaney; we were listening to that stuff a lot. He took what he wanted from that and used his own melodic sense. He came up with something totally unique. Since then, I've heard a lot of people trying to imitate *George's* style.

For this album, he came into the studio with four or five songs, and that was the one he least expected me to choose, 'cause the others were more R&B- or rock and roll–oriented. But it had the solid character that we needed to put in the album, and I just loved the song.

What was it like working with Cecil and Linda Womack on "Lead Me On"?

Fantastic. We spent three or four days together, and they came with all of their family and their grandmother and all the kids. It was just hippie heaven, and they're great people. They really made me feel special.

We tried to do that song completely live. I tried later to improve the vocal, but it's more or less all live. They encouraged me so much.

Regarding the song, the power of the sensation of falling in love can prove addictive for many people. They mistake the tug of the falling with what the feeling of being in love really is.

If you listen carefully to the words of that song, it starts out with one concept with the guy saying, "I know you don't love me but I love you anyway, so you can lead me on and I don't care." And then she comes in and says, "But I wouldn't lie to you!" It's almost about his paranoia. She really does love him. It's like a two-way conversation.

And Robert's guitar-playing! I had no real idea until I saw him how unique it is: his tunings and his style. That acoustic lead that you hear, that's him. It's very rich-sounding, and it's a perfect offset for what I'm doing.

"Before You Accuse Me," the old Bo Diddley song, sounds like something you might have done at the Crawdaddy Club in the old days.

Yeah! We did! I've played that song so many times live and never even considered putting it on a record. It came about because, when Robert [Cray] and Jim Keltner showed up, I in fact had nothing to do! We'd reached one of those awful points in recording where I didn't have any idea of what material we could come up with. Not only that, but I was suffering from third-degree flu and was disoriented and felt inadequate.

It was like a God-given sign when he just put that song into my mind and said, "Do that!" just to pass the time. We played it all day, then picked a take we liked; it was a lifesaver.

Now, the Crawdaddy Club was only on Sunday nights at the Richmond Station Hotel, and when I first went there it was like a traditional jazz club that kinda leaned toward R&B. Georgio Gomelsky was running it, and I said to him, "There's this little band that plays at the Marquee and the Ealing Club called the Rolling Stones. You should get them in." He did, and they played the Crawdaddy for a year. They had no manager, and poor Georgio, it went right by him that he could move in and clean up.

A year after the Stones had been playing this residency, this guy Andrew Loog Oldham came in with a whiz-kid attitude, thought there was some money to be made here, and signed them up. They left the Crawdaddy, and that's when the Yardbirds got *their* opportunity to move in.

The Yardbirds became the house band, and then we lost the use of the premises, and we went over to the Richmond Athletic Club, the rugby club. It became a cult place to go. The Birds with Ronnie Wood, they were in there, and a lot of other groups moved through after I'd split from the Yardbirds.

That club was also an opportunity for you guys to play with your blues idols, like Sonny Boy Williamson.

That's right. He was around for a long time.

And the Yardbirds' second single was Williamson's "Good Morning Little Schoolgirl."

I sang on that, you see! That was an early singing attempt. I think I heard that original song version of that on one of those compilation albums. Boy, I loved it.

That Yardbirds' single was also the first evidence of your violin-like sustain on guitar. Did that feel risky to you, or give you a sense of release, considering the Yardbirds' pop-versus-blues conflicts?

Yes, and I was part of that, because it wasn't ever part of the blues tradition to have feedback guitar. For me to get into that, I guess that was a bit risky. I don't know where that could have come from, though. There were a lot of influences being shoveled around London then. There was the Indian music influence, for instance, and that's the only thing I could put the feedback thing down to. Because I sometimes wanted my guitar to sound like a shanhai, an Indian reed instrument that's almost a cross between a trumpet and a flute. It has a long sustain quality. That's the only thing I could put my finger on. I mean, why would you want the guitar to feed back? And have that long note? Unless you wanted it to sound like something *else*, something that wasn't part of the blues idiom.

As you assimilate such new sounds, they give you a new vocabulary to compose with. What was it like hearing that recording for the first time on playback?

The thing is, if you've gone into the studio with a band like the Yardbirds, first of all you've cut your obligatory B-side, which would be a blues instrumental. Then you know you're gonna do something that's more poppy, so *that's* when you take these risks. As you listen back you think, "Oh, we could probably do that a bit *more* avant-garde!" Like you say, it's the great sense of release in breaking new territory.

I think one of the first times you tried those bent-note, string-squeezing electric blues outbursts was around 1963, playing the Freddie King Song, "I Love the Woman," with the Roosters. Did you own that record, or had you heard it on a jukebox?

It was on the B-side of "Hide Away" in England. It came out on one of the English labels like Pye International. We always got EP compilations of American blues in England that were just bizarre. After the Roosters heard and did "Hide Away," I convinced them that we should also do "I Love the Woman." And that *was* the first I had ever heard blues guitar playing of that style, with the wild bent notes. It blew me away, really, and changed my whole outlook.

Freddie King had such a rough style, very aggressive. It was coarser than that of the other Kings, like B. B. and Albert.

He was my first choice, actually, and I idolized him. I got the chance to play with him on tour—three tours together—and he was my support band! Can you imagine?! This was '75–76, just before he died. He was a great guy to play with.

I can recall going back into his dressing room, and he would show me his gun and his knife, [*grinning*] and then we would finish off a bottle of gin before he went on. The man was a hurricane, he was *unbelievable*, and there would always be a couple of spent women lying around!

And then he'd go on and *play* after this! I thought, "How can he? He's got the constitution of an ox!" He was big, and he made those ES335 Gibsons look like toys as he'd play with the strap on his *right* shoulder. A giant of a man.

Like you say, he had this very brutal style, but sweet at the same time. Before I hung out with Buddy Guy and played with him, this was the guy I closely related to as being a rock and roller. The guy was just as crazy as anyone you'd want to meet—and a gentleman too.

Another early Yardbirds record, "Got to Hurry" sounded like it had a little Freddie King taste in it.

Definitely. He was my number-one influence. He really was. Because he could make albums of instrumentals that were *all hooks!* How many guitar players think like that? Not many, I can tell you.

It's always been a significant tradition in the blues to sit down and learn to play by listening to the records of its most adventurous exponents. Even Magic Sam or Buddy Guy would listen to a T-Bone Walker record, getting themselves ready for a cutting contest years onward when the chance came.

What always seems to happen with me is that I idolize these guys and learn exactly, note-for-note, what it is they do. But when you meet them they don't want to hear you do that! They're very flattered, but they find it slightly annoying that you hang on their coattails, so they want you to be yourself. They want to hear you play the way *you* play. So the first time you play with these guys, it suddenly releases you. It's been very important throughout my career that I've met all the guys I've copied, because at each stage they've said, "Don't play like me, *play like you.*" It's been a very, very liberating experience—and very important I got into that situation.

You also played Muddy Waters stuff from the Roosters onward. Then in the seventies you both became close during tours with him.

Initially I was very shy with Muddy; I was in awe. It was a different situation than with Freddie; with him you felt he was of your own generation and like a colleague. But with Muddy, he was like the father of it all. And so whenever I was around him I tried to be as humble as possible and not start conversations, just let it come from him. As a result, I never pushed him in a researcher's way, I never asked him questions that I thought would be irritable. Like, I didn't want to ask him if he knew Robert Johnson. That to me would be a very disrespectful thing to do; a cold and distancing way of approaching it.

So I talked to him the way a son would talk to a father, 'cause that was the way our relationship grew. I hoped that, by leaving out all this more formal attitude, we could get onto a better understanding of one another. I wanted a natural affection to develop, and I let it come from him. Gradually he would tell me things. He said his favorite song that I ever did was a Big Maceo song, "Worried Life Blues," and that Big Maceo was one of *his* heroes.

I guess my fondest memory of him onstage was the last gig he ever did in his life, which was to come on with my show in 1983. He wasn't with the tour, he just turned up in Miami with his wife, and came on and did "Blow Wind Blow." That was a fantastic tribute and a great memory. The other great memory was me getting involved in a poker game with Muddy's drummer, "Big Eyes" Willie Smith, and realizing that I was being cheated [*grinning*], which is often the situation. Muddy was touring the rooms, going up and down the halls, and I was in the room with the band, playing this dreadful game of poker, and watching my money disappear.

Muddy poked his head 'round the door and *immediately* sussed what was going on. He turned on this power and shut this guy down so hard—I've never seen anything like it— in a terrifying, bellowing voice. Oooo, man, it was scary. He went into dialect, and said things I didn't understand—at all. [*roaring laughter*] It was frightening, but I loved it.

Let's discuss more contemporary associations of yours. You and Leon Russell wrote "Blues Power" together. It was a nice merger of British electric blues and that Tulsa roll.

I had only met Leon through Delaney, and it was while doing that first solo album with Delaney that we once again ran out of material. Leon just said, "Well, I've got this—" [*he sings*] " 'Bet you didn't think I knew how to rock and roll!' " And we just finished the rest of the song from there.

That was the first time I was aware of Leon's talent. Later on, he started making *his* solo albums. And the funny thing is, when I came to sing "Pretending" on *Journeyman,* that's the guy I thought of when I did the vocal. I was thinking of "Stranger in a Strange Land," the way he put his vocal on that, so it was [*sings, with slight drawl*] " 'How many tiiimes . . .' " I tried to adopt the attitude the guy was singing from, as much as the licks I played.

Thinking again of friendships, kinships, and where they lead, people might forget that when Derek and the Dominos were coming together as a unit, you were all doing work for George Harrison on All Things Must Pass, *out at his home studio in the English countryside.*

That's right. We made our bones, really, on that album with George, because we'd just got together and we were rehearsing and living at my house, and we had no gigs, there was no game plan at all. We were just living there, getting stoned, and playing and semi-writing songs.

When George said, "Can I use some of the guys?" I said, "Yeah, help yourself!"

"But," I added, "Let's just make a deal. It'd be nice if we could get Phil [Spector, producer of Harrison's LP] to produce something for the band." George said, "Okay, what we'll do is get Phil to produce an A- and a B-side for you for your first single, and then we'll use the band for my album."

So that was it. I would just go in with the Dominos and watch them play the tracks, and then we set aside a day with Phil Spector and put down two of our songs with him.

"Roll It Over" was one.

Yes, "Roll It Over" was one, and "Tell the Truth" was the other. They're both cowritten with Bobby Whitlock—and Carl Radle too.

"Roll It Over," of course, came out recently on Crossroads.

Did it! Oh, really?! [*laughs*] Well, you see, that single came out briefly in England and then went back in again, very quick. They deleted it. I don't know why. It went out and just died a death, because no one knew who Derek and the Dominos were. It didn't work, so we lost that one.

"Old Love" on Journeyman *doesn't strictly resemble anything from the Derek and the Dominos era, but it's one of the most compelling songs since "Layla." It has a burning emotional quality to it.*

It's written about the same lady. That could be why. [*laughter*] Can't get her off my mind. I mean, that's been a big thing for me for almost twenty years! And for George too. We're talking about Patti, who was married to George and then married to me. She just has that quality of being a Muse. You think about her, and you want to write a song. And that song was about the fact that, having been divorced for almost two years [the legal proceedings having just recently been finalized], I still kept thinking about her. Whenever I'd write a song that I wanted to channel some lost emotion into, it would be about her. That's what the song is saying: I still love you, but leave me alone, get out of my mind!

Sometimes someone can bring out emotions that are so original in another person that time cannot fade them.

It seems like it takes a certain kind of person to push those buttons. All those changes I went through, I would relate them to her. Maybe it wasn't her doing, but things were happening to me then that I would have said, "Well *you* made me feel like this."

The guitar parts you share with Robert Cray on that track almost sound like an angel whispering in one ear and the Devil whispering in the other.

[*Big laugh*] That's right, that's right! Obviously Robert doesn't know that much about the inside story on that song, but he seemed to have picked up on it.

The Last Waltz *in 1976 must have been a nice opportunity in terms of a gathering of kindred spirits. Muddy Waters was there, so many other friends.*

The sad thing about that was that even as we were doing that show, it didn't hit home to me that it was the last time the Band was gonna play as the Band. It was like, "Yeah, you're kidding, guys, right? This is a great farewell tour, but you'll be out again next year." There was a feeling that it wasn't really the last thing, so emotionally it was a very easy sort of thing.

We actually were going to do two songs together. We rehearsed "All Our Pastimes," which was on *No Reason to Cry*—which had the Band involved—and "Further On Up the Road." But I guess we dropped one of them, "Pastimes," for the show. Overall, we had a great time, but I think if we'd been convinced it was the last time the Band were going to play together it would have been a lot more morose.

The late Richard Manuel of the Band was a man you had a very tight friendship with.

I was madly in love with Richard because we were going through a lot of the same difficulties in life. We were on a par, really, screwing around with drugs and drink and everything, and basically getting pretty crazy down deep. I was very insecure and he seemed to be very insecure, and at the same time he was so amazingly gifted.

He was finding it difficult to cope with his talent. I just identified so strongly with him. For me, he was the one I thought was the *light* of the Band. The other guys were all fantastic talents, but there was something of the holy madman about Richard. He was *raw.* When he sang in that falsetto, the hair on my neck would stand up on end. Not many people can do that.

You've written some good material with women. In 1969–70 you did a lot of writing with Bonnie Bramlett. "Let It Rain" is a classic example. Later on, you wrote "Lay Down Sally" and "Innocent Times" with Marcy Levy. Do you like writing with women?

I love doing *anything* with women, to be honest with you, Timothy. I prefer the company of women to men, for a start. I think that usually when I meet a female that I get on very well with, something creative seems to take place. With another man, I find it very difficult sometimes, because if a man is a capable songwriter he's usually got a drive or an ambition that will keep me reticent. And I will let that ride roughshod over me.

That was often the way with Delaney. If he had an idea, I wouldn't challenge it. I wouldn't come back and say, "Well I think *my* idea is better," or "Let's put your idea alongside mine." I would just go with his idea.

In a woman, when you're writing, they don't have that edge. They're much more giving. That's just the way women are.

They have a generous spirit.

Well, they *had.* [*rising laughter*] I mean, things have changed! You're running into a whole different woman these days. There's now a lot of masculinity amongst the female gender. The whole thing of being independent and a working woman has taken a lot out of it.

Describe the writing of "Let It Rain."

That goes back a long way. We were on the road, I think, when we were starting to write that. In fact, it was me and Delaney that started it with the riff to that song. We were touring with Blind Faith; Delaney and Bonnie were the opening act. They were almost instrumental in the breaking up of that band, or of me leaving Blind Faith, because I was so enthused about Delaney and Bonnie, the style of material, and where they came from.

I lured myself into that situation, and I found with Delaney and Bonnie that I was *writing*—they encouraged me to write in a way that I'd never come across before, just by having fun and not making it a job. They'd spend all day on the bus, just singing and playing. So we started writing "Let It Rain" on the bus, and we finished it in the studio. I hadn't been through that in many years; that was a brand-new approach to me. They did that great album called *Motel Shot,* where they recorded it all in motel rooms.

Another musical avenue you've explored over the years is reggae. You did some recording down in Kingston, Jamaica, circa 1974 with Peter Tosh, cutting Tosh's "Whatcha Gonna Do" and "Burial." How did you come to find yourself down at Dynamic Studios?

We were recording mainly with [producer] Tom Dowd then, and Tom's chief thing is that you should go to wherever the source is. If we wanted to play reggae, or we were being intrigued by reggae through Bob Marley, why not go to where it comes from? Tap the source.

I owe all of that to Tom Dowd; he got us down there for *There's One in Every Crowd,* which was almost 50–50 reggae stuff and Marcy Levy songs. When we got down there, people were just wandering in and out of the studio, lighting up these massive trumpet joints. After a while, I didn't know who was in the studio and who wasn't, there was so much smoke in the room.

And Peter was *weird.* He would be sitting in a chair—asleep, or like comatose. And then someone would count it off and he'd wake up and play, with that weird kind of wha-wha reggae chop. And then at the end of the take he'd just nod out again!

He didn't seem to know what the tune was, or it didn't matter. But then we'd get him to sing. He sang the pilot vocal to "Burial," and also to "Whatcha Gonna Do." I couldn't understand *a word.* I literally couldn't! It was hard enough when those guys talked because you'd have to ask, "Could you say that again *slowly* please." But when they sang, it almost completely disappeared. So I had to have it translated to me by someone. So even today, I don't know if I sang the right words on that! I have no idea. And if I did, I don't know what half of them mean.

Any reason those two reggae tracks weren't used on Every Crowd*?*

I think the feeling was that it was getting to be too much of a reggae thing. We'd had the big hit with "I Shot the Sheriff," and it was starting to become an overpowering influence. And there was a feeling of discontent amongst the band, too, that we were going off too much on a sidetrack. 'Cause when we got onto the concert stage we weren't going to be a reggae band, so the albums had to reflect what we were going to do live.

If I'm not mistaken, George Terry, the fine guitarist out of Criteria Studios in Miami, was the one who pointed you toward Bob Marley's music.

George Terry was the one. He had the album [*Burnin'*] that "I Shot the Sheriff" was on. That was my first taste of Bob Marley. It took me a while to get into it, to tell you the truth. I was coming from a completely different place. To break my inherent musical tightness down into this real loose thing was very, very difficult for me to assimilate.

The "Sheriff" track was conceived in Miami, with a Tulsa band. [*grinning*] It was such a weird melting pot. All I could do to stamp *my* own personality onto it was to sing it, and just play the occasional lick. The rest of it was almost out of control. It was a complete hybrid.

You didn't meet Bob Marley until quite a while after the single was a hit, right?

The record came out, and went up the charts, and shortly after that I got a phone call from Bob. I don't remember where I was, or exactly what the circumstances were, but we had a half-an-hour conversation on the phone. Again, half of which I understood and half of which I didn't. [*laughter*] And I kept asking him if it was a true story—did he really shoot the sheriff? What was it all about?

He wouldn't really commit himself. He said some parts of it were true, but he wasn't gonna say which parts. The next I spoke to him, he came to England with the Wailers and did a small tour—until one of them got sick with the flu. None of them had ever had flu before. They thought they had a serious disease. They canceled the tour and went home, 'cause it was *cold* then in England.

But I went to see them at the Hammersmith Odeon, and I walked into this dressing room that I couldn't see the other side of for the smoke. This was in '78 or '79. I sat and talked with Bob, and he was just a *great* guy. He was so warm. A beautiful man. He was serious about what he was doing, but was very gentle. That was the first face-to-face meeting.

We spoke earlier of a long tradition in the blues for cutting contests. Buddy Guy first made his reputation in the 1950s at the Blue Flame Club in Chicago by taking on Magic Sam and Otis Rush in a style that had a link to theirs. Is that demonstration of skill something you've enjoyed?

Given the right kind of guy. If it's a guy who isn't that serious about it. Buddy will always do that to me, and I'll do it to him. We'll go so far, and then we'll both kind of stop. Or maybe he'll beat me. Usually I'll just kinda say, "That's enough for me. You take it from here," because that's the respect I owe him for being who he is.

But there are other guys I wouldn't even want to do it with because they don't have that in-built dignity. They treat it as a serious contest, and they really wanna win. I won't even get into it with people like that. When it stops being a joy to do, then you don't want to do it. You could usually tell, just by meeting the guy, if it's gonna turn out that way.

On the 1977 Slowhand *record you wrote this tender ballad, "Wonderful Tonight," that actually stands apart from most of your guitar-based career. It's one of the nicest songs I've heard a man in rock and roll write about a woman.*

Patti was getting ready to go out. We were about two hours late. I was *furious.* 'Cause I hate unpunctuality. I'm very punctual myself, and I can't tolerate in other people. She was always late.

I was sitting downstairs, and I'd been ready for two hours. I went upstairs to see what was going on, and she was up there with one of her girlfriends, still trying on different things. I said, "Well that's nice—what is it, a *curtain?* You look wonderful!"

I went back downstairs, and while I was waiting I picked up the guitar and I started writing that song. It wasn't in the sense of love or affection. It was written just to pass the time, and I was pretty angry.

That lady can draw a lot out of people. She has that ability. Great lady.

You recently joined your old friends the Rolling Stones onstage during their Steel Wheels *tour.*

The song I played was "Little Red Rooster," and I remember being taught how to play it by the [Howlin'] Wolf himself. 'Cause we did an album together in London [*The Howlin' Wolf Sessions*], and it was quite a hairy experience. I actually did get it together for the Wolf in the end, but it was nerve-wracking. He came over and got hold of my wrist and said, "You move your hand up *here.*"

For the Stones thing, I called up Jane Rose, Keith's manager, to see if I could get tickets. She said, "Sure. Would you like to play?" I got there, and the great thing was they'd actually *thought* about what they'd like me to play. I was really moved by that.

It was easy, I didn't feel nervous. Usually, if you know you're gonna play, you can't enjoy it. You keep thinking, "Will the guitar work?" or "Will something go wrong?" But it didn't feel like that. And to watch those guys up there, it's like they're in a club. They don't worry about it at all. They knock everyone else into a cocked hat. When Keith kicks it off, there isn't anyone else.

It took me back to the fact that we'd been friends so long. We grew up together; I was always ligging around them in the early days, when they had a band and I *wanted* to be in a band.

Let's return to your beginnings. Even in your earliest days on the London music scene, you were always such a sharp dresser. I remember the album jacket for the 1964 Five Live Yardbirds *debut album. You had that sharkskin suit on, and looked like Simon Templar in "The Saint" TV show.*

I was mad about clothes, and I was trying to get the other Yardbirds interested too, but that was a waste of time. It's always been that way. I was just mad about Ivy League then, and there was one shop in Piccadilly that sold imported American suits. And that was it for me, to buy these Ivy League suits—especially *modern* Ivy League suits, the ones with one button. It was unbelievably difficult to find this stuff, and you'd pay through the nose for it. But no one else was wearing it!

It was like the beginning of the mod period, and not long after that everyone had crew cuts and were riding scooters and wearing anoraks. I guess I could have been a fashion designer or gotten into that world because I've always been fascinated by clothes. One of the reasons I think I was edged out of the Yardbirds was because, having had *long* hair—and they were all just developing Beatles-style haircuts—I went and got myself a crew cut. That shook everybody up! Whoa, they could not handle that at all.

Was there a role model for that look of yours?

[*Nodding*] I always used to buy jazz albums on Blue Note, and even when I was just buying blues albums I'd go into the record shops and flip through the bins and pick out something by Miles Davis, and see this guy impeccably dressed. The way these guys presented themselves attracted me to the jazz world much more than the music. They were *sharp.* And people like Ray Charles would go to a session wearing a shirt and tie and a suit. Guys now wear *track suits!* [*laughter*] I mean, what's it all about?!

During your fifteen-odd months with John Mayall, it seemed to me you brought as much public attention to the Gibson Les Paul guitar as Les Paul himself had up to that point. You gave people a sense of the modern possibilities of the instrument. What excited you about it?

The LP cover for *Freddie King Sings the Blues*; on the King label, and he was playing a Les Paul! I went out after seeing that cover and scoured the guitar shops and found one. That was my guitar from then on, and it *sounded* like Freddie King. It had everything;

it was it. But Freddie's particular model, I've never seen. It looks like a Les Paul Standard, but it hasn't got a sunburst top. It like's a dirty red color. If you check that album cover out, it's the weirdest looking beaten-up Les Paul you've ever seen. It could've been hand-painted.

When you were putting Cream together in 1966, in the early stages the trio might have seemed to you like the ideal blues configuration, but the first songs you recorded, like "The Coffee Song" or "Wrapping Paper," they were pretty quirky stuff. I would have thought you'd do "Cat's Squirrel" or "Rollin' and Tumblin'" straight away.

Well, those guys were pretty strong personalities. I hadn't taken that into consideration. At the first rehearsal, most of my ambition to lead that group went out the window, because I realized I didn't have the wherewithal. Whatsoever.

I mean, when it came down to forceful personalities, Ginger was the man. And Jack was vying for the role too. So I just let them get on with it, and I backed off.

My way of introducing material that I thought we should do was to just *play* it. It'd became, like, after the fights had died down at rehearsal I'd start playing a riff, and then one of them would go, "Aye, whot's zat?" I'd say, "Well, it's just something I'm kind of writing." "Aye, well, maybe we could do that."

It was very tense and hesitant stuff, a situation where I hadn't the confidence or the experience to stand up and dictate what we were gonna do.

You did some writing for Cream with a fellow named Martin Sharp. You wrote "Tales of Brave Ulysses" with him. How did that come about?

It was a jokey situation. He was an Australian painter I shared a flat with in '66, and he was constantly saying, "Oh I'm a good writer. I write poetry." I said, "Oh, come on," but he said, "Let's work together!"

So I only once or twice did it, with that one and with "Anyone for Tennis," which I thought was *diabolical.* [*laughter*] Those were the only times we really got it together. I think that "Tales of Brave Ulysses" worked, but when we tried to repeat it, it didn't. It went to his head and to my head a bit.

In talking about painting, you showed some promise in your boyhood as an artist, didn't you?

I was a very early drawer. I used to draw men eating meat pies, for some reason, at the age of six. I don't know why. My grandparents were the first people to notice that I did have a talent for perspective and things like this, which weren't taught to me. They were like gifts.

They encouraged me to go to art school, and I passed the necessary exams without any problems. Usually to get into an art school in England you need a limited number of GCEs, which is like a scholarship. I failed at English and Math and all the other things, but I got through on the strength of painting and drawing.

At about the same time, unfortunately, I was seriously trying to play the guitar, and the one got the better of the other. I was actually thrown out of Kingston College of Art, because my portfolio at the end of the first year had nothing in it. Also, I think I went into the wrong department. There was Graphic Art and Fine Art, and I enrolled in Graphic, which meant that I was going to be a commercial artist. I should have been painting.

I still sketch now and then. I still use my eye as much as possible. That probably comes through in what I choose to wear, but nothing gives me pleasure as much as playing the guitar. I still love to look at paintings, or even paint or draw, and do a little bit of interior design at home, but it doesn't give me the high I get by playing in front of an audience. Nothing would.

Your grandparents were John Clapp, a carpenter and plasterer, and his wife, Rose. Your grandmother helped you get your first guitar on a time-payment plan.

It was a double cutaway Kay electric, and very expensive at the time. And a bitch to play. Had a big thick neck, and very high action which you couldn't lower without touching the fret bars. It was heavy and unbalanced, and sort of a copy of the ES335 that Gibson was making—without the refinements.

Is it true that first guitar cost your grandmother £100?

That's right, which was a fortune then. It just goes to show how much faith they had in my ability. It was wonderful. And I was a bastard, I took the money and ran! [*grinning*] It was only later, when I was in my early twenties, that I realized how much of a debt I owed them, in terms of love and finance. And I did start giving it back in every way I could as I went on.

They were very fun-loving people, and I was always happy to take people back there to Surrey. I'd go to London and hang out with these bums and wandering troubadours who'd go back to Surrey with me and meet my grandparents. And my grandparents would remember them to this day! My grandmother has met all of them. She's met Buddy Guy, B. B. King, Muddy, and they loved one another. It's great.

My grandparents were really understanding; that's the thing. Having been thrown out of art school—and for a year I didn't know what I was gonna do—the disappointment to my family must have been massive. And yet they were happy to send me on my way doing something that didn't seem to have *any* future whatsoever.

Did your grandparents play instruments?

My grandmother plays piano but not really up to concert standard. My mother plays piano too. I guess I first heard anyone playing music at home, around the piano. My mother played standards of the day.

Have you ever found out much about your dad, Canadian soldier Edward Fryer?

I've never really got the true story. The family is very tight-lipped about that. It's difficult for me to approach the subject without sensing a great feeling of hurt. Obviously it was a very painful thing for them to go through when it happened: that my mother would be pregnant at such a young age, and that the guy had gone, and how were they going to resolve this.

For me to dig it all up again, even for my own sake, I don't think it's worth it. All I think I know is that he died quite a few years ago. Even to go and look for whatever's left of his family would open a can of worms that I may not be able to deal with myself.

But you've seen photos of him?

Just one photo. But I was raised very well. I probably had a better childhood than most people.

Did you have many nonmusical jobs in your life?

After being thrown out of art school, I worked with my grandfather as his assistant on the building sites. It was hard work. He was trained in woodworking, in bricklaying, in plastering. He could build a house on his own.

It was magic to watch him work. And to attempt to do it, to get a trowel and lay some plaster in a straight line up a wall was something that very few people could do. He could plaster a room in maybe two hours, and it was phenomenal. It was a work of art.

Did your granddad's skill at his work influence your own sense of the value of adroitness and creative verve?

He did actually teach me that value in a very indirect way. It was by example. He never forced anything on me at all. He very rarely told me off about anything unless it generally had to do with a sense of values. He would guide me in that way.

It was mainly by watching him, and his dexterity, and his skill, that I realized that little things are all-important. He was a true craftsman. [*proudly*] In fact, he was a journeyman.

A gravelly voice crooned, "I took her to an all-night laundry; we watched her bra go 'round in the machine." It could be a lyric from a whimsical Sam Cooke song, perhaps a couplet left off "Another Saturday Night." But no, the line belongs to asthmatic British rock-and-rhythm rasper Rod Stewart. It is his explanation of how he met and courted Britt Ekland.

A gifted raconteur and songsmith, Stewart is adept at such picturesque on- and off-the-record summations of his recreational involvements. It's a bit tricky discerning whether he's jerking one's chain; but that's part of the fun, as well as the problem. Rod *should* be best known for his deeply felt admiration of Sam Cooke, whose gospel passion, soul virility, and pop humor he was able to mirror and even recast. But his reputation, like that of Cooke, has come to rest on his cockamamie run-ins with the opposite sex.

The best known is his years-long dalliance with Britt Ekland, whom he encountered on and off during the early 1970s before getting cozy with her after she came backstage when Stewart and the Faces were playing the Los Angeles Forum in March 1974. Stewart must have liked what he saw in the washer (or was it the dryer?): Britt promptly moved both herself and her laundry into Rod's estate.

Rod Stewart

1988

After a few years of listening to Stewart's vague stories about marriage and keeping some semblance of fidelity while watching him bird-dog anything in skirts (excluding the traditional ancestral male costume of his beloved Scotland), Britt slapped Rod with a $15 million palimony suit. The protracted litigation was a Hollywood horror show, the screen version of which might have been entitled *It Came from Beneath My Kilt.* In the end, he settled out of court and returned to his promiscuous habits, a life-style immortalized in a limited edition foldout poster included with a 1971 Faces LP called *A Nod's as Good as a Wink to a Blind Horse.* The gamy giveaway was a compilation of snapshots showing band members flagrante delicto. The record company regained its senses and deleted the freebee from the second round of packages pouring out of the pressing plant, but the legend of Rod Stewart and the Faces' march-or-die party ethos had been born.

It was with dropped jaws, then, that fans of the singer received the news that "Rod the Mod," as the dandified crooner had been known since his early days in London rhythm and blues clubs, had wed starlet Alana Hamilton in April 1979. While the bloom was still on the rose, Alana assured the British tabloids that "there could never be any question of me suing Rod for money because our marriage is forever. We both know that."

Stewart seemed to take such dictums with a grain of salt—"Da Ya Think I'm Sexy" (the biggest single of his on-and-off solo career) was released that same year. He and Alana had two children, but Rod kept his eye on the passing parade. Rod and Alana tussled, separated, and reconciled with great frequency—something he and Britt had also specialized in. Finally, in 1983, Alana sued for divorce. Stewart's manager, Arnold Stiefel, issued a uniquely exasperated public statement: "God knows this is so confusing—like something out of *As the World Turns.*"

Only Stewart seemed to know what he was doing. He released a new LP that year, *Body Wishes.*

Although he was born in London—on January 10, 1945—Stewart defers to his Scottish lineage. He left home at seventeen and spent months busking with companion Wizz Jones, singing American folk music in Belgium, Italy, and France with a light-hearted fervor. He started to blend the blues and a Gene Vincent–Eddie Cochran rockabilly itch into his folk bag, and, in 1963, he landed a spot as a singing harmonica player with Jimmy Powell and the Five Dimensions. They backed up Chuck Berry, who announced they were his best pickup troop in recent memory, and they got the house-band position at the Crawdaddy Club when the Stones left town with Bo Diddley. After recording some singles with the Five Dimensions, Rod left to do session work, cutting gooey versions of pop hits for drugstore album collections.

Gaining an awareness of his vocal strengths, Stewart put out a solo single, "Good Morning Little Schoolgirl," on Decca, the Stones' label. Next came two more solo singles for Columbia, "Day Will Come" and "Shake." Then came a brief stay in 1966 with Baldry's Steampacket. After a clash of egos with Baldry, he hooked up with future Fleetwood Mac members Peter Green and Mick Fleetwood; they called themselves Shotgun Express. In 1967, "flash" guitar snob Jeff Beck hired Stewart to front the Jeff Beck Group, and two LPs, *Truth* in 1968 and *Beck-ola* in 1969, brought Rod's tortured soul timbre to the attention of a large rock audience. Mercury Records offered him a solo contract, and some superb albums resulted—*The Rod Stewart Album* and *Gasoline Alley*.

After Beck broke up his band, Stewart signed on with the Small Faces, which thereupon shortened their name and cut a number of LPs as the Faces, beginning with *First Step.* In June 1971, Stewart released his own *Every Picture Tells a Story* and became an immediate star, the album being the first record to chart at No. 1 in the United States and Britain simultaneously; the single "Maggie May" followed suit.

He put out an insipid album, *Smiler,* in 1974 to fulfill his obligations to Mercury, and then joined Warner Bros., where his output was by turns deeply felt and doltish. No one could hit all the jagged corners of a song of shattering love ("The First Cut Is the Deepest"), or renew a pledge of faith in the rigors of true romance ("Tonight's the Night"), or lend coloration to a sentimental, back-porch valentine ("You're in My Heart [The Final Acclaim]") like Stewart. But when an arrogant sappiness set in, the best he could manage was such comic-book ribaldry as "Hot Legs."

Stewart seemed destined to become rock's human whoopie cushion, his clangorous music a purple party trick. *Camouflage,* a 1984 pass at reclaiming his storied past, petered out before the first side was over. Circa 1985, he started to rediscover his love of singing, joining old mate Jeff Beck for an austere, insistent study of the Impressions' "People Get Ready," a single that brought needed credit to his eighties catalog. He had a much bigger hit with the silly "Love Touch" theme song from the film *Legal Eagles,* but then his pattern of scoring with rock lollypops for restless housewives was well-established. *Every Beat of My Heart* in 1986 halted his backslide into pandering, and 1988's *Out of Order* was the payoff, with four excellent hits ("Lost in You," "Forever Young," "My Heart Can't Tell Me No," "Crazy About Her") that propelled a fourteen-month North American tour to grosses of $50 million. And the dessert was *Storyteller, the Complete Anthology: 1964–1990,* a voluminous album collection that included the 1989–90 hit, "Downtown Train," and "This Old Heart of Mine," a duet with Ronald Isley.

Now the father of infant daughter Ruby Rachel by companion Kelly Emberg, Roderick David Stewart had seemingly outlived his lapses and follies. His rippled rasp was robust once more as he brayed to the back rows, displaying a pink blazer, polka-dot tie, and hair the hue of champagne. None of his youngest fans could have guessed that he was once the humble, committed preserver of the blues line, so shy and consternated before his initial Jeff Beck Group audience at New York's Fillmore East in 1968 that he sang the kick-off song from the wings.

The following interview took place in a Los Angeles studio early in the summer of 1988, during the same week Stewart's *Out of Order* album was released. Immediately after the interview, Rod went out into a parking lot and stripped down to his slacks. By prearrangement with a local haberdasher, there was an array of expensive silk shirts laid out on the hood of a Mercedes for him to review as possible garb for his upcoming tour. While secretaries cheered from nearby windows, Rod Stewart ran through the casual display of apparel, trying on most of the shirts before selecting a half-dozen of the best and brightest.

You've got a reputation for being fun-loving in the extreme. Is it possible that Out of Order *is such a good album because it was composed and coproduced with former Duran Duran member Andy Taylor, who's one of your drinking buddies?*

[*Smiles*] I do like Andy, he's a good mate of mine. He gets me into lots of trouble. He was a little bitter with the whole Duran Duran thing, but I feel he's coming into his own right now. I don't think he ever got a look in, so to speak, with Duran Duran as a guitar player, and he's got a lot to offer. Our working styles are compatible:

we don't like too much rehearsal when we write or play, and we don't like going to the studio too early to record. We prefer to have a coupla bottles of wine handy and just see what comes out.

"Lost in You" is a Stewart-Taylor song that sounds like it was worked out in a loose, even live setting.

It's funny how that one came about, because we'd been in the studio all day, and we weren't getting anywhere. I had a football match in the evening [*laughs*], and I said to Andy, "Look, I'm gonna leave you here with the guys. Just try and work *something* out to save the day." So I went off and played football and came back three hours later, and he'd started writing "Lost in You." I sat down and wrote the melody and the hook to it. I already had the title, so it was just a question of slotting that title somewhere in the song. We didn't finish that day but came back fresh the next morning and nailed it. I'm not a very swift lyric writer, so it took me a couple of weeks to write the lyrics.

Do you see yourself as a songwriter, a musician, a band leader, or primarily as a vocalist?

I think all of those things. I don't think one of them is more important than the other. I definitely see myself as a band leader, keeping them together, keeping their spirits up when they're on a long tour. There's an art to that.

"Lost in You" is a good example of your unique gift for rocking a ballad.

"Maggie May" was the first up-tempo ballad I ever did, and this one, I think, is very much in the same mold. It might not be quite as melodic, but it's certainly got tons of mandolin on there.

Whose voice is that saying "I miss you too" on the track? Is that Kelly Emberg?

Yes. It took about four months to get her to do that. It was nerve-wracking to her, so I applied tons of wine down her throat, and once she was nicely drunk she couldn't stop giggling. Then it took another three–four hours to stop her giggling!

We'll have a lot of trouble doing that live, actually. [*giggles*] I keep trying to get one of the guys to sing it, and none of them want to. You know: "I miss you baby." "I miss you toooo!"

Yeah, I guess that's not a dialogue you can do with your drummer. "Forever Young" is a more somber example of the somewhat Celtic narratives you seem to be effective at devising.

Songs like "Forever Young" have definitely got that Gaelic quality in the melodies. One of the things I think I do best is try to tell a story in three or four minutes. I think that's quite an achievement if you can do it. I really do enjoy telling a story. Unfortunately, you don't get too many chances to do it. That song was more or less dedicated to my three children, Shawn, eight, Kimberly, nine, and Ruby, one. It's really about the kids and what I wish for them.

Another thing that people haven't given you much credit for is the innovative instrumentation on your records. I'd never heard a mandolin on a rock and roll record until you put it there.

I always thought the mandolin was such a romantic-sounding instrument. It sounds very Italian to me, and I like spaghetti [*laughs*], you know? I found the mandolin guy who played on "Every Picture Tells a Story" and "Maggie May" in a restaurant in London, funnily enough—and the fiddle player too. They were both playing stock romantic songs from the 1930s. In the studio, I would just whistle the parts for them to play.

That's one thing I pride myself on: coming up with melody lines for the instruments, especially in those days. I want to go back and get more into acoustic rock and roll albums again, like John Mellencamp's. He's doing that very well now, I think. So I want to get to that in the next album and leave the electric guitars alone for a little bit.

Speaking of acoustic music, Mick Waller's manic, flustered drumming added to the distinctiveness of the entire Every Picture Tells a Story *LP.*

He used to turn up with just his snare, a bass drum, and sometimes a high-hat—the most humble of equipment. If you listen to "Maggie May," there's no crash cymbals because he didn't use any. The early solo records were made in a random way.

I can't listen to the first solo record anymore, it's far too naïve for me. But *Gasoline Alley* I like. Those few early records didn't sell at all, by the way. Maybe the critics liked them, but you couldn't give them away.

It wasn't until *Every Picture Tells a Story* that I began to satisfy myself, but that record didn't take more than three weeks to make. Woody [Ron Wood] and I would write and rehearse the songs at my house during the day and record them in the evening.

Let's talk about your most famous band. The Faces had a reputation for being a hard-drinking, bawdy bunch that went straight from the pub to the stage.

That was all borne out by the fact that we were terribly insecure.

None of us thought that we could play, so we spent a lot of time drinking to cover up our feelings about the mistakes we'd make in the concerts. It was still one hell of a band to be in, and the most fun I've ever had. But we took it as far as it could possibly go. We were very limited musically in that band. I think Ronnie did the right thing, going off and joining the Stones. I would have stayed with the Faces, I'm a fairly loyal guy. But my solo career was also getting bigger and bigger, and it was becoming Rod Stewart and the Faces, which I didn't want and they didn't want. So ours was a timely end, I thought, but I still love our music, and I still do "Stay with Me" in concerts.

For me, Ronnie Lane was the brains behind the Faces. Once Lane left, that was the end of it. He was like Keith Richards is for the Stones, the *essence* of the Faces, the backbone, the heart of it.

Ooh La La in 1973, the one with "Borstal Boys" on it, was the album that broke up the Faces, because I slagged it off in the music papers when it came out. The other Faces were after me for weeks after that, trying to kill me. I didn't think we'd reached our potential, and I opened my big mouth and told the music papers.

When was the last Faces concert?

Minneapolis, October 1975. And it was pretty much on a par with the rest. I don't think we ever played *terribly* badly. They were all fairly good gigs. We weren't one of these bands where shows clicked or they didn't click. Rather than us getting too rowdy, what we used to get was birds flashing, showing their tops to us; we'd get a *lot* of that commotion. [*big grin*] Although I do remember we did one concert up in New Jersey during our first tour of America, when we were supporting Savoy Brown. The promoter said to us, "I'm sorry boys, but there's no time for you to go on. Savoy Brown have run on too long, and there's a curfew and we have to close the theater." What came next caused a bit of a riot then, because we just went on, took Savoy Brown's instruments away from them, and started playing!

From the first solo Rod Stewart Album *onward, you had a reputation for doing these audacious cover versions of other acts' signature songs. What do you think the boldest one was?*

I loved "(I Know) I'm Losing You," the Temptations' song, but the boldest I ever attempted was the Stones' "Street Fighting Man." That was actually supposed to be, believe it or not, "The Girl Can't Help It," the Little Richard song. I actually began singing "The Girl Can't Help It," and I suddenly changed it all around and went into "Street Fighting Man"—with chords from the other song. I'm just singing "Street Fighting Man" over a set of new chords.

I'd taken it just far enough away from the original that, rather than being criticized, I got a lot of credit for the move. I think Mick [Jagger] likes it too.

There are a number of Rod Stewart songs that are very somber and reflective. Judging from songs of yours like "You're in My Heart," or your versions of others' material, like "Handbags and Gladrags," you seem to prize certain qualities in people. Loyalty seems to mean a lot.

It does. Loyalty and honesty. I think I'm a fairly loyal person too. Although there's probably a few girlfriends who would disagree with me. It actually does mean a lot to me.

Where do you think you got that from?

Good Scottish roots. [*laughs*] Dad's a Scot. He's eighty-five. He was a builder, and then he retired when he was sixty-five and became a shopkeeper; he had a little sweets shop. He's an interesting guy—rotund, about five-foot-ten, and he's got one tooth because he doesn't believe in going to the dentist. A lot of Scots haven't got too many teeth; it's got something to do with the water, apparently. He's very, very thoughtful, fairly puritanical, and a quiet man. But an absolute soccer *nut.* Loves his soccer, as do his three sons. I remember seeing him play soccer as a little kid, and once seeing him get his leg broken. He just was playing a bit too tough, and spent Christmas in a cast in a hospital.

What I do now is all me dad's fault, because he bought me a guitar as a boy, for no apparent reason. I wanted a railway station for me model railway when I was fourteen, and he bought me a guitar! It was an old Zenith that cost about twelve quid. The first thing I learned on it was "It Takes a Worried Man to Sing a Worried Song," in the key of E, and then it went to A and B flat. [*laughter*] "I'm worried now, but I won't be worried long!"

We just celebrated my mother and father's sixtieth wedding anniversary—amazing! I've gotten to know my parents more in the last ten years than the previous thirty-five. Me mum's much more outgoing than Dad. The one thing she loves now is to get the family around and give them a drink and make everyone get up and sing a song. She's what you would describe as being a party girl, really. She's eighty-four and don't go to too many parties anymore, but she likes a drop of Scotch now and then, and likes to sing a song—and she was a very, very good mother.

Incidentally, it's four o'clock! Look at your watch! We have to stop for tea! Could I have a cup? [*breaks into song*] "Oh the factories may be humming / With a doomalanga-loomalanga-we / But when the clock strikes four / We work no more / 'Cause everything stops for tea!"

[*He stretches and waits, resuming after his Earl Grey is served.*]

Are you ever surprised at the amount of material you've generated?

Yeah! I've written, I think, 150-odd songs, which is probably nothing compared to what Dylan writes, but it's a fair old body of work. And I have seventeen or eighteen albums. I was thinking of turning professional. What do you think? [*laughter*] Do you know I was turned down by EMI Records and Decca Records when I went for auditions?!

Decca actually signed me in the end, gave me a quick shot with a cover recording of "Good Morning Little Schoolgirl." That was my first serious record, but the general public went for the Yardbirds' version instead of mine. Anyhow, my early auditions went badly, both of these companies ultimately feeling I wasn't suitable. I did some Sam Cooke stuff for them, and you know what they said? "You're far too rough. Your voice is too *rough.*"

You've always acknowledged Sam Cooke as your hero and primary influence.

I still do listen to Sam Cooke and copy him to a point, and I love Jimmy Reed. In my earliest days of busking on streetcorners, I used to try and sound like Ramblin' Jack Elliot, Woody Guthrie, and the early Dylan records.

Do you enjoy your own voice?

[*Quietly*] Yeah, I do, I really do. I can't stand the sound of my own talking voice, but the singing voice I can listen to. I always think it should be a lot deeper, more butch, my speaking voice. But it's not, it's up there. And my singing voice is *really* up there.

It's kinda reedy.

Reedy is the word, yes.

The first time I heard you sing live, I was surprised at how big your voice is. People who have a whiskey quality to their vocals often don't have a very big instrument, but you have a big instrument.

[*Laughter*] Thank you very much! I must tell me girlfriend about that!!

And you don't sing bad either!

Aha yes, I do take your meaning. It's very strong now, my voice, and when it's really working for me it's good for four or five nights straight at two and a half hours a night. Which is remarkable to me when I think of how high I sing—and every song's got that rasp in it.

Listening to me has ruined a lot of other singers. A lot of singers who have tried to sound like me, they sound like they're going through so much *pain.* There's that girl that had that hit, "Bette Davis Eyes," Kim Carnes. She sounds like she's *straining* to be like that, and you shouldn't have to.

Vocally, one of your best recent recorded performances was your solo version of "People Get Ready" with Jeff Beck.

Jeff had come over to the States on a holiday, and he'd done that track as a demo. He played it for me in cassette form and I said, "Let me do a vocal on it! Just to see how it turns out." So I went 'round to someone's house to do it. The entire track was made in people's houses and garages; it was never a professional studio job. It took me three takes for my vocal, and I never thought anything would happen with it. All of a sudden, I hear it on the radio! I was caught off guard that it would be liked at all, let alone thought highly of. Of course, when we did the *Truth* album with Jeff Beck, that was recorded *and* the vocals were done and mixed in three days!

What's been your most unexpected hit? Is there one that you were initially advised to leave off an album or discard entirely?

[*Giggling*] "Maggie May" was like that! I was nearly persuaded to take that off the album. A mate I was knocking about with at the time said he didn't think it had anything melodic to offer. I sort of agreed with him, but it was too late because we didn't have any more tracks. Even more important is the fact that when it came out on a single it was a B-side; "Reason to Believe" was the A-side. And it was a disc jockey in Cleveland, I believe, that turned it over. Otherwise, I wouldn't be here today. I'd still be digging graves in the cemetery.

What was it like digging graves?

I had just finished playing soccer professionally with a London team called Brenford, and I couldn't make up my mind what I wanted to do with myself. I only dug three or four graves total, but it poured with rain all the time. I remember it like it was yesterday. I took the job because I thought it'd help me overcome my fear of death. When I first went on that job the other guys in the cemetery initiated me by putting me in a coffin and closing the lid. That scared the shit out of me—but I've had no fear of death since! It cured me.

And then I did some paper rounds for me dad once, when I was twenty-one, because I was unemployed again because my music business wasn't going too well. I'd get up at six o'clock in the morning to deliver papers. Can you imagine?

Was there any point in your career when you were fearful and discouraged about your odds of building a life in rock and roll?

Yes, just before "Maggie May." And prior to that, just before I got into the Jeff Beck Group. When I got into the Beck Group I thought this is definitely a foot in the door, because I was playing with great musicians and playing something that *means* something—we were updating Chicago blues. But before that I really thought, "Aw gee, no luck, no luck."

I'd been at it a long time, playing clubs all over Britain for about five or six years, and I thought it was becoming ridiculous. I was twenty-four or twenty-five at that time, and I wasn't getting anywhere. So I was a little bit despondent in the early sixties, especially because there were a lot of bands taking off like the Stones, Yardbirds, and Beatles. These were guys I used to go to clubs and watch, and I thought that there must be a place in there for me, because I could sing as well as that geezer with the big lips in the Rolling Stones.

It must seem a long time since you were so wary of stardom that you had to sing from the wings.

That's a true story, of course. That was the first concert I ever did with the Jeff Beck Group in America, on a bill with the Grateful Dead at the Fillmore East. I suffered that night from the most frightening experience: my voice just went! It was just stage fright, I suppose, but I opened my mouth on the first number, "I Ain't Superstitious," and nothing came out.

In those days, Woody and I used to have a little red bag we'd carry around all the time that had a small bottle of brandy or rum in it. I ran out, got the bag, had a quick shot of brandy, ran back, and picked up the mike again. At first I crouched behind the amps as I swigged, with Beck covering for me by playing a solo. There was definitely a bit of embarrassment all around, with everyone looking for the singer. But sure enough, as the brandy hit the bloodstream, back came the vocals!!

Joni Mitchell

1988

The French poet Alphonse de Lamartine has written, "God has placed the genius of women in their hearts because the works of this genius are always works of love." Yet love, like hate, is a natural exaggerator, seeking outlets but never limits, the unrelenting fire of life that either purifies or consumes.

Like the erotica of Anaïs Nin, the songs of Joni Mitchell have been a move, in a world generally dominated by men, to express the experiences of physical and spiritual love solely from a purposeful woman's vantage point. Through an often-angry admission of her emotional weakness for and dependence on the opposite sex, of her foolhardy miscomprehensions and unrewarded acts of faith, and of her ability, however imperfect, to make the process of self-love and the search for romantic fulfillment compatible, she has forged a fresh image of the autonomous female artist. It is not a political representation, tied to trends or to movements like Women's Liberation, but a forceful announcement of her own singularity. She began by embodying the archetypal fair-haired hippie-chick singer, ornamenting the male folk-rock enclave, taking lovers (Graham Nash, James Taylor) from among her associates, yet making it plain that they were her peers, that she claimed co-ownership of the experiences, and that she reserved the right to think out loud about them. Mitchell, like the rest of the obstinate rock and roll community, was on the way to satisfying herself, and she made no bones about it.

David Crosby—who is credited with discovering her in a club in Coconut Grove, Florida, producing her debut LP *Joni Mitchell/ Song to a Seagull*—is said to have commented once that his protégée was "about as humble as Mussolini." Perhaps, but certainly no more arrogant than David Crosby. She has insisted on having her own mind, and she has flourished in a contest where she found she was "outside the uniform of rock and roll, and it annoyed people."

A native of Alberta, Canada, she was born Roberta Joan Anderson on November 7, 1943. At the age of nine, she contracted polio in an epidemic that swept Canada, and it was thought that she might not walk again. She remembers spending Christmas in a hospital, shouting Christmas carols at the top of her lungs in the polio ward as a gesture of defiance. Regaining her strength, she plunged into social dancing, organizing weekly Wednesday-night get-togethers. Joni was a precocious child, interested in painting and music. She began her art studies in Saskatoon and bought her first record in 1953, a Rachmaninoff theme used in the score of the Ethel Barrymore–James Mason movie *The Story of Three Loves.*

Mitchell took up the guitar and ukulele in order to play Kingston Trio songs at parties (the hootenanny/sing-along fad was then extremely popular). She attended the Alberta College of Art in Calgary, planning to concentrate on commercial graphics, but got sidetracked by folk music and became a regular at the Depression Coffeehouse. After moving to Toronto to have greater access to clubs, she met and married Chuck Mitchell; and they formed a loose duet. In 1966, they relocated to Detroit, where the relationship fell apart as her solo career took off. She headed for New York, where she became known as a songwriter, singer Tom Rush adding her material and that of newcomers Jackson Browne and James Taylor to his sets. In 1967, she signed a contract with Reprise and went into the studio with David Crosby, whom she credits with helping her fight to see that her writing wasn't diluted to fit the current folk-rock trend. A year later, her material had gained wide exposure; Tom Rush recorded her "Circle Game" as the title track of his 1968 LP, and Judy Collins hit the Top 10 with "Both Sides Now." Mitchell's own *Clouds* album, which featured her version of "Both

Sides Now," benefited from the attention, and "Chelsea Morning" became ubiquitous on FM radio. Nineteen seventy's *Ladies of the Canyon* sold 500,000 copies, and "Big Yellow Taxi" landed on the charts.

Her next two records, *Blue* and *For the Roses,* were the sharply confessional works of a woman resentful of her inability to stand loneliness and eager to place the blame on others—even as she denies that she is doing so. But Mitchell's delightful vocal animation was a leavening factor, her trills, ululations, and sandpapery skips along the scale revealing a personality increasingly willing to laugh at its willfulness. Her guitar-playing was also distinctive, the humming heft of her open-tuning chords and hard-strumming style anchoring the whole with impressive authority.

Court and Spark, released in 1974, showed that her overall musicality had matured to a point where she could look beyond herself for input and thereby achieve new dimension. A virtual collaboration with hornplayer-arranger Tom Scott and his L.A. Express, the LP was an immaculate jazz-rock exploration; the wide-open, freeway-entwined vistas of Los Angeles seemed to become aural landscapes in which the singer loses, rediscovers, and surrenders herself. *Court and Spark* was considered a brilliant new direction for both Mitchell and rock, and artists as diverse as David Bowie and Jimmy Page expressed envious admiration of the album.

From there, however, Mitchell became more obscure as she drifted further and further into a jazz-like fringe of her own invention. *The Hissing of Summer Lawns* in 1975 was as overwrought as the title implies, as was *Don Juan's Reckless Daughter,* although they did feature landmark Afro-rock and jazz-rock hybrids. *Mingus,* a 1979 tribute to the terminally ill jazz bassist, was brave but brittle. Two live albums released in 1974 and 1980 were only occasionally winning; while her 1982 release, *Wild Things Run Fast,* found Mitchell returning, almost apologetically, to the conventions of *Court and Spark. Dog Eat Dog* in 1985 showed Mitchell's work acquiring an astute topical faculty as she assailed the smarmy triumverate of TV evangelists, advertising executives, and junk bond salesmen who were brokering America's moral fiber. The lucid, sublimely sung *Chalk Mark in a Rain Storm* consolidated her social concerns while showcasing her ease in shifting between jazz, rock, and folk veins. Coproduced by husband Larry Klein, a distinguished bassist, keyboardist, and arranger, *Chalk Mark* utilized guest stars

Don Henley ("Snakes and Ladders") and Peter Gabriel ("My Secret Place").

Chalk Mark in a Rain Storm was also Mitchell's most captivating effort since 1976's *Hejira,* a work whereby she entered an entirely new realm of creativity, producing a ghostly, ethereal record of stalking, abandon, and flight. Like *Chalk Mark, Hejira* probed a twilight realm in which the dark side of love is directly confronted, the soul subsumed, an otherworldly eroticism achieved. It was the kind of handicraft Henry Miller was pushing Anäis Nin toward when he kept advising her to concentrate on the carnal and "leave out the poetry."

The following conversation took place over chicken salad sandwiches one March '88 evening in a dimly lit studio in North Hollywood, just two weeks before *Chalk Mark in a Rain Storm* was released. Mitchell was lighthearted and charming but involuntarily jumpy because of her "darned hypoglycemia." Once the sandwich had been digested, she relaxed, growing soft-spoken and touchingly sentimental.

Joni, Chalk Mark in a Rain Storm *is a powerful composite statement, so pretty to the ears, but upsetting in its content. Is the title describing something deliberate that's ephemeral at the same time?*

[*Nodding*] It's an image of impermanence. It's also a line from the song "The Beat of Black Wings." A young soldier delivers it, and he's drunk in a tavern somewhere, talking to anyone who'll listen. Mainly he talks to the woman who is serving him his beer, and his outlook is pretty gloomy. He says he's never had anything in his life, so it's from that standpoint that he delivers the line, "I'm just a chalk mark in a rainstorm, I'm just the beat of black wings." An individual is a kind of a chalk mark in a rainstorm in view of the direction we've taken as nonecological animals.

Is that soldier character, Killer Kyle, derived from anyone you've met?

Yes. In the sixties, while all my friends were busily avoiding the draft in any way possible, I was playing a coffeehouse circuit on the Eastern Seaboard which took me down to Fort Bragg in North Carolina. I played for gung-ho boys coming and going from Vietnam.

One person I met there introduced himself as Killer Kyle. He was like a Tennessee Williams character, very young and short. I walked into the room, and he was red in the face, livid, his fists clenched, and he said to me in a drawl, "You've got a lotta nerve sister, standing up there talking about love, because there ain't no love. Not where I come from. Love is gone, love is dead, and I'm gonna tell you where love went."

This is approximately the way he opened up, and he proceeded to tell me a terrible, but I guess typical, story of a Vietnam experience. For a while afterward he wrote to me, but basically all he wanted to do was get strong enough to get over his shell shock so he could go back and kill a Commie for God, although that illusion was broken.

As a matter of fact, Killer Kyle is mentioned in "Cactus Tree," one of my earliest songs. I hadn't thought about him for many years until I started recording this album at Peter Gabriel's studio in the southwest of England, near Bath. On the other side of the valley from the studio is an army base, the base from which U.S. planes attacked Libya. So it crossed my mind when we were recording that if there was retaliation, we might very well be the target. Also, the radiation from the Chernobyl accident was drifting toward us. It was a very pensive time for Yanks in England, and gave everyone an awareness that this planet is a tiny place indeed. Accidents from one country and wars in another now affect us all.

There is no safe or secret place anymore. Yet the notion there might be seems more entrancing than ever. Your duet with Peter Gabriel on "My Secret Place" seems intended to depict the birth of trust and affection between two people, even two strangers.

Exactly. Rather than a duet of a boy singing to a girl—or *at* a girl—it's the beginning of the optimistic one-mindedness at the start of a love affair. You're on the same wavelength. That's the time when you're liable to say the same thing at the same time, and giggle a lot about it. It's a psychic period of bonding.

I prefer to see life as an undulating force—which is more an Oriental process of perception. I disagree with Western thought, with its mind/body split, its good/evil split. You have to cultivate a dialogue with life that's less judgmental, yet has a greater attention span. I'm still living in the days of radio; I'm not a channel-changer. I'll watch anything on TV because moving pictures fascinate me, as does conversation.

Reviewing your career, there's always been a tendency to cast you as a confessional writer and singer, but I'd say your overall approach is more conversational in spirit.

Here's how I look at my songs, and it's very simple: I feel that the melodies, if they're "born" first, require words with the same melodic inflections that English has in its *spoken* forms. So I'm singing with an ear for the music and meter of the spoken word. And then from jazz I took the liberty to not necessarily nail the downbeats all the time. I enjoy dialogue, and I'm a big talker, and my music helps me be a big listener too.

Besides the "confessional" assumption, people assume that everything I write is autobiographical. If I sing in the first person, they think it's all about me. With a song like "Free Man in Paris," they attribute almost every word of the song to my personal life, somehow missing the setups of "He said" and "She said." Certainly, most of the song is eyewitness accounting, but many of the characters I write about—even if their tone is entirely first-person—have nothing to do with my own life in the intimate sense. It's more like dramatic recitation or theatrical soliloquy.

Granted, but you've made albums like Dog Eat Dog, *in which you seemed to function as a journalist, and others like* Blue, *in which you let listeners in on your private emotions.*

Well, we're talking about several things here: the poetry of the lyrics, the reporting in them, and my own emotional makeup. In a certain way, I do see myself as an eyewitness reporter. Some of my things are purely fictional, though, in that I begin from an eyewitness vignette to depict it. Then I find it won't rhyme [*laughter*], or it lacks a certain dramatic quality, and there's a necessity for exaggeration.

We're talking art's artifice here, and it has its own truth. It's not necessarily a literal truth. It's a creative truth, a larger truth.

I have, on occasion, sacrificed myself and my own emotional makeup, singing "I'm selfish and I'm sad," for instance. These are not attractive things in the context of rock and roll. It's the antithesis of rock and roll—which is "Honey, I'm a lover and I'm *bad*!" [*laughter*] You don't go saying these other things in pop circles because they're liable to bring terrible results: unpopularity. Which is what you don't want.

When I started to do this "confessional reporting," partially it was artistic integrity, and partially I wanted to sabotage any worship that was setting up around me. If I was being worshiped, something was wrong. If you're worshiping things, it means you're not really leading a full life. It's healthy to admire; all of my musical growth has come out of admiration. But to *worship,* that's taking it too far. You've got to get yourself together if you do that.

Blue was the first of my confessional albums, and it was an attempt to say, "You want to worship me? Well, okay, I'm just like *you.* I'm a lonely person." Because that's all we have in common. Happily married, there are still lonely moments.

Loneliness is the main thing we have in common with animals. Unfortunately, we have this ability to perceive more strongly—unlike, say, the coyote, who's born and sits in the bushes until one day his mother bites his nose to the bone and says, "I'm not feeding you anymore!" And then sends him cruelly out into the world to be on his own.

We all suffer for our loneliness, but at the time of *Blue* our pop stars never admitted these things. Now, I'm a public person, and my life's an open book.

When did it begin to feel that way for you?

Around the time of *For the Roses.* There was an adjustment period to be made, and that album was that adjustment period. In my teens, I wrote a poem for some class assignment about Hollywood called "The Fish Bowl." It was based on Bobby Darin and Sandra Dee, and having all of your business in the public eye. Sandra Dee was the Madonna of that decade, a cute kid with her blond hair flipped up at the ends.

So this poem went: "The fish bowl is a world diverse / where fishermen with hooks that dangle / from the bottom reel up their catch / on gilded bait without a fight. / Pike, pickerel, bass, the common fish / ogle through distorting glass / see only glitter, glamour, gaiety / and weep for fortune lost. / Envy the goldfish? Why? / His bubbles are breaking 'round the rim / while silly fishes faint for him."

With that point of view as a teenager, it's very peculiar that I ended up in this game in the first place, because I knew that I was more of a private person. And I've always been the ages of three, seventy-five, and twelve all at the same time. As a baby, I was very old, and in my twenties I was very young. It's strange how it seems that you contain all of the people you are and were and will be.

Anyhow, *For the Roses* was a time of withdrawal from society, and intense self-examination. Maybe I don't handle adrenaline very well, but even the applause was hard. I know I have adrenal problems now, and I'm hypoglycemic—but back then I didn't. So my animal sense was to run offstage! Many a night I would be out onstage, and the intimacy of the songs against the raucousness of this huge beast that is an audience felt very *weird.* I was not David to that Goliath.

Fight or flight? I took off in flight, a strange reaction. I didn't know anyone else who did that. I had to adjust to the din of that much attention.

So *For the Roses* was written in retreat, and it's nearly all piano songs. I was building a house in the northern British Columbia forestry, with the rustle of the arbutus trees at night finding its way into the music. There was moonlight coming down on black water; it was a very solitary period. It was melancholy exile; there was a sense of failure to it.

The title itself was facetious. I wanted to use a drawing of a horse's ass for the album cover. I did use it for a billboard ad. It was my joke on the Sunset Strip, the huge drawing of a horse with cars and glamour girls, and it had a balloon coming out of the horse's mouth which said, "For the Roses." But nobody got the message.

I started this thing, all this star machinery "that brings me things I really can't give up just yet." That was the dilemma. And I threatened to quit all the time, but it's, hey, you're in show business until you're in the poor house! [*laughs*] You either stay up there, or you begin your decline and the vultures come and pick the last little bit as you go down. As your money diminishes, so does your ability to buy good lawyers to fight the monsters.

You wonder about people who made a fortune, and you always think they drank it up or they stuck it up their nose. That's not usually what brings on the decline. It's usually the battle to keep your creative child alive while keeping your business shark alive. You have to develop cunning, and shrewdness, and other things which are not well suited to the arts.

Success has an interior and an exterior dimension, and it can also have an effect on your core drive. You're waking up to things you can do, but you seek an audience for each of them.

There are different kinds of success. *Mingus* to me is a successful project from my core, and yet it pretty much cost me my airplay, my radio presence.

Yet it began with the incredible compliment of Charles Mingus valuing your work so much that he wanted to pull you closer to him as an artist.

That's what I'm saying: there are different *kinds* of success. I'm not a jazz musician, but I had the experience of being invited into an idiom with which I had been flirting.

My husband and his generation of musicians didn't exist in my early days. They're ambidextrous and can play hard rock with a light jazz feel, or funk with a rock feel. He can do anything. I loved rock and roll, but I had to make my choice at a certain point, because the rock and roll musicians around when I began were fairly primitive, frankly, and couldn't sense rhythmic nuances; they'd just bruise them. Since I didn't belong to any camp anyhow, I was drawn to people like Larry, and of course to Mingus, which became a great privilege.

It used to be embarrassing to myself and to Laura Nyro in particular to play with technical musicians in the early days. It would embarrass us that we were lacking in a knowledgeable way, and that we would give instructions to players in terms of metaphors—either color descriptions or painterly descriptions.

That feeling of embarrassment persisted until one day when I turned on the television in the middle of the film *Never on Sunday.* The scene was this: there's a drunken American, I guess it's Melina Mercouri's wedding, and he's yelling at the band in his intellectual manner, saying "You're not musicians! You can't even read!" And the bouzouki player or guitar player, he's a sensitive little guy, and he suddenly stops playing because he's injured by the belief that the American's words might be true. And he locks himself in the bathroom.

Mercouri's upset and says, "Now look what you've done, you've ruined my wedding!"—I'm paraphrasing the scene—and she's standing outside the bathroom door, wondering how she's going to restore this musician's confidence, until finally she knocks and says, "It's okay! The birds don't read either!!" And he comes out elated and goes back on the bandstand. That's how I felt, before and then afterward.

There was a smugness to studio musicians in the early days, and I was an illiterate rock musician who had none of the A-chord and B-chord languages. But you can imagine the thrill for me when I first met great musicians like Wayne Shorter, who spoke to me in my language of metaphors for a track like "Paprika Plains" on *Don Juan's Reckless Daughter.* Before he started to play his sax, he said to me, "It's like we're in Hyde Park, and there's a nanny with a baby in a boat on the pond, just *nudging* it, her hand's nudging it." Or sometimes he'd say, "I'm a string section now!"

Tom Scott was also very open to metaphorical instruction on *Court and Spark*. I'd say, "You're playing the Doppler effect: just give me straight lines." And he was a great sport. It was an exciting project, that record with Tom, and so was *Don Juan* with Wayne.

But once you'd get the lexicon down and the album done, you sometimes had to teach your muse to your public. The Hissing of Summer Lawns *had tracks that experimented with mergers of rock and African forms.*

There was a big stink about that. It was taboo, you see. I don't think I realized how culturally isolated we were until the release of that record. In white culture it was problematic, but it got good reviews in the black magazines, where it was accidentally reviewed because there was an illustration of a black person on the cover. I thought it was adventuresome, but it was shocking how frightened people were of it.

I think the record was inadvertently holding up a mirror to a change that people were on the brink of in this hemisphere, and people were disturbed by the teetering they were experiencing. The Third World was becoming more important and they were disoriented.

Another revolutionary record of yours was Hejira, *which was accepted because it had such a strangely pretty sound to it, yet I'm not sure it's been entirely understood yet. It treads on a metaphysical plain in terms of inner experience, dream states, psychic journeys, and flights of imagination.*

Hejira came out of another of my sabbaticals, another time when I flipped out and quit show business for a time. This instance was in '76. I'd been out with Dylan's Rolling Thunder Revue, which was an amazing experience, studying mysticism and ego malformation like you wouldn't believe. Everybody took all of their vices to the nth degree and came out of it born again or into A.A. Afterward, I drove back across the country by myself, and I used to stay in places like light-housekeeping units along the Gulf Coast. I gave up everything but smoking, and I'd run on the beach and hit health food stores. In New Orleans, I wore wigs and pawned myself off as someone else. Meanwhile, nobody knew where I was.

I'd do these disappearing acts. I'd pass through some seedy town with a pinball arcade, fall in with people who worked on the machines, people staying alive shoplifting, whatever. They don't know who you are: "Why are you driving that white Mercedes? Oh, you're driving it across the country for somebody else." You know, make up some name, and hang out. Great experiences, almost like the prince and the pauper.

So whenever possible during these breakdowns in my career I would pawn myself off as someone else, or go to some distant clime and intentionally seek out a strata of society I was sure I would never have gotten near otherwise.

How do you feel about the fleeting acquaintance you've had with the Top 40 via singles like "Big Yellow Taxi," "You Turn Me On, I'm a Radio," "Help Me," and "Free Man in Paris"? Those hits all occurred during the early 1970s, and your impact has since come from other less obvious angles.

I have nothing to do with the choosing of tracks for singles. Generally speaking, I don't agree with the selections, and there are tracks that never get played on the radio that I regret won't get that exposure. So I like the idea of well-received singles and am sorry when they don't get a chance to happen. "Car on the Hill" was one I thought would have been a good single; I wish that was circulating in the golden oldies department because it has a vitality today, it would work. "Troubled Child" too, and "Just Like This Train," which I'd rather hear on the radio than "Raised on Robbery."

I like the song "Big Yellow Taxi" better than I like my rendition of it. I don't think my version is definitive. "Help Me" is a throwaway song, but it was a good radio record. My record companies always had a tendency to take my fastest songs on albums for singles, thinking they'd stand out because they did on the LPs. Meantime, I'd feel that the radio is crying for one of my ballads!

"Ladies' Man" is another song radio missed, and it's a song that Aretha Franklin could have sung. In fact, there's two little catches in my vocal that are out of admiration for her. I also have at least one note I got from Tony Bennett, who I liked as a kid. And there's a lot of the Andrews Sisters in my choral work, although my harmony is different from the harmony of that era.

The Andrews Sisters era, of course, was World War II and its aftermath, a period that's the setting for "The Tea Leaf Prophecy (Lay Down Your Arms)" on Chalk Mark. *It's such a wistful song. Tell me about it.*

That song began as a music track that Larry wrote. For the lyric, I kept thinking about World War II and my parents' courtship, which was unusual in a prophetic way. My mother had been a country schoolteacher, and she had come to the town of Regina in Saskatchewan to work in a bank. It was wartime, and nearly all the men in the town had been shipped overseas. So there weren't many prospects for her, and she was a good-looking woman, thirty years old—which was old for that time.

There was a fancy hotel in that town that served high tea, and you had to wear hats and gloves in those days to get in. One day she and her girlfriend went over there just for the dress-up of it all. When they were finished, a gypsy came over and read her teacup and said, "You will be married within the month, and you will have a child within the year—and you'll die a long and agonizing death." The last part was a horrible and hideous thing for even a clairvoyant to tell anybody.

My mother laughed in her face. She said, "This is ridiculous. Look at this town. There's no men left, just frail boys and babies." Two weeks went by, and a friend of a friend had a friend from out of town, and they put my mother and father together on a blind date and it was instant chemistry. My father had two weeks' leave. He said, "I know this is sudden Myrtle"—her name was Myrtle McKee; in the song it's Molly McKee—"but would you marry me?"

So they ran off to Moose Jaw, Saskatchewan, and got hitched. I was born within the year, and to this day she feels a little funny about the rest of the prophecy, considering the odds of the other parts coming true. She's seventy-six, and she's never been sick a day in her life. I mean, she's a real germ fighter because she's convinced it's a germ that's gonna knock her down. She does yoga, Tai Chi, cross-country skiing, and doesn't even have a quaver in her voice yet.

I say to her, "Don't worry about the gypsy, Mom. Two out of three ain't bad." The gypsy got it wrong. It's *me* who's gonna die the long and agonizing death, with my bad habits.

But I had to ask her, "What made you marry Dad? You were so picky." And she said, "Because he looked so cute in his uniform." So that's in the song too.

In the mid-1940s urban Jamaicans were using an island-rooted colloquial phrase, "beast lick," to describe the punishing physical and psychological blows—such as the bombing of St. Paul's Cathedral—that Hitler's army was then dealing the British Empire. Often the words were used in the context of a metaphorical cricket match, in which the "beast lick" was delivered by Nazi bowlers bowling off the wicket.

During the postwar years, the term evolved to describe the pugilistic prowess of a ghetto tough, i.e., a rude bwai's knockout punch in a street brawl. When the symbiosis of ghetto sportsmen, hooligans, and reggae musicians was reaching its halcyon period with the first full blush of Bob Marley's stardom (thirty years since his birth during Hitler's downfall), a "beast lick" had become hip street jargon for a professional masterstroke, an expression of top-ranking prowess.

In the fall of 1975, Bob Marley was immersed in the creation of a sequel to *Natty Dread*—a "beast lick" of the first order, *well-sharp* in its dread reggae trenchancy. The third album since *Catch a Fire,* the mainstream debut on the Island label that had heralded a bold new international tide in popular music, *Natty Dread* was a seamless meld of raw reggae and modern rock sinew. How to follow it

Bob Marley

1975

up with a truly commercial beachhead without compromising his music's roots integrity?

At the time, Bob was recording at Harry J's Studio on Roosevelt Avenue in Kingston, working to integrate the I Threes into the Wailers' increasingly rock-edged sound and trying to choose between American lead guitarist Al Anderson—who'd contributed fine playing on "No Woman No Cry"—and local axman Earl "Chinna" Smith. Although a great fan of Anderson's, Bob would opt for Smith because of disruptive friction between Al and Wailers major domo Don Taylor, and Anderson would work for Peter Tosh for a spell, although Al's solos on "Crazy Baldhead" would make it onto the completed track. Bob was also listening carefully to the politically sophisticated Rasta worldview being espoused by cohort/star footballer Alan Cole, which would translate into the scaring "War."

This was also a period during which Bob and longtime friend (and early manager) Dickie Jobson were hanging out a lot with Countryman, the legendary "natural mystic" and fisherman who lived on the outskirts of Kingston at remote Hellshire Beach. A descendant of the large numbers of East Indians who had emigrated from their country after Jamaica's slavery days to cut cane and serve as domestics on five-year work contracts, Countryman was the son of George Lothan, an impoverished irrigation supervisor based on a sugar plantation near Spanish Town. As a child in 1957, Countryboy (as he was then known) moved to a remote Hellshire encampment founded by an older brother and lived there in peace as a fisherman, selling his catch at nearby Port Anderson Beach.

Three ensuing events would have a profound effect on Countryman's unfettered life-style and those of the men with which circumstance conspired to acquaint him: the 1958 motorboating mishap that led the stranded twenty-one-year-old Chris Blackwell to Countryman's settlement in search of help; the public-works initiative some fifteen years later to build the first formal roadway out to Hellshire, and the arrival by way of that new blacktop in the early 1970s of Dickie Jobson and Bob Marley, who were hunting for a new spot to swim and party.

The four became fast friends, Countryman and his brethren being Blackwell's first intimate exposure to Rasta hospitality, and Bob fascinated by Countryman's elemental existence (and the two crocodile teeth he wore around his neck as a good luck charm to ward off the fearsome creatures, who often got entangled in the fisherman's swamp nets). For Dickie's part, he thought the Countryman story would make a nicely atmospheric movie, and in December 1975 he wrote the first draft of the script that would become the 1982 Island Films release.

Bob, Dickie, and Country would pass whole days at his neat shack, smoking herb, eating roast fish, and swimming, Bob picking out new tunes on his acoustic guitar. In Bob's imagination, the folk rock of Richie Havens, the hard rock of Jimi Hendrix, the sassy funk of Sly Stone and Stevie Wonder, and the electric blues of B. B. King slowly combined with the rhythms of the surf and sky—and with something more: Countryman's mystic philosophies. A man who lived closely with nature, maintaining a tensile respect for its might, Country liked to swim past Bush Reef, as far out to sea as he could possibly manage, and then fight the current back to shore, his lungs aching as he struggled to cheat death. He also believed he could cause lightning to flash from the firmament and "walk across the sky," and could incite the earth to rumble underfoot.

In a compelling interview with me, the thirtyish Countryman recited what he advised Bob: "If a mon lives upright, ya cyan speak and make lightning, ya cyan speak and it is done, and you will command and it will stand fast, but ya have to live a clean life! People have to try an' live up.

"I've seen a lot of little miracles in the night. I'm a fishermon; I fish for a long while and in the night I see the sky move! Sometime ya cyan see for yourself—ya find t'ings jus' done in front of yuh, and it looks like miracles."

It was in this unique milieu of influences and reasonings that Bob began toiling to create *Rastaman Vibration.* The following conversation took place in September 1975 on the front lawn of Bob's home at 56 Hope Road in Kingston. Bob believed he was born on February 6, 1945, but his often playful conversation contained the allegorial replies and mischievous contortions that would later hinder further inquiry into his personal history.

The early-to-mid-1970s era of the evermounting Wailers campaign was a time span in which everything—from fact checks to sound checks—held a boundless potential for mixup-mixup, but somehow always came out all right. In Jamaica, surrounded by his family and his brethren, Bob was relaxed and expansive as he talked of this process, full of his characteristic "Ya know?"s. Early on in our interview he gave me a reverent assessment of Countryman: "Countrymon is a very *wise* mon. Well-strong. Yeah. In the eyes.

Mon strong with him rights. He's a mon who live out on the beach, and him live like that because him want to live like that. And it's nice. He come here sometime, and bring his youths!"

And then Bob began playing with his own kids as our deliberations moved on to things musical. Six months later, after *Rastaman Vibration* had become a physical reality, I would see Bob again in Island Records' New York City headquarters, then located in the Carnegie Hall Building on West 57th Street. Even though he was in the company of friends and band members, he seemed rather tense, and very concerned about the reception the new LP would get. He was under the impression he had made a very commercial, rock-shaded record, but recognized he had taken a risk by giving himself over to a newfound faith in his support crew. "Jah nuh partial," he said earnestly. "Every mon have a role to play!"

In other words: all things contribute. And through that holy communion of talent, righteous intent, and mystic revelation, Bob Marley fashioned another record that was, from "Positive Vibration" to "Rat Race," an unbridled beast lick.

I'm told your father was a white captain in the Jamaica West Indian Regiment, and your mother was from the interior of Jamaica.

That's what I heard. My mother was from Africa.

How many brothers and sisters do you have?

Right now from me mother, I have two brothers and one sister. At that time I was with my mother. But I don't know what's gone before, I don't know where they all are, ya know?

Where in Jamaica did you grow up?

Me grew up from in the country, in the woods, to the city, ya know? A place named St. Ann's. That's the garden parish, they call it the "Garden Parish," and now me grow in Kingston, from Barry Street, den to Oxford Street, to Regent Street, and then to Trenchtown. Me lived in Trenchtown from 1958 to 1961. Then all over.

When did you start playing guitar?

Well, never I really take it seriously, see? Most times I just take up a guitar and I just play like ah, but I never really used to do no recordin'—until the musicians that was really playin' the music at that time, they get so ripped off that they would play no more. And so was getting no good music again. So we start playin' it ourselves.

Is it true that Desmond Dekker, your boyhood friend, was cheated from the start by the record producers?

[*Nodding*] Quite likely. Quite likely, mon. They steal you every time. Hear me! Mark some album before me, before I knew Island. That was because I in England, and that's why I don't get to meet Island, and yet Blackwell's from here. Well, the thing is, imagine a company like Trojan now, and there's three album from me that me don't know about. Unnerstand? Weird. That's why some guys get knots. Kinky.

When you grow up as a youth, you know, you see people and meet people and talk to everybody and everybody show you a smiling face because you is a youth. But when you grow up come now, it something else that go on, because the same people that used to laugh is the same people that now go "*Urrrrr* [*grumbling*]." You know? So, there's plenty fill up the earth.

Everybody get ripped off. Every time. Three album! I don't think them have any more stuff. They can't do that, 'cause them play out what them have. That was kinda recently, but as yet it's been a lickle while.

What performers did you admire as a youth? Jimmy Cliff has told me about Jamaican kids listening to Fats Domino and New Orleans rhythm and blues on American radio at night when the weather was good.

Yeah, them music it used to pass through, ya know? Most of my music listenin'—ya mon! Yah see, my people was always amongst bars. You have jukebox and you always have music going on. I remember we used to have plenty, plenty music. And one time a show with Brook Benton came down here, Brook Benton and Sarah Vaughan, me saw. Dinah Washington—I think it was Dinah Washington. Like, they all show up: Nat King Cole, Billy Eckstine, ya know? Even Frank Sinatra and Sammy Davis, in a certain period of my time, like when I was living on Oxford Street.

But when I was living in Barry Street I used to hear things like "Jim Dandy to the Res-cue!," "A-Bony Moronie," "What Am I Livin' For," "Don't Break Your Promise to Me." Heavy music. That was Barry Street. We go to Regent Street and me hear things like [*sings*] "Show me-a, show-me-a, gimme look out, bail-me-out." And some work with a guy named Danny Ray. That type of music. Because the type of people me stay with is them time a music them deal with. Then we go down to Regent Street now, and there me hear Brook Benton.

But Fats Domino and Ricky Nelson and Elvis Presley, a whole heap of lickle other music come on one time strong. Then me go to Trenchtown and starting listenin' to jazz. Except me couldn't understand it [*laughter*], ya know what I mean? After a while me get to understand it, and me meet Joe Higgs and Seeco, who schooled me. And me get to understand the feelin'. Me try ta go in the mood of a mon that's blue, to understand the t'ing what them do. To get to understand the feelin' they express.

How many children do you have? Seven?

Yeah, and got one coming too. It don't take plenty, you know what I mean? It just take a nice girl who don't take no birth control. [*laughter*] You know what I mean? Sexual intercourse is an advantage. [*much laughter*] Me have four boys and three girls. The eldest one is about eight, or seven. Sexual intercourse is a lovely t'ing.

Do they like music?

Yeah, them musicians. Them grow up and play music, as a natural thing. Is righteousness Jah will reward us. Children is wonderful, a part of my richness. Important to keep every thing natural. If we live in truth, eat ital food and love.

Aww, but them higher people in the government should clean up the dumps and slums and feed my people, our children! [*looks at front-page story in* Jamaica Daily News *about children in garbage dump on Causeway Road*] I read the paper and I am ashamed. That's why I must leave this place and return to Africa. If Jamaica was my home, then me love Jamaica, I wouldn't feel like I feel: that this place is NOT my home. I want to leave with my children. I don't want to fight the police who help start riots with cruelty and plant guns on helpless people and turn them into the Gun Court. You understand. Evil police business.

Them guys are crazy. The way I feel about the Gun Court is that the mon who plan it, he have so much money and him hate black people so much, see ya walk down the clean street, poor with your feet dirty, and say, "Ah! You must die!"

What do you think of all the urban renewal and business development taking place in New Kingston? Will Jamaica become like the island of Manhattan?

Do you know what you're saying? One time they show me a plan that they had for Kingston—and that's Manhattan, New York, New York! I mean, if you go down to Harbor Street there, and look good, there's some high building, and you say, "What's really happening here? Who's coming in, putting a lot of weight upon the earth?" And big sky scrape—going up.

With urban development comes urban sterility.

That's what's happening mon. Money mon, moneee! Is plenty things them people don't know, you know. Is plenty wisdom them people don't know. Because is few guys know that figures ain't got no end. You can start all over again. Numbers. They don't go more than nine. But they don't have no end. That mean, if numbers is where you get your kicks from—to have plenty—then you're *lost.* Because it don't have no end. So plenty people don't realize that this thing is something happening here. This shit don't have no end. Ya know. It's just *madness.* Weirdness. Weird situation.

What tracks have you completed [for the forthcoming Rastaman Vibration *LP]?*

Yah, we have one called "Jah Live." Them on the news say that our God is dead. But, you know, is them don't understand. Them don't understand. We have a name, "Crazy Baldheads," and we have one named "Roots." We're gonna chase those crazy baldheads outta town. That's about the system and the things what happen around here. Like, for instance, we build the cabin, we plant the corn, our people slave for this country. Now, you know what I mean, today they look upon me with a scorn. Yet, them eat up all our corn! So we have to chase those crazy baldheads outta town, man. Ain't nuttin' else we could do. We can't stand and let them bury us. Enough of that *sheeet!* You know what I mean?

Because we plant the corn, yuh know. We build the cabin, we plant the corn. And we build the country. Yet, you have guys that look for Rastaman and say, "You know *Rasta,* deh no good!" It's our sweat they walk on every day! Our blood and our sweat!

You feel that Jamaicans don't share in Jamaica's wealth.

Is like all that. For two thousand years now.

When will it change?

Does the whole world ever change? Because God shall bound the Devil again, in the Bottomless Pit. Ya know? The Devil shall be cast into the Bottomless Pit. And there'll be no more remembrance of him. Is the people gotta live right, ya know! People going to live right, mon. If all the people upon the earth ever died off, and the generations start again, where the people just have to live right—is no way we can continue like this. It don't pay.

You see, for instance now. Sit down here, right? And I think—you dig it? Good. I move half of what I think, yuh unnerstand? Like other people do the same thing. But if you live right, mon, and you doing right, then—when me come to you me don't supposed to be a bad vibration as you can treat me foolish. You supposed to have so much power that's if you was ever the Devil you'd have to arm yourself and listen to what I say, because I have the right vibration.

It's like, in Jamaica now, you can go into a yard where there's bad dogs. Bad dogs bite ya. Now, you can go in there and this dog, him just glance at yah and him can feel afraid because him can pick up your vibration, and him no want to go on with you right away. So him know if him can attack you [*laughter*] or him know if you're cool. That's just like people.

I mean, no one have the right to do one them things. Righteousness must win. That's why I can't really, I really couldn't go around and say, "Yes them can do that," because them can't do it! Is you make them do it. Ya know? Is you really make them do it. [*laughter*]

When did you become a Rasta?

Well I ever was, ever is, and ever will be, Rasta.

Are you intent on spreading the Rasta creed in your music?

Well, a thing like that. What is righteousness rule the earth. It goes that there are two things on the earth: good and bad. You have the Devil and you have God. Well, if you live right, yar Rasta, and if you live wrong you're the Devil. Yuh unnerstand? 'Cause is just two t'ings, just two elements. One care and one don't care. You know what I mean? But with the Last Days in time, plenty things are happening, you know. Who will hurt; who will decide Rasta and who will decide to be the Devil. There is only two things—good and bad, negative and positive.

Is it possible to be both righteous and *rich?*

The thing is, your mind is the whole thing, because we are the richest people upon the earth. Richer than rich, our father Creator. Who own the mango tree? Who own the pipe? Who own the ladder? Who own everything?

You find that when most people get money them kinda get withdrawn, foolish. Them thing a-no work, mon. Them come and a search and them never have a penny, if money is richness. Money is *not* my richness. My richness is to live, and walk on the earth and bear fruit. And you can grow. That is what richness is. Richness is when your mind can tell you, "Get up and do something" when you want to do it, 'cause you no want to do something your mind can't tell you for do it.

Your music is full of images of struggle, calls for equal rights and revolution. How do Rastas feel about armed struggle?

Armed struggle? I don't want to fight, but when I move to go to Africa, if they say no, then me personally will have to fight. Me don't love fighting, but me don't love wickedness either. My father was a captain in the army; I guess I have a kinda war thing in me, but is better to die fighting for yar freedom than to be a prisoner all the days of your life.

[*Picks up guitar against tree, strums it, humming softly*] Talk about blessing the child, you understand? I write a song called "Children of the Ghetto." When my children are old enough to sing it, I'm gonna record it with them.

Me still working on the words, the way it go: [*talks/croons lyrics*] "Children playing in the streets, in broken bottles and rubbish heap, Ain't got nothing to eat, only sweets that rot their teeth. Sitting in the darkness, searching for the light—Momma scream, 'Watch that car!' But hit-and-run man has gone too far. [*sighs, looks at Rita and Robbie*] Aw, Jamaica, where can your people go? Me wonder if it anyplace on this earth." [*long pause.*]

Have you ever been arrested?

Me go down to jail one time in Jamaica, and me go to jail one time in England. When I was put in jail in Jamaica, I drive a car and somebody in the car was like a—no, a guy was driving the car without a license, and when the police happen he tell them I was teaching him to drive. So them teach me for abidding and abetting [*sic*]. Circumstances in England is that one time some guys who was smoke herb, and them claim some herb was coming into England, and them come check out our place one time and find one of the guys who's seller was there. Them hold him and tell him we was responsible for the house. And them hold me too. But it was nothing; I stay in jail about two–three hours, and them let me go. I stayed in jail in Jamaica for six hours, or less than that. I went to court and they say, "Okay, you can go." [*laughter*]

Someone suggested on the flight down here that you and Toots and the Maytals could team up for an amazing live album, a reggae jam.

Me never really think about that but maybe after a while we can go into that, because Jamaica is a place where you build up competition in your mind. Them feel like, say, you must fight against me, and I must fight against you. You know what I mean? Whatever you do. Is just a big fight going on. Sometime a guy him must feel him must be like that because he might never go a school and mine go a school, so him say, "I think sometime him a wipe me off the market," and him try and wipe you off of the market, and competition is that.

We should come together and create music and love, but is too much poverty. Too much poverty. People don't get no time to feel and spend them intelligence. The most intelligent people is the poorest people. Yes, the thief them rich, pure robbers and thiefs, rich. The intelligent and innocent are poor, are crumbled and get brutalized. Daily.

What does the future hold for reggae?

I think it will get more spiritual, more spiritual. Benefit, ya know? Benefit for the people. American musicians don't really—reggae music too simple for them. You must be inside of it, know what's happening, and *why* you want to play this music. You don't just run go play this music. Because you think you can make a million off of it. But the music have a purpose. You can make a million off it like Johnny Nash but de creative purpose suffers. But the music have a purpose. Why you play this music? And how come you can play other music, and you don't play other music? Why you play this music? Because we like the feeling of this music. This music have great expression.

A different feel from every music. Love it!

You recently met George Harrison of the Beatles, right?

Yeah. Yeah mon. Me sing one of the Beatles song too. Cover one of the Beatles songs—and I love her. [*he sings: "I gave ya all my love, that's all I doooo . . . ha!"*] The thing was we meet and shake hand and say great—them dude they nice. I really like meet them and sit down and chat with them. They're bredrens. Jah just love roots. Them guys are roots. Them guys are all right, ya know. There is like a king and a queen, ya know—those guys are *roots.*

Have you liked the articles on yourself you've read in from the States?

Me read plenty article, 'cause me know plenty article that is joke article. Get plenty article that is just pure foolishness. You have a guy come talk to you for a whole week, and him go an' write something for please the Devil. If want to just please the Devil because him feel, say, "That is the way of the people." It's just a thing where nobody's strong enough to please the ones that you deal with. One and two guys is strong enough to do that. Most guys try to find *something* lickle bit foolish to say. Don't really make sense. You just keep hurting oneself. [*laughter*] There is no mystic place, you know.

Bob, for the record, when were the Wailers formed?

Well, ah, we'd been playin' together for a long while but we were never really doing recording, ya know? Jus' like the musicians who still do lots of recordin' sessions. So we get together and form a group from before 1970 or something like that. One of them deals.

Before that, there were records in the early 1960s by the Wailing Wailers . . .

Yeah. That was when we just used to do singing.

Your voices were higher then.

At that time, yeah.

What is the first record you ever made?

That thing named "Judge Not," a song called "Judge Not." I was singing by myself. 1961. [*He later explains the song was cut late in '61 and released in Kingston in early '62.*]

Leslie Kong cut your first records, right?

Yeah. "Judge Not" and "Do You Still Love Me." I write both-a dem. I meet Leslie Kong at Federal. I was looking for-a Count Boysie, and Desmond Dekker say I should check Leslie Kong. And dat mon rude! Tell me ta sing my song straight out, standing outside. Didn't have no guitar, rass-clot. Dat focker! Him take me inna room, past Chinamon and this guy Ken Khouri, who tek the money and put it inna pouch on 'im chest. No, Kong must pay for the studio time for me. So I sing and Kong pay me two ten pounds note and then push me out. When I sing for him, I say, "What if it a hit?" Him say, "Coo pon," and say I'm trying to rax [*ruin*] the deal. Them blood-clot. Mon-a name-a Dowling make I sign the release form, then them push me out a studio, and I run home. First I wait for acetates, then I run home.

I always loved the African Herbsman *LP on Trojan. Was that a ripoff or an album the Wailers planned?*

An herbsman is a righteous mon who enjoy the sweetness of the earth and the fullness thereof. Him just smoke herb like the Bible say, and commit no crime. Never see nothing from them Trojan recording. I'll tell ya something, mon. Me never thought reggae gonna become popular over the world, reaching many ears, when it was beginning. Was too much wickedness trying to hold it down. The Devil was everywheres.

Are you bitter?

Nah, fuck. Me no bitter. Me *better.* Yes! A better mind!

Besides listening to New Orleans R&B on American radio, what other musical influences were incorporated into your music? Did you listen to jazz?

I don't know, I can't really play so good to play jazz. You know what I mean? Jazz is when you really know plenty things about sensitive plenty sound. Then you can hear the 5th and the 7th and the 6th and the 9th and the 11th, and you can really hear them and put them nicely in a working thing. But me couldn't do it, because me no really reach that stage yet.

You know, I spent my teens growing up in Montclair, New Jersey, the same town that your lead guitarist, Al Anderson, is from. We both played in local rock bands, and he was known for his skill at playing Jimi Hendrix's leads.

You grew up with Al? Yeah! Fuuuuckkk! That's good! He used to play with Jimi Hendrix? Oh, you used to play Jimi Hendrix's *music.* The thing is, I was in England, ya know, for the music; me like music, me love music, I appreciate people who love music, and I meet Al in England while he was doing some overdub guitar. We talk a little and it's nice, ya know? So I ask him to come play with the group. Him think about it for some time and then him decide he would do it. Boy, him great! Fuckin' good mon!

Now, his rock-styled way of playing raises an interesting point, because reggae isn't normally dominated by a lot of lead guitar. You rarely hear a lot of prominent leads of the kind he plays.

Because we never have a guitarist who can do it, ya know? Yeah, just that! We never have a guitarist who can do it! Because you see, he's a mon don't put down music, because me don't like to put down the people or put down music. But me talk like—MIS-PLACEMENT. If I was livin' in America me bet I'd be a *champion guitarist.* Me. Ya know? But being still in Jamaica me now watch it: it don't happen. Instead you play a guitar and smoke some herb and you lean back and your head go oooout! Yuh unnerstand? In America you can do that but there's *plenty* things you can do! If you want to do something. Like me can want to learn my guitar, but a million things back up around my head.

In America now, you go inside your room or your apartment and the beauty is for practice. This, that and you do. You just have a t'ing a-go. You just confine and practice. Up at Hope Road lickle things you do, and make plenty jokes. But to appreciate it still.

Do you think Al's rock guitar style will influence reggae, make it more complex?

Never idea! I have plenty ideas. A wild world of ideas. Ya know? I don't especially like—I like creative guitar. I don't especially dig like, a rock and roll solo or a blues solo, where guitarists regularly play. Ya know? I like creative things. Ya know? Al's guitar has done a lot for reggae music, mon. You can hear it on *Natty Dread,* "Lively

Up Yourself"—him playing the hell outta that one. [*laughter*] Know what I mean? Rude! Good! Good!

So you really like the Natty Dread *album, huh?*

Me like it because Al up on it. An', me hear something me wanna hear. Me hear some *music,* ya know?

Incidentally, several people have recently called you a "Jamaican Bob Dylan."

I used to hear about Bob Dylan plenty. You can say something now; growing up in the ghetto, you don't really got no money for going out and buying recordings. You know what I mean? In time you have money to buy food to eat. So me hear about Dylan's music over the radio. I might go to somebody's house, and they have Bob Dylan and play it. But me never seriously listen to Bob Dylan, until the other day me start, like, listening. Because me have people around me who directly, them love music so them become like music freaks. Them invite me out, and say, "Come! Want you to listen to some music!" We have the best herb, the best food, and so we listen to some music. 'Cause this mon have, like, Richie Havens and them guys there.

Your own career follows the evolution of reggae itself, from the simple ska days, through rock steady into reggae.

Complicated thing happen. Dig it? When I started singing, I couldn't play an instrument. We still have these musicians who play the instruments and are playing better music than we play today. But the guys who used to do the thing, it was a young thing growing. I can remember the first time I hear a record when the thing was going to get popular, when Jamaican singers in Jamaica was gonna get popular like Wilfred Edwards and Owen Grey, and Jimmy Cliff, Lord Tanamo. Plenty of them type a guys, during those times.

What were we talking about? [*laughter; he relights a huge white spliff*]

And then it changed. The guys who used to, like me, go to a studio, and you come to me and say, "You can play?" and me say, "Yes!" and you will want the opportunity. Because there is no work, although you can get work, but who want to work for £5 a week? Not at that time. Music was the thing.

Well, them rip off the people that play music, and music supposed to make you conscious—but you know, you can get conscious with your rights but you can't come conscious with your flesh. You know what I mean? You can go up and drink a whole heap of rum!

The thing was, what happened to reggae music was that you can play a good American music, and when you put on reggae you hear a big difference. And it don't sound nice. When we put on the American music and put on reggae music, one of them sound weak—so the music grew in reggae. Improved.

During the period when the Wailers music was evolving from ska into rock steady into reggae, did you ever go to America to perform? Did you ever do any shows in Brooklyn?

Did I go to Brooklyn? We played there lickle time, long time ago. We played with a band over there—and police stop the show. *Lots* of policeman. First I ever see so much police. All I saw was about ninety police come in, in the place and throw us around. And it wasn't such a big place.

And one of the police come up to me and say, "You have to stop now." I play like me never hear, so still I sing. And him say [*voice rising*], "You have to stop now!" And me still I play, and so some of them kick off the current, the lead coming there. [*laughter*] When we went outside there was lots and lots of big truck, a jeep and cars—police business. Like it was supposed to be a riot or something.

Why had the police come?

Boy, I don't know. Is the guy who was keeping the show was a West Indian, right? And most people think figure, say, them guys are just the ripoff people, that mean any hour them a advertise we're there we are not there. Them want to tear down the place. You know.

And so we was really there, but the guy who had hired we out had gone over to the next place, and then them guys come in and start going rude because them can't see us, who them come to see, and them want see right before we go onstage so them can be sure that their money really paid out. [*laughter*] I feel that the guy who owned the place call in the cops.

Was anybody hurt?

No, everything work out. Nice. Calm. Police was on guard at the gate to see that everybody leave. There was my experience in the likes of a thing like that. Police like *dirt,* all dressed in black. American police. I know some of them guys' style. [*chuckle*]

Has anything like that ever happened to you in Kingston?

Yah mon. Them just don't like to see whole heap a crowd, where we draw. We draw the ghetto, we draw the people ready to fight. We draw the people who are ready to live. We draw the people who love righteousness. And the Devil don't like that! So him send them to come and try and mark me up and things. The Devil don't like that.

I brought a bunch of old singles down to show you. I have a 1972 single here on the Punch label of a Wailers' song called "Screwface." What does screwface mean?

That's a song about the Devil. The Devil is a very generous mon—he'll give you everything for your soul! Hear me, he's a very generous mon, a very tricky mon.

When the thieves took up with reggae music, mon, they have it *made.* It easy in Jamaica for any guy who have a few dollars to rent a studio, go in, get a recording, ask the engineer to mix it. The hustlers move in as soon as he's gone into the street; the record goes into the stores and Jojo knows nothing about what happened! Jamaicans go slow, everything is "soon come," but if there's one thing Jamaicans rush about it's makin' a recordin'. [*laughter*] Nothing is important that much.

Was money a consideration when musicians stopped playing ska and started playing rock steady?

Well, the guys who were in control robbed the older musicians up, and them get frustrated and stopped playin', you understand? So the music changed from the older musicians to the younger, hungrier ones. People like I, we love James Brown and love your funky stuffs—yeah mon—and we dig into dat American bag, you understand? Strong. 'Cause this was rock steady now—du-du-du-du-du [*he mimics a quickened bass line*]. Rock steady going through! It kind get lightened now. The competition come up. We start selling them.

We didn't want to stand around playing that slower ska beat anymore. The younger musicians, this was rock steady now! Eager to go! A change was coming, from the older the younger. We love James Brown, and we wanna play that way, in dat groove. Dig it! But the older musicians no want to speed up the beat. Them wanna keep it down, but it must go through!

I was surprised to learn that the Wailers rarely perform in Jamaica.

We hardly appear here, you know, except when we have something doing, 'cause sometime it don't really make sense. The only places you can play right now is some of the theaters, and you just play theaters at holiday time, like Easter, Christmas, holidays like that.

But next month you and Peter and Bunny are planning a big concert in Kingston with Stevie Wonder, right?

Yeah! We lookin' forward to having a party there! A nice party instead of this big thing, you know. *Dig* Stevie. Never met him personally.

Besides your American idols, who's your favorite Jamaican artist? And I've heard you prefer dub and version tracks to complete tracks.

In Jamaica? In Jamaica we have the Burning Spears! And me like the heavy way them deal. Me like the version, love version. Me love plenty artists, but me don't know some of them names. And me don't really listen plenty.

Living so close together, I would think you guys would all get together and jam a lot. Do you?

[*Nodding*] Me don't know some of them names, we just jam. They just come meet me. Never really jam with no musicians who have a name. Johnny Nash used to like to sit down and play the music and me hear it. And we really get into a thing and jam and feel ready! We jam down there with all the musicians.

I would wonder if jealousies arise in such a poor situation, people like you making money while other ghetto musicians are not.

Moneee, moneee, can't spoil you. They musn't let money spoil them. I'm not to see that plenty people do spoil at your money, because I still know me have good friends. Once money spoil you boy, you ain't got no friends. You friends is your money—that mean that all the people we have around here, them like you because you have money—and then when your money done, you're finished. You have plenty people sing themselves, "When your money done, you ain't got no friends."

That line is from an old blues song by Billie Holiday. She died as a result of her deterioration from heroin addiction.

Died of heroin? Sad. No money. They go-go, but it always come! Plenty people, they just spot truth. Money done, you ain't got no friends. Money done, you ain't got no woman, neither! [*big laugh*] Whyyy-ooooh!

How do you feel about all the sudden interest you're getting from people around the world, all these outsiders like me coming up to this house to interview and photograph you?

It's a funny feeling. Not really a *funny* feeling; it's just like—this is one of the things that happen if you're doing music, if you're in the recording business. You must expect people to ask you what's happening. It is a funny t'ing.

You're most popular in America among white kids. How's that strike you?

Well, to me them have no difference. To me, them coming like [*cordial tone*], "What happening, Bob? What happening?" Wherever, we are friends, just seeing people. It never really no difference. Jah give you the wisdom to understand it. Is nothing can surprise me. And me don't frighten. And me know if I see them, them hold and talk to me.

How accurate is the film, The Harder They Come*? It's supposed to be a mixture of your story, Jimmy Cliff's, and the Jamaican outlaw Rhygin.*

To tell you the truth, I don't really see the film yet. I wasn't even here when the film was down here. I like to travel if I have something doing. If nothing doing, I prefer to stay. Me don' want to travel just because me want to know places. Want to do things to come know everywhere, but if you've seen one place you've seen them all. People might talk about different item, different people, but as for the place, if you've seen one place you've seen them all. [*laughter*] I'll say there is some places in America like Jamaica!

You'll be doing a lot of traveling, touring, once the new album is done. Apart from individual shows here and there, have you done a great deal of traveling before, in the old days?

Yeah, not in England before, but I was in America, 'cause me mother lived there. The pace faster. Definitely. Things go quicker. Difference with America is that you can get things done. Jamaica is a place where you relax and put off things. Jamaica is a place where you relax and *learn* to put off things. [*laughter*]

Ho boy, in America you got to get it boy, you got to get it! Yah mon! We have Americans come down here, mon. Is a help we get them, like, "Don't go so fast, watch this. *Please* don't go so fast." In America, things a *snap!* You hear a young girl say, "Goddamn it! One telephone run Jamaica! I live in a house with twenty telephones and one telephone run Jamaica!"

A sequined Diana Ross started to rhapsodize in front of 2,500 guests at Pasadena's Civic Auditorium in the spring of 1983: "Someday, we'll be together." The high-spirited crowd became positively transported when, from the wings, former Supremes Mary Wilson and Cindy Birdsong emerged to join in. The song was the trio's last No. 1 hit as a group, before Diana Ross departed in 1969 to go it alone. At the time of the breakup, the act was known as Diana Ross and the Supremes, and Diana's departure had been imminent for three strained years. She was replaced by Jean Terrell, sister of heavyweight boxer Ernie; Wilson and Birdsong were gone by the early 1970s, and their replacements disbanded the act before the end of the decade. Florence Ballard, founder of the group and the woman Cindy replaced in 1967 after Motown president Berry Gordy dismissed her, died of cardiac arrest in 1976, a problem drinker living on welfare.

Diana Ross

1988

While the audience was electrified by the reunion—which had been arranged as part of the live taping for Motown's twenty-fifth anniversary gala—the women themselves seemed awfully tense. That feeling might have remained a nettlesome notion, simply an unfounded suspicion, had "Reach Out and Touch (Somebody's Hand)" not been added to the program. That song was a Top 20 hit for Ross in 1970, her first accomplishment on her own. She seemed not to want to relive the memory in the company of the Supremes, however, because partway through the song, Ross gave Mary Wilson a spontaneously spiteful on-camera shove of such force that it caused Wilson to drop her microphone.

Only the hasty diplomatic arrival of Smokey Robinson, offering himself as a gracious, smiling buffer between the two bickering women, saved the evening from further tarnish. It also provided a touch of nostalgia. In 1964, when the Supremes, the Temptations, and other Motown acts first introduced themselves to America through the Motor Town Revue company bus tour, it was Robinson who continually served as a one-man rescue team when acts faltered. And it was Robinson, the senior member, who always closed the show. The Supremes were stuck in the vulnerable position of opening each evening's entertainment, but Diana shrewdly saw the latent advantages in the situation and exploited them to the fullest. "She stole everybody's act," Motown president Berry Gordy once recalled, referring particularly to choreography. "When [the others] came on, they looked ridiculous. They had to change their acts every day. They all hated her.

"There are winners and there are losers, and there are heavyweights, middleweights, and lightweights," Berry added. "Diana Ross has always been a heavyweight. She has been called the plastic queen of soul. That's a fallacy."

Gordy made certain that the shoving incident was excised from the televised version of the special. Diana Ross is far too testy and tough to be mistaken for something so unsuitable for conducting heat and electricity as plastic.

Diana Ross was born on March 26, 1944, in Detroit, Michigan, one of Fred and Ernestine Ross's six children (three boys, three girls). A stable lower-middle-class family, they lived in the Brewster-Douglass housing project in the "Black Bottom" section of the city. Her father was a foreman at the American Brass plant, her mother a maid for a wealthy white family. Diana recalls that, as a child, "all I wanted to do was sing and wear pretty clothes." While studying design at Cass Technical High School, she took a job as a night busgirl in one of the four restaurants housed within J. L. Hudson, one of the city's oldest and most exclusive department stores; as the first black ever hired by the store for a position outside the kitchen, she became a talked-about curiosity. Her salary was spent on weekend modeling and cosmetology classes.

At fourteen, shortly after an unsuccessful audition for a school musical, she was invited to join a singing group by neighbors Florence Ballard and Mary Wilson. Another girl, Betty Travis, was added. Manager Paul Williams approached the girls' parents for permission to use them in tandem with the Primes, a male vocal group; and he got an OK. The girls called themselves the Primettes. Travis dropped out shortly after they were signed to the local Lu-Pine Records label, and Barbara Martin came in to help them cut two singles, "Tears of Sorrow" and "Pretty Baby." The records helped them get bookings, and they worked with the Primes, but the act was shaky. Martin left to get married, and Ballard was pulled out periodically by her mother whenever her grades dipped. Even when her parents agreed to her singing, Florence was a listless, unreliable participant, given to unexplained truancy and disappearances; occasionally, Ross and Wilson had to appear as a duet.

William "Smokey" Robinson of the Miracles, an informal talent scout for Hitsville, U.S.A. Records, later to be called Motown, had been involved in bringing the Primes into the company in 1960. That same year, he arranged for the Primettes to audition for Gordy. The boss was unimpressed, but he said he'd consider a deal after they'd finished school. In the meantime, the girls hustled for recording experience, singing backup on Motown sessions and hanging around the bungalow headquarters on West Grand Boulevard in hopes of pickup work. A few opportunities arose, backing Marvin Gaye, cutting demonstration sides with Martha and the Vandellas, as well as lending handclap effects to rhythm tracks, each at the rate of $2.50 a session.

After Ross's graduation in 1962 (she was voted Best-Dressed Girl), the Primettes were taken on by Motown, and they issued the tepid "I Want a Guy." Then the Primes became the Temptations, and Ballard suggested the Primettes also change, supplying the new name—the Supremes. After a so-so commercial response to their "Let Me Go the Right Way" single, Gordy put the girls together with the Holland-Dozier-Holland songwriting-and-production crew. Eddie Holland shaped their vocals; Lamont Dozier developed their melodies and background vocals; Brian Holland mastered a signature sound in the studio. The molding didn't stop there. Auxiliary tutelage was provided by the Artists Development Department of Motown, a team consisting of musical directors, a choreographer, vocal coaches, wardrobe consultants, and advisers on stage patter and social etiquette.

While Mary Wilson had always been the lead singer of the group, Gordy considered her vocal coloration uncommercial; of the three, Florence had the strongest pipes, but Diana's high voice was the most expressive. Her tart, wily phrasing, although in need of much guidance and goading, cut through the characteristic gospel density of Motown's backing and the pop crispness of its production values. As Diana's role as lead singer grew firm, she gained general dominion over the group. She became engrossed in their image, choosing and even sewing their costumes, devising their hairdos, pushing for the supperclub poise and sophistication she aspired to in her own outside charm-school classes. To her mind, appearances were the coin of ambition, a rococo wardrobe a wise means to a worthy end: come what may, you are not a star until you *look* the part. The results started to show in 1963, when the Supremes scored with "When the Lovelight Starts Shining Thru His Eyes." The careful refining process clicked in 1964. "Where Did Our Love Go" topped the pop charts, initiating a stellar pattern—eight more consecutive No. 1 singles between 1964 and 1967. No female group, white or black, had ever done so well or been in such demand for concert bookings. But the lead singer was dissatisfied on both personal and professional fronts; she found the Diana Ross version of Dale Carnegie training still wanting, and, in 1966, spent the group's only vacation in three years taking a charm-school refresher course.

Later in 1967, a change in the group's billing—to Diana Ross and the Supremes—showed up unannounced on "Reflections," which peaked at No. 2, and rumors and real disgruntlement within the trio began to grow. When Ballard missed dates pleading "illness" (drinking problems, melancholia, and bad blood between her and Ross were the true causes), Gordy put her on suspension. The proud, impulsive Ballard retaliated by firing off a letter to Ross and Wilson, saying that she was quitting. Cindy Birdsong was brought in, but Diana started to squeeze solo appearances into the crowded Supremes schedule, disturbing associates with the stress her acquisitive will was putting on the group and on her own well-being. In June 1969, she cracked. She found her poodle, Tiffany, and Yorkshire terrier, L'il Bit, dead in her dressing room at a New Jersey nightclub; they had eaten rat poison intended to rid the premises of field mice. Diana fled the scene and canceled a week of Supremes' bookings.

Ross's announcement of a solo destiny came in December 1969. For the next two years, she began her own dates with the greeting, "Good evening, and welcome to the Let's See-if-Diana-Ross-Can-Make-It-On-Her-Own Show," and her efforts were bolstered by a high-powered Motown campaign aimed at turning her into a glamorous "personality." Nick Ashford and Valerie Simpson supplied material with a tightly tailored combination of elegance and dramatic content; the studied torchy new arrangement of their "Ain't No Mountain High Enough" is a prime example of the expansive story-song setting they were after.

Ross expanded her activities in the early 1970s to include television and films, particularly *Lady Sings the Blues,* the Motown-backed musical biography of Billie Holiday in which she starred. (Ever vigilant in her unremitting quest for *le dernier cri* and its desired effect, she threw a much-publicized tantrum on the set in protest of the "tacky" costumes selected for the role.) She also eloped with Robert Silberman, an actor's agent who worked under the name Robert Ellis. *Lady* gained Diana an Academy Award nomination as Best Actress and fortified her international image as a glittering clotheshorse. Her second movie was *Mahogany,* the story of a black fashion model's rise and disillusionment; it was plainly a reflection of Diana's own hopes for herself as fashion plate—the character's gauzy regalia was of Diana's own design. While Diana's single of *Mahogany*'s theme song reached No. 1, the film was rejected as a pretentious mess by critics and fans alike. Then, in June 1976, her five-year marriage to Silberman went into divorce court.

"My wife *belongs* to that company," Silberman once said of Motown. He also expressed a weariness with its overweening corporate head, who even accompanied the couple and their children on their family vacations. "She's totally dominated by a man who never read a book in his life. I just can't stand it anymore to hear them calling Stevie Wonder a genius. What happened to Freud?"

Diana signed a new seven-year contract with Motown, and the

company think tank called for a more youthful, sultry persona. She became interested in a film interpretation of Broadway's *The Wiz,* then being discussed at Motown. Sitting up one night with a videotape of the original movie, she phoned Berry Gordy at 4:30 A.M. and insisted on being given the part of Dorothy. "Have you been drinking?" he asked. Ross refused to budge, and she got her wish. Moviegoers were unwilling to accept her as an ingenue in the overblown production, and the movie flopped, but critics took note of her role in the emerging solo career of Michael Jackson, who played the Scarecrow in the film. In their scenes together, especially the dance sequence for their "Ease on Down the Road" duet, his unvarnished adoration of her was blatant.

"He kind of idolized me," she later said, "and he wanted to sing like me . . . everything; people couldn't tell which was me and which was Michael."

After two disappointing albums, she recouped in 1979 with *The Boss,* an audaciously self-assertive album that was produced by Ashford and Simpson. Her next LP, *Diana,* had hits with "Upside Down" and "I'm Coming Out" in 1980. She shared the spotlight with Lionel Richie for one of 1981's biggest singles, the theme from the film *Endless Love,* and then revealed her decision to leave Motown. The news took observers by surprise; Berry Gordy was thought to have an unbreakable hold on Diana's services—and on her heart. He offered her a multimillion-dollar sum reported to be the most offered any individual by a record label, but she turned it down, severing her twenty-year tie. She signed a $20 million arrangement with RCA, purchased a co-op in the Sherry Netherland Hotel and a Connecticut estate, released a new album, *Silk Electric,* and had a sizable hit with "Muscles." It was a brazen song about a woman's craving for well-developed men, written and produced by Michael Jackson.

In 1985, she wed wealthy Norwegian Arne Naess, Jr., bearing him two sons. There had been hits during their courtship, including "Swept Away" and a Marvin Gaye tribute entitled "Missing You," and she graced the black charts with another Michael Jackson duet, "Eaten Alive." But albums with titles like *Red Hot Rhythm 'n Blues* and *Workin' Overtime* could no longer gull a public that had her gauche number. She ended the eighties with her music completely overshadowed by her wardrobe, an inevitability prefigured by a preposterous incident.

Back in 1983, Ross had proclaimed a new era of personal magnanimity by calling a press conference to say she was giving a free concert in New York's Central Park to raise money to build a children's playground named for her. The initial concert and its raindate the following night were chaotic, plagued by a torrential downpour on the first pass and marauding street gangs on the second. It was learned months later that the shows had wound up costing $2.5 million. The city lost $479,000. Not one cent was left over to build the playground, despite the fact that the city had footed all bills for police, sanitation, and other services. When the city asked the Ross organization for a full accounting, they learned of lavish spending for trappings: embroidered gown, $11,035; makeup, $625; limousines, $12,000 (Diana already owned a Rolls Royce). "Shaken and unhappy" with the disclosures, she presented the city with a personal check for $250,000 to get the playground construction under way. The overall fund-raising project was judged a debacle. But then, all Diana had wanted to do was wear pretty clothes and sing.

Paul Simon

1975

"Home run!" hollered young Paul Simon, a small bat in his hands, as the baseball-sized cube, blue with yellow dots, bounced off the top of his bedroom window. "That's the waaay!" he roared with high-pitched, nasal glee. "Didja see that ball go? I gotcha now, Eddie," Paul chided his companion, and then lapsed into an imitation of a Yankee play-by-play announcer: "How about that, fans? A Ballatine blast! And the score is 1-0 as we go to the bottom of the nineteenth."

Eddie Simon smirked, simultaneously amused and annoyed. A shortstop by vocation, he knew his sinking curve ball was his best pitch, but no match, at least this afternoon, for the nimble arch of his older brother's righthanded uppercut. One lousy hit in nineteen innings might not seem like much, but over the last six years the boys had honed the fine points of bedroom baseball pitching to where they could maintain a scoreless tie for as many as thirty innings, neither surrendering as much as a foul tip.

The soft blue cube had fallen to the floor and bounced along noiselessly, coming to rest at the toes of Eddie's sneakers. It was one of a pair of oversized foam rubber dice, hip midfifties bijouterie that the older fellas in the neighborhood liked to dangle from the rearview mirrors of their cars. As far as the Simon brothers were concerned, the dice were ideal bedroom baseball substitutes for the old horsehide: heavy enough for reasonable pitching control; light enough so that a thoughtful swing was required for accuracy—and no worry of broken windows.

Eddie scooped up the "ball" and exchanged it for the bat as he passed Paul on the way to the imaginary batter's box at the far end of the fifteen-by-eighteen-foot room, whose plaid wallpapered walls were festooned with the usual motley collection of oddments gathered by small boys: sports photos, Yankee and Michigan State football pennants, a poster of Johnny Ace . . .

It was late June of 1955; Dwight David Eisenhower was better than two years into his presidency, Senator Joe McCarthy (R-Wis.) was the bane of nationwide Joe-Must-Go clubs; and the Atomic Energy Commission had just reported that a nuclear bomb similar to the one exploded that May in Yucca Flats, Nevada, could be constructed in unlimited size from the cheapest atomic explosives. Albert Anastasia, a Brooklyn racketeer, had just been sentenced to a year in jail for income tax evasion, and Argentine-born singer Dick Haymes, husband of actress Rita Hayworth, had won a three-year court battle against deportation.

Paul Simon, thirteen, and his brother Eddie, nine, couldn't have cared less; baseball season was in high gear and the various trees lining peaceful, almost-suburban 70th Road in Kew Garden Hills, Queens, New York, were in full flower. Indeed, the nation's headlines seemed light-years away from the shelter of their two-story brick home, one of a block-long row of identical, attached cottages.

If the two pale, dark-haired, rather tiny boys were distressed by anything in the newspapers that year, it was the widespread prediction that Cleveland would again edge out the New York Yankees for the American League pennant. Thankfully, the Tribe had nosedived at the end of May, and the Yanks presently had a 5½-game hold on first place. Mickey Mantle, a hero of Paul Simon, was the Yankees' only .300 hitter and led the league in homers.

(Nearly two decades later the two would meet on the Dick Cavett show, and Mantle would privately ask Simon. "Howcum you didn't sing about me instead of Joe DiMaggio in that 'Mrs. Robinson' song?" "Nothing personal," Simon told him sheepishly. "You were always good too, but I needed the syllables.")

Most important of all to Paul Simon at that precise moment in 1955 was that school was out for summer, which meant that he would never again have to return to Parsons Junior High School, which he had attended for the past two years as part of an accelerated program replacing seventh, eighth, and ninth grades.

He hated that place. Parsons was not located in his tranquil, overwhelmingly Jewish neighborhood, but in a tough black/Italian section twenty walking minutes away. Before Paul finally mustered the courage to stand up to the local punks, they had taken considerable pleasure in tormenting him and his buddy Artie Garfunkel, also in the special program.

Morning after morning as Artie and Paul approached the school during their first year, four or five of a loose gang of a dozen "hitters" would descend upon them for an elaborate liturgy of humiliation that including extorting their lunch money, throwing their books over a nearby fence, and then coercing them into vicious fights they had no hope of winning.

Young Paul shuddered at the recollection. In a few days, he'd be leaving for two months at a bucolic summer camp far out on Long Island, and then he'd start tenth grade in Forest Hills High School, located in the fashionable upper-middle-class enclave.

"Forget it," he said to himself, relaxing a clenched fist that had compressed the sponge cube to the size of a walnut. "It don't matter anymore . . ."

Driven indoors earlier that afternoon by a sudden downpour which had caught them at the baseball diamond at Public School No. 165, Paul and Eddie, their jerseys and dungarees still damp, had been absorbed for the last hour in one of a half-dozen events in the "Simon Olympics," a customized two-boy indoor sports marathon which also included wrestling, basement hockey, house basketball, and a curious type of sparring consisting of playfully strategic hesitations and studied jabs that were never (intentionally) landed.

Nobody else was home. Louis Simon, a professional bass player, had left for Manhattan early that morning to sit in with the CBS-TV band for a taping of the Arthur Godfrey show and then do some session work across town. His wife, Belle, was out for a day of shopping. But for the laughter and raucous banter coming from the brightly lit second-floor bedroom, the neat, simply furnished house was dark and silent.

Though the boys were some four years apart in their age, their appearance, mannerisms, and even speech patterns were so strikingly similar that at times their ritual fisticuffs must have seemed like sharp-focus shadowboxing. But besides the age difference—Paul was born on October 13, 1941, and Eddie on December 14, 1945—

there *were* a few other distinctions between the two. Paul was an inch taller than Eddie, had larger, broader features, and though an agreeable, outgoing boy, was decidedly more subdued when compared to his bubbly twin.

In fact, Eddie seemed to take after his mother, a diminutive—four feet, eleven inches in her stocking feet—effervescent woman who taught English at the elementary school level. Paul, however, shared much of the reserved, studious side of his father, Louis, who stood a trim five feet, four inches and, at that time, was a respected professional musician whose career included stints in the studio orchestras of local radio stations and frequent work on the Arthur Godfrey, Garry Moore, and Jackie Gleason TV shows.

Eddie faced Paul and waited, stonefaced, for the first pitch in the bottom of the nineteenth inning, the room silent but for the gray rain tapping on the windows. Baseball, bedroom or otherwise, was of almost religious importance to both boys, but Paul most especially. He was an excellent outfielder and base-stealer, known for his fierce dedication to winning at any cost; he wore spiked shoes even to casual pickup games and had no qualms about thrusting them into the legs of a skinny young infielder while sliding into second base.

(Paul still has bitter memories of his final year in Queens's Five-Foot softball league. The borough was playing Staten Island for the city championship, and just before the game, all team members were measured to make sure none were taller than five feet. Paul, a star player all season, had grown an inch over the summer and was barred moments before the start of the final game; Queens lost, and he was *glad.*)

Paul winked at Eddie from across the room and then went into an abbreviated windup; the pitch was high and inside with a breaking outward spin on it—you really could do a lot with that foam die. Eddie pulled in and tried to bunt it between the beds for a single, but Paul saw his plan and leapt across for a classic one-handed catch: Paul wins, 1-0.

A small victory, but a victory nonetheless—the kind of modest triumph Paul Simon has always found especially satisfying.

Soon afterward, the Simon brothers were down in the basement playing hockey with equal determination—one taking shots with a tennis ball and the other tending goal with a fielder's mitt on one hand and a tennis racquet in the other.

"My brother and I knew how to create fun," Paul Simon later

tells me. "We made up our own sports, depending on what materials were available. When my mother and father would go out, Eddie and I would go into their bedroom and play basketball with a Spauldeen, swinging their door against the wall to form a basket-type shaft.

"We had these crazy made-up names for each other when we played bedroom basketball. I was called George Muffchatiery, and Eddie was Mickey Muffchatiery. We used to do these running commentaries as we played, and I always was 'Coming out of retirement for *one last game!*'

" 'He's playing from memory!' Eddie would announce to the imaginary crowd; 'Old George is playing the whole game from memory!'

"Baseball, though, that was the big thing with me," Simon muses with a low, wistful chuckle. "I can remember, clear as a bell, sitting on my father's lap in our living room and listening to a 1947 Yankee game on the radio: boy, I loved the Yankees. My father once took me to a Dodger game at Ebbets Field—in 1949—and I was so ashamed of being there that I wore a Lone Ranger mask so nobody would recognize me.

"I *always* was good at that game," he details matter-of-factly. "I used to hustle stickball around Queens in the 1950s, deliberately blowing the first game to fool guys and then doubling the stakes on the second. I'd make $15–$20 a day!"

The year 1955 was an important one in Paul Simon's life. His friendship with Artie Garfunkel, begun while both were still back in P.S. 164, had evolved into an extremely close one through an advanced mutual interest in singing. The two had recently braved their first public appearance together, an assembly at Parsons High late in the spring in which they sang an a cappella version of "Sh-Boom."

"Artie always was the best singer," according to Simon. "Once in P.S. 164 he stood up at a school program and sang 'They Tried to Tell Us We're Too Young,' and everybody was talking about how beautiful it sounded.

"I started to sing around the age of eleven," Paul explains. "I remember exactly when I began. I was singing along to this record of *Alice in Wonderland.* [Artie and Paul were in the sixth-grade graduation play at P.S. 164, a dramatization of *Alice*; Paul played the

White Rabbit and Artie the Cheshire Cat.] It was a pleasant little kid's record, and I was sitting on my bed, singing the songs. My father passed the room, and he said, 'That's nice Paul. You have a nice voice.'

"That was it; from that moment on, I thought of myself as someone who could sing."

Eager for some musical accompaniment for his and Artie's vocalizing, Paul followed his younger brother's lead and took up the guitar.

"My father bought me a $25 Stadium-brand guitar for my birthday in October of 1955. He felt that everybody should play a musical instrument and had tried to teach me the piano, but it was no go, so he gave up on me and taught my brother. The guitar was a second attempt on his part."

"Nobody thought that Paul would be very good on guitar," recalls Eddie Simon, who by then was well into classical instruction on the instrument. "The day he got it, he sat down and picked out a one-note tune, 'Rudolph the Red-Nosed Reindeer,' I think. It didn't sound too promising, but he fooled us all and got good quickly."

Paul Simon always has been good at anything he deigned to turn his disciplined attention toward. Those powers of intense concentration have over the years brought him much good fortune, acclaim, and, according to some, a measure of sadness which one friend of his would privately describe to me as "Paul's burdensome, tragic sense."

Paul was fourteen when he began writing songs, at that time collaborating with Artie, who lived three blocks away on 72nd Street. The very first was entitled "The Girl For Me":

The girl for me is standing there
That's the one, flowers in her hair.

"Artie and I got 'The Girl For Me' copyrighted and everything," Simon says. "We sent the form in to the Library of Congress along with the four dollars, and then went into Manhattan after school and on Saturdays to hang around the Brill Building, trying to get it published.

"We were fifteen years old when we signed a contract with Big

Records as Tom and Jerry," Simon went on. " 'Hey Schoolgirl' was the first song we recorded. To go along with the Tom and Jerry thing, I took on the stage name Jerry Landis and Artie took Tom Graph. I picked Landis because I was going out with a girl named Sue Landis at the time, and Artie picked Graph because he used to follow all the current hit records on big sheets of graph paper. 'Hey Schoolgirl' was sold in both 45 and 78 rpm: on the 45 it says by Landis-Graph, but on the 78 it's got P. Simon and A. Garfunkel."

The record was released in 1957, with another Landis-Graph song called "Dancing Wild" on the flip side, and eventually sold 120,000 copies, remaining in *Billboard*'s Top 100 for nine weeks. It advanced as high as No. 54 early in 1958 before disappearing from the charts.

The hits didn't keep on coming. Several other Tom and Jerry efforts were released, among them "Our Song" and "That's My Story," but they stiffed.

Though their early recording career failed to earn them the fortune anticipated—the boys split a few thousand dollars for "Schoolgirl"—it did serve to make their names household words in their own backyard, especially after two appearances on Dick Clark's "American Bandstand."

"You can't imagine what it was like having a hit record behind you at the age of sixteen," Simon confesses with a quick, embarrassed grin. "One month Artie and I were watching 'American Bandstand' on television, and the next month we were on the show. It was an incredible thing to have happen to you in your adolescence. I had picked up the guitar because I wanted to be like Elvis Presley, and *there I was!*

"The first time we appeared on Bandstand we were guests along with Jerry Lee Lewis. He sang 'Great Balls of Fire'! I tell you, it was a tough act to follow. We didn't meet him before *or* after the show, though. Actually, I think we were too scared.

"We were big deals around Queens and the high school for a while after the song hit," he adds softly. "I saved the money from 'Hey Schoolgirl,' and, well, two years later I bought a car, a red Impala convertible, which eventually burned to the ground. It had three carburetors in it, and they caught fire one night while I was driving along. As a matter of fact, it happened right on the corner of Artie's block. I had to leave the car—jump right out—and ended up watching while my whole share of the record burned up."

A disarming stream of anecdotes pour from a reticent man who seldom lets them slip anymore. It's unfortunate; a natural storyteller, he delivers his with a dry, understated élan that reminds one at various points of George Gobel, George S. Kaufman, and Oscar Levant. Downcast at first, he brightens at my amusement with his reminiscences, showing a genuinely friendly smile that all too quickly vanishes.

Paul Simon, dressed in dungarees, a dark blue shirt, and a drab green tweed jacket with suede patches on the elbows, is seated in an overstuffed leather chair in a drawing room–like chamber of his New York offices, located in a stately townhouse off Fifth Avenue in Manhattan's East Sixties.

After some three months of prodding, he has agreed to two concessions to stardom that he admittedly detests: an interview and, during our meeting, photographs. There was a time when he was so self-conscious about his size that he insisted, as have other public figures of short stature like Tom Jones and the late Rod Serling, on being photographed from below, or some other vantage point which would distort any relative perspective of height and depth. It is a testament to Paul Simon's craft and strength of purpose that he has become one of the major singer-songwriters of his age, selling tens of millions of records and generating a considerable amount of popular sheet music, without once resorting to a publicity stunt, a garish stage show, voguish material, or hype of any sort.

A constant innovator, he has been instrumental in introducing to mass audiences the talents of such artists as reggae guitarist Hux Brown, the Dixie Hummingbirds, South American folk instrumentalists Urubamba, bottleneck guitarist Stefan Grossman, the Jessy Dixon Singers, Brazilian singer-accordionist Sivuca, and jazz greats like violinist Stephane Grappelli, saxophonist Phil Woods, and harmonicist-composer Toots Thielemans (author of "Bluesette").

Although his work, and especially his melodic sense, is much admired, Paul Simon has long been the target of criticism: first, during his collaboration with Garfunkel, for songs that many critics felt smacked of Ivy League ennui with a sticky maudlin glaze; and then, as his solo career has progressed, for lyric imagery that some say has become increasingly hostile and/or sarcastically melancholy.

Simon knows that some people think he's running an *angst*-

athon; he appears to read everything written about himself. He admits that he is not undeserving of critical review but has repeatedly maintained that he writes not for a youthful audience desirous of "entertainment for its own sake" but for adults—marred, scarred, hopeful, inquiring grown-ups.

On the gusty, late-autumn afternoon that we talk, he lets me know with subdued vexation that, since I was asking, he wants to explain the nuts and bolts of his artistry at some length: purpose, choice of subject matter, technique—all of it.

In retrospect, it is neither his opinions on nor explanations of his work, fascinating as they were, that linger, but rather his manner: a quietly compelling combination of something both childlike and durably fatalistic. Apart from behaving as if he wished to be anywhere else but in that room talking about himself, he exuded the Saroyanesque air of one alternately triple and then one-third his years; I won't deny that I envied the timeless quality in his demeanor.

One of my first questions concerned the lyrics of "Night Game," a song on *Still Crazy After All These Years.* Set in a gloomy, funereal ballpark, the song apparently concerns the cruel demise of a pitcher. Paul Simon being a person sufficiently fond of baseball to have played it with relish all his life—a broken nose and several public mortifications notwithstanding—and then eagerly accept the honor of throwing out the first ball at the start of the Yankees' 1969 season, I was curious why he would then write a song that dressed the game in such utterly odious raiment.

" 'Night Game,' " he sighs. "That song is about ritual death, like in Roman times when they used to send people out into the arena to fight to the death, fighting animals and so forth, and it would have this cathartic effect upon the crowd. Well, today in our stadiums, people don't get killed, but they fight, and there's a winner and a loser. They're the descendants of those arenas, those games. So that's really what the song's about—death: ritual death."

"A number of your songs sound as if they come from some sort of sad resignation," I tell him. "How about '50 Ways to Leave Your Lover'? It has humorous overtones, but if you read the words without the music, those overtones simply aren't there."

"I woke up one morning in my apartment on Central Park," he says, "and the opening words just popped into my mind: 'The problem is all inside your head, she said to me . . .' That was the first thing I thought of. So I just started building on that line. It was the last song I wrote for the album, and I wrote it with a Rhythm Ace, one of those electronic drum machines, so maybe that's how it got that sing-song 'make a new plan Stan, don't need to be coy Roy' quality. It's basically a nonsense song."

"It doesn't hit me that way," I insist. "It seems more real to me than that."

"It's just the character in the song," Simon minimizes, "that's all."

Eddie Simon, now thirty and an accomplished guitarist who owns a successful music school in Manhattan, would later provide somewhat contradictory background on "50 Ways."

"Paul loves to play these little improvisational rhyming games with his three-year-old son, Harper James," Ed reveals with a laugh. "You know. 'There Goes Rhymin' Simon' and all of that—that's where that stuff comes from. It all started a while ago when Paul was teaching him this 'Fe Fi Fiddle-eye-o' song, and just grew from there. Harper James laughs like *crazy* when he does it!

"I think that's where the song came from. I believe it grew out of those games they play. I know it's Harper James's favorite."

In a similar way, Paul Simon discounts a literal translation of "My Little Town."

"That song isn't about me," he asserts adamantly. "It isn't autobiographical in any sense. The song is about someone who hates the town he grew up in. Somebody happy to get out. I don't know where the idea came from.

"It was originally a song I was writing for Artie. I was gonna write a song for his new album, and I told him it would be a *nasty* song, because he was singing too many sweet songs. It seemed like a good concept for him.

"As I was teaching it to him," Simon recollects, rubbing his razor-neat moustache, "we would be, aaah, harmonizing. So he said, 'Hey, why don't you do this song with me on the record?' So I said, 'Yeaah, sure, why not.'

"I think it was Artie's idea to put the song on both of our albums. He felt it wouldn't be fair to put it on one. We figured there would be a certain amount of commotion about our not having sung together in the studio for five years: we decided if people wanted to buy Simon and Garfunkel, they should not have to buy one album as opposed to the other album."

The year 1975 was a rough twelve months for Simon. His four-year marriage to the former Peggy Harper was breaking up during the making of the *Still Crazy* album, and the songs reflect that strain.

Paul declines a request to speak about that misfortune, but says, when I ask, that the song "I Do It for Your Love," a chronicle of poignantly ordinary occurrences in a crumbling marriage, was "all partly true, but not literally true."

I then say I regarded the title song on the album as a series of personal reflections and that I had been disturbed by the ominous implications of a couplet in the final verse:

Now I sit by my window
and watch the cars
I fear I'll do some damage
one fine day.

"What sort of damage?" I ask him.

"Violent," he replies in an irritated tone. "Something violent; do a violent act, whatever that might be. Killing someone would be the most violent, then take it down to whatever."

"Where does that anger come from?"

"I don't know," he says. "Right then I was writing about the character in the song, and that's how he felt."

That last part surprised me; I had assumed we were talking about Paul Simon, not a character in a narrative song.

"See," he says confidingly, making a cranky face, "I believe it's no good to talk about your songs; it's wrong. You should leave your songs alone and let them say what they say; let people take what they want from them.

"All I try to do in the songs," he explains, "is write about the world that I'm in, and I try to do it honestly. But it's not good to explain. If they were meant to be explained then they wouldn't be written."

"Okay, what's the *artistic* motive behind your music?"

"Well, I think my songs are lyrically . . . grown-up, you know? I've seen some reviews of the last album [*There Goes Rhymin' Simon*, 1973] where they say it's disillusioned or bitter, but I strongly don't feel that it is—nor do I feel that *I* am.

"I think that those guys, those songwriters who grew up in rock and roll and were prominent in the 1960s have to keep writing about their lives as they reach their thirties. There's *no need,*" he emphasizes, "for me to write 'Saturday Night's All Right for Fighting.' It's not in my life anymore. Somebody's gonna write that and write it well, though, and somebody's gonna write 'Born to Run' and write it very well. There's always been that in rock and roll.

"Look," says Simon, "one of the big things that revitalized popular music in the 1960s was the Beatles, who came around and wrote the truth when the lyrics were still based on a 1950s mentality of 'We're not too young to fall in love' and shit like that. The Beatles wrote about their *age,*" he asserts, showing another fleeting smile. "That's what I'm doing. I can't stay writing the same lyrics I wrote when I was twenty-three."

Simon is utterly committed to the task of writing for his age group. As he complained to the *New York Times* in May of 1973, "Nobody's making music for me"—and he says he believes that now more than ever.

"So much of what I hear on the radio is *boring,*" he moans. "I think part of the reason is because it's not real. It may be real—maybe—if you're eighteen, but not if you're thirty. People thirty years old wonder why they're not getting off on popular music the way they once did, and it's because nobody's singing for them. When you reach a certain age you're not naïve anymore. Everything I write can't be a philosophical truth, but it certainly isn't innocent—because I'm not.

"Music is forever; music should grow and mature with you, following you right on up until you die."

"What about the current state of the concert scene?" I ask. "What do you think of the big arena syndrome, the theatrics? . . ."

"An attempt to evoke an audience response, unless it's something that's truthful, is bad," he decides. "Entertainment for its own sake never appealed to me much, and bad entertainment for its own sake is even worse. But if I know that someone's purpose is to shock me, there's no way in the world that they can shock me; if the performer's purpose is to unnerve me, then boy, I'm annoyed!

"That's what's happened at rock concerts, and it's partly due to the fact that concerts moved into those arenas, where you had to make larger strokes to be seen. I don't participate in that."

Simon is currently winding up a concert tour that many—among them producer-friend Phil Ramone, who produced his last two albums and Simon's soundtrack to the film *Shampoo*—suspect will be his last for some time to come. Ramone, a likable, well-spoken man with curly salt-and-pepper hair and a bushy beard to match, also has handled the sound-mixing for Simon's last three tours, a unique carryover for a producer. As he has for nearly all previous tours, Simon booked these shows into auditoriums and concert halls in the 3,000-seat range, a deliberate move that, coupled with his insistence on a sizable supporting cast that included the Jessy Dixon Singers and studio-quality sound equipment, ruled out any possibilities of doing much better than breaking even at the box office.

"Paul's *very* meticulous," Ramone says, "and on the road he looks for a special feeling, a delicacy missing from the normal, blaring rock shows. I apply a recording engineer's concepts to p.a.-system problems to try to bring about something far superior to the norm."

Simon and Ramone have become close as a result of their professional association, and Ramone feels part of the reason is that they share similar opinions on Paul's working pace and what constitutes a well-crafted product.

"Paul Simon is not prolific," says Ramone. "That's not his strength. What makes him great is that he's a craftsman, a perfectionist, and I guess I am too.

"When Paul begins an album, he never has more than one song ready and maybe a fragment of a second one. We take our time and experiment until we get precisely what he wants. The last album took about nine months to make," he grins, "just like a baby. I guess you could call it natural childbirth!

"To work successfully with Paul you must live in the pace he comes into the studio with. A lot of times during the album, we had to stop for a month or so because there was nothing flowing from him. Once they're written, each song matures technically at its own individual speed. When we finally got the concept we liked for 'Gone at Last,' Paul and Phoebe [Snow] knocked that off in about two hours, but that was unusual."

("Gone at Last" was originally recorded with Bette Midler, but never saw release because, as Simon puts it, "We couldn't get through all the haggling with the record companies. The version with Bette had more of a Latin, street feel," he notes. "I changed the concept with Phoebe and tried a gospel approach because she was perfect for it.")

Simon corroborates Ramone's testimony on his studio technique.

"I *never* have songs in the can," he said. "When I finish ten songs for a new album I stop and don't ever start to write again until it's time for the next album. Right now, I don't have anything in the works, not a single tune. I treat each album as a project; I like it better that way."

What's this about a farewell tour? The newspapers and even some of your friends are speculating that, hereafter, you'll restrict your activities to the studio, and maybe a Broadway show.

"The last tour was supposed to be my farewell tour," he says, "and here I am again. I really thought it would be the last, but I changed my mind. Thing is, next to interviews and photographs, touring is my least favorite thing, but then I get drawn into it and the next thing I know, I'm out on the road.

"But listen, I don't feel any need to tour and I'm not worried whether I ever will again. I don't mind performing for people, but I'm not a big showman and never was. It's not as if I've got a show of some kind and need some place to put it on.

"As for the things in the newspapers and other magazines recently about a Broadway musical, that's all bullshit. I have absolutely no plans for something like that and no one has approached me, either. I'm not saying I wouldn't be willing to do it some day, but the only plans I have at the moment are to do a lot of reading and start another album in a year or so."

Between the public and private lives of Paul Simon there lies a portable netherworld in which he volunteers, on a small, intimate scale, to bridge the two.

Over the years, that meeting ground has usually been the studio, where he sits down with a few other talented people who assist him in hammering his musical statements into shape. There have been other situations, however, such as a New York University classroom where he led a songwriting workshop in 1971.

"I once spoke to an old friend of Paul Simon's who told me that the best description of him was one of his own lyrics: 'I am a rock. I am an island.' I was surprised—and I don't think I buy it."

The speaker is Melissa Manchester, one of a group of a dozen or so young songwriters selected, through auditions, to study the craft with Paul Simon in the NYU workshop.

"It was one of the most remarkable experiences of my life," she says. "At the time I was eighteen years old, and my heart was set on writing songs. To have Paul Simon advise me on something so all-important to me was a gift beyond description.

"It was a very loose situation," she explains. "He came in the first day and said, 'Listen, I've never done this before and I'm not sure I know how, but we'll keep at it until it ends itself.' We used to sit around playing our songs, and he'd play stuff he was working on too. He'd walk around discussing our songs with us, telling us to play one passage another twenty times and then taking apart the lyrics.

"He struck me as an explorer," says Melissa. "A little sad, maybe, the way most artists are, but available for a laugh on life and the dumbness of an industry that sells art.

"One of the most fun things he used to do was tell us stories about all his hassles and paranoias as a successful songwriter, and the silly things he'd done. He told us about the first time he ever met Bob Dylan. He said he went over to his house all excited, and the place was a total mess, with junk all over and wrinkled old scraps of paper covering the floors. Dylan kept walking around the room talking and thinking out loud. Paul followed, picking up every loose scrap of paper he could find—anything with words on it—and stuffing them in his pockets. He said he was dying to find out *how Dylan did it.*

"In the end," Manchester concludes regretfully, "I felt I only got to know a part of him, but I think he was one of the most decent, sincere human beings I ever met. As far as his songs went, he seemed to pay penance through them for all the things gone screwy in his life.

"I remember somebody asked him the first day, 'Paul, how does one write a song?' And he said, 'Oh? What makes you want to write a song?' "

A very pregnant Phoebe Snow prepares a 10:00 A.M. breakfast at home in Bergen County, New Jersey, with her new husband, Phil, and reflects on the events of the past few months, most particularly the privilege of working with Paul Simon.

"Doing 'Gone at Last' with Paul was super exciting for me," she laughs. "God! All of a sudden I was in the studio with a genius whose songs I'd loved for years, singing this joyful gospel tune. That session was so crazy; it went by so fast, like an Amtrak!

"Right now I'm just finishing my new album with Phil Ramone," she enthuses with girlish charm. "I'm trying to trim down my songs, but I'm up to my neck in words!

"That's one thing that never happens with Paul. He has this beautiful simplicity, this incredible succinctness. If I wasn't so chicken, I'd ask him how he does it.

"He has a gift for wrapping complex things up in neat little bundles that is amazing," Phoebe offers, "yet he still leaves room for you to wonder. One of the new songs that fascinates me is 'Night Game,' the one about the pitcher dying. It's sad; I wish I knew the story behind it.

"But the Paul Simon song that knocks me out most," she rules, "is 'Something So Right.' I was in Los Angeles when the *Rhymin' Simon* album came out, and people were telling me about this incredible song on it. 'You've gotta hear this,' they said, and they were right. It's the ultimate ballad. So many people can't come right out and say 'Hey I love you!' but we all desperately need to communicate that to each other, and to be told it ourselves. No bullshit, I cried so hard when I finally heard that song; I kept thinking, 'How much more personal can a person get? How much more of your soul can anyone possibly bare?' I didn't tell Paul when I met him, but I wanted to cover that song, and still do, but I honestly don't think I could get through it.

"I think he understands all the emotional levels of the artistic process," she adds. "I think he understands what's at stake. We were in the control room one day listening to the final version of 'Gone at Last,' and he suddenly turned to me and said, 'Isn't it nice to win?' And I said, 'Yeah, it really is—for a change.' "

Winning is what Paul Simon is all about; going as far down in the well as he thinks he needs to, to find out what he must know, risking whatever is necessary, and then climbing back out, bruised and shaken, the humble prize in hand.

"My brother wrote a song on the last album that any thinking, feeling human being can understand," Eddie Simon suggests one day as we sit together in an empty classroom in his music school.

"The title song of his [*Still Crazy*] album tells it all. My brother's saying, 'Look. I'm working every day; I'm trying to do the right thing and get through the best way I know how; I've been famous and not famous, badmouthed and broken up inside; I've traveled, I've seen a shrink, I've been in love and got married, and that bottomed out too. And you know something? After all that work, all that pain and trouble, all these years—I'm still crazy. Still fuckin' *crazy* after all of these years . . ."

As art imitates life, so baseball for Paul Simon has provided both the pluperfect analogy and ultimate achievement of his troubled passage.

It's a sport anyone can play, be they fat, skinny, short, tall, country folk, city people; it's boring, and then, unexpectedly, it's wildly thrilling. You're just one person, lonely at the plate, or on base, or in the outfield, and the whole world is watching, waiting to cheer your best, boo your failures, and dissect your mediocrities.

After all the booing, the cheering, the torments, and small triumphs, what comforts Paul Simon?

"I'll tell you something," he says firmly, near the close of our talk, "I'll tell you something that's really *real* to me.

"One of the biggest memories of my life—the biggest—is stealing home in the bottom of the 11th inning of a high school baseball game when I was sixteen years old.

"I believe," he swears in dead seriousness, "that I *peaked* at that moment; I truly believe that was it and don't think I've done anything greater since. I honestly believe I never came quite that high again in my life.

"And I believe," he continues softly, "that the thought crossed my mind as I came sliding across the plate that I was peaking at that very moment. You just can't do any better than steal home in the bottom of the 11th and win the game for your high school team.

"Here's how it happened," he recounts with painstaking care. "I walked; then I stole second, went to third on a ground out and held. As I stepped a ways off third to get ready to run at the next hit, I could see that the pitcher was going into a full windup instead of a stretch. He was giving me a big lead, and I knew I could steal on him.

"I went almost halfway down the third base line on the first pitch, but it was fouled off. But I knew I could do it; heck, I *really* knew it. So I told the third base coach I wanted to steal, and he gave the batter the signal to bunt. The pitch came bad, high and outside—and I took off.

“And as I was running for home, I could feel how important this was always gonna be to me; I was sliding along in the dirt with my heart beating ’n all, and I could tell in my bones that this was gonna be my biggest shot; and when I slid across that plate—I was completely sure of it. As sure as I’ve ever been in my life.

“The guy never even *touched* me.”

Fat horns, strident and clipped, bray in unison against the dusk, paced by the cool *crack* of metallic percussion. It sounds like the opening salvo of "Choo Choo Ch'Boogie," the 1946 jump blues hit by Louis Jordan, one of the founding fathers of rhythm and blues. But the honkers and shouters out jamming on this early winter evening in Manhattan are just victims of traffic gridlock outside of a truckers' diner in a lonely factory district near the Lincoln Tunnel. Behind the beanery's greasy windows, the wizened waitress tugs at her hair net and slaps several more pairs of silverware against Formica as the horns subside and the hollering stops.

"I'd like a bowl of that clear soup with the rice in the bottom," says a willowy, blond-haired young man as he angles himself into a snug back booth. His tone is meek, his manner demure. The waitress's mouth wrinkles in a maternal smile. The grin her customer returns is disconcerting, jagged milky teeth flashed with vampire grace. The sight is canceled so quickly one shudders, wondering whether it was ever there at all, an unwelcome glimpse at a secret best left intact. "Oh, yes," he adds, gently recapturing the woman's crimped confidence, "and I'll have one of your lovely chicken pot pies—and a glass of milk."

David Bowie

1983

Turn and face the strange: thirty-six-year-old David Bowie, dressed like a librarian in crisp blue shirt, sleeveless argyle sweater, and khaki slacks, his bleached hair schoolboy-short. Savoring his lunch, he enthusiastically discusses the aftermath of the Superbowl, and is coddled by the frumpy counter-lady—"Don't let your soup get cold, hon!"

When she drifts off, he blushes a waxy pink and says he's been coming to this diner for almost ten years, dating back to when he had an apartment in the West Twenties during his days as Ziggy Stardust. He adds that he had bet on the Miami Dolphins even though he's a Redskins fan, and dropped $10 in the process. Such admissions seem suspect. One tries to envision the Magus of Glam-Rock wolfing down homey roadhouse fare, his attention glued to some American football on the tube, but memories of his spectral warpaint and sci-fi drag demeanor make it difficult.

Predictably, it all later checks out: the management of the lunch counter confirms that Bowie is indeed a semi-regular customer of long standing; and the musicians on *Let's Dance,* his first all-new LP in almost three years, explain that they got their boss hooked on the playoffs (and attempted to mold him into a Jets fan) while recording this winter at New York's Power Station studios.

It's always been an entertainingly strenuous chore separating the man from the image, and there have been so many versions of the latter over the last decade that his predilection for elaborate reinvention has long since surpassed mere calculation or ritual self-parody. If only by virtue of its crazy-quilt staying power, the *concept* of David Bowie has achieved an integrity all its own. Lon Chaney would have been envious. Kafka might've been inspired to recast *The Metamorphosis* along rock and roll lines. But not really. Art usually celebrates/imitates life, not artifice. Yet David Bowie has brought artifice within striking distance of art.

There was a time when such goals were a good deal more than Bowie could have dared hope for.

David Robert Jones came into the world at 9:00 A.M. on January 8, 1947, at 40 Stansfield Road, in Brixton, London, the sole child resulting from the marriage of Soho club-owner-turned-publicist Haywood Stenton Jones, whose previous wife had divorced him on the grounds of adultery, and Margaret Mary Burns, a theater usherette. David had two siblings, Annette and Terence, and a family tree fraught with hereditary insanity. Terry—his father's child from his first marriage and David's elder by eight years—was prone to long, fitful bouts of unexplained weeping. Terry was in his early twenties when he returned from service in the Royal Air Force, greatly disturbed. David could only watch as his stepbrother gradually shut out the world, eventually ceasing to talk. Then Terry vanished for a few years; he was later discovered in a mental ward, where he has been institutionalized ever since. Other close relations have been prone to sudden, mysterious disappearances; aunts and cousins have been hospitalized after being found wandering in the streets. His step-sister, Annette, is said to have gone to Egypt with a millionaire businessman and has never been heard from again.

At the age of sixteen, David himself became withdrawn, spending all his free time reading books recommended to him earlier by Terry. But after exposure to Kafka's *Metamorphosis,* he became uncomfortable with his own thoughts and was harried by vivid nightmares of human insects, seeing himself becoming an unrecognizable monster. Breaking away from these insistent images, and haunted by the specter of his own impending lunacy, he endeavored to create an alternative world in his own mind, populated with more inviting figures and—most important—fresh characterizations of himself.

While attending Bromley Technical School, David made the acquaintance of Peter Frampton (future lead singer in the Herd) and one George Underwood, who became his closest crony. Their bond held even when Underwood formed a rival band (George and the Dragons) to David's (the KonRads), and, in an unrelated incident, punched David in the eyes and put him in the hospital. (When David returned to school three months later, his left eye was stricken with aniscora, paralysis of the pupil.)

After graduation from Bromley Tech, Bowie took a job as a "junior visualizer" with a commercial art company and then spent six months working for a London ad agency. In 1963, he formed the King Bees with Underwood. In June 1964, seventeen-year-old Davey Jones and the King Bees released their first single, "Liza Jane," on the Vocalion Pop label. That fall, he appeared on a BBC radio program with members of several local bar bands to lobby for "the prevention of cruelty to long-haired men." He recorded singles with two other bands, the Mannish Boys (who had Jimmy Page on the session) and Davey Jones and the Lower Third.

In January 1966, he changed his name to David Bowie, and his new group—David Bowie and the Buzz—became regulars on the pirate Radio London station and appeared on bills with Long John Baldry, Elton John, and the High Numbers (later the Who). He cut three solo singles for Pye Records in 1966 before signing to Decca Records' new Deram label. He went on to a stewardship with Lindsay Kemp's Underground Mime Troupe, "living," Bowie remembers, "the most degenerate life with this rancid Cocteau-ish theater group and writing odd songs about child abusers and dykes" that found their way onto *The World of David Bowie* LP in 1967. When he'd had his fill of Kemp and company, he joined a Buddhist group headed by Chimi Youngdong Rimpoche, a monk who'd recently escaped from Communist China. Bowie came close to moving to the group's monastery in Scotland and taking his vows. But he changed his mind at the last minute and returned to pop music as a Dylanesque folksinger. He appeared in avant-garde films and made a commercial for Lyons Maid "Pop Ice Cream." In 1969, he formed the Beckenham Arts Lab, a creative arts cooperative. "Space Oddity," a single he wrote at the time of the moon landing, hit big in 1969; he was backed in an album, *Man of Words, Man of Music,* and a tour. Not knowing what audiences were like in rock and roll revues at the time, he found himself doing a Dylan/Anthony Newley–influenced set before droves of belligerent skinheads.

Then, seeing the kind of androgynous shock rock the kids were eating up, he formed a fey, mincing outfit called Hype. His head swimming with opiated hashish, Bowie sat about writing brutal songs about his own bizarre upbringing. *The Man Who Sold the World* was the result; it featured "All the Madmen," a track about brother Terry. In March 1970, Bowie was wed to Mary Angela "Angie" Barnett, the couple agreeing to an open marriage that would accommodate unrestrained infidelities and Bowie's bisexuality. In 1971, Bowie released *Hunky Dory,* a homage to the New York City art-rock scene led by the Velvet Underground.

By 1972, he'd told the British press that he was gay (the brocaded gowns he'd been photographed in over the last twelve months had been a tip-off) and created an ill-starred pop-savior persona—Ziggy Stardust. Like all the false faces in his wake, Ziggy was intended to be a painted nothing, an android from another planet who recognized rock solely as an energy exchange in the rubble of a doomed metropolis.

In the beginning, glitter rock and grotesque grandstanding were not uppermost in his mind. Thinking back to before there was the swishy blunt-cut Beau Brummel on the cover of the 1970 album *The Man Who Sold the World* or the Veronica Lake look-alike of the 1971 *Hunky Dory* LP, recalling an era predating messiah-stud Ziggy, Dada dandy Aladdin Sane, and leering Aryan dilettante the Thin White Duke, David Bowie makes a frank admission about the origins of his exhibitionism: "As an adolescent, I was painfully shy, withdrawn. I didn't really have the nerve to sing my songs onstage, and nobody else was doing them. I decided to do them in disguise so that I didn't have to actually go through the humiliation of going onstage and being myself. I continued designing characters with their own complete personalities and environments. I put them into interviews with me! Rather than be *me*—which I thought must be incredibly boring to anyone—I'd take Ziggy in, or Aladdin Sane or the Thin White Duke. It was a very strange thing to do."

And it nearly proved to be Bowie's undoing, as he suffered through what was essentially the drugs-assisted unraveling of a "hurt, broken mentality; a fractured person," while living in Los Angeles in the midseventies, the period of his greatest commercial success.

In the aftermath of his L.A.-aggravated mental traumas, Bowie resettled in Berlin in 1977, renting a spartan apartment over an auto parts shop and collaborating on two raw, highly impressionistic electronic albums *(Low, Heroes)* with Brian Eno while he convalesced. "Slowly gaining control over *me* again," as he puts it, he moved on to Switzerland in 1979, where he and Eno completed their trilogy with *Lodger,* a tribute to human restlessness in all its forms. While in Switzerland, he finalized his divorce from Angie and assumed custody of son Zowie, eleven, now known as Joseph. In 1980, Bowie dipped back into his nightmares again with *Scary Monsters* (*and Super Creeps*), but this time he appeared to rule the shadow creatures rather than the other way 'round.

He bowed out of music for a spell in order to act, debuting on Broadway as *The Elephant Man* and on TV in Bertolt Brecht's *Baal.* He also landed leading roles in two movies. *Merry Christmas, Mr. Lawrence,* directed by Nagisa Oshima (creator of the controversial 1976 erotic film, *In the Realm of the Senses*), is a study of captives and captors in a Japanese P.O.W. camp in Java in 1942, with Bowie cast as a tough-willed Lieutenant-Colonel who refuses to break under torture. *The Hunger* has Bowie playing opposite Catherine Deneuve; she is an immortal siren who needs human blood to survive, and he is her lover of nearly three hundred years, who is abruptly—and rapidly—aging.

Now an extended hiatus from recording has been ended with *Let's Dance,* a buoyantly commercial effort that heralds Bowie's signing (for a reported $17.5 million) with EMI, a long-term deal that presumably will also allow David to exploit his new company's extensive video and film involvements. In spirit, the record is a distillation of the rhythm and blues craze that swept England in the early 1960s, golden years of exceptional black music that captivated David Jones and his Brixton mates. In content, *Let's Dance,* which was coproduced by Chic's Nile Rodgers, owes a debt to Louis Jordan and a host of other jump blues giants, but the Asbury Jukes horn section and the hard Texas blues riffing of Stevie Ray Vaughan combines with its other components to forge an original party-funk *cum*-big bass drum sound greater than the sum of its influences.

"To tell you the truth, I was not very familiar with David's music when he asked me to play on the sessions," admits the twenty-eight-year-old Vaughan, an Austin-based virtuoso whose blues group, Double Trouble, is known as one of the city's best. His 1959 Stratocaster burns with "a passion straight out of T-Bone Walker; Bowie apparently has damn good taste in guitarists," says veteran R&B producer Jerry Wexler, who arranged the Double Trouble gig at the 1981 Montreux Jazz Festival, where Vaughan and Bowie first met.

"David and I talked for hours and hours about *our* music, about funky Texas blues and its roots—I was amazed at how interested he was," says Vaughan (whose brother Jimmy is one of the Fabulous Thunderbirds). "At Montreux, he said something about being in touch and then tracked me down in California, months and months later, calling at 4:30 in the morning. It was get-up-and-make-sense-quick time! That's sort of the way in which the album came together, actually. It was the most fun I've had in my life. David works quickly because he knows exactly what he wants."

And what Bowie wanted was a sleek, stylish record that rocked with a soul swagger; one that rekindled the joy of R&B, which had long ago helped pull a timid Brixton boy out of himself. Peter Meaden, the renowned British mod who discovered the Who and defined the natty, R&B-*cum*-amphetamines life-style of the hip London teens of the early sixties, once offered a terse description of the mod's nocturnal mission: "Becoming neat, sharp, and cool; an all-white Soho Negro of the night." That line fits *Let's Dance* and this year's David Bowie to a T. The title track, "Modern Love," and "Ricochet" are incendiary ballroom raveups, and the new version of Bowie and Giorgio Moroder's "Putting Out the Fire" (from the soundtrack of the 1982 film *Cat People*) is a sensual sizzler.

David Jones and David Bowie have finally merged, organically, admirably. But the old artifice dies hard. He flew into the diner with a flourish, whipping off his bulky tan raincoat and offering a hale and hearty handshake. "Let's make this as formless as possible!" he exulted. He lit a cigarette, handling it as if it were a conductor's baton. The wispy smoke and the steam from his piping hot lunch swirled around his pale face, the skin so translucent it seemed you could see the blood coursing underneath. The thin lips and pointy, vaguely vulpine teeth punctuated various jests and pronouncements with their secret smile. He was in jocund spirits; he seemed at ease. And when he'd talked enough, he withdrew with a strategic suddenness that was masterful in its deft execution.

Without a doubt, David Bowie is once again in control.

Let's Dance *has a lot of interesting early R&B shadings, bits of Bill Doggett, Earl Bostic, James Brown, and a helping of Louis Jordan.*

Yeah, you can probably say that. What happened was that over the last year or so, as I've been doing filming, going to places like the South Pacific, I took tapes to listen to, not really knowing if there'd be much local radio, or indeed what the music was like over there anyway. I realized that in what I'd picked out, I'd gone back twenty or more years to stuff that meant a lot to me when I first started playing saxophone; there was a lot of Johnny Otis, Red Prysock, that organic rock and roll orchestra sound. So I think there's a degree of those other influences on the new LP. It certainly doesn't sound anything like a revival record.

When you got together with Nile Rodgers, your coproducer, was it casual at first, the two of you just playing records for each other socially?

That's really what happened, because I had met him a few months ago in a club in New York, just after I'd come back from doing the *Merry Christmas, Mr. Lawrence* movie with Nagisa Oshima. We started talking about old blues and rhythm and blues stuff and found we'd both had the same artists as strong influences. I guess that triggered me off thinking it might be fun working with him. I admired some of his work in the areas of his bass sounds and drum ideas; he was very instrumental in pulling those sections together on the album. I felt that with the kind of European influences I've had, it might be interesting to see what could result from our working together.

How do you hear the musical textures on the new LP?

I like the horns—but they're not an overly predominant feature on every track. It's kind of a mixed bag, really. And—not for any elitist reason—[*laughter*] there are no synthesizers on it. I really wanted that same positive optimistic rock and roll big band sound that was very inspiring for me back when. It's got a hard cut, very high on treble—it sears through.

You assembled an entirely new group of musicians for the record. How did you select the personnel?

The guitarist, Stevie Ray Vaughan, denotes where I was coming from in terms of putting the band together. [*drawls*] He's from Austin, Texas! Plays in a blues band down thar!

When I saw him a year or so ago at the Montreux Jazz Festival, his trio was the support act for somebody like Muddy Waters. Stevie is just dynamite—he thinks Jimmy Page is a modernist! Stevie's back there with Albert King. He's the wiz kid.

Also, I wanted to have a little relief from the guys that I usually work with. I wanted to try people that I'd *never* worked with before, so that I couldn't predict how they were going to play. They didn't have much idea of how I worked in the studio. And as I hadn't recorded in two years, it seemed perfectly natural 'round about now to try new people. Nile picked up most of the rest of the band for me: Omar Hakim from Weather Report; Carmine Rojas from Nona Hendryx's band; Stevie and Nile played guitars, and that was the nucleus.

Surprisingly, you don't play anything on the album. Not even sax.

I don't play a damned thing. This was a singer's album.

Since the new music marks a return to your very beginnings in rock and roll, both career-wise and in terms of your earliest exposure to certain acts, let's talk about your background. You were a well-known night-crawler as a teenager, haunting the West End pubs. Is it true that your father owned a wrestling club?

Yeah, at one time. It's part of my family mythology. His father died and left him a lot of money, so he put it into a traveling theater troupe, which lost most of the money. What was left he put into a London club for wrestlers in Soho, a nightclub that was gangster- and wrestler-oriented. I don't know *how* he got involved in that!

Then he went into the army and when he came out he started working as a P.R. man for a charity organization [Dr. Barnardos's Children's Home], and stayed there for the rest of his life. He met my mother when she was working as an usherette in a cinema.

Were your parents much in evidence as a kid?

My father died when I was about twenty years old. He was instrumental throughout all my teenage life; as I got older I got more and more support from him. My father bought me my first saxophone. I was not particularly close to my mother, but I've gotten closer to her over the years. I think the recognition of the frailty of age makes one more sympathetic to the earlier strains of any child-parent relationship. The problems are never ultimately on one side or the other—it's a shared responsibility and you get more mature about it.

Is that your mother in the Scary Monsters *video?*

[*Grinning*] No, that's just a mother figure. She's a well-known British actress. That was an inevitable question, and people in London ask her the same thing.

Tell me about adolescence, your early teens.

I had the usual desire to break ties with home and parents, the general anger of youth. I have a half brother and a half sister, neither of whom I've ever been particularly close to, because they've never lived at home. I was brought up ostensibly as an only child, and they put in these lightweight appearances. I lost contact with my stepsister Annette when I was twelve—that was the last time I saw her. She was quite a lot older than me and went to Egypt to get married. We've none of us heard a word from her since, and we've tried to trace her.

I was living up in Brixton until I was eleven years old, and that was enough to be very affected by it. It left great, strong images in my mind. Because the music that was first happening in my early teens was happening in Brixton, it was the place one continually had a relationship with. All the ska and bluebeat clubs were in Brixton, so one gravitated back there. Also it was one of the few places that played James Brown records, other than two French clubs in town, La Poubelle and Le Kilt. A friend of mine, Jeff McCormack, who ended up as Warren Peace in the Diamond Dogs band, had the big ska record collection, and it just wasn't worth competing with him, so I went straight into buying Chuck Berry, Little Richard, and the blues stuff.

Were white teenagers welcome at the "shebeens," as the West Indian clubs in Britain are known?

At that time it was cool. If you expressed an interest in the music and got off on what was happening in the clubs, it was a lot easier, I guess, than it is these days. Although I don't know; I haven't been to those clubs in years. I've hardly been in London in a social, living way for so long that it's almost an alien city to me now—which is unfortunate in some respects, but you lose some and gain some.

At the start of your career you spent a lot of time around the legendary Marquee Club on Wardour Street in London, which had weekly R&B nights featuring twin bills like Sonny Boy Williamson and the Yardbirds. What was that scene like in the early 1960s?

I got friendly with the owners; for me there were no rules at the door, so I used to creep in and watch what was happening. The Marquee, the Scene, Eel Pie Island in Twickenham, they were all a circuit. At the time—sixteen years old, for me—when I was frequently in those places it was during the era of the first batch of mods. There were two batches of mods in England, the first lot being in 1962–63. The initial crop called themselves modernists, which reduced itself down to the mods. That was excessively peacocky. These weren't the anorak (quilted, gabardine raincoat) mods that turned up later on motor scooters. The scooter thing wasn't quite as big with the early mods at that time; it was still trains.

But the first mods wore very expensive suits; very, very dapper. And makeup was an important part of it: lipstick, blush, eyeshadow, and out-and-out pancake powder—not Clearasil. It was very dandified, and they were the James Brown–lovers. Elitist. Pills always played an important part; everything was fast.

You weren't supposed to like bands like the Rolling Stones, and especially the Action, the Who, and all that crowd who came along later—these were the anorak boys in the later sixties—because they weren't *real* mods. I did—secretly. But I felt sad the former fashion had died out.

I dressed the archetype: mohair suits, two-tone suits; the shoes were highpointers; Billy Eckstine shirts with big roll collars. You either had a pinned collar or button-down or roll collar.

How would you earn the money to dress up?

[*Snickering, with a wink*] You earned the money somehow or other, wheeling and dealing. Also, a popular thing was to go down the back of Carnaby Street late at night and raid the dustbins.

Because in those days if anything showed the slightest sign of deterioration, or a button was missing, or there was the least thing wrong with it, they used to throw it out, so you could pick up the most dynamite things down there! This was just as the street was becoming popular. Indeed, there were only about four shops along there that sold clothes of that nature, so it wasn't a tourist thing at that time.

Also, you could get some good suits made in Shepherd's Bush. There were good tailors there that would knock up a suit quickly and inexpensively, out of material [*big grin*] which you didn't ask how they could get so cheaply. So you'd get dressed, go 'round to the Marquee Club, and just get loony and listen to rhythm and blues. Fundamentally it was a rhythm and blues period, which had just hit the underground in a big way.

I wasn't a hundred percent into *performing* music at the time of the mods, but I'd been playing saxophone since about thirteen years old, off and on. The things I'd considered doing once I left school were either to continue being a painter, start working in an advertising agency, or be a musician if I could possibly get that good.

Entrepreneur Kenneth Pitt had seen you at the Marquee Club around the time you were eighteen and led the band called Davey Jones and the Lower Third. What kind of group was the Lower Third?

I guess it wanted to be a rhythm and blues band. We did a lot of stuff by John Lee Hooker, and we tried to adapt his stuff to the big beat—never terribly successfully. But that was the thing; everybody was picking a blues artist as their own. Somebody had Muddy Waters, somebody had Sonny Boy Williamson. Ours was Hooker.

It also was the first band where I'd started writing songs. I think the first song I ever wrote—there might be others but this is the only one that sticks out—was called "Can't Help Thinking about Me." [*breaks up laughing*] That's an illuminating little piece, isn't it? It was about leaving home and moving up to London. "The London Boys" was another one about being a mod. It was an antipill song; I wasn't particularly pro the thing—after a bit.

Wasn't there a point in your late teens that you were into Buddhism for a while?

I've always been a great fan of diversification, eh? At one period I had the whole *lot* going. I was a Buddhist mime songwriter and part-time sax player, or it became like that. I just couldn't see the wood for the trees. I was trying *everything.* I mean, my whole life is made up of experimentation, curiosity, and anything that seemed at all appealing.

Was that around the time that you hooked up with Lindsay Kemp's Underground Mime troupe?

[*Nodding as he gulps down chicken pie*] Lindsay was the man who I ended up studying with, and working for, and living the most degenerate kind of life with. It was all wonderful, incredible. It's a great experience living with this sort of rancid Cocteau-ish theater group in these bizarre rooms that were decorated and handpainted with elaborate things. The whole thing was so excessively French, with Left Bank existentialism, reading Genet and listening to R&B. The perfect bohemian life.

Pitt got you your first recording contract in 1967, didn't he? You were signed to Decca for an album, The World of David Bowie, *in an era when most deals with new artists were for singles.*

I did an album that ended up sounding like a baroque Tony Newley, more than anything else. They were little vignette songs. I guess it was around the time that I was learning to formulate songs out of observed points of view and story lines, trying the bit of standing back and looking on at things. They were very narrative, odd things about child abusers and dykes.

That was all Lindsay's influence—that the everyday is not as interesting as the curiosities of life, and that they can eventually bring you back to the everyday again.

Had you read any Isherwood at that point in your life?

I think I'd read everything by the time I was eighteen or nineteen that I would yet read again, from Kerouac to Isherwood to Kafka to Marcel Duchamp. They had all passed through my life at some time or other. On the second pass I just honed in on a very few of them and sifted and filtered the stuff that was, for me, affectation rather than something that actually meant something. And indeed, that's what I still do.

When "Space Oddity" hit in England in 1969, weren't you suddenly faced with a weird juxtaposition in live performance—something the later Bowie might have conjured up—where you'd be doing Dylanesque shows in front of pissed-off skinheads?

It was *odd.* I was not prepared for that at all. It was, unfortunately, a very good song that possibly I wrote a bit too early, because I hadn't anything else as substantial at the time. What I was involved in to a lesser or greater extent at that point was what were known in England as the "Arts Labs." The idea was to encourage people locally to congregate at this meeting house in Beckenham and become involved in all aspects of arts in society. To come and watch strange performances by long-haired, strange people. They started out with altruistic aims. We'd all contribute to the funding, but those things were always broke, owing money left, right, and center. You'd hire Bunuel films like *Un Chien Andalou* for people to see and not be able to pay for the rental. Then you'd have poets who'd come down from Cumberland in their transit vans to read, and so on.

In the midst of all this, I'd written this little thing about Major Tom and gotten it recorded, and I was told I had a concert tour if I wanted it! I thought, haughtily, "I'll go out and sing my songs!" not knowing what audiences were like in those days. Sure enough, it was the revival of the mod thing which had since turned into skinheads. They couldn't abide me. [*laughter*] No! No way! The whole spitting, cigarette-flicking abuse thing by audiences started long before the punks of 1977 in my own frame of reference.

During 1969, you also made a little-known film which I've never seen, called The Virgin Soldiers. *Was that your first?*

Actually I'm in it for about twenty seconds as an extra. I don't know how it developed into a thing I've done as an *actor.* I've never seen *The Virgin Soldiers* either, so I'm not sure I'm actually even in it still. I know that I was thrown over a bar in it. That was a film put together by a guy in London named Ned Sherrin who was one of the leading satirists of the time and worked on things like *That Was the Week That Was.*

My first true film appearance was years earlier in a movie called *The Image,* an underground black-and-white avant-garde-type thing done by some guy. He wanted to make a film about a painter doing a portrait of a guy in his teens, and the portrait comes to life and, in fact, turns out to be the corpse of some bloke. I can't really remember all the plot, if indeed it had a plot, but it was a fourteen-minute short and it was awful.

What was the first film acting you've done that you felt was worth a damn?

I suppose *The Man Who Fell to Earth.* I was more than optimistic about it, and then I really thought it was a great movie. I couldn't *but* think that, because everything that Nick Roeg had done up to that point I thought was great. And I think it's even better now than

I did then. I think it's surely taken on other qualities over time and is a most intriguing science fiction movie—especially in relation to a lot of the stuff that's out at the moment.

The uncut version is the best.

Quite definitely. That's the only version we knew about in Europe. I was floored when it came out over here and had twenty minutes cut out of it—*hacked* out of it. It brought the thing to its knees; a bad thing to do to Nick's movie. But the best thing about it is that it did achieve critical acclaim at the time. It's still often playing places.

I've always wondered how long it took to apply the slimly body makeup for your role in The Man.

That was a good four or five hours, much like *The Hunger*, which was another four or five hours. The skin of my character in *The Man Who Fell to Earth* was some concoction, a spermatozoon of an alien nature that was obscene and weird-looking. I think it was put together with the whites of eggs, food coloring, and flour. Nick does revolting stuff that creates such challenging vignettes! Nick's love scenes must be some of the most perverse ever filmed. There's a quality to them that is so cruel. There's something about Nick's films which is awfully worrying but I think the magnetism of his movies is the wariness and worry they create.

Incidentally, they kept putting the release of *The Hunger* back because they were trying to get the rating changed. These Hollywood people, they got themselves in trouble with some sex scenes, which they were probably stupid to put in in the first place.

Do you feel, in retrospect, that Tony DeFries and his MainMan organization were helpful in your rapid rise to notoriety as Ziggy Stardust?

No. I think he oversold me. Looking back on it, I think he did a lot of things far too early and tried to overkill with everything.

I recall the infamously lavish and indulgent 1972 press junket, when hordes were flown over to London from New York to catch the debut of your Ziggy stage show.

Insane. The most ridiculously crass thing to happen. There was too much happening at once. The attitude of more is better, I quickly learned, is just the wrong thing to do in music. If you think your work matters, and if you want some kind of understanding between the audience and the work, then you can't throw it away like that. All those things came to be the friction between Tony and me near the end. I wanted to approach the thing from a much lower profile than all this hyperkill.

You've said that the Ziggy character overwhelmed your personality for a while, drove you to the brink. Did you feel like you were getting out of touch with your own craft and losing control of your performing identity?

No. That was the thing! I was getting *more* in touch with it near the end, and that's why I wanted the whole MainMan thing away from me. It was circusy. I was never much of an entourage person—I *hated* all of that. It's a relief for all these years I've not been MainManned to be on my own, and to not have a constant stream of people following me around to the point where, when I sat down, fifteen other people sat down. It was unbearable.

I think Tony saw himself as a Svengali type, but I think I would have done okay anyway. Now, I look back on it with amusement more than anything else. Everybody was always going to get their *teeth* done or something, brand-new people appearing in the office, having changed their appearance completely from the day before, and so forth.

When you said in July of 1973 that you had "rocked your roll" and were going to retire, did you actually feel that way?

Absolutely. [*smiling*] I do *every* time. Only living *at* that moment and thinking *of* that moment, and being too young to recognize anything else, it never occurred to me that there were periods when you just got tired of what you were doing and possibly took a rest. So for me it was conclusive: "It's all gone wrong; I don't like what I'm doing; I'm bored; therefore, I'll always be bored; therefore, I'll retire now—that's what I'll do! It's gone! The spark's finished!"

Nowadays, if things start getting on top of me, I just step back for a few months. I would never be so foolish again. It's very important to sort out the star trip. The idea of fame was an obsession—until it happened. Since those years, it's been a redefinition of why I wanted to make music in the first place. That's the continual thing I go back to when I'm feeling a little confused about what I'm doing or why I'm doing anything.

Was the stark 1978 Station to Station *album and tour the result of a reignited interest in the German Expressionism of the early twentieth century and the output of people like film director Georg Wilhelm Pabst, or was it merely a result of mounting disinterest in theatrical overkill?*

The reasons for doing the show and record were many-faceted.

The overriding need for me was to develop more of a European influence, having immersed myself so thoroughly in American culture. As I was personally going through a very bad time, I thought I had to get out of America and get back to Europe. So it came out of that.

You're referring to your notorious wig-out period, after leaving MainMan and making The Man Who Fell to Earth, *while living in a house in Los Angeles around 1976–77?*

That's right. That was the wipeout period. I was totally washed up emotionally and psychically, completely screwed up. I was fed up hallucinating twenty-four hours a day.

What's the story on that incident Cameron Crowe wrote about in 1976, in which you interrupted your interview with him to pull down a window shade, which had a star and the word "Aum" drawn on it, and light a black candle, claiming you'd just seen a body fall from the sky?

[*Cackling laugh*] That used to happen *all the time.* I was one of those guys that you see on the streets who suddenly stops and says, "They're *coming!* They're *coming!*" Every day of my life back then I was capable of staying up indefinitely. My chemistry must have been superhuman. I'd stay up for seven or eight days on the trot!

Keith Richards would blush.

[*Moans*] Ohhh, the Stones would be absolutely floored by it. They'd see me a few days later and find out that I hadn't been to bed! It was unreal, absolutely unreal. Of course, every day that you stayed up longer—and there's things that you have to do to stay up that long—the impending tiredness and fatigue produces that hallucinogenic state quite naturally. [*chuckle, wink*] Well, *half-* naturally. By the end of the week my whole life would be transformed into this bizarre nihilistic fantasy world of oncoming doom, mythological characters, and imminent totalitarianism. Quite the worst.

I was living in L.A. with Egyptian decor. It was one of those rent-a-house places, but it appealed to me because I had this more-than-passing interest in Egyptology, mysticism, the cabala, all this stuff that is inherently misleading in life, a hodge-podge whose crux I've forgotten. But at the time it seemed transparently obvious what the answer to life was. So the house occupied a ritualistic position in my life.

It's amazing the things David Bowie can get himself in and out of.

Pulling myself back out of that was not quick, it was a good two- to three-year process. There was a flashback effect. I must have put myself through the most bizarre physical ordeal, apart from anything else. For the first two or three years afterward, while I was living in Berlin, I would have days where things were moving in the room—and this was when I was totally straight. It took the first two years in Berlin to really cleanse my system. Especially psychically and emotionally. I really had to find myself again.

Did you get any psychiatric counseling?

I've always had an immature attitude toward mental health detectors. There was a stigma attached to the whole thing which I felt was inhuman and just didn't want to become involved in. Also, I had a slight impression that I might go to a hospital and not get out again. I felt *that* imbalanced at the time. This was late in 1976. Fortunately, I was able to pull out of it with the help of two or three friends who either came to Berlin with me or were in Berlin. I realized how close I was to either completely screwing myself up or just not being around anymore.

Is there something in your personality that craves change for its own sake, an obsessive side where the performer overtakes the nonperformer?

Well, I think it's more because of the success of the early few years in the seventies. I'd always had the natural instinct to be curious about life in all its forms—the arts, whatever. But I had an increasing tendency not to recognize the future. Everything became more and more just living from day to day. Then this parallel thing happened, where as I came out of that last bad period, I grew more aware of my son's life and the responsibilities I have toward my son.

I guess it's aging, getting older, but I now have a very direct link with the future. My son, just because of his presence, keeps telling me there *is* a tomorrow, there is a future, and that there's no point in screwing up today; because every day that you screw up is going to have an effect, karma-wise, on the future. One just adjusts.

Without reservation, I think it's very important for youth to have anger and an awareness of *now*-ness. I think all those things are part and parcel of being young. But I think that's just a passing grace, and then you shift to another viewpoint in life that's tempered by experiences, and the future becomes very important. But you *need* all the rest, that vortex of mess and misbehavior, to then straighten up and see where the future can go.

How old is Zowie now?

He's eleven years old. He lives with me. I have complete responsibility for him. I'm a single parent with a son, and more than anything else over the last five years, that fact has honed my outlook generally, and will continue to change my approach to music and whatever else I do.

How did your loosely collaborative relationship with Brian Eno on the Low, Heroes, *and* Lodger *records evolve?*

Well, it's 1977, and we're now in Berlin, my first year there. I'm throwing away everything in terms of what I'd done before in music, and I don't give a hang if I never make another record that has any appeal to it whatsoever.

I phone up Brian, who's somebody I've long been excited by in terms of his approach to music, little areas of which I'd touched on in terms of William Burroughs–inspired cut-ups—and disorienting ways of putting instruments and things together. I knew that Eno had a different approach to the studio than I'd ever had before, and I felt that this was the time to work with him—especially if I was going to start *examining* what I want to do and if I ever wanted to go back to America or England again. I thought: let's see *why* I like his music.

Brian recognized my own desperation for wanting to understand if I should go any further with music or not. It's wonderfully easy to produce a workshop atmosphere when there's nothing to lose, and nothing to gain by resting on your laurels. I didn't care if RCA sued me; just didn't care. And, indeed, they were very dissatisfied with what we produced for those three albums.

Let's speak of Low, *for instance.*

Terribly important album for me personally. And the position we adopted on *Low* colored what was to happen in English music for some time. What Eno and I achieved was something that would be filled out and fleshed out over the years that followed in terms of ambiance and drum sounds. That "smash" drum sound, that depressive, gorilla effect set down the studio drum-fever fad for the next few years. It was something I wish we'd never created, having had to live through four years of it with other English bands, until it started changing into the "clap" sound we've got now.

You see, there was no longer an interest by myself, and certainly not with Brian, in writing anything that had anything to do with narrative, other than in setting up atmosphere completely for atmosphere's sake. That music can be *used* as atmosphere, and listened to in many different contexts.

What sort of an atmosphere were you attempting to create aurally, musically?

For me, a world of relief, a world that I would like to be in. It glowed with a pure spirituality that hadn't been present in my music for some time. Mine had in fact almost become darkly obsessed. There was a degree of the Lower Elements that it occurred to me had been in recent previous songs and in the structures of the music.

There was a cleansing for me in *Low.* I find it has a *clean* feeling as an album. That album, more than any of the others we did, was responsible for my cleaning up musically, and my driving for more positive turns of phrase, if you will, in my music. Except for a slight relapse in *Scary Monsters.*

On Heroes, *songs like the title track and "Joe the Lion" sounded like fierce, flush-the-pipes music. Yet the free-form* Low *sound had now been codified into more comprehensible song structures.*

The content of the album, which was the looking at the street life in Berlin, had a lot to do with the feeling of "Joe the Lion" and "Heroes." It's like the street life in New York but without the emphasis on consumerism. Politically, it's a lot more radical in its expression; everybody has a very definite political view, either far right or far left. That kind of friction produces a wonderful . . . they say *Zeitgeist.* There is a *Zeitgeist* of the future, there is a feeling of social responsibility that's overpowering. There's not the kind of lush, decadent thing that's thrown about concerning Berlin—that's entirely wrong. There's a young population there and the middle-aged and the family people have moved out into West Germany because there's no industry left.

So the people who are in Berlin are older stoics who have no intention of ever moving; or students, because there's still a great emphasis on education in Berlin. Because of that, there's a serious quality to the people, a resistance to silliness. They want change to come about positively for the *people.*

Observers sometimes tend to interpret the German people too directly through their art and music. They see the harshness and rigidity of some of their celebrated painters, for instance, and believe that's how those artists see the world, rather than recognizing that, in fact, these are anticipatory images, ones the artists are creating to alert people to impending realities that can be warded off.

Yes, there's very little nihilism in German art. The Expressionists cared. Even the later Expressionists like Otto Dix and George Grosz, the satirists; they possibly didn't have the same tender feelings toward life, but they damned well knew what was going on in Germany and they tried to point it out with the very aggressive little portraits they did of the worst sides of Berlin life, which was a *small* life. That worst side occupied the *Kurfurstendamm,* and that was it.

Undivided Berlin was eight times bigger than Paris, and people here talk about one or two streets that took on national prominence in the late 1930s, as if Berlin were the seat of some great decadent cabaret life. That's absolutely not true.

These days most Berliners are people who want good, strong family ties and a good strong social fabric where people care for each other. That's why I was drawn to that city after Los Angeles, which is the antithesis of that. Berlin was my clinic; it brought me back in touch with people. It got me back on the streets; not the streets where everything's cold and there're drugs, but streets where there were young, intelligent people trying to get along, and who were interested in more than how much money they were going to make a week on salary. Berliners are interested in how art means something on the streets, not just in the galleries. They wonder how a painting can help them in their lives.

In terms of your own painterly Zeitgeist, *will you ever do a public show of your own paintings?*

I'm tempted in terms of my own ego and self-flattery, because I've just seen the new exhibitions in Berlin of the new young artists, and I've suddenly become aware of how close what I started painting in Los Angeles is to their work. I was in tune! I don't know if there's any real substance in my painting, but certainly from a form standpoint I was excited to see how close I was to what's been happening in Dusseldorf and Munich, and with the new Italian Expressionists. I've seen it in New York, too, with David Salle.

That's kind of scary [*nervous chuckle*], because look what happened to the world the last time people felt the need to work in this kind of form, with the feeling of: "Let's strip everything away, 'cause we've got no time to muck around with decorative art, and there's just-about-enough-time-to-paint-*this!*" But any fool can see the two going hand-in-hand: the advent of nuclear destructiveness and that kind of art.

How did the "Fame" session with John Lennon for the 1975 Young Americans *LP come about? I'm asking not for the sake of nostalgia in the aftermath of tragedy but because it was such an intensely solid collaboration, an amazing song.*

After meeting in some New York club, we'd spent quite a few nights talking and getting to know each other before we'd even gotten into the studio. That period in my life is none too clear, a lot of it is really blurry, but we spent endless hours talking about fame, and what it's like not having a life of your own anymore. How much you want to be known before you are, and then when you are, how much you want the reverse: "I don't want to do these interviews! I don't want to have these photographs taken!" We wondered how that slow change takes place, and why it isn't everything it *should* have been.

I guess it was inevitable that the subject matter of the song would be about the subject matter of those conversations. God, that session was fast. That was an evening's work! While John and Carlos Alomar were sketching out the guitar stuff in the studio, I was starting to work out the lyric in the control room. I was so excited about John, and he loved working with my band because they were playing old soul tracks and Stax things. John was so *up,* had so much energy; it must have been so exciting to always be around him.

Funny that such an urgent record as "Fame" would be so danceable too, but maybe, at the root of it, that's all of a piece.

[*Nodding vigorously*] Look at the blues! I mean, you keep having to go back to that. In our music, rock and roll, the blues are our mentor, our godfather, everything. We'll never lose that, however diversified and modernistic and cliché-ridden with synthesizers it becomes. We'll never, ever be able to renounce the initial heritage.

Keith Richards has said that rock and roll is about two things: sex and risk.

They're a foundation of it. *Life* is about sex and risk, but that doesn't mean that's all that life is. I think he's quite right that they will always be a strong element of it, but they're merely a starting point. [*chuckling*] I think it can expand its horizons a little more than that—but I think that a life of sex and risk can be very satisfying as well. I've had a lot of it myself. But I would add *relationships* to that.

Humanistic glue.

Yes, indeed! Humanistic glue. [*wistful smile*] That reminds me of something. You know, John Lennon had such an incisive point of view and a way of capturing just what was going on around him or anybody else with five or ten words or one sharp line that was a précis that didn't need to be fleshed out. I once asked him, "What do you think of what I do? What do you think of glam-rock?" He said [*imitating Lennon*], "Aww now, it's great you know, but it's just rock and roll with lipstick on."

Nobody has ever said it better.

Dr. Isaac Taylor is nervous, apprehensive. Not finishing his sentences. He wants to talk about his celebrated son but doesn't want to give away any "nuggets." He phones his son's wife to make sure I'm "clean." He starts to talk, and he wants to be upbeat and easygoing about his boy, but it's not coming out that way. He knows it's mostly sounding sad, wounded.

We get on the subject of "Jamie's" latest record, *Dad Loves His Work,* and suddenly Dr. Taylor knows what he wants to say: "This dad certainly loves *his* work. I've been very happy with my career."

Isaac Taylor was dean of the University of North Carolina's medical school before retiring in 1971, but he still holds a part-time post there. Now he has an administrative job at the Boston University Medical Center. He's busy, but he also has a lot of time to, well, think.

"Looking back, I wish I had found work that could have kept me at home." His voice trails off, and then he asserts, "I made a *point* of taking the children to my laboratory to see what I did all week, perhaps just as James is trying to do with his new album. I was doing experiments with heart tissue, and I had a colony of hibernating hamsters. I feel sure Jamie and the other children enjoyed seeing them."

James Taylor

1981

There is an awkward silence.

"It was just a conscious attempt to get closer to my children. On *Dad Loves His Work,* I think Jamie wants his children to know that although he's away a lot and seems very burdened by his life, he loves his work, and they shouldn't worry about him. As for me and him, I don't contribute to his life now, except when he needs me or when somebody's ill. When his son, Ben, was sick with kidney problems last year, James called for advice, and I got a great deal of satisfaction out of being able to help."

He adds that when James was two years old, he got out a wire recorder—this was before the days of portable tape recorders—and had James sing along with him on "Little Red Wagon Painted Blue." He says it was James's first recording, right? He says he's sorry he lost the damned thing.

"You know, I tell my friends, in jest, that I didn't want James to be a doctor and that I'd tell him to get on back to his guitar and practice, because that's where his future would lie. But that's not true, really. I didn't do that."

I first encountered James Taylor in the flesh one chilly July night in 1980, at a house not far from Taylor's own on Martha's Vineyard. I was visiting Timothy Mayer, a friend of James's who wrote "Sugar Trade" with Taylor and Jimmy Buffett for *Dad.* When I strolled into the living room, it took me a full minute to realize that the tall, gangling man hunched over on a couch was James. He and Mayer each had an open case of Grolsch beer next to them. When they rose in unison, stepped over to a walk-in freezer, and extracted yet another case and a half, I stole a second glance at the open boxes and discovered they contained empties, their white ceramic tops all neatly reclamped.

The two men were engaged in a lively, rather erudite conversation about public comprehension of "popular" music through the ages, from Bach's private clavichord recitals to Strauss waltzes to Frank Sinatra. It's amazing what people will fixate on when they're shitfaced.

Mayer praised James for the internal rhymes in his songs.

"This year, I'm gonna work on the externals," he said with a smile.

As the evening flowed onward, and great insights stumbled into muddled pronouncements, James was politely asked to clear the air with a song or two. I had heard that he was not overly fond of holding court with his guitar, but he gingerly lifted his Martin to his lap and called for a request. I suggested "She Caught the Katy," and his tight lips broke into a scamp's smile.

"Oh, I *do* know that little tune," he said with mock innocence and began to pick and sing. It seemed remarkable, considering his intake of beer, that he never slurred a word or flubbed a note, but that feat was soon overshadowed by his ability to sustain interest in the song for a solid hour and a half. Eventually, he moved on to material as diverse as the Sam and Dave hit "I Thank You," Walter Robinson's "Harriet Tubman," his own hilarious "Is That the Way You Look?" and a few Hoagy Carmichael tunes.

The sun was winding its way through the snarled scrub forest pressed against the windows when the guitar was finally, carefully, laid in its case. Then James stood with a studied steadiness and said, "I certainly want to thank you gents for your company, and I wish you all a good day."

With that, he made his way through the labyrinth of beer crates, electric cables, and amplifiers and disappeared around the bend into the guest bedroom. There was a crash, a wheeze of bedsprings, and the birds began to chirp.

Driving away, I decided he was not the James Taylor I would have expected to meet. I was unprepared for his animation, his good humor, his cordial manner. And then I began to think back on what I had read about the man and his family background, tormented past, painful professional ascent. Despite much press about his problems over the last decade with drugs and married life, Taylor remains a cryptic personality, a maddeningly shy man surrounded by protective friends and relatives. One day, I wanted to hear this guy explain himself.

"James is a dreamer," says wife Carly Simon. "He dreams a lot about being where he's not, doing things he isn't doing, seeing things he hasn't seen. He's not well organized and usually lets people plan his day for him, especially in the city, though in the country he'll get up and say, 'Okay, I'll sail or row today,' or 'I'll ride my bike or swim.'

"He is an odd mixture of dependence and independence—quite

a paradox. He seemed to be independent as a child because he could, and still can, be aloof and closed off. But when James was sent away to school, his great need to be connected to a home and his parents became critical and traumatic."

Quiet, reclusive, James enjoyed his boyhood years in the picturesque college town of Chapel Hill; he felt "centered" by the family home. When he wanted to be alone, he would walk out the front door of the tasteful manse and down the great knoll on which it was built, disappearing into twenty-five acres of encircling woods.

The South was a special place to him; he loved the lazy pace of its people and their tendency to back off when they weren't wanted and draw near when they were. North Carolina was an elemental environment where the lushness of the landscape, intensity of the sun, fury of the thunderstorms, and the brittle sounds made by insects at night culminated in a powerful, benign *presence.* For James, the countryside was a constant companion.

In the perpetual absence of his father, James clung to the rest of his family the way he hugged his big cello during the Taylors' "kitchen concerts"—informal recitals at which Alex played violin, Kate and Livingston manned the piano, and Hugh and mother Trudy sang. During the summer, the clan migrated to Martha's Vineyard, and James was particularly fond of the fact that it was an island.

When he needed to open up to people, he had friend Stan Sheldon to turn to. But he would avoid that kind of intimacy until it was nearly too late.

James's unfettered existence disintegrated when his parents decided he ought to choose a direction in life; so at the age of fourteen, he was packed off to a Massachusetts boarding school, Milton Academy, where he was expected to cultivate a new independence, succeed academically, and get his ass into a good college.

For anybody else, it might have been the best move in the world, but for young James, it was, as he says, "wrong, wrong." The school was "high-powered"; it functioned by means of "fear-tactic stuff," and there were "no girls in sight." James was jolted; he began to realize that he was not wrapped tight enough for this kind of jostling, and he left school and returned in his junior year to Chapel Hill, only to be confronted with another unsettling reality.

"I'd lost touch with everyone in Carolina," he says with a shudder. "I thought, 'What the hell, finish boarding school and aim for college, because the past has nothing more to offer.' "

Milton Academy took him back—his grades had been good—but he felt as if he were ambling across an abyss. It didn't help matters that he was assigned a small room by himself in the schoolmaster's house. He'd always preferred to be alone before; why was it so fucking frightening now?

"I got more and more depressed," he says, "and I was sleeping twenty hours a day. Finally, at Thanksgiving, I started thinking about suicide."

Home for the holidays, he grew panicky at the prospect of returning to Milton but was too paralyzed by fear of failure to speak of it. Vacation ended. It was time to go. He walked out the front door, down the knoll, and went over to Stan Sheldon's house. He told Stan that if he went back to school, he was afraid he was going to take his own life.

"He sent me to a shrink," says James, "and I broke down in the shrink's office. He said, 'Listen, I'm gonna put you under observation for a while in a local psychiatric hospital—McLean.' "

Taylor's tenure at McLean lasted several months and was a numbing routine of medication, drab meals eaten with plastic forks (confiscated afterward), and weekly consultations with conservative psychiatrists. He didn't relish the time he spent looking out through 2,000-pound-test security screens on the windows, but he had willingly committed himself to McLean because he saw his "certified crazy papers" as his best exit from Milton Academy—and the draft.

When the army finally beckoned, Taylor asked a husky attendant named Carl and a similarly formidable friend to dress up in the trademark white suits and accompany him to the draft board. They flanked James during his entire interview, answered all the questions for him, and ensured that he received a clean bill of poor mental health.

Taylor eventually slipped out of McLean in a friend's truck and sped to New York, where he renewed his boyhood friendship with Danny "Kootch" Kortchmar and composed such bleak ballads as "Don't Talk Now," "The Blues Is Just a Bad Dream," and "Rainy Day Man." Together their spirits soared in a four-man group called the Flying Machine—until James's wings were clipped by a mounting heroin habit with which he would struggle for the next nine years.

"It was a dreadful, stressful situation James got into when he was seventeen," says Dr. Taylor. "He called me, and I flew into New

York, rented a station wagon, loaded it with his stuff, and we went back to Chapel Hill. Six months later, he went to Europe to seek his fortune."

That trip resulted in his being signed to Apple through the good graces of A&R man Peter Asher, now his producer and manager. In 1980, James returned to London on a vacation with his wife and children, feeling, as he sings in "London Town" on *Dad*, "I do believe / I must believe / I think I can begin again / Become again the man I was back when."

"I saw some of the places where I used to live, a basement in Beaufort Gardens," he says. "It had a machine that you would put a two-shilling piece into in return for a few minutes of gas heat. I explained this to Carly and the kids. It was a great time for me back then because I was totally free.

"I think of that early time in London when I sing 'Carolina in My Mind.' I was homesick when I wrote it, and the 'holy host of others standing 'round me' refers to the Beatles. The lyric dealt with being somewhere else, which has always made me feel real good, and it encouraged me that I could write a song that strong. I can always count on a goose pimple or two when I sing it."

Famous for the artful *angst* in many of his songs, Taylor is also one of rock and roll's reigning eccentrics, and he concedes that he's capable of "monumental silliness." Indeed, his sense of humor about his own existence has fortified him against his fears, and even his wife marvels at how "spontaneously goofy and verbally witty" this customarily retiring man can be.

Has James ever composed any screwball songs he wouldn't dare commit to vinyl?

"Oh, sure," he says. "I wrote a song called 'I Guess I'll Always, Always, Always, Always . . .' that went on forever. It had a few chord changes but no word changes. And I wrote 'Mona,' a tune about a pig of mine. I was thinking about killing the pig because she was old. I had a new baby [Ben], and my brother Alex noted that the pig sometimes got out and was rambunctious. In fact, I once saw it kill another little pig. They can get ornery in old age. So Alex said, rightly, 'That pig might kill one of your kids. You gotta be careful.' I was afraid it was true, so I was considering bumping her off, and I wrote a song about it. I occasionally play it at picnics."

Drummer Rick Marotta, a longtime friend and one-time neighbor of James and Carly's, offers more evidence of Taylor's peculiar levity. When he hears I plan to take the red-eye flight with James, he offers some counsel.

"I'm warning you," he blurts. "You won't believe it till you see it, but he'll talk your ears off, and he can drive you crazy when he calls for stationery and starts drawing to explain his points. His sense of humor gets pretty bizarre; he takes those airline cards with the emergency instructions and writes on them: HAVE A NICE TRIP. HOPE YOU DON'T DIE."

"Your brother's an architect?" James exclaims after we've taken our seats in the plane's first-class lounge. "Let me get some stationery. I want to explain this dream house I've been thinking about building for about three years."

James Taylor wasn't aware of it at the time, but the cover of his 1979 *Flag* album, the modest-selling record that preceded his success with *Dad Loves His Work,* was the nautical symbol for "man overboard." And in the months that followed its release, Taylor sank into as difficult a period as he's experienced in his notoriously troubled passage.

"This past year has been the worst in my life," he says bluntly. "I see myself, basically, as a depressed person who tends to hole up and shut systems down. And a lot of things have been happening at once."

Taylor's troubles in 1981 included a crisis in confidence concerning his career ("I *am* a little scared") and strained relations with his wife, both of which have led to serious doubts about how he rears his own children.

"I was recently telling a friend how much I loved my father, and how much I missed him when he made a two-year-long trip to Antarctica when I was young, and how much I missed him whenever he went to work. I'm a traveling father now, and when I leave, my son cries.

"See, *Dad Loves His Work* is a little whimsical but also sad. Wanting to do your work, wanting to be responsible, loving your father for wanting to be responsible and good and then having work take him away from you when you want him most—it's like a curse.

"But I think it's important for children to get the feeling that you enjoy yourself and that *life* is enjoyable. I see some people—including myself—frequently saying, with a moan, 'I'm sorry, Daddy *has* to go to work now.' And my son is crying and my daughter is removing herself from me, and I'm saying, 'I don't *want* to go.'

"Well, *that's not right.* I want them to know I'm gonna *enjoy* it. They miss me, but I'm having a good time. I'd like them to think fondly of me."

"James loves to travel," says Carly Simon. "He has a great love of mobilization, and I've given him a hard time for that. I've never spent a night away from Ben and just a few away from Sally. James's own father's absence was very painful to him, and he felt slightly responsible. He had the grandiose and very mistaken idea that because he loved and admired his mother and got to know her better than he did his dad, his father was jealous of their relationship and left all the time for that reason. James had built up an Oedipal dilemma in his mind.

"James's work is extremely good for him," Carly continues. "It holds him together. And he's usually most healthy physically and mentally when he's on tour. But while he feels justified by his *Dad Loves His Work* philosophy, it's still difficult for his children, especially Ben. James is really a country boy, likes being on the loose and disorganized, and it's one of our incompatibilities. When he comes back from the road, there's always a feeling of anticlimax, of relief followed by 'Jesus! *Now* what?' It seems that sons cannot help following in their father's footsteps, whether they like the path or not."

After ten albums, numerous hit singles (the latest being "Her Town Too," his duet with J. D. Souther), near-constant touring for adoring audiences, a movie career *(Two-Lane Blacktop, No Nukes),* and some composing for the screen and stage (Studs Terkel and Stephen Schwartz's *Working,* the films *Times Square* and *Brubaker*; his songs were not used in the latter two), Taylor, at thirty-three, is assured a place in the entertainment-industry pantheon.

In 1969, with the release of his debut LP, *James Taylor,* on the Beatles' Apple label, he achieved instant prominence and drew considerable praise for the confessional boldness of his dark folk narratives—inky, anguish-wracked songs that would have made for unnerving listening had they not been structured around the bright resonances of his nasal North Carolina twang and the clipped, suspended chordings of his ringing acoustic guitar. He crooned about confinement in a mental institution, about nervous breakdowns and dungeon-deep depressions, and somehow he left such disquieting realities a little gentler on our minds.

He was handsome in a spindly, lantern-jawed way—his friends in boarding school called him "Moose"—and everybody wanted to embrace and unravel his cool, crisp mysteries. By the time he scored a No. 1 smash in 1970 with "Fire and Rain," a song partly written about a friend who had committed suicide, he looked to be a talent capable of great things but destined for self-destruction before he had barely developed his gifts. (Brother Livingston and sister Kate, like James, have spent time in McLean Hospital, the mental institution outside Boston.)

Suddenly, this fragile young man with the gothic Southern lineage was a mainstream superstar. He was on the cover of *Time.* He was twenty-two. He seemed doomed.

Now, on a Thursday afternoon in the spring of 1981, he just seems a little tired—and anxious. Rawboned and lanky as ever, dressed in baggy jeans, rubber-soled canvas slippers with rent seams ("Whoa," he says with wild eyes and a manic grin, wiggling his protruding toes, "these here slippers are trying to be sandals!"), and a rumpled white dress shirt with a large jelly stain below the pocket, James is plunking out "Fire and Rain" at a TV soundstage on Cahuenga Boulevard in Los Angeles. He's whipping his band (with guest star J. D. Souther) into shape for yet another road show, and the spring and summer dates are to be taped for a live album, tentatively titled *Bicycle Built for a King.* (Debilitated at the beginning of the tour, Taylor would grow so weak with pneumonia he would be in danger of collapsing while doing his shows.)

James steps down from the raised platform he's playing on and extends his hand in a firm greeting. I see that he's balding, and the condition seems incongruous with his adolescent demeanor. When I express surprise at what a sturdy old warhorse "Fire and Rain" is after all this time, he smirks and says, "Well, sometimes when I sing 'Fire and Rain' at a show, I think someone in the audience is thinking, 'Aw, you poor guy. You got so upset you had to take *two* Valiums, eh?' "

He excuses himself to confer with his road manager and then hurries back. "Hey, ah, I don't mean to make this interview problematic for you," he says nervously, "but are your bags in the car?"

Huh?

"Well, instead of flying back to New York tomorrow morning as I'd planned, I'd like to fly back tonight. If you can get your stuff, we can talk on the plane. That way, I can spend about twelve hours in New York with my son before I fly to Berkeley for the first show of the tour on Saturday night."

I nod, slowly comprehending the urgency of his request. He must read the puzzlement in my face, because he confides, "Yeah, it amazes me that, with only twenty-four hours off, there's nothing I'd rather do in the world than sit on an airplane. I'll spend fifteen hours in transit during the next thirty-six; then, the rest of the time, I'll watch TV with the kids or read them a story or do whatever silly thing they want to do. It just pleases me."

He shrugs. I leave to get my luggage.

He calls for the steward, asks for paper and pencil, and sits back sipping beer until the man returns. Comfortable in a gray felt fedora and a blue *Gangster Chronicles* promo jacket that hides the jelly stain, he takes the paper and begins to sketch in broad, hasty strokes.

"It has three floors and a duct running under the house that pushes cool air out and draws warm air in on a seasonal basis," he says intently, referring to floor plans that become almost indecipherable in their complexity. He remains engrossed in the dream house until a casual mention of the space shuttle voyage plunges us into a discussion of its shortcomings, which somehow segues into the "kinks" in the origin of prehistoric species, and, at length, his own evolution.

During the last year, James has evidently been thinking a great deal about the road behind him, as well as the uncharted course ahead, and as our plane hums on through the night, the talk turns both introspective and retrospective.

"For a long time, all of the album titles were names for myself," he volunteers. "A large amount of the stuff I was doing was self-definition, exercises in trying different aspects of myself on for size—sometimes fanciful, sometimes serious, sometimes happenstantial.

"People will see me write a song that they think is about Carly," he says, popping another beer, "or people I know hear themselves described in a song I write, and they say, '*How can you do that?!* The song you've written about me makes me feel terrible!'

"It's taken so out of form," he maintains, exasperated. "You can't really nail down a person that way, ever. What it comes down to is, if somebody chooses to let this obvious encapsulation or distortion or angle on them supercede the relationship itself, then what does that say for the friendship?

"Although I did not write 'You've Got a Friend,' I sometimes expect someone to come up to me after I've sung it and say, 'You call yourself a friend?!' "

I ask for another example of a song that has elicited this kind of reaction.

"The song 'B.S.U.R.' on *Flag* was inspired by the cartoons of William Steig, who has a book out called *CDB!* about how to take letters and numbers and turn them into sentences, like 'IMAUMBN'—'I am a human being'—or 'URNNML'—'You are an animal.' Well, my sister and I used to play that game. So I wrote 'B.S.U.R.' [which contains the verse: "She's been holding on too long / Hoping I'm gonna change / Giving it up just a little bit more / Each time I come home / Looking and acting strange / Putting her down for putting up with me"], and Carly was fine about the song, *sang* on it, but other people were appalled that I could put our relationship on the line that way. She's written a song called 'Fair Weather Father' that seems to paint me pretty ugly, but I sang backup on it, and I don't take it seriously.

"For an intimate relationship with one's mate, the only really important thing is *feelings.* That's the main thing; whether or not someone's right or wrong doesn't make a damned bit of difference! You can be seething about something that's so petty you hardly dare bring it up, but the fact is that you *must* say, 'I am furious.'

"There's always a risk. I mean, your wife may call up your friends and say things about you that you trusted her with, or in a loose moment, I might say something about Carly to a reporter, or she might say something to magazines about me. Well, I accept that as a possibility. A close friend called me about a recent article on Carly. I haven't read the article, because I don't want to take it seriously when I know I shouldn't. My friend said, '*Read* it. You've been dealt roughly with.' I said, 'I don't think Carly had any intention of hurting me, and I'm not going to indulge.' "

Is there a threshold there that shouldn't be crossed?

"The threshold is whether you are betraying a confidence that is still valuable to you. It has to be looked at in terms of whether or not it damages *you.*"

I ask about the great solitude of the character in what I have always considered one of Taylor's finest songs, "Walking Man."

"It was about the coming of winter and the way I feel about it," he says somberly, shifting in his seat. "I panic a little bit when I feel it coming on. It's always reminded me of having to go back to school, and maybe it's a primal thing of realizing that winter means you're going to have to put up with a tough time—the dark, difficult, cold times you have to be prepared for."

"I didn't know James felt that way about winter," Carly later says, "but winter seems to remind him of the rejections he felt as a child. He always wants to spend winter on the Vineyard, which is a sore point between us, because as a city person, I find it harsh, boring, desolate, while he enjoys the isolation.

"He also has a fear, a great dread of imminent catastrophe, and he wants to have his own self-contained oasis on the Vineyard, where we can farm our own land, draw water from our own well, and so on. He often talks about how we'll live in safety when 'the catastrophe' comes.

"All of that aside, I've always felt awfully guilty that I'm not in the Vineyard in winter—that I'm not capable of doing what my husband expects of me. After all, he's spent so many winters in New York."

James has his own pangs of conscience concerning his marriage, and as he begins to talk about "Hour That the Morning Comes" on *Dad,* a good deal of his guilt comes to the fore.

" 'Hour That the Morning Comes' is about people at a party," he says. "The first one is Carly, who doesn't get drunk and has a good time without hurting herself. The second guy, with his head 'kacked'—that's a junkie term—in his lap, is just someone who's miserable. The next person, the fool with the lamp shade on, is somebody else I know, and the 'secret-agent man' is a dealer, or someone with an angle he has to play out at the party.

"I don't have much moderation in my drinking," he states firmly. "If I get intoxicated, I lose control. And I've sometimes made mistakes when I was too high that I deeply regret. I can get real sad thinking about things I've said to people and ways I've made people I love feel because I was so out of it. But those are in the past."

Yet they haunt him still, as with the tale behind the terrifying "Sleep Come Free Me" on *Flag.*

"Bob Rafelson, the director, came to the Vineyard one time and asked me if I wanted to act in *Brubaker,* which he started making before something took him off the project. He said he was also looking for a song for the movie, and I came right out with this line 'Ten lonely years without a woman,' which was part of the original lyric. Then, to make it rhyme, I made it 'Ten lonely years of my life taken.'

"A couple of weeks before that, I had gone on a bender, and I got *so* drunk that I blacked out a whole rampage of awful behavior. I don't know where I got the energy for it. I can remember that I played 'She Caught the Katy,' which I love, at a party for something like eight hours straight, and when someone finally threatened, or offered, to beat me on the head lest I keep playing the song, I actually bit a big hole in the guitar. And this guitar belonged to a good friend of mine, so it was a *bad* thing to have done.

"I had also recently watched a TV program on angel dust, where some poor bastard killed a man and couldn't remember afterward. So I began to think of how some person could end up with no memory of what he had to pay for with his time in prison.

"When *I* came to, I heard for days about my behavior—some people just gave me dirty looks—so I wrote that into the song":

Now the state of Alabama says I killed a man
The jury reached the same conclusion
I remember I was there
With a tire iron in my hand
The rest is all confusion.

When I remind him of his lengthy rendition of "Katy" that night at Tim Mayer's house, he shakes his head.

"I go on and *on* with that tune."

Has he always had this outrageous nature?

"You bet," he says. "A long time ago in London—when I was nineteen or twenty—I took an acid trip with a friend. There was a candle burning in the middle of the table, and we were peaking. It melted down into the dish it was sitting in and made a great pool of wax. And as it did, I took some matchsticks and made a little cabin out of them. Pretty soon the wax was vaporizing inside the cabin and giving off a nice light.

"I went out the window at this point, and I swung from one fire escape to another on these buildings. I used to get crazy on this drug. Then I walked along a ledge, stories and stories up, and jumped into a tree in a park along Baker Street. I climbed out of the tree, hopped into my car, a Cortina GT, and blasted around the West End, doing about eighty—just screaming. It was a golden time, and I was right *in the pocket.*

"When I came back to the apartment, I came up the fire escape and in through the window. I found that everyone was kind of spooked and dragged. This plate of matches had become a nova and blown up. The plate was in shards; there was a hole in the table and a big hole in the ceiling. I later thought of that as being pretty irresponsible.

"That same year, I spent about two days on the island of Formentera drinking Romilar and riding a bicycle, just chanting. It was a hypnotic, antipsychedelic experience. It was nice."

Gravely concerned about the quality of his fatherhood, the detrimental effects of his wanderlust and personal excesses, the significance of his work, and the security of his family life, James Taylor is seeing old patterns and images he thought were long dispersed flooding back into the here and now. Like the bedeviled millworker he wrote about in the song of the same name, Taylor finds himself riding home in the evening, staring at his hands, perplexed as to what he's ultimately wrought.

"Perhaps I'm at a contradictory point," he says softly. "I'm trying to be a public figure and at the same time be average. It's like *proclaiming* my ordinariness.

"One of the things that's positive about Japanese culture is that people strive to be ordinary," he continues. "In other words, what in this country would be displayed as a status symbol—a piece of art, for instance—well, I've heard of an industrialist in Japan buying a Monet and hanging it in the bathroom, loving it, but not wanting to be presumptuous about owning it, or not letting possession of it rock the boat. Maybe it's a Zen kind of thing.

"Being a celebrity is not so great a gig, and it's not as good as being a good musician or having a particular skill. Celebrity always misses the point, and you end up disappointing the people who thought you were what you never said you were. And from this, people approach your children not only for who they are but for reasons beyond their knowledge or control. To be a celebrity raising children is tough.

"Now for me, I really don't ever have any problem walking on the street, going to a restaurant, walking away from a concert.

"This is a bit of what 'Walking Man' tries to say. I've seen a lot of high-flying people hit the big time and then wonder why the fuck they don't feel special. Everybody's *calling* them special. That's one of the things that I think makes stars tend to take drugs, drink too much."

As our plane begins its descent into New York, James reaffirms his vow to curb his own vices, especially drinking. I ask what dreams he has in store for the future.

"Well, my brother Hugh and I have been considering a little undertaking for some years now, and this may be the summer we finally get started on it."

What undertaking is that?

"We want to open our own brewery on the Vineyard. How does Taylor's Lighthouse Lager sound to you?"

Bob Seger 1983

Every morning, Bob Seger wakes up to the image of a ghost. It sits on his night table, a creased and ashen photo of a broad-featured man in a smart suit and vest, his thick hair brushed into an upswept pompadour. The impish, wounded expression on his craggy face calls to mind a playful James Cagney or Victor McLaglen; the phantom holds a ukulele in his hands in a strumming pose, but the jaunty gesture does not convince—his dark eyes are stark in a haunted cast. The ghost, it seems, is a specter even to himself.

"That's him, that's my father," murmurs his graying but still indefatigably boyish son, smoothing his silver-streaked beard as he squints at the small, battered snapshot. "I suppose I should do something to preserve that picture, especially if I'm gonna have it along when I'm away from home. I don't really have all that many memories of my dad as it is."

Bob Seger was ten years old when Stewart Seger, a former

bandleader and failed medical student-turned-Ford Motor Company medic, abandoned his family in Ann Arbor, Michigan, and lit out for California.

"I was never too close to him, unlike my firstborn brother, George," says Bob, indicating the nearby framed portrait of a successful business executive and his own family, "and then I only saw my dad three times between the time I was ten and about twenty-four, my age when he died."

Bob Seger, forty-one, slim and fit in leather jeans and black boots, is moving restlessly through his rented canyon-top Bel Air hacienda, an expansive pool-and-patio-encircled complex located several miles and nearly two decades from the site where Stewart Seger met his demise. Toiling as an itinerant male nurse in Los Angeles, the senior Seger had been assigned to keep an alcoholic patient sober, but actually was sharing drinks with his charge. He perished while apparently intoxicated in a freak fire in his apartment house.

"When my father died, my mother had never divorced him—and they were separated fifteen years," says Bob, shaking his head in puzzlement. "During the 1930s, when they courted, it was traditionally accepted that you were married for life. My mom is seventy-two years old, and she still wears his wedding ring. The memory of love is a powerful thing; it's a tangible possession in and of itself, and I guess that's been a theme running through my whole personal development as well as my career. Nothing can ever correct and make right the stunt my father pulled. You have to forgive him for it and *then* you have to live with it."

Bob Seger is but a few days past okaying the master pressings of *Like a Rock*, his fifteenth album and the most wrenchingly wrought (three probative years in the process) of his solid quarter-century in rock and roll. Among the most difficult tracks to realize was an epic five-and-a-half-minute ballad entitled "The Ring," which he cut and recut on four separate occasions since spring 1984 (in Michigan; Muscle Shoals, Alabama; Miami, Florida; and Capitol Studios in Hollywood) before deciding the last version was a keeper.

"The original song was eight minutes long," he offers, "and I guess it was real special to me. It starts out with a guy totally in love with his wife and what they share, but by the middle of the second verse the story has shifted to her point of view, and she reveals how she came to give up all her youthful dreams during the course of accepting her fate. When you're in a relationship, you're always surrounded by a ring of circumstance—joined together by a wedding ring, or in a boxing ring."

He lights a cigarette and takes a deep drag. "It's so scary to commit to one person, to depend on or rely on someone in particular, because you can end up mighty disappointed. I'm by myself now," he allows bluntly, referring to the breakup in 1983 of his eleven-year bond with lover Jan Dinsdale, as well as the recent denouement of another two-year romance. "Odd thing is, for the first time since I was in this foolish impulsive marriage back in 1968 for one day short of a year, I would definitely consider marrying again. [He would shortly wed actress Annette Sinclair; following ten months of marriage, Seger filed in August 1988 for an amicable divorce, he and Annette continuing to date.]

"The most important things in my adult life have been my commitments to certain women. I always tried to put them first. And in every relationship that lasts a long time, someone always has to give up more than someone else."

This rueful sentiment could hardly be more directly explicated than in the gripping verse ultimately deleted from the finished recording of "The Ring," which Seger softly recites:

He came on so strong
He hit her full force
Like a storm raging out of control
He touched something deep in her soul
She gave in, and let herself go . . .

"Sooner or later, we all sleep alone," Seger rules with a hesitant grin, "and it's my turn. Music means a lot to me, and people close to me have told me—with a certain amount of uneasiness in their voices—that *Like a Rock* is the most intimate and soul-baring album in a pretty candid stretch of work. But I can't help it, 'cause for me everything flows from my relationships, and I've come to believe that, creatively, to make yourself totally open is the bravest and, hell, the best thing you can do. I learned that from what happened with my parents," he says, nodding to himself. "They became for me a lifelong model of what *not* to do."

Robert Clark Seger was born on May 6, 1945, his family moving from Dearborn, Michigan, to western Detroit, and eventually to Ann Arbor. The freshly inaugurated John F. Kennedy was plotting the Bay of Pigs debacle and Moscow was preparing to put the first human in orbit on the frigid evening in 1961 that Bob took his own first bittersweet shot at immortality, cajoling a kindly DJ at Ann Arbor's WPAG radio into spinning an acetate demo of his song, "The Lonely One." The primitive guitar, bass, and drums treatment of the awkward ballad had been recorded in the basement of one Max Crook, then gaining notoriety as the nimble keyboardist responsible for the skedaddling Musitron solo—"It was the first rock synthesizer riff," Seger maintains—on Del Shannon's fleet-selling chart-topper, "Runaway."

As his song seeped out of the dashboard console of a car aimed down Stadium Boulevard, fifteen-year-old Seger gulped a Hamm's beer and let his mind gallop with a peculiar longing. But Bob Seger quite pointedly had no designs on thrilling the lily-white crowds at the Walled Lake Casino resort where Jamie Coe and the Gigolos performed for jammed weekend hops, and where a generation earlier, the thirteen-piece Stewart Seger Orchestra had been a featured postwar attraction. The otherwise introverted father had been a skilled swing clarinetist in the classic Benny Goodman mold, but his mounting insecurities at the bandstand found expression in too-frequent trips to the beer gardens and jealous rages with his attractive wife, Charlotte, a coquettish ballroom dancer whose outgoing nature at his gigs he came to detest.

When Stewart Seger walked out on his wife and his sons, he pulled the rug out from under their middle-class existence and submerged them in a world of seedy studio flats to which they were virtual rent slaves. Radio was the only escape available to the mortified boy, the sole source of accurate solace.

"Living on the poor side of town, I not surprisingly had *greaser* tastes," he recalls with the vibrantly husky haw-haw that is his version of a chuckle. "So after my mom and brother turned in for the evening and the Michigan stations had shut down or reduced their power, the 50,000 watts of good ol' WLAC in Nashville would come beaming through on my teeny transistor earphone. I'd listen to John R. the Horseman getting down with James Brown and the Famous Flames, or Garnet Mimms and the Enchanters doing "Cry Baby." Then Ernie's Record Mart from Gallatin, Tennessee, would urge you to mail in $1.25 for any single ever pressed anywhere, or Music City Songcrafters would do their pitch about sending in a poem that they would write a song around!

"It was my R&B and raunchy rock and roll obsessions that

pushed me off the Honor Roll after tenth grade, really, but maybe it was the Songcrafters that got me into writing all that poetry in English class. I discovered I had a natural gift for rhymes that weren't dumb-sounding. My main thing school-wise was cross-country, and even though I was a big smoker I cleared five feet, six inches to place third in the high jump at the Ann Arbor–Ypsilanti High meet—which was my biggest nonmusical moment as a kid. I needed to blow off all my general resentment any way I could."

Seger's track-and-field prowess also came in handy when he and his well-to-do friends from the upscale side of the Michigan college town began breaking into the exclusive Barton Hills country club. There were other incidents of petty hooliganism and flirtations with the shadowy side, among them a memorably delinquent 1961 Detroit weekend in which he and six other chums took turns (his less successful than some of the others—"a pretty *nasty* scene") plying their inaugural night moves with an unflappable black hooker.

It was the entrepreneurial preppie scion of a prosperous Michigan produce distributor who introduced Seger to a world beyond the borders of cheap adolescent thrills. Eddie "Punch" Andrews first collided with Seger during University of Michigan Delta House frat blowouts fueled by Bob's three-piece Decibels band. Andrews and partner Dave Leone had seen the overnight boom of British Invasion–instigated teen bands as a potential gold mine and begun renting a network of halls dubbed "Hideouts" in suburbs like Harper Woods and Southfield. They charged underage Beatles and Kinks fans a buck admission to sip Cokes and frug to the Top 40 repertoire of fledgling combos.

As the bands improved, so did their commercial potential, and the five Hideouts' receipts funded the launch of the Hideout and Punch labels, whose early releases included sides by Brownsville Station, a Glenn Frey–led act called the Mushrooms (whose record, "Such a Lovely Child," was written and produced by B. Seger), and something called Bob Seger and the Last Heard.

"The Last Heard—*whooo* what an awful name that still is!—were formed from remnants of the two post-Decibels bands I was in, Doug Brown and the Omens and the Town Criers," says Seger. Most hardcore Seger fans are aware that Bob's 1965 "Gloria"-derived "East Side Story" was picked up by Cameo-Parkway and became the calling card that led, by a tangled route, to a deal with Capitol.

"But most people don't realize that I was almost signed to Motown as one of their first white rock artists! The band that originally cut 'East Side Story,' the Underdogs, they got a Motown deal and then the label was pursuing me. Motown actually offered Punch more money than Capitol, but he had friends at Capitol and was unsure how much exposure we'd get with the Supremes, the Temptations, and all those other acts taking off. Also, I don't know if 'Ramblin' Gamblin' Man,' my first Capitol hit in '68, would have fit on Motown. It was more in a Wilson Pickett rather than a Smokey Robinson vein."

And how about "Sock It to Me Santa," his sizable 1966 Midwestern holiday hit on Cameo-Parkway?

"Haw!! You know that tune! Shit, what a riot! Listen, I want you to know that single came out a *full year* before Mitch Ryder's record; plus I had a nice little tribute to James Brown with the line, 'Santa's got a brand new bag!' And on the flip side was 'Florida Time,' where I praised the Florida surfing scene out of sheer gratitude for that state being my only loyal market outside of Michigan. I was giving everybody the best of both climates!"

Seger is in stitches, howling so hard he begins gasping for air. "Whew! All that stuff will always come back to haunt you. I also had a track Punch put out on the Are You Kidding Me? label in '66 called "Ballad of the Yellow Beret." I did it under the pseudonym the Beach Bums, and it was catching on with college kids when Sgt. Barry Sadler sent a telegram threatening a lawsuit. I guess we were lucky Capitol was willing to take us on."

Well, yes and no, if you consider the initial behind-the-scenes identity problems Punch Andrews, still Seger's manager after twenty-one often lean years, had with what he used to call "the Lettermen Factor."

"We love Capitol, they're like family now," says Andrews, "but at the time they were quite conservative. In fact, everytime I asked for anything they would tell me, 'The Lettermen don't get that, and so *you're* not about to get it.' They were the standard at the company, and you have to remember that Capitol was forced by EMI to take the Beatles; that signing was dictated by the mother company.

"So in the beginning it was the Lettermen, the Beatles, the Beach Boys—and us. And we seemed like fucking cuckoo birds. When I brought the "2 + 2 = ?" anti-Vietnam single in, I conveniently didn't reveal what it was about until it hit the stores. They literally threw me out of the office when I told them it was questioning an illegal war, and they half-suggested we should be thrown into jail! Of course, it was immediate curtains for the [1968] single.

"The period around 1972 when he left Capitol for [the *Smokin' O.P.'s*, *Back in '72*, and *Seven* LPs on] Reprise and then got dropped was the hardest time. Nobody knows this, but Warner Bros. rejected *Beautiful Loser* outright, and Bob and I were dead broke. I had to find a way to borrow $1,000 to remix the tape to play it for Capitol at a time when I had $4,000 worth of $3 bounced-check charges against me. Nobody also knows this, but after Capitol welcomed us back for *Loser,* they turned around and rejected *Live Bullet,* thinking it was a cheap excuse for *Frampton Comes Alive.* It was a long, long argument."

But all's well that ends well, eh?

"Not exactly," says Andrews, "because after *Live Bullet* hit, Capitol rejected *Night Moves!* I hope I don't get into trouble for revealing this, but they thought it wasn't as exciting as *Live Bullet* had been!! No wonder Seger has so much heartache these days deciding whether he's got a finished record or not."

"Which is the gospel truth," Seger concedes sheepishly as we leave the house, heading for friend Don Henley's ranch house compound in the coyote wilds high above Mulholland Drive. "I wouldn't even let the Capitol execs hear a note of anything until late February, and they were *concerned.* I wrote twenty-five songs for *Like a Rock,* had a series of false starts in Miami and Muscle Shoals, and threw out a whole heap of interesting songs—'Wildfire,' 'Star Tonight,' 'Days When the Rain Would Come,' 'Living Inside My Heart.' I had an antidrug song called 'Snow Today,' which I shelved in favor of 'American Storm,' and I'm glad I put 'Storm' out as a single.

"I'm not saying I'm a saint, but I've never had a drug problem. Yet I saw the cocaine thing become this insidiously destructive juggernaut in the lives of friends. When I thought the whole coke mess couldn't get worse in the late seventies, that's when it exploded as a hemispheric plague, wrecking governments in South America and threatening to ruin a generation here. Next, I pick up *Newsweek* and read about grammar school kids buying crack with their allowance!

"Somebody has to let them know that it's not hip anymore to do drugs, that there will always be pressures and times in your life when you'll need answers, but that coke and the rest offer nothing—

no outlet, no information. And, believe me, you're only as good as your information."

While Henley shaves and gets dressed for dinner, Seger cannot resist a short testing of the handsome grand piano in Don's splendid modern adobe living room, and he plays an abbreviated rendition of the poignant "Star Tonight," an ambition-versus-ardor adult lullaby that actor Don Johnson has requested for his forthcoming solo album.

"It's an interesting thing about love," Seger mulls. "You have to choose who you want to love, because you get a lot of different chances. My mother made her choice, and I think a lot of her for sticking to it. She's had some health troubles with her heart in recent years, and I almost lost her in '85 . . ." He doesn't finish the sentence. "She's still full of spunk and optimism."

Henley appears, playfully chiding Seger about his irresolute dating habits—"Don't make any hasty decisions now, Bob!"—and then it's off to a meal at Helena's, a chic private supper club in a remote pocket of Los Angeles. On arrival, it's discovered a number of the regular patrons have stopped by to take in "Tango Night," an evening of lessons being offered on Helena's dance floor by Argentinean experts. Actor Harry Dean Stanton, a kindred spirit, shifts his meal over to the Henley-Seger table and sparks a semi-whimsical discussion of what could constitute superior "tango rock." " 'Hotel California' is something you could do the tango to," Seger muses. "The Eagles had a bit of tango potential on that one."

Stanton concurs and Henley grins, ordering another round of beers by way of thank you and asking a lovely raven-haired wallflower at an adjoining table if she'd like to join the glowing gentlemen for a drink.

"Did I hear somebody mention Eagles?!" she says in a shrill Italio-Spanish spew of broken grammar as she plops herself down. The social butterfly launches into a ringing denunciation of all things American, but particularly rock and roll and the Eagles. Both Seger and Stanton look to Henley with embarrassed apprehension . . . but he's beaming.

"Well, if you knew more about American culture, madame," says Don, "you'd know that the Eagles were not a big group here. Like most people in rock and roll, they all became junkies and died in pathetic obscurity." The woman snaps her tresses over one bare shoulder and eyes the speaker suspiciously.

"You toy with me," she decides coolly. "Are any of you rock and roll?"

"Him," says Henley, patting Seger on the shoulder. "Why, many years ago, he used to do it as a hobby, an outlet."

"But I eventually changed all that," says Seger, lifting a glass of chilled cerveza. "And now, I'm proud to say"—a toast, followed by a slow, satisfied swallow—"that I do it for a *living.*"

Stepping out into the Hollywood night, Seger leads the way to his siren-red Stingray. He tucks a cassette of Jackson Browne's *Lives in the Balance* in the car's deck, and we head onto the freeway. "I used to actively dislike the past," he says, "because the memories of struggling were always so painful, I wanted success and legitimacy so badly it was tearing me apart. The first 1975–76 compositional trilogy of albums, *Beautiful Loser,* the *Live Bullet* collection, and *Night Moves,* took that on. But when I gained some ground publicly and in my own mind, I was a little terrified of losing it. I had an almost crippling dread about the idea of growing old in rock and roll. Then the two anxieties got intertwined, as if they were the same threat, and they became the undercurrent of the material I wrote for the second 1978–83 trio of LPs, *Stranger in Town, Against the Wind,* and *The Distance.*

He's reminded of the chorus of "No Man's Land," the song that was supposed to be the title track of *Against the Wind:* "The haunting and the haunted / Play a game no one can win / The spirits come at midnight / And by dawn they're gone again."

"It was spooky stuff," he affirms. "Then I tried to confront the aging process in 'Can't Hit the Corners No More,' my [unreleased] baseball player–inspired allegory about a publicly acclaimed phenom who's faced with the private *instant* when he suddenly doubts he still has his peak faculties, his power edge. I was in that head when I was saying good-bye to the days of the original Silver Bullet Band with the *Nine Tonight* live set of 1981.

"I almost put a new version of 'Corners' on the flip side of the 'American Storm' single, but the point is that I wrote that paranoid tune about cashing it in back in 1979—*seven years ago!*

"Both 'Corners' and 'Like a Rock' are about the loss of innocence regarding ideals and what you make of it. 'Rock' was the song I wrote in the spring of 1984, several months after the *Distance* tour ended. It was a reexamination of my unguarded days in this business, the time when no stroking mattered, and when ten years of a $7,000 annual salary and a life-style of traveling a hundred thousand miles in a station wagon were something I just enjoyed doing instead of a conventional day gig.

"I played bump-and-grind joints, where the stripper genuinely had a goddamned horse in her act. We also did time in dockside dives in New Orleans where the owner got a .357 Magnum stuck in his stomach, and an underground cave in Festus, Missouri, in '72 where I fronted a band called Julia on a bill with Ted Nugent. The cave was foul, with water dripping through the fissures shorting out the amps, and I was freaking out backstage when an infuriated Nugent walked in and barked, 'Shit or get off the pot, Seger! No crybabies allowed in rock and roll!' I never got better advice.

"Unfortunately, the phoniness you more regularly get showered with colors you, or at least creates a big wariness, and in my tune I'm singing about 'the weight of all the hustlers and their schemes,' the industry types who urge you to 'stay confident' about your success when what they're really saying is 'keep working fella, and stay available to us.' The vision of that fresh and bold beginning also has a ghostly quality to now, but I can draw strength from the musical contribution I've made and the bit of influence I've had.

"People talk about me, Springsteen, Tom Petty, Don Henley, John Mellencamp, a few others, as being part of a family tree in a sort of modern American rock heritage. And I definitely like the idea of being a prime link, just like I enjoy giving enormous credit for my growth and approach to James Brown, Otis Redding, Mitch Ryder, and most especially the master himself, Van Morrison."

Without pose or pretense, prone to mistakes but incapable of false moves, onstage never anything but his restless, caring self, Seger has meant every syllable of every song he's ever recorded. His catchy proletarian heart-pounders swing like lunch pails and have broadened the parameters of rock dreams to include every untimid Midwestern factory boy who's ever longed to aim his fuel-injected designs at the heart of the night. Whether detailing his teenage loss of virginity on a backroad in 1962 in "Night Moves," the dull ache of another Ramada Inn rollout in "Turn the Page," or the working stiff's susceptibility to self-corruption in "Hollywood Nights," he speaks for the spunky pilgrim. Bob Seger is the man who made rock and roll a blue-collar profession of ballsy merit.

"What I try to do, which is a very American thing I guess, is to dig in and try to find the truth in an idea."

In 1964, Seger spent time on a Ford assembly line and then quit, refusing to give up on rock and roll but wanting to make the kind of music that would help his co-workers feel good about themselves, too. Thinking back on it almost twenty years later, with the auto industry facing the most dubious future since its inception, he sat down at the piano in his Michigan home and wrote a song about a bygone, intractable pride in one's labor and in an impeccable finished product. "Making Thunderbirds" was truth-telling rock and roll of superior car-radio vintage. We made Thunderbirds once, he sang, and if we bust our asses hard enough, someday, in some way, we might rediscover the secret of doing it again.

Like Bob Seger. The Keeper of the Gearbox.

Don Henley

1990

He was born during a whirlwind.

The only child of C. J. Henley and his wife, Hughlene, he came into the world on an oddly chilly July 22, 1947, in Gilmer, Texas, as a tornado tore through the piney woods of Upshur County, ripping the roof off the local gymnasium. Harry Truman was in the White House, the inhabitants of Gilmer were huddled in storm shelters carved from the east Texas clay, and Donald Hugh Henley was in his mother's arms in Ragland-Fenlaw Clinic, sleeping soundly as the twister howled outside.

When the storm had passed, the Henleys took their infant son home to Linden (population 1,700), some forty miles to the northeast. Don grew up restless and distracted, scanning Farm Road No. 1399 in anticipation of postmen bringing *Car and Driver* magazine or a mail-order "Rat Fink" T-shirt, and tuning into New Orleans's WNOE in search of Fats Domino. He taught himself to sing, took up the drums, and in high school formed a diverse succession of garage bands whose common denominators were boyhood chums Richard Bowden (on guitar) and Michael Bowden (on bass). Don wrote bittersweet songs with titles like "I'm Gone" and "God Is Where You Find Him." By late 1969 their rowdy country-rock had landed them a record deal with a small Los Angeles–based label and they headed farther west.

Henley settled in Los Angeles in 1970, the summer when south Florida's Flying Burrito Brothers issued their *Burrito Deluxe* album and a Tucson-bred girl of German-Mexican extraction named Linda Ronstadt was saturating the airwaves with the wistful "Long, Long Time." Writers back East were beginning to identify these performers as part of a "California Sound," something of an absurdity to the artists themselves, since they were fiercely proud of their regional roots. But critical ignorance did help reinforce a loose sense of community among the migrant musicians, and they hung together as they welcomed each new kid in town. Rallying points for that crowd in the early seventies included the Topanga Corral, the Palomino, the Troubadour, and, next door, Dan Tana's restaurant, one of the first bistros to let long-haired rockers sign a tab for their meals.

One band, the Eagles, would rise from this sunny conclave in 1971 to gain an audience so vast they'd be called the "American Beatles." Still, under the leadership of drummer/singer Henley and guitarist/keyboardist/singer Glenn Frey (with Bernie Leadon playing second guitar and Randy Meisner on bass; Joe Walsh replaced Leadon in 1976, and Timothy B. Schmit took over for Meisner in 1977), they created what seemed an indigenous, post–Beach Boys brand of romance.

Over the course of eight years, Henley cowrote some of the most popular songs in the history of rock and roll, among them "Witchy Woman," "Desperado," Tequila Sunrise," "James Dean," "Best of My Love," "Lyin' Eyes," "Hotel California," "New Kid in Town," "Life in the Fast Lane," "Victim of Love," and "Heartache Tonight." To many of these, Henley supplied an eloquent sense of longing, displacement, and loss, his literate lyrics undercutting the illusions of this or any other Promised Land.

When the Eagles dissolved in 1981, the members moving off in different solitary directions, observers pegged disciplined, driven Glenn Frey as the most likely to succeed solo. Yet upon the release of Henley's album *I Can't Stand Still* in August 1982, with its barbed "Dirty Laundry" and "Johnny Can't Read," the sad-voiced singing drummer emerged as the more mature recording artist.

For a new composing collaborator, Henley had chosen guitarist Danny "Kootch" Kortchmar, an East Coast pilgrim from Larchmont, New York (born April 6, 1946), who'd come to California at roughly the same juncture as Henley. Kootch was a cornerstone of Carole King's sound (helping make her classic *Carole King: Writer, Tapestry,* and *Music* albums); then James Taylor's music (nudging him toward rhythm and blues and writing songs for him like "Machine Gun Kelly" and "Honey Don't Leave L.A."), and also Jackson Browne's records (helping conceive his live *Running on Empty* album, writing "Shaky Town," and cowriting "Tender Is the Night" and "Knock on Any Door"). As a guitarist, Danny expanded the modern rock vocabulary with his distinctive arpeggio picking and roaring vibrato Stratocaster.

Henley and Kootch pooled their producing, arranging, and songwriting skills, and added a vast appetite for aural experimentation. At the Actress, Kootch's home studio in the Hollywood hills, Danny ransacked and revamped the best of eighties recording technology. The two men aimed to merge a socially responsible topicality with music as taut, edgy, and ominous as the times. *Building the Perfect Beast,* their *Bladerunner*-like rendering of technocracy run amok, was released in 1984 to rave reviews. Some five years later, after various side projects (Henley guesting on albums by Joni Mitchell and others, Kortchmar producing Neil Young), their partnership was renewed for *The End of the Innocence* (1989), critically praised as a record that was novelistic in depth and acuity. Like much of Henley's music, it dealt powerfully with voluntary or forced separation from one's roots and the often forlorn search for new footings.

The following interview with Henley and Kootch was conducted over strong coffee and an ample breakfast on a June 1989 morning at Danny's home studio.

What was the first track you did together for I Can't Stand Still*?*

KORTCHMAR: When Don decided to make a solo album in 1980, people were coming up to his house and jamming. He had one song at the time, "Nobody's Business," which ended up on the first solo album. We played that together, and then I came back with a little piece of mine which I thought sounded like Don's music. He agreed. That tune turned out to be "Lilah."

Wasn't that song recorded with the Chieftains playing on it?

HENLEY: I think it has four or five Chieftains on it. I'd been reading a lot about Ireland and the war in the North. The song's about that conflict, although at least one writer took it as the story of a man on his deathbed.

Don, your family has an Anglo-Irish heritage, correct?

HENLEY: The Henleys came from England. Henley, as far as I can tell, is a place name. It means "where the hens lay," hens meaning pheasants or wild game birds. So it means my father's ancestors came from a field of tall grass somewhere. [*laughter*] My mother's the Irish side, she's a McWhorter. They came from County Cork.

Danny, it's interesting how you and Don have collaborated, borrowing from each other's pasts. Isn't the melody of "Sunset Grill" taken from unrecorded material you had when you were with the Section, a jazz-rock band that recorded alone and with James Taylor?

KORTCHMAR: Yes, it was something I had started with the Section, but back then it was in 6/8 time. I was trying to be Joe Zawinul back in the early seventies and had momentarily forgotten about the blues, which mean so much to me. Don wanted to write a song about the Sunset Grill that was modern and sleek, but also told the story from a street point of view. So I went back and pulled this piece out, and started to develop it in 4/4 time.

"Sunset Grill," of course, is about Joe Froehlich's hamburger stand on Sunset and Gardner.

HENLEY: Right. It's now dwarfed by the Guitar Center, this giant store filled with heavy metal guys with poodle haircuts.

Basically it's a song about accountability in these nameless, faceless times in corporate America. These days you can't find anybody in government or business who's responsible for anything. Everybody you talk to is "just working here." Joe's responsible for what he makes. You can find him. He's right there, behind the grill.

The song is also about a sense of place. Kootch came up with a clean urban feeling for the track. Ever since I moved out here from Texas I've been in the Twilight Zone. I don't feel like I really belong here, and yet I can't go back to where I came from, so I'm floating somewhere over New Mexico. [*laughter*] And "Sunset Grill" also grumbles about how deteriorated the urban landscape has become, but then it says that everybody I care about lives here, so what the hell.

There's been strong social commentary on Don's three solo albums. "Johnny Can't Read" made it plain how important both of you feel literacy is. The song tackled a worthy issue.

HENLEY: My record company didn't see it that way, but thank you. I think it's a valid statement for a song, kind of a dangerous thing to say.

KORTCHMAR: See, we're suggesting that it might be *Johnny's* fault that Johnny can't read.

HENLEY: Randy Newman always thought that was a brave, even Republican, stance to take: to actually blame it on the kid instead of the system or society at large.

KORTCHMAR: All of it set to this cheerful go-go beat. Randy liked the irony of it.

You're both voracious readers. How did that come to be?

HENLEY: If you're gonna write songs, you've gotta have a life. It's as simple as that. Words and language are the most important things we have. They're the root of civilization, the way we communicate. My mother had a college degree, taught elementary school for several years, and bought me books all the time. Before I was old enough to read, my dad would read aloud to me every Sunday; he read me the funny papers and articles that interested me. I was reading before I started school.

Tell me some of your favorite books.

KORTCHMAR: *Money* by Martin Amis, *The Bonfire of the Vanities* by Tom Wolfe, a fantastic book. Another would be *Landslide,* by Jane Mayer and Doyle McManus, about the Reagan Administration.

HENLEY: My list would include *All My Friends Are Going to Be Strangers* by Larry McMurtry, and Harry Stein's book, *Ethics (and Other Liabilities)—Trying to Live Right in an Amoral World.* One I read in college that's still a favorite is *Jude the Obscure* by Thomas Hardy. There are two women in the book who are total opposites, one very earthy and lusty, the other very pristine and spiritual. And this man is torn between these two extremes—which is what [*laughter*] a lot of my writing is about. "How Bad Do You Want It," a song from *The End of the Innocence,* is a perfect example. It examines the age-old conflict of a guy drooling over a beautiful woman and calling it love instead of lust.

I also love *Walden, or Life in the Woods,* and anything else by Thoreau. And Mark Twain. And Ralph Waldo Emerson's *Essays.*

Emerson's essay on self-reliance was literally where I got the nerve to become a songwriter.

Would it have been roughly June 1970 when you started to pass an evening or two at the Troubadour?

HENLEY: Yeah, and we were also doing some gigs around the San Fernando Valley. Kenny [Rogers]'s wife became our temporary manager, booking us at the Goose Creek Saloon in Northridge. And I was starting to hang at the Troubadour, which is where I became friends with Glenn Frey. I had met both Glenn and J. D. Souther down at the offices of Amos Records, which was distributed by Bell Records.

Glenn and I slowly warmed up to each other, and one night he bought me a beer and asked if I wanted to go on the road with Linda Ronstadt. My band was going nowhere, and he and J.D. had broken their duo up.

I was broke, and it was an opportunity to make two hundred bucks a week and get out of town, so I immediately accepted the offer. I knew all her songs anyhow, and passed the audition with flying colors.

Kootch, you've worked so much with Linda Ronstadt too. How did you make your own trek out to L.A. and her band?

KORTCHMAR: I was playing in Greenwich Village with the Fugs, and left them to go to L.A. with a band called Clear Light, and I also began spending time at the Troubadour.

HENLEY: You know, the Fugs are another cosmic connection between us. Ed Sanders of the Fugs was a good friend of Glenn's and J.D.'s, and he stayed at their apartment in Echo Park when he was out here doing research for his book on the Manson Family [*The Family*]. They used to take turns sitting up all night with a pistol, in case any Manson-oids came in through the window.

Ed Sanders subsequently wrote the unpublished Eagles biography, which is 900 pages long, and is sitting at home on my shelf. Where it will remain.

Do you think the Troubadour has been overromanticized as an important rock and roll watering hole?

HENLEY: I'd say it's been *under*-romanticized, if anything, because it was a key part of a musical and cultural revolution going on at that time. I suppose it was a coffeehouse and folk club to begin with, and then grew into something unique. More than being a good-time place, it was a spawning ground for a great many artists throughout the sixties and seventies. It was a place of germination and creativity.

I understand you've gotten some of your best lyric ideas for your solo hits during long car rides.

HENLEY: Yes, I was driving up by Zuma Beach when I got the lyric ideas for "The Boys of Summer." And for "The End of the Innocence," I was driving home from Bruce Hornsby's house in the San Fernando Valley in the summer of '87. He'd had the basic musical track for a while and couldn't seem to do anything with it. He lived way out in the middle of the valley, on a street called Hartland, which was near this big cornfield on federally owned land that they let these two Mexican-American farmers plant. It was all too perfect: Bruce Hornsby, heartland, cornfield. The rest was just like channeling. [*laughs*] I could get into Shirley MacLaine territory here, wondering where the actual lyric came from, but let's *not.*

The car *is* a nice little creative capsule. Nobody bothers you in there, you have a sense of forward motion. It just works well for me. But sometimes people miss the lyrical twists cars help me think up. I got a letter from a woman who corrected my spelling of the "Mercedes bends" line in "Hotel California"—she thought I muffed the automobile reference.

Where'd you get the idea for the title of Building the Perfect Beast*?*

HENLEY: I'd read an article about genetic engineering, and how it would put an end to a lot of suffering. We would be able to cure a lot of diseases, but on the other hand it would open a Pandora's Box. When you start fooling with the basic building blocks of life, you have the potential to create monsters. There's a futuristic insidiousness involved in trying to play God and getting down into the very core of human beings. We want to conquer nature rather than live in harmony with it.

Don, I think you threatened at one point to record all of the Building the Perfect Beast *album here in Kootch's studio.*

HENLEY: I always loved the way Danny's demos sounded here. They have a quality to them that you lose some of when you go to another more complex and well-equipped recording facility. But we've all been programmed into thinking you have to record in a place like that for fidelity. I'm not sure that's true because Kootch's demos from here meld amazingly and have an off-the-cuff quality.

Building the Perfect Beast *took listeners through some horrific sci-fi landscapes, but then it ended on a hopeful note with "Land of the Living."*

HENLEY: I always try to end things that way. That's how I see them. I've seen this city become a great deal more crowded, dirty, and violent than it was when I came here some nineteen years ago, and there's always that conflict within me between the urban and the pastoral. But I still have faith in tomorrow.

"Gimme What You Got" on The End of the Innocence *seems to be a song about the idea that values and ethics are ordinary and immediate. They're not something you need to have a clean shirt on for.*

HENLEY: There has to be something more. Greed's so pervasive in this society. You see it, like we say in the song, from Wall Street to Washington. It's every man for himself. It's about "Me, me, me and damn the rest of the nation."

We need to look deeper, especially into ourselves. A lot of the latest album is about the way things *appear.* In "Little Tin God," we chant "World of appearances!" We don't look further than the surface, and that goes right down the line from the men and women we choose to go out with or marry to the presidents we elect. We're caught up in the way something seems to be, or looks, or is presented. If someone is very articulate, very beautiful, or very handsome, they can really get away with murder.

Let's talk about "I Will Not Go Quietly" on the new album.

HENLEY: Kootch did that entire track here, and when he played it for me I almost fell down. He actually played or programmed every single instrument you hear on the record. Together, we wanted to prove we could write something like that, a real kick-ass rock and roll song, bordering on metal but based on the blues. In keeping with what Led Zeppelin used to do.

KORTCHMAR: Metal has gotten too many generations removed from its roots. To me, the original heavy metal music was Howlin' Wolf singing "Forty-Four" or "Tail-Dragger." It's everything metal claims to be.

HENLEY: Lyrically, our song is about raging hormones. It's about a young man who's being spurned by a young lady. It's about not giving up. It's about pluck. And having a fighting spirit. To that end, it was Kootch's idea to bring in Axl Rose to sing harmony.

I was having a lot of flashbacks when Axl came into the studio, because I know how I felt when I was twenty-two or twenty-three and went in to sing on other people's records who'd been doing it for a long time. I was scared to death sometimes, but I also had a lotta nerve and so does he. He stood out there and sang for hours, until he got a migraine headache. We had to make him stop singing. His voice is like a chainsaw.

I'd like to talk about [both of] your childhood[s]. Don, weren't you involved in Future Farmers of America?

HENLEY: I was a Future Farmer of America, yeah—F.F.A. It had another name, but we can't go into that. [*laughter*] It was a high school course you took for credit, like wood shop. You had to have a project your senior year in order to graduate.

My project was an acre and a half of cucumbers. They came up nicely, and boy was I sorry. It was hell, pure *hell*! Because cucumber vines have little prickly things on them that irritate your hands. I had to get up at five o'clock every morning to harvest them and take them to the pickle-processing plant and sell them. There were just so *many* of them, and it was so early in the morning! I hated it. But it was good exercise, and it taught me some things—[*laughs*] it taught me to move to the city!

My father had an auto parts store after World War II, but he grew up farming, and he always planted a gigantic garden anyway. The older I get, the more I appreciate what I learned from my father. He taught me a lot about appreciating the earth, and growing living things. In fact, some years I still plant a vegetable garden myself in order to keep that value system. You can't buy a good tomato around here, anyway.

Kootch, when you were growing up, didn't you have the nickname of "Happy"?

KORTCHMAR: [*Sheepish*] That's right, I did.

HENLEY: [*Whooping laughter*] Ooooh! I hadn't heard this one! This is a new one.

KORTCHMAR: Yeah, my neighbor Mitchell Wilson used to call me Happy, because I was the most miserable kid he had ever seen in his life. I never smiled, I always wore black. He'd see me during the summer, and I'd go to the beach dressed in full black, with biker boots.

Don, your singing often has this rooftop soul-tenor quality. "If Dirt Were Dollars" shows peaks and high points in your voice I never knew you had.

HENLEY: We always try to put songs in a key that puts me at the top of my range, so I have to strain a little bit to get it. I don't like relaxed vocals. My voice changes a lot when I'm warming up, and it confuses recording engineers. [*laughs*] They think the microphone is breaking up, or some module in the mixing board is bad.

"New York Minute" is like a novella, with its urban images of dissolution. The tableau of the ruined man's scattered clothing on the railroad tracks is chilling.

HENLEY: We wanted to leave that open. Maybe he threw himself under the train, maybe he threw his clothes off and just kept walking. You don't really know. I'd always wanted to write a song called "New York Minute," which oddly enough is a Southern expression. It means quick, like "I'll have that done in a New York minute!"

To me, the song is saying that we go through life thinking we can give love and receive love on our own terms, and then one day we wake up to realize that we can't have love on *any* terms at all.

Don, "You Can't Make Love" from your second solo album makes the point that anything meaningful requires time and humility to develop. I know that you were about thirteen when your paternal grandmother died. You once told me that you were startled by how soon afterward your grandfather also expired. Did that influence your outlook?

HENLEY: Yes. He pined away. And prior to that, he'd been in excellent health. They had been together for more than fifty years, and it was a very profound thing in my life that the absence of my grandma would affect him so much. When my grandfather died, they really couldn't give a cause of death except for the loss of her. The lyrics are memos to myself about these issues and insights.

Modern rock ballads usually cast the narrator as someone who's an embittered emotional casualty, but "The Heart of the Matter" makes the point that love can't be love if it's conditional.

HENLEY: It's hard to put those kinds of things out there, but the older I get, the more ability I have to do it. I was determined to get this song out, because I'd been planning on writing it for years. A few cocktails later [*laughs*], it came out.

KORTCHMAR: He's doing what, as an artist, he's supposed to do in that song: which is to reveal himself.

HENLEY: It's obviously a very personal song to me. And it took me almost forty-two years to get to that place where I could say what I said in that song about the importance of forgiveness. I think it's another step in my growth as a male human being.

Joey Ramone's father has never been too big on his son's peculiar brand of rock and roll. Until recently, exposure to the Ramones' spare, howling blare would promptly reduce Dad to a headbanger (his own, of course) or leave him feeling as if he wanted to, well, be sedated.

"The music used to drive me up a wall," he admits wearily. "I tried to get my son interested in good music—his grandmother, Fanny, used to sing for Macy's; you rented a piano from the store for a party, and she came with it—so I got him an accordion when he was a child. He loved the goddamn thing, but he squeezed it until there was nothing left of it—I think he loved to hear the wheezy noise it made. As a teenager he was fairly good at the drums, playing 'em in the basement with his friends, but it got so I really had a hard time standing the racket.

"But say, I got a question for you: *How the hell did you find me?*"

Ramones

1979

It wasn't easy. Precious little is known about the backgrounds of the various Ramones, save the customarily mumbled information that original members Joey, Dee Dee, Johnny, and Tommy Ramone all hail from Forest Hills, Queens, New York, and formed their one and only band circa 1974 after graduating from, or "growing out of," high school. They had been together for less than a year when they debuted to a virtually empty house at CBGB's, the notoriously seedy Bowery club where a blank generation of distinctively raw rockers first gained a foothold. Hammering out a numbing, seventeen-minute set consisting of about eight three-chord, two-stanza songs, the Ramones were instrumental in spawning an aggressive national groundswell of back-to-basics rock bands whose defiant individualism inspired a horde of disaffected young English snots simultaneously rallying together as the Sex Pistols, the Clash, Generation X . . .

New York music writers like Danny Fields of the *Soho Weekly News* began devoting passionate columns to the four Forest Hills rockers. Mop-haired and sickly looking, with faces so acne-caked they resembled pink peanut brittle, the Ramones were as appealing as their hasty repertoire of head splitters: "Blitzkrieg Bop," "Chain Saw," "Loudmouth," "Now I Wanna Sniff Some Glue," and so on.

Meanwhile, on the other side of a widening No Band's Land, the trenches were full of contemptuous mainstream rockers and their fans, not to mention radio programmers, concert promoters, and even some critics, all of whom denounced the Ramones as no-talent sacks of shit. Incensed that four mysterious creeps with the same last name (the Ramone Brothers?) had come out of nowhere to release one remedial record (*Ramones*, Sire Records, 1976) and subsequently generate as much press as the last Rolling Stones tour, the tradition-bound opposition demanded an explanation: *Where do these punks get off?*

Four years and four albums later, Joey Ramone's father is still pondering the same question. "I gotta be honest with you," says a bemused Noel Hyman, chatting in the office of his Manhattan trucking company, "I was surprised, very much so, when Jeffrey [a.k.a. Joey] and the band started putting out records and getting a little popular. I was always hearing him say, 'We got something here,' until it rang in my ears. And I didn't believe in it *at all.* I would have liked him to come into the business, really.

"The first coupla times I saw the group play, I must say I didn't like 'em, but I got used to it—although it took some time. But then,

I guess the first time some people taste champagne they wanna spit it out, right? Still, I think they oughta put more different things in their music, 'n' complicate it up a bit, if they wanna get high up on the whattayacallit—the lists, the charts? I dunno, I'm an old square. Guess it looks like he may do okay after all, right?"

"I'm *sick* of not selling records," Joey mutters to himself as he peers into the mirror in his cramped upstairs dressing room at Philadelphia's Walnut Street Theatre. "I want to draw more people to the shows, make *something* happen. If the new album isn't a hit, I'm gonna kill myself."

Recently returned from a well-attended tour of Europe, the Ramones are back on the road in '79 to promote their LP *Road to Ruin.* The album has been almost universally praised as the band's most ambitious and engaging effort to date, demonstrating as it does an impressive growth in musicianship and an expanded compositional flair. Dee Dee has blossomed into a deft, distinctive bassist; Johnny's brisk, chunky riffing has given way to some canny, if restrained, leads; new drummer Marky (a replacement for Tommy, who bowed out last year) provides a solid bottom and a powerful forward thrust; and Joey has evolved—with the help of voice lessons—into a rather spry, inventive vocalist. None of these developments has lifted the band anywhere near the Top 50 or the lofty status of an arena-filling attraction, however, so the Ramones have dragged their equipment out to Philly by van to headline a modest program on the site of the historic first presidential debate between Gerald R. Ford and Georgia Governor Jimmy Carter.

Snapped out of his dressing-room doldrums by a pat on the back from baby-faced Johnny Ramone (alias John Cummings), the spindly, knock-kneed Joey is summoned into a back room for an impromptu preconcert conference. Timing and pacing are discussed, the meeting chaired by the authoritative Johnny, who clearly is the de facto perfectionist of the group. He's also the most business-minded of the four, momentarily putting their huddle on hold at the appearance of sandy-haired manager Danny Fields, the Ramone's longtime booster. Johnny registers a stern complaint with the straight-faced Fields about the absence of posters in the theater's outside display cases and requests some information on current airplay and record sales in secondary markets, before returning to his cohorts to drill them on the evening's songs.

"Watch the beginning of 'Cretin Hop' tonight," he scolds the lantern-jawed Marky (Bell). "You came in wrong again last night. You're just not hearing it."

"Okay," Marky says meekly. "Tell it all to me again."

"No, we'll *play* it once quickly," Johnny rules as he plugs his white Mosrite guitar into a small practice amp.

"Hey, I don't want to play too much, John," Dee Dee (Colvin) whines, scratching the arrow-through-the-heart MOTHER tattoo on his biceps. "Look at my nail. It's split! I want as little pain as possible."

Johnny ignores the bassist's plea, and they launch into the song.

His presence not required for the run-through, Joey has slipped into the dressing room and is bent over the dirty sink, rinsing his purple eyeglasses under the faucet. He remains locked in this position for an extended period, oblivious to the ebb and flow of awed fans and curious members of the other groups on the bill.

Ten minutes later, diminutive Linda Stein, thirty-two-year-old wife of Seymour Stein (the president of the Warner Bros.-distributed Sire label) and the other half of the band's managerial team, strides in, and Joey lifts his head and whispers to her urgently. She nods and then issues a booming command to all assembled: "Excuse me everybody! Please clear the room! Joey wants to be alone to wash his face!"

As the throng moves toward the door, Joey's furtive eyes meet mine—a rare moment—and his face erupts in a crimson blush that temporarily obscures the swollen zit nestled against his pug nose. But the awkward instant is suddenly dispelled by the appearance of a bold devotee who bursts through the stream of departing fans and starts jabbering into Joey's ear.

"I really loved 'California Sun,' man, I really really did!" he gushes. "Could you write an autograph for my friend?" Joey nods shyly and dries his hands on his grimy, sweat-soaked shirt. "Say, 'To Ian, from Joey Ramone,'" the fan insists as the skinny star begins scribbling on a scrap of paper. "And, er, could you please *print* it, cause he only understands printing."

The Ramones are DUMB—and so is their public.

You read it everywhere—this magazine [*Rolling Stone*] included—and hear it at parties whenever someone dares to play one of their records. Throughout the recording industry their enemies are legion, many dismissing the four as hopeless mooks. Joey Ramone in particular has frequently been singled out as a Grade A Fancy ninny whose motor responses supposedly were so atrophied by adolescent glue-sniffing that now he can't even find his ass with both hands.

Those allegations seem to take on a certain gravity when Joey's viewed in concert. During the show at the Walnut Street Theatre, he clutches his tipped mike stand with abject desperation, weaving around the unsteady axis like a drunk looking for the keyhole. As always, his deathly pale visage is almost entirely hidden by a curtain of matted hair, and his bird legs are locked with spastic rigidity as his jeans droop past his hipless waist.

The set has opened with Dee Dee roaring his ritual "*One, two, three, four!*" countdown to kick off the Ramones' biggest (No. 66 in *Billboard*) chart single ever, "Rockaway Beach," as their large red, white, and blue eagle banner is lowered behind the drums. Following in quick succession are astringent treatments of "Blitzkrieg Bop," "I Don't Want You," "Gimme Gimme Shock Treatment," "Don't Come Close," and "Sheena Is a Punk Rocker."

By this time, the packed house—a surprisingly diverse mix that includes the safety-pin-through-the-nose crowd but also a host of Ivy Leaguers and even some middle-aged longhairs in down parkas—is in a flat-out frenzy, thrusting their fists in the air as Joey leads them in between-songs chants of "Hey! Ho! Let's go!" "Needles and Pins," the latest single, lifts the proceedings to a fever pitch, and a wildly flailing Marky purses his lips as if he's going to puke from the exertion.

Combining the stunning attack of the early Kinks with the energy, flamboyance, and spectacular pacing of the Who, the Ramones give of themselves with a kooky totality that is strangely moving. Witnessing the event, even one who is not really an avid fan has to wonder whether the Ramones' harshest detractors have ever seen them in live performance. Thematically, songs about decapitation, teenage lobotomies, headbangers named Suzy, sniffing Carbona spot remover, and wanting to be sedated may be an acquired taste, but it's difficult to understand why more hard-rock enthusiasts—especially the heavy-metal helots—cannot find a place in their hearts for the Ramones' explosive sound. No concerts so well executed as their own could come off without *some* lucid thought being paid to musical craft and presentation, and it's a genuinely triumphant moment when a roadie rushes out at the climax of the Philly date to hand Joey a black and yellow banner emblazoned with the exhortation: GABBA GABBA HEY!

"GABBA GABBA HEY is from the 1930s horror film *Freaks,*" Tommy Erdelyi (formerly Ramone) explains to me one evening over sandwiches in an East Village eatery. "There's a party going on in the film, and one of the midgets has married this pretty woman—she's not a freak. During the celebration, they start chanting, 'Gooble gobble, we accept her, one of us!' Or something like that. So when we wrote the song 'Pinhead' [on the *Ramones Leave Home* LP], we decided to use the chant, but we changed it to give it more power. We were trying to tell the audience that we're all one."

Unfortunately, Tommy and the other band members are currently estranged. Fed up with the grind of the road ("I couldn't stand it; my nerves were shot"), he left the group after the release of the Ramones' third LP, *Rocket to Russia.* Born in Budapest, Hungary, Erdelyi, now twenty-eight, immigrated to the United States with his older brother and parents when he was four.

Tommy served as manager of the group during the period when the nucleus was Joey on drums, with Dee Dee and Johnny splitting the lead and rhythm guitar chores. The boys auditioned several bassists before Dee Dee agreed to give it a try, and Joey was drafted as the vocalist, because, as Tommy admits, "He had the best voice." That left the drummer's slot open, and Tommy eventually shrugged, sat down, and started pounding the skins.

"The truth of the matter was that my function with the Ramones was as a producer and an organizer," Erdelyi reflects. "My least contribution was as a drummer." He began his career as an assistant engineer at various Manhattan studios, working on John McLaughlin's *Devotion* album and some of the later Jimi Hendrix sessions that would resurface on *Crash Landing* and other LPs reconstructed after Hendrix's death.

As producer of their legendary sixteen-song demo and coproducer of all four Ramones LPs released in the States (a live collection entitled *It's Alive* is due to be issued overseas), Erdelyi sees himself as the Ramones' seminal theorist and the man who played the chief role in honing their musical concepts.

"There was never anything like the Ramones before," he assures me. "It was a new way of looking at music. We took the rock sound into a psychotic world and narrowed it down into a straight line of energy. In an era of progressive rock, with its complexities and counterpoints, we had a perspective of nonmusicality and intelligence that takes over for musicianship.

"Going back to the first album, which was the seed, we used block chording as a melodic device, and the harmonics resulting from the distortion of the amplifiers created countermelodies. We used the wall of sound as a melodic rather than a riff form; it was like a song within a song—created by a block of chords droning.

"I'll tell you what else was distinctive," he says, gathering steam. "The hypnotic effect of strict repetition, the effect of lyrics that repeat, and vocals that dart out at you, and the percussive effect of driving the music like a sonic machine. It's very sensual. You can put headphones on and just swim with it. It's *not* background music."

Was all of this conceived beforehand or are these just Tommy's accumulated afterthoughts?

"Well," he demurs, "it was *always* a combination of talent and intelligence."

"Wait a minute," I say, "Johnny told me that the first LP sounded so primitive because that was the best you guys could play at that time."

"Yes," Erdelyi concedes, "but there was *always* intelligence behind it. If every untrained musician doing the best he can decides to make a record, he's *not* going to get a Ramones LP out of it."

Intrigued by this high-minded analysis, I decide to schedule a symposium down at Joey Ramone's dingy Lower East Side loft to give the other members of the Ramones the opportunity to explain themselves and their rock perspective. The band assembles around a rickety table at one end of the long rectangular room.

Flopped across a corner mattress is bleary-eyed Danny Fields, who says he's "a young thirty-five" but looks a bit older. A Phi Beta Kappa from the University of Pennsylvania and a Harvard Law School dropout, Fields is a veteran of the rock wars, having signed the MC5 and the Stooges to Elektra while working there as director of publicity. After being fired from Elektra, he says, for defending the MC5's right to have the word *fuck* on their album jackets and in their print ads, he moved to Atlantic Records as a publicist—and got fired again, he says, for openly detesting Emerson, Lake, and Palmer.

He subsequently resurfaced as the editor of *16 Magazine,* wrote a music column for the *Soho Weekly News,* and then—Gabba Gabba Hey!

A raconteur of considerable renown, Fields maintains a curious silence during the talk.

As I gaze across the table at the current Ramones lineup, I am struck by the great differences in their personalities and backgrounds. All are twenty-six years old and similarly dressed, but that's about all they have in common apart from their music.

Johnny Cummings, the authoritative, business-minded guitarist, was born on Long Island. An only child and a self-confessed teenage reprobate, he drifted from one military academy to another during his secondary-school days, searching for some sort of "discipline" in his life. The son of a construction worker now retired in Florida, Johnny has since found inner peace as a Ramone, a Betamax junkie, and an avid reader of film biographies and history books.

Dee Dee (Douglas) Colvin, who is secretly married, was born in Virginia but spent fourteen years as a service brat in Germany, where his father, an army career officer, was stationed. Hard-jawed, with dark chilling eyes, his meek, courtly manner cannot conceal the streetfighter's savvy that earned him the ugly knife scars that mar his upper torso and—he later reveals—his buttocks.

Marky Bell is a timorous outsider from Brooklyn, where his father labored for eighteen years as a longshoreman before becoming a lawyer. He is the most seasoned musician, having drummed over the years with transsexual Wayne County, Richard Hell and the Voidoids, and a defunct group called Dust that recorded two albums in the late sixties for the Kama Sutra label.

Joey (Jeffrey) Hyman, the lovable scarecrow, is a native of Forest Hills. His father and mother have been divorced since the early sixties. He has a younger brother named Mitch, who is a guitarist with rock critic Lester Bangs's band, Birdland. Contrary to popular belief, Joey is the most clever and quick-witted of the Ramones.

We begin by discussing Forest Hills, which Johnny describes as "a middle-class, mostly Jewish neighborhood—if that means anything." He then mentions that Michael Landon, the star of TV's "Little House on the Prairie," is from the same area. I interject that Paul Simon also lived in Forest Hills, and Marky corrects me: "Paul *Stanley*—of Kiss." When I say no, I mean Paul *Simon,* he gives me a blank stare.

"Aw, you know Paul Simon," Johnny chides the drummer, but Marky replies with another blank stare.

"Don't mind him," Johnny tells me with exasperation. "He's from *Brooklyn.*"

How did you pick the name Ramones?

JOEY: It had a ring to it, like "Eli Wallach" does. Just sounded good.

JOHNNY: We thought of Spice and other names but felt, "That's ridiculous."

DEE DEE: We never gave it *too* much thought.

Where did your American eagle logo come from?

JOHNNY: I don't know if what we've got is the American eagle, but that's what we thought of at the time.

DEE DEE: It looks good up there. I mean, Patti Smith has the American flag . . .

JOHNNY: . . . and we have a kind of presidential seal.

MARKY: Yeah. "In God We Trust."

JOEY: [*Snickering*] We *weren't* thinking of God.

JOHNNY: You want a strong symbol, and that's it.

DEE DEE: [*Earnestly*] We want to make it clear that it has nothing to do with fascism or anything like that.

JOHNNY: [*Alarmed*] Nobody asked ya!

DEE DEE: [*Continuing*] It's just a sign that I think . . .

JOHNNY: [*Firmly*] *Nobody asked ya!*

You still look like teenage troublemakers, young thugs. Were you?

JOHNNY: I guess we were sort of juvenile delinquents, but Forest Hills ain't the South Bronx; it's a nice neighborhood. So if you walk around like this [*he indicates his leather jacket, T-shirt, jeans*] you're already looked upon as a hoodlum. I mean we were just general *nogoodnicks.*

DEE DEE: But we didn't have an organized gang.

JOHNNY: We *once* tried robbing a drugstore on Queens Boulevard—unsuccessfully. It was in a whole row of stores, and we broke into the laundromat from behind by mistake. The next time we tried robbing a bakery on 63rd Drive; somebody climbed in the window above the door. The police came to my house the next day and asked somebody to identify me, but the person said I wasn't the one. The other kid finked on me—but I don't care 'cause he's gotten killed since then.

I didn't become bad until I got out of high school. Sniffing glue was probably the start of my downfall. My first drug experience was sniffing glue. We tried it and then moved on to Carbona.

That's why we wrote songs about it. It was a good high, but it gave you a bad headache. I guess it destroys your brain cells, though.

JOEY: Then "Carbona (Not Glue)" got pulled from the *Leave Home* album because Carbona was gonna sue us for using their name. We thought it was a substance, not the name of a product or company.

Speaking of songwriting, I thought in the beginning that the brevity of the songs was tongue in cheek, a gimmick.

JOHNNY: [*Bewildered*] The what of the song was *what?*

The brevity of the songs was . . .

JOHNNY: What's *brevity* mean?

Shortness, conciseness.

JOHNNY: Oh, well, we were new at writing songs and new at playing our instruments, so we couldn't write anything too complicated, really. It was nothing intentional. We decided to sing about something that we found amusing.

DEE DEE: And *daring.*

JOHNNY: All our songs are written by all of us. We wrote two songs the very first day we were a band. One was called "I Don't Wanna Walk Around with You" and the other was called "I Don't Wanna Get Involved with You." "I Don't Wanna Walk Around with You" made it on the first album, but "I Don't Wanna Get Involved with You" didn't.

You never recorded it?

JOHNNY: No. It's very much like "I Don't Wanna Walk Around with You," almost the same song. We might someday record it.

What's the basic lyric?

DEE DEE: [*Blandly*]

> *I don't wanna get involved with you*
> *That's not what I wanna do*
> *Come knocking on my door*
> *I'm gonna knock you on the floor*
> *I don't wanna get involved with you*
> *That's not what I wanna do.*

How would you describe your own music?

DEE DEE: We're playing at our level of ability.

JOHNNY: We're playing pure rock and roll with no blues or folk or any of that stuff in it. And we try to be entertaining and bring back the feeling of kids coming and having a good time—united with us. But we never considered the whole local new-band scene here or in England. We never had the weird pointy haircuts. These are our regular haircuts.

Linda Stein said she felt that the Sid Vicious murder case has caused you to lose bookings.

JOHNNY: We've had a lot of job rejections. We had a lot of radio stations taking us off and rejecting us. We just had a job offer at Notre Dame with Foreigner, and Notre Dame turned us down. We got pulled off stations after the *Weekend* show with the Sex Pistols. It had nothing to do with us. We don't look or act like them. We weren't out to ruin the music business. There's room for everybody. When we started, we were more or less looking at the hard-rock groups of America like Aerosmith and Ted Nugent and Kiss as our competition.

JOEY: [*Brightly*] Alice Cooper helped my life because he was my first hero. I related to the guy—until I found out he really was the way he was.

You mean before he started playing golf with George Burns?

JOEY: Yeah, right.

JOHNNY: [*Serious*] Joey, wouldn't you like to be playing golf with George Burns?

JOEY: [*Sheepish*] I dunno, but I guess I respected Cooper because that's all he wanted to do in the first place: get big so he could play golf with the stars.

JOHNNY: It's nice to play golf with George Burns, if you wanna. I played golf in military school for about a year.

The other night Joey said that he would kill himself if the new record didn't do well. Things have been rough, eh?

JOHNNY: Yeah, but we've been on salary since we started recording. It's not much, it's meager, but it's been okay. When we started it was about $50 a week. Now it's $150 a week—actually that starts next week, a raise from $125. We get $10 a day when we're traveling, and occasionally get a royalty check for songwriting.

Why did Tommy leave the band?

JOHNNY: He just couldn't take touring.

DEE DEE: It's very hard to tour.

JOHNNY: He was getting to be catatonic.

JOEY: [*Chortling evilly*] Tommy cracked like an egg!

Say, Dee Dee, when did you get the knife wounds?

DEE DEE: [*Embarrassed*] That was something stupid I did. I don't want to say it 'cause it was bad.

JOHNNY: But now we're nice.

How did you fellas manage to change your dispositions?

JOHNNY: We got into a group, and we became nice.

They *are* very, very nice boys," says Joey's mother, Charlotte, as she serves me milk and cookies one afternoon in the pleasant East Village apartment she shares with her second husband, a psychologist.

A slim, attractive woman in her late forties, the former Mrs. Noel Hyman is an accomplished artist and an avid collector, as evidenced by the tasteful arrangements of paintings that cover every wall of her home.

"Forest Hills is a very conservative, conventional place. I think we were the black-sheep household of our street," Charlotte muses. "It was a meeting place for both of my boys' friends because we also had the basement there open to them, and there was always a lot of music going on.

"You know, they taught me how to smoke pot when they were about thirteen. I realized they were doing *something* down there, and I didn't want them to do it outside where they could be busted."

Did Joey's father ever smoke pot with the boys?

"*I don't think so,*" she says evenly. "I don't think he would like to hear that I allowed them to do it at home, either. But at that time we were divorced."

Was the house basement also a haven for glue-sniffing?

"Not that I know of," she says with a laugh, "but I'm sure there were things that they did that I didn't know about. It's very possible. The little devils tried everything."

It appears her tolerance was as unique as her sons' behavior. Was she upset when Joey quit school to play his music?

"Uh huh. Naturally, like any good Jewish mother, I would have wanted my son to finish high school and go to college."

Does she recall any early songs that Joey wrote and showed to her?

"He showed me *everything,* but there were so many. I know

they all had that little anger in them, and I thought it was a great release for him to get it all out of his system."

Where does she think that anger came from?

"Naturally, it was anger against his parents. Probably his father more than me," she adds with a nervous chuckle. "When he'd come upstairs from the basement after playing the drums, I used to say to him, 'You just beat the hell out of me, didn't you?' He'd say, '*Yeah.*' "

Is Charlotte a Ramones fan?

"Don't you know I'm known as Momma Ramone?" she asks, a little hurt. "I really like them. I guess I have to confess that the first album sounded a little *strange* and unprofessional, but I caught the energy and I found that fascinating."

Does Joey/Jeffrey ever speak to her about his career?

"No, nothing in particular. Occasionally he lets me read some of his fan mail; all these little girls from all over the country writing to him, telling him they're madly in love with him, and that they can't wait to see him.

"And then he gets these *propositions,*" she confides breathlessly, "from forty-year-old women who want his fair body. I think he gets a charge out of that."

"A long time ago I used to get drunk and hang out a lot around mental institutions, because the girls there are all loose and they are . . . fun, you know?" Joey tells me later that evening, by way of detailing the parameters of his love life. "So I kind of fell in love with this girl, and every week they took her upstairs to the fifth floor to have shock treatments. They would strap her into a wheelchair. Before they took her up she was fine. Then she came down, and she was like a zombie and didn't even know who I was."

"Have you seen her since?" I wonder.

"No. She turned into a real alcoholic. I think that's what happens to you when you have a lobotomy. You have to escape all the time."

"A lot of what you've experienced is recounted in the band's songs," I tell him. "Johnny told me earlier that when you guys were growing up, you could never get any dates with girls."

"Well," Joey explains, "there's a lot of people that really get into being in high school; they go to dances and all that shit. I always hated those people. At that time you didn't really get much—nobody really had any girlfriends and there was just like one Brooklyn chick, named Lois, that everyone was going to and she'd give me a blow job down in the basement.

"Everyone would go there on a Friday night, and the guys would line up. She was also the kind of chick that was hideous-looking. She was about twenty-seven, and, well, it was very hard to get her to fuck. So I'd turn her on to LSD and shit like that."

"Sounds very romantic," I offer.

"Oh yeah," he laughs. "I used to like, on Sundays, take her to my house. At that time I was living with my mom. It was very rough trying to get her down the street to my house without anyone seeing."

"Ever have a long-term romantic relationship?"

"I never had any, like, ones with girls that really liked me. Most of them were short-term. These days we get a lot of weirdos coming to a show. We get all these kids who are loners."

With their fortunes currently on the upswing, the Ramones are sure to attract a lot more lost souls. *Road to Ruin* is the group's biggest-selling album, with worldwide sales just above the 250,000 mark. But the real breakthrough for this beleaguered band has been in concert bookings; the Ramones have made significant strides in landing lucrative gigs since signing an agreement with the powerful Premier Talent agency. The deal, Danny Fields points out, was made on the same day that Elvis died, and it's just now paying off, with the Ramones finally opening for big acts like Black Sabbath.

In addition, the group recently completed the starring role in a Roger Corman film tentatively titled *Rock & Roll High School.* An epic that concludes with the student body blowing up the school building, the movie is slated for spring or summer release, along with a soundtrack album that—barring legal complications—will include a song by Paul McCartney (a big hero of Johnny's) and Wings, originally written for *Heaven Can Wait,* called "Have We Met Somewhere Before?"

But all these exciting developments raise an inevitable question: Will success spoil the Ramones?

"Well, it's all a game," says Johnny, "but you gotta play to win. We're gonna do it our way though, 'cause we don't wanna disappoint our fans."

"Like, it's weird, you know?" says Joey. "We're very influential. Once when we played in Minneapolis, I think, there were all these kids in the club, and everybody was tripping on LSD or something.

And they all started banging their heads against the floor, just like in the song ["Suzy Is a Headbanger"]. *All* of them; it was like, really sick. About 300 people were there."

"Maybe some of your fans will send you their heads when they're done banging them?"

"That would be great," says Joey with a wry chuckle. "It would spruce up my bathroom."

PROGENY

Childlike playfulness and tempered mettle have rarely blended so well in a performer's facial features: bright, sparkling, manchild eyes gazing out from beneath feathery eyebrows and fairly illuminating the gently rounded caramel lineaments. A gracefully sloping, mildly puggish nose strengthened by high cheekbones and a strong, angular jaw. A symmetrical halo of wiry hair hovering confidently over it all. Utterly beguiling, brimming with boundless curiosity, good humor, and clarity of purpose—and it is gone forever.

In its place is a disturbing mask, stark and skull-like, the physiognomy flattened and hardened in deference to a pinched skeletal nose that seems a hasty reconstruction, as artificial and undistinguished as the plucked eyebrows that form pencil-line arches above the now-cold stare. The mouth is a sullen fissure, unconvincing when smiling, ungainly when set in a frown.

No natural development could have so cruelly eradicated the former subtlety and charity of this countenance. It is a visage reassembled after a tragedy, or one deliberately distorted in a grotesque act of

Michael Jackson

1977/89

self-conscious folly. In the 1980s, for better or worse, a plastic surgeon forever changed Michael Jackson's face as Michael Jackson irrevocably changed the face of popular music.

It is August 1977, the end of the beginning, or the beginning of the end.

"I've never been scared of any kind of performing, even when I was the littlest kid," rules nineteen-year-old Michael Jackson, seated at a shadowy corner banquette in Georges Rey, a frayed old French restaurant on West 55th Street in New York City. His hands tremble as they hold the menu.

"I don't feel right in these places," he murmurs to a member of his party. "Do you? I don't know how everything works. Help me not mess up, okay?"

We are a party of four, including Michael, the vice president in charge of publicity at Epic Records, and her husband. None of us has much previous acquaintance with the guest of honor, or his meek mien.

"Oh no! I better not do anything like *that*," Michael asserts when asked if he'd like to order wine or a drink. When his Caesar salad is placed before him, he looks down at the plate, then at his silverware, and begins eating each dripping leaf with his spidery fingers, oily dressing accumulating on the tablecloth.

Jackson tucks his linen napkin deeper into the collar of his charcoal T-shirt, and then shrinks from the maître d's solicitous main-course inquiries—"Some excellent chicken cordon bleu? Or escargot? Quiche lorraine?"

No reply. Around the table, there is a long moment of overlapping miscomprehension. Finally, Michael fills the silence with a breathy, barely audible question: "What's *qweech*?"

A previously ordered wedge of the cheese-and-custard pie is rushed to the table. Michael, stabbing his fingers into the steaming wedge, gathers up a gooey hunk and ingests it in one hasty gulp. "It's like ham and eggs!"

Michael Jackson has been in New York City a mere two weeks—the longest stretch he's ever spent in America's urban Oz—and it is having a discernibly profound effect on the fellow. The matter that lured the starved man-child to Manhattan from Los Angeles in August 1977 is *The Wiz,* the Universal-Motown film production of the long-running black Broadway musical that was based on L. Frank Baum's 1900 book fantasy, *The Wonderful Wizard of Oz.* Michael has been selected to play the Scarecrow, the acutely insecure stuffed effigy who comes to life—and to the realization that he possesses a serviceable intellect—under the auspices of a lost little girl named Dorothy.

Shooting for *The Wiz* is set to begin in four weeks at the freshly renovated Long Island City, Queens, premises of Astoria Studios, where such twenties and thirties cinema classics as Rudolph Valentino's *Monsieur Beaucaire* and the Marx Brothers' *Animal Crackers* were filmed.

In the interim, it is Michael Jackson who seems a stranger in a strange land.

"I don't drive," he volunteers when some solo sight-seeing is proposed. "But I *love* cars. I like big old ones that make you feel protected. Not just some new Ford. I like the old Continentals."

He wants a Lincoln, not a Ford—just like the last president, a member of the dinner party quips, referring to Gerald Ford's defeat by Jimmy Carter in the last White House election race.

"Excuse me?" Michael probes in his tiny-tot treble. "Vice President Ford was a *president?* Really? Boy, I gotta keep up on these things!"

He is similarly unapprised of recent events that shook the foundations of the republic.

"I don't know much about Watergate," he concedes when asked, picking at the crust of a dinner roll. "It was terrible, wasn't it? I guess it was. Have you met Nixon? Is he happy? I saw him on TV last year, and he looked so unhappy!"

What are the ingredients for woeful isolation in the waning twentieth century? How does one become stranded in the center of a cyclone? Back in 1977, Michael Jackson lacked both the proximity and the presence of mind to compare notes with Richard M. Nixon. And Elvis Presley had been found dead in his bathroom only the week before.

Certainly the Jackson clan lacked the mettle to give Michael any counsel. By her own admission, mother Katherine Jackson had been too frightened of his precocious will to insist he do so much as *eat* on a daily basis! So he turned inward. Which means he postponed generous portions of his own maturation. Which means he became his own worst enemy.

The Jackson 5 were never given the critical attention of more sophisticated Motown stars like the Temptations. Yet they were surely the most original act on the label. Their hyperharmonic cadences, paced by Michael's piercing falsetto, were an ingenious rhythm and blues merger of streetcorner soul-caroling and the drills of the black drum-and-bugle corps that were an inner-city staple in the Midwest. Capping this hybrid was a sassy dash of the histrionic funk normally seen in the rowdier of the Chitlin Circuit saloons.

That numberless kids had cottoned to the Jackson 5's physical cuteness was secondary to the incendiary adult verve of a track like "I Want You Back," whose ticklish cross-rhythms would pose a vocal minefield for singers less adept than the Jackson boys. Despite a glut of imitators, few have even bothered covering the actual Jackson 5 repertoire, because it's too damned difficult to approximate, let alone rival. Like them or not, there was no yardstick for the Jackson 5's art but their own output.

It was openly deliberated by the record people handling Michael Jackson back in 1977 whether his demeanor was an intricate put-on. Upon realizing it was not, their posture shifted to discreet alarm, and a screening mentality toward the media took hold. Susan Blond, the Epic executive at the Georges Rey dinner, was chary about further press access to Michael.

By 1983, when Michael Jackson was well on his way to becoming a phenomenon, there was too much control on the inside and too much wrongheaded protectiveness on the outside to help matters. Everyone with entrée was treading lightly as the singer was beginning his surreal ascent, and few wanted to further addle a human cash register. As the twig is bent, so the tree inclines, knots and all.

Reading the reputable accounts of Michael's progress through the pop wilderness as sales of *Thriller* soared, one felt that, in their gauzy descriptions of his E.T.-like status, they were often fueling the problem. The most widely circulated comment on Michael's strange daze was Steven Spielberg's kindly obfuscation: "It's a nice place Michael comes from. I wish we could all spend time in his world." Oh? If so, why didn't anyone accede to Jackson's alleged plea to reshoot all of his scenes in Disney's *Captain Eo* to include his umpteenth physiognomic alteration—an odd chin cleft?

Not since Elvis has there been such a cautionary tale of one performer's inky dance with illusion, or one with a more unfathomable ending. All anybody knew for sure at the time was that Michael was off to see the Wizard.

The Dorothy character in the *The Wiz* was due to be embodied by the thirty-four-year-old Diana Ross, the foremost black performer of the era, and a triple threat (recording artist—nightclub diva—Oscar-nominated screen actress for *Lady Sings the Blues*) who appeared primed to merge her accumulated skills into megastardom in the $20 million movie musical. Yet from the first lavish New York press conference for *The Wiz,* something was unavoidably amiss in the star-stoking machinery. Just before Ross made her entrance from the side of Astoria Studios serving as the urban sweatshop of Evilene, the Wicked Witch of the West, an Afro-topped spindle named Jackson sauntered into the photographers' view. Gliding with a heel-clicking casualness under the brick and granite portico where Groucho Marx and Gary Cooper had once passed, Jackson bestowed a bell-like "Hello!" and a buoyant wave to the thronged correspondents.

His unaffected charm shattered the pervasive aura of practiced glamour like a thunderclap—and it shamed the pretentions of the painted lady sweeping in just behind him. No one present will likely forget the precise instant the former juvenile shouter from the Jackson 5 eclipsed the rapacious ex-Supreme. Crossover soul had its beguiling new cynosure, a nonchalant arriviste who was part camp scamp, part funky will-o'-the-wisp.

Throughout the Big Apple, the buzz around this bean pole was deafening. Everybody had known the adenoidal R&B bantling of yore, but who was this Thin Black Duke?

It was an open question, and so it remains. No entertainment figure in modern times had reached the threshold of mainstream fame with greater gifts of enthrallment. Unlike Elvis at his early peak, Michael was not an intuitive novice, near-oblivious to the depth of his own skills. Rather, he was an acutely polished veteran of the footlights. His ten years of roadwork fronting the Jackson 5 soul calliope had seen them forge new standards of hit potential: four straight No. 1 singles out of the box in 1969–70—"I Want You Back," "ABC," "The Love You Save," "I'll Be There"—with a dozen other chart successes to follow.

But the fifth son of arc welder–crane operator Joseph Walter Jackson and Katherine Esther "Kitty" Jackson's nine children was a textbook case of arrested personal development, adroit to a fault on the high wire of his own ambitions, yet utterly hapless as a social being in the slack pulse of ordinary existence.

After an initial four-hour conversation at the handsome, mirror-walled Upper East Side apartment being rented for Michael and younger sister LaToya, I talked with him by phone and in person three more times during *Wiz* director Sidney Lumet's thirteen-week shooting schedule.

The Michael Jackson of 1977 was a wholly untempered individual, as oblivious to national and local headlines as he was to etiquette in a public eating establishment. Separated from the tools and terrain of his expertise, he had little sense of himself. Indeed, he regarded the offstage Michael Jackson as a phantom, a formless creature who cast no reflection, left no worthy trace.

Seeking to get to the basis of his exquisite detachment from all things earthbound, I interviewed Joseph Jackson, who proved as dour and forbidding as Michael was benign.

A native of Fountain Hill, Arkansas, Mr. Jackson was raised in Oakland, California, and settled in Gary, Indiana, in his late teens, marrying at age twenty. He and wife Katherine made their home at 2300 Jackson Street, rearing the kids according to the harsh Lutheran rubrics inherited from his own schoolteacher dad, Samuel Joseph Jackson.

"My father was very strict," the broad, muscular Joe Jackson explained brusquely. "He really went to us. I'm glad that happened. I might not have been able to do the things I do without a strict raising."

What Mr. Jackson had done was act as chief taskmaster and field marshal for the Jackson 5, coaching them since 1967 in musical skills he'd acquired while heading a bar band in his youth.

"I saw the potential in them being stars," he said, "*big* stars. And so we worked toward that goal, and they had to be talked to all the time, with a skillful hand. With an iron hand. There's other interests in life other than just singing and dancing, and the Jacksons used to play a lot of team sports. All of them, in fact, except Michael, who was strictly show business.

"They had entertainment," he concluded curtly, "and they had me to rehearse them. Everybody can't be as lucky as the Jacksons."

But the professional and domestic tranquility of his brood had been ruptured in March 1976, when the Jackson 5 exited Motown (and moved to Epic Records) in a climate of mutual acrimony. Fourth son Jermaine had elected to stick with "The Corporation," since he'd recently wed Motown President Berry Gordy, Jr.'s daughter Hazel. The youngest Jackson boy, Randy, was recruited to fill Jermaine's slot, and Motown's ownership of their original stage name compelled them to become the Jacksons. Lawsuits erupted. Motown sought $20 million in damages from Epic parent company CBS Records. Eventually they received $600,000 in damages and sole rights to the name the Jackson 5.

When I met Michael, he and his brothers had just completed *Goin' Places,* the crucial sequel to their much-ballyhooed 1976 Epic debut, *The Jacksons. Goin' Places* was only the second LP to contain songs by group members (during the Motown years, song material and publishing were consigned to a corporate writing staff). While their Epic debut yielded such favored radio fare as "Enjoy Yourself" and "Show You the Way to Go," *Goin' Places* was a stiff—as Michael had privately dreaded—from the day it was pressed.

After two albums, the Jacksons broke away from the tutelage of independent Philadelphia International producers Kenny Gamble and Leon Huff (who'd done so much for the O'Jays) and produced themselves on *Destiny,* a superb 1978 release that included the radiant rug-cutter "Shake Your Body (Down to the Ground)." It climbed as high as No. 7 on the *Billboard* survey, then stalled.

For Michael's part, he was proud of *Destiny* as it took shape, but from the day we were introduced in the summer of 1977, he made it plain that his first priority was a pathfinding solo album that would erase any popular memory of the ones (*Got to Be There*; *Forever, Michael*; etc.) he did for Motown. "I hear an ideal record in my mind, maybe with Quincy [Jones, who produced the original-cast-soundtrack LP of the film version of *The Wiz*]," he mentioned at the tail end of one of our phone conversations. "We'll see."

That "ideal record," released the week before Michael Jackson turned twenty-one, was the Quincy Jones–coconstructed *Off the Wall.* It would go on to sell some nine million–odd copies on the strength of the singles "Don't Stop 'Til You Get Enough," "Rock with You," "Off the Wall," and "She's Out of My Life," the first (and best) of which was written entirely by Michael.

Off the Wall was just as startling for the portrait photo on its jacket cover: a suddenly thin-nosed, squared-jawed Michael Jackson had surfaced, his revised visage resembling an amalgam of the Scarecrow's features and those of *The Wiz*'s female costar. The surgical hunt was on for a mask Michael could live with, and all natural development in his personal and professional life had come to a grotesque close.

After nearly two years of relative seclusion, Michael reappeared as a solo performer, peddling a torrid album that boasted intoxicating terpsichorean fare about illegitimate children, gang violence, and youthful seduction. When *Thriller* hit the stores in 1982, its presence proved incendiary, luring legions of buyers into record shops. Vivid, dramatic videos shot for "Beat It" and "Billie Jean" helped accelerate the stampede to the cash register when they were shown on Warner Amex's twenty-four-hour MTV cable network. Consumer obsession with the lanky new superstar expanded beyond measurability after he appeared on a reunion-like 1983 TV special marking Motown Records' twenty-fifth anniversary. The gala program was taped and aired for the press, but not one reporter foresaw the reaction viewers would have to Michael Jackson's performance. After a Memory Lane medley with his brothers, he launched into a breathtaking song-and-dance rendition of "Billie Jean," his narrowed eyes flashing near-sinister sparks as he slithered through a sexually ambiguous *danse de force* highlighted by slippery "moon walk" pantomime, breakneck spins, and balletic toe stands. (Michael's choreography seemed influenced, to a startling—moon walk-included—extent, by Bob Fosse's portrayal of the Snake in the 1974 film version of *The Little Prince.*) Home viewers' awe with the unexpected number swept the country by word of mouth, and kids flocked to buy the single.

His young fans screamed and swooned and bought more albums when director John Landis unveiled the *Night of the Living Dead*–inspired video for "Thriller." Then Michael's hair caught fire while filming a pyrotechnic sequence of a Pepsi commercial. He was rushed to the hospital with second- and third-degree scalp burns. Over 700,000 copies of the album were sold in a single week following the accident.

By the middle of 1984, *Thriller* had sold more than 30 million records worldwide, earning a place in the Guinness Book of World Records that demanded an almost daily update. He signed a $1 million deal for a biography to be edited by Jacqueline Onassis. An eleven-inch replica of himself was the sensation of the American Toy Fair. At the twenty-sixth annual Grammy Awards, Jackson collected an unprecedented eight awards for *Thriller.* During commercial breaks, millions saw the finished Pepsi ad. There was no place left to hide from Michael Jackson, and, very nearly, vice versa.

In a climate of extreme expectation, anxiety, envy, greed, and desperation, strained ties of old began to cut deeply, while more recent ones were broken off. Ron Weisner and Freddy DeMann, the management team hired by Joe Jackson, were summarily dismissed. Joe made racist asides about no longer needing "white help" as go-betweens with CBS Records. Michael denounced his father's remarks in a statement to *Billboard* magazine: "To hear him talk like that turns my stomach." Promoter Don King got flagrant in his boasts of control over Michael's destiny; he too was brought up short in a pointed epistle from Michael's office. He could take no actions concerning Michael without advance formal approval from the singer himself. Period.

Even Michael's heroes and role models faded into insignificance: The Emotions . . . Jackie Wilson . . . Sly Stone, whose funk-rock dance stylings fascinated Michael. Cynical comparisons of wealth, canniness, impact, and artistic contributions were drawn in the international press; the defunked Sly Stone was relieved of his connections to his musical legacy as Michael Joe Jackson officially acquired the rights to the dissolute soulrocker's publishing catalog.

Resounding through all these actions was the icy echo of doors being slammed shut and sealed over, of the engineering of an autonomy and an exquisite isolation that beggars description. Michael passed more and more of his idle hours in self-enforced confinement. Michael was a Jehovah's Witness; but problems inherent in the public proselytizing his religion requires soon rendered the practice all but prohibitive; there were fewer and fewer neighborhoods whose residents didn't own his records, didn't display posters of his likeness, didn't give their children miniature Michaels to play with.

After the Jacksons' chaotic 1984 *Victory* tour satisfied any perceived obligations to his brothers (actually, while the *Victory* LP sold adequately, the shows near the tour's end would fail to sell out), Michael withdrew from the fold. Some of his precious few friendships would be snuffed or worse by insensitive business attitudes, a case in point being the cunning outbidding of Paul McCartney for the $47.5 million ATV Music publishing company, which owns the Beatles' songs. (After a lifetime of work and financial reorganization, it was probably McCartney's sole shot at owning his own compositions.)

Why Michael Jackson embarked on his irreversible path is difficult to grasp. There may be clues in his complex relationship with his parents. (He's left the town of Encino—long the family seat—buying a home in Sycamore Valley, California, and no longer speaks to his father.)

Michael had sought for years to conform to the ascetic, proselytizing regimen of his mother's Jehovah's Witness faith, but the violence and sexual imagery in his music precipitated a parting with the denomination. He also gave up grappling with his dad's overbearing management tack.

Jackson located fresh career guides in (short-lived) major domo manager Frank Dileo, and recently replaced attorney John Branca—both fiercely tough men who excel at keeping the world at bay on their clients' behalf. Michael has announced that he will never give another interview, and contact with the bulk of humanity will henceforth be confined to what few personal appearances are required to smooth business deals.

Early in 1990, CBS Records presented Michael Jackson with a plaque to commemorate worldwide sales of over 110 million units for Jackson's *Off the Wall, Thriller,* and 1987 *Bad* albums and their numerous hit singles. The company also announced the proposed fall 1990 release of *Decade 1980–1990,* an album anthology (with companion home video) that will include five new songs Jackson himself describes as "some of the best things I ever recorded."

If the goal is fame, the battle is won to a fare-thee-well. If the aim is music, Michael Jackson has never made a "bad" record, and his latest output has been crafted to almost soulless perfection. If the intent is happiness, it can only arrive in realms of mundane risk and chance, places Michael no longer frequents. And yet if someone so well-known, admired, and essentially harmless (to others) as Michael Jackson cannot find a full measure of cheer and contentment during his allotted span, then the human equation in our culture has been diminished to a degree more deplorable than any rearrangement of his facial features.

The mysteries of Michael Jackson's sexuality, or the reasons why he owns a hyperbaric chamber and covets the Elephant Man's remains, are minor puzzles. The important riddle is: Why has this young man labored tirelessly to fix everything but the facets of his life that do not work?

As Michael continually repeated to me when detailing his ongoing fascination with the Scarecrow role, "My character knows that something is wrong with the way he sees things, but he can't quite put his finger on it."

In my time with him during 1977, he seemed to bring out the nanny, big brother, and baby-sitter latent in everyone, particularly in catering to his mercurial mood swings, which ranged from bubbly to contritely depressed. His retainers, hired or spontaneously self-appointed, were never actively solicited or dispatched by him, because he gave them little notice.

Those people in his largely professional circle of awareness who were acknowledged were either "good," "great," or they were nothing at all. The two words were spoken as sound, logical appraisals, without shades of meaning. In his polite tolerance of new arrivals or short-time visitors to his claustrophobic sphere, there was an air of condescension, awkwardly assumed. And beneath that, something more: an icy, largely distracted resolve, and a drive beyond ambition.

Michael Jackson earned international fame, respect, and affection as a symbol of enlightened self-discipline. Now he earns perverse notoriety as a paragon of elaborate self-denial. Within and between the lines of this interview are some of the roots of one battered spirit's blind search for love and dignity. In his own bewildered way, Michael Jackson has always known that you simply don't stop till you get enough.

Are you happy with the new Jacksons album, Goin' Places?

[*Cautious, nodding*] Umm hmm.

Your last album was the first one called The Jacksons, *right? It got a lot of play in discos.*

Yes. It did very well. They released a single ["Show You the Way to Go"] from that album in London, and it did very well. Went to No. 1. It was No. 1 for like two weeks in a row. And now they released "Dreamer" from that album. It's one of my favorite ones from that album. It's a ballad 'n' all.

"Goin' Places" is supposed to be the single from the new album?

So far, they've chosen it.

Who chooses it? You?

Kenny Gamble, the producer, and the president of Columbia [Walter Yetnikoff].

Do you have any influence?

We talk to the guys and everything, you know, and tell them. Because they know we know what's good, and we know what the kids wanna hear. We dance, and we're out there all the time while they're in their offices. [*grinning impishly*] So they know they better listen to what we say.

Are you hot for dance singles these days?

Yes. Both—ballads and dance singles. I just love to see the kids have a good time when the music come on. Sometime I sneak into this skating rink when they put them jams on. And you can tell when something dirty: the kids be kicking in. Soon as there's something hot—*ow!*—they break out. Which is important, because people like to dance and have a good time.

Speaking of ballads, I think back to "Ben." ["Ben" was written for the 1972 horror film Ben *(the sequel to 1971's thriller about befriending rats,* Willard) *by composer Walter Scharf and lyricist Don Black. The recording session was coproduced by Freddie Perren, Fonce Mizell, Deke Edwards, and Berry Gordy, Jr. Michael Jackson had no credited role in creating the song.] Even though it was No. 1 in 1972, a lot of people don't know the song's about a rat. They haven't seen the film, so they see the song as a ballad about friendship.*

Umm hmm. I like it both ways.

How do you mean?

I mainly like it as a record. I *love* rats. And I like it as a friend, too, as if I'm talking to a guy that's a friend of mine—[*blushing smile*] but none *other* than just a friend! Some people see it the rat way. Some people see it the friend way. It works both ways.

You're big on rats?

I *love* them. I used to raise them.

White rats? You raised them at home?

Yeah. In cages and things.

You've gotten out of it now?

[*Nodding*] You know, 'cause rats have weird characteristics. [*very sheepishly*] They start eating one another. They really do. It just got sickening to me, and I just said forget it. I came home one night and looked in the cage, and the rats had started eating each other. The *father* was eating the babies. I got sick of looking at it all and left their cage outside. I didn't realize how cold it was. The rats, still alive, froze to death. [*laughs*] I don't mind talking about it, if you don't. Do you?

Plus, in Beverly Hills there's a lot of snakes. I almost got bit by one rattlesnake because of the rats. See, when you live up in the hills, that's what happens.

The rats draw snakes?

Umm hmm! Tremendously.

And it was cold enough in Beverly Hills one night to freeze the rats?

Yeah, oh yeah. See, it's high *up.* There was a strange mist around, a rainy type of coldness, and the snakes started coming out of the ground to get the rats. I guess I got caught in the middle of this thing. It was awful! [*laughs*]

How many rats did you have?

Oh, I had quite a few. A lot of them. My mother hated it. I was up to about thirty rats.

Do they reproduce quickly?

[*Grimaces*] *Weirdly* quickly! You wake up one morning, and you see all these little things crawling around. It's fun, anyway.

Nobody clued you in on the rats' habit of eating each other?

Nope. I just saw it when they ate the babies. I shoulda separated the father from his children. I'd never see that deal. I had no idea, no idea. I don't think anybody knows the reason why—it doesn't exist; if they did say it, it's not a good enough reason.

Well, let's go back to the film. How were you approached to do the Scarecrow in The Wiz?

I was sitting at home one day, and the phone rings.

Home in Beverly Hills?

No, we don't live in Beverly Hills no more. We moved. See, we built this studio. And where we were staying we had a lot of room, but it wasn't enough. We always wanted to build a studio, 'cause we were rehearsing in our garage in Beverly Hills and the neighbors complained. And so we moved to Encino, in the San Fernando Valley, got a lot more room now, and we built a studio in our house, and so now we record and do a lot more stuff in that house. That's what it's great for.

But anyway, getting back: I was sitting at home and the phone rings from our office, and they say, "Hey, Michael! How would you like to do *The Wiz*?" I said, "Well, where'd you get this news from?" He said, "Well, in New York City Rob Cohen and Sidney Lumet called." I said, "Yeah! I'd like to do it!"

The only reason why I said yes was because I knew a lot about the production and getting it together. And I knew it was some of the best people in the film industry working on this thing. Sidney Lumet is the hottest director of the time.

Had Diana stepped into the project at this time?

[*Laughing*] Oh yeah. I had called Diana up in Las Vegas, and she was telling me that she was gonna go to New York and film it, and I said, "Well I hope the best for you!" Next thing I know is I'm *in* the film!

So what sort of preparations have you made to play the Scarecrow? I assume you saw the old Wizard of Oz *movie?*

Oh yeah, I have it on videotape. I watch it sometimes and just turn the sound down and watch the moves. When you see the old one, you realize—I had to say this—but you realize that they didn't bring out what they should have brought out. That's what *The Wiz* is all about—it's bringing out what Frank Baum, the writer, was really trying to say, in this movie. You can see where a lot was thrown out. We make it more recognizable to people what the story is all about.

Give me an example.

Well, the different characters, the Scarecrow with the brain thing. He *think* he doesn't have a brain, but he does. All the time it's there, but he don't know it. The whole thing is bringing *it* out.

What I do as the Scarecrow is, I don't think I'm smart and everything. And all through the movie I be bringing out these quotations from out of my sleeves 'n' all. See, I'm *garbage* instead of straw; I'm filled with the stuff. And I'm reading these quotations from all over me about such and such: "Confucius said this." But I *still* think I'm ignorant.

So it will have a larger social impact than a whimsical kid's story?

[*Solemnly*] *Umm hmm.* It's a *strong* movie. Some people will see it as a kid's film, but it isn't. You can follow it as you go through your life. That's the main answers to life—with that whole movie. I mean you can just follow life with that movie. It's deeper than what people really think it is.

Have you read the original book?

[*Embarrassed*] I know I should. I was supposed to read it, but I haven't had the time.

If you do, you'll find it's not precisely a children's book. Diana Ross recently made the point that it never mentions how old Dorothy is.

Dorothy's not really in the story at all. Not that much. It's just the way MGM did it that makes people think she's a big part of it.

[*Excited*] You can find so many great things in *The Wiz* about life. There are so many smart people walking around that don't know they're smart, don't *believe* in themselves. It's helpful for that too.

That's what the Scarecrow is all about. He's a smart guy! There's these crows that come every day and jive me and say I'm dumb, I'm ignorant, I can't walk, I can't do this. And they're so cool they just walk into my garden and take advantage of me. I'm begging them, "Can't I get down just for one second and walk in the garden?" They say, "Man, you can't walk!"

One day my break comes when Dorothy helps me down. I've been reading all these quotes that show how smart I am, but I really don't know it. I know something's wrong with what they're telling me, but I can't put my finger on it, and something's still wrong.

It just brings out more. It's more of a city story. Instead of straw, it's garbage. The tin man is all kinda cans: peanut butter cans, and this and that. Toto is like a German shepherd puppy. It's really great; this is great!

It's a fantasy look, too. When I say we're gonna be on location, a lot of people think we're just gonna look real-to-life. With a sky like this one [*points out the window*]. No, we're gonna give it a real fantasy look. Some of the scenes will have 600 dancers! It's a $12 million production! That's how much they're spending.

What do you enjoy most about the filming?

[*Very softly*] I love the amazing makeup and all the costumes and all the excitement. And I love the dance sequences. We got some dance sequences gonna knock people down! [*giggles*]

Are they working you too hard?

Not at all. It's just the opposite. I never want to stop. Sometimes I even come home in my makeup!

You're that attached to the character?

[*Nodding slowly*] It takes a long time to put it on my face, but I like how *different* it feels. I can be in a whole 'nother place with it. Sometime I wear it home, and people—kids—I look out the back window of the car and let them see me. Whoa, they get frightened! They don't know who or what it is! It's a trip, it's really a trip. [*softly, guardedly*] It's a secret; that's it. I like that it's a secret.

[*Relaxing*] It's just a warm feeling inside, like I can do anything he does, and everybody will dig it. Because once he comes down from the pole in that corn patch, everybody appreciates the Scarecrow.

You've never done a film before, have you?

I've done so much acting but never in a film.

How do you mean?

Well, all the variety I've done, and different sketches on TV shows. I've done so much, you know, long sketches. I've done "The Flip Wilson Show" and "Carol Burnett," all that stuff, "Sonny and Cher." But I've never done a movie. This is the first one.

Are you scared?

No. Not at all, not at all. Honest to God, I'm not. I'm challenged. I love it. I'm not scared at all.

Even when I was very small, all I wanted to do was get into this performing kind of thing. But no matter how many movie offers come to me, music will always be my No. 1 thing. Because it's inside of me, and it's something that has to come out. And it's still in there.

[*Smiling shyly*] Like when I'm going over my script, music just comes into my head, and songs, and I run to the tape recorder and put melodies on tape. *Constantly.* Not to wait for a piano for stuff, because I can't help it. I can't. I *got* to have it.

What was the first time you performed?

It was in a shopping center, the Big Top, in Gary, Indiana. It was at a grand opening. All the people come around and buy the season fashions. We agreed to be in front of the mall, in the middle of it, and sing. And that's what we did.

You must have done some performing before that, to have that come about.

[*Mulling*] Yeah, but you know, I can't remember. I wasn't even thinking about that. I just *did* it. I was about six. I got started around five.

What is your earliest memory of performing? Did someone, your father maybe, take you by the hand and ask you to sing?

No, we were just singing around the house, old folk songs, "Cotton Fields Back Home" and [*sings*] "Down in the Valley . . ." We used to wake up singing.

We had bunk beds, and I would shack up with Marlon, and Tito would shack up with Jermaine, and Jackie would have his own on top. We would just sing every morning.

See, my father had a group, with his brothers, the Falcons. And Tito would sneak his guitar and play it when he'd go to work.

When he got caught, Tito would get in so much trouble for playing Dad's guitar. One day Tito broke a string, and my father got so mad at Tito, he got so mad at him, so angry, he said, "Lemme see what you can play! If you can't play that, I'm a really *beat* you!"

Tito was scared, but when he *could* play, my father was shocked. He was so good, by just sneaking and playing. My father thought, *Well, there's some kind of talent here,* and he started saving up money, buying instruments and microphones and amplifiers.

We would do talent shows in the neighborhood in Gary, and later at the high school. [*proudly*] We would always win every one. We have all these trophies in our house, all over the place.

One day Gladys Knight told a guy named Bobby Taylor at Motown about us, and Motown got ahold of us. We did a show on

Berry [Gordy]'s gigantic estate in Detroit, around the poolside. *All* the Motown stars were there: Diana Ross, the Temptations, everybody. They loved us, and we recorded our first record, "I Want You Back," a three-million-seller. And we went on and on.

How old were you when you got the first hit?

On "I Want You Back" I was ten, but our *very* first one was a record [in 1968] called "I'm a Big Boy Now" on Steeltown, and it was a Gary, Indiana, company. It was a local hit.

Who wrote "Big Boy"?

[*Frowning, shrugs*] Boy, I don't know.

Do you remember how the song goes?

[*Brightening, smiling*] Yes. It's a good melody! It goes: [*sings*] "Fair-y tales, fair-y tales, have lost their charm. Da-da-da, da-da-da, a-da-da-da. 'Cause I'm a big boy now!" It's a good melody. It'd be a hit today, really. [*insistent*] It could! You know, a lot of these people, they take these old songs and say the same thing, thinking, "The *kids* don't know it."

Sure, Rita Coolidge has a hit now with "Higher and Higher."

That's right, that Jackie Wilson hit! People don't know, but they take those old songs and bring them back, and everybody think it's something new—when it's *old.* And I'm just listening to them and thinking, "My *mother* usta put on these records!"

So your father had a band called the Falcons, right? How much do you know about his band?

Well, it was his three brothers [the band had five members], and they were a little group from the South, with guitar, bass, and drums. Dad's from the South—Arkansas. I don't know what city.

Did he ever tell you any stories about the early days playing with the Falcons?

No. I don't think he needs to talk about it. We haven't talked about it. He's *never* talked about it. All we know is that he had a group. We know he was a good player, because they played in Gary when we were little. Then they were split up, but he would just grab his guitar and start playing . . .

. . . around the house?

Uh huh. And his brother played guitar very well, too. They would be jamming at the house, playing the blues and stuff. They all helped Tito learn how to play.

How many people in your dad's family, meaning brothers and sisters?

I think it was about four. I think there's three left.

Was your mom from Arkansas, too?

No. Alabama.

How did your dad meet your mom? Did they ever tell you that story?

[*Shy giggle*] They won't! Kitty starts blushing over the whole thing. I mention it, and she starts blushing. She says, "Now, why you wanna ask that?" I think it was in high school or something, when he was young.

You really don't know anything about how your parents met and courted?

[*Softly*] I don't know anything about it. They won't discuss it. [*giggles*] It's hard to *picture.*

How do you get along with your father?

[*Glancing away*] He's—he can be very hard . . . sometimes. You don't wanna be gettin' him mad. He's strict, but we never object. That's how he wants it, so we go along. He shows us the value of work and hard effort.

So your very first public performance was in a shopping center?

Well, I sang at my school, a long, long time ago. At a P.T.A. meeting I sung "Climb Every Mountain." And boy, did I hear some applause. Those claps, I can still hear them now—really. All the teachers were there. I felt proud. I was five. I think my music teacher taught me the words.

I had a music class, but I never paid attention in that class. [*laughs*] I went to the Garnet Grammar School on Garnet Street. We lived on Jackson Street. Pure coincidence.

What was it like being so young and traveling around performing in those early days?

We had our own van. It was some great times. I would sit in the wings and watch the other acts, on and on. I would watch every step Jackie Wilson made on the stage. I'd hear them say, "Jackie Wilson!" And he would take that coat off and strut around! I would sit there and watch every step and just *learn.* Every show, I would run down just to watch him take the stage.

We had our own band, and we would tour with the O'Jays when there used to be four O'Jays, and the Emotions—we been knowing them girls for *years.* We always knew they were great, and now they're just happening. People say, "Oh them. A new group." I'd say, "That's what you think. They been around a *long* time."

Were these tours package deals a record company put together?

I don't think they were on our company [Motown]. They just did the shows. We'd tour the East: We did the Regal Theater in

Chicago, the Apollo in New York, the Uptown in Philadelphia. That's mainly the ones I remember.

Where do you play now when you tour?

We just finished a big concert tour; we were in England. We did a command performance for the queen in Scotland, and we went to Germany, to Paris, to Holland. I wish we could have filmed it, because we keep a catalog of shows. I'll never forget my first "Hollywood Palace Show"—or the first time we were on "The Ed Sullivan Show." I got it on tape. I'll show you.

[*He gets up from his chair and goes to his large, shelved tape library.*]

Is that a Star Wars *cassette you've got there?!*

Yeah! Barry White, who's on 20th Century Fox Records, got it for us. It's so hard to get into that movie.

But anyway [*cuing up 1970 "Ed Sullivan" tape*], Motown would tape all their TV shows, but CBS dubbed this one up for me.

I'll never forget the day I was walking the halls at the Ed Sullivan Theater. I walked past his dressing room—see, I'm always known for just looking around and seeing what each place is like; I always do that. And he calls me in, and he says he saw our rehearsal that day, and said, "No matter what you do, never forget to thank God for your talent." He looked me in the eyes. He was unique, he was really kind. Such a nice man.

[*Tape begins. Ed Sullivan, a bundle of nervous ticks and furtive movements, stands at stage right and announces, "From Gary, Indiana, here's the youthful Jackson 5, opening with a medley of their hits that have sold over a million, each, er, skit—hit!" The group begins performing "I Want You Back."*

Michael stands and stares at his younger, diminutive self on the screen, dressed in a garish citrus-colored vest and bell-bottoms, executing a series of intricate dance steps as he sings. Watching himself, the modern-day Michael appears riveted.]

Do you remember this song?

Are you kidding? Of course I do.

How old are you there?

Eleven.

The music was prerecorded, wasn't it?

[*Still watching as group goes into "ABC"*] I was singing live. The background is prerecorded. I always had to do that. I was always worried about these shows, because if you mess up, everybody see it. You had to be really on your toes.

[*The on-screen Michael goes into a superbly dexterous dance break, dipping, whirling, and shouting, "Sit down, girl! I think I love you. No! Get up, girl! Show me what you can do!" The other Jackson brothers lip-synch the backing chorus: "Shake it, shake it, baby." Then Michael sings the final refrain: "A-B-C, it's easy, it's like counting up to three. Sing a simple melody. That's how easy love can be!" The music stops, and Michael shouts, "A-B-C, girls!"*

Off-camera, throngs of little girls in the studio audience shriek.

ED SULLIVAN: *On July 7, these five brothers will begin their summer tour of one-nighters at Madison Square Garden, and they're gonna bust every record in the country. Wonderful to have you on our show!*

MICHAEL AND BROTHERS: *Thank you.*

ED SULLIVAN: *Right now, here they are singing "The Love You Save" from their new album,* ABC*!*

Little Michael's on-screen steps are spectacular during the opening instrumental passage of the track, the routine a tightly plotted explosion of springs, spins, shimmies, and jitterbugging fandangos. The real Michael looks bored, and shuts off the tape.]

When was the last time you watched this video clip?

[*Long, nervous pause*] I've watched it . . . before.

I recall seeing the Jackson 5 on TV in 1974, at the time of "Dancing Machine." You had a dance routine that was so wickedly hot. Do you put those things together yourself?

Do you mean the robot moves and all that? We always do all our own choreography. Michael, Marlon, and Jackie, us three do it.

You always had great moves. I'm sure you had a lot of people coming up to you and saying you were very skilled for your age. I don't know of any eleven-year-old kids who had that kind of poise.

[*Glum, exasperated*] For so many years I've been called a midget, a forty-five-year-old midget, and I was, like, six and five. And they would tell us how "great, great, great" we were, but could "never get the big head." We heard that so much. "*Never* get the big head." They were saying don't get too big for your shoes.

Have you ever gotten a big head?

Oh, no. No way. No way I could deal with that.

Why do you think that is? Because your father tells you to be cool? Or your brothers do?

Yeah. Good parents, and just, you know, how can you think you're better than somebody else? I mean, I do certain things that millions of kids out there will never get to see or do, but I shouldn't think I'm better than them. [*In a hush*] We're all human.

Have you ever had kids your own age approach you and remark on your amazing abilities? How would you react?

I'd just listen—and then get better and better.

I don't know what I was thinking back then. I'd just listen, say thanks, and keep on going, and not let it affect me terribly anyway. [*suddenly tense*] I'm just always trying to get better. That's all, really. I'm just telling you that all I'm trying to do is get better and better. Which I never stop doing. 'Cause when you stop growing—[*he cancels the thought*]. Boy, you *never* can stop growing. But some people do.

On TV you look sharply accomplished, even shrewd. And tough, almost like a grown man. But I meet you now, and there's a striking difference.

[*Smiling strangely*] That's true. People always tell me that. All the kids at school say, "Man, you're so much different onstage. I can't believe it's the same person." But I'm not really recognizing what people are telling me.

When I get onstage, I don't know what happens. Honest to God. It feels so good, it's like it's the safest place in the world for me. [*warily*] I'm not as comfortable now as I would be onstage, because I was raised onstage. That's all I did: travel and sing and dance and watch other people that were trying to do it.

At school, I didn't know how to *be* in class. Teachers would write home and say [*giggles*], "Michael comes to school to sleep." Because we would be up all night in the nightclubs, doing our acts and tours. When I'd get to school, that'd be my sleeping hours.

[*Confidential tone*] And my pockets would be *loaded* with money. Because people would throw money on the stage—the money, the change! We would have $300 lying on the stage, and we would make just $15 from the manager paying us. We'd go to school—whoa!—with all this money.

It was great, great times. [*dreamily*] I'll never forget those times. I write about them in songs.

I'm writing a *lot* now, too.

These days you're writing a lot of songs?

[*Nodding*] In the studio. I love to go into sessions and listen. Whenever Stevie [Wonder] has a session, I'm always there. I sit and listen and *learn.* He's a great friend of mine, and I think he's one of the greatest guys around. He so much farther ahead of everybody; he's so good.

What kinds of topics are you writing about these days?

[*Cool, pensive*] I just *hate* everyday love songs. I'm interested in a different type of love song. I want a brand-new thought. That's what I love about "Ben." There's a mystery to it. You wonder, "What *is* this about?" I even got sick of it [*snigger*], so many people come up to me and say, "Why did you create such a song about a little stinkin' rat? But it's so beautiful! How'd you make it so beautiful if it's about a dumb rat?"

I said, "I don't know. I just felt it, because rats, they got a mind, they got a heart as well." I don't look at it that way. I *love* animals. I said, "*You* may not look at it that way, but I love animals."

I write about all kinda things. I write about an old man, a tree, what's happening in the world, a deer. I love writing so much I'd *eat* it, really. I love it!

Have you ever written a song about one very specific incident? You met someone, something very specific occurred, you wrote about it—and maybe it went on to be a hit?

Oh yeah. A song I'm writing now about traveling the world. It mentions, in the song, all the different countries and, to me, what they're like. And there are so many people around the world that *don't* get a chance to travel. And there are some that *do* want to travel but can't. And some that think the whole world looks like New York City, that the whole world is what *they* just picture. There are a lot of people like that.

Well, some do say that Europe is looking too much like America, from McDonald's hamburger stands on outward.

Oh, not to me. Did you go out in the country and stuff? Now, business *will* do that, but that different country and their society and their culture just creeps in anyway. The governments are different, and there's no way that could be like America. Of course, business will remind you—you look at McDonald's sometime and you forget that you're in England. But they even have McDonald's stands that look different! So there's no way: The culture is different, the government is different, the countryside is different.

Nonetheless, other countries put such a value on the American system—the way we think, the way we dress—because they consider us the most current in a lot of ways.

Americans got it made. They got it *made.* I don't think the different governments would let that happen. I know they have their ways of doing things, and they're completely different from what Americans do.

Have you ever been to Holland? Holland is the Europe that you *dream* about—I'm not just saying this. London, England's city, *can* look like New York—a little—but if you go to Holland, man, you know it's real Europe. And Scotland is—oh, I could eat it, it's so beautiful! You know *it's* not America.

Back to your records: Is there a big hit that came out of a personal experience I might not necessarily pick out from the song itself?

If so, I would write it out on the album jacket, and talk about it. See, we just started writing songs on our albums. Before, those songs were all by Motown producers. We would help in, but we would never mainly write the stories or anything. With our singing, we would help in. That's what so great about what we're doing now. We *will* be writing our own stuff, completely.

How about "Goin' Places"?

That was a tune Kenny Gamble [and Leon Huff] wrote. We wrote "Different Kind of Lady" and "Do What You Wanna." But they wasn't specific to something that happened in our lives.

See, I love the folk type of style music, the soul, and the rhythm going out funky. I like to mix those things. And I like easy listening. I like Bread, the Carpenters. I love Stevie Wonder and the Brothers Johnson—they are smelly, they are really *smelly.* "Strawberry Letter 23," that track is bad, isn't it? The lyrics are—*cripes,* they're so way out, they're crazy! I'm still trying to figure them out.

Have you ever seen Parliament-Funkadelic with their flying saucer–Dr. Funkenstein show? They're pretty off-the-wall.

I'm 'posta see them in concert. I *know* they crazy. But I'm gonna watch carefully to see if it's them that's good live, or just the scenery and special effects.

Was there one person who was a model or hero of yours when you were forging your own particular style?

I had those that I admired, like James Brown, a man that today don't get the credit he should get from the music industry. Look what he did to music: all these funky tracks that you hear today, that's where it came from. Sly Stone, James Brown, these are people that started funky music. They stood between the gospelly soul and the dance music. And that's *funk:* Sly, James Brown, and people like that. Wilson Pickett, Otis Redding. And of course in rock and roll, there's Little Richard and Chuck Berry and all those guys. That's who I would always watch. And Jackie Wilson—*yeow!*

Have you met James Brown?

I know James Brown. I met him long time ago at the Regal Theater. I don't remember exactly how—[*fretting*] how could I forget? I just remember him onstage gettin' down.

I talked with him during rehearsal at a Dick Clark music-awards show last year. He said, "I remember you back at the Apollo Theater. I'm the one who got you the gig! One of your biggest breaks!" I said, "Thank you." He read me the cash receipts from his last tour, and then he broke out into the aisle, sliding and doing the James Brown dance. And then he walked off. [*laughs*]

But you know, rock and roll, at one time, nobody even wanted to hear it. [*laughs*] They said, "What *is* this?"

Elvis was considered white trash for singing so-called race music in his billbilly style.

See, but when the blacks did it, they really wouldn't accept it. It's only a fact, and it's true. It turned around when people like Elvis did it, but it was there all the time. Blacks had been doing it for years.

Mostly everybody made fun of it. There's this book out called *Blues: The Devil's Music,* and it talks about the origination of blues, and how people just talked so *bad* about it. And look what it is today! Even with the rock and roll, as well. And jazz.

When did you go over to visit with Jackie Wilson?

When we did our album; we just finished it. Not too long ago, in Philadelphia, at the hospital. He really don't get the credit he should get. He's the man the big people of today in the music industry copy after. [After years of hospitalization following an onstage heart attack in 1975, Wilson died in 1984.]

Does that bother you?

Yes. I think it's an *awful* thing. 'Cause I like the people who really do something; they sweat and work for it and go through hell bringing it about. And the guy who takes it so quick [*loudly snaps his fingers*], he comes along and gets all the credit for it. I'm glad at least it took somebody to bring it about, but real people should get credit.

Same thing with artists that paint. It happens the same way—till they die, and *then* they get the recognition.

Have you ever felt that way about things you've done?

Yeah, a lot of things. [*giggles*] You know, I don't have to mention names. How do I feel about it? I feel it's a compliment in one way, and in another way [*voice drops to a whisper*] you be kinda *angry.*

[*Aggressive*] Because it's *yours.* We were the first young group out there with that style, making hit records. There were nobody out there at our age. We came across it, and then all of a sudden along came the Osmonds, the Partridge Family.

Now you have groups like the Sylvers! The Sylvers have the same producer that wrote all our hits, Freddie Perren. That's why they sound so much like us.

A lot of people that worked with the Osmonds said they would have videotapes on us and study us. They really patterned themselves after us, because they were singing barbershop on "The Andy Williams Show." They never were recording jams, poppin' soul, then—boom!—they were.

I heard "One Bad Apple" several times before I found out it wasn't you people.

[*Grinning fiercely*] I know! One lady walked up to me and said, "I got your new record." I said, "What?" She said, " 'One Bad Apple.' " I said, "Lady, why don't you *read* who's on the label?"

Did you know that record was ours at first? But Motown turned it down. George Jackson is the producer, and he came to Motown with it, and Motown turned it down. Because we were in a funky, strong track–type bag, with good melody. George's song was good, but too easygoing; we were striving for something much stronger. So he went and gave it to the Osmonds. [*Annoyed*] They sang it, and it was a smash—No. 1.

He had you in mind when he wrote it?

Sure! That's why it was mainly like us all the way. They sounded so much like us. I don't mind if somebody takes it and go farther with it. The only thing I *hate* is they take it and make like they started it. It's like a dog-eat-dog type of situation. I think it's *aw-ful.*

At least the Beatles did mention where they were influenced. They were great writers, on their own, but they *did* study black music.

'Cause Chuck Berry—who was it, Chuck Berry or Little Richard?—when the Beatles were coming up he saw them and he introduced them to a lot of people. A long time ago, the Beatles were on an all-black label [Vee-Jay]. The guy's name is [Ewart] Abner—I know him, he was president of Motown Records—and a long time ago, he had them! Then, after they went on from there, they were gigantic.

I love Paul McCartney. With his own records he proves he's the most talented Beatle. When you take any one of them away, it gets kinda weaker and weaker, but as a whole, it was always the best Paul—him and John Lennon were dynamite. I've been to two of Paul's parties, and we get together and talk.

He wrote a song for me, and I never get a chance to record it. Him and his wife were telling me about it. It's called "Girlfriend." ["Girlfriend" was included by McCartney on Wings' 1978 *London Town* album. Michael finally recorded the song in 1979 for his *Off the Wall* LP.] They were singing it to me, and they say they want to do it, too.

[*He sings*] "Girlfriend . . . boyfriend"—it was an easy thing. I remember him singing it. I'll never forget the melody. I can forget all kinds of things [*giggles*], but I never forget a melody.

This was a year ago. I've got some pictures here of the party. It was a *gigantic* party at the Harold Lloyd estate. It was a very good evening. All the stars were there! [*He pulls a voluminous black scrapbook off a nearby shelf and leafs through it.*] Lemme see. . . . This is when we met the queen. . . . This is at Paul's party at Harold Lloyd's estate, right around the time when Paul and his wife and I, we were talking about the "Girlfriend" song, and exchanging numbers and addresses.

That was one of the greatest parties I've ever been to, because when Paul gives a party he believes in just *going out!* It was a whole schedule: nine o'clock, you get to see the ballerina act. Ten o'clock, Chuck Norris, the karate expert, put on a show. At four o'clock in the evening [the Broadway company of] *The Wiz* would put on a show. There were all kinds of food! You want Mexican food, they had a Mexican stand, a Mexican lady. Italian, an Italian stand with an Italian man. American food, a buffet! Oh, man!

And that's more at Paul McCartney's party, where they had the *Wiz* show. . . . And John Belushi doing his Joe Cocker imitation at Paul's thing, too. Did you see the robot on summer TV specials? That was the same robot that was at Paul McCartney's party! That was the first time I had seen it. I said, "How does he work?" People went crazy over him. And that's my friend Tatum O'Neal. . . . And that's my nephew on my brother's side.

I left kinda early, but the party went on and on . . .

Do you keep a lot of scrapbooks like this?

[*Flashing a confused glance, continuing to thumb through it*] Not really. We have somebody in the business office who makes them up for me, and our own photographer to follow me and take the pictures. . . . That's my father's father, Samuel Jackson. . . . And that's the three brothers that had the band the Falcons: Lawrence, Joseph, and Luke. . . . Samuel Jackson still around the house; he sings and sings; he's still alive in Arizona. . . . And that's the first monkey on the moon! She's still alive today. Her name is Miss Baker. [*He points to an odd scrawl below the shot of the chimp.*] See, she "autographed" it. . . . It's good to look back and think. . . . There's Fred Astaire . . . and Minnie Riperton. . . . [*He puts scrapbook away.*]

Tomorrow, from when you wake up, what will your schedule for the day be like?

I get up at 9:00 A.M. or 8:30, and I work on *The Wiz* at the rehearsals until 5:30 P.M. Then I'm free, unless I have other appointments. I'm going to the Parliament-Funkadelic concert tomorrow, which is a form of freedom, but there's no way I can get away from the stage completely. I got to have it!

Certain people were created for certain things, and I think our job is to entertain the world. I don't see no other thing that I could be doing.

So many people do so many different things that they're good at. It seems like "He was meant to do that!" or "That's her job!" because of how they enjoy it. It's that way with me and entertainment, and it's strange, because our whole family is in on this thing. We *all* do it.

I notice the Bible over on the coffee table. Is your family especially religious?

We all believe in God, of course. [*giggles*] I study and read the Bible with my mother and sisters. I know there's a true and breathing God. A lot of people don't believe in that, but I know there's no way it can't be. There's *no way* it couldn't be; it's so true that there is a God, when you break it down: the universe, the beauty of the world, the sun.

But there's a lot of ugliness in the world, too, a lot of cruelty. Did God create that?

No! That's because of man! Man is because of the fallen angels. It says in the Bible that all this would happen, and it's all coming true.

It's easy to judge the world from the privileged safety of America. If you'd been to India, say, and seen the ugliness there . . .

I can't wait! That's what I *want* to see! I've seen the very rich and the very poor, but I'm mainly interested in the poor. I don't wanna think the whole world is just like what's around here. I want to appreciate what I have, and try to help others.

I know what the rich are like. I've studied that country India so much, and when I go to other countries, people say, "You wanna see the ugly part of it?" [*Nodding*] That's what I want to see!

What are you looking for?

[*Smiling*] I want to see what it's really like to *starve.* I don't want to hear it, or read it. I want to see it.

Why?

It's a whole different thing when you see it! All the things I've read in my schoolbooks about England and the queen were okay, but my very eyes are the greatest book in the world. When we did the royal command performance, and then after it I actually looked into the queen's eyes, it was the greatest thing! And it's the same thing with starvation!

[*Dreamily*] When you see it, you just receive a little more.

What would you say is the worst thing you ever saw in your life?

Well, can it be anything?

Sure.

It was probably during the hard days onstage. Some of the things I use ta see when we use to do nightclub acts. [*giggles*] You'll probably say, "Aw, that ain't nothing," but to me, especially at that age, I had never seen anything like it.

Seen what?

[*Giggling harder*] See, we used to do club shows, and there was this one lady—you probably know what she did—but I thought it was awful. I was around six, and she was one of those stripteasers, and she would take her drawers off [*giggles*], and a man would come up, and they'd start doing—aw, man, she was too funky! Ugh! That, to me, was *awful!*

Looking backward and forward, how do you feel about your body of work?

All those records in the past are our songs, and we've sung them, and we put our hearts into the *singing* of them, but they're really not from *us.* They're not *our* thoughts and what we think should go on that plastic, on that wax.

When I get into writing my own stuff, I'm gonna just let it *all* out. It's something I always wanted to do: Make it really *me!*

Speaking of your thoughts and your heart, do you have any girlfriends?

I'm too busy for dating and girls right now. I'd like to try, maybe. What do *you* think? Think I should, yeah? Well, I'll think about that. I'll think about what you said. We'll see. . . . But I'm happy.

You've certainly got the power to make yourself happy. People live their whole lives and don't find that power. Do you think you'll use it well?

[*Grim-faced, listing his thoughts on his fingers*] Okay. For starters, there's nothing inside of me that wants to come out but don't know how. I just let it all come out.

If there's something I'm not, I'll mention it.

I love children—crazy 'bout 'em.

I love music.

I'm looking forward to writing lots of songs and good material and putting it out and just doing my best.

So nothing's bothering me, because I got things that I want to do, and I know I can do them.

[*Adamant*] There's nothing inside killing me.

Filming The Wiz *and playing the Scarecrow seem to be the high points of your life thus far. Will you be sad to see it end?*

[*Musing, almost whispering*] Ohhh yeah. Sometimes, when I come home with my makeup, I keep dancing in front of the mirrors here as the Scarecrow. Or I get out of bed at night and do a few moves in front of the mirrors.

When I get into it, I forget everything else but the Scarecrow's world. It's a feeling of peace. It's just like . . . magic.

The Bee Gees

1979

Ahh, yes, *Saturday Night Fever.* I remember it well." Bee Gee Robin Gibb lifts a goblet of Perrier into the fiery sunset on Biscayne Bay. "*We* thought up the name," he boasts, swaying in time with the yachts tied up at the edge of his patio as he sits in the glass-enclosed living room of his rented Miami home.

"Robert Stickweed, er *Stigwood,* rang us up and said, 'Look, I need some music for this film I'm making with John Revolting and Olivia Neutron Bomb and'—oh, no, that was *Grease,* wasn't it? Okay, no harm done; I mean *Saturday Night Fever* with *no* Olivia. So anyway, Robert said, 'I haven't got any music!'

" 'Hmm,' I replied. 'That's a *nice* place to start.' "

Gibb doubles over in nasal cackling, greatly pleased with his impersonation of a pompous, disdainful rock superstar. Gibb can afford a few guffaws at his own empire's expense. He and fellow Bee Gees Barry and Maurice Gibb, working with the octopus-like entertainment network that is the Robert Stigwood Organisation, have risen, fallen, and risen again over the course of their twelve-year partnership. And now, the trio is one of the wealthiest, most successful, and certainly most pervasive musical forces in what group leader Barry solemnly calls "the pop wilderness."

The Bee Gees first attracted national attention in the late sixties with their mordant, adenoidal hymns to mining disasters, hapless lovers, self-delusion, and broken hearts. They have released more than thirty runaway hit singles, their output since 1975 consisting mostly of the buoyant, uptempo toe-tappers that helped spawn the billion-dollar disco industry. "Tragedy," the second No. 1 hit from the Bee Gees' *Spirits Having Flown* LP (their twenty-first U.S. album), is the British group's fifth chart-topper in a row, the longest such string since the Supremes had five in 1964–65 and the Beatles notched a streak of six in 1965–66. And when the Bee Gees themselves aren't ruling the nation's airwaves or commanding its cash registers, Barry Gibb and the Bee Gees' producers, Karl Richardson and Albhy Galuten, are doing as much for such singers as Frankie Valli, Samantha Sang, and especially baby brother Andy Gibb, all of whom have had No. 1 singles.

Whether it be through the *Saturday Night Fever* or *Grease* soundtracks, their own albums, or those of their beneficiaries, the Bee Gees' slick, bleating harmonies and pendulant rhythms have become an unignorable presence in our culture. All of which seems of only passing interest to Robin Gibb, twenty-nine, as he sips the wine brought to him by a sylphidine, redheaded secretary named Liz and surveys the golden sea lapping at the estates of his millionaire neighbors. Contrary to widespread assumptions, the Gibbs are not constantly obsessed with disco hooks, megadollar record sales, and platinum certification. While a winning lyric and catchy commercial melody are never far from Robin's mind, his interests are truly manifold. Attired in crisp aqua slacks, pure white patent-leather slip-on loafers, and matching cotton sweater, he is a tanned picture of near-angelic deportment as he warms to his favorite topic—pornography.

"To me, *Saturday Night Fever* sounds like some sleazy little porno film showing on the corner, second billed to a film called *Suspender Belts* or something," he says, going on to recount that the Bee Gees were holed up in Château D'Hérouville Studios outside Paris in 1977, mixing *Here at Last . . . Bee Gees . . . Live* and writing songs for a studio LP when Stigwood phoned with his immortal soundtrack assignment. As Robin tells it, the group had at that point already recorded "Stayin' Alive," "Night Fever," "How Deep Is Your Love," and "More Than a Woman," a revelation that contradicts the legend of the one-week marathon writing session that neatly filled Stigwood's tall order. Robin has been known before to get chronologies muddled, however, and Barry later disputes his younger brother's recollections with the calm assurance that he is "quite incorrect." But it's all neither here nor there as far as Robin's concerned, since his most vivid memories of the famed interlude in France are slightly offbeat.

"You know, years ago there were so many pornographic films made at the Château," he says intently. "The staircase where we wrote 'How Deep Is Your Love,' 'Stayin' Alive,' all those songs, was the same staircase where there've been six classic lesbian porno scenes filmed. I was watching a movie one day called *Kinky Women of Bourbon Street,* and all of a sudden there's this château, and I said, 'It's *the* Château!' These girls, these dodgy birds, are having a scene on the staircase that leads from the front door up to the studio. There were dildos hangin' off the stairs and everything. I thought, '*Gawd,* we wrote "Night Fever" there!' "

For the record, this unsettling discovery in no way precipitated Robin's studio hobby of scribbling highly imaginative, smutty line drawings. That was honed long ago and currently runs to grotesque, elf-like creatures who scurry about with enormous genitals and ravenous stares.

Somehow, the conversation segues into an appraisal of the recent Grammy Awards show, and Robin rolls his eyes as he reflects on John Denver's stiff-hipped rendition of one of the winning songs.

"When he started singing the nominations, I thought, 'Oh, no, he's *not* gonna start singing "Stayin' Alive"!' He was all right singing the ballads, but Denver didn't exactly have the same moves as John Revolting, did he? But he did go for two hours without saying, 'Far-out.' "

Speaking of awards, I note that "Last Dance," Donna Summer's scorching single from the *Thank God It's Friday* soundtrack, has been nominated for an Oscar, and in the process I reopen an old wound.

"Yes," Robin rejoins, "and that film was just a copy of *Saturday Night Fever,* wasn't it? Robert raised a helluva stink last year when they didn't nominate any of our songs from the film, but, well, they nominated *Grease* this year. They're trying to make up for what they didn't do last year, and you must remember that they are all very long in the tooth at the Academy and full of excuses. They said the album had only just come out back then; it was only 23 on the charts or something. But *Saturday Night Fever,* which sold 15 million copies in the United States, was to change music the way the Beatles once did. Before the Beatles, Mitch Miller had three or four albums in the Top 10!" He counts them off on his fingers. "Let's see, there was *Sing Along with Mitch, Hum Along with Mitch, Scratch My Balls with Mitch, Here's My Ass, Mitch* . . ."

Once again, Robin erupts into uproarious laughter, then dismisses the last half-hour's talk with a gulp of water and clearing of the throat. As night falls and the housekeeper begins to set the dining-room table for dinner, Gibb's mood turns somber and he details another of his nonmusical pastimes.

"I like to break boats up," he says with an uncertain chuckle. "I take a boat out and smash it up, or so far that is all I've succeeded in doing."

Come again?

"I have boat accidents all the time. A couple of weeks ago I ran aground. Both my engines cut out. I just got to the front of the boat, jumped in and swam. The current took the boat to that breaker down there," he says, pointing into the pitch blackness beyond the patio, "and smashed it up. I had a hard time getting in; me against the sea you know, battling the whitecaps. But I made it to the dock.

"And I got caught fifteen miles out at sea about three months ago—for seven and a half hours. It was awful, a nightmare, right in the middle of the Bermuda Triangle."

It appears that Robin is repeatedly involved in harrowing incidents from which he somehow emerges unscathed. The most terrifying occurrence, he tells me, was the well-known Hither Green train wreck outside of London in 1967. At that time, the Bee Gees were working on their *Horizontal* LP. Robin and wife Molly were returning from a holiday weekend in Hastings when the train jumped the track at seventy miles per hour. Forty-nine passengers were killed and seventy-eight more seriously injured, but Robin and his wife survived without a scratch.

And then there was the day in 1966 when the boys and their father were speeding along an Australian highway and a tire blew out on their Ford Falcon. The car flew off the road into a pasture and turned over several times.

"The car looked like a concertina when it stopped rolling," says Robin, "all smashed and squashed. But none of us were hurt. It's very strange."

That evening, we feast on broiled beef chops, string beans, squash, and baked potatoes, and I watch with polite curiosity as my spindly host eschews the meat and green vegetables in favor of the potatoes. Within fifteen minutes, he has devoured the insides of no fewer than five spuds and is reaching for another when he abruptly joins the sedate chat I am having with his secretary about the current state of the world.

Railing against the rising crime rate and rampant decadence, Robin denounces the "weak minds" of those drawn into cults and cites Charles Manson, now eligible for parole, as the embodiment of an unspeakable evil loose in the land. There is no argument at the table, yet Robin pursues the thought with great vehemence, ruling that Manson and his ilk "should have been hung in a sack and beaten bloody."

Attempting to change the conversation to something less grim, I ask him about his earlier remarks concerning the Bee Gees' poorly received *Sgt. Pepper's Lonely Hearts Club Band.* He is very critical of both the film and soundtrack album, saying that the project was "too innocent for these times." What did he mean by that?

"It should have been more like *Superman,*" he explains. "It should have had more excitement poured into it. As we were making it I was thinking, 'I hope they are going to put some visual effects in here.' When I saw it, it was exactly as we shot it, nothing was improved. On the set the camera is pointed at you, and you're thinking to yourself, 'It's gotta be more than just me sitting here in this room, 'cause nothing's happening.' But then you see the film and that's all there is."

What approach would he have preferred?

"Well, *Saturday Night Fever* had fucking in the back seat, you know," he observes evenly. "I mean *that* is the kind of film people are seeing these days. *Sgt. Pepper* comes out, and people sort of expect to see fucking every now and then. After *Saturday Night Fever* they expect to see a little bit of sex, but there were no fucks, you know? It was too goody-goody.

"I knew the film wasn't going to be a big hit," he concludes with a swallow, dropping another empty potato skin on his plate. "Well, better luck next time."

If this exotic discourse seems a mite jarring coming from a clean-cut Bee Gee, well, that's understandable. When they first emerged in England in the late sixties, the then five-member group (with Australians Vince Melouney on lead guitar and Colin Peterson on drums) seemed more than a little bit precious. Toothy lead singer Robin warbled urgently in his drainpipe vibrato about some willowy girl who was "such a holiday," while the rest of the band, clad in quasi-Edwardian garb, posed like footmen behind him. From the calliope harmonies to the index finger glued in Robin's right ear, the Bee Gees' image was one of unrelenting sweetness underscored by queer epic fare like "Craise Finton Kirk Royal Academy of Arts," "Lemons Never Forget," "Seven Seas Symphony," and "Paper Mache, Cabbages & Kings."

Bizarre settings and subject matter notwithstanding, the tone of each song was breathless wonderment, and the poor *angst*-ridden pups were so unswerving in their perspective that even the most devoted Bee Gees fan occasionally longed to give them a shot in the collective head. *Jeeze,* you had to mutter, *what a sappy, humorless bunch of dinks.*

And the maudlin hits kept on coming through 1972: "Words," "I've Got to Get a Message to You," "I Started a Joke," "Lonely Days," "How Can You Mend a Broken Heart," "Run to Me"—each a well-honed pop tool that slowly, surely turned the Bee Gees' hyperromantic rut into a trench. Their quandary was uninterrupted by the sibling strife in 1969 that caused the group, now down to a foursome, to disintegrate, leaving Barry and Maurice in one camp, Robin in the other, and the disenfranchised drummer making the screwy claim that he had a right to their name ("Bee Gees" is shorthand for "Brothers Gibb"). Amid rumors of bitter battles, manic spending sprees, hard drinking, and drug abuse, the estranged brothers released two undistinguished solo albums, Barry and Maurice's effort (under the Bee Gees banner) being *Cucumber Castle* and Robin's entitled *Robin's Reign.*

A year and a half later the brothers reconciled, carrying on as a trio, and a subtle evolutionary process began. The lads started to loosen up, grow scruffy beards, and trade their velvet morning coats for jeans and body shirts. Their album titles shifted from high-minded handles like *Trafalgar* to the lighthearted *Life in a Tin Can.* And whereas Robin had previously been the frail, quavery focal point, now Barry assumed center stage with a more aggressive, flamboyant vocal tack.

In late 1973, after years of producing themselves in conjunction with manager Robert Stigwood (and occasionally with one Ossie Byrne), the Bee Gees put themselves in the hands of Atlantic's veteran R&B producer/arranger, Arif Mardin. The first collaboration, *Mr. Natural,* was a syrupy disaster, but the second, the funky, falsetto-driven *Main Course,* placed these most unlikely trend-setters on the cutting edge of the disco craze. Conveniently, Barry Gibb, with his chiseled bronze visage, snug-fitting leather and satin outfits, and hairy, medallion-festooned chest, seemed the ultimate dance-floor dilettante. Flashing a smile as dazzling as a mirrored ballroom globe, his grace, canny charm, and utter confidence became the hallmarks of the Bee Gees' metamorphosis. And yet they were every bit as misleading as any of the earlier trappings, for the *real* Bee Gees, you see, are something else again.

"There's *three* of us and there's always been *three* of us, and since school days it was *us three* against the world," says Barry Gibb, thirty-two, stretched out on a snowy white couch in his castle-like Miami Beach villa as he remembers the Gibbs' earliest days in Manchester, England. Born on the British Isle of Man, the boys shuttled back and forth between their first home and England as their band-leader father, Hugh, bounced from job to job. "We were always foreigners in a foreign school, and in Australia [where the family lived from 1958 to 1967] the kids called us Yankees. It was always us three fighting somebody else in the school, or us three being picked on by a mob."

Music was as much a refuge as an avocation, and the brothers were singing together and performing publicly before they reached their teens. Known first as the Rattlesnakes and then, for no apparent reason, as Wee Johnny Hays and the Bluecats, they performed Everly Brothers tunes and played ditties composed by Barry, such as "Turtle Dove," "Let Me Love You," and "Twenty Miles to Blueland." On the oceanliner to Australia they were Barry and the Twins, but by the return trip nine years later they had become the Bee Gees, with one big hit Down Under ("Spicks and Specks") and two LPs on the Festival label, *The Bee Gees Sing and Play 14 Barry Gibb Songs* and *Monday's Rain.*

En route back to England to expand on their success, the trio (then considering a name change to Rupert's World) entertained on board and found they got the biggest reaction when they played Beatles songs. Galvanized by the response, Maurice even went so far as to purchase a sitar à la George Harrison during a stopover in Ceylon. From the start, the Bee Gees sound has been compared—usually unfavorably—to the Beatles' early work, and it is only recently that the Gibbs feel comfortable enough to mention both groups in the same breath. But far more striking are the Bee Gees' deep, across-the-board insecurities and regrets, feelings they have been masking with cutup comedy since their vaudeville days.

"We had to get to know each other again," a somber Barry says of the brothers' reconciliation. "We knew when we came back together that it would take us five or six years to become anything like what we were before we started on the drugs, and before we got fame and huge egos and all that. And six years is what it took. We had to become brothers again and forget those little things that aggravated us about each other. It was an awful lot to get rid of.

"Robin and I were the people who really fought, and Maurice was always on the outside getting the flak. We two were at loggerheads with each other 'cause he was a songwriter and I'm a songwriter, and his voice and my voice are different. We're two different people, but we're both creative, and at that period it was too much for us: who was getting credit on the songs, who was getting voice credit, who should be *singing* what song. Nowadays we don't care, we just discuss and then do. But our problems then were very destructive.

"It's nice to see Robin in the shape he's in now," he confides. "If you'd have seen Rob six years ago you would have gotten a fright, and I've gotta say that about all of us. We got into pills—Dexedrine—and liquor too. The only thing that we never got involved with was LSD."

("I was the piss artist," says Maurice later, "Barry was the pothead, and Robin was the pillhead.")

"We ended up in—have you ever heard of Batley's, the variety club in England?" Barry asks. "It was a little club up north, and if you ended up working there it can be safely said that you're not required anywhere else. In those days [1974] that was the place *not* to work in, and we ended up working there.

"I remember us talking about it backstage at that place, and I said, 'If this is the bottom, there's no further we can fall. Something's gotta happen for the positive.' I think it was positive thinking that got us back to where we are now, refusing to accept anything negative. Like, making a three-week album became a negative thing. It was time to start working on three-month albums and making the very best of them. It was a frightening time."

But when it's mentioned that the Bee Gees should now feel vindicated and secure in their success, the leader of the band is incredulous.

"In this position," he argues, "we are constantly up against the wall with people saying, 'Please us!' It's an invisible thing, but you can feel the wall behind you, and you can hear the whole industry saying, 'Give us a surprise, we *expect* you to outdo yourselves.'

"Whatever this new album is, I can tell you the pressure was mountainous to follow up *Saturday Night Fever.* And we felt that there was great pressure to follow up *Children of the World* with *Saturday Night Fever.* And *Children of the World* followed *Main Course,* which everyone was talking about!

"It always goes on that way." Barry nods to himself in exasperation, wringing out his sweaty palms. "I mean if *Spirits* is a monster—pray that it is—then once again we'll be against the wall."

Now it's my turn to be incredulous. This seems like an unusually joyless attitude, especially considering that *Spirits Having Flown* has presently produced three hit singles and sold more than 4 million copies in the States alone.

"We spent ten months doing this new album," he explains. "You've gotta believe that a lot of times we cut a track, then said, 'No! No good!' A lot of tracks we cut a *dozen* times. We just did not want to go wrong with this album. And a few critics say that we did. Our father always said, 'Look, no one ever criticizes you when you're down; you only get the criticism when you're up, so *shut up.*'

"So we try and live like that, or at least live with it. But I've never gotten over harsh criticism. I can never pick up a review and finish it if the guy doesn't like the album, 'cause the rest of my day is screwed up. It's so painful.

"*Spirits* is really a listener's album—if you can stand the falsettos long enough," he says with a sheepish laugh. "You have to listen to it four or five times, *if* you like it enough to listen to it that many times.

"You see, success like we have now was just a very distant dream in 1971. I mean, we thought it was all over for us then. And now we can't really accept what we've done and where we are when we read magazines saying, 'The Bee Gees are hot.' But sooner or later these bubbles burst anyway, and I would like for the Bee Gees to stop before we wane. I don't know if it's easy or accurate to say that in the next two years the Bee Gees will decline or continue at this pace. None of us can say," he frets with a bowed head. "But all bubbles have a way of bursting or being deflated in the end."

This last soliloquy is punctuated by a blast from the horn of a tour boat surging past Barry's seaside estate, a full load of tourists hanging over its railings as it moves extremely close to the grounds. Security is tight around the walled residence, a Moorish complex that includes gardens, bubbling fountains, and a spectacular pool surrounded by cabanas. It would be an idyllic tropical retreat except that, as Barry puts it, "It's like living in a bloody goldfish bowl.

"We've asked them if could they please keep the boat at least 200 yards out, but they don't," he explains, sinking low in the couch opposite mine as if afraid the shutterbugs can see through his veranda windows. "The boats come past every hour on a nice day, and the people all have cameras and binoculars.

"They have a Universal Tours–type bus that comes down this road every hour with loudspeakers. It's getting to the point where I'm going to have to get out of here. Seriously. The *Miami Herald* did us a real nice favor last year: they printed our address [actually, they just named the street], with a picture of the front gates. You can't stop the press from doing these things. They can say, 'Oh, who do they think they are? They've got everything they want. So let's play a little game.'

"But *they* oughta try playing that game for a while. Imagine sitting in a house like this, nice as it is, and not being able to go outside because of all these people coming past. I'm very fortunate to live well, but on the other hand, if you've got a family, including kids [Barry is married with two small children], there's just *got* to be a little bit of privacy."

Much as Barry says he loves this home, it's clear he regards it as one of a series of indiscretions—some more serious than others—that have plagued him and his brothers over the last five years.

Among the missteps that pain the eldest Bee Gee most was the group's stubborn early-seventies insistence (prior to hooking up with Arif Mardin) on recording album after album of gooey ballads. It was a wrongheaded direction in an era dominated by hard rock and finger-poppin' roll.

"Wrongheaded is right," he laments. "We had an album tentatively called *A Kick in the Head Is Worth Eight in the Pants.* Seriously. It's easy to laugh about this, 'cause it was never released. One song on it was called 'Harry's Gate,' which was about a gate we used to swing on when we were kids. It was *definitely* a wrong direction."

When I ask Barry about the great contrast between *Main Course* and the preceding, ballad-burdened *Mr. Natural,* he is somewhat embarrassed, merely acknowledging that on the second, record producer Arif Mardin's guiding input was "total," and "he pulled the falsetto out of me."

"The *Mr. Natural* album was done in London and New York, and the songs were in the old Bee Gees style," Mardin recalls later. "When they arrived [at Criteria Studios] in Miami the following year, we started to record, and some of the songs were *still* in their old ballad style. But the Bee Gees were listening to a lot of American groups, especially R&B groups, and since my background was R&B, I was well suited for the affair.

"They started writing different songs, like 'Jive Talkin',' and we had a fantastic rapport. We spent fifteen or eighteen hours in the studio every day for two months, and it became like something out of a movie, with everybody being incredibly creative and dynamic. We would try many things, like synthesizers, and probably because of my background with Aretha Franklin and all the R&B greats, I said, 'Hey Barry, why don't you sing a *high* note here?' He said, 'Okay, let me try it.' And that was the first falsetto, which he sang on 'Nights on Broadway.'

"It all just happened in the course of a day's work. So when people say, 'How did you bring it about?' I must say we all did it together. It shouldn't sound like *The Glenn Miller Story,* or something where someone discovers a new sound overnight. The Bee Gees have always had an unmistakable sound. It's their collective singing and beautiful vibrato and their unique solo vocal strengths. And what happened was that there was a happy marriage of their sound and the orchestral strings punctuated by a strong beat, which is part of my style."

When RSO Records announced in 1976 that it had signed a worldwide distribution pact with the German Polygram Corporation, thus ending its relationship in the United States with Atlantic, the Bee Gees found to their distress that they could no longer have the services of Atlantic staff producer Mardin. The subsequent *Children of the World* LP, the work of the Bee Gees in tandem with Criteria producer/arrangers Karl Richardson and Albhy Galuten, proved successful. But earlier there had been a false start with Richard Perry.

"We were in the studio in L.A. for three days with Richard," says Barry. "His constant position of sitting in this studio was this." Gibb slumps over and narrows his eyes to sleepy slits. "And he had a phone on his console that he always talked on, so things were either constantly out of it or constantly disturbing. What he does, I'm told, is that he's out of it most of the time, but when it comes time to cut the tracks and actually *function,* he gets it done. And then he goes back to being out of it again. It's a system he's worked out."

(Richard Perry declined to be interviewed concerning his brief association with the Bee Gees.)

"I think they're in extremely capable hands now—their own," says Arif Mardin with the tone of a proud father. "They're doing it now with Karl and Albhy, who are great musicians and engineers, and I'm very happy for all of them."

Unfortunately, there's no relief for the driven, and Barry Gibb feels that he had scarcely slipped out of one potential noose only to get strung up by another, namely the Stigwood-sponsored film and record productions of *Sgt. Pepper's Lonely Hearts Club Band.*

"It was a battle all the way for us," says Barry of the film. "Robert had verbally promised us the starring roles, and then this red-hot young man named Peter Frampton came along and Robert wanted him to play Billy Shears.

"The film didn't work for the Bee Gees. It worked for Peter but—and I think you'd have to be blind not to see it—the Bee Gees had no place in the story. We just weren't consequential to the story line, and we tried to point that out along the way. I just wish they'd given people a chance to act."

Whose idea was the absence of dialogue?

"Probably Robert's," he concedes. "But he's suffered enough from the whole thing. All he hears is 'Robert's Folly!' My main criticism of *Sgt. Pepper* is that the music shouldn't have flowed consistently through the film, and they should have used only *Sgt. Pepper* music. It seemed like the idea was to shove as many Beatles songs in there as was humanly possible."

As for the album: "I don't think that George [Martin] should have produced *Sgt. Pepper* again, and I think George knows why. George was religious with the original arrangements; he didn't want to change them. What the people were looking for was something totally new. 'A Day in the Life' I thought was a little bit insipid."

(George Martin replies: "I didn't want to do the project at first, but I was persuaded because Peter Frampton was riding so high back then and I admired the Bee Gees very much. The premise was that it was a film score and not a record album. I did the very best job I could, and I *was* faithful to the arrangements, but they were not mere copies. The music was right for the film but wrong for the Bee Gees—and their disco sound would have been unsuitable. I think that with all the different songs we used, it's a pity the film wasn't called *Sgt. Pepper's White Abbey Road.* I have no regrets, though.")

Throughout the conversation, Barry has been leaning forward at various intervals to turn up the volume discreetly on a large portable radio tucked under the coffee table. I am about to ask him what he's up to when I realize that he's been reacting to every faintly pumping bass tempo that catches his ear, checking to see if it's "Tragedy." Unfortunately, in the last three instances, the martial rhythms were those of Sister Sledge, Leif Garrett, and Peaches and Herb, and right now it's Rod Stewart asking "Da Ya Think I'm Sexy?" Seeing that I'm on to him, Barry's face turns a bright red and he nudges the radio to one side with a clipped chuckle.

He begins telling how he was startled to discover there was the thematic thread of reincarnation, which he fervently believes in, running through *Spirits Having Flown.* I am wondering whether he'd rather check out of this woeful world and take his chances in the next, when the gloomy mood is lifted by the appearance of a grinning Maurice, who comes bounding into the room, followed by a somewhat sullen Robin.

To understand the Bee Gees' brotherly chemistry, it's essential to observe them together on their own turf, Maurice making fun of his balding head and filling every moment of dead air with a quip, while Barry encourages him coyly; Robin all the while sitting off in a corner, appearing distracted but actually waiting for the precise moment to deliver a devastating barb.

Concerned about the prospect of a third world war now that China has invaded Vietnam, Maurice, twenty-nine, expresses the fear that he could be eligible for an emergency draft call since he is a U.S. resident. Barry tries to reassure "Moe," but Robin kicks the legs out from under his counsel with a well-timed, "Oh, *bollocks.*" Unruffled, Maurice goes on to relate that his house on the Isle of Man is up for sale, adding that the Isle has the oldest parliament in the Western world. Barry supports this learned tidbit, and Robin expands on it with the straight-faced assertion that the ancient ruling body is made up of "Saxons, body bandits, and fuckin' *fairies.*"

An infectious giddiness fills the room, and Barry volunteers some anecdotes about the making of *Spirits,* most notably the detail that, as the result of two days of trial-and-error sound-effects experimentation, the "explosion" before the chorus of "Tragedy" is actually him belching into a microphone.

"Deep down we are songwriters first and foremost," Maurice interjects. "We can write a beautiful ballad and then turn around and write . . ."

". . . A load of crap!" Barry finishes gleefully.

"Right!" Robin concurs with a snort. "Absolute bloody *rubbish*!"

As the Gibbs slap their knees in hysterics, I ask if they've ever recorded any jocular compositions that never appeared on record.

"We did one called 'Mr. Waller's Wailing Wall,' " says Barry, singing a snippet whose melody vaguely resembles "Penny Lane."

"And we did a song called 'Baby You Can Break My Back,' " adds Maurice with an oblique wink.

"We did this limited edition record for the fan club about Prince Wally, a mad Scottish nobleman," Barry continues. "Our sense of humor is very influenced by the old 'Goon Show' and 'Monty Python.' We had to cut out sections of 'Wally' where we shit all over the castle floors, and that kind of behavior."

Are these sorts of outbursts unique?

"Oh, no," says Barry. "We have a serialization called *The Adventures of Sunny Jim.* It only happens at recording sessions, and no one else ever hears them. We do them to relax ourselves when we're singing. So we do them first, have a bit of a laugh, and then we're ready. We start the stories off the tops of our heads and call them [*booming voice*] 'The Continuing Adventures of Sunny Jim'—and there's always an echo-chamber effect there. Then we go off into 'Sunny Jim in Brazil,' 'Sunny Jim Joins the Army,' and strange stuff like 'Sunny Jim Steals Surgical Instruments.' "

What sort of a guy is Sunny?

"A lunatic I suppose," Barry mulls. "He's just an imaginary character."

"Hey," says Maurice, "do we have a tape of Sunny Jims here?"

"Ahh," says Barry warily. "Somewhere, somewhere. But I don't know where . . ."

"I think Karl [Richardson] made a cassette of a bunch of them," Maurice exults. "I think I know where it is!" He jumps up excitedly and scurries into the next room.

"Er, Moe," Barry calls out with some trepidation, "I don't think it's around here. I don't know if Timothy has the time, really!"

Maurice reappears a moment later brandishing a cassette. "Sunny Jim!" he crows, laughing evilly. Barry suddenly looks pale.

"They're sick!" Maurice says triumphantly. "Wonderfully dirty and sick!"

He places the cassette on Barry's tape deck and cues it up as Barry shrugs helplessly with a frozen grin.

" 'Sunny Jim on Safari'!" says the announcer, whose voice I recognize as Barry's. There are rustling sounds, as if some souls are moving through dense jungle foliage, and then:

BARRY: I say, Sunny Jim! Would you like to borrow a pair of my cotton shorts? I see you're so ill-equipped!

ROBIN: [*Vacant, high-pitched whine similar to that of the hapless clay tot on the Mr. Bill segments of "Saturday Night Live"*] Oh, I really hadn't noticed.

BARRY: [*Voiceover*] Yes, next week more encouraging adventures with [*echo chamber*] Sunny Jim!

BARRY: [*Voiceover*] This week, "Sunny Jim Discovers Incest and Has Love with His Older Sister"! A sister examines his dong with a tape measure. Then calls for their mother to appraise it.

ROBIN: [*Squeaky female voice*] Ummm. Not like your father's. Father! Come here! Get out your dong and show Sunny Jim how big it is!

BARRY: [*Voiceover*] Next week, "Sunny Jim Goes to a Male Gynecologist"!

The tape continues in this vein for about fifteen minutes, each episode lasting no more than sixty seconds and running the gamut from "Sunny Jim Goes Down into the Mines" and "Sunny Jim Goes to the Himalayas" to "Sunny Jim Goes to a Massage Parlor," "Sunny Jim Gets Jock Itch," "Sunny Jim Gets Hemorrhoids," and the showstopping "Sunny Jim Develops a Third Tit":

ROBIN: Doctor! What'll I do?!

BARRY: Aww, I don't know. I don't want to cure it; it looks too good.

ROBIN: And what about my hemorrhoids!

BARRY: Aw, fuck yer hemorrhoids!

The tape ends with three familiar voices crooning: "Please give it a chance / It's almost like Christmas / Dishonest romance / All those discharges at midnight / All over the bed / Send me outta my head."

By this time, the boys are whooping so convulsively that tears are rolling down their cheeks. How long have they been doing these routines?

"For years," says Barry, gagging with laughter. "It started around the time of *Main Course*!"

The Gibbs have scarcely caught their breaths when Maurice slips away again, returning with a videotape he calls the "Collected Items." He inserts it in the Betamax and stands back expectantly.

What ensues is about an hour of blackout stunts coordinated to simulate an evening of TV programming. Obviously taped at Criteria Studios, the skits include a *cinéma vérité* minidocumentary about an inept band cutting its debut record, entitled "Wankers by the Moonlight"; a Don Kirshner–style conversation-at-the-piano with an effeminate pop-schlock songwriter; a current events talk show called "The Eugene Shitass [pronounced "Sheit-arse"] Report"; and "80 Minutes," a TV news-magazine that features an interview with a noted surgeon (Robin) after the first successful penis transplant. Wearing a blood-smeared white smock, the good doctor is pressed for information by the hard-nosed host (Barry):

BARRY: [*Surveying the surgeon*] It wasn't a neat operation today, eh?

ROBIN: [*Shaking his head gravely*] No, no. In an operation like this we need to know what the patient's thinking, his every move.

BARRY: [*Outraged*] As far as I can tell, this doesn't sound like something that's normal. What it sounds like to me is that you performed some horrible act on another human being.

ROBIN: On the contrary, the man wanted some new private parts, so we helped him.

BARRY: But what about the private parts he already had?!

ROBIN: They were very small.

BARRY: [*Seriously concerned*] What state is the patient in right now?

ROBIN: Well, when I left him he was unconscious.

BARRY: Do you think he'll have a longer future because of this?

ROBIN: [*Nodding sagely*] *Much longer.*

As the host signs off, the surgeon leaps onto a couch and begins singing at the top of his lungs in an unintelligible falsetto.

Before I can react to this tour de farce, I am ushered out to make way for a script meeting the group has scheduled with the crew filming the Bee Gees' forthcoming TV special. As I say my goodbyes, Barry is back fiddling with his portable radio, trying in vain to locate a Bee Gees song.

"*Damnit,*" he hisses to himself, shutting it off.

Arriving the next day at Maurice's palatial spread (some six blocks down from Barry's house), I am admitted inside to find his pretty blond wife, Yvonne, and his in-laws sunning themselves by the pool. Moe escorts me indoors and, at my request, puts *Spirits Having Flown* on the stereo. (He's the only one of the three brothers to have a copy of the LP in his house.)

Maurice is bopping back and forth in shorts and a terry-cloth windbreaker, straightening the family photos on the walls, when "Love You Inside Out" bursts from the speakers: "I ain't no vision / I'm the man who loves you / Inside and out / Backwards and forwards with my heart hanging out."

He joins in by the second chorus, singing, "Inside and out, backwards and forwards with my cock hanging out!

"That's the version we sent to Robert," he says with an impish laugh.

When I ask him about the great disparity between the Bee Gees' wholesome image and their raunchy sensibilities, he eyes me quizzically and replies defensively: "We are just normal people."

Does he share Barry's belief in reincarnation?

"In a way I do believe in it," he says cautiously, saying that he and his brothers are particularly prone to strong feelings of *déjà vu.* The Bee Gees are also known to share a slight telepathy, but Maurice maintains that the psychic bounds between them are much greater than people suppose.

"Robin and I are twin brothers," he reminds, "and I definitely have a kind of ESP with him. One time when he was a boy, he was riding a bicycle and he had a crash. I didn't; I was at home, but I ended up aching and I wondered what the hell I was aching for.

Robin came back, and he had bruises in exactly the same places I had mine.

"When Robin was in the Hither Green train disaster, he was late for a press conference and I said, 'There is something wrong. Something has happened to Robin.' And Barry said, 'What do you mean?' And then we found out. We watched the news, saw the train disaster, and I went, 'Robin was on it!' We went to Hither Green Hospital, and there was Robin—his wife was in having X rays—sitting there going, 'I didn't think I was going to see you guys again.'

"He pulled six people out of a carriage, and he said, 'I never knew I had that much strength.' He laid them on the lawn, and they were all dead. I knew he had been through a strenuous thing—my arms were aching."

Though the Gibbs have uniformly skittish gazes, each has a wholly distinctive spark in his eyes. Robin's are hard and self-absorbed; Barry's are open, inquiring, and vulnerable; and Maurice's are kindly but pained, melancholy. As he hurries around his house, showing me his new outdoor Jacuzzi, his video projector, the specification sheets for the jets he's purchased, the photos of boats he covets, and the brochures for the English manor house he is interested in buying, I get the eerie feeling that I am more comfortable as a brief visitor to his world than he is living in it. There are rumors that Maurice's involvement with the Bee Gees in recent years has been minimal, but before I can ask about it, he tells me he hurt his back just as work on *Spirits* was getting under way. "I had to sit there and tell the bass player [Alan Kendall] what to play," he says, averting his gaze. "It was a bitch."

He explains that most recently his time has been taken up coproducing the new Osmonds album, *Steppin' Out,* and puts on a test pressing of the record that he received in the mail just this morning. A bright, sinuous funk sound oozes forth, with arrangements every bit as inventive as the very best Gibb/Galuten/Richardson efforts.

"Congratulations," I say. "It sounds superb—but absolutely nothing like the Osmonds." He laughs so heartily that I later question sources close to the project; they allege that only Wayne and Merrill Osmond sing on the record and that the tracks were almost entirely reworked in Miami. As for future production challenges, Maurice says he would like to take a crack at Gerry Rafferty or Emitt Rhodes.

As I depart, Maurice is standing out by the dock, wondering aloud when his new speedboat is going to be delivered.

As both a musical force and a family unit, the Bee Gees and their close-knit relatives seem to stand well apart from the rest of the world, playing an isolated waiting game in which they are forever on the lookout for the one sign of success or approval that will convince them to drop their bunker mentality. The Gibb brothers give no firm indications that they themselves know what the sign might be, but it certainly hasn't come yet.

Their isolation breeds a unique brand of creative innocence, which in the past has both benefited and betrayed them. When discussing their records, the Gibbs have individual perspectives that are quite discrete, yet they share a bewilderment about their overall worth and impact. If you congratulate them for their well-crafted disco hits, they confess rather contritely that they were unmindful of the genre in which they were working. Such an admission seems suspect until one realizes, for example, that not once in any conversation about their craft do the brothers mention the terms "rock and roll" or "rock." The Bee Gees recognize only one outlet for their efforts, and they refer to it, with a mixture of awe and ruefulness, as the "Pop Business." They view this business as murky, treacherous, and cruel. The best strategy they have devised to survive it is one in which their own artistic impulses are consistently supplanted by the desire to "please other people."

"We never completely do a song just to please ourselves," says Barry solemnly. "We bring everybody we can into the studio, even the receptionist, so that we can get their opinions. We put about 30 percent of what we consider to be our art into our records and about 70 percent of it is us writing for the public. You've got to include both, and that's how we do it. And we don't dwell too much on deep stories, because today people want to hear songs about love. Each song in the Top 20 is about love. Every album in the Top 10 is based on love."

As for the division of labor, Maurice Gibb bristles when confronted with the hearsay regarding his diminished contributions.

"I'd like to clear this point up," he says firmly. "I know there are rumors that Barry does more on our records than Robin and I. I don't know how that rot got started, but I hate and resent it. It's a load of shit. People get that impression because Barry's out front a lot and gets quite a bit of attention for his work with Karl and Albhy on other people's songs, and for his work with Andy. But as far as *our* records are concerned, we all contribute *equally* and all produce *equally.*"

("I think everybody knows that Barry is the idea man and leading light of the three," says George Martin. "And when he is too overt about that they tend to rebel a bit.")

But Barry considers it paramount that the trio never be divided again along any lines, adding that "the Gibb family is *not* a family that is *all* pointed toward business and success. We're a family that's rediscovered ourselves. Being a family means so much to us now because we lost it all, threw it all away."

The next two years are going to be the busiest for the Bee Gees since the period following the fateful day in 1967 when they auditioned for Robert Stigwood in the same Saville theater where the Beatles' concert sequences for *A Hard Day's Night* were shot. The group's David Frost–hosted TV special is slated to be a semidocumentary of the last year's activities, possibly including re-creations of the songwriting sessions that led up to *Spirits Having Flown.* And the last part of the show will be live concert footage from the forthcoming summer tour. Next will come the preproduction for a non–Bee Gees film about drug smuggling in Miami that Barry Gibb has written with British screenwriter David English.

If there are no *Sgt. Pepper*–like snafus, Barry himself has been promised the role of Che Guevara in the Stigwood film version of *Evita,* Tim Rice and Andrew Lloyd Webber's rock opera about Eva Peron. Barry says little brother Andy Gibb may portray "Olivia Newton-John's Australian brother" in *Grease II,* and there's also an outside chance that Andy may play an active role in the next Bee Gees LP. But not before he has completed his own follow-up to *Shadow Dancing* and his older brothers have issued a *Greatest Hits* package. In addition, Barry seems likely to coproduce the next Barbra Streisand LP with Richardson and Galuten this winter.

For all the hard knocks, trials, and disappointments they must endure, it's still a good time to be a Bee Gee. But there is much uncertainty ahead. Chief theorist/strategist Barry Gibb is acutely conscious of maintaining the Bee Gees' well-scrubbed "image" as he maps out future merchandising ventures with the sober, detached air of a Madison Avenue advertising executive. The Bee Gees frequently draw comparisons between themselves and other "family" groups like the Beach Boys and the Osmonds, and they are determined to avoid the public infighting that has marred the former band, while eschewing the religious (Mormon) proselytizing that colors the latter group's approach.

"People have come up to us and said, 'Do you realize how much power you have now?' " Barry says. 'You could change the world with some of the things you say.' And I say to them [*bitterly*], 'Leave me *alone.*'

"Power is fleeting; so is ego," he cautions. "When you start putting religion or whatever into it and tell the world how it can be saved, it just rubs against people. Politicians have no idea how to save the world, so why should pop stars? Instead you can do things like the UNICEF thing [the Bee Gees donated the potential multimillion-dollar publishing revenue from the song "Too Much Heaven" to UNICEF], which is just a positive move to help children."

And there are a few other commercial pitfalls that the Bee Gees are intent on avoiding.

"If you're an innovator, you've gotta be real careful not to get involved with all the spinoffs, because they're highly dangerous," says Barry. "We have our own merchandising company, and it's done with taste, I hope.

"We're doing things like nice T-shirts. We deal in jewelry but only real gold plate. We're doing a little electronic piano with Mattel Toys that'll be available soon. And we don't deal in wristwatches because if watches break, children tend to blame the artist who's on the face of the watch."

Sounds as if Barry has thought of everything, and so long as Sunny Jim retains his low profile, the Bee Gees are assured of maintaining their "G" rating. Following in the footsteps of Donny and Marie Osmond, the go-ahead has been given for the manufacture of a cute Andy Gibb doll, but Barry wisely rules that Bee Gees dolls are out of the question.

"I don't think I would want some little girl to have a Bee Gees doll in bed with her," he says with a crooked grin. "With Osmond dolls, the clothes are the skin—there's nothing under there. With a Bee Gees doll, let me tell you, you're *asking* for trouble."

"Is there anything more sad and unjust than a *fake*?" frets radically flustered British rock legend Roger Waters, seated in his Spartan loft offices in London. His fervid question fairly scars the afternoon air with its savagery. "Can you imagine the disappointment in learning you'd spent your savings on a false Magritte or a fraudulent John Lennon manuscript? Not to mention the spiritual trust and emotion people invest in the symbolic power of any name."

Indeed, Waters allows, in many ancient cultures names were sacred things that could never be changed, transferred, or falsely assumed. To tamper with a name, much less manipulate it in the marketplace, was to desecrate the spiritual force it contained. It was like spitting on the soul.

"And it was the struggle *against* these kinds of attitudes," adds the wiry Waters, his square jaw stiffening, "that helped John Lennon create the sense of artistic decency that I like to call 'the Lennon Instinct.' "

The fight that Waters is discussing is closer to home than any cunning exploitation of the far-flung Beatles legacy, but the stakes are still plenty high. Indeed, one of the biggest and most bitter battles in the annals of the billion-dollar rock

Pink Floyd 1988

business concerns the much-coveted legal custody of a quirky musical trademark: Pink Floyd.

In the beginning were the words, and the words were the Pink Floyd Sound. Derived from the first names of two obscure Georgia bluesmen (Pink Anderson and Floyd Council), the term was applied in 1965 to a certain experimental British rock band; and over the course of two decades it has become synonymous with a magnetic, edgy music in which its pervasive chilling mood is the star.

The man at the center of the ugly contest for control of this potent rock presence is songwriter Roger Waters, a lyricist *extraordinaire* whose spiky meditations on death, madness, and apocalypse were pivotal in leading an obscure British psychedelic group to the pinnacle of commercial preeminence in progressive rock. In particular, Waters wrote all the words and the better part of the music for Pink Floyd's 1973 album, *The Dark Side of the Moon.* One of the most successful records of all time, the hypnotic *Dark Side* has lingered for a staggering 725 weeks on *Billboard's* pop charts; yet its spooky cover image of a prismatic pyramid is the closest its faceless creators have ever come to icon-like stardom.

Waters's legendarily fertile imagination yielded another phenomenal blockbuster in 1979, the epic autobiographical ode to postwar alienation, *The Wall*—and under his leadership the band would ultimately move more than 55 million albums. But the focus of fans' adulation remained the anonymous banner of "Pink Floyd."

The Floyd broke up in 1983—notwithstanding all flamboyant appearances to the contrary—and now Waters and longtime Floyd lead guitarist–vocalist Dave Gilmour are locked in a fight over rights to the name. Waters wants "the reigning trade-emblem of rock" to be permanently retired, pleading, "Let's be fair to our public, for pity's sake, and admit the group disintegrated long ago!"

Gilmour vehemently rejects such notions, raging, "I've been working on my career with Pink Floyd for twenty years—since 1968. I'm forty-four now, too old to start all over again at this stage of my career, and I don't see any reason why I should. Pink Floyd is not some sacred or hallowed thing that never made bad or boring records in the past. And I'm not destroying anything by trying to carry on!"

Actually, these pitched acrimonies evolved out of a 1985 management rift, in which Waters ended his representation by veteran Floyd manager Steve O'Rourke. Their falling-out was over contractual agreements for future Floyd output—a matter Waters deemed moot since the band was, to his mind, defunct. When O'Rourke bridled, calling his termination by Waters a violation of his own formal agreements with, and responsibilities toward, the entity known as Pink Floyd, Roger sought support from former band members Gilmour and drummer Nick Mason. (Roger even rashly proposed to cede the band's rights to Pink Floyd if they'd close ranks against O'Rourke's claims; neither Gilmour nor Mason accepted Waters's never-to-be-repeated offer.)

As Waters tells it, when he calmed down and took the long view on both the deepening breach with O'Rourke and his estrangement from Gilmour, Mason, and Floyd orphan Rick Wright (who Roger says was fired by mutual consent of the rest in 1980), he decided the sanest course of action was a writ to nullify the name Pink Floyd.

In 1986, on Halloween, Roger Waters filed suit in London against Gilmour and Mason. Last year, the dispute spilled out of the offices of the principals' attorneys and onto the world's concert stages. Roger Waters mounted a massive tour in support of *Radio K.A.O.S.*, his second solo LP, while Gilmour, Mason, and Wright performed the *A Momentary Lapse of Reason* LP under the Pink Floyd flag.

Waters's record drew wildly mixed reviews and sold modestly; yet his much-praised *K.A.O.S.* concert pageant, while pitted against the rising tide of pseudo-Floyd promotion, slowly prospered to where Waters could sell out solo shows in England's gigantic Wembley Arena on two consecutive nights. Meanwhile, the product of Gilmour's Floyd facsimile drew similarly mixed notices but triumphed in record stores, sparking a hefty three million purchases in the United States alone; and the lasers- and props-packed *Lapse of Reason* dates proved a steady sellout internationally.

On both tours, crowds were treated to the bountifully foreboding sweep of the Pink Floyd aesthetic. Hits and FM favorites like "Welcome to the Machine," "Money," and "Another Brick in the Wall" were lavished on all comers—but it was only during the *Radio K.A.O.S.* concerts that noted Los Angeles DJ Jim Ladd (performing as the voice of the mythical KAOS station) deigned to declare, "Words and music by Roger Waters!"

While Waters's authorship of the best of the Pink Floyd repertoire was plain from the start, it was opponent Dave Gilmour who won the crucial first round at the box office. While savoring the bounty from *A Momentary Lapse of Reason,* Dave permitted himself a bit of boasting last November in the pages of *Rolling Stone*: "We never sat down at any point during this record and said, 'It doesn't sound Floyd enough. Make this more Floyd.' We just worked on the songs until they sounded right. When they sounded great and right, that's when it became Pink Floyd."

Roger Waters read that "arrogant soliloquy" down in Nassau's Compass Point Studios last spring while at work with Paul "Don't Shed a Tear" Carrack and the Bleeding Heart Band on the then-untitled follow-up to *Radio K.A.O.S.*

For Roger, Gilmour's assertion was the last straw. "That's an outright lie, absolute and barefaced," he seethed, slamming the magazine down, "and someday the world will know the depth of this entire hoax!"

Waters saw Gilmour's quote in *Rolling Stone* as the rock equivalent of the Iran-contra crew and their droll demurrals concerning official misconduct, despite a damning paper trail to the contrary. The Gilmour statement emboldened Waters to come forth for the first time with details of what he sees as the behind-the-scenes disloyalties and double-dealings that gave rise to *A Momentary Lapse of Reason.* "I must say," Waters quips, "that under the circumstances, it's a superb title for a so-called Pink Floyd record."

Granted, anyone can say anything in the press to justify his position to Pink Floyd's legion of rabid fans. However, the intrigues that emerge from six months of independent inquiry into this epic test of rock and roll wills differ shockingly from all previous accounts.

What emerges is a saga of greed, cynicism, and misrepresentation in the modern music business. Over the last twenty years, rock has grown from the simple expression of a spirited singer and his song into a gigantic entertainment juggernaut in which even the most splendid displays of "talent" and "vision" can be of synthetic origin. Thanks to the convolutions of current recording technology, a musician needn't play, a band needn't assemble, an artistic bond needn't exist. A songwriter-producer can adopt the focused traits of an assembly-line foreman as he brings the illusion of a supergroup and its latest album into being. This is the story of a massive controversy, centered on the marketing of two seemingly foolish words: Pink Floyd.

"You learn nothing from a lie," says Roger Waters, stretched out in the Billiard Room, a home studio that has supplanted the game room of his spacious house in Barnes, West London. It's been a troubled six months since our initial Pink Floyd–related talk, and the sinewy Waters looks distinctly world-weary. "Even as you discover a deliberate untruth, it always only confirms what you already knew but refused to face."

This blunt observation is at the core of Roger Waters's outlook as a composer, since unsentimental confrontations with delusion form the fundamental themes of his work. Like many old-guard rock practitioners, Waters values the unconditional openness of the best rock as a public expression of a personal truth. Naysayers claim that rock no longer requires any creed or substance beyond the brazen announcement of itself.

"In Aldous Huxley's book *Brave New World,*" mulls Waters, nursing a cup of strong tea, "he warned about every human being conditioned to accept his lot so that the bosses arrive at a nice smooth situation where nobody questions anything and everything is supposedly 'taken care of.' This is the deluded scenario I put forth in *Radio K.A.O.S.*—which was my doomsday-bound vision of a 'soap-operatic republic' in which nobody gives a shit, if, for instance, Oliver North did the right thing or was wrong, or what effect it had on anything else. All that many viewers still care about concerning the indicted Mr. North is whether he gave a good, solid John Wayne television performance. And because North's airtime suddenly became entwined with the American networks' sickening concept of what constitutes great television, it was literally excused!

"What it comes down to for me is: Will the technologies of communication and culture—and especially popular music, which is a *vast* and beloved enterprise—help us to understand one another better, or will they deceive us and keep us apart? While there's still time, we all have to answer for ourselves. But neither Huxley nor Meese nor Ollie North could have prepared me for the creative, technological, and moral issues I'm facing with the Pink Floyd sham—a grand display that's also being excused in public because it makes for great arena rock.

"Naturally," he chuckles, showing a handsome, seldom seen grin that merits more exposure, "all of this solemn contemplation is turning up in my music. *Radio K.A.O.S.* was hopefully universal in its pained concern, but my new album's themes involve anguish in my very own backyard."

Indeed, one day last winter [in 1988], as the personnel calling themselves Pink Floyd were moving across the map from San Diego to Sydney in fierce pursuit of ticket sales, a pensive Roger Waters went to the Billiard Room and began writing stanzas for what became a song for his new album. He offers an excerpt:

We watched the tragedy unfold
We did as we were told
We bought and sold
It was the greatest show on earth
But then it was over

We oohed and aahed
We drove our racing cars
We ate our last jars of caviar
And somewhere out there in the stars
A keen-eyed lookout spied a flickering
star
Our last hurrah

Waters gradually realized the two verses were a requiem for the fragile integrity of the Pink Floyd reign. And yes, tens of thousands of spectators *were* at that moment crowding arenas to hear a band calling itself Pink Floyd. Yet the most devout fans surely were aware that the whole presentation could not be further in fact or intent from the aims of the idealistic school chums who forged the Pink Floyd Sound.

When a title for his bittersweet new song eventually occurred to Roger Waters, it also seemed an apt name for both his latest scheduled solo album and the tragic creative destiny that it summarizes. "I didn't know what else to call it," he shrugs, "but *Amused to Death.*"

Among ultra-hard-core Pink Floyd zealots, the period of mourning for the band commenced way back in 1968, when another Roger—Roger Keith "Syd" Barrett—was booted from the psychedelic act he'd named. A fellow student of Waters's at Cambridge High School for Boys, Syd Barrett was invited by Roger in late 1965 to join a combo he'd formed with two other architecture majors (Nick Mason, Rick Wright) at London's Regent Street Polytechnic. Blaring barrages of feedback-*cum*-Chuck Berry chords during Sunday-afternoon "Spontaneous Underground" sessions at the fabled

Marquee Club, Pink Floyd quickly became the vanguard experimental outfit on the London underground scene.

Unfortunately, young Syd too quickly became high-priest-without-portfolio of a surreal strain of hallucinogen-fueled rock songcraft, whose golden era was as hazy as his own cerebrum. While still sufficiently grounded in January of 1967 to author Pink Floyd's first British hit, "Arnold Layne," Barrett soon tired of the rigors of reality. He was halfway to the laughing house when *The Piper at the Gates of Dawn,* the debut Floyd LP, emerged from Abbey Road Studios in August 1967.

Cambridge High School alumnus Dave Gilmour, fresh from gigs as a male model in France, was brought on board in February 1968, to serve as backup guitarist and vocalist for the dangerously balmy Barrett. When too many visits to the pop-star pharmacy paved the way for Syd's inevitable on-tour mental collapse, Gilmour got the nod as new guitar hero. Waters, Gilmour, and Rick Wright went on to assist Barrett in two loopy solo LPs *(The Madcap Laughs; Barrett),* and then Syd retired to his mum's house to preserve his premier rank as acid-fried rock savant.

With Gilmour the appointed front man, Waters gripped Floyd's artistic reins and steered them into years of exotic progressive-rock reveries. The electronics-drenched albums had titles like *A Saucerful of Secrets*; *Ummagumma*; *Atom Heart Mother*; *Meddle.* And the spacey songs followed suit: "Set the Controls for the Heart of the Sun," "Astronome Domine." The band also provided soundtrack scores for a few of the more outré late sixties–early seventies art movies, notably *More* and Michelangelo Antonioni's daffily desolate *Zabriskie Point* (1970), in which the Floyd song "Careful With That Axe, Eugene" soared over the closing sequence of desert explosions.

The Pink Floyd stage productions of the era were the forerunners of the modern rock extravaganza, featuring elaborate special effects and one of rock's inaugural light shows, plus protracted instrumental suites served up via a remarkable 360-degree sound system called the Azimuth Coordinator. At one U.K. concert, a fifty-foot inflatable octopus rose from an adjacent pond during a climactic number, the Floyd playing so loudly the decibel level actually decimated the real aquatic life in the water.

For all its bizarre overkill, the Floyd had no impact on the American market until 1972's relatively subdued *Obscured by Clouds* was embraced by FM radio. From there it was a short step to a commercial blast-off courtesy of *The Dark Side of the Moon,* with its immaculate instrumentation, ominous phonic mumbles, and jarring sound effects (ticking clocks, ringing cash registers). Each band member contributed something to the mix of *Dark Side,* but lyrically, musically, and conceptually it was Roger Waters's coming-out party. While the rest of the group basked in the glow of their abrupt mass acceptance, Waters busily exorcised his ingrained demons, expounding throughout *Wish You Were Here* (1975, dedicated to Syd Barrett), *Animals* (1977), *The Wall* (1979), and *The Final Cut* (1983) on gloomy human themes rooted in grief for his airman father's World War II death.

"My father was a schoolteacher before the war," Waters explains evenly. "He taught physical education *and* religious instruction, strangely enough. He was a deeply committed Christian who was killed when I was three months old. A wrenching waste. I concede that awful loss has colored much of my writing and my worldview."

It has also shaped Waters's intense sense of protectiveness toward Pink Floyd's recording heritage, since it encompasses major developmental horrors in his life—whether they involved coping with the death of the dad he never knew, or witnessing the psychic dissolution of adolescent companion Syd Barrett.

"Syd and I went through our *most* formative teen years together," Waters shyly admits, "riding on my motorbike, getting drunk, doing a little dope, flirting with girls, all that basic stuff. I still consider Syd a great primary inspiration; there was a wonderful human tenderness to all his unique musical flights."

From his alternately slack and hypertense body language to the crackling clarity of his discourse, Roger Waters, forty-four, is the epitome of the overly bright man for whom intellect, self-awareness, and social conscience are a decidedly mixed blessing. The hardness of his chiseled visage and flinty gaze are leavened, however, by the disarming vulnerability of his nature.

"There's something to be said for disastrous business miscalculation and failure in the marketplace," he says with a hapless chuckle. "They send you back home to ponder your value systems, and at the same time they reward you with a new freedom to follow your creative heart without worrying about commercial tyrannies.

"I've also discovered that the law is not interested in moral issues so much as the cold factors of ownership, treating the name Pink Floyd as if it were McDonald's or Boeing! On a personal level, I have nothing against Dave Gilmour furthering his own goals. It's just the idea of Dave's solo career masquerading as Pink Floyd that offends me!"

Gilmour is the polar opposite of his adversary in both appearance and opinion. Round-faced, smiling, with a teddy-bear torso, he projects amicability and approachability—until his darting eyes sense weakness in their vicinity. At which point, the smile turns to a fixed leer and a fabled sarcasm spills forth.

"I don't share Roger's sense of angst about music and the world," he banters scornfully, speaking at dusk in a Providence, Rhode Island, hotel room shortly before another concert stand. "If I did, maybe we would have come to an agreement on our dispute. While Roger's acted dumbly and isolated himself, I've discovered new strength with the extra work load I've had to put on myself in this last year. But like him, I did several solo LPs myself and made no demands on anyone when I did. Granted, I did less work with Pink Floyd back in the old days, but that was something Roger was forcing. And now," Gilmour adds with glee, "the poor chap has lost his whip hand!"

Perhaps. But David Gilmour is singing a vastly different tune than he did back when his solo future seemed brighter.

"Roger comes up with the concepts—he's the preacher of the group and spends more time home writing with Pink Floyd in mind," a breezy Gilmour told *Rolling Stone* in 1978, as his *David Gilmour* album was being issued. "We get along fine. I know what I give to our sound, and he knows it, too. It's not a question of him forcing his ideas on us. I get my ideas across as much as I want to. They would use more of my music if I wrote it."

Gilmour took an aggressive stab at writing his own music for his *David Gilmour* and 1984 *About Face* collections, but it appears that only Pink Floyd cultists bought them. It was after his second solo album that he began to press the Pink ploy.

"From there, the story takes a sordid turn," says Waters, "and after long thought on this mess and the mountain of falsehoods that this scheming bunch has created, I'm now going to divulge the cold, hard, indisputable facts. Please do feel free to go back to any of the parties mentioned about their side of the story. I think you'll stop them dead in their sneaky tracks."

The first bombshell Waters drops is that Bob Ezrin, who served as coproducer on *The Wall* as well as *A Momentary Lapse of Reason*, was originally supposed to produce *Radio K.A.O.S.*

"That's right," Waters says with a grim nod. "We met in New York City in February of 1986. This was after Gilmour had been spouting for a year about how wise it would be to get Pink Floyd back together in any passable form—with me always refusing that scam.

"So I see Ezrin for a two-day meeting and give him cassettes of the *K.A.O.S.* material I'm working on. He said he was interested in doing the record. We shook on the *K.A.O.S.* agreement, and we agreed to start work in England on April 16 of 1986."

Come early April, Waters found it impossible to contact Bob Ezrin.

"I couldn't reach him," says Waters. "Then, exactly ten days before my first scheduled *K.A.O.S.* session in England, I manage to catch him at home in the wee hours of morning. He picks up the phone, is startled to find it's me on the other end, and he blurts out, 'My wife says she'll divorce me if I go to work in England!' I was stunned. I said, 'Couldn't you have told me that three months ago?'

"I'm in a state of shock, and the minute I put the phone down after the conversation, my wife, Carolyn, says to me, 'I'll bet he's going to do that pseudo–Pink Floyd record David wants.' All I could reply was, 'I can't believe he'd do *that.*'

"I discovered exactly one week later," Waters says, "that he had indeed been hired to do a Pink Floyd record."

After having Waters's detailed accusations read to him, Bob Ezrin replies, "I was in Los Angeles in the midst of a Rod Stewart album when Roger called from London in February of '86, and I set two days aside at Roger's insistence and we met each other halfway, both of us flying to New York to talk about *K.A.O.S.* At the time I met with Roger, I said I wanted to do the album, but I had an instinctive sense that he was being too rigid and intense in his attitudes about the project. And believe me, I know how rigid Roger can get from doing *The Wall* with him.

"See, Roger was completely inflexible about when and where he wanted to do *K.A.O.S.* I have five kids, and he was wanting to move my whole family to England for a minimum of three months. My wife was against it because she felt it would disrupt our children's school schedule. And so after I thought it through, I exercised my right as a potential employee of Roger's to decline.

"It was a *full month* afterward," Ezrin proclaims, "that I was approached by Dave Gilmour about producing a Pink Floyd project. I hadn't been in touch with Dave since producing his *About Face* solo album."

So why, after rejecting a three-month Waters-related stay in England for the good of his family, did Ezrin wind up spending almost seven months in London recording *A Momentary Lapse of Reason* with Gilmour?

There is a long pause. "Dave didn't demand things like Roger did," Ezrin finally replies. "While Roger was thinking only of *his* family's schedule, Dave was willing to work out a more flexible calendar plan that would accommodate the school schedules of both our sets of kids. Also, Dave flew to L.A. to hang out and play his work tapes—rather than insisting I go to him."

Ezrin's disclaimers sound peculiarly prissy coming from an itinerant veteran whose studio dance card has regularly included heavy-metal hell-raisers like Alice Cooper and Kiss. However, giving him the benefit of the doubt, we move on to the artistic integrity of *Lapse of Reason.* Roger Waters's outspoken ire, you'll recall, was triggered by Gilmour's assertion to *Rolling Stone* that "we never sat down at any point during this record and said, 'It doesn't sound Floyd enough. Make this more Floyd.' "

On the contrary, according to Waters, it was Bob Ezrin who rang just such an alarm at the halfway mark in the *Lapse* sessions.

"After four to five months of constant work with Gilmour and company," says Roger, "Bob spoke to Michael Kamen, who did orchestral arrangements on *The Wall* and also coproduced my first solo album, *The Pros and Cons of Hitchhiking.* Bob told him the tracks were 'an absolute disaster, with no words, no heart, no continuity.' " (Michael Kamen, who had declined involvement at the start of the project, confirms Waters's account of the conversation with Ezrin.)

"Ezrin was so depressed," says Waters, "he took a cassette copy of the tapes home to his house in Encino, where his teenage son Josh discovered it and played it with his friend. Both of the kids got angry, and Josh told Ezrin, 'Dad, it's *not* Pink Floyd!'

"What happened next," says Waters, gathering steam, "was that Bob Ezrin, David Gilmour, and CBS Records executive Stephen Ralbovsky had a confidential lunch meeting at Langan's Brasserie, the famous London bistro in Hampton Court, in October or November of '86, wherein both Ezrin and Ralbovsky told Gilmour, 'This music doesn't sound a *fucking thing* like Pink Floyd!' And according to what Dave told me, they had spent $1.2 million on it!"

Back to Bob Ezrin. Is Roger Waters's account of this secret meeting correct?

"*Omigosh!*" gasps Ezrin in dismay. Then, in a quavery tone: "How Roger could have known that we all had that meeting is remarkable to me! Okay, fair enough; the point of the meeting was for me to tell David that what he had thus far was not up to Pink Floyd standards.

"Wait a minute, let me rephrase that: I said it was not up to *our* standard of a Pink Floyd project, and that we should start over again. And David was open and willing to do that.

"But the fact, amazingly, that Roger has become a *detective* to learn about that meeting says to me that this thing has become . . . er, it's gone too far past, er. . . . It's not about the music anymore! It's about the simple 'making' of the *Lapse of Reason* record—as well as the fact that Roger's not on it."

Precisely. Roger Waters's most vociferous charge has always been that the intention on the part of Gilmour, Ezrin, et al., was never to create music that succeeded on its own terms, but instead, from the corporate estimation on down, to endeavor to fake the Pink Floyd Sound. Right?

Another uncomfortable pause. "Well," Ezrin murmurs, "I won't tell you that there weren't times when I didn't say to David, or David didn't say to me, 'This would be easier if Roger were here,' or 'Roger would know what to do,' or 'Roger could give us that flavor.' But both David and I knew that that would mean contending with the rigid, intense, obsessive, and *artistic* Roger—which we didn't want."

And which Roger had closed the door on, anyway.

"Er . . . yes. So we had no choice but to go our own route and start over—and we did."

Which brings us to the question of exactly whose fingerprints are on (and *not* on) the version of *A Momentary Lapse of Reason* that reached the marketplace. Scanning the fine print on the inside of the expensive gatefold album jacket, one discovers—in addition to Gilmour, Nick Mason, Rick Wright, and Bob Ezrin—a guest list of fifteen noted session musicians. No fewer than eighteen *more* musicians and technical experts are acknowledged and thanked in the sub-fine print. And the songwriters tucked away on the record's label include, besides Gilmour and Ezrin, Messieurs Anthony Moore, Phil Manzanera, Jon Carin, and Pat Leonard.

This mysterious multitude is discreetly substituting for an act that last consisted of Waters, Mason, and Wright, with Roger doing the overwhelming majority of the songwriting. Does Dave Gilmour still presume to call this army of hired guns and mercenaries Pink Floyd?

"Listen," Gilmour fumes, "the band is bound to change! It must, regardless of the external or internal climate it faces. But Nick and Bob Ezrin and I ultimately sat down with the material and decided what worked and what didn't!"

Notice there is no mention by Gilmour of the fourth "member" of the unfathomable Pink Floyd, Rick Wright.

"That's because Rick Wright is merely on a wage on this entire Pink Floyd world tour," Waters explains. "Rick has been burned out since September 1979, when Gilmour, Ezrin, and myself unanimously decided to fire him.

"Ezrin was the person to first call Rick during Rick's odd little vacation that fall to Greece—just as *The Wall* was being completed—and said, 'You're no longer pulling your weight.' And Rick told him, 'Fuck off!' It was then we all discussed the matter, and Gilmour said, 'Let's get rid of Nick Mason, too!' Eventually Rick did some *Wall* shows, but he only received a wage, and then in 1980 we fired him for good." (Gilmour corroborated these charges of Wright's failings and "severance" arrangement in a 1984 interview, in which he said of Wright, "He wasn't performing in any way for us; he certainly wasn't doing the job he was paid to do. On *The Wall* . . . Rick didn't play many keyboards.")

"On August 4 of '87," Waters says, "I had a meeting with Dave on the *Astoria,* his houseboat–recording studio that's anchored on the Thames, because we were still trying to settle our differences. Dave told me himself that he still had no respect for either Wright or Mason, but that they were useful to him. The man who was most useful, however, was Bob Ezrin, which is why Dave and Bob now each split three points right off the top from the gross retail sales of *Lapse.* The remaining twelve or so points are divided among a sea of other participants like Mason. As for poor Rick Wright, he's on a weekly salary of $11,000. I know, because I've seen his contract with my own eyes.

"At least Rick knows it's just a payday. Nick Mason goes around acting like Pink Floyd might really be a functioning tour band. And once again, I invite and urge you to go to Wright and Mason and repeat all these charges."

Unfortunately, Wright and Mason refuse all requests for interviews, which are repeatedly tendered through both the press offices of CBS Records (which also remains Roger Waters's label) and those of JLM Public Relations, Waters's own Manhattan representative.

However, two Floyd sources in a position to know allege that Mason is only "a figurehead" in concerts, with even his live parts actually played by drummer Gary Wallis, who was listed in the tour program as a percussionist. And Roger Waters says that most of Nick's apparent drumming onstage "is actually sampled stuff that he triggers or mimics!"

Reached by phone in his room at Manhattan's U.N. Plaza Hotel on August 18, 1988, while in town for a Floyd performance, Gary Wallis denies these charges, saying, "No, Nick Mason plays, Nick plays as well. It's a 50–50 thing, and we usually play in unison, one right on top of the other. The point is, I'm also the percussionist, so you see me running about the stage doing that too.

"But Nick is certainly playing his own drums," he adds edgily. "We're playing together, you see."

Asked if any of the drumming was sampled, Wallis replies, "No, nothing is sampled at all." Wallis offers no explanation for the curious fact that his concert equipment—as confirmed by a formal list supplied to the American music press—includes an Akai S900 sampler as well as two DW trigger kicks. He also gives no reason why he has three times more acoustic and electronic drum gear onstage than Mason.

Unswayed by Gary Wallis's side of things, Roger Waters states, "The only time Pink Floyd ever had two drummers in concert was during the *Wall* shows, when we had the 'decoy band' onstage to make the point about the phoniness and nonconnection of massive stadium shows. And, for those shows, we had hired Willy Wilson as a drummer to keep time because we needed a drummer who could *keep* proper time."

If, as Waters alleges, the erstwhile personnel of Pink Floyd merely function as potted phantoms and paid-off tour props, who can be counted on to propagate the Pink Floyd Ploy beyond the '88 world tour?

"That's the most scandalous facet of this whole ruse," Waters rules, "because Gilmour has built up an entire cast of backstage characters that he's sought to enlist as sources of material for the *next* so-called Pink Floyd album. Many of them are leftovers from the first abortive try, when he and Ezrin were pulling their hair out in vain efforts to concoct a concept album. Failing that, they just established relationships with anybody willing to cook up songs that resembled something Pink."

Could Waters reveal the names of any of these other phantom Floyds?

"Oh, sure. One is Eric Stewart, a founding member of the original 10cc band and a very talented British musician and songwriter who's collaborated with Paul McCartney, for instance, on Paul's 1986 *Press to Play* album. Another lyricist David has waiting in the wings is Roger McGough, the Liverpool poet, who was a member of the famous experimental midsixties rock group Scaffold—which also had Mike McGear, McCartney's brother. And then there's Carole Pope, who's one of the finest contemporary Canadian songwriters. I'll give Gilmour credit: When he devises a fraud, he goes to first-class talent for assistance."

"Yes," Eric Stewart confirms, "Dave Gilmour and I got together around August or September of 1986 to work on a concept that was definitely intended for the next Pink Floyd album. We sat around writing for a period of time, but we couldn't get the different elements and ideas to gel. The songwriting itself was acceptable in certain parts, but not as a whole; so the concept was eventually scrapped.

"I don't want to divulge the concept because, especially knowing Dave, he may want to go back and revive it. It may well be used in the future."

Peter Brown, former director of the Beatles' NEMS Enterprises management company and present manager of Roger McGough, is happy to give similar confirmation of his client's Pink Floyd–related collaborations with Dave Gilmour.

"Dave worked with Roger McGough late in 1986 on original ideas for the Pink Floyd project," Brown explains, "but those ideas remain a gray area. We're waiting for Dave to finish his Pink Floyd world tour to see what will come of it all."

"The idea to contact me came from Bob Ezrin," says Carole Pope. "It was January of 1987, and they were looking for somebody to rewrite a batch of Dave Gilmour's material, so I went over to England for a few weeks to lend assistance. Bob and David also asked me if I had any suggestions for concept albums in the Pink Floyd style. By the time I left England in February, they still couldn't decide what to do. They did have one song, though, which

I thought was quite nice, though it never surfaced on *Lapse of Reason.* It was a mid-tempo thing about Roger Waters, called 'Peace Be With You.' Seems strange that they didn't use it."

And so, while the genuine creative alliance of the Pink Floyd Sound lies in an unquiet grave, David Gilmour has contrived a ghoulish farm-club system designed to generate prolific stand-ins and impostors. As you read this, the current Floyd cavalcade is fulfilling its last global concert commitments, the whole 1988–89 North American and European tour having grossed an estimated $135 million. But peace is not at hand. Once Gilmour completes the tour, perhaps he'll contact those collaborators currently on hold for whatever Pink Floyd roles stand vacant. It's as if a surviving Beatle—say, Paul McCartney—had instituted an employment agency for Beatles clones, and found it worked efficiently enough to dare call the fickle roster the Fab Four.

Bob Ezrin, who could be at the helm for the next episode of this pop chicanery, has his own convoluted rationale for the enterprise.

"I think Roger is brilliant, but he's a tough guy to disagree with, and he can be overly passionate and uncompromising. It's those qualities that go into making him a great artist, but neither Dave nor I would ever consider ourselves great artists. We're more interested in creating something that's popular and fun. Actually, I *hate* the word *artist,* but I would definitely concede that Roger is a great artist—as well as a total obsessive and a psychiatrist's dream. I love Roger, and I truly love most of what he does, but not enough anymore to go through what's necessary to be a part of his process. It's far easier for Dave and I to do *our* version of a Floyd record."

For Gilmour's part, he will press on unless a court decision prohibits him from such activities.

"I don't see any reason why I should stop," he states tersely. "It took decades of care and feeding for Pink Floyd to find its loyal audience, and I won't throw in the towel, especially after *Lapse of Reason* has been such a huge success. Roger doesn't have the right at present to tell me what to do with my life, although he believes that he does. And he'll not ruin my career, although lately he's been trying to."

Actually, apart from the ongoing legal fray, Roger Waters is pouring his energies into completing *Amused to Death*—plus a hoped-for live LP from a benefit staging of *The Wall* in the Potzdamer Platz between East and West Berlin.

"Things change so drastically, and yet they remain the same,"

Waters assures, leaving his chair in his West London home to begin another afternoon of trial-and-error songcraft in the Billiard Room. "The Lennon Instinct tells me that, as with John's song of the same name, my approach to the Floyd fight is 'just like starting over.' Yet I'm also pleased that I've got a new career, a solo career, that I've been nurturing since 1984.

"The main difference between me and Dave Gilmour is that, when it comes time for him to finally confess his dishonest . . . venture to the world, I'll at least have the justice of a solid, credible head start on him."

Waters shows a fatigued grin. "That's the benefit of putting your *own* good name on your work. If people do decide they enjoy it, they always know who to thank and where to find you."

I get along without you very well
Of course I do
Except when soft rains fall
And drip from leaves, then I recall
The thrill of being sheltered in your arms
Of course I do
But I get along without you very well . . .

—"I Get Along Without You Very Well,"
HOAGY CARMICHAEL, 1938

Autumn has come to Martha's Vineyard. A stiff wind cuts through the dense, copper-colored stands of trees that shelter the clearing where James Taylor built a home in the early seventies for his wife, Carly Simon, and their children. A maze of porches, quasi turrets, and windows with frames painted in luminous pinks and yellows, the large, shingled retreat is a cross between some cockeyed farm boy's idea of the perfect honeymoon cottage and a rustic castle worthy of a C. S. Lewis children's fantasy. Even on the bleakest day, to approach it from the winding gravel road below would surely make anyone smile.

Well, almost anyone. According to Carly—sitting outside the house, heavily sweatered against the chill—these are not

Carly Simon

1981

the happiest of times in the Taylor-Simon household. She is now facing a formal separation and likely divorce from her husband of almost ten years.

The breakup had been imminent for nearly two years. Both Carly and James were seen in the company of other escorts. And the couple often lived apart. Recently, James set up his own residences close to the house on the Vineyard and their apartment in Manhattan so that he could be near their two children: Sarah, seven, and Ben, four. The basic bone of contention: Was James ever going to stay home and be a full-time husband and father?

"There are good reasons for the decision," says a tanned Carly with a pensive nod. "Our needs are different; it seemed impossible to stay together. James needs a lot more space around him—aloneness, remoteness, more privacy. I need more closeness, more communication. He's more abstract in our relationship. I'm more concrete. He's more of a . . . poet, and I'm more of a . . . reporter."

She smiles weakly, her full lips somehow appearing thin. "Basically, he just wasn't willing to dress up like Louis XIV before we went to bed every night. I really *demand* that of a partner." She bursts into what is apparently much-needed laughter and then grows serious again, smoothing out her corduroy jeans and pulling her long legs up under her.

"I feel as though I have to get on with the rest of my life and that if I start thinking, 'Well, I'll wait for James to get it together and wait for us to get back together again,' then I'm not going to approach my life the same way as I would if I were thinking, 'Well, that phase of my life is over and now I'm entering a new phase.'

"Sometimes we get along very well and sometimes we don't get along at all. What you have here are two people who have made up their minds that they can't stay together, but who are dedicated to raising their children together. Underneath it all there's a tremendous feeling of . . ." She searches for the right word. "I would call it love."

When they first met, it hurt Carly to learn that James was unfamiliar with her music. Almost ten years later, after all her albums (with their notoriously erotic covers) and all her hits (some of which James sang on), she still seems doubtful that she was successful in getting his attention. He was already living with her when he first saw the cover of her inaugural *Carly Simon* album (Elektra, 1971).

"Hey, that's a fine-looking woman," he said to a friend.

"That's *your* girl," said the friend.

"What?"

"That's Carly."

"Oh," said James, looking closer. "*So it is.*"

Taylor first glimpsed his future wife on the Vineyard in the midsixties, as she and her sister, Lucy, performed at the legendary Mooncusser folk club. But it was not until some six years later that they had so much as a casual conversation. Carly remembers the exact date that she first spoke to her future husband: April 6, 1971. She was performing at the Troubadour in Los Angeles when "Jamie" Taylor came backstage to say hello. She was attracted to Taylor and let him know it.

"If you ever want a home-cooked meal . . ." she said.

"Tonight," he answered.

When they married, in 1972, he was twenty-four and riding high with the commercial and critical triumph of the album *Mud-slide Slim and the Blue Horizon* and its single, "You've Got a Friend." Carly, then twenty-seven, was soon to rival her spouse's successes with "You're So Vain," the monumental hit off her third album, *No Secrets.*

Considering her flirtatious ways and his roustabout inclinations, they seemed a plausible showbiz pairing. Stepping out of limos, locking arms in nightclubs, they were two lanky aristocrats—he from the South, she from the East—embodying the talent, intelligence, self-conscious style, and sex appeal that characterized soft-rock stardom in the seventies. James was the slyly reluctant ladies' man, sauntering around in the spotlight with an "Aw, shucks" self-deprecation that amplified his magnetism. And Carly was the brainy siren, the ultimate catch. But while everyone was chasing Carly, she was running after the one guy who just kept on walking.

A perplexing man whose charisma cried out for closer scrutiny, Taylor was the right guy for all the wrong reasons. Clever, shy, reckless, aloof, gentle, and romantic in his own unreliable way, he was as casually self-absorbed as a man hooked on heroin for the better part of nine years could be. Drawing him out of *that* relationship and into theirs, Carly found, was like pulling a grown man through a knothole. She never wanted to be a rock and roll vamp; that was just an act to build up her courage. But she found herself living the script that vamps get stuck with. Sadly, she realized that you've got to walk it like you talk it.

Now, what it has all boiled down to is a dreadful disparity

between Carly's relatively austere existence (she can, occasionally, be a firebrand and a hell-raiser) and what she calls James's "extravagant life-style." He does drugs. She *hates* them. He drinks and parties with abandon. She is embarrassed for both of them. He roams where he pleases, slipping away on the Vineyard to carouse for days with his brothers, or flying off to St. Maartens and St. Bart's to go on benders with singer Jimmy Buffett. She also follows her own impulses, but they always lead her straight home to her children and her wifely responsibilities, i.e., away from him.

For a while, however, they managed to keep the relationship from flying apart. There was a steady ebb and flow. Then, James became more elusive, departing on bike rides that turned into weekend binges and long walks that led him around the world. His behavior was not unlike that of his father, Dr. Isaac Taylor, former dean of the University of North Carolina medical school and a workaholic who traveled widely for research purposes, often virtually ignoring his family. "It seems," said Carly last winter, "that sons cannot help following in their fathers' footsteps, whether they like the path or not."

And what of daughters?

In the spring of 1950, Richard Simon, founder and president of the powerful Simon & Schuster publishing house, and Andrea, his wife of some fifteen years, packed up up their four children and moved from Manhattan to reside in a stately red-brick Georgian mansion in the Riverdale section of the Bronx. It was the sort of house, thought Andrea, into which a capable, well-married woman installed the family of a powerful, refined man—a man whose literary and business acumen had made him a millionaire by his midtwenties and a respected national figure. Throughout Riverdale, it became known as "The Simon House," its expansive lawn an impressive stage where the talented children would play instruments and sing, pose for their father's pictures, and act out their aspirations. Inside the house, the large living room functioned as the family agora for group entertainments and solo concerts on piano by Dick Simon, as well as the social rallying point for the father's friends and business associates—noted writers, artists, thinkers, composers, and even baseball players, such as Dodger Jackie Robinson. The pine-paneled library in the right wing of the house was Dick Simon's room. Period. He would sequester himself there to read manuscripts, have informal, quick-witted talks with clients, and hold solemn closed-door conferences with Andrea. It was a warm house, full of fireplaces and crackling expectations. And it was an often-troubled house, rife with undercurrents of frustration and grave apprehension. The Simons, a family blessed with beauty, intelligence, and social grace, were entering a dark period that their fine home could not protect them from.

Richard Simon was a shrewd editor and executive who also possessed abundant artistic sensibilities. But these qualities were offset by a bad temper, hypochondria, and intransigent attitudes about what he perceived to be a well-ordered home life.

"Being six-five and very handsome and commanding, when he entered a room everybody sort of quieted down and he became the focal point," says Andrea Simon, now seventy-three years old. "He was a very witty person but full of anxieties. He suffered a great deal from them. He worried a lot, largely about his business. It involved much of his time because publishing is very social."

When Richard Simon first encountered Andrea Heinemann, she was the switchboard operator at Simon & Schuster. Beautiful and dignified, she had grown up poor but proud in Philadelphia. It was all for the better that she was not to the manner born when Richard Simon ushered her into his genteel world. She was a fierce student of refinement because she *chose* to be.

Mrs. Simon was consumed with the future, but her husband was consumed by the past. She explains that although Dick seemed well-suited to the shark-filled waters of the publishing industry, he had originally wanted to be a concert pianist. But his father, a dull, strict man who imported maribou and ladies' hat ornaments from Europe, forbade him to enter such a "back-door, undistinguished profession." As a result, Simon, at twenty-three, became the next best thing—a piano salesman. While attempting to sell an Aeolian piano to businessman Max Schuster, Simon began discussing a biography of Beethoven lying on Schuster's desk; their mutual interest in books led to a publishing partnership that started in 1924, modestly enough, with a lucrative crossword-puzzle trade that capitalized on a craze in the twenties.

"During the course of our relationship," says Andrea, "Dick frequently mentioned the fact that he was a successful publisher because he was bound and determined to get back at his father and show him he was a better businessman than he was."

The publishing whiz quickly became circumspect in showing

affection and concern for his offspring. "Dick was very much a guest in his own house, rather than a member of the family," says his wife. "But he made it understood that he was to receive certain attentions, and one of them was *no children around* when he got home from the office. He went to the library and closed the door."

As Dick Simon grew increasingly preoccupied with the shifting fortunes of his publishing house, he became more obtuse in his attitudes, quirkier in his behavior. Something was amiss. Festering. And it was destined to evolve and infect Simon and those closest to him. By 1957, the man of the house was a semi-invalid, and his career was in jeopardy. In the midforties, he had been pressured by his partners to join them in selling their interests in Simon & Schuster to department store magnate Marshall Field after the unprofitable acquisition of the pioneering Pocket Books paperback company. He did, for $1 million. And because he hadn't been in favor of the deal, he was eventually shunted aside. It was a severe blow to his already precarious emotional state. During the tragic personality disintegration that ensued, he paid little attention to his children, especially Carly.

"I was only close to my father for two years, you know—1952 and 1953," she says. "We used to drive out to Ebbets Field almost every day the Dodgers were home and watch them play. We'd sit and talk about RBIs, Texas Leaguers, and Carl Furillo's batting average. I did it to cultivate a relationship with my father. My mother was often giving me hints about how to win his love, because I felt he didn't love me. People have told me I'm wrong, but I didn't *feel* it.

"As for my other sisters [Joanna, nicknamed Joey, and Lucy] and brother [Peter], I think that my father was very excited by Joey, the first child, and he was very charmed by Lucy, the second child, who was very demure, beguiling, a princess. She was his favorite. By the time I came along, he wanted a boy. He wasn't too pleased with my sex from the beginning. So, perhaps during an Oedipal phase in my life, I went after him in a very matter-of-fact way, thinking I *had* to win this man's love. I may even have felt that it was going to be important for *all* my relationships with men."

Carly persisted in trying to capture her father's affection. She doggedly performed cartwheels for him, made funny faces, and flashed Dodgers baseball cards, imploring him to guess the batting averages and uniform numbers of the players. Her overtures became more urgent and less fruitful as he grew more eccentric, walking around the house in the evening turning out lights, unable to differentiate between night and day.

Carly was about ten and her father was about fifty-five when he initially got ill. The first night he was hospitalized by a heart attack, she knocked on wood. Somehow, she had learned of that superstition, and because he didn't die that night, she kept it up. From the time he got sick to the time he died, she would knock on wood—on the night table or the headboard or on the wall—five hundred times every night before she went to sleep.

"In that ritual, I felt I was doing my part to keep him alive," she says.

Unfulfilled personally and undone professionally, he revealed the depths of his own anguish in an incident that occurred during the last three weeks of his life. His wife was driving him down Fifty-seventh Street one day to visit friends, and as she turned into the driveway of their Manhattan apartment, he tried to seize control of the steering wheel, nearly causing a serious accident, while yelling, "Where are you going? We're going to Carnegie Hall, and I'm playing the Rachmaninoff Concerto!"

Richard Simon died of a heart attack on July 31, 1960. Carly, then sixteen, recalls that her mother woke her in the morning with the news; she crawled from bed and padded numbly into the bathroom, frantically trying to "arrange her attitude" and decide how to react to the fact that all her feverish wood knocking had been for naught. She was neither angry nor sad—she had been anticipating it for too long. But she was envious when she saw Lucy doubled over in tears.

"With Dad's death," says Lucy Simon, "my sense of anguish was for the loss, because I had achieved all I hoped for in terms of being satisfied that I had his love and respect. Carly's relationship with him was never totally established, so his death made it impossible for her to complete her task—that's where *her* anguish came from.

"Looking, comparatively, at our relationships with men in our lives, we could probably find strong parallels to this. I've been very happily married for fourteen years. Carly's marriage is full of turmoil."

Lacking emotional stamina, Carly was, by her own admission, "a fairly neurotic kid" who grappled from an early age with agoraphobia (literally, "fear of the marketplacc"). She had a strong aversion to leaving the house to go to school, and often made the inevitable trip with stomach aches and a gagging constriction in her throat that she and her mother referred to as the "worry lump." In class, she often stuttered so badly she could scarcely utter a sound, let alone recite or read aloud. Carly needed extra attention, a lot of lap-sitting, and constant reassurance just to function. She was about ninc when the emotional dam inside her finally broke.

"I was eating a bowl of Cheerios," she remembers, "and I suddenly started shaking all over, feeling clammy and faint and utterly panicked and lapsing into palpitations—I didn't know what they were then. I ran upstairs and started whirling around the bathroom, thinking that I was gonna die, and telling my mother to call an ambulance and get a straitjacket—somehow I knew about straitjackets when I was nine. This episode lasted for half an hour, and Mom somehow subdued me and got me into bed. I think I cried it out."

The worry lump kept recurring, as did the stuttering, the anxiety, and the agoraphobia. At age eleven, Carly saw her first psychiatrist. She would have to be excused from school each Tuesday and Thursday for her appointments, and the disruption in the classroom routine became a source of mortification that she feels undermined any benefits the experience might have offered. It was the fifties. Psychiatry was for misfits and malcontents. She was indelibly stigmatized. And it eventually corrupted her own image of herself.

"There were teachers who explained to the kids that I was more *complicated* than the other children, as opposed to *sicker,*" she says. "Of course, I knew it meant that I was sicker."

She also felt ridiculed for her "unusual" looks and her awakening interest in the opposite sex. "It seemed like a very long period in my life where I felt ugly," she says, noting that she still feels homely one day out of three. "It was in sharp contrast to the way I saw my two older sisters, which was as great beauties. People would come to the house and say, 'Oh, Lucy, you've gotten so *beautiful.* And Joey, you look so *elegant.*' And then they'd turn to me and say, 'Hi, Carly.' I took that to mean I wasn't even in the ballgame." Moreover, her father's blunt criticism and caustic wit did little to alleviate this notion of her undesirability.

"He could be very thoughtful, but he could also be very cruel," says Carly. "One day I said, 'Daddy, do you have any good-looking friends who could come to the house?' because I was reading *Gone with the Wind* at the time and was in love with Clark Gable. He said,

'There's a man coming today who, in fact, looks just like Clark Gable!' I was so excited and got all dressed up, put on makeup, did my hair, the works. When the dinner guest showed up, I came down the stairs Scarlett O'Hara–style, and he was just a little old man with glasses. I saw my father laughing at me, and I was crushed."

Carly's early sense of herself as the ugly duckling in a bevy of swans was cemented in later years when Sloan Wilson, author of *The Man in the Grey Flannel Suit* and a frequent visitor to the Simon house, wrote a book of memoirs in which he remembered *all* the Simons to be strikingly attractive—except for Carly.

"There it was, the horrible truth, finally confirmed," she says glumly. "On the days when I now feel homely, it doesn't mean that I don't think that I'm attractive. It's just that I don't want anyone to concentrate on my looks, 'cause I don't think they'll like what they see."

This might sound odd coming from a woman who has spent a good deal of her public life advertising her physical attributes in snug jerseys and jeans, low-cut dresses, and black lingerie. Some critics have likened the covers of Carly Simon's albums to the lurid covers of forties dime novels, which regularly depicted a scantily clad temptress or fallen angel ensnared by WANTON LUST! or UNSPEAKABLE DESIRE! Actually, they're more like postcards from a woman in search of her beauty, her "core," as her mother puts it. Andrea Simon doesn't think her daughter has found it yet, but she remembers when Carly first began looking in earnest. She was a young coed, winning new friends and an uncharacteristic self-confidence at Sarah Lawrence College. Eager to test her wings further, Carly left school at nineteen for the south of France, to live for six months with boyfriend Nicky Delbanco in the tiny town of Grasse. "It was a blissful setting; we were alone together and it was marvelous," she says. But there was soon trouble in paradise. She began to have nervous problems again; strange body tremors would awaken her in the night.

She phoned her mother, who urged her to return to New York to see a psychiatrist. Carly began what proved to be four years of costly Freudian analysis ("I spent all my inheritance"). After "graduation," she went out to a little French restaurant on Forty-ninth Street with Delbanco to celebrate. For old time's sake, they ordered a bottle of wine from the same district of France they'd lived in.

That night, for the first time since she'd left Grasse, the tremors returned.

"It wasn't difficult to put two and two together and realize it was due to an allergy to the wine," she says with a shrug and a small smile, moving indoors and seating herself on a velvet couch in the cozy, wood-paneled den of the house. "There can be a lot of things which will spur you into analysis. And for that reason, I very often distrust that a lot of my anxiety symptoms are purely psychosomatic, and I look for chemical, including hormonal, reasons why I may be feeling out of sorts, terribly depressed, or vaguely suicidal."

Carly insists she never planned a career in music, that it had been Lucy who dragged her, over the course of Carly's summer before college, into the spotlight. Dave Kapp caught the Simon Sisters' act at the Bitter End, and in the early sixties, he signed them to a deal with Kapp Records that produced two LPs *(The Simon Sisters, Cuddlebug)* and a regional hit single, the syrupy "Wynken, Blynken and Nod." They even appeared on the popular "Hootenany" TV program. But Carly, being prone to sudden acute anxiety attacks, disliked performing.

"I can't remember when it began exactly," she says, "but it would certainly happen every time I would try to go onstage, which is what made me think I had stage fright, when in fact it wasn't. It can get to me walking in the woods and in other nonstressful situations. It can attack me anywhere, and I'll be in a helpless state of anxiety. It was just easy to focus my agoraphobia on one thing—the stage."

"It never surprised me that performing became such a terror for Carly," says her brother, Peter, who confesses that he consciously "blotted out" most memories of his dad. "Her need to perform, the tremendous expectations she has when she does, and the fear she feels, just seem logical extensions of her having to perform for my father to get the slightest reaction from him."

And she usually didn't garner the desired response. For instance, when Carly recounts the long hours of piano practice her father demanded of her as a child, she adds that "he would come in and say, 'Well, that's very nice, but let me show you how *I* would phrase it.' He'd sit down and play this Schubert waltz so beautifully and just forget I was even there. I would slip off, using him as an excuse not to practice, but also he intimidated me with his talent."

"In later years," says Peter, "Carly and I grew quite close for a span of time, and when she had to go solo and project herself alone in order to gain acceptance from record companies and the public, she became very down on herself, awfully negative. Between 1967 and 1969 she was just bouncing around New York, recording commercial jingles and demos, and being very depressed."

After Carly split from the Simon Sisters, John Cort, a partner with Albert Grossman in the firm that also handled Bob Dylan, was determined to guide Carly to a new professional plateau. "I remember feeling that I was being groomed as a female Dylan," she says. "They asked Dylan to rewrite Eric von Schmidt's 'Baby Let Me Follow You Down' for me, so I met with Dylan in Albert's office after Bob had rewritten some of the words. This was about a week before his famous motorcycle accident, and he seemed like he was very high on speed, very, very wasted and talking incoherently, saying a lot about God and Jesus and how I would have to go down to Nashville [*mimicking Dylan's nasalbleat*]: 'Hey . . . you know . . . oh . . . you . . . Nashville . . . the players . . . are just . . . you gotta . . . just . . . just believe me . . . *believe* me!' And he stretched his arms out as if he were nailed to a cross—*truly*—repeating 'Believe me!' over and over."

The "Baby" track was cut with most of the Band, Mike Bloomfield, and other session cats. Columbia declined to release it. Cort and Grossman made another halfhearted attempt to advance her career by creating an act called Carly and the Deacon—"He was going to be some short black man from the South who was going to sing duets with me." Fortunately, it never made it off the drawing board.

Signed to Elektra in 1970, Carly Simon first tasted acclaim with the significant sales and airplay of "That's the Way I've Always Heard It Should Be," the single from her first album, and she found herself "driven" to acquire another dose. And another. "It made me feel in awe of myself," she says. The flip side of that sensation came many years later with the release of *Spy* in 1979. It promised to be the biggest album of her career: the timing seemed right; she had a nice body of work behind her; she was fairly aggressive about her career; she had worked hard and created a well-crafted product; she had even made a racy videotape to tout "Vengeance," the blatantly commercial single from the record. But nothing happened. Nobody seemed to care.

"It plunged me into depression and a serious ego quandary," says Carly. "I really couldn't find myself. I thought, 'Well, Jesus,

I'm not hitting the mark. Why aren't people appreciating it? Is my opinion of myself totally based on what other people think? Do I *have* a sense of myself?' I was just floundering. I didn't know if I was any good as a person. It seemed to hit me at a time when my self-esteem was precarious anyway. And it toppled it."

The concept and failure of *Spy* seem to say more about Carly Simon than she might suspect. The turning point that hastened the burning point, the record had both a provocative premise and fascinating undercurrents. As Carly describes it: "I've always been intrigued by spies and read the biographies of Mata Hari and Tokyo Rose. But then I read Anaïs Nin's book *Spy in the House of Love,* which was so wonderful because she saw herself as a spy on herself, on her own intrigues, and on the very thing that *is* love. The book was filled with a lot of extramarital associations, trysts, liaisons, and assignations, and I liked the image of her in the black cape. It corresponded with my own feelings of being a spy.

"There was a time in my life, for about three years," she continues, "when I wanted to be a detective. That was my main interest in life—to find out things about other people in a secretive way. When I was twelve or thirteen, I would do things like set the alarm clock for midnight, and I'd get up very quietly and put on my trench coat. I'd sneak downstairs to the living room with a spyglass, look through the keyhole, and keep a notebook on, say, 'Joey's Date with Mark.' I'd make a list of things I could see or hear: heavy breathing, tie over the back of the chair, ashtray filled with cigarettes, glass half-filled with Scotch on the table. Since then, I've always felt that a lot of my songs deal with spying on myself."

Just as her playful voyeurism had its poignant side—a need to know if her sisters' lives were progressing any better than her own (they were)—her artistically motivated "peeks" at herself in later years eventually took their toll. She grew uncomfortable with what she saw: a person trying desperately to live up to a glossy fabrication of herself, in the midst of a failing marriage. While on tour in October of 1980 to promote her *Come Upstairs* LP, everything seemed to be falling apart in her life. She got weaker and weaker with each concert, became overwrought with self-doubt, and eventually developed a deep dread for her own physical well-being. The grotesque denouement occurred as she was about to take the stage in Pittsburgh.

"I felt as if I couldn't stand up straight—and then I couldn't catch my breath. When I got out onstage, I was having such bad palpitations that I couldn't breathe at all and I couldn't get the words to the songs out. I seemed to go to pieces in front of the audience. They were incredibly supportive, and a lot of them came up onstage to sit by me. They were massaging my back and legs and saying, 'Hey, Carly, we're with you, take your time.' They would have taken anything; they would have accepted my *dying* onstage. It made me feel as if I owed them even more—that I should either pull myself together and do a great show or *die* and fulfill their expectations, so it just didn't seem to get better. Right after the show I collapsed, and cried and cried. My sister Lucy was there with me and said, 'There's just no reason why you ever have to put yourself through this again. There are other ways of getting yourself out in front of the public.'

"I started seeing a psychiatrist again, and I decided that at this time in my life, when things are so difficult for me in other ways, I shouldn't aggravate my nervous condition anymore."

In the meantime, Carly Simon's fans will have her latest album, *Torch,* to scrutinize. They can analyze the choice of tracks and marvel at the torrid jacket photos and their implications. Truly ardent sleuths operating in Carly Simon's own clandestine style will discover a more liberated artist who says that after the ordeal of making her latest record, the victory was in its release and the rest is anticlimactic. "Regardless of how well it does commercially," she says, "it was a success to me in the first place."

Torch is Carly's eleventh solo LP and the first record devoted almost entirely to the kinds of songs she grew up hearing: bittersweet love ballads that such tunesmiths as Arthur Schwartz and Richard Rodgers used to play at the piano in the Simons' living room, back in the late forties.

"I remember going to bed singing those songs instead of nursery rhymes," Carly says with a faint grin. "They were songs from the heart, emotions that were easily expressed. While recording them, it was rare that I got through a song without crying because, well, they did have a certain amount to do with what was going on in my life, both then and now."

Perhaps the most upsetting track on *Torch* for Carly was the one composed by Hoagy Carmichael in the autumn of 1938; the lyrics were adapted from a poem mailed to him by a woman mourning the death of her husband. Carmichael desperately tried to find the woman for the song's first public performance on Tommy Dorsey's radio show, but she'd died just days before he located her. It's said that listeners wept when band singer Helen Ward sang it on the air.

And James Taylor, for one, has always been crazy about the music of Hoagy Carmichael.

I get along without you very well
Of course I do
Except perhaps in Spring
But I should never think of Spring
For that would surely break my heart in two. . . .
—"I Get Along Without You Very Well"

Winter's coming on. It's a good season to come to grips with mistakes, to shatter old patterns and reaffirm commitments. Carly Simon's primary concern these days is that she be there for her children, taking them to school in the morning, playing with them in the afternoon, soothing them at night when they ask her difficult questions about the future. She gives the best answers she can, the few she actually knows.

"Having children brought about enormous evolutionary struggles in Carly," says Lucy Simon. "And one of the things that makes her such a fine mother is her amazing memory of her own past situations. Recalling the pain of her own childhood in minute detail, she has a wellspring of empathy and compassion for her own children. She's one of the most devoted parents a kid could hope to have."

Such are the kindnesses of time. But time is also a villain. The problem, for instance, with many families is that parents often die or disappear before the children can reach an age where they can accept or reject them as equals. The families aren't able to *mature.* It's the same with marriages.

"I think James and I both learned a lot about each other," says Carly. "When needs *aren't* met is when you learn about what needs are. We failed in the context of marriage, but not as people. James taught me what I needed to know about myself *and* him and made me a better person for the next person I'll want to love. Funny thing is, if I met James now, I would know so much more and be a better partner, but that sounds a bit unrealistic, huh?

"On my *Boys in the Trees* album, I had a song called 'Haunting.'

'There's always someone haunting someone' was part of the lyric. Basically, you don't have to see somebody for a long, long time for them to still be inside of you. There's no way of killing it off; it's a kind of obsession. And some people do have that effect on me. I have a good memory, especially for emotions, and I don't get over strong feelings."

From the other side of the house, Sarah is crying and Ben's calling out for attention. Carly gets up to leave.

"Sometimes, if you're in a complete relationship, feelings have a chance to die out," she concludes, a wistful gleam in her eyes. "But if a relationship has ended prematurely for some reason, or it can't be fulfilled for another reason, the haunting goes on, the obsession, the dreams about the person [*she stops, sighing heavily*], and the feeling that he is forever locked inside."

Bryan Ferry

1985

Three hundred thousand bewildered Britons were surging down the darkened Strand, trying to get their bearings. Panic and violence erupted in various pockets as people, many of them small children, were toppled or swept away by the surly hordes and thrown against park railings and cars.

It was approximately 10:30 P.M. on an atypically balmy and unclouded July night in London, 1981, and the throng was attempting to distance itself from Hyde Park, site of a massive fireworks display mounted on the eve of the Royal Wedding. The panic in the streets had been growing for half an hour, when disgruntled spectators had begun to leave early after realizing that most of the highly touted pyrotechnics display would be taking place at a forty-foot facade on the *ground*—hence, out of their view. Now they were discovering that no arrangements had been made by the police or the Palace to guide them home, and most of the entrances to the Underground were barred and locked as on a normal evening. Large numbers of petrified tots became separated from their parents in the ugly melee, with more than a hundred still unclaimed by the following morning. It was a royal mess.

"It's all very depressing in England now," commented Bryan Ferry, a debonaire sentinel in an impeccable tuxedo, as he took small sips from a sweaty, vine-stemmed glass of Bollinger. He was standing in the shadows of an English garden, taking the night air under a stately tree while twenty yards away, beneath a striped, circus-sized tent, dozens of titled gentlemen in Turnbull & Asser eveningwear spun bejeweled ladies to the strains of "Cabaret," courtesy Lester Lanin's society orchestra.

The two sharply contrasting London crowd scenes were at that moment unfolding simultaneously only a short limousine drive from each other, but they could have been taking place on different planets. Ferry shifted his elegant stance, ran his fingers through his gleaming black hair, and scanned the faces of London's *jeunesse d'orée,* and added, with the merest trace of his trademark irony, "The British people desperately need an evening out on the town, a humble bit of fun to break up the drearies." He was a guest at the ultra-exclusive pre-wedding romp being thrown in a fine home off Fulham Road in the Little Boltons by Serena Balfour, the Duke of Marlborough's niece and daughter of Lady Sarah Spencer-Churchill. The great brick mansion and garden, originally built by Lord Beaverbrook for his mistress, was a far cry indeed from the cramped cottage Ferry knew as a child, born September 26, 1945, and growing up in the farming and mining country of Washington, County Durham. Yet he suited the refined setting with greater élan than the majority of those assembled.

How Bryan Ferry, who has never made the slightest attempt to conceal or downplay his hardscrabble working-class beginnings, could rise to take his place among England's leading best dressed, become one of its most celebrated pop figures, and be accorded toast-of-the-town status among the most tony movers of aristocratic British society, is no small riddle. He is not a fawning fop, nor the sort of fellow who could be content with his narrow nose pressed up against the glass for a glimpse of the high life. With considerable ease he has achieved intimate access but preserved his distance—and his balance. Not even when girlfriend Jerry Hall, the famed model and social butterfly, left him in 1978 for Mick Jagger, did he allow his uncanny dignity to be in any way diminished.

On the contrary, he kept his own counsel and put a temporarily uncertain solo career on hold to re-form Roxy Music, the distinguished British pop group he'd founded in 1971 to record six consecutively successful albums of, in the main, his own incomparable songs. From the appearance of *Roxy Music* (1972) onward, Ferry treated the hypercritical Anglo-rock scene to an eerie/magical music that fused a sublime primitivism with a coolly disquieting brand of avant-garde cocktail lounge blues. And on such solo outings as *These Foolish Things* (1973) he cut a reverse-camp figure of saloon-crooning surrealness, a Dada Sinatra—who sounded utterly sincere! It provided more perplexing magnetism for the already-enthralled—plus an intriguingly sophisticated step beyond the painted, preening pop culture puppetry a leering Bowie embodied.

At the time of the Royal Wedding, *The First Seven Albums,* a handsome boxed set of the Roxy catalog, was about to hit the shops. *Manifesto* and *Flesh and Blood,* the first LPs following the band's reunion, were both extremely well received, and Roxy had also recently scored a No. 1 U.K. hit with "Jealous Guy," a tribute cover of the late John Lennon's classic soliloquy. Once the Wedding Week festivities had faded, Ferry toiled on with his then-current work-in-progress: *Avalon,* the ghostly and poetic Roxy masterpiece that would yield a sizable British hit with "More Than This" and a Top 30 U.S. single with the title track—the group's first since "Love Is the Drug" clicked in the States in 1975. Ultimately, Roxy Music was disbanded in 1983 after an extended, much-lauded, and artistically draining tour.

Now Bryan Ferry is again on his own—for good, he assures—with the new *Boys and Girls.* He sidestepped the fast life to marry three years ago, and he and wife, Lucy, have two baby boys, one of whom is named Otis (as in Redding), but the proud father's enigmatic self survives intact.

Yet, his newfound personal happiness, coupled with an unexpected personal sorrow (the death of his father) that prompted an introspective reevaluation, have for a brief period of time conspired to make this uncommonly private and elusive man more accessible than ever before. On the breezy summer afternoon we met and talked, Bryan Ferry had just arrived in New York City from England by way of Toronto. He showed the jaunty and slightly lightheaded bonhomie of a jetlagged tourist too overtired to sleep, and seemed pleased and excited to be back in the Apple. A tall, slim man with a boyish stride, he explored the Manhattan streets dressed in white cotton slacks and matching shirt and shoes, an outsized blue blazer completing the sporty look, and selected a sedate Italian restaurant on East 52nd Street for what proved to be a very leisurely late lunch.

Hunched over a steaming plate of pasta with pesto, his chiseled features bent in a many-angled smile, he was witty, genial company, his soft, sonorous voice often erupting in throaty mirth. Poised and thoughtful, Bryan sipped lightly at his wine as he had in the summer of 1981, emerging shyly but surely from the shadows.

It's a question you have always dodged, but how would you describe your music?

My music has always been very deeply felt. That's the only thing that I can vouch for as being of any value in what I do. I've done some rubbishy things in my career, mainly on my solo albums, although recently I think everything I've done has been good.

The early Roxy output had a hard edge, flirting almost with the sinister. But Flesh and Blood, Avalon, Boys and Girls, *are in a much different vein. They are warm, sensual, but vaguely eerie music that can transform the mood of a room.*

[*Smiling*] For my part, I wouldn't dare *play* my records with anyone else in the room. I don't play my own music much anyhow. I actually meant to listen to everything of mine before I began work on this album, thinking, "I must get a day to take stock . . ." but I never got around to it.

You broke up Roxy Music after the Avalon *tour that resulted in the live* The High Road *EP, yet* Boys and Girls *expands on the* Avalon *aura.*

I didn't want the album to be *Avalon, Part Two,* but it does have a continuity in that at least ten of the musicians on both records are the same. And I'm the same composing-wise that I was on the previous album. But it has some differences as well. I've always seen my Roxy catalog as my main body of work, as opposed to my solo career, and I do see *Boys and Girls* as coming from my Roxy work.

Was this record done recently, or in dribs and drabs following the breakup of Roxy Music?

It was an ongoing drab. Sometimes I'd take a week or two weeks off to work on the lyrics. I'd do the verses at night, go to bed thinking, "Leave it in the typewriter, I've got it now," and the next day: "Ohh, hell!" I usually write freehand, but when it's looking right I put it in the typewriter to make it more real.

Most of the work on *Boys and Girls* was done in The White House, a little demo studio on Kings Road in London owned by Mark Fennick, my manager, and E. G. Records, Ltd., the people I've been with for all of my career.

Let's run through the history of the project.

I'd been working on this record since July of 1983. All the tracks were started on an eight-track system that I rented—not having a studio of my own—and brought into my home in Sussex. They all were started on keyboards with my chief engineer, Rhett Davies, programming a rhythm machine. And then Andy Newmark or Omar Hakim or a combination of both would play with it at a later date to get some sort of human element.

The guitar at the end of "Slave to Love," with all that spiky stuff and those little licks, is Neil Hubbard, and the backwards stuff in the beginning and in the central solo is Keith Scott, who plays with Bryan Adams's band. Bob Clearmountain suggested him during a time when the Adams band was in London doing concerts.

"Sensation" was begun six to nine months before the last Roxy tour. Guy Fletcher, a keyboard player who was on the road with Roxy, and who has since been snatched up by Dire Straits, played on that track at Phil Manzanera's Gallery Studio in England. What you hear there, with all those changes and settings that sound like steel drums, is his audition!

"The Chosen One" was started as a kind of raga thing, with Chester Kaman playing acoustic guitar because I'd thought it'd be unusual to have a dance beat *set* by such an instrument. The chords of "Valentine" to me always had the feeling of a Brecht-Weill Berlin cabaret thing with the la-la-la-la chorus of European street songs, and I deliberately contrasted it with a reggae mood. "A Wasteland" was a reprise of "Valentine" and I kind of moved it away from that song and gave it space of its own. I like "Windswept" for the South American rhythmic elements, and it's Mark Knopfler's semi-acoustic guitar that provides the heavy, beautiful solo there, although it doesn't sound like him. And I get to play a keyboard solo, finally, after several years, on "Stone Woman," and it sounds a bit like a guitar, interestingly. "Don't Stop the Dance" began with a chord sequence that Rhett Davies devised and I wrote to it. That's how collaborations with Roxy always were, and I used to like that.

David Gilmour adds the strong licks on "Boys and Girls," and

I want to play with him more in the future. I made it the title track because I thought it was the central piece, the meat and bones, musically and thematically, of the record. The principal song, for me, is never the single, yet I name the record after it to spotlight in people's minds when they think of the album as whole cloth.

Overall, to me it has a steamy feeling, of the jungle almost, the concrete jungle. It has a sensuality thing, like a snake, which I like very much. A vividness.

Speaking of things vivid, do you still paint as you did back in the midsixties as an art student at the University of Newcastle?

No, not at all, but possibly in the future. I don't see any point in doing it if I don't do it seriously, and I really don't have enough time to shift my artistic field to that one now; I think it would dilute my energy. The one thing I have always been involved in was the designing of the LP sleeves. I especially like the covers for *Roxy Music* and *For Your Pleasure.* But I have trouble with sudden creative shifts, as a rule.

When I was on the last lap of mixing on the record last year, a songwriter in L.A. sent me a tape of a certain song, asking if I'd like to record the track as the theme tune for a film called *The Breakfast Club.* I heard the tape, thought the song was great ["Don't You (Forget About Me)"] but I couldn't bring myself to change gears. So Simple Minds picked it up, and it became huge in America! But that's the way I am. I can't adapt or adjust quickly to new input or whatever.

You also seem to work more slowly, perhaps more carefully, on your records than ever before.

It took a while to get started on this go-round because I was trying to finish off this special office-study-workroom room in my house in Sussex. It's a funny house I've got; all the windows face south, the north side is all bricked over. I had to build a big wing off the back of the house, and it has huge floor-to-ceiling Venetian windows, and a skylight. I built it so I could put all my things in it because previously all my stuff, my cassettes and papers, had been scattered all over the place.

I'm the best daydreamer; I'm quite happy sitting and drifting away. I do like when I have something specific to do. Going to the studio means that I can go to work. I like that feeling of doing a day's work. I'm not one of those people who likes his own company, and the discipline of going to the studio is very good for me.

Do you prefer country living to city living?

My wife and I are attempting to divide the two, spending more time in New York in order to appreciate the differences and contrasts between the two settings. I'd like to do some fishing this year. My wife, Lucy, was brought up fishing; her father was always off in Scotland, Ireland, Iceland, on fishing trips with the family. So she taught me to fish while I was doing the *Avalon* album.

The region shown on the cover is where I conjured up some of the songs; it's near Galway, on the west coast of Ireland. It's a very old-fashioned corner of the world, fifty years behind the times. It's very austere, very rocky, barren, but relaxing. And you hear wonderful Irish folk music on the radio, these Celtic pipes and fiddles skipping around and interweaving. I was there last year and had hoped to get there again this year.

[*Somber*] I took my dad and mother to Ireland last year for a week. They'd never been on a holiday before. He caught the flu . . . and then he died four days later, of a heart attack. Most of my father's people are dead, and what family is left came down to the funeral, a big gathering of the clans in Sussex, and I saw people I hadn't seen for thirty years.

I haven't been back to Galway since I buried my father.

Boys and Girls *has a dedication: "For my father, Frederick Charles Ferry, 1908–1984." There's so little known about your upbringing, your background. Let's talk about the Ferry family.*

I must tell you straightaway that I've never been too good at intimate talk per se; I'm a withdrawn type, but the wine, which is good, may help. I'd like to try, frankly, because I've been thinking about my life a great deal over the last year since losing my father.

He was seventy-six. The strangest man; I loved him very much. He was unique because he was so simple in his ways. According to the popular press and the rock encyclopedias, he was a miner, but he wasn't at all, really. Actually, he was a farmer, as his father, Alfred, was a farmer. They worked some land for a man in Penshaw, about four miles from Washington, where I was born. My dad, who was one of nine children, used to get up every day at 4:00 A.M.

In the northeast of England, you see, there were and still are networks of mining villages, with lots of green belts of farmland around them. It was interesting to have this industrialized society and these Thomas Hardy–type villages existing side-by-side. My mother worked in a chemicals factory in the region. She and my father met on a blind date; they went out for ten years.

He was born in 1908, so he would have been twenty, and she

was a year younger. They got married and moved into this farm cottage without any electricity. She was scared of the rural environment, with the cows putting their heads through the windows and that sort of thing, but she adjusted. They didn't have any money and wanted children, so he found he could make extra money—by looking after the horses that used to pull the coal carts underground in the nearby mines. His position as horsekeeper was a rural job, yet underground, and for thirty-odd years, he worked shoeing and grooming and caring after the teams. As a young lad, he used to box in a bar for money; once, a miner made the mistake of physically mistreating one of the horses, and my father knocked his teeth out!

Sounds like he was as tough as his environment.

Tough but gentle and quiet when not provoked. When he worked in the pit, he got little money, because it wasn't a highly skilled industrial type job like even drilling. It was a curious profession for someone who loved the outdoors as much as he did.

He kept a vegetable garden; he used to spend much of his free time over at his allotment—a designated section in the housing development. He would give my mother his wages every Friday, and she would give him a pound out of which he had to buy his tobacco. He smoked that thick, ropy twist of tobacco, the cheap stuff that you cut a plug from with a knife, until his dying day. But he had to smoke it outside because my mother wouldn't allow it indoors. He also kept racing pigeons there, which were his only luxury.

When he died, he was still as simple in his personal ways as ever. He couldn't and didn't use the telephone, and he couldn't drive a car or anything. My parents lived with me for the last eight years, in a cottage next to my house in Sussex. They would look after things while I was away, and it was great. If I had said, "I'm going to live on Mars. Would you like to come and look after things with me?" they would have said, "*Sure!*" My mother has always lived through me, and my incredible father, he was so calm and at one with nature. He didn't know anything about music, we never discussed it. It was a different world he had no conception of, yet he was a big influence on my work.

Tell me about the house you grew up in.

The first house, which I lived in until I was five, was called No. 5 Model Dwelling. It was a terraced, connected house like the row houses in the British "Coronation Street" television program shown in the States. Then we moved to a development, a council-house estate, which was a step up. It was a semi-detached house with a garden on Gainsborough Avenue in the town in County Durham, about eight miles from Newcastle.

I've two sisters: Ann, who's older and played classical piano, and Enid. I was a quiet kid, not a lot of friends, and I read a lot. Later on we got a phonograph record player, which was always in the living room, which we all shared. Later on, when I was thirteen, we also got a television, so we took turns with the one or the other. At night, I always listened to Radio Luxembourg before bed. My bedroom was very small, and I had poems on the walls, things I cut out of the Sunday *Times,* like Sylvia Plath. I don't know why they printed poems in the newspapers, but they did. I also taped up these postcards of famous paintings, or reproductions from art magazines.

Who are some of your favorite poets or authors?

Someone I go back to again and again is T. S. Eliot. That was possibly reinforced when I discovered we shared the same birthday. He was one of these American anglophiles, who'd worked in a bank in London, not secure in the belief in his own powers. The first thing I read of him was *The Wasteland,* when I was in school in Newcastle; I was sixteen and had become absorbed in literature, poetry, and art more or less at the same time.

Prior to that I'd just been bobbing along. I was a Boy Scout in the first Washington Troop, Curlew Patrol—that's a kind of bird with a long, thin down-curved beak. I remember carrying the flag about, going camping. I stayed with the troop for two years and got a badge for woodsmanship, chopping trees in the correct way and so forth. There was quite a bit of adventure in all that in my young mind; as we told our fireside stories I saw myself akin to David Livingstone and the great explorers and missionaries.

How, then, did you accomplish the jump from Scouting to the arts?

Through music—reading about Charlie Parker and his drugs when I was about eleven. I started buying records at twelve; a Charlie Parker EP was the first record I remember being crazy about. It was *The Immortal Charlie Parker,* and it had four tracks: "K.C. Blues," "She Rote," "Star Eyes," and "Au Privave." I used to go around singing all the solos by him and the young Miles Davis. There was something strange and difficult and beautiful about him.

What did you imagine Charlie Parker to be like?

Someone unlike anybody I knew—which was enough then, I suppose—and sad most of the time, because you can't be *hot* all the time, and when he was creating and on a good run, a good solo that was soaring somewhere, how could the rest of his life match up to that? And the rest of his life, with the drugs and all, was so tawdry in comparison to when he was up onstage cutting it. The same with Coltrane. I believe that a performer sometimes lives in this netherworld for the benefit of those who can't go there; the listeners' lives are made richer by getting the feeling from the artist, but they can't join him at his source.

I can recall sitting in a booth at J. G. Window's record store in Newcastle and trembling as I first heard this music, wondering, "Why do I get this sensation. Why do I positively shiver? *Why? Why?*" I got a similar thing when listening to old blues people like Leadbelly, Blind Lemon Jefferson, Big Bill Broonzy, and then later, with Billie Holiday. Her sound was a painful thing, steeped in an awful stress and yet exquisitely beautiful as well. I was touched by it, whereas pop music meant nothing.

Were you listening to any live music?

Oh yes! When I was eleven, I remember clearly the day I won a ticket for a show, because it was the day I had to take my exams to determine if I would go to a grammar school or a secondary modern. If you passed your exam, you went to a grammar school; if you didn't, things were going to be hard for you. That morning, I had won two tickets from Radio Luxembourg to see Bill Haley, and a Bill Haley album. So after the exam, I went to the Empire Theater in nearby Sunderland to see Haley, who was decked out in his tartan jacket. And his saxophonist, Rudy Pompilli, was leaping about wildly.

But did you pass that exam?

Yes, yes. So I went to the Washington Grammar School and got a really good education, provided by these old characters, many of them ex-army officers. The enrollment was boys and girls, thank God, boys and girls together. Academically, it was good, and if you worked hard you had a good shot at going to university—and if you *did* get into university then you had made it out of the working-class malaise. You had taken a step toward becoming classless, which was the ideal. Only then could you start creating your own life, as opposed to being a bricklayer who lives his life on building sites, or a fitter in some steel factory.

You see, for six weeks during each summer holiday I *would* go to work on a building site or in the local steel factory. I also had two paper routes, delivering both papers and magazines. I covered one route in the morning before school and the other in the evening.

Also, I would go around to the pubs on Saturdays selling the special pink football sheets.

On Saturdays, after I had done my morning paper route, I would put on my smartest suit and get on the bus for the ten-mile ride to Newcastle, where I worked in a tailor's shop, Jackson the Tailor, on Northumberland Street, the main street in Newcastle. I was expected to write down measurements and fetch bolts of cloth and the like.

[*Laughter*] I guess that's where I got interested in clothes. I used to love to look through the shop's old catalogs of clothes, each of them filled with wonderful drawings of fine suits, pictures of vintage sartorial elegance. Later, I'd go over to the local billiards room, where all the Teddy Boys used to hang out, and they had these remarkable clothes: bright peacock-blue or deep scarlet suits with velvet-collared jackets that ran down to their knees, and thick, crepe-soled shoes. I stood there in my school blazer, amazed.

Were you spending your wages on records or clothes?

Both, but later on I spent them on bicycle parts. I'd joined a racing club of the Tour de France sort, meaning these were not motorbikes. The bike thing was a scene I explored for about two years, beginning when I was fifteen. I *had* to have the best bike, and the only way to do that was to send away for these special parts. As in mod culture, where you had to have exactly the right length of hair and type of shoe, in cycling there was only one sort of brake you could have, only one sort of ten-gear unit. You had to have a very short crew cut, a certain cap, short white socks, perforated black racing shoes, and tight-fitting black racing shorts. I was quite dedicated and used to do a lot of training after school.

Were you any good at the sport?

Good? I was utterly useless! [*huge burst of laughter*] Never any good at all.

After cycling, then, your next predilection was rock and roll?

[*Wide grin, shaking his head*] No, no. Next was rock-climbing. I formed a mountaineering society in my school when I was seventeen. Four of us used to do our climbing in the Lake District, in the Cumbrians; they have some very good crags there. Also in Northumberland, near the famous Roman Wall which runs for some hundred miles or so. I did the climbing thing to the limit, with the whole Matterhorn aesthetic: camping out on various summits in mountaineering tents, dressed in leather boots and heavy corduroy breeches, smoking a clay pipe and reading poetry. Ridiculous.

So where the hell was rock and roll when all this was going on?

I really don't know. I think it was hardly there at all. The big thing was passing my exams and interview for university. But during the ten-week break between leaving school and going to university, as I was contemplating the usual building site/factory work stint, I bumped into this guy in the street who used to be in the old cycling club.

He said, "Can you sing?" I said, "Sure I can sing!" [*chuckles*] having never done it in my life. He said, "I've got a group. Do you want to get together with us?" So I went up and this fellow had a back-to-back fish and chips shop and hairdressing salon, and the band, the Banshees, was rehearsing in the back room. So I joined up with these guys, who were factory laborers who did this in the evenings, and we began playing an itinerary of ballrooms and workingmen's clubs. We played R&B, Chuck Berry, all that, and the workingmen loved us. We finally graduated to a hip club in Newcastle, the Club Au Go Go, a legendary place where Cream, Jimi Hendrix, Captain Beefheart, and others played. Then it was time for me to go to university, and I said good-bye and began a new chapter.

Were you a big man on campus?

Not as such. Everyone wanted me to go to Oxford to study English, because I'd acted in this Shakespeare production at school, playing Malvolio in *Twelfth Night*, and got rave reviews. It was my first stage experience, and though it was very scary I quite enjoyed it—I'd do it again. People are always telling me to get into acting, but I wasn't interested in Oxford or the theater. So in 1964 I went to Newcastle University, and I had various rows there, because they wanted me to be the head boy there if I'd cut my hair, but I said absolutely not because I was still into this poetic, Byronic nineteenth-century Romantic mountaineering phase.

After I'd been there a month or two I found people from different parts of the country who wanted to form a group and started the Gas Board with a bass player friend, Graham Simpson, who would later be on the first Roxy Music album. He had a wonderful collection of jazz records, every Blue Note album ever, each in immaculate condition. But we didn't play jazz, though ours was more sophisticated material than the Banshees: Bobby Bland, Otis Redding, B. B. King, Freddie King, Albert King. Our guitarist, Ian Watts, a physics student, was quite good and helped make us a hot band. We all lived in a house on Cheltenham Terrace in Newcastle. We bought a van, got publicity shots taken, the whole thing. We continued for my first year and part of my second, and they went on to become professional while I decided to stay and finish my courses. I was too much into art at the time, studying with a gifted conceptual artist named Richard Hamilton, and though I enjoyed the music greatly it wasn't an expression of myself.

In 1968 I graduated and moved down to London, where I got work driving delivery vans, working in an antiques restoration shop on Walton Street, driving a truck for a removal company, moving people's furniture, and taking pianos down steep stairways—plus teaching art. Eventually I got myself an old piano and tried to teach myself a few chords, and started writing songs. I also tried to meet other people interested in the same thing.

After about a year, I had enough people to form a group, and that was Roxy Music. After a few months of odd little gigs I had enough songs, like "Ladytron" and "Psalm"—which didn't turn up on record until *Stranded*—to do a first album. I started carrying the tapes around, and I sent one to Richard Williams, who worked for *Melody Maker.* He called me back the same day, and said, "Great! Can I do an interview with you?" John Peel, the big underground DJ for the BBC, he got one of the same tapes, and asked me to come on the show. It all happened so quickly it was like, *zooom.* I started writing songs seriously in 1970, and now I've been at it for fifteen years!

Throughout, there's always been a churchy aura to your music. Are you religious? Do you pray in times of stress and loss?

I was raised in the Church of England and sent to Sunday School. My wife's a Catholic; we were married in a Catholic church. I don't go to church at all, but I'm somehow sure I'll become more interested in it later in my life, as that seems to be the general way things go as you age.

The only time I have strong feelings about religion is when I'm writing, and people have always said to me that there's a strong, oddly religious mood that comes through in much of my later work, which I don't consciously generate or put into it. What I'm trying to do is reduce words and images and sounds down to the bone.

And yet, you've long been identified as a leading trend-setter in the decidedly unaustere cult-of-fashion scene in England.

I've always gone through different phases of style consciousness. While in my teens, the idea of being an artist appealed to me long before I was an artist, the whole image of the bohemian Left Bank painter wearing a black cloak and calling for "more wine!" Later,

I switched to the Jackson Pollack New York loft look, with his T-shirt and jeans.

England is a fertile place for fashion; it's a small country, it's an island, it has hordes of young people, it has a great past, and there is a genuine depth to its culture. From America, it's seen as being provincial, but information passes through its borders very quickly because it's very tightly focused, especially in terms of music. When Roxy first appeared in England in 1972, everybody in the country knew about it at once, whereas in America there still are regions where the band's music is on the outskirts of radioland.

I suppose the network of the English art schools, which now sadly are being phased out, were very important to the growth of the British music scene. So many future rockers attended them before and during my time—and many kids followed suit afterward *because* of us. The attraction was obvious when you consider that, in a society where a traditional trade is customarily *the* thing, young people could leave a conventional school, get a government grant to go to an art college—due to my parents' limited resources I got a full grant—and spend a few years being trained as sculptors or painters. And each town had an art school even if it was just part of a technical college.

Actually, I assumed that everybody had art schools. They've always been a hotbed of talent, where the influence is greater than what they make out of it themselves. A lot of the fashion ideas come out of these colleges and into British street culture among the young, but the money is never there to capitalize on the ideas, so they're pinched by Paris, New York, and Japan. One of the most significant individual fashion exponents is Antony Price, one of my oldest and most eccentric friends, who took the pictures for the sleeve of *Boys and Girls* in his living room, and has done artwork for Roxy albums. He's been a huge influence as a designer on a vast number of people, whether it's been with his women's tube dresses with the spiral zippers, or the squarish, big-shouldered suits adapted from 1940s men's clothing—so many, many things.

With my own musical and performance work, I've always been asked why so many people are influenced by me. But actually, both with Roxy and on my own, I was always *implying* a lot of things. I would hint at and suggest but never entirely pursue an idea, an attitude in making music, a visual image, or a sense of style to its conclusion, so they were all rich avenues that were there to be explored further by others. For someone starting out in the music business, all these slices of stimulation proved to be attractive directions to take.

I guess it's been a kind of philosophy on my part, but there have been times [*laughter*] when it's crossed my mind to go back to one of those avenues to explore it more, and I've discovered, "Oh, oh. Too late. Someone else is well on with it now."

Currently, I don't listen to what anybody else is doing in music because there are so many things that seem to remind me a bit of what I do or have done. It gets incestuous. [*laughter*] At the end of the day, you just have to know that no one can be you, and at best there can only be superficial similarities. I'm just getting further and further into myself.

Maybe you've come full circle from the early, struggling years when you were trying to isolate time to think for yourself.

It does feel cyclical, in a sense. Back then, around 1970, I felt I was getting nowhere, spending all my time at jobs I didn't like, so I applied to the London Education Authority for a part-time job as an art teacher. I did it three days a week, and it gave me enough money to live on. On my days free, I began to write songs in a flat I shared with my girlfriend Susie on Kensington High Street. Then I took them around on cassettes to record companies.

The demos were made on a big gray tape recorder that Brian Eno owned. I'd met him through Andy Mackay, and he'd come over to the apartment on Kensington High Street with it, and he'd tape Andy fooling with his oboe, and me on keyboards, and him twiddling on synthesizer. We advertised in *Melody Maker* for a guitarist and drummer and got Roger Bunn and Dexter Lloyd. And then they were replaced by Paul Thompson and David O'List—a lot of shuffling about!

One of our first gigs was in 1971 at a pub on Kensington High Street called the Hand and Flower, playing all the songs from the first album. After a few more personnel changes we were a band making a record, with Phil Manzanera on guitar and Pete Sinfield producing, of course.

I fell in love with the idea of something called Roxy Music. I had sat down one day to write and had fancifully made out a list of the names of cinemas—like Plaza, Odeon, Regal, Ritz, Rivoli—because I liked the idea that they were important sounding but didn't really mean anything. When I got to Roxy I stopped, and mused: "Roxy . . . Rox-y . . . Rox . . . Rock." I thought it'd make a fine name for the band. For a couple of months we were just Roxy, and then someone said there'd been a band in America with that name so we added "Music," which seemed even better.

And then John Peel at the BBC and Richard Williams at *Melody Maker* pitched in with their critical enthusiasm. That kind of thing could never have happened in America. People read the piece in the *Melody Maker,* heard the session we did on the BBC, and we were off and running. E. G. Management gave us an audition in a cinema in South London, and they asked me if I wanted to sign by myself and use better musicians. Being very retiring by nature, I was terrified of being onstage alone anyhow.

You conquered your reserve quickly, however. Because it was less than two years before you were building a solo career.

The first two Roxy albums had been hits in England and most of Europe, and the whole thing was going great. But I was exhausted from the work, particularly on the *For Your Pleasure* album. I'd felt I'd made a reputation as a songwriter playing fairly weird music, and I thought it'd be interesting to do an old-style Sinatra-like album of standards and material I'd admired from Goffin and King, Lieber and Stoller, the Beatles, and the Stones. I felt that the songs I like aren't really ever going to get out there to the mass public, and you get a bit bored being limited to a cult audience. I was hungry to make more records, but also hungry to learn more as well, and *These Foolish Things* fit those ambitions. The solo would just be a one-off record on which I was just a singer/stylist/arranger. Some of the songs were more successful than others, but that record was also a European hit. In America it just confused the issue, since the Roxy Music thing was complex and odd to begin with. Nonetheless, I realized, "Gee, I've now got two careers!"

These Foolish Things influenced Roxy's *Stranded,* both of which, like *For Your Pleasure,* had been completed during 1973; I was moving very fast, learning very fast. And then I did *Another Time, Another Place,* which showed me in the white tuxedo, which it was so strong, that image, that it stuck to me for years and *years.* Previously, I had been wearing these vaguely futuristic, showy, neo-1950s costumes with lurex and tiger stripes, which Antony Price had done for me. We felt that the music *needed* some kind of presentation to attract attention, and also it made it easier for us to perform, since we weren't particularly showy people. To get dressed up in a different guise made it much easier to carry it off.

The solo thing went on in tandem through the mid-1970s, with Roxy's *Country Life, Siren, Viva!* and my *Let's Stick Together* and

In Your Mind. My solo career grew so big there was a *lot* of friction from the band, and it became a very unpleasant place in which to work. I went on a world solo tour and then lived in L.A. for six months in 1977 just as the punk movement was coming on. I took a combination of English and American players to Montreux, Switzerland, to do *The Bride Stripped Bare.*

And that's when your luck ran out.

[*Nodding sheepishly*] Precisely. But I must say that up to this point the previous *In Your Mind* album had been my least favorite record, and I was looking for a dynamic new combination of elements. None of the musicians I'd brought along with me had ever worked with each other, and it was all very weird. We were in Switzerland in the winter, with a lot of snow, everything very bleak—the perfect environment for what became a cold, bleak record. [*He shudders.*] Uhh! My girlfriend [Jerry Hall] ran off with somebody [Mick Jagger], and the music turned into blues, very sad.

I was after a kind of Duchamp thing, inspired by one of his most famous works, "The Bride Stripped Bare By Her Bachelors, Even," known popularly as "The Large Glass." Richard Hamilton, my teacher at Newcastle, had done a reconstruction of it in 1964; and I had always loved the mystical, intellectually convoluted qualities of Duchamp's work. I also liked the idea that after being one of the most important artists of the twentieth century, with his dadaist brilliance, and then jumping into cubism, futurism, and all that, Duchamp finally gave up and played chess for the rest of his life, until he died in his eighties. [*laughter*] He used to do things he called "ready-mades," which was signing bicycle wheels and urinals and objects that were already made. I felt I was doing the same thing on the album by putting my signature, if you will, on other people's songs.

And suddenly, I was faced with my first commercial failure. It was a bunch of firsts: my first time with American players; the first time I tried for a laid-back, behind-the-beat sense of space on a record; the first time I had no single; the first time I had a flop.

Therefore, partly due to the punk thing, and partly because I felt my image had gotten so out of control, I decided I'd better put Roxy back together again. So we did it with Manzanera and Andy Mackay and a few people who'd also been on *Bride.* It felt like a whole new phase, and I decided I'd make a go of it under the group name, and *Manifesto, Flesh and Blood,* and *Avalon* were the results, along with what was a lot of touring for us.

In truth, I find each album to be exhausting, because I don't consider what I do to be disposable pop music. I get very serious about it. I want to *share* it in the present. I may even start out trying to make the song difficult, but then melody overtakes me, and funky guitar, and traditional body rhythms. So I figure that while I can still groove, I should, while I can still feel this sensuality, which *is* a part of me. And I'll maybe wait for the day when I'm in a wheelchair before I get into nonrhythmic atonality. Although I'm a white, European, very English sort of person, I do understand and love the rhythms of black music. The combination of rock and roll, Celtic things, and black music that I've been experimenting with lately has been quite good, I think, so I'll keep with it.

Frequently people expect the artist to be the embodiment of his work. The fan and devotee look forward to meeting someone they admire because they expect to see his art in him, but that's never so. What you paint or compose or write is never who you are. Rather it's an expression of who you would like to become, the growth you hope for, the personal reach you envision. It's always a full length ahead of who you know yourself to be.

Yes, yes! That's exactly it. My work is *not* me. Creating is a touching thing, it's a hurting thing. You're trying to discover how you *really* regard things and there's pain in that, an intensity, because with that recognition as the starting point, you're then trying to make something that is extra to yourself, that is better than yourself.

Did Boys and Girls *live up to your own revised expectations?*

I was nervous until it went into the charts at No. 1 in England, but over here, I get a bit of the "Who do you think *you* are?" reaction, being asked why I'm not more successful here, but I'm game to make an even greater go of it. It's been a fascinating journey thus far, and I suppose I've taken a crack at just about every goal I can think of.

Except acting, interestingly enough. It's curious that someone as image-aware as yourself wouldn't want to expand your suave persona on, say, the big screen.

[*Brooding*] I don't know that I'm cut out for it. I'd love to surprise myself by doing it well, but it would have to be a very special project, because it's an art form that has become too subject to commercial pressure. I wouldn't want to trivialize a lot of the heartfelt effort of the past by doing it badly. That would crush me.

I guess it's a matter of someone imagining me doing something in film that would be a natural and perfect fit.

Hmmmm. I could see you as a great, very spectral romantic lead playing opposite some haunted beauty, you a shadowy figure of desire who has absolutely no dialogue.

[*Face brightens; he grins slyly*] Ahh! See, that's why I never say a total no to the prospect! So now, have you any more ideas on how we can bring off this inspired little role?

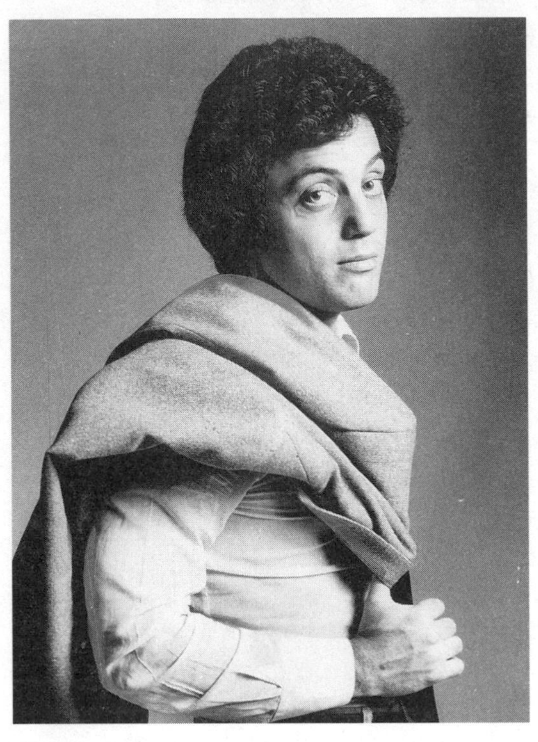

William Levitt had an American dream. He wanted to strike the first bold blow in defeating the massive housing crunch of the years 1945–49. Men who had risked their lives to eradicate the Nazi threat were returning home to rebuild their lives, get married, and detonate a baby boom—but there was no shelter for the swarm. These men, who by now had learned to fight more than one kind of battle, were being forced to live in coops, lean-tos, and stables; and a nationwide revolt of disturbingly uncertain proportions was in the air. Politicians warned of the impending shame of new Hoovervilles, the Washington, D.C., shantytowns from which General MacArthur's tanks routed thousands of unemployed and impoverished World War I veterans and their families in July 1932. The Senate held hearings on the problem but did little.

Billy Joel

1982/89

William Levitt seized the initiative. Looking at the massive stretches of potato fields on his native Long Island, he saw land easily convertible to housing developments and conceived the idea of mass preparation of the site, putting in all the utilities, hardware, and so on, for some 17,500 Cape Cod houses, the same way a spud farmer might install a sprinkler system for an anticipated crop. There would also be ball fields, village greens, schools, and even a shopping center to make the community self-sustaining. Paring the construction schedule of the entirely uniform homes to twenty-six steps, he trained his civilian crews accordingly, convinced the government to underwrite the mortgaging for the strapped vets, and the greatest tract-housing sprawl known to man was born—Levittown, New York.

That was the good news. The bad news was, as William "Billy" Martin Joel, who grew up in the West Village Green section of Levittown, phrased it, "The houses looked so much alike that if you stumbled home drunk, you never knew where you'd end up." Once the vets got over the thrill of owning their own homes, while at the same time not having to fret about keeping up with the Joneses (who had the same house right down to the daintiest detail), they began to be oppressed by the stupefying and terribly alienating sameness of the development. This reaction took a while to take shape. It was the children of the vets who really hated Levittown, and they hated it with a flagrant, sometimes fatal vengeance. One native elevated his ire to the level of a lively art, turning his characterizations of suburban American alienation among the products of the postwar baby boom into superbly acerbic anthems: this was Billy Joel.

Billy's father took the long way home from the ravages of Hitler and the war. A Jew born in Nuremberg, Howard Joel survived confinement in the Dachau concentration camp and escaped to New York City by way of Cuba. He married, fathered two children while he and wife Rosalind lived in the Bronx, then got sold on Levittown.

Billy was born on May 9, 1949. At the age of four, his mother lost patience with the boy's constant banging on the Lester upright piano in their tiny living room and dragged him to formal lessons, so that he might emulate his father, a classically trained pianist. The Joels' economic status was mildly middle-class until the parents divorced when Billy was seven, leaving his mother to muddle along on a meager secretary's salary, supplemented by small support checks from her ex-husband, who'd moved to Vienna.

By his early teens, Billy's thorough disdain for the impersonal landscape of Levittown and his fury with the way in which he stuck out in it, had hardened and found expression in crime. Attired in the standard night-spree garb of leather jacket, purple shirt, chinos, and matador boots, he and other members of the Parkway Green Gang took to robbing stores, fighting with rival gangs, drinking wine, and sniffing glue.

During Billy's high school years, the Beatles arrived in America, followed by the Dave Clark Five and the scruffy, defiant Rolling Stones. Playing in a band was now as important as being ballsy in a punchout. The time he'd spent at sissy piano lessons became valuable, and he formed a group called the Echoes. Dressed in blue jackets with velvet collars, the Echoes were the hit of the Teen Canteen at Hicksville High. The group changed its name to the Emerald Lords, then the Lost Souls. Sneaking backstage after a Young Rascals concert to meet keyboardist Felix Cavaliere, Joel became a convert to their blue-eyed Long Island soul. Staying up all night playing bars and roadhouses became a routine, and the 7:00 A.M. wakeup alarm for school became a nuisance. Scheduled to graduate from Hicksville High with the Class of 1967, he was informed that spring that his diploma would be denied because of absenteeism. Running away from home, he found himself sitting on the stoop of some anonymous home in Hicksville, wondering where he'd sleep that night, when a patrol car pulled up. The house had been broken into earlier that day, and he was arrested on suspicion of burglary. Spending the night in jail, he imagined what it must have been like for his father in Dachau and panicked.

The charges were dropped the following morning, but Joel's sense of being trapped, in Levittown, in shabby economic circumstances, took root. Just turned eighteen, he saw that many of his friends in the Parkway Green Gang were in jail, strung out on drugs, or dead from toppling off train trestles while intoxicated and playing "Chicken." An offer came to join the Hassles, a major club band, and he took it; the band recorded two albums for United Artists Records, *The Hassles* and *Hour of the Wolf,* in the late 1960s before being dissolved. Joel found work dredging oysters from a barge. At roughly the same time, his longtime girlfriend broke up with him. He attempted to commit suicide by drinking a bottle of furniture polish, then committed himself to the mental ward of the Meadowbrook Hospital in East Meadow, Long Island, for three weeks of observation.

Convinced by his stay "with a cast of characters out of *One Flew over the Cuckoo's Nest*" that he was not crazy, he redoubled his efforts to make it in rock and roll. He and Jon Small, the drummer in the Hassles, formed Attila, a two-man psychedelic band inspired by Cream and the Lee Michaels Band. The two were pictured on the album jacket dressed as Huns and standing in a meat-locker.

In 1971, he fell in with entrepreneur Artie Ripp's Family Productions and cut a solo album, *Cold Spring Harbor*, for ABC-Paramount Records. When it was released in 1972, the mismastered LP made Joel sound like one of the Chipmunks. Worse, Joel had sold off much of his publishing royalties to Ripp. Embittered by the consequences of his naïveté, Joel left town, hiding out in Los Angeles for almost two years under the pseudonym of Bill Martin.

Ripp realized the blanket contract with Joel would have to be renegotiated if either party was to get anything out of it, so a settlement was reached wherein Ripp's Family Productions would receive twenty-five cents from every dollar Joel made from all subsequent albums. Joel signed with Columbia Records, and "Piano Man" was released in October 1973. Although it rose no higher than the Top 20, it established Joel as a songwriter. "The Ballad of Billy the Kid" also received considerable FM attention. The song was a deliberately inaccurate retelling of the outlaw's life story, the singer's point being that anyone has the power to reinvent himself if he dares.

Piano Man was the work of a completely novel rock practitioner. Unfortunately, though it sold over a million copies, Joel reportedly made only $7,763 on the album. Appalled, he asked his wife, Elizabeth, a graduate of UCLA's School of Management, to sort out his affairs. She did well by him. His next album, *Street Life Serenade*, yielded a Top 40 hit in 1974 with "The Entertainer," a song simultaneously cynical and stirring. Then, in 1976, Joel issued *Turnstiles*, which contained "New York State of Mind," a song he wrote on a plane returning to the city; he pictured Ray Charles singing it at Yankee Stadium—the quintessential pop standard. Instead, Joel himself made it a standard, and Frank Sinatra sang it at Carnegie Hall.

The Stranger arrived in 1977, with five huge hits, all of them omnipresent in the American pop music repertoire. This album accentuated Joel's uniqueness in rock and roll—he'd successfully merged the vernaculars of Hollywood sound stages with those of Shubert and Tin Pan Alley, along with the warm ambiance of

Sinatra saloon albums, 1950s car-radio pop, the sound of the Beatles-led British Invasion, and the rich melodicism of post–New Wave rock. It was a remarkable feat, making his piss-off, polyglot music the most widely accepted since that of the Beatles, yet completely his own.

Glass Houses and *52nd Street* produced more hits, and *Songs from the Attic* did well in 1981 with its reprise of little-known songs from the early stages of his career. In 1982, Joel unleashed what was generally considered to be his masterpiece, *The Nylon Curtain*, which contained "Pressure," "Goodnight Saigon," and "Allentown." At the beginning of 1983, Joel and his manager-wife, Elizabeth, filed for divorce, and he began dating model Christie Brinkley. *An Innocent Man*, released in 1983, was Joel's final farewell to the reckless romanticism of his youth, distilling the distinctive sounds of the acts he thrived on when he was a glue-sniffing gang pug—the Four Seasons, the Tymes, Little Anthony and the Imperials.

The Bridge (1986) was an elegant and emotive look at his second marriage, to Christie Brinkley, and its fruits (daughter Alexa Ray, named for Ray Charles), while *Kohuept* (1987) was a live memento of his tour of the U.S.S.R. In 1989, Joel released *Storm Front*, the diary of a baby boomer's doubts about his generation's vanity-diluted values. The superior record contained themes of personal uncertainty as well, notably the distressed "I Go to Extremes" and the near-disconsolate love lament "And So It Goes."

Joel also had serious doubts about his business management, firing former brother-in-law Frank Weber on August 30, 1989, after an audit of Billy's Frank Management organization allegedly uncovered thefts of millions of dollars, with still more millions lost to risky investments such as horse-breeding. In a $90 million suit against Weber, Joel charged misuse of power of attorney and misuse of funds through interest-free loans. Ironically, the singer's feelings of breached faith were reflected in a statement made seven years earlier regarding the grim national legacy his peers seemed saddled with.

"Here we are, having fought our way to adulthood in the aftermath of the baby boom, while rising up through the traditional values of our parents, protesting and testing them," said Joel. "Now that we're prepared to go forward with our heads screwed on straight, all the possibilities are being closed off. An unspoken promise has been broken."

The following interview was done in autumn 1982 at Billy Joel's house in Oyster Bay, Long Island. He was living alone in a large waterside mansion after separating from his first wife, Elizabeth, and he was recovering from a motorcycle spill in which he'd badly injured his left hand. Joel was soon to fall in love with Christie Brinkley and start a new life, but at present he was passing the hours reading Betty Friedan's *The Second Stage* and John Erlichman's *Witness to Power,* as well as puttering with the melodies that would comprise *An Innocent Man.*

Much of our talk took place at his Baldwin grand, on which he'd intersperse full songs from *The Nylon Curtain* and unfinished new fragments with bursts of "Sh-Boom" and "Appalachian Spring." His manner was easygoing and unaffected, the playing vigorous and sure. Gazing over Joel's shoulder as he illustrated some Aaron Copland chords, one could see a small etching on the piano easel just above his scarred left hand. Its inscription read: "We carry within us the wonders we seek."

Well, you went and did it this time. Made an album your old pals the music critics actually admire.

[*Grinning*] You know, I wanted the album jacket to look like a book cover, the latest novel from Ludlum or Michener, a paperback you'd find in the racks of any airport shop in the country. That kind of accessibility. CBS wanted my picture on the front, but I'm sick of my face. I was a little worried about the sequencing of the songs, though. The album opens with four songs about, respectively, unemployment, guilt, pressure, and war—the Four Horsemen of the Apocalyptic American landscape. Whew!

But man, I like the straight-force piano resonance in "Allentown," an Aaron Copland–influenced arrangement of major 7ths that's percussive and stirring. Gives *me* goosebumps, it's got so much classic, shoulder-to-the-wheel Americana in it. I love Copland's majestic kind of coloration. The original melody for "Allentown" I started writing about ten years ago, while hitting the circuit of colleges in the Lehigh Valley of Pennsylvania. That region is such a pretty pocket of the country, so spacious. A feeling of the good U.S. earth rolling around you. Coming from the direction of New York City, you pass through the Lehigh Tunnel and you're suddenly in the heartland. Allentown: the name echoes "Our Town," or sounds like "Everytown." When I was in grammar school I had this reader called *Your Town,* and in it you were told about the doctor and the grocer and the butcher. It taught you about storybook democracy in action.

Next to Allentown is Bethlehem, lying right off the Pennsylvania Turnpike on the Double Deuce—U.S. Route 22. I think Allentown is where everybody lives and Bethlehem is where they all work. A decade ago, I rode through the area and thought, "So this is where Bethlehem Steel is—Steel City, U.S.A. And off the top of my head I got the opening couplet, "Well, we're living here in Allentown, and they're closing all the factories down." But the song stayed frozen at that stage for the longest time.

So it wasn't originally tied to Reaganomics and the bottoming out of the economy?

No, but I had a kind of premonition about what would happen if all this industrial might was somehow silenced. I left the song alone, and every couple of years the band and I would go into the studio and try to write "Allentown," but it wasn't coming because the mood in it was of a trivial "my town, your town" generalness. Then, when the series of reversals happened in the steel world, bringing on the plant shutdowns in Bethlehem, I suddenly knew what I was going to write about. It was literally the fifth time I had sat down to write it, and it became a song about the solitary anguish of unemployment and the current climate of diminishing horizons. I picked up the daily newspapers, and the lyrics were in the depressing headlines; proud, decent, bewildered working people found themselves stuck just killing time, filling out forms, standing in line.

I've never heard you discuss your songwriting in detail. How did you develop a theme like "Allentown," once you'd gotten the germ of the song?

I always write at a piano, largely in the studio. I started "Allentown" at home, and I wrote the bridge in the studio, which is common for me. Honestly, I love having written a catalog of songs, but I *hate* the writing process and I don't want to waste any of my creative energy if the band isn't going to like them anyhow, so I take them into the studio to get a reading. If they really like it, which is rare, they'll go, "Yeah, yeah! That's *solid*!" and I'll finish inserting the bridge, which is always something of a Chinese torture device for me. They'll be standing there all the while, very much a jury, and they can really be a nasty bunch of guys. They really nudge me with their "show-us" routine, spur me on.

Thematically, I wanted "Allentown" to tie into the postwar baby boom and what happened to our generation in the aftermath. Now that we're prepared to go forward with our heads screwed on straight, all the possibilities are being closed off. It's like, "Huh? What happened to the everyday workingman's dreams—small, modest dreams, not big ones—that always came true in America?"

Surprisingly, the song breathes and manages to galvanize the listener; it's especially skillfully wrought in that it doesn't feel claustrophobic like the dilemma it describes.

[*Pensive*] I dunno; I believe it's a little piece of the American puzzle, like it or not, and I wanted it to have a sense of hope, but I didn't want to push it on people. I thought I'd let them discover it and accept or reject it without a lot of fanfare.

You and me, we grew up in the fifties. Our parents had a sense of boundless possibilities and certain rewards for strivers. After World War II, it was wide open. Now it's locked up tight. Especially for our generation. So we have to go back to where *they* were to get a sense of perspective of where we are now. So I figured, "Let's build to this task in the structure of the song." The lyrics emerged naturally, almost organically.

Our fathers fought the wonderful war to make the world safe for democracy and hot homemade pie, and we got stuck with the Vietnam ugliness, where the issues weren't cut and dried. That was the monkey wrench tossed into the mechanism of our spirit as a nation. They threw the American flag in our faces, saying "Well it's time for *you* guys to take up guns and go to war." Like taking a number in a deli. So we did it, and what did we get for the misery? Isolation from ourselves.

With "Goodnight Saigon. . . ." you didn't go to Vietnam, yet it seems that you caught the murky rock-and-roll-underscored unreality of the waking nightmare.

I researched the way the battles were fought, reading books like *Rumor of War* by Phillip Caputo, an amazing and upsetting book that may be the definitive one on the war. They'd load the troops into these big metal insects, drop them into this battle zone, and then pick them up at the end of the day; it was a nine-to-five war. How *sick* is that?! The song is framed the same way the parameters of the days were: by the sounds of the choppers leaving and returning.

For the sound effect of the rotors, we got a recording of the actual "Huey" [UH-1E] choppers. But I came to understand that the Huey sound didn't reproduce on record the way the ear hears it, so I used a synthesizer effect that had more highs. So it's a two-part re-creation: the highs are the synthesizer and the bottom is the Huey. It gave the end product greater ambiance, a sense of it buzzing in your ear like a gnat; an annoying, chilling metallic sound that wouldn't let you relax, that pestered and haunted like a recurring, unwelcome dream.

I knew a lot of people who went to Vietnam. In Levittown and Hicksville, Long Island, where I grew up, everybody went. People with my lower-middle-class background didn't attend college. You either had a job waiting for you after high school, went to a vocational technical school, or joined up in the Marines. So many went the last route, winding up in 'Nam. Some didn't come back, some came back screwed up, some came back as normal people. But they weren't encouraged to talk about their experience. They got shafted because they desperately needed day-to-day catharsis from our society, some aid and comfort like any shell-shocked soldier does, but people didn't want to hear about the war or the Vietnam vets' physical or psychic wounds. Now, we have to confront these survivors and the war still in their heads before we can go on as a people. Whether safe at home or in a rice paddy in Asia, it was *our* war, our generation's trauma, fought, and fought against, by us. What did it do to us? How did it scar us?

I would ask my friends to tell me about 'Nam for the song, but, again, it took years and years. So many images finally emerged though—"I was dropped into this quiet, steamy swamp . . ." Imagine going from a sunny street in suburban Long Island to a crazy, sinister city like Saigon, and then into a quiet, quiet swamp that was in the center of no place; stoned, with an M-16. Where/who was the enemy?

These guys told me, "We had no home front; the war was anywhere and everywhere. But the countryside was beautiful over there." Yet I began to notice that almost no one had pictures and I asked why. They said, [*bitterly*] "We had no Instamatics, we had automatic rifles. We shot bullets, not photos." They played the Doors and Hendrix, passed a bong of hash, spaced out as best they could, and kept their heads down.

There are strong, visceral themes in The Nylon Curtain. *It's about growing up estranged in America, wanting to embrace it but realizing that even something as massive as America can be mercurial. For our generation, no place is home. I don't mean that in a nihilistic way. We've got to learn to be comfortable on the run.*

Right! That's part of the American tradition. We're constantly in a state of flux, craving incessant change. You go to Europe, and people have lived in the same valley for hundreds of years. Americans are always on the move, for better or worse. But we live behind a veil, a nylon curtain, separated from the goals and sorrows of the rest of the world.

That's another American ambition: the individual desire for separateness. The fun of living way out in Long Island is partly the feeling I don't belong in this "old money" environment. I come from Hicksville; people from my background don't end up here. My friends come over in their beat-up Volkswagens. The WASP ghosts in the house are probably moaning, "There's a Jewboy in here with us!"

But I'm constantly bouncing back and forth between here and the city. I usually get drawn in there to record, and I feel most at home anywhere when I'm recording. To me, where I record makes no difference. People say, "Go to Montserrat, London, Caribou Studios." Why? Once you're inside, it doesn't matter. It's an office, a factory.

It wasn't until I was on the road with your band that I understood how much their aggressive musical support and keep-Billy-honest camaraderie has to do with your music.

Listen, I write the way they play! They were there when I was nothing. We all grew up together, personally and musically. And their presence gives me an invaluable sense of perspective on my work. They look at me as the writer-nebbish in the band. And, uh, I happen to sing, too. They can walk in and go, "Shut up, schmuck. I *know* you; don't give me that dopey garbage." They are *not* impressed by Mr. Billy Joel one measly bit.

As the albums have come and gone, we've worked out a unique studio strategy centered around the Chinese food we order in when we're working. The recording is very scientifically divided into pre- and post-Chinese food takes. [*smirking*] Don't look at me that way! This, unfortunately, is not a gag.

Sorry. Please continue.

So in terms of inner-band diplomacy there is a schism between those who feel the pre-Chinese tracks are superior to the post-Chinese variety. It has to do with the grease on the egg rolls and the effects of the monosodium glutamate on blood sugar, on the left side of the brain and its conceptual strengths. We've actually had some half-serious arguments, complete with hurt feelings afterward, concerning this question. Liberty got up at one point during the sessions for the new LP and gave a speech about respect for the ancient Chinese civilization, their culture, their art, their gunpowder . . .

Then we have a trio called the Mean Brothers, which consists of me, Doug [Stegmeyer] on bass, and Liberty [De Vitto] on drums. We always lay down the basic tracks. Then the guitars and the horns come in and do their thing. The Mean Brothers have their own satin road jackets with Doberman pinschers on the back. I'm MB No. 1, and so forth. We are the elite corps, and we give the other guys, especially the guitarists, "The Ear." We sit there like Cheshire cats while they tune up and construct their parts, making taunting comments like, "Go ahead, pal, play with your toys. We're waiting. Just want to mention that we're only gonna give you *twenty minutes* to get this take before we move on." And they'll be frantic, fiddling with their cords and buttons, trying to shape up. We can really be mean.

And how rotten can the band be to you?

How rotten? I'll tell you a story. I sat down at the piano one show on the last tour, and I did the whistling intro for "The Stranger." I'm in darkness and my spotlight slowly comes on. Now, I'm not a great whistler, and it's taken a lot of practice to stay on key. Gradually each of the band members is spotlighted, and they turn to face me. Each of them is wearing a black paper eye patch or a moustache, their teeth blackened. I blow the sensitive whistling in front of 20,000 people, the romantic mood of lovers cuddling close shattered. My signature song, right? Humiliated, I plunge into the song and discover that the keyboard is stuck together with long strips of white adhesive tape. The gentle, melodic intro sounds like I'm walking across the keys wearing snow shoes.

Believe me, any time me or anyone else is vulnerable, these fucking guys are guaranteed to go for the jugular. Take writing: I really get on edge, very high-strung and raw-nerved and way out when I'm trying to compose; extremely wound up and handle-with-care fragile. Recently I was out at the piano working through an intricate problem and wearing my headphones so that I could hear any supportive thoughts and suggestions from Phil and the engineers in the control room. I'm watching the band involved in what looks like a grave discussion on the other side of the glass. They're facing each other, and one casually props himself against the board and pushes, accidentally, I guess, the talk button on. I begin to hear a solemn conversation that went like this:

"You know, he really worries me. I've begun to wonder if, well, if he has the knack the way he used to."

"God, please, let's not go into that."

"Then you've noticed it too?"

"Ummm, yeah, I have. Who hasn't? It's tragic. I mean, poor Billy, he used to have such a grasp of melody, such instinct . . ."

". . . It's kinda been burned out of him."

"Boy, I hate to admit it, but it looks that way."

"So what's gonna happen when we have to play this wimpy stuff on the road?"

"Well, out of loyalty to Billy we'll just have to bite the bullet and act like nothing's wrong."

"You know, he doesn't even *look* so together anymore."

"You mean the swollen eyes, the pasty face?"

"Yeah, and the blank stares. But we can't let it get to us. We can't let him know we know. It would be too cruel."

"He used to be able to knock out a song—hell, a hit!—in half an hour."

"Pretty sad, isn't it?"

I'm sitting out there, my nerves completely shot to begin with, and I'm really starting to freak, wondering if they know that the talk button is on, thinking, "Are they serious? Are they *right?* My God, am I really totally off the mark?!"

Just when I'm about to lose it, they break up laughing and shout some crap in my phones: "GOTCHA THAT TIME DUMBO!!"

It's unbelievable! But it's all intended to keep me *on my toes.* That kind of screwball camaraderie gives me the inspiration to want to knock those guys out with a great song. They don't like *anything.* They're big on Elvis Costello, Squeeze, the best of the best, and they respect craft in songwriting. If I walk in with something below par, they jump all over it. I honestly believe that a lot of what's good on this album came from wanting to jolt the band, to get more out of *them.* When you can move and touch a jaded, cynical crew like that, it's a step forward artistically.

Are you and Phil Ramone studio perfectionists?

[*Laughing*] If it sounds right, apart from a tempo screw-up, we usually leave it in. In "Allentown," and "Scandinavian Skies," there's a din down in the mix that resembles 10,000 storm troopers marching through a foundry that's going at full tilt. I kept telling Liberty that I wanted this massive noise of robot hordes clanging in unison. In exasperation he ran over to two huge percussion cases filled with tambourines, maracas, cymbals and traps and hardware, and began hoisting them in the air and smashing them against the floor, yelling "Is *this* what you want, dammit? Is *this* good enough for you?"

"That's it!" I said. "That's it!" And it was, too. Luckily the tape was running at the time, and we caught it for the record—it sounds like the Krupp munitions plant going full blast. Unfortunately, everything inside those cases was shattered to bits, completely ruined. I guess it was worth it.

There are foul-ups all over the *Glass Houses* album; they're easy to hear when you're told they're in there. You can hear strings breaking in the middle of a hot lead, with that amazingly resonant, stinging *pic-coooowww*! coming right in the middle of a phrase. It's an effect you could never plan on. There's other treats in there too, like drums falling over, high-hats crashing into amps, mikes shorting out.

If you want to hear a really big blooper, check out "Room of Our Own," on *Nylon Curtain.* There's a part where I sing "Yes, we all need a room of our own" before I go into the final vamp. We were cutting it live, and Liberty forgot where he was and started to play the beat backward; he was still in time, but he's suddenly turned the time signature inside out. There was this look of horror on his face, and Phil was waving his arms frantically to tell us "Keep going! It sounds great!"

I love this approach to recording. The Stones used to cut records like that. We call the flaws "clams," and even though it's painful for the culprit to hear his part in the playback, you know you've got to keep it if it works. Technically, we don't go by the book. It's all ear-to-heart.

On "Pressure," that noise like the horn of a French taxicab, that strange breathless staccato beep, is actually a tape of me singing every note in my repertoire, which was then programmed into an Emulator—it's similar to a Mellotron. Then I overdubbed me hollering "PRESH-AR!" like a RAF captain would bark "TEN-HUT!" While the master tape was running, I impulsively hit all the buttons to punch out everything but that yelling. Phil was dumbstruck, saying "God! What'd ya just do? You erased part of the song!" It was true. For that one segment, everything just stops dead but my voice, but it was just what the track needed.

Does the band ever openly object to material?

"Just the Way You Are" is a good example of that. First of all, we weren't even serious about the song. Everybody was down on it and thought it was too goofy and sappy. Liberty didn't even want to play on it. "I'm not Tito Puente!" he said. "I won't play that oily cocktail lounge cha-cha/samba crap!" I couldn't explain the tune to anyone. The track never really made much sense until I added the wordless vocal that winds its way through the track, giving it some glue and some texture.

When we were cutting "Big Shot" for *52nd Street,* that fake Rumanian accent I use on the chorus was done solely as a joke, a stunt to crack up the group. I'd written the song completely differently. When we ran through the basic track, the accent and the bitchy stutter—"You-you-you had to be a *beegshot*!"—just popped out. We always said that we'd go back and fix that up one day, but I decided to leave it as it was because I'd gotten so much joy out of succeeding in catching the band off-guard and busting them up.

"Big Shot" sounds as if you're having fun actually telling someone off. The vocal tonalities in your best records aren't stagey.

The human voice has all this nuance, and I like to use humor to drive home points. I don't think of myself as a singer. I don't have a lot of confidence in my singing voice, so I'm constantly fooling around with it. When I have to listen to my voice cold in the studio, I cringe. I try to give it a live-in-the-arena setting on record because I think it's pretty boring. I like to compose and play in such a way that I don't have to sing all that many round notes, keeping the emphasis on syllabic bursts filled in with drum beats and guitar licks and whatever. I sound better when I'm socking out a tune to one degree or another than when I'm crooning.

You don't especially enjoy your own singing?

Not particularly. I think of myself as a piano player and songwriter; my singing is all tied to my piano playing. I do all my vocals live while I'm playing, which results in leakage between the vocal and piano mikes. There's never the total separation you'd get with a first-rate mix, but that's become an aspect of my sound, a distinctive trait.

And if I must overdub sometime, I'll literally sit at the closed piano and pound my fingers on the lid. Guess the piano bone is connected to the throat bone.

From a production standpoint, Nylon Curtain *is an extremely eccentric Billy Joel LP. You and Phil have put more invention into it than perhaps any other you've collaborated on. Was that part of the overall game plan?*

Very much so. Every song on the LP has a different vocal effect and various tricks and conscious quirks, because we decided from the start that we were going to make the studio itself work for us as an instrument, like the Beatles used to do. We wanted it to be a good headphones album, more suited to those great big Koss headsets rather than the Sony Walkman types, which have a big sound but lack torque.

On "Goodnight Saigon," I aimed for a sweet high innocent and youthful voice, using an echo chamber but with a noise gate to cancel out the normal ringing effect. The combination of the two makes the voice seem out-of-breath, frightened, and agitated.

We used a lot of the panning and phasing I loved on albums like *Electric Ladyland,* and lots of exotic touches layered on top of layers. For the tag line of "Pressure" we laid six synthesizer tracks over each other, and then Phil got four Russian balalaika players from Brooklyn to come in after they'd done some orthodox wedding to play from charts we gave 'em.

Are you serious?

Damn straight! Phil found these four old Russians and pulled them in for a day. They spoke in broken English. They didn't know me from Adam! [*extended laughter*]

Getting back to a more sober plane, do you hope to elicit an emotional response with your music, to move people?

[*Nodding*] Let's face it. These details I'm revealing are amusing to know, but we take the end product we're moving toward *seriously.* I worked harder on this album than any other. I agonized over the message. "Where's the Orchestra" was an attempt at communicating what moves me about the difficulty of getting through this life. I've come to realize that life is not a musical comedy, it's a Greek tragedy. I'm an adult now; I've paid my admission fee to this ordeal, and I'm disappointed I didn't get a brass band in the deal.

You know better than to believe there'll ever be a brass band backing up your struggles and celebrating your victories, but you never stop hoping, and that's part of what keeps life so sad, so bittersweet. For me, music is this magic acoustic element that makes perfectly rational people who have come to realize the unalterable fact that they are truly alone in this world somehow feel for fleeting moments that maybe they're *not* after all. It's this pleasant, soothing vibration we can send out or take in that keeps us company. Chopin, Gershwin, the Beatles, the lyricism in their music chases that sadness, makes me feel like part of the human family. It's a chemical reaction of some sort. A very odd thing.

Was there ever a point in your life when you suddenly recognized with great urgency that there's only one Billy Joel and that he is never going to come again?

That's been understood with me from the very beginning. I don't think there is an afterlife or a reincarnation. So I try to fulfill every margin of potential I've got. If I complete myself, I'll improve the quality of the lives that intersect with mine. When I wrote "Surprises" on the new album, I got very choked up by it, because I didn't know what I wanted to say at first; I discovered that I was thinking these angry, frustrated, violent thoughts: "Break all the records, burn the cassettes." And it became a song about human finiteness, and the rage and hurt it can bring on. Every minute really does matter to me.

The act of realizing that is the closest I get to spirituality. It's being touched by a quality within myself that I can't reason out or understand but that, when it's set in motion, *finds* me. I can't say it any other way.

I've talked with you in the past about your flip-out in your early twenties, when you flirted with suicide and then committed yourself briefly to Meadowbrook Hospital on Long Island, only to realize that you were romanticizing your own pain, and were much more together than your mental wardmates. Have you had any other traumatic rites of passage?

[*Somber*] When I was seventeen, I spent one night in jail, an overnight lock-up for suspicion of burglary. I had just run away from home, deciding I had had it with the arguments with my mother and sister, the disappointment about my dad being gone, the tension from money being tight at home. I just wanted to break out in general.

I split that night, and I was sitting on the stoop of this anonymous house in Hicksville in the darkness, pondering my fate, when this patrol car pulled up. Now, unbeknownst to me, this particular house had been robbed earlier that night. The cops came up to me, grabbed me, and threw me in the clink as a prime burglary suspect. Sitting in the tiny cell, I felt, "They've got me. My world is now three walls and a floor and a mattress and a stinking sink." I couldn't sleep, couldn't do anything but be scared out of my wits. I couldn't bear the sensation of loss of *control.* It really made me realize what life is and isn't.

Have you ever seen that movie, *The Fixer,* or read the book by Bernard Malamud? It's based on the true story of a Jew in Czarist Russia during the reign of Nicholas II who had been unjustly blamed for the ritual murder of a Christian child. He was imprisoned, chained, tortured, poisoned, and by the time the determination that he was innocent was made, the authorities had decided the wheels they'd set in motion against him couldn't be stopped. He had to be a victim to preserve the corrupt and inhumane social order. I had recently seen the movie, and I knew of course that my own father had spent time in Dachau. All I could think about—when you're young, your mind has no discipline—was that they were going to shave my Jewish head, beat me, slap the soles of my feet bloody, and force me to live on gruel.

The experience and the confrontation with my own fears made me see that I was willing to fight like hell to hold on to my life and my mobility. I like that in myself. I'm gonna claw, scratch, bite, kick, and kill if I have to in order to stay alive.

You're an atheist, I know. When did you settle on that philosophical position?

Well, I wasn't raised a Catholic, but I used to go to Mass with my friends, and I viewed the whole business as a lot of very enthralling hocus-pocus. There's a guy hanging upon the wall in the church, nailed to a cross and dripping blood, and everybody's blaming themselves for that man's torment, but I said to myself, "Forget it. I had no hand in that evil. I have no Original Sin. There's no blood of any sacred martyr on my hands. I pass on all of this."

I had some Jewish guilt in me already—which must have been genetically ingrained since I wasn't raised in a Hebraic religious setting—so I knew I definitely had no room for Catholic guilt too.

Then my mother took my sister and me to an Evangelical church, the Church of Jesus Christ. I was baptized there at the age of twelve, and it was strictly hallelujah time. But one day the preacher is up in the pulpit unfolding a dollar bill and saying, "This is the flag of the Jews." Whoa, fella! We left that flock.

Now my grandfather, whose name was Phillip Hyman, had always been a staunch atheist, and my sister, Judy, and I were very frightened for him, always saying, "Grandpa, believe in God! Don't die this way and wind up in Hell!"

But I was very, very close to him. He was the most inspiring presence in my life. He was a very proper, very well-mannered, and well-read Englishman, although none of his breeding had brought him wealth or position. He was a jeweler for a little while; his family in England were tinsmiths. But he didn't have a dime because all of his energies were funneled into the pursuit of knowledge. He used to sit in bed at night and read books on trigonometry and paleontology. He didn't respect anything but knowledge, and you'd better know what you were talking about or he would devastate you. He could be a pain in the neck, but he was a happy man, the only self-fulfilled soul I've ever known. He made a science out of doing only what he wanted to do.

As a result, I was motivated to become a voracious reader, which I am. And I gradually decided that just because I didn't have or couldn't find the ultimate answer didn't mean that I was going to buy the religious fairytale. As an atheist you have to rationalize things. You decide first of all that you will *not* ask Daddy—meaning God in all of his imagined forms—for a helping hand when you're in a jam. Then you have to try and make some sort of sense out of your problems. And if you try and find you can't, you have no choice but to be good and scared—but that's okay! When animals are afraid, they don't pray, and we're just a higher order of primate. Mark Twain, a great atheist, said it best in *The Mysterious Stranger*, when he stated, in so many words, "Who are we to create a heaven and a hell for ourselves, excluding animals and plants in the bargain, just because we have the power to rationalize?"

Death is death, and the ego can't handle the consequences. We should all struggle to the last to hold on to life, and religion encourages people to give up on making this life work because the supposed next life will be fairer. Religion is the source of too many of the world's worst problems.

I once wrote a love song that contained, as it turned out, some insights into Catholic guilt. But the point of "Only the Good Die Young" was not religion but lust. "Come out, Virginia!"—and I'll tell you anything you want to hear so I can get in your pants!

As a kid, I actually did go into a confessional booth in a local Catholic church, and I made up all these terrible things. I said, "Father, I felt up my sister, I robbed money from my mother, I hit my grandmother." The priest on the other side of the screen just said, "Well then, you will say seventeen Hail Marys and fourteen Our Fathers," and I said, "You mean that's *it*? I can go out and do it all again and come back next week?" He said, "Who is this?! Are you a member of this parish?!" I said, "I'm not even Catholic!" And I took off in a hurry. But I was curious about this confession thing. Jewish guilt is very popular; there're books and movies about it. But Catholic guilt seemed Gothic and shadowy.

I believe that all important matters have to be settled *here,* not in the clouds somewhere after we kick off.

Speaking of the preciousness of life and of personal fulfillment, was there ever any private dread following your motorcycle accident that your hand injury would seriously impair your ability to grow or even go on as a pianist?

You know, it didn't even occur to me, which seems like nonsense, but there's a reason why. I used to box as a teenager, and I literally broke many of my knuckles—not to mention my nose—and suffered dislocated fingers, sprains, all sorts of hand injuries. To this day, I get pain in my fingers from those old wounds. My fingers curl up at times and become slightly arthritic.

Not to be ghoulish, but could I have a close look at your hands?

[*Holding them out*] They're kinda weird up close. See, there's a scar over every single knuckle. I didn't realize my hand was hurt after the spill on the bike until I tried to drag it out of the intersection. I got up off the asphalt, shook my head to clear it, remembered that I'd hit a car broadside that had run a red light—my bike's brakes had just been fixed, idiotically—and I got up and went over to pull the wreckage to the curb. I found I couldn't and glanced down to see that my left wrist was the size of a grapefruit and my thumb was split open with the bone and all of this red junk hanging out. I was plenty upset, naturally, but I just thought, "Broken wrist. Broken thumb. Need a good surgeon and time to mend."

There was a metal pin temporarily inserted through the knuckles of the left hand after the accident to hold the bones in place, and it healed fairly well. But look at my thumb: looks like a hammer head, right? Crooked and rigid. I could probably drive nails with the damned thing now. In concert I used to snap the bass strings of my piano with that thumb. No joke. One night in 1980 a bass string broke, lashing out and almost decapitating Doug Stegmeyer—they whip out with such force! So now we tape the ends down so they can't fly around if they break. I don't know if I'll still be able to do that little feat, but so what—it's hardly a criteria for playing well.

Dexterity is not a problem, but stamina may be. As a result of the damage that was done, certain muscles atrophied while my hand was in a cast. As the bones and muscles mended, they grew back in a different way. It's just not the same hand anymore. When I tour during the fall and winter, I still plan to do a two-and-a-half-hour set, and pump the keys to reach the kid in the last row of the arena, but I won't know my new physical shortcomings until I have to face them.

One thing's certain: I'm not going to stop riding cycles. I rode my bikes when my hand was still in a cast—I'm a firm believer in getting back up on the horse after a fall. From now on, I just have to drive defensively and not assume that people will obey red lights at intersections. I won't give up the thrill of cycles because I need the outlet, the escape, too much.

As for my injuries, I'm getting used to being injured. Nearly every tour I break or sprain an ankle tearing on and off stages. Two years ago in Pennsylvania I did an encore with a fractured ankle after I got hurt running down the steps leading offstage.

Do you regard yourself as an accomplished keyboardist? Are you proud of your piano playing?

Most of the people who play piano in rock and roll aren't pianists, they're piano bangers of some quality, and I fit into the latter category. My approach to the instrument is a very athletic one, because I get off on that in concert, but in my quiet moments I'll play almost anything. I like Bach, Chopin, Copland, Traffic, Ray Charles, good Top 40 killers. I've got enough equipment to cover all the territory: a Baldwin nine-foot grand in my living room, a five-foot Howard "studio grand" in my home studio, Fender Rhodes Stage Model 73, the classic Hammond B-3 organ with the Leslie tone cabinet, two Minimoogs, an Oberheim OBX synth, a Yamaha CP-80 electric piano, a Wurlitzer D-40 electric piano, an Emulator, a Mellotron, a Baldwin electric harpsichord, a Parrot accordion—the brand name having no relation to the Zombies' old record label—a Hohner melodica, and an acoustic electric Ovation guitar, which I play way down in the mix of "Goodnight Saigon" because I'm a terrible guitarist who has bizzare substitutes for decent bar chords.

You used to accurately mimic Leon Russell and Elton John's piano styles in concert. How would someone go about mimicking you?

That would be tough because I have no particular style, I think. I'm too absorbed in the music to be concerned with the musician. I've always sublimated whatever virtuosity I might possibly have in favor of the song. The material I write requires the involvement and friction of the band members rather than the ability to play extremely well. Technically, my band is better than the demands of the material, but that makes for a nice dynamic tension.

Many see you as a macho cheerleader for the tough guy in all of us, but you're not really such a hard-ass at all. You've written a lot of songs about and also for women, and I hear a good deal of tenderness toward feminine sensibilities in your songs.

Well, I come from that lower-middle-class, suburban background. I think that it's noble to strive and view the working man with the romantic eyes of, say, a painter like Thomas Hart Benton. As for writing for or with females in mind, I was raised by and in the company of women, so I'm empathetic but also feel I can address them very directly. "Laura," a song on the new album, seems to be inspiring a fair amount of controversy in this area. I've seen it compared to "Stiletto" on *52nd Street,* as another of my misogynist songs. I don't agree. "Stiletto" was a song about a bitch, and there are women like that, just as there are men who are bastards. I've known a few of both varieties. "Laura," which has been described as my "Lennonesque" song—and I would say that he's definitely in there—was actually a song meant to explore the guilt that any relative or close friend can give you. The sex of the main character or the exact nature of the tie was irrelevant as far as I was concerned when I was writing the song; it could easily have turned out to be a man. Actually, the ideal peg for the song would have been a parent, particularly a mother. The definitive bomb-the-mom song has yet to be written, and would exorcise a lot of demons for a lot of people.

Also, people seem to think that every time I mention a woman in a song it's a thinly veiled reference to Elizabeth. That's not fair. I've got a vivid imagination and have known more than one woman in my days.

It's common knowledge that you and your wife are divorcing. I know you're reluctant to discuss it, but it seems unfair to simply sidestep the subject. It must be uniquely awkward and painful to be estranged from someone who was so supportive during an absolutely critical period in your life.

I understand what you're saying. My wife and I have split up, and it's not something that happened all of a sudden. It was a gradual thing. Around late spring of 1980 we were talking about a transition for both of us; it was evolving as far back as that. We just slowly, steadily grew apart, and it's definitely a sadness in my life right now.

She's a good friend, and I hope not to lose that. I don't want to fight about the change in our lives or be unnecessarily distant from someone I was married to for nine years and lived with for over eleven.

In the last three years, I was touring for six to nine months each year, and that may have contributed to the change, but it happened in dribs and drabs, bits and pieces, until we realized we were not together as one, we were together as two.

I certainly don't have anything bad to say regarding her. It's not a Hollywood soap opera. I'm sorry that it had to occur because I'm one of these people who wanted to be married just once and for the rest of my life; one commitment, with one common goal. Our marriage was not something either of us took lightly, and we're both unhappy it didn't work out.

Professionally, many people don't realize that Elizabeth hasn't managed me for over three years—not since 1979. It was always on a temporary basis. She was going to put things right for me contractually and administratively—which she did—and for the last three years I've managed myself in terms of career moves, with business management handled by a firm that was later set up called Frank Management.

Now, I just have to get used to being on my own. I'm dating people, but I don't expect bachelorhood to change my life-style much. I'm not Errol Flynn; I live quietly and mostly hang out with old friends. I'd make a bad playboy. But I also want to emphasize that I'm not soured on marriage. When Elizabeth and I got together, I wanted it to be forever—I bought the dream. But I'm still open to buying it again someday. I would never knock the institution; it's still worth it to me.

You've had a notoriously rough-and-tumble relationship with critics. They assert you're neither a rocker nor a pop tunesmith, or that you're both, and they think you have an artistic obligation of some sort to choose sides. Do you still read the reviews?

Anybody who says they don't is a liar in almost all cases. Sometimes I do get some constructive insights through them, to tell you the truth. Suspicions I have about my weaknesses can be confirmed. On the other hand, some reviews are so esoteric or so literal rather than musical in their outlook that they just confuse the issues involved. It must be hard for the critic and the journalist to define or describe a melody, to convey a musical idea in a literal way. I know that I don't write the words to my songs as poetry, I write them as lyrics. They are, hopefully, irrevocably tied to the tune, embellishing the notes and vice versa.

As for the rocker-versus-pop-singer thing, I'm just a musician. I grew up listening to my dad play classical music at home on a beat-up old upright; my mom took me to see Gilbert and Sullivan, and my grandfather took me to the symphony; I've had formal training in jazz improvisation and once made noise in a superloud psychedelic band [Attila]. It's better to fail at different things and build up the lessons that result than to stop taking risks. I want to keep this whole business interesting for me, too. I don't want to limit my diet, sampling only one vegetable in the garden.

What angers you most about critics' assessments of your, uh, musical menu?

[*Shaking his head wearily*] The fact that the criticisms sometimes amount to a public rank-out. I'll read one and feel, "Aww, man, not in front of all my friends, my relatives, my own ego, for the damned *world* to see!" I need to get angry at times in order to lose the anger I feel. In most cases there's no context available for me to come back at the attack.

If I have a philosophy in life, it's to keep a solid grip on your belief in your own potential, to make sure that it doesn't get worn down by setbacks or hard times or mistakes. Don't let anyone or anything take it from you. A lot of good could come out of our ability to get through this bleak period. You have to keep fighting the good fight but recognize that there's more than one way to do that. We can think up *new* ways of doing it.

In time—if you live long enough—you come to realize that it's not always appropriate to play tit-for-tat and trade blows. It's embarrassing to be called out in public, for instance, even if it isn't justified, and my capacity for embarrassment has been a problem for me. But in the last few years, I've tried to listen to the critics, and they have really helped me grow, have given me a lot of pushes, and helped keep me challenging myself.

See, it took me a long time to accept that, to pay attention to the points behind the criticisms. It's an old Hicksville tradition to just get your basic shots in too, to be damned sure to land just as many punches as your opponents do. I'm learning, though, that the world *isn't* Hicksville or Levittown.

[*Small smile, nodding to himself*] But then I knew that all along, didn't I?

Do you believe in magick? It's a question at least as old as rock and roll, which originally was the hell-raiser's synonym in the rural South for untempered music, unbridled sex—and potent sorcery.

For Daryl Hall, one-half of the renowned singing duo of Daryl Hall and John Oates, the answer is yes. And it's an intriguing admission not entirely isolated from the fact that Hall and Oates have swiftly risen since 1980 to become the most popular duo in the history of the record charts, easily eclipsing such fruitful forerunners as the Everly Brothers and Simon and Garfunkel on the strength of such huge hits as "I Can't Go for That (No Can Do)," "Maneater," "Out of Touch," and "Adult Education."

It's no accident, as far as the slim, fair-haired Hall is concerned, that the enshrinement of his distinctive silky-sharp vocal style in the rock and roll pantheon overlapped with his initiation into the realms of magick. Indeed, his greatest professional strides coincided with

Daryl Hall

1987

his decision six years ago to finally put his protracted metaphysical inquiries to practical, dynamic use.

To understand what this means, it's useful to imagine, as does Daryl Hall, a world in which the will holds absolute sway. In such an environment, there are no accidents of any kind; all occurrences, no matter how monumental or microscopic, take place solely because some singular human presence wills them to happen.

This concept is called magick. Before Christianity, before paganism, before religion, before belief itself, it is said to have been the primary spiritual instrument of existence, a supernatural order of things more real than reality.

"It has to do with the development of the brain, from the lowly swimming lizard to that of modern man," says Hall. "As the physics and metaphysics of intelligence evolved, the brain retained an awareness of all these stages—and their source of power. If you can get in touch with those parts of the brain—the 90 percent human beings never use—you can perceive, function, and really flourish in different levels of reality.

"You can establish a connection between your internal power and that of the living world surrounding you—a lock that triggers a remarkable flow.

"Like any source of power, it's got potential for bad or good," he continues, arranging his rangy frame in the backseat of a stretch limousine as it slips through Manhattan's Central Park on a sunny day in the autumn of 1985. "But that personal power is definitely there if you want to find it. As a kid, I used to devour all the books on King Arthur and European history and fantasy; I tried to learn from their essential philosophy, which was: Mold your world, don't let it mold you.

"Around 1974, I graduated into the occult, and spent a solid six or seven years immersed in the cabala and the Chaldean, Celtic, and druidic traditions, [and] ancient techniques for focusing the inner flame, the will that can create unimagined things and truly transform your individual universe. I also became fascinated with Aleister Crowley, the nineteenth-century British magician who shared these beliefs.

"I ran all of this through my own brain, discarded anything my intuition told me was crackpot or crazy, and after 1980 I began applying all these concepts, focusing the power of my own soul."

Hall pauses, his head bowed. His thin fingers draw his dense blond mane back from his face to reveal a smiling expression of enigmatic serenity.

"And, I mean, look at what's just happened," he asserts, referring to an afternoon spent shooting a cable TV special at Harlem's legendary Apollo Theater with former Temptations Eddie Kendrick and David Ruffin. "When I was a teenager breaking into singing back in Philadelphia, all I wanted to do was meet the Temptations and play the Apollo! By the midsixties, I was actually *friends* with the Temptations—and Paul Williams, their lead singer, bought each of the guys in my group a magenta sharkskin stage suit! After another admittedly uneven ten years or so, John Oates and I were making our own contributions to rock and soul as Hall and Oates—with the big breakthrough, as it turns out, coming in 1980 . . ."

Which was when the commercially faltering Hall and Oates, following a string of coolly received LPs, elected to produce themselves for the first time. For his part, Hall put every ounce of psychic determinism he could muster into the material. The result was *Voices*—and four hit singles.

"And now," continues Hall, "we've just finished headlining the Apollo with the Temptations' two top vocalists. My dreams have come full circle, and I figure I've somehow learned how to harness the mind-over-matter equation."

So it's all a testament to the applied power of positive thinking?

"Well, it's a bit more than that," he says cautiously. "I had to pinpoint what the 'it' I was seeking to channel was, and I did, although there's no word or name for it."

He later details that "years ago, I once described myself as a Fortean phenomenalist Thelemite anarchist. The Fortean part refers to Charles Forte, an eccentric mailman who became known for collecting offbeat information and newspaper clippings about weird phenomenology like rains of frogs, fireballs, and ghosts. As for Thelema, it was a place envisioned by the sixteenth-century French writer Rabelais, where 'Do what thou wilt' was the only rule."

And in 1904, Aleister Crowley, the hugely controversial British master necromancer, formulated what he called the "Law of Thelema," a new religion of "force and fire." Believing himself to be the prophet of a new age, the Great Beast 666 foretold in the Book of Revelation, Crowley devised a new occult system that he called magick, the final *k* intending to differentiate it from all other modes of magic. The Thelemic religion was itself a complex amalgam of the "Imagination + Will = Magic" dicta of the Order of the Golden Dawn (an occult fraternity founded in Europe in the 1880s whose initiates included W. B. Yeats); the Yoga disciplines of ancient India and China; and the Germany-based Order of Oriental Templars, whose sexual magic aimed to transform the orgasm into a supernatural experience. To all these conjoined arcane codes Crowley added the overriding principles "Every man and woman is a star" and "Find the way of life which is in accordance with your inmost desires—and live it to the full."

Hall is quick to point out that while he personally did spend considerable time studying magick prior to 1980, he pursued the world-traveler, poet, and graphic-artist sides of Crowley while bypassing the roles of bisexual satyr and heroin addict that helped make the always notorious Crowley an outrage in Europe until his death in 1947.

"But I was fascinated by him," Hall declares, "because his personality was the late-nineteenth-century equivalent of mine—a person brought up in a conventionally religious family who did everything he could to outrage the people around him as well as himself."

Hall acknowledges he's not the first entertainer, inside or outside of rock, who's sought a deeper meaning to the raw, uncommonly ferocious energy that roars through him when he takes the stage before hordes of adulatory celebrants. Throughout recorded history, there have been avid students of magic, many of them also pursuing careers in the fine and lively arts. And most of them have never quite fit the conventional image of a devil-currying conjurer, their number including men like the prophet-king Solomon, the philosopher Plato, artist-poet William Blake, and physicist Sir Isaac Newton.

What all magickians have in common is a view of the universe as a living being, the physical manifestations of the cosmos obscuring the true import of the powers that animate it. Each daily tableau, all the world's mundane facets of nature, and even the visions swirling in one's sleep are perceived as physical allegories or mental reflections of cosmic principles. The machine and the computer, for example, are deemed as temporal imitations of ideal mechanisms that already exist in the invisible eternity that surrounds us.

"I don't believe in the dictionary concept of the occult," says Hall, "because there's no reason to make anything secret. Secrets were for oppressive societies where people had to go underground to literally keep their heads—which unfortunately may not be that far away from recurring. But at least in this point in time we can say whatever we want and share it and feel it."

Magick's contemporary agents are committed to the creed that through the focused might of one's will, a person can accomplish absolutely anything, ranging from "a communion with the Divine Man latent in himself," as Crowley once declaimed, to, well . . . a smash-hit rock and roll record.

And so in 1977 Daryl Hall took time out from his commitments to Hall and Oates to attempt a solo musical synthesis of his personal philosophies. Entitled *Sacred Songs,* the record explored the ancient Gnostic Christian concept that, as Hall puts it, "the act of creating reality corrupts it; the minute you sing a song you've diminished it, because it goes from pure idea to profane, material fact." His record company seemed to be on the same wavelength. *Sacred Songs,* produced by gifted guitarist Robert Fripp (another musician with a mystical bent), was to languish in the vaults of RCA Records until 1980, when a massive influx of letters from disgruntled fans moved the label to release it—to critical raves.

Now, on this breezy fall afternoon in New York City, Hall revealed that he was about to put Hall and Oates on hold for an indeterminate time to once again "outrage myself, break out into a new beginning, redefine my imagination."

Hall had arranged a rendezvous in Paris in October of 1985 with producer-composer Dave Stewart, partner with Annie Lennox in Eurythmics and also a sober inquirer into cabalism. Hall and Stewart puttered in Paris's Studio de la Grande Armee, weeding through the material that would become Hall's second solo outing, *Three Hearts in the Happy Ending Machine.*

Upon its completion a year later, there were no corporate misgivings at RCA about Hall's experimentation. Released immediately, *Three Hearts* was an instant hit. And few, if any, of his biggest fans were aware of it, but the pounding, insistent first single from the album was initially inspired by the mystic plane, accessible to men in their sleeping state, that the Australian aborigines call "dreamtime." It is a sphere of complete awareness, of great joys but also of grave jolts, because it is filled with ominous insights about the waking world.

"Rock," wrote novelist-occultist William Burroughs in 1975, "can be seen as one attempt to break out of this dead and soulless universe and reassert the universe of magick." Hall agrees with

Burroughs, and his musical outlook is no less urgent: "You're living on dreamtime, baby / It's time to shape up!"

"Whenever something has needed to happen to me, it always has," says Daryl Hall, seating himself on a low velvet couch in a corner of his expansive but comfortable Greenwich Village apartment. "The weird way 'Dreamtime' came about illustrates that, as well as encompassing the method in which the album and much of my overall success has occurred. It's always been a series of happy accidents, serendipity."

It's yet another bracing autumn in New York, exactly one year since this ongoing discussion of music, magick, and Hall's career commenced, and "Dreamtime" and a follow-up single "Foolish Pride" are currently flooding the airwaves on both sides of the Atlantic.

Surrounding the singer in his Village apartment are neat rows of volumes on art, cinema, music, philosophy, and the hermetic sciences (he owns a signed and numbered copy of Aleister Crowley's *The Book of Thoth*—Thoth being the Egyptian god of writing, wisdom, and magic), as well as glass cases enclosing exquisitely preserved pieces of medieval armor and antique weaponry. It could be the home of an N.Y.U. history professor, and the grinning Hall, attired in white sweatshirt, tight black jeans, and boots, is overflowing with discourse that suits the bookish setting.

"The title for 'Dreamtime' came from a long-forgotten notation in my journals," he says, "put there in reference to Peter Weir's film *The Last Wave,* which was about apocalyptic religious beliefs among the Australian bushmen. I just loved the sound of the word.

"I came across it again one day while I was in the recording studio in London with Dave Stewart. We had gotten bogged down and needed a breather, and so Dave rolled this tape he had lying around, which had a series of guitar chord progressions on it. It was some rough but very appealing guitar ideas given to him by this guy John Beeby, who owned an instrument-repair shop across the street. Dave told me the guy used to back up Motown acts during their British tours.

"I thought, *Motown, hmmm* . . . , and something instinctive clicked in my mind; so I immediately wrote a new song using Beeby's chord progression and the first entry—'Dreamtime'—in my journal's list of unused song titles. The lyrics were stream-of-consciousness stuff, and through the whole process I felt like I was a convenient channel for some unconscious energy that wanted to surface and bloom. I felt like a mechanism that allows something good to happen—a happy-ending machine."

As for the refrain about needing to "shape up" and "shake up," they were references to the frame of mind Hall was in before undertaking his second solo album—but also concerned the "nearly shattering emotional experience" he'd gone through at the same juncture. After twelve years, he and his lover Sandy "Sara" Allen had almost ended a relationship that had endured the early, painful years of Hall and Oates, as well as the fulfillment of their first hits ("Sara Smile," the 1976 smash, was written for her), many of which she coauthored.

"It's fair to say that *Three Hearts* is an autobiographical record for Daryl," says Tom "T-Bone" Wolk, the skillful bassist and arranger for Hall and Oates since 1981 and the third member of the *Three Hearts* production team. "For someone so tapped into the spiritual and magickal aspects of music, the album represents a major leap forward in terms of capturing the difficulties he's gone through recently, as well as the sense of gratification he'd struggled for so long to grasp.

"He was much more open during the making of this record than I've ever seen him," Wolk adds, "and it has continued over to his everyday life. When you delve into his background, you realize he's got a remarkable story to tell."

And Hall's willing, perhaps for the first time, to do the telling. A guarded, prudent personality, he feels he's been burned frequently in his encounters with chroniclers of his professional passage. There was the "fag baiting" he and Oates were subjected to in 1975 because of the ill-advised effeminate silver-and-black face painting on their *Daryl Hall and John Oates* LP. Then came outright critical dismissal during the fallow period prior to *Voices.* Most recently, it's been the allegations that best friend John Oates is the lesser among equals in their collaboration.

"I don't appreciate praise at John's expense," Daryl states bluntly. "We know how hard we work together, and our separate paths for now will just help keep our special bond special.

"The underlying theme of all my lyrics with Hall and Oates has been 'Let things go; move on to fresh territory.' John is off considering his own solo record and some movie and producing projects, things he wanted to discover about himself. Neither of us fear change—and I can't stand to live without it. It's significant that I get along with John, because as a kid I couldn't get along with *anybody*, felt like an outcast, hated school. I thought I was from Mars, so I came to loathe the past. There always seemed a good reason not to remember any of it. Now I can go back into it, as far back as it's possible to go and then some. Now the past makes me strong."

He was born Daryl Franklin Hohl on October 11, 1949, in Pottstown, Pennsylvania, the only son of Walter Franklin Hohl, a foreman-turned-administrator in a dye-casting factory, and the former Betty Mae Wanner. Daryl grew up in Cedarville, a small village abutting the Amish farm country of Chester County. On his mother's side, he was descended from the Huguenots of Alsace-Lorraine and Bavaria, whose ancestral line can be traced back to A.D. 790. The Wanners were the elite officers of kings, mayors of towns that bore their name, traders of gold and silver, and honored churchmen in the cathedrals of imperial Germany.

On his father's side, the family tree encompasses still more noblemen and preachers, plus innkeepers and undercover agents who were active during the Revolutionary War.

"Our great-great-great-grandmother was a famous spy in Pennsylvania," explains Daryl's younger sister Kathy, a designer in the art department of the CBS Records Group. "Her name was Molly 'Mom' Rinker, and when she wasn't converting and baptizing the Leni-Lenape Indians, she used to sit knitting on a fifty-foot rock overlooking the Wissahickon Valley in what is now Fairmount Park. After watching the British troop movements, she'd hide her information in a ball of yarn and drop it over the cliff to George Washington's men. She was killed when she later fell from that rock in unexplained circumstances."

Daryl jokes that "being addicted to risk-taking," he "may have drawn unconscious inspiration" from Molly's saga for the song "Private Eyes," Hall and Oates's hit of 1981.

Yet the figure in his family tree for whom Daryl Hall reserves the greatest admiration is his namesake Benjamin Franklin Hohl. "Benjamin, my great-great-grandfather, was a warlock, a mojo man," says Hall with a thoughtful grin. "In rural societies in the region, especially—surprisingly—in Pennsylvania Dutch society, it was common to have a faith healer, or powwow doctor, as they called them in Berks and Montgomery counties, where he was active. People went to Benjamin Hohl for everything from curing cattle, dowsing for water, and banishing warts to matters concerning curses. My grandfather was equally gifted at removing *and* putting curses on people. . . .

"And just as I got my musical gifts from my mom and dad—she was a vocal teacher, he sang in gospel harmony groups as a young man—so I also inherited this"—he gropes for the word—"personal *force* from my earlier forebears. All my life, I've had these unusual things occur in my head and happen to me, things I'm still not ready to discuss freely. I've had to learn more about these things that I feel are innate in everybody but more pronounced in me, to focus this power and make the best use of it."

He blinks shyly, and looks away as a sudden breeze races through the small park below his apartment window, stately spirals of yellow leaves rising from the sooty sidewalks.

When he looks back, there is an eerie fire in his gaze, lending him the vaguely calculating air of a cornered animal. Up close, Daryl Hall's complexion is ruddier and his flaxen hair thicker and heavier than they appear in photographs, both qualities hardening his almost excessively boyish features to where, at first encounter, they have a jarringly impervious impact.

In European folklore there is the legend of the changeling, the strange child substituted by forest sprites for one they have stolen away. Daryl almost seems like a canny elf who dared substitute himself for the kidnapped offspring, and then decided he enjoyed that role enough to remain in it.

During his boyhood, Hohl regularly slipped away from bucolic Cedarville and across the Montgomery County line into the industrial snarl of Pottstown, or, more specifically, the illicit pulsings that emanated from its black ghetto, Chicken Hill.

Throughout his youth he had watched his starstruck mother (she'd named her boy for dashing movie producer Darryl F. Zanuck) go from vocal chores in the choir of the local Methodist church to her featured spot in a forty-piece dance orchestra called the Pottstown Band. A sometime choirboy himself, Hohl sought out his own grittier outlet by forming a quartet at Owen J. Roberts High School he dubbed D. and the Originals.

But it wasn't until Daryl explored Chicken Hill that he discovered deeper and more satisfying pleasures in the sounds of native Philadelphians like jazz drummer Joe Jones and tenor- and soprano-saxophonist John Coltrane. And something more: the rhythm and blues that surged from such Philly radio stations as WDAS and WHAT.

By the early 1960s, the City of Brotherly Love was producing such national smashes on the native Cameo-Parkway label as Chubby Checker's "The Twist," the Dovells' "Bristol Stomp," Dee Dee Sharp's "Mashed Potato Time," and the Orlons' "South Street" and "The Wah Watusi." While a music major at Temple University in 1964, Daryl Hohl was shadowing R&B shows at the chitlin circuit's prestigious Uptown Theater and hanging out with recent graduates of Overbrook High, the fabled "Rock 'n' Roll High School" that was alma mater to the membership of the Dovells, the Delfonics, and other hot West Philly talents. Daryl's own fivesome, the Temptones (named for the college, not the Temptations' songs they covered) was soon second only to the nationally known Magnificent Men as the city's best blue-eyed-soul unit.

All of the aforementioned acts cut their teeth in Uptown Theater talent shows, and the Temptones got tight with the Temptations themselves through several seasons of backstage bull sessions. After beating out the black Delfonics in an Uptown contest hosted by WDAS deejay Jimmy Bishop, the Temptones scored what became an important two-singles pact with South Street's Arctic Records.

Late in 1967 at a raucous WDAS-sponsored dance at the Adelphi Ballroom, Daryl Hohl met John Oates. The hop had been ripping along nicely until one black gang member elected to answer a rival's smart lip with a taste of hot lead, the gunshot sending the teen revelers scattering. Oates and Hohl (who several months later decided to change his name to the smoother-sounding Hall, making it legal in 1972) ducked into a freight elevator, and got to talking as the doors closed. Oates, another Temple student, led a top local act called the Masters, and he knew Hall by reputation. Both were then hustling studio backup gigs with black groups like Kenny Gamble and the Romeos (which included Leon Huff and Thom Bell, Gamble's future cohorts in Philadelphia International Records—home of the O'Jays and the Stylistics).

After a brief stint student-teaching music at Stoddart-Fleisher Junior High on Thirteenth and Green streets, Hall quit Temple University and eloped in 1969 with Overbrook High graduate Bryna Lublin. John saw Temple through to graduation, then split for a summer in Europe. In Oates's absence, Hall recorded a grim album for Elektra with a group called Gulliver. When John returned, the reunited pair snared a deal with Atlantic Records through the salesmanship of Tommy Mottola, a twenty-one-year-old Bronx-bred executive at Chappell Music. The wryly titled *Whole Oates* debut LP was a bust in 1972, its earnest folk tack a tactical faux pas in a nihilistic rock era heralded by David Bowie's *The Rise and Fall of Ziggy Stardust and the Spiders From Mars.*

At Mottola's urging, Hall and Oates consoled themselves by writing more material; the already depressed Hall promptly began a song to describe his recent divorce from Bryna, titling it "She's Gone." John added guitar as the words came to his partner. It would be the centerpiece of the elegantly textured R&B that propelled *Abandoned Luncheonette,* their second LP. When Tavares's cover of "She's Gone" became a No. 1 hit on the R&B charts, Hall and Oates were accorded their first taste of national songwriting credibility. Nonetheless, Atlantic Records dropped the duo after their third album, the caustic Todd Rundgren–produced *War Babies.* (But Atlantic went on to release the Hall and Oates version of "She's Gone" in 1976, and it belatedly conquered the Top 10.)

The sinuous Hall and Oates sound has customarily been described as "blue-eyed soul-pop" or "rock 'n' soul," but actually it's a bit more distinctive than that. Finer than the total of its influences, the pair's best output, from signature smashes ("Rich Girl," "One on One," "Say It Isn't So") to FM standards ("When the Morning Comes," "Back Together Again," "It's a Laugh"), has a curious mood of apartness that eludes facile categorization, an enticingly spooky undercurrent that lends it a quirky, even surreal allure.

"I guess that they have just a touch," Hall offers wryly, "of a sort of musical alchemy."

Alchemy, the transmutation of natural elements through the use of a catalytic agent—the philosopher's stone—has always been regarded as a branch of magick that speaks to one's creative intuition. Plato believed music to be a force of nature that is perfect in its mathematic structure (he even had a tonal theory of numbers), peerless in its properties of enlightenment, and supreme in its magickal might. As Plato stated in *The Republic,* "Argument mixed with music . . . alone, when it is present, dwells within the one possessing it as a savior of the virtue throughout life."

And for Hall, the music he composes is indistinguishable from what he has come to call soul.

"Soul," he says slowly and evenly, leaning forward on the couch in his living room, "is *not* about black or white music. Soul is a physical manifestation of a higher consciousness. It's a going from the right lobe straight out to the world, using the physical body as a springboard for an insight.

"In terms of the black musical experience, it comes from gospel music and preaching, but in every culture there are those feelings," he continues. "Soul is howling at the moon—and having the moon respond. When I'm singing and in touch with the energy I'm generating, I sometimes literally have no awareness of where I am. The ego disappears, and me and my surroundings with it. I've learned how to be able to do that in public, but I do it in private, too. And, frankly, that's the reason I'm in music—to achieve that feeling."

It was during the recording of his *Sacred Songs* album that Hall came upon a book that directed him toward further inquiries into these mystical avenues of the spirit. Robert Fripp gave the singer a copy of *The View over Atlantis,* a book by British writer John Michell about the mysteries of geomancy, the universal alignment of natural and man-made structures throughout the world. Simply put, the book posits that the planet is a living repository of electromagnetic energy that travels along set paths more ancient even than the concept of permanent roads.

"The book is concerned primarily, as far as case studies go, with earthworks, megalithic sites, and unexplained monuments in the British Isles," Hall says. "There is a lot of research devoted to ley lines, as archaic footpaths, church paths, and prehistoric roads are called. Some of the theories concerning the interrelations of ley lines are spurious, but the evidence of a unified pattern to all of these sites, from Stonehenge to the renowned ruins at Glastonbury to monuments whole countries away, is quite compelling."

By himself, or with Robert Fripp, or, more recently, Dave Stewart, Hall has spent years visiting each of the myriad geomantic sites discussed in the book.

"In postdruidic times, when people built churches on top of the foundations of old pagan temples, it may not have been just to blot out the old religion with the new one," says Hall. "There could have been an awareness that the site on which the places of worship stood was important for itself."

Those sites were reportedly selected, when necessary, by dowsers, men and women somehow empowered to assist farmers in finding underground streams on their lands. And since the European colonists in North America were, according to *The View over Atlantis,* perhaps the first to exterminate the native inhabitants without learning of, or respecting, the secrets of their geomancy, any American dowsings are grossly inadequate stabs at resurrecting a buried mystical heritage in this country.

Nonetheless, says Daryl Hall, where there's a will, there's a way to set things right. To at least lay open to scrutiny, and intuition, the notion that there may have once been a time when the natural forces of the earth were dramatically in accord—when, for instance, the real importance of cabalistic geometry and their corresponding musical tones was appreciated.

It's a lot for anyone to consider, Hall concedes, especially for those with minds clogged with too many lurid Hollywood depictions of witches and pagans, or those whose latter-day prejudices are formed by half-dressed heavy-metal howlers with pentagrams painted on their Stratocasters.

But Daryl says it'd be a dreadful mistake to dismiss rock and roll as a mere font of decadent frolic.

"I think that rock and roll, in its best, purest, and most positive form, is a completely different way of composing, one that after thirty years has achieved some maturity," he relates, lifting his willowy frame from the couch and pacing pensively before the bookshelves as the afternoon sunlight fades.

"The end of World War II and the way the world changed in the wake of those cataclysms is what caused rock and roll. It was human conflict and rebellion that created rock and roll—*not* the other way around," he goes on to explain. "After seeing what happened during the last World War, the antihuman madness of Hitler's holocaust, and the ghastly nuclear legacy of Hiroshima, the world could never be the same again. Its people, especially its youth, had to and did go through a change in human perceptions. When you combine that with a complete revolution in technology, communication, and the thresholds between science, physics, and metaphysics, you've got a new kind of renaissance.

"Rock and roll deals with the acting out of your emotional, conscience-oriented, and sexual feelings in front of someone," he continues. "That's a big step in self-realization, because once you get in touch with your body that way, you can't go back, whether you're the performer or the audience reacting to it. And feelings expressed that directly can prove offensive to some people.

"These things have always been built into tribal society, but they were never before part of mass society. In his time, Bach did it for twenty people in a drawing room on a portable clavier because there was no way to do it bigger. But Liszt did it in concert halls, from his *Faust Symphony* to his *Christus* oratorio, and Paganini was the Jimi Hendrix of his day, rolling around on floors during his dazzling, virtuoso violin performances. Unfortunately, at the time such works could not be recorded for future generations to witness. You had to set it all down later on paper, on sheet music, where it fell prey to endless analysis.

"Now," Hall exclaims, "paper isn't necessary, and music no longer has to be overly analytical, subject to formula—even in its acceptance by others. True rock and roll has no form, it's nebulous. And if rock and roll happens to sometimes also be a rebellion or a reaction to something, that is never its primary purpose. The main purpose of rock and roll is celebration of the self. And the only evil in rock and roll is deliberately directed mindlessness—which is a good definition for evil in general.

"The danger today with rock is that, as with religions, it can lose its power when its rituals become formalized—and therefore empty of personal spiritual meaning."

He smiles, sighs, and extends his hand to say good-bye.

"Whew," he says softly, tossing his blond hair over one thin shoulder in a gesture of relief. "I guess we really got into some abstract controversies here."

And he certainly sounds dedicated to sorting them all out.

"Yes! But I warned about the sensitive, radically motivated tradition in my family tree. I've even got a cousin who's a pro-Sandinista Methodist minister, and, of course, he's got *me.* We're a rare bunch, but then, my great-great-grandfather had to be unique to be a witch, and dedicated, too."

So would Daryl Hall attribute his success in rock to dedication—or to magick?

He shows the slyest smile of the last twelve months.

"Well, the answer may be in a line from 'For You,' a song on *Three Hearts in the Happy Ending Machine,* where I say, 'Attention's essential, analysis not.'

"Maybe," he chuckles, "I'm reaping the rewards of paying very close attention."

Everywhere he looks, he sees the high and haughty giving short shrift to the humble American, and John Cougar Mellencamp is in a slow burn.

Within the space of two weeks, the rock singer has shuttled from the stifling hearing rooms of the United States Senate to a simmering back alley in the poorest black neighborhood in Savannah, Georgia, and the things he has seen have inflamed his notorious Hoosier ire. (It is not without reason that the thirty-five-year-old singer and songwriter has awarded himself the sobriquet of "Little Bastard.")

"This street, one of the last unpaved places in this thriving town, is a sad comment on the local government," he states flatly, surveying the dust-strewn shanty site for the video of "Paper in Fire," the ferocious first single from his new album, *The Lonesome Jubilee,* which has risen promptly to the Top 10. "Do you know a film crew came through this area . . . and dressed a block of this lane to look like a shambled Vietnamese village! Talk about lending insult to injury."

For his part, Mellencamp arrived the day before at this hoveled tract between Price and Broad streets, asking door-to-door permission of the locals to depict in the video their neighborhood and its inhabitants exactly as he found them. They

John Cougar Mellencamp 1987

could participate in any manner they cared to, he explained, and would be paid generously for their time and contributions.

Suspicious and frightened at first, but drawn to the rough-hewn warmth of the singer, they discussed the offer among themselves for several hours and ultimately—and enthusiastically—agreed.

So it is that on a cloudy and sultry day, filming is about to commence. All told, there are perhaps forty citizens, crew, and band personnel gathered around Mellencamp's small microphone stand. "O.K., everybody settle down and listen in!" hollers the puggish Mellencamp. "There's no script," he assures with a beguiling grin, "so just be yourselves, enjoy each other's company, and have some damned fun."

"I ain't left this ol' street for forty years," remarks one elderly gentleman, looking on in amusement as the music commences, "and this is the first *pleasant* surprise I seen on it in that whole time."

Meet the new John Cougar Mellencamp—the former enfant terrible of heartland rock. This is the man who once stormed out of a CBS "Nightwatch" interview because of what he considered baiting questioning. This is the same man who, in 1982, threw an equipment-clearing tantrum onstage in Ontario, Canada, when technical problems became disruptive (he later gave a free concert by way of apology).

He did all this, however, when he was known as John Cougar—a name foisted on him by his first manager. Today's Mellencamp (he restored his Dutch-German surname in 1983) has retained his wildcat moniker. "I was wellknown as a failure," he explains, "so I figured I'd fight to fix, rather than deny, my sorry reputation." It is a fight that the singer appears to have won. Late in 1986, *Billboard* magazine, the music-trade bible, announced the three top pop artists of the year: glamorous Whitney Houston, sexy siren Madonna—and craggy-faced John Cougar Mellencamp.

Last June 18, it was the new Mellencamp who appeared before the Senate Subcommittee on Agricultural Production and Stabilization of Prices. The singer is a member of Farm Aid, a movement based in Cambridge, Massachusetts, to help alleviate the economic crisis facing small family farms throughout the nation. Once a year, since 1985, he and the country singer Willie Nelson have headlined a Farm Aid benefit concert. It was as representatives of Farm Aid that the two singers were testifying in support of the Family Farm bill, sponsored by Senator Tom Harkin, a Democrat of Iowa.

"I am an entertainer playing rock music," Mellencamp told the committee in his intense, raspy drawl, "and Willie asked me to be involved in Farm Aid about two or three years ago. In Seymour, Indiana, the town I grew up in, there used to be a John Deere dealership—it is no longer there. . . . When I am out on tour and I am talking to people, they are afraid. Their vision of the future is: What is going to happen to my children in twenty years when, all of a sudden, three farmers are farming the state of Indiana and they also own all the food-processing plants!

"It seems funny and peculiar," he continued, "that, after my shows and after Willie's shows, people come up to us for advice. It is because they have got *nobody* to turn to."

As Mellencamp spoke, there was a steady exodus of those against Harkin's Family Farm bill. Shortly before the singer began speaking, Senator Rudy Boschwitz, a Republican of Minnesota, leader of the farm bill's opponents, had taken the floor to inform Mellencamp and Nelson: "I thought I was going to come here and listen to Willie Nelson and his friend Mellencamp sing. Instead, I am listening to the senator from Iowa, whose song I have heard before."

"You know," whispered Mellencamp into Willie Nelson's ear, "this kind of behavior really brings out the *juvenile* in me." But the Little Bastard held his temper.

It is this new self-discipline and focused fire that have enabled Mellencamp to reclaim rock—which has in recent years become largely frivolous—as a vehicle for social commentary. Rock and roll is a billion-dollar industry, so such a move by a singer of Mellencamp's status is nothing if not provocative. Politically, the songwriter is a left-of-center populist with no love for what he views as the current "monolithic forces" of big business. "They're willing to exploit John Doe," he says, "and let America become a third-world country economically if it benefits them."

The current rock scene has been largely dominated by the working-class fervor of Bruce Springsteen, whose showmanship and compositional splendor have been offset by an ambiguous thematic voice and an equally enigmatic personality. A Springsteen hit such as "Born in the U.S.A." greets the ears like the sound of Caesar entering Rome, yet its lyrics are actually the lament of a Vietnam veteran who sees himself as a beaten dog. Springsteen is a melodramatist whose personality is deliberately disguised by his theatrics. He carefully restricts contact with the public and is rarely seen offstage. Mellencamp, on the other hand, is an open book, with no larger-than-life bravura—even though the deeply personal side to his music has been little known. Springsteen's formidable sound is all flesh, but Mellencamp's more accessible rock is all bone.

Mellencamp has gained stature as a scrappy musical spokesman who doesn't broadcast mixed signals or an underlying message of defeat. Like Springsteen, he declines to permit his defiant brand of rock to be used for car commercials or ketchup ads. He was particularly pungent when aides of President Reagan considered the use of "Pink Houses"—Mellencamp's paean to the simple economic hopes of the heartland—as a campaign song for the President's 1984 reelection drive.

"I made it clear from day one that he just had to *forget* it," Mellencamp said at the time. "I couldn't bear gettin' involved that way with any politician, least of all Reagan, and corrupt what is essentially a basic, humble dream of contentment he can't even understand."

Mellencamp himself understands that successful rock stars have customarily retreated from controversy as their fortunes have risen. Yet the songwriter is taking a bolder approach. In *The Lonesome Jubilee,* he says, "I want to create songs that include a lot of ordinary people, that raise their self-esteem." This album, his eighth, is his most ambitious attempt "to report on my boomer generation's bruised optimism," as he puts it. "The title refers to ordinary victories, the private ones that are usually very solitary. In the past, I've tried to sing about overlooked Americans. On the new album, I'm trying to speak *for* them."

Mellencamp's previous three albums of grass-roots social commentary—*American Fool, Uh-Huh, Scarecrow*—each sold a solid three million copies. The singer himself believes that their appeal lies in his merging of two major influences—James Brown and the Rolling Stones—plus a folkish enthusiasm all his own.

In *Lonesome Jubilee,* which has won immediate critical acclaim for its artful instrumentation and searing imagery, Mellencamp takes heartland rock one step further. He augments the larger intent of this album with a new musical vocabulary. At his behest, his eight-member band has expanded its flinty hard-rock approach by employing such traditionally rustic instruments as fiddle, hammered dulcimer, autoharp, accordion, banjo, mandolin, and lap steel guitar.

"With John's music, you work on the emotional essentials," says Larry Crane, Mellencamp's guitarist and righthand musical confidant for twenty uninterrupted years. "He always insists on an authentic band sound when he's recording, which has become unusual in this time of endless studio gadgetry. He's also not willing to sacrifice that band feel for the sake of an idea, or vice versa, so he makes it our responsibility to keep up."

Crane practiced tirelessly on a lap steel guitar. Kenny Aronoff, a classically trained percussionist, was dispatched to consult with Malcolm Daglish, the noted hammered dulcimer expert, to tackle that vintage instrument. Mike Wanchic was urged to master the dobro.

"Some critics have said these instruments on *Jubilee* have an Appalachian flavor, but that's wrong," says Crane. "Appalachian music, as John and I both know, is a certain cross between folk and bluegrass. What John said he wanted was a 'real spooky sort of gypsy rock,' and he used trial and error with us to find it."

Lyrically, the bulk of *The Lonesome Jubilee* seems an extension of the underdog themes of Mellencamp's preceding album, *Scarecrow.* Titles such as "Hard Times for an Honest Man," "Down and Out in Paradise," "We Are the People," and "The Real Life" reflect a continuing interest in America's troubled countryside. However, the heavily atmospheric musical settings have an eerie vividness that makes them more than topical.

As with *Scarecrow,* whose association with Farm Aid encouraged oversimplified interpretations, *The Lonesome Jubilee* also threatens to be understood only on a superficial level. Mellencamp readily concedes that *Scarecrow* was a "double-barreled shotgun." "Farm Aid," he says, "made it easy for people to deal with the title track poetically, romantically, but they often didn't hear the personal shots fired on the record's other ten songs."

"See," he adds bluntly, "a lot of the time I write in the third person, but I'm mostly describing my own ordeals. When those unsettled struggles prey on your mind, you become haunted. To get free, you must defeat your ghosts."

In that light, "Paper in Fire," the first hit single from *The Lonesome Jubilee,* takes on an ominous immediacy:

There is a good life
Right across this green field
And each generation
Stares at it from afar
But we keep no check
On our appetites
So the green fields turn to brown
Like paper in fire.

Is Mellencamp perhaps singing about his own past?

"Let me put it this way," he murmurs, seated on the brick stoop outside his beachside summer house, less than an hour's drive from downtown Savannah. "Remember that sweet old guy in the alley who said he hadn't been out of there in forty years? Well, he took me aside to tell me he'd also been *drunk* for most of those forty years. Because if you come from that place, people mark you for life, won't hire you, want no part of you. That's a lot of pain to surmount all by yourself.

"In my corner of the world, I've experienced those attitudes, and the rage they create. *The Lonesome Jubilee,* like *Scarecrow* and the rest of my best stuff, is about me and my family tree grappling against both the world and our own inner goddamned whirlwind."

At birth, on October 7, 1951, John J. Mellencamp was found to have a potentially crippling defect of the spinal vertebrae known as spina bifida. A corrective operation was a success, but Mrs. Mellencamp would later wonder if the trauma had a lingering effect on her cantankerous offspring.

Not that the Mellencamps were known for their benign dispositions. The former Marilyn Joyce Lowe, a runner-up in the 1946 Miss Indiana pageant, first encountered her handsome brawler of a husband, Richard Mellencamp, during a hectic Saturday afternoon in the late 1940s.

"Dad knocked Mom over as she was walking out of a store," says the singer with a wide grin. "He and his big brother Joe were running from the cops after pummeling four guys in retaliation for a whupping my father had gotten earlier. The police caught Joe, but Dad pitched Mom on her butt and kept on going. It was love at first sideswipe."

And it was of a piece with the temperamental exploits of John

Mellencamp's elders. "I've often wondered where the family got its anger from," he says. "I can tell you that, for as far back as anyone can care to remember, there has been a rigid, petty, small-town class system in Seymour." Seymour, Indiana, has long been a tough agricultural town with some light industry. It was in the outlying farmland where Mellencamp's great-great-grandfather, Johann Heinrich Mollenkamp, a German-Dutch peasant farmer from outside Hamburg, Germany, settled in Wayne Township in southern Indiana's Bartholomew County in 1851.

In the town's social hierarchy, at the top "were the people who made their money during the Industrial Revolution," continues Mellencamp. "In the middle were the sometimes poorly educated wage earners, and at the bottom were the folks in shacks. The elite didn't like any meddling with this pecking order.

"My Grandpa only knew one solution to any belittlement or perceived slight—a fight. A guy who comes on macho is probably the most vulnerable person in the world, and he was. After the sudden death of his father, the family farm had to be sold, and Grandpa was forced to quit school in the third grade to make his way as a carpenter. He was barely literate, couldn't speak English well, and felt deeply ashamed. Grandpa went to register to vote as a young man and told the clerk, 'I'm Harry Perry Mellencamp.' She laughed, poked fun at his name, and he walked out. He never voted in his life, due to that mortifying incident.

"We were always hearing talk that 'You low-class Mellencamps will never amount to anything,' so from the instant he was able to swagger, Uncle Joe did," says Mellencamp. The six-foot, two-inch Joe became a star running back at Seymour High and Indiana University, and he built up a successful concrete and construction business. Women and brawling were Uncle Joe's undoing.

"Joe married, but he . . . was never faithful to his wife," the singer continues. "In 1967, he got so bored he was briefly involved with the John Birch Society. That woke me up to the ugliness of his overall outlook."

Meanwhile, Joe's younger brother Richard—an electrician's assistant—was crafting his own future, moving from contracting jobs to Robbins Electric, a company with customers as diverse as Disney World and the nuclear-power industry. His bullish ambition served him well, but he could not buck Seymour's rigid hierarchy.

"My Dad went into the Cadillac dealership to buy his first nice car, and the salesman refused to wait on him," says Mellencamp.

"Their attitude was 'You Mellencamps can't afford these.' " Undeterred, the senior Mellencamp moved his wife and five children to nearby Rockford.

Richard Mellencamp, recalls his son, was "a complete tyrant." "Dad and I would have fist fights, and then we stopped communicating altogether." At fourteen, John Mellencamp was a beer-swilling truant. The next forbidden plunge was into rock and roll, "particularly the popular music of blacks, which—since the region still had signs reading 'Black man, don't let the sun set on you here'—was something my friends and I calculated that the right people would *hate.* I was raised with a near-oblivious disregard for racial differences, but when I learned the town elite frowned on these viewpoints I embraced them all the more."

His first record purchase was Chubby Checker's 1960 hit "The Twist," but at fifteen John Mellencamp found grittier fare. He and Fred Booker, a seventeen-year-old from one of Seymour's twenty-eight black households, formed a boisterous eight-man band called Crepe Soul. As 1960s teen culture evolved from the Beatles and rhythm and blues to acid rock and the sexual revolution, John discovered dizzying new avenues for parental aggravation. "A narcotics agent came to school and busted my friends and me for amphetamines—we'd been high for the whole week when the principal got suspicious."

Back home, Richard Mellencamp administered the ritual drubbing, then stripped his delinquent charge of his long tresses and hippie mufti. John retaliated by parading around the neighborhood with a hand-lettered sign around his neck that read: "I am the product of my father!"

When he was eighteen, John's twenty-one-year-old girlfriend, Priscilla Esterline, became pregnant. Indiana law did not permit an eighteen-year-old to get married without parental consent, so the couple eloped to Kentucky. John enrolled at Indiana's Vincennes University, a two-year institution willing to wink at his D average. After commencement, he found employment installing equipment for Indiana Bell, but was discharged after he accidentally disconnected all the phone service in Freetown, Indiana. The failed lineman returned to his first passion: music. His early albums, Mellencamp recalls, were full of "selfish, reckless, boy-wants-girl stuff, songs I meant then but surely wouldn't write now."

In 1976, the singer allowed his manager at the time to recast him as John Cougar—a midwestern clone of the glittering pop surrealist

David Bowie. The comparison was ludicrous. Four lean years later, John was in Los Angeles cutting his last-ditch LP *Nothin' Matters and What If It Did*, when reports trickled in from Australia that "I Need a Lover," an earlier single of his, had gone No. 1 Down Under. Shortly thereafter, the same single went Top 30 in the United States.

Meanwhile, John had fallen in love with Victoria Lynn Granucci, daughter of a veteran Hollywood stuntman. He was hurriedly divorced from his first wife, and two months after he and his new love were married he became the father of a daughter, Teddi Jo Mellencamp.

By the close of 1983, Mellencamp was a family man living with his wife and two daughters in Bloomington, Indiana. He was also one of America's most successful rock stars. But life remained unsettled. He was changing management again, searching wearily for a business plan to solidify his belated success. What was worse, his supposedly indestructible grandfather—the man he always turned to when he had a problem—was succumbing to lung cancer.

"Just before his death," the singer remembers, "he called everybody into his bedroom, and although he wasn't a religious person he said, 'You know, I'm having a real bad *beating* of a time with the Devil.' He was saying that the Devil wouldn't let him say a prayer to save himself. He'd built up this 'I am a rock' pose and where had it gotten him? It stopped me cold to see my Grandpa so scared. Six hours later, he was gone."

A bleak early-morning breeze penetrates the stand of trees surrounding John Mellencamp's split-level home in Bloomington backcountry. The summer is spent, and the family is back to its normal routine. The kids fret over homework, and Vicky Mellencamp prepares for a board meeting at the area's progressive primary school. John Mellencamp sits in the tiny kitchen that is his lair.

"Let's face it, you *are* your parents, whether any of us like it or not," he says. "I believe the personal history I address on *Scarecrow* and *The Lonesome Jubilee* is the same. I think it's tragic when families don't grow up, when they don't get past adolescence."

Mellencamp wrote a lot of songs over the summers of 1983–85, good-time material with titles such as "Smart Guys" and "The Carolina Shag," but none of it found its way onto the album that became *Scarecrow*. Instead, he began to sift through his grandfather's legacy, wondering what it would take to call a halt to the Mellencamps' undeclared war within themselves.

"My Dad changed completely when we buried Grandpa, went from being a screaming dictator to the nicest person you ever met, and he apologized," says the singer, his voice unsteady, "with his whole heart for the way he'd behaved. Even Uncle Joe grew up at the age of fifty-four, and became the kindest soul you could imagine." Richard Mellencamp left his job as an executive vice president of Robbins Electric to become his son's financial manager.

Thinking of his troubled family and his own untempered nature, John Mellencamp wrote a song for *Scarecrow* titled "The Face of the Nation," with the stark refrain: "You know babe I'm gonna keep on tryin' / To put things right / If only for me and you / 'Cause the devil sleeps tonight."

Just as *Scarecrow* was haunted by the specter of his grandfather, so *The Lonesome Jubilee* is shadowed by the death last year of his Uncle Joe. " 'Paper in Fire' is about Joe and the family's ingrained anger," says the songwriter. "I figure rock and roll's a far better way to blow off steam."

"Paper in Fire" is the sound of a soul in desperate flight, running either from or toward its destiny. The choir of screaming fiddle, banjo, and squeezebox creates a chilling aura of suspense—but leaves the conclusion to one's imagination.

"My uncle wasted fifty-three years," says Mellencamp, his subdued tone slowly intensifying, "and he only left himself another three to be a complete human being. I don't want that to be my story. I want to keep myself in check . . . even though I sometimes babble stuff that I regret, or wrestle with an impulse to tell off the U.S. Senate."

Mellencamp rises to prepare for a band rehearsal, then pauses.

"You know, my smallest girl was born two summers ago in Bloomington Hospital. Vicky had gotten awful sick with chicken pox, and the doctors said the illness might result in deformity of the fetus. We were so terrified—maybe the way my parents were with my spinal problems at birth—that we never had time to think up a damned name for the child. As the doctor began the delivery, we decided that if there was any justice in the world the baby would be healthy.

"So now," he says, smiling faintly, "as I think about family truths and consequences with *The Lonesome Jubilee,* I try to remind myself that there really is a little Justice in this world."

The High Priestess of Pop-Rock is spitting mad.

"Mark my words," says Stevie Nicks, a furnace in her gaze, "tomorrow, in this very room, is the final reckoning, and if Lindsey Buckingham *dares* to insist his own projects are more important than the future of Fleetwood Mac—that's it! New beginnings have always been the best part of this band. I swear it to you now: If there needs to be a new Fleetwood Mac, we'll start all over again!"

It is Wednesday, July 8, 1987, and the wild-hearted head siren of rock and roll's longest-running passion play is storming around the art nouveau–packed living room of her hillside Los Angeles home, attired in full Good Witch of the West Coast finery. Stevie's startling fashion statement builds upwards from white lace anklets and black spandex hose to a vision of cemetery seduction. And there is disorder in the dark lady's realm.

"If that man tries to hang us up," she vows, regarding

Fleetwood Mac

1989

Fleetwood Mac's errant lead guitarist, "he is *not* gonna have the last laugh!"

The matter at hand on that fateful afternoon was the future of Fleetwood Mac, which rose to musical prominence in the 1970s as heir to the pop throne vacated by the Beatles and the Beach Boys. The British-American unit was the prolific purveyor of such transcendent hits as "Over My Head," "Rhiannon (Will You Ever Win)," "Dreams," "Gypsy" . . . the list is endless, with another bumper crop from 1987's hit *Tango in the Night. Tango* was five years in the dawning, and it arrived nearly a donkey's age after *Rumours,* 1977's 20-million-selling alloy of Brit blues-rock and California acoustic pop. *Tango*'s appearance hinged on a belated mating dance with Buckingham, the band's eccentric studio Merlin. It is he, along with former inamorata Nicks and sultry songbird Christine McVie, who has generated most of the band's output. And it is he who frequently shaped that often "rough" yield in the control room until it shone from a light within. Buckingham was the resident alchemist in this medieval court intrigue, and the man who wound up stretched on the rack of his cohorts' frustrations.

And so, two weeks after the July '87 ultimatum expressed by Nicks and company, Lindsey Buckingham was dismissed from Fleetwood Mac. He was replaced seemingly overnight by Billy Burnette, accomplished (seven solo LPs) son of rockabilly legend Dorsey Burnette, and by Rick Vito, former Bob Seger/Jackson Browne lead guitarist. Burnette had once backed Lindsey in his extracurricular concerts and also played in Mick Fleetwood's spinoff combo, the Zoo. Vito served a hitch with Fleetwood Mac mentor John Mayall's blues infantry. As further evidence of the durability of the Mac tradition, the band issued *Greatest Hits* (1988), a compendium of modern Mac chart successes—plus material cut by the latest lineup, with "As Long As You Follow" currently filling the airwaves.

As promising as the new group appears, the challenge of overcoming the loss of Lindsey Buckingham looms large. It's strange that 1987 brought both the comeback *and* the dissolution of the most famous Fleetwood Mac lineup, yet their swan songs on *Tango* boasted all the star-crossed struggles and pop enigmas for which they had become renowned. "Big Love," the first single from *Tango,* carried a hint of foreboding with its inscrutable choruses of sweaty *ooohs* and *aaahs.* Who, the rock rumor mill wondered, was responsible for such outbursts? With a wink and a shrug, Buckingham is now happy to 'fess up.

"It surprised me there was a whole lot of interest in who was doing the female side of the song's 'love grunts,' or whatever you want to call them," says Lindsey, with a nasal laugh, while seated in the Slope, the cluttered twenty-four-track home studio inside his quasi-oriental Bel Air home. "That was actually me—with VSOs, variable-speed oscillators. There's a lot you can do in terms of your arranging and your voicing with slowing and speeding tape machines. It was odd that so many people wondered if it was Stevie on there with me. I guess it just follows the same thread as everything that was brought to the public in *Rumours*—you know, the musical soap opera."

Buckingham is referring to the romantic taffy pull among the band's personnel that turned brittle after the formidable success of *Fleetwood Mac,* the 1975 album on which the L.A. contingent of the twenty-year-old Mac debuted. By the time the follow-up *Rumours* LP was completed, Lindsey and Stevie's four-year romance was asunder; ditto the marriage of Christine McVie and bassist John McVie, as well as founder-drummer Mick Fleetwood's with Jenny Boyd. (Mick and his spouse divorced, remarried, and then in 1979 divorced again, Jenny's penchant for rock wedlock being shared by sister Patti Boyd Harrison/Clapton/Harrison/Clapton.)

"While *Fleetwood Mac* took only two or three months to record," says Nicks, "*Rumours* took twelve months because we were all trying to hold the foundation of Fleetwood Mac together, and trying to speak to each other in a civil tone, while sitting in a tiny room listening to each other's songs about our shattered relationships. It was very, *very* tense—a room full of divorced people who didn't dare bring anybody new into the same room, because nobody was gonna be nice to *anybody* brought into the circle."

Back then, at least, there was a strained consensus that the circle be unbroken. No such unity of purpose still prevailed in the wake of *Tango in the Night,* which only came about after Christine McVie recruited Buckingham, Fleetwood, and her ex-husband to help her cut a new version of the Elvis chestnut "Can't Help Falling in Love" for the score of an aptly titled Blake Edwards film, *A Fine Mess.*

"There were no ulterior motives to try and get the band together," Christine maintains, yet the abrupt momentum of the project, begun in late '85, served to weaken Buckingham's hard-won new independence from the supergroup.

"At the beginning of *Tango,* we hadn't spent a lot of time together," explains Buckingham, a slight, delicately featured man whose diffident look is countered by an intense discourse. "So, because there was no real central organizing force, people on the periphery started to get into the picture. Lawyers started to construct a situation that would get this thing off the ground, and their perception of a creative situation to inject something 'new' was to bring in a young guy from New York to engineer/produce. It took us a week to realize this guy was in a little over his head."

The inorganic methodology backfired as it became obvious that Lindsey and engineer–best friend Richard Dashut, who had been studio maestros for the Mac from the audacious *Tusk* onward, could not contribute to the fold in a compartmentalized fashion. In order to steady the foundering *Tango,* Buckingham and Dashut saw no alternative but to plunder the best assets of Lindsey's beloved third solo LP-in-progress. "I used everything that I liked for *Tango,*" he moans, a total of four songs commencing with "Big Love." Then it came time to either farm out wordless music tracks to the other members, or buff the rough gems they proffered.

"If I had to choose my main contributing factor to the band," he says, "it wouldn't be as a guitarist, a writer, or a singer. It would be as someone who knows how to take raw material from Christine and Stevie and forge that into something. That's a nice gift to have, and to be able to help people with.

"I think I'm coming into the most creative period of my life," he rules, "and whether that has to do with Fleetwood Mac or whether it doesn't is not really important. My solo work is back on track, Warners has already heard and liked some fruits of my latest labors, and the public will shortly be able to judge for themselves. [The album is expected in 1990.] Meantime, I've done my best by this group of people!"

They had wanted more. Not out of selfishness so much as simple need. They expected Buckingham to set aside his own aims and press on with a world tour in support of the nine-million-selling *Tango.* While Lindsey was neither the star of this outfit (Stevie has that slot), nor its leader (don't let the sunken stare fool you; manic flailer Mick Fleetwood has always stayed in charge), Buckingham was its strategist, theorist, and master mechanic. He's always been most adept at devising high-minded artistic maneuvers, while the rest of his colleagues have clung to a humbler purpose: survival. Now he was history.

"On August 5th, 1987, the new history of Fleetwood Mac began," stated Stevie Nicks at a secret September band rehearsal in Venice, California, just before the revised Vito-Burnette edition embarked on its baptismal concert trek.

According to Nicks, the original July '87 meeting in which the band was to have it out with Buckingham proved anticlimactic. All personnel arrived at Nicks's house in the afternoon, arranging themselves on the semi-circular ivory leather couch in her living room. The atmosphere was taut, but Lindsey diffused the tensions by announcing that he might still be open to the road trip. A low-key dinner for final deliberations was scheduled for that evening—and Lindsey failed to show.

Nonetheless, a call came from his management several days later, informing one and all that Buckingham would indeed tour. "We all got really excited," Nicks recalls. "It was like, 'Well, he's gonna do it, even if it's only for ten weeks. It's gonna be great, we'll get to play, and we're gonna make some money; everybody needs to make some money.' " Instantly, all of the members' separate management offices aligned to spend a frenetic week booking an intricate itinerary that more properly should have been arranged six months earlier.

The night before the final production meeting to settle on additional backup musicians, lighting and staging, etc., Buckingham's representatives rang Nicks and guest Mick Fleetwood at her main manse in Phoenix, Arizona, to tell them Lindsey had rescinded his agreement. In collective shock, but unwilling to face the humiliation of informing the nation's top concert promoters that the band was in dire disarray, the rest of Fleetwood Mac demanded a confrontation in Los Angeles with their delinquent whiz kid.

That conference on August 5 lasted a matter of minutes before Nicks was on her heels, tongue-lashing her old boyfriend. The duo's mutual harangue culminated in an outdoors tiff in an L.A. parking lot that grew more deeply felt than either party ever intended or feared.

"It was horrifying for both of us," says a somber Stevie Nicks, describing her August altercation with Lindsey Buckingham, a shouting match extraordinaire. "We said too much to each other. We said all the things that we had wanted to say for the last ten years, and we *screamed* at each other. Those things in a relationship that you try to never say just in case you do get back together—we *said* those things. Lindsey and I had been going together from about 1971 to around 1976. But we never really broke up until that moment. We've since patched up our friendship, because Lindsey is far too important to my life not to do that, but the creative ties are behind us.

"The thing about Fleetwood Mac is that everybody wants everybody to be free," Nicks now reflects, "everybody wants you to be in this group because *you* want to. I think that in his heart Lindsey didn't want to say, 'I quit, I'm leaving.' Everybody believes in dreams and fairy tales, and we all hoped he'd change his mind. I knew he would *never* change his mind.

"He just wants to concentrate completely on his own music, recorded and played on *his* terms," she summarizes. "And I admit he's certainly earned that right."

Not surprisingly, Buckingham concurs. "In the past," he says, "what I've done is given over the commercial side to Fleetwood Mac, and tried to make, hopefully, more artistic statements on solo records." And how would he describe those statements? "Ah, just lust, longing, loneliness," he answers with a subtle grin. "Same old thing you always hear from me."

Hours after the parking lot blowout with Buckingham, Nicks asked Mick Fleetwood if she could join him for dinner. Mick had reserved a table at the chic Le Dome bistro on Sunset Boulevard for himself, Zoo guitarist Burnette, and free agent Vito. Mick and his manager, Dennis Dunstan, wanted to invite the two musicians to a Fleetwood Mac band rehearsal slated for the following afternoon.

"I walked into the restaurant," says Nicks, "sat down, and was introduced to Rick Vito, who I saw play with Bob Seger, but had never met before. What really happened was that everybody just started to smile. And as I sat there I thought the same thing I did at the beginning of Fleetwood Mac, when Lindsey and I joined; I thought these are going to be *very* close friends of mine.

"And I want this to work out, I want us to *converge,*" says Nicks, who invited the fresh lineup to her house for the August 16, 1987, Harmonic Convergence, "so if there is something happening up there we'd be first on that priority list. You don't ever replace anybody, or their soul or their historical value to Fleetwood Mac, but you *do* go on."

What has always rescued the band from artistic dissolution, as well as tatty backstage sordidness, is its candor about individual sins and shared illusions. Rock and roll was once synonymous with scathing honesty, but in an era when the music is rife with hypocrisy and specious accommodation, the family tree of Fleetwood Mac continues to bare its fairest foliage as well as its gnarls. You may elect to go your own way, but it's how you travel the twisted route that makes the destination worthwhile.

In the beginning there was hot-wire limey blues, and the brisk hoisting of lager that blurred the band's rainiest days. Peter Green, né Greenbaum, Eric Clapton's replacement in John Mayall's Bluesbreakers, quit that crew in 1967 and invited sometime interior decorator Mick Fleetwood—who had been dropped from the Bluesbreakers for chronic drunkenness—to join his own fledgling outfit. To flesh out the sound, Green chose guitarist/prankster/Elmore James impersonator Jeremy Spencer and so-so bassman Bob Brunning. Sensing a good time was brewing, veteran Bluesbreakers bassist John McVie—also temporarily ousted by Mayall for excessive intoxication—came swiftly on board to replace Brunning.

"I was playing with John Mayall in a pub in East Anglia," says McVie, "and I was a full-on blues bigot. We had just put horns in the band, and I felt the Bluesbreakers were getting too jazzy." During a twenty-minute break, the disenchanted McVie fetched a pint of the best from the bar to stiffen his resolve and slipped out the back door. "I went to a phone booth across the street, called Pete, and said, 'I'm in!' "

Fleetwood Mac's debut album was cut in three days, and lingered on the British charts for thirteen months. Green was as gifted at songwriting as he was at bending his Gibson Les Paul guitar to his dexterous whim. He composed a slew of influential hit Mac singles in the United Kingdom, among them "Man of the World," "Oh Well," and the reverb-soaked 1968 chart-topper "Albatross"—the song which caused the envious Beatles to create "The Sun King" for *Abbey Road.* Green also wrote the Santana staple "Black Magic Woman."

The Mac's prowess as a live act—further augmented with the addition of third guitarist Danny Kirwan—became the stuff of legend. Numbered among the band's loyal following was self-described "Fleetwood Mac groupie" Christine Perfect. She came from a musical brood, father Cyril being a violinist with the Birmingham Symphony. Back in art college, her first boyfriend had been Birmingham

University German teacher Spencer Davis, soon to gain fame with the group that bore his name. Moving to London, she found daytime wages as a department store window dresser, night work as a pianist and singer with Chicken Shack, and a new musician-admirer in John McVie. Shortly after they were married, a 1969 *Melody Maker* poll named Christine top female vocalist of the year, and she left Chicken Shack at her manager's insistence for a halfhearted solo LP and tour.

Christine had all but given up music, settling into life as a housewife, when Peter Green made the astounding declaration in May 1970 that *he* was quitting rock. In a series of turgid testimonials, he babbled about the decadence of the road, with its tempting virgins, poisonous victuals, and assaults on his immortal soul. Green claimed divine intervention in his life, and his remorse led to a vehement repentence during which large chunks of his income were dispatched to charities for African famine relief. While his heart was in the right place, his psyche was not—owing, in the minds of many of his colleagues, to a massive acid dose he suffered one evening while on tour in Germany.

Peter Green finally bolted the Mac to become a disciple of a small fundamentalist denomination in the States, releasing a quasi-religious solo record *(The End of the Game)* in 1970. (Several other solo albums would follow, mostly on smaller labels.) His subsequent appearances were those of a private citizen with an addlepated demeanor, refusing his backlogged record royalties while toiling as gravedigger, publican, and petrol pump attendant. To this day, it is difficult for Americans to comprehend the jolt Green's mental collapse gave his British audience; had Eric Clapton not recovered from his heroin-induced exile of 1971–73, the public sorrow would have been comparable.

Mick Fleetwood, the band member to whom he was closest, still views Green's unraveling as a crisis of conscience, but remains profoundly disquieted by the founding member's farewell rant: "He said it was all evil, he had to give everything away."

If Green was hellbent to divest himself of all rock transgressions, Fleetwood Mac seemed just as eager to distance themselves from the vacuum left by Green's exit. Fleetwood, Kirwan, and the McVies retreated to the south of England, renting an ancient oast house—that is, a farm building containing a kiln for drying malt or hops. It was in this humble dwelling that the band not only mended its spirit with the moving *Kiln House,* but also absorbed Christine as a full participant. She had been greatly saddened by Green's deranged grief, and the wistful landscape of self-colonized enchantment that she drew as the record's jacket illustration had its own personal subtexts of loss and metaphysics.

"My mother, Beatrice Perfect, had recently died," Christine remembers. "A remarkable, very psychic lady, she was a medium and faith healer. Her strange talents and interests used to concern me, because she belonged to these psychic research societies and would go off ghost hunting. As for her faith healing, I had a rather nasty wart underneath my nose when I was about eight. My mother just put her finger on it one night before I went to bed, and when I woke up the next morning it was gone!"

Seated cross-legged before the fireplace in her antiques-appointed Beverly Hills cottage, the comely, husky-voiced McVie chuckles mischievously at this anecdote and doles out another. "I distinctly remember a time when a friend of my father's had leukemia and was told she had virtually no time at all to live. I remember my mother being sent a white kid glove that belonged to the sick woman, and my mother wore it in bed several times. Within a month, there was a phone call from this sick lady's companion, saying the doctors couldn't understand it but she was completely healed, not a thing wrong with her!"

Pity the remarkable Mrs. Perfect couldn't have ministered to the bedeviled souls in Fleetwood, for they were multiplying. Jeremy Spencer was a confirmed scamp notorious for stunts like taking the stage of London's prestigious Marquee Club with a wooden dildo dangling from his gaping fly. But the tawdry sideshow in the City of Angels seemed to shock him into a paranoid Puritanism. When in Los Angeles with Fleetwood Mac in February of 1971, he left the hotel prior to a performance to purchase a newspaper—and promptly disappeared. Four days later, he was discovered in the local commune of the born-again Children of God sect.

Once more, Mick Fleetwood was the patient listener to whom all scarifying sorrows were divulged, Spencer's consisting of an "evil" cloaking L.A. that was out to "get him," the dreadful proximity of the San Andreas Fault, and a guilt that embraced everything from the band's increasing divergence from their blues charter to the mounting gate receipts they were banking. Spencer's midtour denouement meant the loss of not only an underrated talent, but also a much-needed sense of humor. John McVie reveals that his favorite Fleetwood Mac album is a 1969 Spencer-sponsored masterwork still unissued.

"It was a parody album, which was *very* funny and technically perfect," says John with a reflective snigger. "It was done as a whole show with different bands in it. It started off with your typical gross MC who introduced this acid band, a blues band, a jazz fusion band, and one doing some fifties Fabian-esque cutie music. We'd be playing in each different style, and Jeremy was very much a mimic with a beautifully sarcastic sense of humor. It was full of wanker jokes, vulgar gags, and very outrageous stuff. I don't think the record company thought we were serious, but it was great!"

Spencer's shoes were ably filled by singer/guitarist Bob Welch, who made strong contributions to four Mac LPs. But more trouble loomed. Not long after the band axed Danny Kirwan in 1972 (reasons given by the rest were that he had been "a nervous wreck" and the source of an "intolerable" professional climate), there was indeed a fake Fleetwood Mac on the hoof.

For Mick Fleetwood, the phony Mac was a source of anguish on multiple levels. In the early phases of a sizable U.S. tour in autumn 1973 to promote *Mystery to Me,* Mick Fleetwood found that Kirwan's successor, Bob Weston, had become romantically involved with his wife, Jenny. Distraught, Mick bounced Weston, after which the band went on an uncertain sabbatical and Fleetwood repaired to Africa by himself to contemplate his options. Band manager Clifford Davis, reluctant to let all that box-office cash evaporate, quickly assembled an anonymous pickup crew he christened the "New Fleetwood Mac" and hustled them out to exploit the uncanceled bookings. The genuine article sued Davis and his fraudulent ensemble and won, although the case took years to adjudicate.

Meantime, Mick Fleetwood patched both his marriage and his band back together and moved the entire crew to California. He also began managing the Mac himself under the whimsical banner of Seedy Management. In December 1974, just as Bob Welch was bowing out to form his own group, Mick was shopping around Los Angeles for a fit studio and new troops to comprise the next Mac attack. It was in a modest complex called Sound City, while listening to a tape in order to demonstrate the control room hardware, that Mick chanced to hear a duo known as Buckingham-Nicks.

Lindsey was a scion of a Palo Alto family who had distinguished themselves over several generations as savvy coffee growers and

Olympics-caliber swimmers (Gregg Buckingham earned a silver medal in the 1968 games). The youngest of three boys, Lindsey was the clan misfit who had squandered a $12,000 inheritance from a dead aunt on an Ampex four-track tape console. His father gave him a tiny room in the bowels of the coffee plant where he could tinker. And when he wasn't holed up there, he was off trying to get another recording deal for himself and girlfriend Stevie Nicks.

The combination of a privileged background and an overachieving parent had conspired to make Stevie into a markedly stubborn and strangely distracted teenager. Seeking a safe magnet for their teen's intense inattentiveness—and hoping to make restitution for a childhood novelty act with her country crooner grandfather that they'd forbade—her parents presented Stevie with a Goya classical guitar.

"It was my sixteenth birthday," says Stevie, who was then under the spell of Bob Dylan and Judy Collins, "and I wrote a song the day I got it. It was 'I've Loved and I've Lost, and I'm Sad but Not Blue.' I was recovering from my first—I thought—love affair," she details with a throaty giggle. "I was crazy about this very popular kid at school, and I made this whole thing up.

"I realized right away I could write songs because I could have experiences without even having them!" Explosive laughter. "And I'd run to the guitar, and I'd cry, and my parents would leave me alone because it was like, *Don't come in the door. A great artist is at work here.* I kept a guitar at the foot of my bed." And she kept her fantasy world working full throttle.

With her family constantly uprooted owing to her dad's incessant corporate promotions, she made few lasting friends, so the formation of little bands became a device for fast-forward connectiveness in each suburban enclave where she was deposited. While in high school, she formed Changing Times, a folk group named for the Dylan standard, but it wasn't until she was enrolled at San Jose State that she located the structure and the mentor she required to make her quirky designs more real.

Fritz was Lindsey's rock combo, playing music he concocted in his four-track lair in the coffee factory. Stevie was the catalyst for its modest goals, and then some. After three and a half years of experience together, which Stevie helped fund through work as a dental assistant (for one day) and a hostess at a Bob's Big Boy, Lindsey and his gal lit out for Los Angeles. They shared a house, much as Lindsey does now, with Richard Dashut, and peddled their demo tapes. Polydor Records bit, and issued the *Buckingham-Nicks* LP in November 1973. An exquisite folk-rock miniature just a tad ahead of its time, it could still be mistaken as modern Fleetwood Mac product.

When the LP bombed, Stevie resumed waitressing on the lunch shift at a Beverly Hills restaurant called Clementine's, and Lindsey hit the road with a group Warren Zevon threw together to back Don Everly. On New Year's Eve 1974, at a party at their house, Lindsey and Stevie were wondering if 1975 was worth welcoming in when Mick Fleetwood phoned with the invitation that made their dreams, and nightmares, come true.

It's been said that the worst thing you can do for talented, sensitive people is to permit them to pursue anything they please. Besides the music, for John McVie it was liquor; for Christine McVie it was unrequited love; for Lindsey Buckingham, it was workaholism; for Stevie Nicks, it was the Grand Slam.

And for once, Mick Fleetwood was too overextended himself to pick up all the surrounding pieces.

"If anyone doesn't know it," Mick volunteers, "I ended up stark broke," alluding to an early 1980s personal bankruptcy proceeding, tied in part to ill-advised investments in Australian real estate which left him owing some $2 million to two California banks, his record label, and his attorney. He was also fired as the band's manager for intemperate spending. Fighting back from these reversals, plus a freak illness related to his blood-sugar levels, left Mick drained in every sense. His prospective recording plans for his adjunct band, the Zoo (they had one RCA LP), have been shelved, since his star guitarist Billy Burnette is now an asset of the Mac. But Fleetwood wants to record a sequel to 1980's *The Visitor,* his own pre-*Graceland* hybrid of hard rock and African roll. And he's completing what he calls "a transcension album, working my drums into spoken-word tapes of the quite wonderful poetry readings of my late father."

While these initiatives are closest to his heart, he's also hot to make his mark in Hollywood. "I've done a bit of acting, appearing early in '87 in *The Running Man,* that Arnold Schwarzenegger film based on a Stephen King story. I played a character named Mick, who was myself, really, at eighty-five years old. I was a mad professor, obsessed with the ideals of the sixties and the deterioration of the social structure. I enjoyed the *shit* out of it!"

While Fleetwood was lost in his harmless Tinseltown reverie, fellow Mac stalwart John McVie was in a near-lethal stupor. "I woke up on the bathroom floor," is how the bassist begins an unsolicited soliloquy about his bleakest bout with the bottle in the spring of '87. "I had a seizure, an alcohol-induced seizure, which scared me and scared my wife. It was time to stop because it was destroying everything. There's nothing constructive comes out of being an alcoholic."

This conversation had started out being about sailing, John McVie's sole interest outside of Fleetwood Mac, and the hobby he plunged into with a vengeance following his divorce from Christine McVie in February 1978. Sailing can be both solitary and social, McVie preferring the convivial side. By the end of 1978, John had remarried to former secretary Julie Ann Rubens and was well into the inebriated joys of high-seas yachting jaunts from Los Angeles to Maui. McVie sails out of Newport Beach these days, most frequently to and from a haven he maintains in St. Thomas—which is where his pre-*Tango* idleness took its alarming toll.

"I sat around," he says, "and it didn't help my alcohol problem. I sat in St. Thomas for a *long* time, and it being a duty-free island, for $2.98 you can get well-twisted." He simpers to himself, his droopy eyes showing a subdued twinkle. "It turned into a constant problem, which I'm trying to beat now."

While McVie views touring as an antidote to his idleness-aggravated dipsomania, Buckingham detests the drab motel-to-motel cycles of nationwide concertizing. While on a 1977 sprint in support of *Rumours,* Buckingham passed out in the shower of a Philadelphia suite and was diagnosed as having a mild form of epilepsy. He's sought thereafter to be more vigilant against undue stress. His greatest detriment, of course, is his own penchant for marathon studio servitude, the turning point being 1979's *Tusk* LP. Taking its name from Mick Fleetwood's code word for the male sex organ, the two-record *Tusk* cost a cool $1 million to realize and was composed in the main by Buckingham. Executed with all the fanfare of a seventies response to the Beatles *White Album,* there has been a tendency in the decade since to depict the lavishly eclectic *Tusk* as "Lindsey's Folly," or an outright debacle, but actually it's a sublimely produced pop cornucopia that sold a respectable four million copies, and its two Top 10 singles (the title track and "Sara") are among the band's best.

Fleetwood Mac responded to *Tusk*'s post-*Rumours* commercial shortcomings with abject contrition, as evidenced by the far more conservative *Mirage* (1982). Buckingham still sounds resentful of the defensive attitudes: "I felt that it's a danger zone when people stop really looking at what the *work* is, and start noticing the phenomenon per se: the sales, all of that. In this business you have a responsibility to constantly be cultivating what you're doing, rather than just watching yourself in action."

Does this mean his third solo album will be a double one? "Quadruple," he quips sheepishly. "Hey, I've got about sixty songs!"

Meantime, Christine McVie's struggles with her art are concerned more with emotional objectives than physical volume. "I like to write songs about love," she says. "Music and love go hand in hand to me, but I like to find an unusual way of phrasing it all." She notes that the wistful "Isn't It Midnight," one of her *Tango* tracks, "goes back directly to a guy that I met a long time ago; it was a concrete situation that didn't work out." Elsewhere on *Tango,* critics found the refrain "Little Lies" ("Tell me lies, tell me sweet little lies"), which Christine penned with new husband Eddy Quintela, to be borderline perverse, but she discards such carping.

"The idea of the lyric is, 'If I had the chance, I'd do it differently next time. But since I *can't,* just carry on lying to me and I'll believe—even though I know you're lying.' "

While there is no attempt to pin the song to a specific relationship, it fits the pattern of her woebegone bond with the late Dennis Wilson of the Beach Boys, who had replaced Fleetwood Mac lighting director Curry Grant as the object of her affections. The likable but profligate Wilson moved into her large Coldwater Canyon house just prior to Christmas 1978 and by all accounts took advantage of her good nature and financial largess. In one celebrated incident, he hired a flock of gardeners to plant a huge heart-shaped flower bed in her backyard as a birthday token. Less well known is the fact that he had the bill for the landscaping sent to her.

For two years, she forgave his every childish falsehood and infidelity, but with his drinking and drug use escalating by the close of 1980, she finally called a halt to the love affair. (An intoxicated Dennis Wilson, thirty-nine, later drowned in Marina del Rey on December 28, 1983.) Christine made her peace with the past and went on, marrying Portuguese musician Eduardo Quintela de Mendonca on October 18, 1986, in London.

For now, Christine's outlook on her own life and career is sufficiently optimistic that she and Lindsey blocked using Stevie

Nicks's downbeat "When Will I See You Again" as *Tango*'s closing selection.

"That was a little too down and depressing," McVie says, so its position on the album was shifted. To fill the gap Christine took an existing instrumental track of Lindsey's and wrote "You and I, Part II," a song that echoes her new beginning with Eddy Quintela. "There's a hopeful, optimistic vibe to the song, of a new tomorrow," she believes, pointedly adding, "It's pop, but it's *mature.*"

Christine McVie doesn't mention it, but another lighthearted track that could have been selected to close *Tango* was a Stevie Nicks rouser called "What Has Rock and Roll Ever Done for You?" Stevie has no rancor about the song's total elimination, asserting with a sigh that Fleetwood Mac usually prefers her "stranger, more demented rock and roll."

Ms. Nicks remains a believer in ghosts and witches, a devotee of the occult who is capable of conducting entire conversations about the modern import of Halloween (her favorite night of the year), the usefulness of the Tarot, and the significance of maya, which in Hindu embodies the illusory world of the senses. In a more concrete sphere, Nicks endures as the most formidable of Fleetwood Mac's solo draws, with a trinity of smash albums to her credit and another one nearing completion. Nonetheless, there are those who persist in dismissing her recordings as—in her words, "musical spaciness."

"It bothers me," she says, "because I would like to know how spacy *these* people are, or if they ever really listened at all. I don't care, even if they say things that aren't very nice, if I feel they had a valid reason. But when people get needlessly cruel it really hurts my feelings. I don't read many reviews because I start questioning and think maybe I ought to get out of this business if I'm such a space cadet.

"I write about true experiences, and if the song isn't about me, it is absolutely about someone around me. Everything I do is a concept: the way I dress, wear my hair, do my makeup, write my songs, live my life. If everybody has such trouble understanding what I'm saying, then I wonder how come I'm still in rock and roll after all these years? I start getting nervous and questioning my concept. I don't *like* to question my concept. I very seldom make a decision and change it."

For instance, she insisted on dedicating her 1983 *Wild Heart* album and the song "The Nightbird" to her best friend, Robin

Anderson, who died of leukemia in 1982. Robin had given birth to a child the week before her death and Stevie was the godmother, so Nicks's mournful/devotional gesture was understandable. But Stevie's decision to marry Robin's bereft widower, Kim Anderson, caught many off guard.

Kim Anderson was a member of the Hiding Place Church, whose born-again Christian liturgy emphasized the supernatural and the charismatic. Philip Wagner, the minister who officiated at the January 29, 1983, Anderson-Nicks nuptials, was outspoken in his "trepidation" concerning the pairing, stating he did not know "where Stevie was at with God." Separation papers were filed several months later, the formal divorce coming through in April 1984.

After two years of relative seclusion, Nicks reemerged in 1986 with *Rock a Little* and the hit single, "Talk to Me." However, the reclusive rock diva declined to talk with the press. Seeking an escape from prying eyes, Stevie joined buddy Tom Petty's winter '86 Australian trek with Bob Dylan and the Heartbreakers. She managed two concert guest shots before immigration authorities Down Under nailed her for rocking, even a little, without a work visa.

"I'll go on any tour!" she exclaims. "I got to sing 'Knockin' on Heaven's Door' with Bob and Tom! I'll never forget in my life walking out to perform and having Bob Dylan turn and do a little bow. It made everything all right—all the pain, all the trouble, all the hassles that come along with this kind of a life in rock and roll. They all went away at that moment."

But they soon came crashing back, in all their alcohol- and drug-beclouded fury. While on a modest, much-postponed tour in support of *Rock a Little,* it became plain Stevie's life beyond the klieg lights was in disarray. The high point of these disturbing stage excursions, preserved for posterity on feature-length home video, is an emotionally harrowing, but ultimately exultant appearance at the Red Rocks amphitheater in Boulder, Colorado. Nicks agrees. "I could have looked better, and played the set a little better, and been a little less tired, but I *cared* that night."

But she cared nothing about the morning after. Compelled in a private intervention by those closest to her to acknowledge her problems, she committed herself to a chemical dependency recovery program at the Betty Ford Center at the Eisenhower Memorial Hospital in Rancho Mirage, California. Giving herself over to a daily regimen of group therapy, lectures, strict diet, and "therapeutic duty assignments" to build self-esteem, she spent twenty-eight days at the comfortable eighty-bed residential campus facility beside the San Jacinto mountains.

The "recreation" segment of her $180-a-day treatment regimen was frequently spent opening the minimum of seventy fan letters she received each morning—an astounding amount considering her stay was a secret until it was nearly completed. "I was amazed," she says with a weak grin. "It flipped me out to see so much affection in my hour of crisis. What I learned was that I pushed myself way too hard, *and* I tried to tour and I tried to do a Fleetwood Mac record at the same time. I'd go on the road and then I'd go home to Fleetwood Mac, and I just decided at the end of the *Rock a Little* tour that I couldn't do it all. *Anymore.* And I decided that the easiest way to readjust my way of thinking was to go to Betty Ford.

"All I can say about the Ford Center is that it's an amazing place, and it makes it pretty easy to readjust your life. I haven't had a drink or anything else since I left. Life goes on, and I still write and still sing, but it's just different now. I'm really excited about what I have to do in this life—and now I *can* do it. I don't think I really could have done it before.

"They say that from tragedy comes great art. Well, I think there is some great tragedy in all of the people who are still around in this band after the thirteen years since Lindsey and I joined. Sometimes I think I should go back to being a waitress; maybe I would enjoy life more. But if I led a perfectly existing life, where I didn't try the universe or dare anybody or take any risks, I would never have written all those songs! So in all of us there's some great tragedy that has gone on, and that is what we write about."

By way of example, she recounts how her "huge" admiration for Tom Petty and the Heartbreakers led to a creative outpouring. "The relationship I have with Tom started with 'Stop Draggin' My Heart Around' in 1981. I can call Tom late at night and say I'm freaked out or I need somebody to tell me everything's all right or this too will pass, and I can depend on him. And that is what makes our musical relationship happen. Tom is one of the only people who can look at me and say, 'Listen Stevie, this is *stupid,* you're fine!' and I'll believe him. Because I know that Tom Petty walks out in front of that microphone every night and plays for all those people, and handles that audience, and handles his home life and everything he does. That's kind of what he and I are to each other: If he's all right, I must be all right.

"Without rock and roll, he'd still be my very good friend," she concluded, "and I don't have many of those kinds of friends." Indeed, all the members of Fleetwood Mac share a detachment from the madding crowd, with the band serving as their sturdiest connection. "It's a living thing, this Fleetwood Mac," says Christine McVie, "a source *stronger* than its various members." And for Stevie Nicks, it is a wellspring of "magical" sparks that spill over into the rest of her career.

Because of the support system of Fleetwood Mac, Nicks dared go public with the thoroughly surreal "Rhiannon," and "followed her intuition" by asking Prince to help her complete "Stand Back," the 1983 solo single that became *the* showstopper on the new Fleetwood Mac's 1987–88 *Shake the Cage World Tour.*

"I phoned Prince out of the blue, hummed a melody, and he listened," says Nicks of the latter hit's gestation. "I hung up, and he came over within the hour. He listened again, and I said, 'Do you hate it?' He said, '*No,*' and walked over to the synthesizers that were set up, was absolutely brilliant for about twenty-five minutes, and then left. He was so uncanny, so wild, he spoiled me for every band I've ever had because nobody can exactly re-create—not even with two piano players—what Prince did all by his little self.

"But these kinds of mystical accidents just happen to me all the time. The first song I gave to *Tango* was a demo my good songwriter friend Sandy Stewart had played for me called 'Seven Wonders.' I gave the tape to Fleetwood Mac at a Halloween party in L.A., to plant a seed, and when it came time for me to sing it live in the studio, I was somehow inspired to sing very different words that instantly transformed the song for all of us. In 300 subsequent takes, I could never sing those unwritten words of mine again, and the original live version we luckily preserved became the second hit from *Tango*!"

What all this serendipity means in terms of the *next* two decades of Fleetwood Mac is anyone's guess. Yet an offbeat solidarity prevails, as evidenced by the festivities in Malibu in April '88 when Mick Fleetwood took longtime companion Sara Recor as his new wife. John McVie served as best man, and the guests included a beaming Lindsey Buckingham.

On the musical front, the next solo expressions of Buckingham's independence from his friends must compete artistically with Fleetwood Mac's own threatening LP of all-new material [*Behind the*

Mask]. Meantime, other Mac expatriates carry on in varying degrees of obscurity. Bob Welch is living a quiet life of film-scoring in Phoenix. Jeremy Spencer was last seen fleeing a Children of God settlement in Sri Lanka after nearly being killed during the nation's political riots; rumor has it he's safe and sound on an atoll in the Indian Ocean. Pity the same cannot be said for Peter Green. After a January 1978 marriage at Mick Fleetwood's home to one Jane Samuel, Green relapsed into mental turmoil and presently sleeps in deserted rail depots of Richmond, North Yorkshire, England. When asked about his attitude toward his guitar, the bloated, disheveled Green says, "I had one a while ago, but it broke." He currently wanders around the English countryside, sporting three-inch fingernails and shouldering the forbidding sobriquet of "the Werewolf."

Certainly the two newest additions to the Fleetwood Mac fold are the most grounded and stable fellows thus far, free of ritual rock vices and exotic angst. Rick Vito's impeccable guitar has been the linchpin of records like Bob Seger's *Like a Rock* and Jackson Browne's *Lawyers in Love.* As for the boyish, immaculately groomed Billy Burnette, besides his own solo catalog, he has generated much well-crafted country, rhythm and blues, and rock material for Charlie Rich, Conway Twitty, Loretta Lynn, Irma Thomas, and Levon Helm.

Both Vito and Burnette showed grace and polish under pressure throughout the *Shake the Cage* expedition, and with *Greatest Hits* in the stores as a commercial buffer, they are eager to put their songwriting stamps on a new Fleetwood Mac studio LP.

"Five years ago, when I met Mick Fleetwood in the audience of a Dick Clark TV special, I wouldn't have guessed it'd lead to all this," says Burnette. "The funny thing is, there was a band I was forming a few years back called the Cholos that Lindsey was seriously thinking of joining as an outside thing! Now that I've dealt with all these surprises, I want to provide what's expected of me."

"This is an astonishing honor that I'm still just trying to keep pace with," says the bashful Vito. "A month before I was invited to join, I was gigging with my own band, Rick Vito and Blues Moderne, at a funky club in Sherman Oaks. At this point, I suppose I've gotten my high school and college degrees in rock and roll, but Fleetwood Mac represents my Ph.D."

Vito's tone is one of rational self-confidence . . . until an ominous air of metaphysics creeps in. "As a studio musician, I'm used to learning other people's song catalogs, yet I can't shake the eerie feeling I've known all these people before."

Stevie Nicks chuckles when Vito's musings are repeated for her. "What would Fleetwood Mac be," she joshes, "without a little psychic phenomena. Some things should never change, right?" Perhaps. The best question for any crystal-gazer might be: Is the future worth the past?

"Absolutely," she assures, "and *each* of us has the skills to prove it. I've been writing songs again like mad, and I've got a killer one I put together with Mike Campbell, the guitarist in the Heartbreakers. Like I say, I always write songs about the truth, and this is definitely one of those. Hell, if it can't keep until the next Fleetwood Mac studio album, I might even make it the *title* of my next record."

What's the name of the song?

"Oh! I call it 'Whole Lotta Trouble.' I mean, what else?"

He's sweating like a stevedore, running hard, and sucking wind as he traverses a broad, sun-scorched street in London's West End, dodging tourists, spinning free of snippy shopgirls and seeming almost in the clear until two infernal lorry drivers decide to hit their accelerators and aim to flatten him. Truly. Good God, these devils wanna ruin his red shoes!!

"Aaaaye!!!" Elvis Costello wears the fear-frozen gape of a haunted man who's just awakened in a shooting gallery as he jumps back onto the curb. Dressed in a midnight-colored suit and matching tab-collar shirt, he has spared his life with his quick reflexes—but not his smart crimson floaters, as the predatory trucks splash a squalid puddle of black water down upon them. "The cheek of those wankers!" he hisses as they roar past. Only momentarily shaken, he picks up his hectic pace again, hurrying from newsstand to newsstand, searching, searching.

"Damn, damn," he mutters, his unexplained efforts apparently fruitless, and abruptly suggests catching a hack to his favorite Japanese lunch spot. The car is cruising through Covent Garden when Elvis—"Aha!" he whoops—suddenly begs the cabbie to pull over and then he leaps out, returning a few moments later with the new issue of *Melody Maker*, hot

Elvis Costello

1983

off the presses. "Excuse me a minute while I look into this," he says and whips through the venerable British rock journal until he reaches the record review section. He eases his glasses back up the bridge of his pug nose and peers anxiously at a piece headlined IMPOSTER UNMASKED (The Imposter having been his alias for a limited election-time release of the scathingly anti-Thatcher/ruling class "Pills and Soap" on the independent Demon label).

"Ummm, ummmm—my God!! They like it! They like it!" he exults, waving aloft the magazine's glowing assessment of Elvis Costello and the Attractions' new album, *Punch the Clock.* When we reach the restaurant, the husky rocker wearing the tinted horn-rims disappears into a phone booth and emerges moments later to announce that the first new single issued in the United Kingdom, the shimmering soul bopper "Everyday I Write the Book," has just hit the Top 30. As a result, a scheduled band rehearsal for an imminent U.S. tour will be shortened tomorrow so that Elvis and the Attractions can hold forth as guests on "Top of the Pops." This calls for sashimi.

It's a steamy ninety-degree day in London in the summer of 1983, but it obviously feels like a deep-freeze for the former Declan McManus when compared with the pop purgatory in which he's been roasting since 1979. That was the year that Elvis and company hit the road for the third time in the States, at that stage in support of their acclaimed *Armed Forces* LP. Cocky and largely incommunicado offstage, the characteristically taciturn leader of the band got into a drunken bout of fat-mouthing in a Columbus, Ohio, gin mill with a belligerent Bonnie Bramlett and other members of the Stephen Stills band, and wound up odd lout out for his highly publicized racial slurs about Ray Charles and James Brown. Costello has long since apologized for his grievous utterances, stating that he was pie-eyed, perversely petulant, and just trying to irk his barmates with the most gratingly nasty remark he could muster. People do a lot of foolish things at the age of twenty-four, and Western civilization rarely takes much notice, but this time a fair chunk of the world was watching, greatly unamused.

It was, of course, a bizarrely self-destructive move for the leading, most critically beloved figure in the new wave hierarchy after the stunning originality of his first two albums (*My Aim Is True,* 1977; *This Year's Model,* 1978) had established him as a rising rock craftsman *sans pareil* (he was twenty-two when he debuted)—and one of the few seemingly destined for mass acceptance. Ironically, he was also one of the few in his sphere of influence who had gone out of his way to reaffirm the enormous debt he and his young colleagues owed to the R&B, blues, and soul greats, in addition to being quite active in the Rock against Racism movement and a sworn enemy of England's fascist, antiblack National Front (his "Night Rally" was an unequivocal denunciation that put him in personal jeopardy with its rabid membership). In short, the Angry Young Man image which Costello cultivated had backfired, severely crippling his career's momentum.

Following the 1979 tour, the Attractions—Steve Nieve, keyboards; Pete Thomas, drums; Bruce Thomas, bass—broke up for a time, while Elvis weathered squalls in his personal life. When the group reunited in 1980 (thanks to manager Jake Riviera) it was to release *Get Happy!* a twenty-song celebration of rockin' R&B that demonstrated enormous energy and invention but little direction. That same year, *Taking Liberties,* a score of obscure B-sides, unreleased masters, and cuts previously relegated to U.K. LPs, was shipped into the States. Like the previous record, it contained many fascinating tracks and was a testament to Costello's prolificacy, but was too diverse to digest and sold poorly. The year 1981 was a gloomy period that showed an even more reclusive Elvis come together with longtime producer Nick Lowe for their sixth LP, *Trust,* notable for the single "Watch Your Step," and a duet with Squeeze's Glenn Tilbrook on "From a Whisper to a Scream." The record received no radio response and a lukewarm sales reception in the U.S. market, and Elvis shifted gears dramatically, heading down to Nashville in May to do an album with veteran country producer Billy Sherrill. A grossly underrated effort by a canny fan of George Jones, Don Gibson, and the best of modern country, *Almost Blue* did well in the United Kingdom, but only served to confuse Costello's loyal (and somewhat dwindling) following in America.

It took the bold, highly impressionistic *Imperial Bedroom,* with its elaborate orchestrations by the brilliant Steve Nieve, to regain mainstream attention for all of the right reasons. Produced by Geoff Emerick, it was a record that was fierce in its desire to flex new muscles and take freshly focused chances, and even the most dogged detractors were forced to unclench their fists and applaud a noble and sagacious compositional effort.

Now, with *Punch the Clock,* Elvis Costello has a shot at an organic popular breakthrough as well as total access to the airwaves on both sides of the Atlantic, and it was clear as he took his place before the sushi bar that he was not going to blow it again. A highlight of the new album is "Mouth Almighty," on which Elvis asserts: "I know I've got my faults / And among them I can't control my tongue." Candid admissions of weakness are the first signs of real strength, and this year's model plainly has come to like himself for himself. Open, vulnerable—and unescorted—he exhibits an easy poise leavened with an engaging self-deprecation. Gone are the defensiveness and hair-trigger fulminations of the untempered, ninety-eight-pound weakling who once cooed "my aim is true" behind Coke-bottle lenses. He's been replaced by a broad-shouldered, affable, articulate, acerbic-within-bounds, and enormously likable adult who laughs heartily at other people's jokes, offers to share his octopus and squid (no thank you), and during the course of a long, lively talk was at one point unable to suppress—I swear it!—a full-blown blush.

No longer a man out of time, Elvis Costello is learning how to make the most of whatever the clock still holds in store for him.

How do you see the evolution of your songwriting style?

Evolution isn't a word I'd use, but I'd constantly move from one style of writing to another as I felt I'd exhausted one or was selling my ideas short. I largely thought that the songs on *Armed Forces*—which coincidentally is my most successful album to date, and I hope won't be by the time this appears—were rather *glib.* I've since adopted a style of writing that's a bit more direct and honest. On *Get Happy!* the songs were shorter, very immediate; I didn't allow as much excess.

I'm a bit of a magpie—I don't play any instrument particularly well, so I do things by feeling rather than by technique. If I think, "Now I'm going to write a Four Tops song or an Erik Satie song [*laughter*], obviously it's a bit limited as to how close I can get. But it's not important how close to somebody's musical ideal it is. It's only important how well the song works, and if I've gotten something I'm satisfied with because it did the job. So I started using lots of other *styles* of music, if you like, quite consciously, but always trying to keep my musical identity in them. That culminated in the *Imperial Bedroom* album, where there are lots of loose ends and lots of potential directions. In each song there's some fake psychedelia or a forties-style riff or things written with a strict format after the fashion of a standard ballad. I wanted to see what effect I could achieve.

Were these later records regenerative projects or exploratory ones?

Well, the last album was exploratory. There are a lot more deliberate obscurities in the lyrics on that one to allow them to work on the listeners' imaginations rather than making a specific point every time. I sometimes like to make an impression rather than a statement. "Kid About It" is an example, and "New Amsterdam" on *Get Happy!* Almost unconsciously, they give off the feeling of an event without describing it.

What was the first song you ever wrote?

I couldn't tell you what it was called. I was writing back when I was fifteen, so I should imagine it was all about the trials and tribulations of being fifteen—not to knock that. I'm just damned glad that I wasn't discovered then. A song I wrote before the first album which didn't appear until later should give you an idea of the sort of songs I didn't choose to record at first—it was "New Lace Sleeves," on *Trust.* The arrangement was a later thing but that less direct kind of song was written in its entirety before my first album. "Ghost Train," which I've done a solo version of, was also written before the first album.

You appear to have a very fitful attitude toward the supposed war between the sexes. It's very Thurber-like, acting as a jocular conscience of human folly.

James Thurber's one of my favorite writers. I never thought about it all along those lines, but maybe there is an element in that sympathy to Thurber's attitude that comes through. I've read a lot of his writings, and I love his cartoons, so it might filter through.

Thurber's view is one of "I see you all doing this, and I give up! I don't know who's in charge here, but dammit, I do see patterns, so I'm going to throw them all back at you!"

I think that's quite it, really, and people sometimes make the mistake with the songs of presuming that every one is written about my life. They say, "*This* has happened to him," but it could have been something I just saw in the same way that Thurber did. [*grinning*] But my life's not a cartoon. For instance, I didn't really meet my wife by finding her crouching on top of the wardrobe!

Could you at least detail how one of your better-known songs, like "(The Angels Wanna Wear My) Red Shoes," was built up?

That's an odd one to pick, because I occasionally get visions in my head that I just write down, and there's no experience of having worked upon them—that being one of those instances. I wrote it all in ten minutes.

I go into a trance when I'm writing, and can remember very little, like, except sitting down once with the newspaper. It can just be a mass of print, or at other times a mass of one-liners that stick out as possible parts of songs. With "Pills and Soap," I had written the title down as something that had come off the TV, and it suggested all these ideas. The substance of the later verses came from reading a newspaper, and these other things leaped out at me. It was as mundane as that.

That's a pretty angry tune. There's a cutting edge to most of your music that makes it dart and stab out of the radio. Would you say that most of your songs are angry?

Well, even if the emotions in my songs are negative, they are *definite* emotions. That's the main thing about them. To some extent I'm satisfied with the songs that give only an impression of an emotion instead of adamantly saying, "This-is-the-way-I-feel," but they're the ones that are the least memorable. They're passive songs—you have to come to *them.* The other songs, whether negative, positive, angry, or glad about something, come at *you.*

There aren't any passive songs on this new record. There was one passive song called "The Flirting Kind" which is on the B-side of one of the singles here in England but was left off the album. I made a conscious effort to be as brief as possible lyrically. I try not to have so many superfluous things in a song but also take care not to strip them of any images that make them vivid and exciting to listen to. Chiefly, I want to keep the ultimate point of the song uppermost.

To my ears, virtually all the songs on Armed Forces *seemed to have a definite quality to them, while the 1981 country album,* Almost Blue, *had a passive feel, as if you were basically in the act of warming up to them.*

Yes, but it's not so much that on the country album as, "Why am I *doing* them?" To view somebody being that unhappy, or to be in sympathy with songs which portray that amount of unhappiness, requires a degree of resignation on the part of the person carrying that out. You can't go in there and give those songs *stink,* you know, you can't give them *hell.*

But I was in that melancholy attitude. I was disillusioned with my own writing and therefore chose to sing those songs. Those songs reflected my frame of mind as well as any others I could have written.

You were disillusioned in what sense? You thought you weren't hitting the mark?

I think there was a period of a hangover from the *Armed Forces* era, which was very successful. So it was on the one hand not enjoying that, making rather a mess out of it in terms of my life and my career, and on the other hand, feeling that I'd squandered an opportunity to have a large audience. I was feeling that I didn't have anything to say for myself, and then when I did have something to say—on the *Get Happy!* and *Trust* albums—I no longer had the means of the medium with which to communicate with a larger audience. The fact that the audience was getting smaller at that point sort of led me to the conclusion that I should stop writing songs.

I decided to do a record of other people's songs to bring some other *talent,* if you like, to the fore—which was the ability to sing rather than just have my words out. It had gotten to where the reviews were just concerned with, "What's he saying on this one? Who's he having a go at now?" I mean, I like to be my own most vitriolic critic about what I'm bleeding on about, 'cause there are always those people who are not convinced by you at all and think you're a terrible sham.

Do you think that critics put too much emphasis on your words rather than the total composition?

Sure, but there's no point in being false about the fact that there's more substance to my lyrics than quite a lot of other writers—not to say that there aren't others who write interesting lyrics. But overall, there are a lot of very poor lyrics on records. I always used to say that the minute that the critics found somebody who *could* string three words together, they immediately called him the new Bob Dylan, they called him the new Bruce Springsteen. It's a very dangerous thing to pay that much attention to someone who perhaps can't withstand it. Whatever happened to Elliot Murphy? Whatever happened to Willie Nile? These people never had a chance because, when they came out, the critics presumed one exalted thing about them and so much was expected. It's extremely unfair.

It's been said that the reason so many American rock critics love Elvis Costello is because they look like Elvis Costello.

[*Barking laughter, blushing*] That's quite a good one. But they don't, you know. Again, that's the thing: they just look the way they *think* I look! I don't look anything like they think I look!

You spoke to me earlier, in the taxi, about the incestuous, elitist qualities of the British press as opposed to the rock-crit self-importance of some of the American press. Do you think the music press makes any significantly positive contributions to the overall environment?

If they're not actually informative—which in different ways they are, I guess, on both sides of the Atlantic—and merely negative, then they set up something to work against. Fighting the American press is like disobeying your parents, because they're so pompous. Critiques in the States usually have the tone of book reviews a lot of the time. In live concert reviews they treat you like opera!—"*Mister* Costello did this" . . . and so forth.

There's the famous instance of Meat Loaf being referred to in the New York Times *as "Mr. Loaf."*

[*Laughing convulsively*] Aaah! Mister Loaf! Mister Loaf! That's *fantastic!* Mister Loaf! [*catching his breath, wiping his eyes*] The rolling buzzards!

It must be incredibly frustrating to constantly have your gradual development, your emerging muse, sharply criticized. A lot of times, just at the stage when artists are beginning to reach a big audience, they are not necessarily doing their best work.

I felt that I was at the time with *Armed Forces,* because I hadn't been one who simply stuck around a long time and suddenly gained a massive audience when they'd made their worst record. I actually felt that I was still ascendant artistically, but in retrospect I think that because everything happened so quickly my judgment wasn't at its best. My great enthusiasm for elements of the way my work went in the light of that initial burst of acclaim was misplaced. I'm not totally denying all the work, though. There were some damned good songs in that transitional period.

Do you have any absolute favorites thus far?

There are songs I still enjoy playing which are not necessarily our best-known songs. "Big Tears," which was the B-side of "Pump It Up" in England, is probably one of the best songs we've made. I still like "Pump It Up" as well. I couldn't imagine going in and making that record now, but I'm glad I made it then.

Your range of focus is an uncommonly wide one. How did you come to put "My Funny Valentine" on the back of the 1979 "(What's So Funny 'Bout) Peace, Love and Understanding" 45?

I'd always liked the song, since I was a child. My parents played Sinatra's rendition around the house, and the band just needed another B-side, really. It was one of those situations where I was available and nobody else was, so we just did the guitar and voice and it seemed okay to me. I ignored all the criticism of it at the time, people saying that I had a lot of bloody cheek singing a song like that because, after all, I was a *punk* [*sly grin*].

It seems that you're really concentrating on your vocals this time around. In "The Invisible Man" in particular on the new LP, you seem to be paying a lot more attention to your singing. There's almost a delicacy to the vocal on that track—I also hear a bit of a Ray Davies influence in there.

[*Delighted laughter*] That sort of became the standing joke when we were recording it! We were not actually copying anything, but without any conceit at all—just an in joke among the band—a song will often become known as "the Al Green tune" or whatever because it has some little lick in there. While we were recording "Invisible Man" Clive Langer said, "That's like the Kinks!" and once he'd said that, I couldn't get it out of my head. You know, I'm not a bad mimic when I want to be.

On the *Get Happy!* album we consciously abandoned the arrangements we were working on and rearranged everything based on a load of soul records I'd bought to refresh my memory. "King Horse" had the "Reach Out" guitar part, for example, along with a long "Poppa Was a Rollin' Stone" intro which we chopped off the record. There were a lot of little jokes on the album, and I think that's quite good fun. You shouldn't be afraid of making those kinds of jokes between yourselves—it helps to deflate any conceit that you have.

The horns on "T.K.O. (Boxing Day)" on the new album have a nice Stax soul review quality.

It's funny, in America folks tend to treat Stax as a vaudevillian throwback. We have a lot more . . . I don't want to say reverence, but more . . . respect for soul and R&B overall. A lot of big bands in the States seem to be frighteningly ignorant of stuff that is really their own heritage. They have this rock and this heavy metal music in America that doesn't have any roots in rock and roll and soul or *anything.* It's a creation of the 1970s. I'm talking about the Totos and the Rushes—those groups that sing, "*We're a rock and roll band!*" or "*We're rocking tonight!*" And they don't have anything to do with rock and roll, and wouldn't know it if it bit them [*laughter*]. I think there are very true rock and roll bands in America, such as the Blasters. The people who have the least clue of what's really good about rock and roll hold it as a god that must be bowed down to. I think it's so bloody old-fashioned, behind-the-times. I can't understand why anybody would be the slightest bit interested in "We're-going-to-do-it-all-night" kinds of songs.

In terms of your style of composing and playing, I sense that you like to hurry the melody and rush the hook. Are you conscious of that? Sometimes it's almost an examination-in-progress of how mannered rock and roll can be.

Well, more recently I tend to sing behind the beat instead of ahead of it, except on some of the uptempo songs. On the last album, I sang very consciously behind the beat, but I don't think I understand what it is you're saying.

There's a hurry-up quality to the structural resolution of your recorded material and to its live presentation that makes me as a listener hear with new ears. It's one of the things that I enjoy most about your music.

The music is built around my singing, and there is a particular tone in my voice at the register I sing at most of the time which tends to sound—some would say *urgent,* others would say *agitated,* depending on whether it jars you or is pleasing. So that might be it. My voice is very powerful in that certain register, and it's the one that is most effective at harassing the listener. [*chuckling*] You know what I mean? It cuts through backing and cuts through the beat as well, so perhaps that's what creates that effect. I've never really analyzed it.

I try not to get too self-conscious about my singing, for instance, and the only time I'm conscious of my singing is when I feel I've been consciously trying to eliminate sounds I don't like from my style. Over the years, I've dropped certain inflections and phrasings, but getting analytical about it is the worst thing you can do. In a few instances, I've allowed records to go out when I was unhappy with the vocal style, particularly on the last album, on which I indulged my experimentation. Normally, excepting the country records, I've always been produced under the disciplines of Nick Lowe, but because I wasn't producing myself on *Imperial Bedroom,* I was going overboard.

What was it like working with Nick Lowe?

I first knew him as a fan of Brinsley Schwarz, and he was the first person I ever knew who was in a professional group that made records and things. I knew him socially from around 1973, before I was a professional musician. I met him in a pub opposite the Cavern in Liverpool—this sounds like something a press officer would invent but it's true. He was playing there just before the club finally closed. I was in a little group, all of us working under our own names, and I met him at the bar. Then he was the first artist signed to Stiff and became the house producer by the time I was signed.

What specific contributions has Lowe made to your sound?

[*Smiles*] When I first knew Nick, his attitude was, "Hell, it's no big deal that I'm in a group! You bang three chords together and you write songs!" Up until then, because I had no experience in recording, I always thought that the more complicated the song was, the more merit it had. To some extent, he was instrumental in making me see the benefit of simplicity—and I adopted that as a creed from there on.

As a singer, I always had an understanding with him that he would let me go so far with a vocal, but if he thought I was going past it and becoming too considered and losing the feeling, he'd stop me and use the earlier, imperfect take. He'd always allow me one or two wild takes beyond what he thought was it, in case I did something extraordinary that he wasn't expecting. He taught me a lot about craft *and* noncalculation—and that they needn't be in conflict.

Is Punch the Clock *a title meant to comment on the drudgery of the work week or a rage concerning age?*

No, but I like titles with double meanings, like *Trust.* It's got a great double meaning to it: you could say, "Trust *me*!" or "Trust *them*!" *Punch the Clock* could mean stopping time, or let's punch in and get to work, but it's not a manifestation of rage about getting old. We were going to give a deliberately pretentious title to the last album just to irritate people—we were going to call it *Music to Stop Clocks.* And then we were going to call it *This Is a Revolution of the Mind,* which comes from "King Heroin" by James Brown—but I discovered that *he* did call one of his albums that! But I'm not a prisoner of time. [*crooning*] "Time is on my side. . . ."

The first time I played "Love Went Mad" from Punch the Clock, *I cracked up laughing because I thought I caught a certain ingenious obscenity in the lyrics that I believed I must have heard wrong, but I checked and, yes, the lyric read: "I wish you luck with a capital F."*

Hmm. I don't think that's a particularly good line. I think it's a lousy one, actually. I prefer the line before it, "With these vulgar fractions of the treble clef." That's just my personal preference. The other one's a bit of an untidy payoff, one of the worst lines on the record.

Seriously? I love it! It's a line I'd use in a pub.

Well, yeah, I suppose you're right. See, that's a song about complacency from a comic opera that will never exist. The detail in it about Piccadilly being turned into Brands Hatch refers to a racing car track in this country that's like the Indianapolis Speedway.

The song is about Mr. Complacency being down in the fallout shelter, totally resigned to his fate just seconds before he's obliterated. There he is down there, playing his family favorites on a tissue and a comb and thanking God he won't have to be tempted by young girls dressed as older women anymore—"There'll be no more lamb dressed as mutton rather than mutton dressed as lamb." [*laughter*] He's counting his few blessings that are left, 'cause he's lived such a good, saintly life.

Your writing has always seemed especially concerned with a stark kind of political commentary that's almost Kafkaesque. There's a line in "Pills and Soap" that goes, "You think your country needs you but you know it never will." Do you have a sense of cynicism about these things?

First of all, concerning how much you belong to your country or your country belongs to you, definitely so. I think it's a really false belief when they tell you, "Your country needs you." Yeah! A great nonsense, isn't it? They only need you as long as they've got a particular function for you. It's not *your* country or *my* country—it doesn't belong to *me.*

Do you vote?

Yes, I do. I voted for the Labour Party in the last election. Why I would not vote for Thatcher is easy: I think that it's an insensitive government, it doesn't have any compassion for people who are not self-made business people. They have no feeling for people who haven't got any money or a job. They're quite prepared to *damn* large portions of the population to miserable lives. I don't think there's any way that you can justify voting any other way but Labour. I suppose you could say that's a very high-handed attitude to take toward any political party, but I should think it goes beyond politics—it's actually morally wrong to vote for the Tories.

Well, I would think that a country is only as good as the quality of life that its working class is experiencing, but do you see yourself as a champion of the working class?

No, I don't see myself as a champion of anybody. I've never stressed it enough that I write from my own point of view. I'm not writing for *anybody* else. What people identify with in the songs is their business. That's what *use* they make of the songs, the same way they make use of something they've read in a book or see in a film. I don't make any demands on the audience in terms of them seeing me as a spokesperson or a champion. I don't cast myself in any roles like those. I'm just an individual.

I think the atmosphere in the United Kingdom makes for a much more vital rock scene. In America the scene is so diffuse.

When you live in a spread-out country, you can't have it any other way. Still, you've got little close-knit creative cliques in particular towns and cities, like the New York community that gave us Talking Heads and the Ramones—that's an unusual scene that can spawn *both* those groups, even though they're both very arty in their way. But I don't put the vitality over in England down to class. Class is a depressing element of this society, and I don't think it has any positive aspects except that it gives you something to kick against. And, of course, there's currently a much larger middle class—at least in their own minds—than there's ever been in this country. But in truth there're only three types of people in the world: people who work, people who are not allowed to, and people who don't have to.

Speaking of your own work, does it bother you that you haven't had any hit singles in the States?

[*Pensive*] I don't know. It obviously bothers me that we seem to be able to have a degree of success, and the hit single is the key to a larger market. If reaching a larger market means that you have to sound like Christopher Cross, then I'd rather stay the way I am. I'm not going to make a record which I think is consciously intended to get the desired effect of a hit in America, a hot single which is gonna break us through so that we then are up there with Bob Seger and all the good ol' ones. I want to reach there when it's on the terms of making good music. Coincidentally, quite a lot of the people who are held in almost obscene reverence in America, like Bob Dylan and Van Morrison, don't sell that many records.

What are your feelings on the music video boom and its relative importance to your group?

We've done one video for this record, and we'll probably do another. We've done loads of them, but you won't see them on MTV—except only at three o'clock in the morning. I don't think we're a particularly visual group, which is a drawback, but we've made some quite good videos over the years; at least one for each album since *Armed Forces.* They're fun, but usually trite; the current English school of the "mysterious video" genre is to wear trench-coats on them and walk through dry ice smoke—you've got to look like you're in *Murder on the Orient Express.* Or was that last year? God, I can't take them seriously. I think it's a big mistake to interpret the twenty-four-hour record company and its bored-brat indulgence in the shape of rock videos as some kind of innovation—that's very self-congratulatory. Actually I think it's a retrogressive step. It takes a lot of music out of it all, so you see what ugly, boring bastards most rock chaps are. I'd rather that you waited all week with some feeling of anticipation for one program that was genuinely great, in which you saw good bands that were exciting, than have twenty-four-hour access to a load of idiots with too much money and not enough sense. I'm afraid that's the standard of most of the videos that I saw when I watched MTV. That's not indicative of the idea; it just shows the paucity of imagination and genuine inspiration, and of the vanities of a lot of the groups.

Say, were you modest and well-liked as a kid?

[*Laughter*] Oh, I never thought, "My God, I'm so much brighter than everybody else." Or [*dreamily*], "I knew from an early age I was special"—one of those kinds of remarks, or "I used to see things other people didn't." I did average work at school—but I don't think that's a reflection of intelligence.

I'm only curious if you had close companions with whom you could really confer as an adolescent.

I don't have very many friends, period—let's put it that way. I just don't choose to have many. I had few friends then and few now, meaning a few I value a lot rather than a lot I don't value at all. I don't worry about how sophisticated the relationship is, I just worry about whether it matters to me. It can be quite *inane,* because a lot of things that matter to you are not often sophisticated. In fact, the things that matter to you generally are things that *lack* sophistication, or what we laughably call sophistication—which is our ability to drown our real feelings in the *cologne* of sophistication. There you go! There's a good one! They're rolling off the tongue today, folks!

Getting back to music: what role does keyboardist Steve Nieve play in shaping songs?

I think it would be unfair to the other two Attractions, Bruce and Pete Thomas, to say that Steve has a greater say overall. Obviously, he has the most scope with his instrument because he's the main melodic interest on most tracks, and from the nature of his instrument he has more range than the bass or the drums. But I think overall it's a fairly even input. On the last album, we had songs which he arranged for outside players, as in the case of ". . . And In Every Home" and "Town Crier." That's a different matter. He contributed quite a lot to ". . . And In Every Home" because I gave him the song, said "give full vent to your imagination," and he gave it this deranged setting. It's marvelous that he has the technical, musical ability to write things down, that he can communicate complicated ideas to players that can only work with written music. I don't have that ability. I don't write or read music at all. I have to describe things to people if I'm working with a writer or arranger; I have to communicate by humming the lines, which can get very tedious.

Still, that's a great rock and roll and R&B tradition.

I suppose it is. I wrote all the main horn refrains on this new album. I sang, "da da da da," and the phrasing and the harmonies of it were worked out between myself, Steve, Clive Langer, Alan Winstanley, and the horn section. Other punches, turnarounds, and modifications came from a communal effort. With the song, "The Greatest Thing," we left a huge gap where we just vamped from E to C sharp minor in the middle of the song and said that when we did the backing track, we'd put some sort of horn bit in there. We just cannibalized a well-known Glenn Miller tune and threw in a bit of Kool and the Gang for good measure. You can do it literally like that, have fun, instead of thinking, "What are people going to think of this?" or "What's the *significance* of this?"

Is there an album of yours that you believe was the turning point, in terms of your doing the work you'd hoped to hear yourself doing?

Get Happy! was it. I'd written about half the songs on it during the 1979 *Armed Forces* tour, which had ended in a lot of disarray both personally and professionally, for various reasons which I think have been well-covered elsewhere. I took quite a lot of time off to recover physically and emotionally, and I went off and did a bit of production, like the Specials' first album. Meanwhile, I had earlier been writing material for the next album, and we rented a studio.

We put about two tracks down, and I realized right away that the arrangements we'd worked out on the tour were going to come out sounding very clichéd, like a parody of ourselves. The sound we'd developed was rather a rootless new wave sound; it sounded like the very things I criticize modern rock music for, yet it didn't relate to glitter rock, nor any of the modern trends, nothing at all. It completely stood alone. Some of the music for the album dated back to 1975; it was really ancient, and the arrangements lacked the character that the songs required. I rewrote a few and others we just rearranged—to varying degrees of success—after I'd gone out and bought some fifty soul records to refresh what I'd liked about that style and the strength of the vocals. If you have a love for the style, the song will often carry it along. You could cast "Many Rivers to Cross" as a country and western song and it would stand up—providing the singer matches the commitment. [*smirking slyly*] Or you could do a Linda Ronstadt on it and fall flat on your—oh, no, I mustn't get into attacking her again!

Despite your wisecracks, I get the distinct impression from both Punch the Clock *and this conversation that you are taking yourself more seriously as a singer—and hope others will too. The growth is there. Is the intent there also?*

Maybe I'm getting better as I get more experienced. Sometimes my intentions would blind me to some of the effective subtleties of singing. Before, I'd be singing with a tremendous amount of conviction, but sometimes it would come out sounding very hectoring. There was usually a lot of feeling there, but I hadn't considered how best to express it, so some of the songs sounded rather like rants. I've learned I can get a point over by using more tonal range.

In the studio, I used to put the vocal to the fore when I was more involved in my own production. This time around I wasn't involved in production decisions beyond being asked my opinion, and I wanted the discipline of that to help shape the arrangements and the structure of the overdubs. The band had its usual arrangement meetings, but then Clive Langer and Alan Winstanley came along and they had their say as well, aiming to give us a more concise approach.

Is that kind of power and involvement on their part unprecedented in your recording history?

It was completely unprecedented, certainly, compared with the last album, where I took every blessed idea I had, more or less, to a logical or illogical conclusion, and the job of Geoff Emerick, who produced *Imperial Bedroom,* was to try and make some sense out of my efforts. A lot of times I was pleased with the results, because you got a dense, sometimes conflicting, sometimes contrasting array of instruments and vocal devices which repay many listenings. But in some cases I buried the songs in a maze of contradictory musical ideas and even emotions.

Your music is intensely emotional, and thematically it often dissects or critiques relationships. I'm still intrigued about your personal perspective on sexism and the current quality of the female-male relationships you encounter.

I tend to treat each person or situation I've observed solely for the individual value, rather than have some preconceived idea about the larger scheme of things when it comes to women and men. I don't think I'm wise enough to make broad statements because I'm still finding things out myself. Chronologically some people might say I should be old enough to know better through experience, but I don't necessarily think I am. But I think the things that bring us to grief are plain to see: jealousy, lack of faith, lack of trust. I'm not a great believer that there are deeper secrets behind the distance between us that are locked up somewhere waiting to be discovered. Generally, I don't think people talk very much, regardless of who they are. They might say more words these days, but whether they're talking to each other is another matter.

In your experience, do you find that people our age currently are more or less guarded in their relationships?

Personally *I'm* much less guarded, not just in the sense of my professional relationships but just generally. I have an interest in being much more open—[*smiling*] as a result of exhausting the opposite possibilities. It's as simple as that. But I don't think in large schemes; I'm very much absorbed with the moment. I think it's more important to deal with life as it comes along than sit around pondering one's personal philosophy. You'd be dead before you ever had a chance to implement it! What useful things you find out in this world, you invariably find out on foot, on the move. You can't *wait.*

Do you have any bitterness about the manner in which you've been dealt with in the press, whether it be the Bonnie Bramlett–Ray Charles incident and your resultant mea culpas or your overall reticence of the recent past?

No, but I eventually was concerned with explaining myself, and I do feel that I did in that case. On another front, I think it's one of the conceits of the business that the record companies worry about what you think of them, and the music papers worry about what you think of them. I don't sit around in my house worrying about those things at all.

My main interest in this business is *music,* and if I'm not concerned with the making of my own, I'd much rather just be thinking, "God, this other person's record is great" and enjoying it for what it is. I don't think, "What am I getting out of this? How is this changing my life?" One of the greatest joys I've yet found in life is to listen to Bobby Bland—it doesn't have to have any further point than that, unless I want to tell someone else they should perhaps check him out for themselves. Framing all the great music out there only drags down its immediacy. The songs are lyrics, not speeches, and they're tunes, not paintings. Writing about music is like dancing about architecture—it's a really stupid thing to want to do.

Oddly enough, you seem totally accessible to me as a person, not at all the crusty character everyone else describes. I wonder if your new, more cordial relationship with the press is merely due to the fact that you've finally become more adept at dealing with them?

No, I think it's because I've done enough work that there is something to talk about, rather than conversation just based on one press release. In the beginning, I did a few interviews, and I didn't feel they went very well, so I just stopped doing them. Why be a conspirator in this nonsense they're writing?!

You mean, say, the corporate formation of a public personality?

Yeah! In the beginning there wasn't enough work there to really talk about, and no substance to the articles, so why should I be involved? They're going to write this nonsense anyway, so why be a party to it? It's as simple as that; I chose to stop doing it. And then when the time went by, and I felt there were some things that were perhaps necessary to explain, I changed my mind again.

What new artists have excited you?

Funnily enough, the group that's supporting us on the U.S. tour, Aztec Camera, I like a helluva lot. I heartily recommend you go and buy their album *High Land, Hard Rain* right now. I quite like Prince, though not all of his stuff, and I think Paul Young has got a great voice and his *No Parlez* album is terrific. I really like the Style Council, which Paul Weller formed since he left the Jam. I like a group that's called, would you believe, Prefab Sprout. They've only got one single out, called "Lions in My Own Garden," which is excellent. There's another group on Rough Trade called the Smiths, and I like Robert Wyatt, obviously, having worked with him. Rough Trade, I must say, has put out the best records of the last two years. I also like "You're in My System" by Robert Palmer—a brilliant record. Recently Johnnie Taylor and Lamont Dozier have gotten their courage back to make great soul records and not conform to the less imaginative end of the disco market.

Every artist and group that hopes to enjoy longevity must go through a continual process of reinvention. You've got to remain close to what made you want to make music in the first place and let that be your motivation.

Quite true. Look at Aretha Franklin—a singer of enormous stature who now largely just sings riffs, and although she's incapable of bad singing, she does what Otis Redding often did, harrying the phrase and so forth. Luther Vandross's production of her has only helped her in terms of setting, not reinvention. You know, Dusty Springfield recorded one of my songs last year, "Just a Memory," which I wrote with her in mind three years ago but made no attempt to get to her because she hadn't been recording. I'd dreamed in the back of my mind that she'd one day make a comeback and record it, and last year she did on her *White Heat* album. Unfortunately, the production left a lot to be desired, and the vocal treatment was bland; it wasn't what it could have been if I'd produced it. We've all gotten used to the politeness of overdubbing as opposed to *captured* performances in the studio.

So what helps you to plug into that?

For me, it takes time, and that's difficult because the longer you record, the harder it gets. I went past a few things on the new album and had to leave them for a couple of weeks and then go back. There are some cases of songs I've *never* gotten right on record, like "Clowntime Is Over," which is now an integral part of our live show. A fast version was on *Taking Liberties,* but we never truly finished the song in the studio. A good version of it doesn't exist on record because I insisted on cutting it live in the studio and wouldn't overdub. To make one of the less flippant comparisons that come to mind, that song was supposed to be our Impressions song, that was to be our "Keep On Pushing"; it was very important for me to get it down, and yet I failed.

In some instances, I've found that what I know to be the important songs of an album, the *weight* of an album, have been the hardest songs to record. I knew that "Kid About It," "Pidgin English," and "Man Out of Time" were the crucial songs to *Imperial Bedroom.* They also posed the most problems and are the most ragged and incomplete recordings. The arrangements and the vocal direction that I took destroyed "Kid About It," which is five times the song live, because I sing more honestly and don't fool around with different octaves and affectations. In the studio I was trying too hard to avoid sounding like a white soul singer, a Michael McDonald. Not to knock him: I think he's a very good singer.

Have you ever thought about working with a classic soul or R&B producer?

I did approach Allen Toussaint to arrange the horns for our shows at the Albert Hall last Christmas. The previous year, I'd done a show with the Royal Philharmonic Orchestra at the Albert Hall—an enjoyable, nerve-wracking, on/off experiment that had mixed results. I wanted Toussaint and his people to take us in a new, less grandiose direction, but their pace of working proved to be too slow to make it come about, and so I had to pull out. It proved to be fortuitous because it could have only worked in the *friction* between his and our arrangements, since Toussaint comes from a part of the world with very different musical criteria. What ultimately came about was that I stuck with the idea of horns and sought out the best players I knew of in this country, the TKO Horns. Because they're English and we share the same relationship to R&B, it worked. To expand on something I alluded to earlier, I find that many contemporary American musicians have a peculiarly patronizing attitude toward R&B, as if it happened a million years ago, whereas to us, Tamla-Motown is *folk music,* not a museum piece. You still hear it played regularly on radio here.

Elements-wise, I worry that Americans might see some of *Punch the Clock* as a novelty, and it isn't—it's dead serious, *alive* music. With the presence of the TKO Horns we're developing a sound, and the tour is an exploration for us. On our first tour of America in 1977, we learned so much about how to play—it was our first experience of a wider audience outside of British clubs—and the same will happen again because now we're effectively eight pieces.

You're nothing if not a risk-taker. The risks just need to be germane ones.

I've decided not to go in for lucky-bag approaches like we did with country music on *Almost Blue,* where I threw myself in with Billy Sherrill, not knowing what was going to come out of it. The best things that came out of it were the frictions, not the complementary stuff. Americans generally dismiss that record as being an insult to the music [*grinning*], but it's just heartbreak drinking music; it's not that mysterious.

The fact that most of the songs come from a particular geographical area makes no difference to me. As for my claim to emotional authenticity, if you compare my record to any of Barbara Mandrell's, I think we might come out better. *Almost Blue* isn't made by a gifted amateur—it's a sincere, genuine record. The fact that we don't have the geographical credentials to make it is completely irrelevant. If you really want to split hairs, most of those songs are ripped off from English, Irish, and Scottish folk songs anyway, so you haven't got a leg to stand on! [*laughter*].

In rock and roll, enthusiasm and focus can almost always transcend technique and environment. But sometimes you can stumble into a marriage that's too eager, too neat. You're in it for all the wrong, external reasons. Zeal can overshadow instinct.

I understand what you're getting at. Let's pick it apart. Peter Green, say, is a great blues guitarist; it doesn't matter that he wasn't born in Mississippi. Quite a lot of other white players who have been lionized, like Eric Clapton, don't hold up as well. The best intentions are the unconscious ones. One of the reasons I'd be reluctant to work with a classic soul producer is that I think whereas there was something to be had from the friction in country music of working in an alien environment, I suspect the orthodox soul attempt would wilt from the lack of it.

Also, you've got to bear in mind that I'm not making records only for America. If I were only making them for America, perhaps I would go and do a record in New Orleans with Allen Toussaint and aim it at the tasty, semi-middle-of-the-road FM market. But I'm not dead and buried here yet; I haven't finished with the English public. I think it's important if you write in one country to keep up a relationship with that native audience.

There's a lot of rubbish that goes in this country but a lot of good things too. I would rather be involved with the good things than desert the country. Five years ago, I could have chosen to leave for financial reasons and been a much richer man. I've elected to remain here not for any patriotic considerations but because it's a more interesting place musically than any other I know of.

Well, I think you appreciate the organic dynamic tension you find in the United Kingdom, although it might not necessarily exist here for another artist.

It's here for others, but it's not here for those insubstantial people who'll come and go. I'm here because I *choose* to be. It's a marriage, as you put it, that's working because I'm in love with the music—not with the marriage.

In the beginning, Bruce Frederick Springsteen was a loquacious public celebrant of the mechanized American landscape of his adolescence and its niftiest attraction, the car. He came of age in a generation where any guy could own or at least temporarily control a car while still in his teen years, acting out rites of freedom and fulfillment while cruising the Miracle Mile. In the past two decades, Springsteen has perhaps written more songs about late-model jalopies and the untrammeled mobility of the kids that drive and ride in them than any other rocker. His first album, 1973's *Greetings from Asbury Park,* introduced a dialogue-starved young parkway philosopher who could not hold back his observations on the suburban curbside buffet. In songs like "Growin' Up" and "Blinded by the Light," the music was a muddled mix of folk-based English rock and starchy blue-eyed soul. *The Wild, the Innocent and the E-Street Shuffle* appeared later the same year, almost as a vociferous afterthought, smoothing out the contradictions of the first record, straining to make its musical intentions clear, the singer's vision of the workingman's urban ballad now pleasantly stylized, thanks to able instrumental support from a show band in the Memphis-soul tradition of Otis Redding and Sam and Dave. It was the work of an

Bruce Springsteen

1990

impatient, suddenly lucid romantic who had stayed up all night to square it away, an impulsive visionary with plenty of time to kill.

Two years later, after much anticipation from fans and dread from overcommitted American critics, Springsteen let go of *Born to Run*, an ambitious album he had been reluctant to release. The dreamy zeal with which it had been created was apparent in cinematic songs like "Meeting Across the River" and "She's the One," the writer's *West Side Story* plotlines providing the singer side of himself with ample room to act them out in the studio and (with greater, grander improvisation) onstage. The staunchly unkempt Springsteen became well-known for his last-ounce-of-effort performances, which demonstrated enormous energy and warmth toward his highly appreciative fans.

He was equally renowned for the legal hassles surrounding his songwriting and recording. His career was stalled when a lawsuit was filed against manager Mike Appel for "unconscionable exploitation" of his career and writing output, Springsteen charging Appel with fraud and breach of trust. The case was settled out of court, and music critic Jon Landau took over the guidance of Springsteen's career as well as production chores (Landau had assisted on *Born to Run*). Springsteen also branched out as a songwriter, writing hits for other artists, or seeing their covers of his work do well. The Hollies charted with "Sandy," Manfred Mann scored with "Blinded by the Light," the Pointer Sisters did well with "Fire," and rock poet Patti Smith reached the high point of her short singing career with the success of the cowritten "Because the Night."

Between 1978 and 1982, Springsteen released three more albums, *Darkness on the Edge of Town, The River, Nebraska,* each one progressively more bleak, barren, distraught. In the broadest sense, the songs addressed with histrionic "road warrior" metaphors the OPEC oil embargoes and the gas crisis they precipitated. The resignation in his music remained after the OPEC threat had faded. Some interpreted Springsteen's austere outlook as a back-to-basics approach to rock and roll; others, focusing on the themes of defeat and disjunction, saw the man as running out of ideas and a fresh perspective on his own very finite concerns.

He was born on September 23, 1949, in Freehold, New Jersey, his father, Douglas, a bus driver, his mother, Adele, a housewife. Bruce was their first child, followed by daughters Virginia and Pamela.

His parents would have preferred their son to pursue a career in law, but he'd been bitten by the garage-band bug and then got a salty taste of provincial glory in the clubs (most notably, The Stone Pony) on the boardwalks of the Jersey Shore. His early groups had names like the Castiles, Earth, Child, Steel Mill, Dr. Zoom and the Sonic Boom. The E Street Band, its personnel changeable, became his V-8. Dates were secured along the Eastern seaboard and on the West Coast, and he dropped out of a local community college to explore the band's showcase potential. The record contract came from Clive Davis at Columbia Records, under John Hammond's patronage. It was June 1972.

In 1984 Springsteen released *Born in the U.S.A.*, a record about cars and nightfall, one that aimed for a commanding depiction of their modest potential for conquering new horizons. He sang in gravelly bursts, like a souped-up Chevy skidding away from the soft shoulder of the road, and on the album jacket he stood before a massive Stars and Stripes like a puckish Patton; but his music was the sound of a defeated rebel, stuck in a small town, afraid to leave home.

Few noticed this depressing fact, however, because from the album art outward, this was a package seemingly contrived to deny its content. *Born in the U.S.A.* and its marketing campaign appeared as imposing as the fifty states, delivering fist-waving bombast in the service of mass appeal. After the careful bleakness of *Nebraska*, *Born in the U.S.A.* was poised to provide the ideal MTV dinner from Springsteen's commercial menu. The moves were studied, but they were not cynical; it simply seemed the best moment to capture megastardom for a perennial comer. Regrettably, *Born in the U.S.A.* proved the perfect complement to the blurred jingoism and let-the-big-dogs-eat imperiousness of the Reagan White House.

In 1986, Springsteen chose to issue *Bruce Springsteen and the E Street Band Live/1975–85,* a five-record collection of concert highlights that was also intended as a living history of his trek from artistic adolescence to creative manhood. Whether owing to the strength of the shows, the choice of recording sites, or the final winnowing process, more than half of the retrospective's tracks were culled from performances in the New York–New Jersey metropolitan area. Steeped in his collegial passion and pep rally theatricality, Bruce's live songs were a dashboard memoir of a decade of concert enthrallment.

There had been times over the years when Springsteen's material seemed to be more *about* rock and roll—its R&B-rooted tall talk, folkloric image, and drive-in movie fanfaronade—than rock and roll itself. But the bold connection documented between performer and public on the live records ratified Bruce's ability to bring even his most trite or claustrophobic material ("Backstreets," "Independence Day," "Racing in the Street") to powerful life onstage.

Thus, *Bruce Springsteen and the E Street Band Live/1975–85* became the one indispensable album for nonconverts. Yet while the anthology's forty tracks traced the exuberant advances of Bruce and his best band, even dropping hints and clues to his formative past, they disclosed surprisingly little about the inner man.

Those encountering him during his first few years (1973–76) at Columbia Records usually found a kind-eyed, unkempt young fellow who was diffident in the extreme. It was then that he often caught a bus up from Asbury to drop by the old *Crawdaddy* offices at Fifth Avenue and 13th Street on the edge of Greenwich Village, visiting the two editors (Peter Knobler, Greg Mitchell) who were his actual discoverers and earliest boosters in the national music press. The hardest part of the trip was getting past the receptionists, who assumed from his wispy Che beard, shapeless polo shirts, and spent jeans that he was a bicycle messenger. Disinclined to correct such conjecture, Springsteen would dawdle in the waiting area, mumbling a string of stalling remarks, until somebody recognized him.

He could be equally chary in more inclusive and festive settings, sitting through entire Yankee games with the *Crawdaddy* staff while offering little more than a grin and a grunt at the seventh-inning stretch. In backstage gatherings a decade onward, Springsteen's shyness had been replaced by a boyish formality, his banter as circular and unspecific as his periodic parleys with reporters.

Most information that circulated about Bruce Springsteen in the 1980s was confined to minutiae concerning his recording career, his management direction, and his intermittent concert guest shots and Stone Pony drop-ins. But for a handful of tightly structured vignettes offered by him during shows and then retold in major interviews, his boyhood was likewise unchronicled. Apart from an avid early interest in surfing, little is also known about his activities outside of music. And even the most commonplace aspects of his recording-era romantic relationships with Jersey Shore girlfriend Karen Darbin, actress Joyce Hyser, photographer Lynn Goldsmith, and others are unlearned—apart from the oft-repeated tale of Goldsmith being lifted out of the crowd by Springsteen during a September 1979 M.U.S.E. (Musicians United for Safe Energy) concert at Madison Square Garden. The two had recently broken up, and she was taking photos against his wishes when he became annoyed, pulling her from the photographer's pit and having her escorted from the show.

As a result of this blanket ignorance of Springsteen's personal life, even hardcore disciples were startled by the news just before Christmas 1985 that Bruce and twenty-four-year-old model Julianne Phillips (whom he'd met that September) had become inseparable. His band members were only slightly less jarred. Clarence Clemons later believed he'd seen the look of a smitten future family man in the Boss's gaze when Bruce stood as godfather to Clemons's third son, Christopher, during the infant's 1984 Hawaii baptism. Two weeks later, Springsteen phoned his saxophonist and said, "Big man, I'm getting married." "I know," said Clemons.

Springsteen wed Phillips fifteen minutes after midnight in May 1985 in a Catholic ceremony (minus the Mass) at Our Lady of the Lake Church in the Portland, Oregon, suburb of Lake Oswego. Clarence Clemons, former E Street guitarist Little Steven Van Zandt, and manager Jon Landau were best men. The bride's attendants were Pam Springsteen, Mary Lepschat (Julianne's sister), and Julianne's best friend, Ann Stuckey Bickford. After a brief honeymoon, Bruce opened the European leg of his *Born in the U.S.A.* tour in Ireland, playing to 65,000 people at Slane Castle outside Dublin. Throughout the tour, Springsteen would sing an affecting version of Elvis's "Can't Help Falling in Love" to Julianne, who stood in the wings.

It was October 1985 before Bruce and Julianne had a chance to settle into married life, dividing their time between a house in Rumson, New Jersey, and a place in Los Angeles. Their days seemed contented, Julianne generating most of the press for her film career (*Fletch II*, etc.). But in the spring of 1987, as ballads demoed at Springsteen's home studio in Rumson received a polish, it became plain they were personal and pessimistic.

When *Tunnel of Love* and its somber first single, "Brilliant Disguise," appeared in August 1987 it made fans and salaried spin-doctors uneasy. The song was the saga of a newlywed panicked by his own promises, his married life airless and cold now that the glory of its public rites was past. Superstition had masqueraded as devotion, and folly wore a sallow face in the bathroom mirror. The singer doubted his love, her love, and their capacity to dispel the vacuum of their unease. The stifling shadow of Robert Johnson's "Stones in my Passway" had fallen across Bruce Springsteen's career, recasting the rock entertainer in the unaccustomed role of nightbringer.

Listening to the entire *Tunnel of Love* album made its scheme sorrowfully explicit. The flamboyant infatuation of "Ain't Got You" could barely be sustained by "Tougher Than the Rest," a braggard's plea for borrowed time and special consideration. The next three songs, "All That Heaven Will Allow," "Spare Parts," and "Cautious Man," were fables of delusion, disintegration, and moral dismay. Springsteen addressed his own nuptials directly on "Walk Like a Man," confessing fear and bewilderment at a false world of his own making.

"Tunnel of Love" spun an ominous new fantasy to mock the original myth of found love. The remainder of these songs—all of which were the finest Bruce Springsteen has ever written—probed his conscience in a way he'd never previously risked. "Two Faces" admitted the presence of good and evil, principles and bullshit, brilliance and banality in his stillborn spirit. "Brilliant Disguise" peered into the hollow existence of a person who would squander integrity. "One Step Up" explained the magnetism of adultery for the emotional drifter; once doubt sets in, vanity exerts a far stronger tug than virtue. The album concluded on notes of self-pity ("When You're Alone") and isolation ("Valentine's Day") as the singer tasted the death-in-life that his actions had spawned.

The faithful didn't know how to take *Tunnel of Love.* It was real in its ugliness, honest in its anguish. Unlike *Born in the U.S.A.*, whose title track couched a patriotic disgust in a clarion arrangement that aped Caesar entering Rome, *Tunnel of Love* could not be conveniently misinterpreted. It held the courage of one person telling the plain truth on himself.

Springsteen's audience had grown so mammoth he was able to sell several million copies of the mournful *Tunnel of Love.* But fan discomfiture with its motifs was so widespread that even disc jockeys would mutter that they weren't much fun to hear. Still, almost no one dared say they sounded like the musings of a man whose matrimony was in desperate turmoil.

Springsteen's marriage did come asunder, reports circulating in May 1987 that he had separated from Julianne and vacated the Rumson house. While in Paris during the *Tunnel of Love* tour, he was seen showing open affection for backup singer Patti Scialfa, the lone female member of the E Street Band since 1984. Formerly a vocalist with Southside Johnny and the Asbury Jukes, the trim, red-haired Scialfa, thirty-five, had also been a member of Tone, a band that contained early E Street alumni. A native of wealthy Deal, New Jersey, Patti was the outgoing and well-liked daughter of a prosperous businessman.

Female fans were especially cool to the affair as it became more flagrant. Bruce began playing concerts without his wedding ring, and his separation from Julianne was formalized before he embarked on a world Human Rights Now! tour with Sting, Peter Gabriel, Youssou N'Dour, and Tracy Chapman in support of Amnesty International. Julianne filed for divorce in California on August 31, 1988. By December 1988, Bruce and Julianne had agreed to a settlement and a division of property. The divorce decree became final on March 1, 1989.

In commemoration of the Amnesty shows, Springsteen released a special EP that included a live version of Dylan's "Chimes of Freedom." His exposure to Eastern Bloc and Third World nations had a marked effect on him. The EP was also rumored to be a fond summing up before a protracted hiatus from the E Street Band (a move Jon Landau confirmed in November 1989). In January 1990, a spokesman for Springsteen confirmed that Patti Scialfa was pregnant with Bruce's child.*

It was also announced that Patti was assembling a solo record, tentatively titled *Burning Love.* And Bruce was finishing a new album after cutting a version of Elvis's "Viva Las Vegas" for a British benefit LP. But the work that continued to simmer in the imagination was *Tunnel of Love.* The E Street Band had been used sparingly on that record, much of the instrumentation provided by Bruce himself. As such, in the minds of many, it was those songs (little played on the Amnesty expedition) that had robbed the Boss of his rank as preeminent rock standard-bearer.

Such grousing seemed silly, but it was prevalent. After years of perceptual engineering by proselytes, Springsteen's persona had become so suffocatingly puritan that it could accommodate no flaws, self-doubts, or missteps. Doomed to be politically correct and scrupulously ambiguous, he had seemingly surrendered the privilege of original behavior.

*A son, born July 1990.

But the true aims of *Tunnel of Love* towered above any public relations obfuscation. Springsteen was waking up to the meaning of his own messy existence, and his prickly insights had an authenticity that outstripped all the roistering rock psalms of the recent past.

The spiritual value of *Tunnel of Love* was so substantial that it gave the artist the freedom to literally begin his life *and* career again, refreshed by his own candor, unimpeded by the qualms of handlers. Few such public figures are ever accorded that chance.

Zz Top

1986

The grandmotherly desk clerk at the HoJo's Motor Lodge opposite Get Down Brown's Bar in Beaumont, Texas, presses the door buzzer with grave reluctance. The greasy glass portal opens to admit a sunglassed man with pennant-length whiskers and his slick-looking entourage.

Across the narrow highway, the teeming gin mill's large gravel entryway is a study in shadowplay, as shifting headlights catch partial glimpses of intoxication, sexual horseplay, and the wages of rock and roll.

"Would you look at that mangy bunch go at it," says the mysterious bearded man in the blue serge suit, momentarily lowering his Ray-Bans to better appraise the murky frolics, as he signs the motel's guest register. His sudden smile shows two rows of aristocratically even pearly whites as he adds, "There'll be nothing but flat-out beer drinkers and hell-raisers at Brown's for *this* soiree."

Inside the spacious tavern,

there are plenty of strapping young men and long-legged women pressed hip-to-hip at the beer taps and chest-to-chest before the smoke-beclouded bandstand. It's an older crowd, ranging in age from midtwenties to triple that, most of them attired in Urban Cowboy mufti—jeans with gleaming oval belt buckles, Tony Lama boots, cotton plaid shirts—and most are agreeably soused. The Cotton-Eyed Joe, Texas Two-Step, and a host of other postmidnight mating dances are getting under way.

Beaumont is an often-sinister city that's been manufacturing its share of dashed hopes and delusionary windfalls since the discovery in 1910 of limitless oil deposits at Spindletop; most of the rewards from these oil strikes went to investors and speculators in far-flung locales, while the defeated hands who worked the rigs sedated themselves in honky-tonks. Around such mundane sorrows there grew up a network of dives and strip joints between Beaumont and Port Arthur (four miles down the coast), featuring country and western, Tex-Mex, blues, and rhythm and blues performers, and, in the sixties, an electrified, agitated brand of white man's combo blues that borrowed heavily from the Linden, Texas-reared heart of Aaron "T-Bone" Walker. Later in the decade, the rawboned rock and roll of the region merged with all of the above and a double-dose of psychedelics to addle the timing of a new and otherwise bored-to-the-bone generation of bar bands: Fever Tree, Thursday's Children, the Clique, the Countdown Five, Horace and the Snakes, and Moving Sidewalks.

The ride was a wild one while it lasted, leaving a lot of sordid police blotter dispatches and half-inch obits in its wake. Several talented participants actually crossed over into some corner of the motley underground media corona that was the rock big time of that period, bringing their colorful excesses along with them. The most ravenous, like Port Arthur's Janis Joplin, succumbed. Others burned out and returned to day jobs. But a very few bit the bullet and bided their time until another decade's worth of wild rides began . . .

"Oh my Gawd!" yelps the head barkeep. "ZZ Top just walked in!"

Sure enough, palming his HoJo's room key with one hand and the wire waist of a comely, raven-haired lady named Debbie with the other as he strides into the heart of the fray is Billy Gibbons himself. The lead guitarist for That Little Ol' Band from Texas strokes his beard in the eye of the tumult, shoots an idle glance in the direction of the loudmouth tending to the thirsty patrons, and then moves onward, guiding his guests through a maze of beaming well-wishers.

Although there was no mention of it in this month's installment of *Texas Monthly*'s hip "Around the State" entertainment guide, tonight marks the reunion of the Boogie Kings, among the hottest white soul bands in the South in the late sixties/early seventies. Billy and company have made a sentimental sojourn all the way down from Houston to catch the ten-piece Kings, a Beaumont legend led by singer-trumpeter G. G. Shinn and Jerry "the Count" LaCroix. The former gent, who boasts a five-octave vocal range, is a onetime member of the jazz-rock trumpet band Chase, while the latter is one of several Kings who are alumni of Edgar Winter's White Trash. Indeed, Winter was born and raised in Beaumont (his and Johnny's parents still live off Thomas Road), and as Billy Gibbons makes his way through the throng, old cronies and drinking partners shout out anecdotes about the local exploits of Billy and the Winter brothers during the heyday (1968–72) of the Beaumont club scene.

"Mind you, these folks are mighty, mighty ripe for a blow-out," warns a gleeful Gibbons, talking out of the side of his mouth as broad-shouldered buddy Jimmy Hammond runs interference to wedge Billy's party into a row of tables beside the dance floor. "See that bald-headed fella over yonder?" Gibbons asks, tipping his crumpled khaki golf hat in the direction of a graying bespectacled codger with a drink in each hand. "That guy's Al Caldwell, a deejay at KAYC in Beaumont. When ZZ Top was getting started down here, he used to introduce us at the Knights of Columbus dances! This was our primary territory, a town where we could always draw when no one else would have us, and just about everybody in this place caught our act in one or another Beaumont hall or hole. Before that, I had my psychedelic band, Moving Sidewalks, and we had a straight R&B and rock act with no horns—which was unheard of in Beaumont then!"

"That's the truth," says Jimmy Hammond, who was the bassist in such rival bands as Horace and the Snakes, and Sage. "They had a row to hoe when I met Billy on his birthday [December 16] in 1967 during a Sidewalk gig at the Crown Room at the King Edward Hotel, because a soul horn section was an absolute must if you wanted to avoid trouble. They had two singles out [on the Wand label], '99th Floor,' which was Billy's response to what the 13th

Floor Elevators were doing with songs like 'You're Gonna Miss Me,' and another tune he wrote called 'Need Me.' They were hippie weirdos, but they were tolerated because they were known."

"It was a rerecorded version of '99th Floor' that got us on a cool 1968 tour with Jimi Hendrix and the Soft Machine," says Gibbons. "We were trying to go the 13th Floor Elevator thing one better with a blues edge, and we topped the Houston charts. We tried to do everything the English guys were doing, with Carnaby Street striped suits and epaulets, but the Elevators were the most freaked-out act Texas had seen, and you didn't dare say you disliked them. They were a bunch of nuts from some tourist trap in central Texas, and the word was they drank Listerine all the time. Every band was in a race to be crazier."

"We all used to hang out at the old Get Down Brown's, which eventually burned down, and then we'd move on to Our Place, a real shitkicker's bar," Hammond continues. "One Christmas Eve Billy and Johnny Winter swung into Our Place, and the usual brawl between rednecks and longhairs broke out—only that night things got outta hand and Our Place burned down too!

"ZZ Top clicked from the git-go though," he says, " 'cause of the nasty sound of the guitars. I knew Billy had gotten it down right, same as when I first saw Merle Haggard at Port Neches in 1963."

The reminiscences are interrupted by two barmaids who bring no less than thirty-two brimming cans of beer for a party of six.

"Good Lord," says Billy, strikingly slim after a strict diet that enabled him to shed thirty pounds, "we've got our hands full 'n then some!"

"*Everybody* wanted to buy you a round, honey," says one of the buxom, micro-mini-skirted waitresses with a slow wink.

"Oooh boy, this reminds me of when Billy owned a saloon in Durango, Mexico, in the midseventies," says Jimmy. "It was called the El Dorado Bar—there's pictures of it in the inside sleeve of *Tres Hombres*—and John Wayne and all these other actors used to drink Tecati and tequila there and check out the house *norteño* band when they made western movies in the area."

"Good times," says Billy, nodding and patting his luxuriant chin-warmer, "*good* times. Why I—"

Gibbons is interrupted by the Boogie Kings, fresh from their first break of the night and eager to exchange bearhugs. At length, a frail, snow-haired grandmother of one of the band members is eased to the head of the line and introduced to the guest of honor.

"Billy my darlin', I got a personal question I have to ask you in front of your girl," she says solemnly.

The crowd around the table is hushed.

"Do you sleep with your beard *under* the covers or *over* the covers?"

ZZ Top is currently one of the biggest bands on the planet and unquestionably among the most beloved. Domestically, the Texas brio trio has sold nearly six million copies of *Eliminator*, released in March 1983, with overseas numbers at four million. The LP has once again begun climbing up the *Billboard* survey as their tenth installment, the incendiary *Afterburner*, blitzes both the record charts and, across the board, the formats of national radio, where five to six of its tracks are being added to playlists. And since Warner Bros., ZZ Top's label since 1978, has acquired the group's 1970–77 London Records catalog *(Z.Z. Top's First Album, Rio Grande Mud, Tres Hombres, Fandango!, Tejas, The Best of ZZ Top)*, there is every possibility that sales of the fabled old product and the subsequent Warners albums (including *Deguello* and *El Loco*) will also be reactivated.

Nobody doesn't like ZZ Top, from yuppies who admire their renegade marketing (there are over forty items in the band's merchandise catalog—"All of them created as a result of specific letter campaign-type demands from fans," according to Lone Wolf Productions Minister of Information J. W. Williams, "and we'll do a half-million in the keychains alone with *Afterburner*"), to hippie holdouts, heavy metal rooters, techy connoisseurs of rock guitar invention, and any observers who get a rise out of the Ghosts of Christmas Present persona they evoke on their ongoing Keys-to-the-Eliminator video series.

What prevents ZZ Top from disintegrating into mere comic book familiarity are the self-depreciation and coy wit with which they invest their ferocious musicality, the elusive nature of the men themselves, and the treacherous Texas rock 'n' boogie brazos from which they emerged.

Their appeal is as universal as the thrust of their message: It's all in fun, pardner—'cept for the music.

"Dusty and me, we just got back from a vacation in Cairo," says Billy Gibbons one sunny Houston afternoon, he and his cohorts arranging themselves on sofas and stools in the living room of a friend's house.

"Billy and I zoomed over there to relieve the tension after we finished the record, but we couldn't find any Cleopatras with headphones and shades," Joe "Dusty" Hill chimes in with a toothy chuckle. The beefy blond bassist is referring to the sexy Egyptian collage art on the sleeve of "Sleeping Bag," the *Afterburner* single that exhorts listeners to "sleep beside the Pharoahs in the shifting sands."

"I couldn't make the trip," says the muscular, clean-shaven Frank Beard with a Jack Nicholson smirk, " 'cause I had myself a prior commitment that wuz just as ancient."

"We'd been planning the visit for quite a while," says Gibbons, smoothing out the wrinkles in one of the loose-fitting, expensive European suits he enjoys when off-duty. "After doing Bobby 'Blue' Bland stuff forever, we figured it was high time we checked out the *original* Memphis, the tomb of the Boy King and the Great Pyramid at Giza, because we'd always been fascinated by the general fascination others have with these things. The morning we hit the G.P. on camels, this young Egyptian kid comes over to beg some money, stops, stares, and whips out this bag with a cassette of *El Loco* in it. He even had a Walkman! But the local stuff the boy played us lacked, we thought, a heavy backbeat and was a bit nasal—" All three men lapse into a unison, four-second whining drone that resembles a fakir's pipes.

"Yeah, it wasn't awfully commercial," Gibbons deadpans, his eyes gleaming with suppressed laughter, "so they were anxious for a helping of our moving groovin' beat. They're not really keen on dancing, that kind of social activity being taboo, yet they were curious about our latest material. But I don't see Egypt as a place where a heavy backbeat fits in; time is irrelevant over there, particularly in light of the fact that the Islamic faith dictates that prayers to Allah occur at midnight and then again at 4:00 A.M., in addition to three other times during the day. They've got these cheap exponential loudspeaker bullhorns mounted on roving vehicles that remind you it's time to drop to your knees and pay homage. Man, it's jarring."

"Screwed onto the dressers in the hotels are these metal discs with a welded arrow on them pointing East," says Dusty intently. "That's to remind you where Mecca is at. The morning we were leaving Cairo it was just before sunrise, and as I was packing my gear the whole city started to wail, a huge portion of the city's twelve million chanting until it became a weird wash of sound. It was the strangest chord I ever heard.

"We had a guide named Sahib—we called him Sam—who was worn out one afternoon and depressed with a sick headache. He took his shoes and socks off, washed his hands and feet, went off and did a prayer wail, and came back completely rejuvenated. Looked years younger; it was amazing."

"That routine could come in handy for you after some of those long nights in downtown Houston," cracks Frank Beard. "Texas has its own funky deserts and rejuvenating wails."

"No *shee-it,* " Dusty nods, twirling his golden moustache around a stubby index finger. "After all I've learned 'tween here and Dallas over the last twenty years about the art of reviving myself, I could go on back to Cairo tonight and be the next King Farouk!"

Dusty Hill was born on May 19, 1949, in East Dallas, the son of James Ernest Hill, a truck driver who divorced Dusty's mother when the boy was eight. He was raised by his mother, "a Kate Smith–type singer with big bands before I was born," and stepfather T. C. "Top Cat" Allen, an assembly-line worker in the local Ford plant. One of five kids by both fathers, Dusty had an independent bent and at thirteen was a familiar paleface at the all-black Ascot Ballroom on Hall Street, sitting in with Freddie King, the Gilmer, Texas, electric blues great. Dusty had already taken up a Harmony solid body (boasting but three strings for an extended period) to earn a slot in the Deadbeats, a combo formed by his guitarist brother Rocky, but within the year he was spending as much time backing bluesmen.

"There was an after-hours club in Dallas called the Kay-Jon that got going after the beer joints closed," says Dusty, "and I started frequenting it because you could meet the main black musicians there. I got to know Freddie King and his wife pretty well, and I'd go over to have dinner with them and their fifteen-odd kids in South Dallas.

"At the time, I was going to Woodrow Wilson High, which was in a nice area called Lakewood," says Dusty. "But I didn't fit in. I was up every night at 1:00 A.M. listening to blues and Tex-Mex stuff from this Mexican station down in Del Rio. There were no regulations or restrictions on stations south of the border, and the show was incredibly raunchy with commercials advertising goat gland operations to restore your sex life. The next day after school I'd go from Sampley's, the old general store where the East Dallas kids hung out, to Harold's, a drugstore and soda fountain in a shopping center in Lakewood where you could corner cheerleaders.

"But these kids would be talking about some stupid pop singer and their virginity when I'd been up to no good the previous evening until Kay-Jon shut down. It was bullshit, it made no sense. My mother, who was a waitress in some of the beer joints I played in, would say, 'You gotta get an education!' but I took care of the school problem in tenth grade and my free time expanded."

Dusty promptly filled his newfound unstructured hours by joining up with Frank Beard, a native of the Dallas suburb of Irving (birthplace of Jimmy and Stevie Ray Vaughan) and the son of the office manager of a Ford dealership. Frank had been the quarterback for the Irving Tigers, but at fifteen he was barred from all extracurricular activities after school administrators learned of his shotgun marriage to a classmate; his pregnant wife was expelled. It was the summer of 1964, and he had just gotten himself a $200 set of blue pearl Lyra drums from Montgomery Ward, a move inspired by the sight of Ringo Starr's casual rimshots on "The Ed Sullivan Show."

"I knew the marriage wasn't gonna last that long," says Frank, another devilish Nicholson grin growing on his thin lips, "and I was looking for a new way to get pussy. I thought, 'These Beatle guys get a lot of pussy; I'm gonna take this up.' I was going to school half a day, and then working in the sporting goods department of a K-Mart kinda chain called International Super Stores from 1:00 P.M. to 8:00 P.M. for $100 a week. Within six months from the time I got that set of drums, I was working in Fort Worth at a strip joint called the Cellar for $15 a night. Things started dropping out of my life, school first, then the sporting goods job, and finally my marriage."

These involvements were replaced by drinking problems, a drug habit (that would later lead to years of heroin addiction), and Dusty and Rocky Hill. Frank blew into the Cellar one night in 1967 and caught the Warlocks, a band fronted by Dusty and Rocky that had issued two singles "Splash Day"/"Life's a Mystery" and "If You Really Want Me to Stay"/"Good Time Trippin' " on the Paradise and Ara labels, respectively. "Another Year"/"Poor Kid," another Ara 45, which aped the British rock of the era with the help of an English siren named Lady Wilde, caused a small stir in the area.

Beard was impressed with the Warlocks and signed on when their drummer left to tie the knot. After the band lost its limey singer, it reformed as a hard rock outfit, American Blues, and opened at a quasi-sister club, the Cellar Door, up in Houston. A band member named Phil Vickery suggested they dye their hair blue as a gimmick, and everyone but the keyboardist, who opted for a wig, acceded.

"We didn't mind that the keyboard guy, whose name was Sharkey, wouldn't go along with the dye job," says Frank, "since he was good in a grocery store when it came to stealing steaks. As for the rest of us, we were all blonds, and we had to bleach our hair white before this Roux No. 10 would take hold. I had to do seventeen bleaches, and it burned like hell."

The Cellar Door proved a source of steady work, and a curious twilight life-style evolved as American Blues took up residence in the Wilby Hotel, a fleabag hostel located four blocks from the gig.

"Depending on finances and fiancées, we rented rooms by the day or the week," says Dusty, a blissful expression blossoming on his broad face, "and so we changed rooms a lot. The blue dye in our hair would wash out, but it stained anything our heads touched, so it rubbed off on the pillowcases and the hotel tried to make us pay for the damages. Then they'd go, 'Wait a minute, there's only five of you guys. How come we found dye in fifteen beds last night?' "

"It was because all the waitresses in the club lived there too, and we were aces at hopping up and down the hallways," Frank explains, popping another can of the diet soda he sips incessantly since he swore off alcohol.

"Before long, we got bounced from the Wilby," says Dusty, "and wound up on the North Side on Airline Drive in the Northline Drive Hotel, which was *whoa*—three dollars a night and grossly overpriced. The Cellar Door, which was one shaky place, started getting to us too.

"Like in a lotta Texas clubs, the stripping and topless dancing were an impromptu thing. The waitresses at that time were *rilly* risqué; they just wore panties and a bra, and my eyes usta pop. You couldn't get liquor by the drink in Houston, so you had to buy a bottle and the house provided the mixers, and the crowd would sit there and get fuck-faced as the night wore on. Funny thing was, they dug the music, but not without the stripping.

"Sometimes we didn't go on until 12:00 P.M. so we'd ride thirty miles down to Dallas to do a quick gig and then turn around. One night we got back, and everybody in the bar was plowed, especially the girls. Frank had gotten hisself a new set of drums, and as we started playing a fat girl jumped up on the bandstand and started to wiggle. He leaned over to me and hissed, 'If she falls on these drums, I'll waste her.'

"Sure enough," says Dusty triumphantly, "she lost her footing, went backward, and drums and cymbals flew everywhere out of the path of her enormous ass."

"I whupped her," Frank recalls. "But I did it more for her being ugly than anything else. It's bad enough doing thirty-nine choruses of 'Walking the Dog,' without dealing with a huge ugly tush in your face, half of it sticking out of a giant hole in a sad pair of bloomers. *Shee-it!*"

American Blues put out a single in 1968 on the Karma label, a cover of Tim Hardin's "If I Were a Carpenter," which KLIF, the key Dallas Top 40 station, spun a few times. *American Blues Is Here*, an album on Karma, drew the interest of Uni Records, then doing well with a psychedelic pop act from California called the Strawberry Alarm Clock ("Incense and Peppermints"). An attempt was made to recast American Blues in the beads-and-Indian-kaftans mold of the Clock, and Uni floated a single, "Melted Like Snow" as well as an album, *American Blues Do Their Thing*.

The high point of the whole hopeless exercise came when the group landed a guest shot on KTRK-TV's "Larry Kane Show," a popular Saturday teen program in Houston. They had done three post–Witching Hour sets at the Cellar Door the night before and then scattered, Dusty awaking that afternoon in the arms of a female acquaintance who lived outside the central city. Naked and terminally hung over, he lurched over to the TV set and clicked on Channel 13 to see the happy host boasting that American Blues would be on right after the next commercial. Despite having no idea where the TV studio was located, Dusty and his predawn sweetheart somehow dashed over just in time for the assembled membership to deliver an abysmal performance.

After an uneven stint at the Fillmore West, backing up Freddie King on a ten-day split bill with the Electric Flag, Blue Cheer,

Buddy Guy, and the Ike and Tina Turner Revue, American Blues disbanded, all personnel flying off in separate trajectories. Dusty landed the most memorable employment, supporting Jimmy Reed for a series of dates between Houston and Galveston. Because Reed liked to suck up the sauce and then tumble keister-over-harmonica clamp into Dusty's bass amp, club owners adopted a word-of-mouth policy of no booze for the gravel-voiced Mississippi blues harpist/guitarist.

"I always used to carry a little bottle in my guitar case," says Dusty, "and when Jimmy walked into my makeshift dressing room on the third night of the road trip and saw that whiskey, it was 'Dusty ol' buddy o'mine, *com'eer* boy!' From then on, I played bass, carried the bottle, and answered the hotel room door when the manager screamed about the drunken all-hours jammin'.

"Although," Dusty adds, "a coupla nights when these backroads Texas innkeepers peered in and saw that it was Jimmy holding court, they actually said, 'You just go on the way you been, Mr. Reed. I'll throw the res' of the goddamn lodgers out if they complain again!' "

While all this was transpiring, Billy Gibbons was coming of age in an upper-middle-class family in suburban Houston. Father Freddy Gibbons was a pianist and orchestra leader who had relocated to Texas from his native New York because of his wife's failing health. Mr. Gibbons graduated from bar mitzvahs to society galas and conducting the Houston Philharmonic, and Billy and his sister Pam often found themselves in the presence of Hollywood royalty, from Dick Powell to Humphrey Bogart. Billy's mom revived and went on to become a member of President Johnson's Texas staff. Billy himself got a leg up on the Christmas morning in 1963 when his pop presented him with a Gibson Melody Maker and Fender Champ amp.

The family maid, nineteen-year-old Stella Matthews, steered the lad in the direction of Little Richard, whose all-Houston band was pounding out "Bama Lama Bama Loo" in a Fourth Ward hooch parlor two blocks from her house. Billy tuned in to soul station KYOK and never looked back. Before long, he was picking out the Wayne Bennett leads on Bobby "Blue" Bland songs like "Ain't Doing Too Bad" and "Blind Man."

Both those midsixties Bland singles were issued on the Duke label, a Memphis-based record company owned by a hard case named Don Robey. On Christmas Eve 1954, while backstage at the Houston City Auditorium, twenty-four-year-old Duke star Johnny Ace reportedly drew the losing slug in a game of Russian roulette and died the next day.

Gibbons, who later had contact with the imposing Robey while leading such green bands as the Saints, Billy G. and the Ten Blue Flames, and the Coachmen (who cut the first version of "99th Floor"), does not hold with the usual account of the demise of Johnny Ace.

"I heard it wasn't Russian roulette that kicked [Ace] and that that was just a version that got trumped up later," he counsels, discussing an alternate scenario widely accepted in Houston inner circles. Namely, that Johnny Ace, riding high with the success of "The Clock" in 1953 and "Please Forgive Me" the following year, had informed Robey just before he was due to take the City Auditorium stage that he was quitting Duke and going to New York to secure a deal with Atlantic. Robey reportedly decried such ambitions and produced a pistol, which he pressed against Ace's temple. With his girlfriend Evelyn still seated on Johnny's lap, Robey splattered the singer's pipe dreams across the dressing room wall.

"I'll tell you this," says Gibbons of Robey, who ran Duke until two years before his death in 1975. "He was a tall *mean* albino. You'd take your demo tapes over to his nothing-much studio off Erastus Street, where he'd cut stuff with Gatemouth Brown, and he'd bark: 'Show me your damned song!' "

Houston was still a wide open town record biz-wise in the fifties and sixties, and if you didn't watch your step somebody else would do it for you. Eager to keep his own head low, Gibbons hooked up with booking agent Bill Ham shortly after Moving Sidewalks' 1969 *Flash* LP fell by the wayside. Ham was handling an appealing but less than flashy singer from Lubbock named Jay Boy Adams, and when Vietnam ensnared several of the Sidewalks, Ham and Gibbons hatched the idea of a new group, built around Billy, Sidewalks' drummer Don Mitchell, and keyboard player Billy Ethridge. They knocked out two tracks, "Salt Lick" b/w "Miller's Farm" for Ham's Scat label. After more auditions, in which Ethridge recommended Dusty Hill, who in turn tapped Frank Beard, ZZ Top (a nonsense name reflecting such blues appellations as B. B. King) was pared down to the current threesome. Late in 1969, Ham took the boys to London Records, proclaiming, "I've got the next Rolling Stones for you."

London gave them a contract, pressed "Salt Lick," and provided some seed money that the group used to purchase a pair of Marshall Super Lead stacks, model 1959. They swept through Louisiana, Oklahoma, New Mexico, and California, getting louder and prouder with each tick of the odometer. Their first sizable hit came in 1973 with *Tres Hombres'* "La Grange," an ode to the brothel off Rt. 95 between Austin and Houston (later immortalized in the stage show and film, *The Best Little Whorehouse in Texas*).

By 1974, they were drawing 80,000 rowdy fans in Austin (and getting themselves banned for another eight years). By 1975, they were breaking Rolling Stones' attendance records at arenas in the deep South with the help of the unsubtle "Tush" off the live *Fandango!* More odes to nooky, lowriders, and dipsomania ensued: "Nasty Dogs and Funky Kings," "Mexican Blackbird," "Arrested for Driving While Blind." Come 1976, Ham devised a ZZ Top World Tour featuring a menagerie consisting of a live buffalo, a longhorn steer, buzzards, and sidewinders that grossed $11.5 million, outselling Elvis, Led Zeppelin, et al.

When extricating themselves from the modest London Records contract became problematic, ZZ Top went on sabbatical for three years. Dusty did some fishing in Mexico. Billy traveled around North Africa and Western Europe, pausing in Paris to assist a group called Artiste Contemporaire in composing ambient electronic music for a show of Xerox art. Frank sought to improve his personal life.

The group reemerged on Warner Bros. in 1979 with *Deguello*, scoring a hit with "Cheap Sunglasses" and dominating FM radio with "I'm Bad, I'm Nationwide," and then "Pearl Necklace" (yes, a sharp-dressed man's euphemism for a blow job; from *El Loco*). But it was MTV that raised ZZ Top to their current august profile.

Gibbons and Hill had been hazy on the concept of a twenty-four-hour rock channel, but Frank Beard was initiated into the phenomenon as he and his third wife, Debbie, were home tucking themselves in for the evening:

"It was a Friday night and we'd just gotten into bed. I was flipping the dial and saw a music video. We thought that was cool, and then another came on. And another. An hour went by, and we wondered how long the show was. Four hours went by. We looked at each other and said, 'When in the hell is something like this gonna be on again?!' We kept on watching. The sun was coming up, and videos were still coming and we were freaking out. It was like a telethon—except nobody was giving us a number to call!"

MTV was less than a year and a half old when Ham and company went out to Burbank, California, a few weeks later to screen the output of leading video directors. They settled on Tim Newman (Randy's cousin) to illuminate *Eliminator*'s "Gimme All Your Lovin' " and thus inaugurated what would be the music network's nearest answer to a quality sitcom. At about the same time, the gods acquired their chariot, the 1933 Ford three-window coupe with the Cadillac-dynasty-red enamel paint job. . . .

As a boy, Billy Gibbons had been obsessed with automobile culture, building scale models of designer Ed "Big Daddy" Roth's Monster dragsters and devouring issues of *Rod & Custom, Car Craft,* and *Hot Rod.*

"It was in 1978 during the layoff period," says Gibbons, puttering around his half-million-dollar townhouse in a swank enclave of Houston, "that I realized that I could finally afford the toy I'd always wished for."

He sits down before a coffee table in his living room on which is laid a just-completed goldleaf scale model of the Robert E. Lee paddle wheeler. Scattered around his digs, a two-story habitat dominated by a stone and wood-paneled atrium, are various other gewgaws ranging from an antique shotgun mounted on the mantelpiece to a surfeit of western memorabilia. In the foyer stand two lifesize mannequins in meticulous mummy wrappings, one holding a skull in its outstretched hand. Taken together, the tableau seems like a best-forgotten sub-basement at Neiman-Marcus.

"So what I did," says Gibbons, pushing his slippery red-framed tinted shades back up the bridge of his long nose, "was fly out to Los Angeles with a friend for the L.A. Roadsters' Father's Day Show with the intentions of buying a hot rod and driving it back to Houston. A guy on the grounds of the fair directed us to Don Thelan of Buffalo Motor Cars of Paramount, California, and I told him I wanted a facsimile of a car I'd seen on television, Peter Campouris's famous California Kid. Thelan talked me into keeping the project totally original, and he promised me a finished car fashioned from scratch within six months.

"Four and a half years later," he says with a sigh, "the cost was up to $100,000 with no end in sight, and it was too late to turn back. At the same time, a fella contacted us about writing music for a hot rod movie he'd done, and it was then that we thought of naming the car and the next album after a drag-racing term. The month before the record was to be released, Thelan phoned to say the coupe was done. We wanted to use the car in a photo shoot for the album cover, but because we still owed Don money, it had to stay where it was, and we settled for a drawing of it on the jacket. By the time we took possession of the coupe, it had become our 'Top Eliminator,' our 'Top Icon' and our top priority."

Back in 1978, Houston, Texas, was at the top of its game—tops in the oil boom sparked by the OPEC scam, with the price of a barrel of crude soaring to $36; and tops in real estate peddling, with farmers north and west of the city getting $100,000 an acre as sleazy Mexican politicians sought to stash fortunes in pilfered government treasury funds in the security of high-rise hotels and condos.

Now, Houston is tops in home foreclosures, with 3,000 posted in Harris County during the week that *Afterburner* hits the stores. Crime is up, unemployment too, and Gibbons concedes that, "unfortunately, it wouldn't be wise or even possible to take the Eliminator out on Highway 610 for a zip around central Houston." Indeed, James A. Michener's best-seller *Texas* is rife with telling exchanges about the fearsome state of the frontier metropolis's thoroughfares:

"Six-ten is a jungle, worst highway in America. You know that during the rush hour the police won't even enter it to check on ordinary fender-benders. They got beat up too often by enraged motorists, sometimes shot and killed."

Realizing that he couldn't take his prize toy out for joy rides, Gibbons bought himself a '66 Chevy Impala lowrider with a remote control riser. He'd head out onto 610 with his pals, gun the engine, and drop the skid plate so that roostertail sparks shot out the back to lengths of twenty feet. But just a short spell ago, some troopers witnessed the whole elaborate display and nailed him. Seeing that both his registration and his out-of-the-state plates had been expired for five years, the patrolmen were about to haul Billy off to the lockup when one of them recognized him and offered a proposition.

"It was late at night, they had a newly promoted sergeant down from Chicago that they hated," says Gibbons, "and they wanted to bust his balls. So they called into headquarters and said they might have a highly suspicious stolen lowrider on their hands and needed his assistance."

Gibbons and friends were stowed in the trooper's patrol car, along with the remote control button, and when the boss pulled up the cops suggested he take off his spanking new sergeant's hat, place it on the road, and check under the chassis to see if it held any contraband. After he had done so, he was rising to his feet when the trooper gave the signal to Billy, who pushed the riser button, the car crushing the good officer's expensive chapeau into the asphalt.

As the hatless and choleric sergeant drove off, the troopers and Gibbon shared a hearty guffaw before they let him go—but not without delivering a stern admonishment to assure him that the hardassed character of east Texas endured intact: "Y'all better head straight down to Westheimer Road from here and use this heap to harass some queers, or you can bet we'll be comin' to get *you.*"

As the sun sets on another unsettling year in the Lone Star State, its car radios simmer with the sensuous strains of "Sleeping Bag," as well as news bulletins that two former friends from greater Houston are battling in court over the $10,000 reward posted by loved ones seeking information leading to the arrest of the murderers of a local folksinger and his girlfriend. They were shot and slashed to death in the house where they ran a large-scale drug operation.

The fifteenth anniversary of ZZ Top is drawing to a close, the band having outdistanced or overcome every demon and obstacle time and Texas could hurl at it. Heading out to Japan on the first leg of yet another world tour, they are content and satisfied with the path before them. Dusty Hill has recovered beautifully from the intestinal damage he suffered in December 1984 when, as girlfriend Jane Ellen Henderson was pulling his boot off, the .38 caliber Derringer he kept in it hit the floor, and a bullet pierced his abdomen wall. Frank Beard, blissful father of a four-week-old infant, has recently been reunited with two daughters from whom he was long estranged, and is at the peak of his golf game. Billy Gibbons is determined to stay slim, is mulling over some independent producing prospects, and is looking at a film property for the group.

All ducks are in a row, all debts are paid—with the possible exception of a roots-related one that cuts to the core of ZZ Top's musical credibility: the blues. Many months onward, during a drive to Clarksdale, Mississippi, to pay a visit to Sid Graves at the dawning Delta Blues Museum (presently little more than a few rooms of displays in the old Carnegie Public Library building on Delta Street), Billy Gibbons and company were detoured to a piece of hallowed ground. Graves advised the band that he was heading to Stovall Plantation, twelve miles up the road, to inspect the boyhood cabin of Muddy Waters, which the Mississippi highway department had requested be dismantled for safety reasons after being struck by a tornado. ZZ Top accepted Sid's invitation to tag along.

While inspecting the damage, Gibbons was handed a cypress timber from the remains of the roof. On the way back across the Tennessee border to Memphis—the site of much of ZZ Top's recording since their 1974 *Tres Hombres* album—Gibbons decided the cypress beam should be turned into two memorial guitars. One would be on permanent display at the Delta Blues Museum, the other to serve as a traveling exhibit to help attract donations for a Muddy Waters Memorial Fund. Deciding to postpone the recording of the sequel to *Afterburner* in order to clear their schedule, they relegated the next full year to a fund-raising campaign which they hoped would culminate in the construction of a Muddy Waters Wing in the new Delta Blues Museum Building.

On a balmy April evening in Memphis, Billy Gibbons, Dusty Hill, and Frank Beard gather at Memphis's Ardent Studios to explain, in round-robin fashion, why they elected to put their own careers on hold to pay tribute to the Father of the Electric Blues. Attired in tailored suits and seated in a casual half-circle in one of the control rooms, the three gentlemen fondly reminisce about their initiation into the blues and their friendship with Muddy. All the while Billy picks and strums, for the very first time, on the gleaming Muddy Wood instrument, just delivered from the nearby workshop of the Pyramid Guitar Company.

"Feels pretty good," comments Billy, meaning both the guitar and the commemorative gesture it represents.

From the beginning, circa 1969, ZZ Top was a regular attraction on the southwest blues circuit, sharing bills with blues greats like Muddy Waters. How come?

BEARD: When we first got started we just got booked out on tours with so many of these people. We had cut our first record, which was "Salt Lick," and the people putting this tour together obviously thought we were a black band. It was great; I mean, it was a poker game that traveled, and when it was your turn to go up and play, you left the game, went up and did your thirty minutes, and came back down to the cards! [*laughter*] Everybody, Bukka White, Freddie King, and the rest, each had a big wad of money and a gun.

GIBBONS: That was the first time we *met* Muddy Waters—in Burlington, Iowa. This was a show that was part of a regular blues itinerary we were booked on, but some of the other Delta bluesmen [on the Memphis Blues Caravan] had come to Burlington for an appearance that was college-sponsored at a time when blues was making its way across the country's campuses. This was in 1973.

We were driving ourselves and actually we were late arriving, and we hustled into the basement. Our fears of being late were instantly allayed because the card game was still in full swing, and *nobody* was willing to stop the game to go up and start playing yet. When we got there Freddie King recognized us and stood up, quizzing us about where we'd been last. As we looked around and peered into the next room, we recognized Muddy Waters and his band, playing cards on a guitar case stretched across a coupla chairs.

BEARD: It was a Fender Bass case.

HILL: If you're gonna play poker backstage, you *got* to play on a *bass* case, know what I mean?

GIBBONS: We were so excited because it was our first face-to-face meeting with Muddy Waters, and we asked Freddie King if he could introduce us 'cause we had a coupla records out that were doing okay and we were feeling pretty good about it. So Freddie—after showing them his wad of cash to let them know who was boss—he ushered us in and said, "Excuse me, Muddy, but these are several fellas who are on the show tonight. I'd like you to meet them. ZZ Top."

Muddy smiled for about half of a second, turned and said, "*Pleased to meet-cha*" . . .

HILL: . . . And then he immediately went right back to the poker game—which was, after all, the business at hand. [*laughter*] That'll get your ego in proper perspective!

BEARD: Another interesting thing about that night's show was that we learned the Freddie King Method of Motivating a Drummer. We were standing beside the stage, and Freddie had done his final song, which was a shuffle. He didn't feel that the drummer was pushing it quite hard enough, and after the curtain went down

Freddie walked over and just kicked the bejesus out of him. So when the curtain came back up for the encore, this guy was now cookin', he was *really* shuffling [*booming laughter*], and had certainly picked up a lot of tempo!

Me, I was just hoping that Billy hadn't been paying too much attention to this technique of Freddie's.

What was your original, individual exposure to the blues?

HILL: Probably like a lot of people, when I was young I'd listen to radio, especially late at night. Some of the X' stations out of Mexico reached all the way past Dallas, and they had a lot of blues shows with everybody. They played all the records you obviously couldn't hear on the Top 40 stations. It was an extremely strong influence on everybody that I knew who played rock with some blues in it. My brother Rocky and myself played a lot of it. The stations were very powerful, especially late at night when you're in bed and you're not supposed to be listening.

That's when the airwaves are real clear so the signal's coming in real strong, eh?

HILL: It came in like a sledgehammer! I mean, it was somewhere deep in Mexico, and it was driven through your head so you didn't forget *any*thing.

On those stations you had an opportunity to hear a lot of the songs that weren't played on most of the radio stations—except maybe WRR in Dallas on Kat's Karavan. The music was underground, yet it wasn't.

You guys came of age when the Texas music scene was wide open in the best sense. You got the blues influences both over the radio and in person-to-person connections.

HILL: Right. In the local Dallas bands, all the musicians gave each of the best blues songs different distinctive treatments. That was a good environment to jam in and sharpen your playing. Then later on I had an opportunity to play with Jimmy Reed and it was great. I also played for a good while with Freddie King.

Frank, what's the first Muddy Waters record that you heard and got a big kick from?

BEARD: Oh, it was probably "Hoochie Coochie Man." I guess I was three-four years old, crawling across the fields. [*laughter*]

Muddy Waters cut that song in the winter of 1954. Actually Willie Dixon wrote it and figured it'd be a good tune for Muddy.

GIBBONS: Willie Dixon served up a wealth of material for a lot of the Chess artists, and Muddy Waters certainly had a heyday while dipping into the bucket of blues tunes that Willie had. They're some of the most colorful poetry you could ask for, just to read them. Very inspirational.

We've done a number of his things, like "Mellow Down Easy" on *Fandango!* In fact we played *with* him; we opened a little club date for Willie in 1971 at Liberty Hall in Dallas.

Now, how did Muddy Waters come to open for you on a number of dates during your 1976 Worldwide Texas Tour?

GIBBONS: We had kept up a loose friendship through the years, and when Muddy would play at a place down on Rush Street in Chicago called Mr. Kelly's, we'd always take time to go and see him. It was a real uptown scene, a concert setting that was far removed from the Southside clubs. But we caught him a number of times because we'd work up the street . . .

So when we came down to Texas to do some home dates that year, we were just wondering what flavorful addition could we include to really embrace the feeling that we were trying to give back to our home state. And the blues being such a big part of not only our music but everybody's music in Texas, Muddy Waters seemed to be a logical choice. He was just doing some of his best playing, and it was really a moving experience.

Billy, was there an opportunity at any point to sit down with Muddy informally and have him show you a few things about his guitar style?

GIBBONS: There was always moments to catch, and back in those days it was thought to be questionable who could wear the badge of the blues. And I think the motivation for us was "Well, we're gonna get this thing but we better watch." So every chance you got you'd sneak a peek when you could. One of my favorite licks of Muddy's was on "Rollin' Stone" . . .

BEARD: . . . And you can hear it on our "Brown Sugar," from our first album.

GIBBONS: That was our best stolen riff, directly out of the Muddy catalog. See, not only was his singing the most powerful thing you could ask for, but he had a top-flight band at all times, and really employed the inventors of this stuff. Some of the inversions of his, like that famous reversed seventh chord [*he illustrates on the Muddy Wood instrument*]—all of that was so definitive in his work.

Another contribution that Muddy made to the blues and rock and roll was his brilliant slide guitar.

GIBBONS: The slide coming out of the Delta had a number of

faces. Muddy seemed to prefer a stinging approach. Later on, when the Telecaster was his main ax, he'd grind on the back pickup and just *sting* it. It was in direct contrast to Elmore James, who had a rounder, fuller sound which was a little more mellow.

The vibrato, that left-hand wiggle that Muddy Waters employed, was enough to make your blood run cold. It did just what he wanted it to do. Whether or not he invented it was beside the point. He had a thing that was definitely his, and it worked. For those fortunate enough to have seen *The Last Waltz,* you can actually see him at work on "Mannish Boy," and all I can say is watch the left hand closely, because it's *fast.*

As for ZZ Top, the brief slide track on "Sharp-Dressed Man" is the flip side of Muddy's stinging bit. It would be the slow, oozing quality that the slide can give you. We have not only been fans of the blues for a long time, but we've really tried to study and deliver with some kind of forceful feeling. And then there's "Just Got Paid" [on *Rio Grande Mud*], which slides around considerably.

But Muddy had the pathbreaking gift, with his slide style and with his inversions. As simple as it all is, it gets you where it needs to, and causes your foot to start tapping.

Frank, did you have a favorite drummer that Muddy Waters played with, Francey Clay or somebody like that?

BEARD: More than Francey, it was probably Fred Below.

GIBBONS: Is that "Five Below Zero" Below?

BEARD: Oh yeah, and he's the most noted of Muddy's drummers. I think he did "Hoochie Coochie Man," and he also did "I Just Want to Make Love to You," which are the definitive Muddy songs. So I guess he'd be my favorite.

Dusty, how about a favorite bassist in Muddy's bands?

HILL: [*Winking*] Well, since I wasn't playing with him, I'd say Willie Dixon. He played on "Just to Be with You," and it was pretty heavy.

GIBBONS: Johnny Winter certainly deserves mention in this conversation because he led the way for so many with his own blues guitar interpretations, and certainly with what he was experiencing firsthand as well. We were immediately able to grasp the music through Johnny's performances in Beaumont and elsewhere. The way he did it was something; he ripped it up.

Of course, Johnny went on to make the Hard Again *and* I'm Ready *albums with Muddy in 1977–78.*

HILL: Great records. Johnny has always been a supportive guy. Johnny and also Edgar Winter jammed with Frank and me in Houston clubs way back when we had blue hair for our old band, American Blues. Between our blue hair and their white hair, it was a very visual thing.

BEARD: During that time there was a little folk club we went to a lot. Lightnin' Hopkins used to come in, and Dusty and I would sit in with him. I kept trying to figure out how to play with Lightnin' and make it sound like I wanted it to. I never could, until I went to the store and bought a thirty-dollar set of toy Remco drums, and that night played those instead of a real drum set. For sticks, I used the rolled-up pieces of cardboard pulled from a drycleaner's hangers. Lightnin' loved it!

See, his drummer, Spider Kilpatrick, was one of my heroes. He invented the "fall-apart roll." It was like somebody walking down a set of stairs; they would make the first three stairs, and then fall and tumble down, and suddenly regain their feet and walk down the last three steps. That's how his rolls were—they'd start out on time, completely disintegrate, go to Hell and back, and then come right in on time at the end. It was amazing how those two worked together.

HILL: The first time I sat in with Lightnin' I was intimidated. It was difficult to fall into the groove with him, even though I knew all his stuff; you needed to just feel it. I got through playing and I sat down at this table, and I didn't know Lightnin' was sitting right behind me. This guy asks, "How does it feel playing with Hopkins?" and I said, "It's great, but it doesn't seem like he's changing at the right points." Lightnin' tapped me on the shoulder and said, [*solemnly*] "*Lightnin' change when Lightnin' want to.*"

BEARD: That's the only reason Dusty and I can play with Billy, because he's never changed time the same way twice in his life!

GIBBONS: That's 'cause *Billy change when Billy want to.* [*laughter*]

Sounds like the blues are composed of feeling, finesse, and fear.

HILL: [*Nudging Frank*] And fear definitely has its place in there, especially if you're a drummer playing with Lightnin' or Freddie King.

Can you fellas think of another ZZ Top song that was shaped by Muddy's music?

GIBBONS: Well, Muddy's "Long Distance Call" with the "another mule kicking in his stall" line, that imagery wound up as part of a long string of influential blues bits and pieces we played in concert. I think it was finally released as the ZZ Top creation known as "Long Distance Boogie," on the live album *Fandango!*

How about ZZ Top and the Memphis music scene? Didn't you learn a little something about rhythm as well as blues during certain early gigs down here?

BEARD: Actually Ike and Tina Turner were very instrumental in ZZ Top's dress mode for a long while. The one show that Billy Gibbons ever wore hot pants on took place right here in Memphis, and it was inspired by Ike Turner!

HILL: Ike Turner and his guys wore these hot pants and big boots, and we played a coupla shows with them. Billy thought that was real hip, but he didn't bother to say, "Hey Frank, Dusty, I'm gonna . . ." No, he just shows up *in* them as we're about to play, and we just kinda looked and said, "Do you think you can pull this off?"

GIBBONS: They were a personal gift from Ike. It was 1973. We had worked the night before with the Ike and Tina Revue, opening the show, and Ike took me aside afterward and said, [*whispers*] "*You fellas got a good band, but you need some uniforms.*" They were black velvet pants.

BEARD: With fishnet stockings!

Did Billy have the legs for them?

HILL: Well, no.

BEARD: Ahh, but he did have the guitar chops, so it was okay.

When was the last time ZZ Top was together with Muddy Waters in a performance setting?

GIBBONS: The Texas dates we did in 1979–80. I think it was a total of eight Texas cities: Houston, Dallas, San Antonio, Austin, Lubbock, Amarillo, and so on. He played as long as he wanted, and by this time he had arranged a concert set which was about an hour and fifteen minutes long. It fluctuated by maybe a half-hour, and when he felt good he'd just play on, saying, "Let's do a little more!" He was very professional, didn't take no jive, and had a low threshold for BS.

When was the final time you saw Muddy Waters?

GIBBONS: We saw him in Chicago, about six months before he died in 1983. It was at the Hyatt hotel at the airport. He was passing through with Jim O'Neal of *Living Blues* magazine, going to a show. We got to say hello, "Pleased to see ya!" and he was in good spirits as always.

The guy was grooving, man, probably up till the end.

A good many of the thousands of female runaways who pass through Los Angeles each year want to become models, movie stars, rock singers, something like that," says Officer James Gilliam, assigned to curtail juvenile crime in the Hollywood division of the Los Angeles Police Department. "We had one eleven-year-old girl who came to town to become a movie queen," he recalls grimly. "She ended up doing nude still photographs for some child pornographers, and the saddest thing was she said she didn't mind doing it if that's what it took to become famous.

"The ones who are picked up are placed in nonsecurity facilities called 'soda homes,' " says Officer Gilliam, thirty, who has been patrolling the sleazy side of Hollywood for almost four years. "As a result, the kids are free to flee again. The girls usually wind up as hookers, drug pushers—just the opposite of what they wanted to be. But some of them are taken in by the local 'boule-

Rickie Lee Jones

1979

vard people,' and the ones who still want to be stars will hang out at discos, music clubs, places like the Troubadour and the Starwood. But as far as talent goes, most of them don't have any talent—or at least they don't show it."

Gilliam, who writes country and western songs with his patrol partner in his spare time, says he has never heard of any onetime runaways who later made it big in show business.

"Rickie Lee Jones?! Was *she* a runaway? Hey, I hear her song, 'Chuck E.'s in Love,' on the radio. I think her delivery is kinda unique; I mean, she's not just singing the words. She sounds like she's pulling them from deep inside herself."

"I've always liked to run away," Rickie Lee Jones confides as she sits slumped down opposite me in the front seat of my rented Plymouth. "It's my favorite thing to do. 'Night Train' is about a girl trying to get out of a situation, making her getaway. As I was about to record that song in the studio, I was looking at what was about to happen to me, and hoping I got out with what was *mine,* with my 'child,' so to speak, when everything was done."

She flicks her long blond hair away from her face to reveal a mischievous grin as we head down La Cienega Boulevard in Los Angeles. It is approximately 9:30 P.M. and Rickie Lee Jones, twenty-four, is just beginning her day. A self-described "night owl on the prowl," she has spent the better part of the day—and the last three weeks, for that matter—holed up in a messy suite of rooms in an aged hotel just off Sunset Strip. She's been undergoing a "period of adjustment" ever since her sultry Warner Bros. debut album, *Rickie Lee Jones,* and the spirited hit single, "Chuck E.'s in Love," combined to make her one of the current top-selling female vocalists in the nation. Normally, Rickie Lee lives by herself in a humble little cottage out in Santa Monica. Since her recent success, however, her doorstep has been darkened by a small army of neighborhood rubbernecks who want to know what she's *really* about. So, once again, Rickie has had to make a run for it.

"I run away at the most peculiar times," she says. "But now I don't run away so much physically—I don't always *go* anywhere. But inside I'm probably always running a little scared."

When she's onstage, she seems anything but anxious. An acoustic guitar slung low from her neck, she struts and sashays with the easy rolling beat, cooing her parables about the tragicomic underbelly of urban life. She has been said to resemble Joni Mitchell musically and visually, but in person Jones looks more like a dishy Burbank carhop than some swank, doe-eyed Lady of the Canyon. Buxom and big-hipped, with the wisecracking self-assurance of a hussy, she can be mighty intimidating when first encountered.

"The first time I saw Rickie Lee she reminded me of Jayne Mansfield," says sidekick and sometimes beau Tom Waits with a lustful growl. (Jones is the mysterious blonde on the back cover of Waits's 1978 *Blue Valentine* LP.) "I thought she was *extremely* attractive, which is to say that my first reactions were rather primitive—*primeval,* even. Her style onstage was appealing and arousing, sorta like that of a sexy white spade.

"She was drinking a lot then [1977] and I was too, so we drank together. You can learn a lot about a woman by getting smashed with her. I remember her getting her first pair of high heels, at least since I knew her, and coming by one night to holler in my window to take her out celebrating. There she was, walking down Santa Monica Boulevard, drunk and falling off her shoes.

"I love her madly in my own way—you'll gather that our relationship wasn't exactly like Mike Todd and Elizabeth Taylor—but she scares me to death. She is much older than I am in terms of street wisdom; sometimes she seems as ancient as dirt, and yet other times she's so like a little girl."

Fabled chum Chuck E. Weiss concurs. "She's all woman, and seems tough—I remember when she was broke and used to sleep under the Hollywood sign. But she's also real soft and playful. She and Waits and I used to steal the black lawn jockeys from homes in Beverly Hills and hop freight trains together. Once we three were at an exclusive party in the Hollywood Hills, invited there by Tom's lawyer, and Rickie went right in, sat down, and put an avocado between her legs. Tom was embarrassed but got a great kick out of it. Nobody would talk to us after that, so we spent the evening going up to people with cocktail dip hidden in our palms and shaking hands with them."

Near the bottom of La Cienega, Rickie Lee and I make a pit stop in a tiny roadside greasy spoon whose clientele is so unsavory that the joint features its own resident rent-a-cop. Rickie Lee, dressed to kill or maim in a skintight, black nylon stretch suit and spike heels, enters with relish, and she creates a minor stir among the night stalkers clustered around the grill when she leans over the counter to place her order.

"I love places like this," she whispers. "Anything can happen in them, and usually does. I like taking *any* kind of a risk. I've done every kind of drug you can do: STP, pot, cocaine, everything but junk; I was in an amateur rodeo in 1965 and got a tooth knocked out while breaking a mare. This is the kind of atmosphere," Jones says, surveying the seedy layout, "that I feel most comfortable in."

How comfortable has she felt since her sudden fame?

"The attention that the public starts paying you scares me," she says. "I think that maybe fame scares away a lot of friendships, because people just assume that you're getting what you need. When you walk into a performance situation or a record-company office, people really like you, they pay a lot of attention to you. But then, your normal life is the same as anybody's—just as lonely. You can't get anyone on the phone, and you can't get a date.

"The place I feel most comfortable these days is onstage; I can cut loose, and I'm so damned glad to be there. As for the audience, I get a lot of strong reactions from girls, much more than from men. The other day a girl ran four blocks down Sunset Boulevard just to catch me. She was about to cry. And I just sat down on the curb and talked to her. What I try to do when I see that kind of desperate look in people's eyes is to try 'n' bring 'em back into a real situation. I understand those feelings . . . because I've been there myself."

Rickie Lee's face clouds over for the merest moment, and then she springs back into a familiar pattern of wry jibes and smart-alecky lingo. Although she strives to obscure it, I sense something melancholy about Rickie Lee Jones.

After recharging her batteries with a gooey cheeseburger and a Coke, we ride back to her gloomy hotel room. She is still in a frisky mood, and a chat about the late hipster-comedian Lord Buckley inspires her to reenact a singsong jive rap reminiscent of Buckley's frenetic style, called "The Signifying Monkey."

"It's very dirty," she assures me. "It's an old New Orleans routine that goes on forever, and it begins [*she lapses into a low rasp*] in the jungle deep, when the badass lion steps on the signifying monkey's foot. The monkey gets madder and madder, provoking the lion." Brandishing an open bottle of Jack Daniel's, she offers a sampling of the saga:

Monkey said, "Your sister is a prostitute and your mama is a whore
And your grandpa goes round sellin' asshole from door to door
And you know that little baby sister that you hold so dear?
Well, I fucked her all day for just a bottle of beer!
I cornholed your uncle, fucked your mama and your niece
And the next time I see your sister, I'm gonna get me a 'nother little piece
And you know your sister did the damnest trick
Why, she got so low she sucked an earthworm's dick!!"

Rickie Lee tumbles to the couch in laughter, spilling a generous amount of bourbon on her clothes in the process. She excuses herself to change and when she returns, dressed in a white DOYT-DOYT T-shirt (a reference to a line in the song "Danny's All-Star Joint"—"They got a jukebox that goes doyt-doyt") and snug, blue sweatpants, her demeanor is somber. She decides to return to the subject of her days as a runaway.

"The first time I ever ran away I was fourteen," she says with quiet intensity, stretching out on the couch with a glass of ice and pouring herself two fingers of Jack Daniel's. "I think that was about 1969. A friend and I had been walking around all night, all over Phoenix—where my folks and I lived at the time—just having fun, and we decided we wanted to go somewhere—to San Diego. I got in a car and my friend drove. We neglected to tell the owner that we were taking it," she says, laughing with a gurgle. "It was a GTO or something, and it made a lot of noise as we pulled out of the driveway. We got caught the next day.

"When we took that car," she exults, "that was the first time I was in love! He was a little Italian boy. I think people never get over the first time they fall in love. It killed *me.*"

As she gulps her whiskey, she explains that she and her boyfriend spent the night in a juvenile detention home before being brought back to Phoenix. Meeting with a tempestuous reception at her own household, Rickie Lee ran away again and moved into a shack behind a friend's home. One night later that week, she made love for the first time with her seventeen-year-old boyfriend: "It was spring, it was hot, and it was very, very dark. There was a little light from a furnace in the shack. *Ooooh.*" Suddenly her blissful smile droops. "Then, one evening, he all of a sudden decided he didn't like me anymore. He took too much acid, I think, and he looked at me and went, *'Oh Jesus!'*"

A "traveling adventure" the following year took her from her new home base in Olympia, Washington, where her family had relocated, to various cities up and down the coast of California. That year, she managed to attend three high schools, being asked to leave the last, Timberline High in Olympia, or face expulsion for her insubordinate ways.

"I was a smartass," she says contritely. "I had a big mouth with teachers who I thought were wasting my time. I would tell them, 'I don't want to sit here and learn to sew dresses. I have *better* things to do.' And I'd walk out of class.

"I just had a bad attitude, I guess. What I got kicked out of school for, it's the same thing that I see myself doing onstage now. It's just a lot of high-powered feelings, a lot of emotion, and now I can work it to my advantage. The same thing I got hired for, I got fired for."

Which is a rather succinct way of saying that Rickie Lee Jones's life became her art. Arriving in Los Angeles in 1973 at nineteen, she held a series of waitressing jobs and basically lived hand-to-mouth. "The low point of my life," she remembers, "was when I'd been working in an Italian restaurant near Echo Park, in an area where the Mexican lowriders hung out. I'd been living with somebody for a year, a guitar player, and he left me with a bounced rent check and no car, and I got fired from my job.

"It was hard times," she says with a shiver, "but being that far down inspired me to go to work."

Work in this case meant returning to her longtime goal of playing music for a living, a notion she'd been carrying around in her head since she wrote her first song at seven, entitled "I Wish":

I wish, I wish
That wishes would come true
And then I know
That I will be all right.

Destitute but determined, she slept (when she was lucky) on various benefactors' couches during the day, and passed the evenings playing for a pittance in places like the Comeback Inn in Venice, California, and the A La Carte and the Ivar Theater in Hollywood. Eventually, she played the Troubadour on Hoot Night. A good deal of her act consisted of rhythmic "spoken-word" monologues told in street jargon. In time, her hipster tale-spinning was interspersed with her own songs. One of the first was "Easy Money," which Rickie Lee says was written in 1976 in a now-defunct coffeeshop in Venice called Suzanne's. The eatery had a piano, and Jones would sit at it for hours on end, drinking strong coffee and struggling with lyrics and melodies. After completing "Easy Money," she did not write again until the fall of 1977, when she knocked out a bunch of songs that included "The Last Chance Texaco" and "Chuck E.'s in Love."

She confesses a special affection for the latter effort, because the period when it was written was a momentous one in which she made not one but *two* lasting friends.

"I didn't have any real friends back then," she recalls, "and I didn't have any place to live. I didn't have any money. So I'd go sit over at the pool at the Tropicana motel [on Santa Monica Boulevard] and rest. A guy I know, Ivan Ulz, was performing at the Troubadour one evening, and he asked me to come over and sing a couple of songs. This fella Chuck E. was working back in the kitchen of the club, and that's how I met him. I sang 'Easy Money' and a song Ivan wrote, called 'You Almost Look Chinese.' A little later on, Tom saw me there, and he and Chuck E. and I started hanging out together.

"That was a high point in my life. Before that, I guess I had learned not to depend on anybody else, 'cause once people start affecting what happens to you, it's trouble. But I think Chuck E. and Tom have been my family for a while now. It seems sometimes like we're real romantic dreamers who got stuck in the wrong time zone. So we cling, we love each other very much."

And who was Chuck E. in love with?

"His cousin," she says, blushing. "I mean, that's what I heard. There was a telephone call from Denver one day, and it was Chuck E. And Waits hung up the phone and said, 'Chuck E.'s in love!' I just made the rest of the song up."

As Rickie Lee tells it, she landed a contract with Warner Bros. after her now ex-manager, Nick Mathe, had sent the label a four-song ("Company," "Young Blood," "The Last Chance Texaco," and "Easy Money") demo tape she had cut under the auspices of A&M Records. Warners was interested, but she insists the clincher came when Ivan Ulz sang "Easy Money" over the phone to Lowell George. George immediately visited Rickie Lee to hear her rendition, and recorded the song several days later for his *Thanks I'll Eat It Here* solo album. Warners staff producer Ted Templeman and A&R man Lenny Waronker (who had seen her Troubadour act) were intrigued, she was auditioned, signed a month later, and the rest is rock and roll.

During her rapid rise (the album was released April 1979) to the top of the record charts, Rickie Lee has appeared on "Saturday Night Live" ("It made me feel very uncomfortable; I had no control"), done a limited-showcase tour of small clubs in key U.S. cities, and has scheduled a more extensive summer road trip that includes a concert at Carnegie Hall. She's been a headliner since her record first reached the stores, and Jones's performances thus far have received considerable press coverage, the published reactions ranging from wild raves to caustic pans. Most of those who were sharply critical have assailed Jones for her bawdy swaggering, salty language, and her bohemian "pose."

Rickie Lee is not without her own harshly critical inclinations, although they are largely reserved for her female contemporaries in the recording industry. She has taken a number of outspoken potshots at Linda Ronstadt, Phoebe Snow, and especially Joni Mitchell.

"It's a genuine place where I'm coming from when I write or sing my songs. They're certainly more lyrical and genuine and less full of crap than any of the other girls I see singing songs these days in their disco wet suits or whatever. How many female singer/songwriters are very active now? *Three*—Joan Armatrading, Joni Mitchell, and me. And Joan is so good, it's a flip of the coin in terms of success. I wonder, 'Why me and not her?' Her music seems more accessible than mine."

Why is she so hard on Joni Mitchell?

"Because of my expectations of her. She sings jazz but she's *not* jazz, she's not a jazz artist. She doesn't come from jazz roots. Consequently, for me it comes off like Barbra Streisand singing a pop song. Barbra can sing the fuck out of a ballad and nobody can touch her, but when she comes out and does 'Stoney End,' hell, why don't we get Olivia [Newton-John] instead? She can do it just as good. I respect somebody's need to expand, but at the same time you ought to take into consideration what you do *well.*

"I get compared a lot to Tom Waits, and I can understand it only from the point of view that we're both writing about street characters. Our writing and our singing styles have nothing in common, I think. But we walk around the same streets, and I guess it's primarily a jazz-motivated situation for both of us. We're living on the *jazz* side of life, the other side of the tracks, and it's a real insecure, constant improvisation."

All this is told to me with great reverence and tenderness, but also with considerable trepidation. The evening before, I had picked Rickie Lee up at her hotel, and we discussed over dinner whether she could bear to go through this process at all. "Once you give up a piece of your life to people in print and let them all take a close look at it, you can never take that information back," she said nervously. "You can never re-create that privacy." She also admitted that she had been deliberately obstructive and/or deceptive in many of her previous interviews. "If you talk to magazines, that becomes important to you. Then you're vulnerable, and it'll fuck you every time. I think that whenever I'm vulnerable to anybody or anything, it'll hurt me."

There is a great curiosity concerning Rickie Lee Jones's stories about her supposedly threadbare background and vagabond upbringing. The many, muttered rumors about her broken home, private traumas and tragedies, and a family tree full of rounders, drifters, and errant vaudevillians have whetted everyone's appetite for the truth. Is Rickie Lee's past indeed rooted in the jazz side of life?

Her mother should know.

"It was a great feeling of defeat for me whenever Rickie would leave home," says Bettye Jane Jones, fifty-two, seated in the kitchen of her modest home near Olympia, Washington. "She and I were always so close up to that time. Until she got in her middle teens, she was a really good girl, but then she became a bit wild or restless. She was always a different child, more quiet and within herself. She always had a few friends, and she never needed a best friend as she got older. She just stayed in her room all the time and wrote poetry and played a guitar her older brother, Danny, gave her.

"I know she had a hard time finding herself, but I didn't know that children did these kinds of things when they got the *proper* love and attention at home. See, I was raised in an orphanage, so I wasn't a typical mother, but . . .

"Oh, excuse me," Mrs. Jones says with a sad smile. "I guess I should start at the beginning, shouldn't I?"

Rickie Lee was born in Chicago on November 8, 1954, the

second of three daughters (and one son) resulting from Bettye Jane's marriage to Richard Loris Jones, after whom Rickie was named. During Rickie's early childhood, she and her parents, older sister Janet Adele (now thirty-two), and brother Daniel Michael (thirty) moved from Chicago to Los Angeles and back, then to Phoenix, where sister Pamela Jo (now sixteen) was born, and finally to Olympia.

"My husband was a traveling man," says Mrs. Jones with a weary laugh, adding that she and Mr. Jones have been separated for about eight years. "I don't know why we were always moving, or why he was always leaving to go to places like Kansas City, Denver, wherever. I didn't think of ourselves as vagabonds then, but looking back now I guess we were. He was a waiter and I was a waitress, and he also worked as a furniture mover, a longshoreman, and a gardener.

"I don't know what he does now," she apologizes, stating that she has since become a practical nurse. "I don't keep in touch with him. But it was Rickie's father's dream to someday be what she is now. He studied acting at the Pasadena Playhouse and wrote songs and tried to break into show business but did not succeed. From the time she could talk, my husband started teaching Rickie to sing and play music. I know there's some resentment on his part now, and there's been some strong words between them. I'm sure he felt he was as good as Rickie is now, 'cause that's the way he is."

Mrs. Jones relates these thoughts and observations in a gentle, kindly tone, any possible bitterness supplanted by a spontaneous onrush of the remorse she feels for the difficult legacy she and her husband brought to their offspring.

"You should understand that my husband came from an entertainment background, and it was important for Richard to have a try at it himself. His father was a one-legged vaudeville dancer named Peg Leg Jones. He did a blackface routine, and we have scrapbooks of his clippings that show he played all the best theaters around the country."

After Mr. Jones's mother, a chorus girl, was killed in an auto accident, Peg Leg put his infant son into a succession of boarding institutions, eventually leaving him behind in an orphanage in the South.

Mrs. Jones grew up in the Richland County Children's Home in Mansfield, Ohio. "It's probably still standing," she says, mulling ruefully. "My mother put her four children there after my father passed away. He was bombed with poison gas in World War I in the Battle of Argonne in France, and he was never the same after that, drinking and carousing till he died. My mother remarried, but she couldn't raise us all, I guess. She's still living, but of course I'm not in contact with her.

"I met Mr. Jones when he was a soda jerk at the Sheraton Plaza Hotel in Chicago. He was twenty-four, just out of the army, and I used to stop in there for coffee on my way to my waitressing job. Both of us being raised the way we were, when he and I got together that didn't make for good roots.

"I'm telling you all this, I guess, to shed some light on why we weren't a typical middle-class family and why Rickie is who she is," Mrs. Jones says softly, her well-modulated voice wavering slightly. "If my children and the people who read this article can understand this, maybe they can learn from their own parents' misfortunes and hardships in raising children."

In the years since leaving home, Rickie Lee has reconciled whatever misgivings or differences she might have had with her immediate family and has made a point of reaching out to all of them, accepting their encouragement and inviting their counsel. While assembling the material for her first album, she regularly sent tapes of the works in progress up to Washington for scrutiny.

"The kids—my little sister Pam and my nieces—loved 'Chuck E.' and 'Danny's All-Star Joint,' " Rickie Lee bubbles. "Kids hear with a true ear. 'Danny's All-Star Joint' has part of a nursery rhyme in it that I got from my nieces, sort of a jump-rope song. The original went like this." She recites:

Hey boys, how 'bout a fight?
'Cause here comes Rickie with her girdle on tight
She can wriggle, she can walk, she can do the Twist
But most of all, she can kiss-kiss-kiss.

Unfortunately, not all of the Jones brood responded so positively to Rickie Lee's creative output.

"I played 'Coolsville' and another real motherfucker of a song called 'So Long, Lonely Avenue' for my father. And he looked at me and went, *'That's awful!'* It destroyed me so much I almost didn't put 'Coolsville' on the album, and I erased the original tape version of 'Lonely Avenue.' " (Despite that rebuff, Rickie Lee still performs one of her father's songs, "The Moon Is Made of Gold."

"It's a lullaby to a child," she says, "how beautiful the night is and not to feel sad that the sun went down, because the moon is made of gold.")

"She is hurt so easily," Mrs. Jones later says. "She gives so much and expects it in return, but people just aren't like that. I think that Rickie's very lonesome. She could have as many friends as she wants now, but she won't ever be that way.

"My son Danny feels that the one thing I could tell you about that would give you the most insight into Rickie is the imaginary friends she had as a little girl. They had strange names like Baslau and Sholbeslau. She would take them with her to church and everywhere else, and make places for them on benches and talk to them right out loud. At one point when she was still small, I told her to stop doing that, to forget such nonsense and never pretend to talk with them again, 'cause I was really worried about her.

"Every once in a while I'll ask her about her imaginary friends and what happened to them, and she'll smile in a funny way and say, 'But Mom, they're *still here.*' "

"God, what time is it?" says Rickie Lee, jumping up from her chair opposite mine to check a clock down the hall. "Damnit! It's almost midnight! Come on, there's someplace you have to check out with me to get the whole story."

Grabbing her heavy wool coat, we leave her hotel room and hurry out to my car.

"Where're we going?" I ask.

"The Troubadour!" she barks. "It's Hoot Night. I think it's important that you see what goes down over there."

As we stroll into the murky environs of the legendary L.A. folk club, a few people wave to Rickie Lee but there is no fanfare. After a few minutes, we are collared by a local guitarist who wants to talk in private with her. I fetch some beers for us as they huddle in the corner, and then Rickie and I move from the outer bar into the main room to watch the last show. After about a half-hour, we go back to the bar and take a small table by the door, where the musician and another male pal of his join us. We all chat about nothing special over several rounds of beer, until Rickie suddenly asks the guitarist if he'd like to go with her the day after tomorrow on a short vacation in Mexico she'd scheduled.

"Whattaya say?" she presses. "I don't wanna go alone. I really need somebody to go with." I am startled. She has been planning this trip for weeks and yet has no one to accompany her.

The musician says he'll think about it, and shortly thereafter he and his buddy depart, leaving Rickie and me to converse alone. We begin talking about her success again, its illusions and disappointments, when a curiously helpless expression fills her face.

"You know, I haven't told you so many things about me," she says sadly, touching my arm. "I don't know why exactly, but I think I want to tell you about my older brother, Danny." There is something in her tone that makes me feel she is stepping over some intangible personal threshold, and I feel a strange chill as she begins to speak.

"Danny was about sixteen when he was in this accident. He was driving his motorcycle; he was on his way, actually, to pick up a new driver's license. On the morning that he got hurt, I had this horrible feeling that something was going to go wrong. He was going out the door, and I begged him not to go. He wasn't gone more than a few minutes when the phone rang, and I screamed at my mother, 'It's Danny! I said he shouldn't go! I told him not to!'

"He had been making a turn when a car came by going in the other direction and sideswiped him. His leg got caught on the bumper of the car, and he was dragged along and his leg was torn off."

She draws a labored breath, and then continues:

"He was in a coma for months and nobody thought he would ever talk again. He lost the leg and was partially paralyzed on his other side. Danny was always an athlete, so that took care of that. My mom and dad were totally freaked out. That's when everything in the family came apart.

"I used to sit in the hospital every day, and I'd talk to Danny and read to him, 'cause even though everybody said he couldn't hear, I *knew* that he could. One day I was there watching television with him and I was going to change the channel or something, and he screamed out, '*No!*' That was his first word in months, and he grabbed me here, on side of my neck, and said '*No!*' out of hatred for the life he now had, the life he was trapped with."

("Danny and Rickie were very close," Rickie Lee's mother would later tell me. "The accident was a terrible blow for her, but it was also worse because she got shunted aside and was sent to live with her aunt when all of this happened. That really hurt her. But she'd spend all her free time with Danny at the hospital, and whenever she'd take a break, she used to ride the elevator to the top floor, get out, and then stand up there singing into the elevator shaft. You could hear it all around the hospital. It was the eeriest sound I think I ever heard. After Danny got a little bit better, he used to joke that Rickie Lee was a witch.")

"My brother still lives at home," Rickie Lee says, her eyes downcast. "My mom didn't kick him out or anything. She taught him how to talk again, and it was sort of a happy time around the house whenever Danny spoke.

"It all just made me realize how things can go totally wrong on a moment's notice," she murmurs, suddenly looking up at me. As she does, the houselights go on. I turn around to see that we are the last two people left in the club, and when I turn back Rickie Lee is on the verge of tears.

I suggest we get some night air, and we walk over to a little park across the street, seating ourselves on the edge of a silent, inky fountain in the center of the grounds. The evening is cool and the sky is very clear, and as we glance up at the stars, Rickie Lee begins talking again.

"I depend on my imagination to keep me happy," she says, her voice trembling. "That's why I prefer the nighttime to the daytime; it's easier to picture life in different ways. *You* fill in the darkness, and L.A. is very quiet and empty at night. Things I saw as a little girl convinced me I need to be this way to survive. I never knew that life was so serious and hard and cruel. You can't depend on anything at all."

She picks up a twig and slowly stirs the black water with it.

As we're going back to the hotel, she begs me to stop by the Tropicana motel to see if we can find Chuck E. Weiss, who lives there. But he's not around, and neither is fellow resident Tom Waits, who is presently finishing up a European tour. Still, Rickie Lee leads me into Waits's ramshackle apartment to show me the battered piano in the back room where Tom lets her write. Despite the awesome, pervasive clutter, the apartment retains a lot of warmth. Yet it feels hollow without the presence of Waits, and we both seem to know it.

"I just thought you'd like to see this nice, crazy little place," she says with a shrug. "Now you've seen just about everything in my world."

Back at the hotel, I drop Rickie Lee off and she takes my hand as she's getting out of the car, gripping it briefly and then turning away. As she slips off into the shadows I reflect that, in many ways, she's still a young girl on the run, and this transient address is little more than another soda home.

I recall something she had said to me earlier in the evening.

"You know, I hope I never forget that incredible time of evolving from a girl into a woman. You start wearing hair curlers, and your breasts are growing, and you're climbing up into some tree to kiss some boy. . . . It's so important to always keep that innocence.

"*God,*" she had whispered, in a voice like a child's, "*it's so important, no matter what.*"

Sting

1985

60° west longitude, 16°45′ north latitude—"Captain sir, permission to break out the vodka and orange!" whoops the handsome blond helmsman as he hugs the ship's sleek steel wheel, an impish gust suddenly sending some briny spray into his smirking face. "And the gods have spoken!" he asserts, wiping the bracing water away. "Aw, yes, this certainly beats the coal fields of Newcastle!"

We are approximately one hour out of Old Road Bay, two miles off the leeward coast of Montserrat, the proud prow of the forty-four-foot *Queen of Scots* sailing yacht slicing the teasing swells at about eight knots, the rocky island of Redondo rising in the misty middle distance off our port side like a miniature Gibraltar. From this privileged early morning vantage point, sun-mottled Montserrat resembles a cozy merger of Hawaii and Ireland, with its serrated volcanic peaks plunging from their collars of fluffy clouds into dense jungle valleys and sloping, emerald glens.

In the spooky, incorporeal Caribbean, there are few things more dependable than the east-west tradewinds, and as they oust the remaining cloud cover from the path of the blazing sun, the impish pilot loses all sense of composure. Hastily relinquishing the wheel to wiry Captain Ken Armstrong, he lunges for the drinks being served. After downing two of them in as many gulps, he improvises an addled jig on the foredeck.

"I love the boys," Sting sings, "I love the navy! I love my biscuits dipped in gravy!"

The eight passengers scattered amidships explode with laughter. Sting and the others take turns reenacting snippets from the famous "Raging Queen" seafaring skit on "Saturday Night Live," as well as naughty revisions of *H.M.S. Pinafore.* A half-hour later—and it's still well before noon—everyone is thoroughly buzzed on Finnish vodka, Monserratian ganja, and their own shared joviality. On board for the day's sail around the thirty-nine-square-mile island are siren-voiced rock singer Sting, a.k.a. Gordon Matthew Sumner, the slim, bronze, and strikingly fit eldest son of Ernest Sumner; Ernie himself, box-jawed, genial to a fault; actress Trudie Styler, the mother of one of Sting's three children and pregnant with another (due in May); shy, lank-limbed Joe, Sting's nine-year-old boy; three guests, and the captain's female first mate.

It is several days after New Year's, and Montserrat has barely recovered from its annual month-long festival, which traditionally culminates with a three-day revel that includes the Calypso Finals (King Reality aced out defending champion King Hero in the Road March) and the frenetic Last Lap Jump-Up, a dusk-till-dawn parade and street dance held in the rustic port capital of Plymouth (pop. 1,267). Sting and his tribe went largely unnoticed in the happy commotion, and those who did recognize him were unfazed.

This day we are in quest of Montserrat's semi-secret natural treasure—its only white sand beach. Because of the island's volcanic origins, the precious few beaches on its western coast are composed of black and silver-gray sand. However, there is one crescent of pink and white coral sand at remote and relatively inaccessible Rendezvous Bay, located near the isle's northern tip. As we press on in our mission, Sting's lively conversation ranges from West Indian politics and the legacy of Bob Marley to Coptic mysticism and Freemasonry, Sting recommending several books that touch on the murky underside of the secret fraternal organization: *God's Banker, The Brotherhood,* and *Holy Blood, Holy Grail.*

"They're sometimes a bit difficult to obtain," he admonishes, "perhaps because the Masons and the Catholic Church, whose loyal defenders are legion, aren't particularly thrilled with their presence in bookstores. For myself, I'm always intent on discovering the story behind any story, the structure behind the facade. Separating the nonsense from the few new facts that might ring true is a constant process I just accept. New ideas replicated are sacraments—meaningful rituals that turn nonsense into relative order.

"And new actions are the same way," he says, momentarily shielding his piercing azure eyes from direct solar assault as he accepts another iced screwdriver. "Apart from my family, which means the world to me, I've nothing firm in my life; everything is flexible—increasingly so." He glances down at the foamy water rushing past the bulkhead. "I feel I'm moving at the speed of light, relative to most people. And when you move that fast, reality distorts and things slow down, grow loose and flowing, and become somewhat mystical. That kind of velocity and mood feeds my vast curiosity, my craving to know and to experience and to test." At this stage in his remarkable passage, the thirty-three-year-old (born October 2, 1951) Sting is demanding a dramatic new independence in which to realize his wide-ranging ambitions. The Police, the reggae-laced, buoyantly melodic power-rock triumvirate that emerged in 1977 from the cacophonous tumult of the British punk upheaval, has not recorded since completing their 1983 album, *Synchronicity.* After touring throughout the following year in support of the record, drummer-founder Stewart Copeland and guitarist Andy Summers went their separate ways for assorted solo projects, among them some film soundtracks (*Rumble Fish* and *2010,* respectively). Sting continued with his own meandering screen acting career, spending seven weeks in Mexico City filming what proved to be a brief, fragmentary appearance as the hateful Feyd-Rautha in the interminable *Dune.* His next two roles, as Baron von Frankenstein opposite Jennifer Beals in *The Bride* (summer 1985) and as a black-marketeer/lover of a French Resistance sympathizer (Meryl Streep) in *Plenty* (fall 1985). With *The Bride* and *Plenty* in the can, his chief concern on this idyllic Caribbean afternoon is a project that promises to postpone any possible reformation of the Police until 1986 at the earliest: his first solo LP.

Rumors mount that his album sounds the death knell for one of the most sagacious groups of the last half-decade, but he discounts such talk.

"The Police and my solitary projects are logically very separate," he says. "We haven't broken up, but we've become separated by our own plans for ourselves for the time being. It's nothing more than that."

After spending several months writing the songs for his solo flight, he brought some kith and kin down to this, his ideal workspace and playground, for some dynamic respite. The Police recorded both *Ghost in the Machine* and *Syncronicity* in Montserrat at the notoriously splendid AIR Studios hilltop villa complex, and this trip is Sting's fifth to the mountain getaway. In between water sports, tennis, and nighttime carousing in the sleepy island's few clubs, he's been revising lyrics and getting the final arrangements in order for his new material, portions of which—"Children's Crusade," "Set Them Free," "Consider Me Gone," and "Bourbon Street"—date back to a writing spurt Sting had in the summer of 1984.

The boat is coming about and easing into the shoals of the deserted Rendezvous Bay as Sting saunters down into the stateroom below. He pops up again, a red baseball cap over his tousled, straw-colored thatch. Sprawling out on the aft deck, his squarish head propped against the mast, he begins detailing the inspiration for "Children's Crusade," a song for which he has cut an exploratory demo track at AIR's forty-eight-track digital board.

"On the surface, it's a song about human folly and the ravages of war," he says quietly. "Americans look back on the First World War as a kind of glorious adventure, a mechanized breakthrough in defending the world against bullies and tyranny. But in England, it's drummed into all schoolchildren that it was an utter disaster, a grotesquely tragic waste of an entire generation of young men. Tens of thousands of them were continually sent over the top of the Western Front to be riddled and dismembered a few feet later by a hail of machine-gun bullets. The lemmings-styled charges were all for naught, gaining not one inch of ground. British World War I memorials contain endless, horrifying lists of the dead. That war became a symbol of the end of the invincibility of the British Empire and shattered the people's faith in the wisdom of their generals and politicians.

"The actual Children's Crusade was a mythic army of kids sent to the Holy Land to convert the Saracens, but the truth is that it was a corrupt plot hatched by monks in the eleventh century. They rounded up street urchins on the pretense of recruiting them for some pious purpose—and then they shipped the helpless children to North Africa. Those that survived the journey in spite of starvation and shipwrecks were sold as white slaves. I tell you, history is, in part, a series of madmen deluding people into parting with their children for loathsome and tragic schemes."

The intense mood lifts when Trudie gives the call for lunch, and she breaks out a mighty Tupperware bowl of her superbly gooey, *al dente* macaroni salad while Sting slips into the galley, reemerging with a basket brimming with cold roast chicken he'd prepared the previous evening. As Sting and the witty Trudie josh each other about their "appalling domesticity," Ernie Sumner chats about his brood of two boys and two girls, who had a strict Roman Catholic upbringing in the Wallsend district of the north England city of Newcastle. Located on the Tyne River, it was once a thriving center for coal mining, shipbuilding, and heavy industry, but the port never recovered from a recession it suffered in the thirties.

"My wife, Audrey, and I, we raised them well enough, tried to give them a bit of good advice," he says with pride. "We were never poor, but life in Newcastle was sometimes difficult. I delivered milk, and then I later got to where I took over the dairy business myself. I'm retired now, and Gordon's brother Philip, he runs the dairy, and also has a nightclub in town." Ernie's face is creased with a crooked grin. "Hey now," he calls to "Gordon," indicating the boat with a sweeping gesture, "when you were a lad I told you to get yourself on a ship and see the world, didn't I?"

Sting nods, blushing, and chuckles as he recalls aloud applying for a seaman's card when he was seventeen. He had landed a job with the Ronnie Pierson Trio, a shipboard dance band contracted to Princess Cruises, playing bass with the group on the summer circuit in the Mediterranean.

After lunch, there is a brief siesta, the boat swaying in time to a radio tuned to the calypso of Radio Antilles. The steel pan and percolating trumpets suddenly segue into the sinewy tick-tock of "Every Breath You Take."

"Goodness," Trudie quips, "that sounds like Daddy working!"

With that, the radio is switched off, and we pile into the rubber Zodiac motor raft tethered to the end of the boat for the short trip to the beach. The broad ribbon of sand is as soft as it is ultra fine, and the sheer, orange clay cliffs looming over it rise at least thirty feet to a plateau of gnarled scrub forest. Sting remarks that the stark beauty of the spot's extreme isolation would be appropriate for a cinema remake of Robinson Crusoe. When he returns to the theme of "Children's Crusade," he says:

"I remember how, around 1980, I got catatonically depressed about the future. Now I feel better, perhaps because I'm on the offensive in terms of sounding an alarm in my music or at least daring to consider the implications out loud, hoping people are listening. 'Children's Crusade' is an appeal to reason."

Joe runs up to snugly whisper something in his dad's ear, a recurring tableau during the course of the sail. Sting cocks his head, takes in the confidence, and then pulls the skinny boy close to kiss him on the cheek.

"Joseph is a bundle of secrets," he says, cupping his hands over the boy's ears. "He doesn't speak to anyone but his dear old dad when he's out in public, and even then he does it under his breath. I don't want *him* to hear this, but I will reveal nothing of his words. Not even upon pain of torture most grievous!" His son begins to giggle, which Sting encourages with a round of rib tickling, and then Joe breaks free of his grasp and spins off toward Trudie. She sits some fifty yards away, gazing out at the glistening water, lost in her thoughts. On the boat she'd chatted about her love of acting, her work with the Royal Shakespearean Company, and the play she'd happily completed just in time to concentrate on her pregnancy.

"You know," says Sting, his tone placid, "I sometimes think of all the turns I've taken. I was the Northumberland champion in the 100- and 200-meter sprints when I was in private school, which meant that I was ranked No. 3 in England in my age group. But having reached that point, I gave up. I decided there was no gain in being part of the pyramid. I was to be the best at something else.

"All my life, the process of forgetting myself and clearing my mind has gone against every conditioning I went through as a boy. I was *conditioned* to plan, to plot, to scheme, to worry. That was the only route out of the working-class world I was raised in, a Catholic boy in a Protestant universe where the class structure blocks your dreams rather than assists them. If you're not wealthy or part of the aristocracy, rock and roll *is* one possible way out of the suffocating British system.

"I just finished reading *One Hundred Years of Solitude,* by Gabriel Garcia Marquez, and I wept at the end of the book because it had a heart and an eloquent genius to it that seemed beyond human ingenuity. It was about how close dreams and long-term realities can be. As it charts the strivings of a family over a century, predictions and visions come true, for better or worse, but you see them taking shape from the start. It takes enormous courage and belief to meet your destiny in life; you can see it so closely, and yet you still have to struggle toward it. Once you're aware of its existence, it's more a hard-fought objective than a preordained fact. That's why many people miss their calling, their destiny, or allow themselves to get beaten down on the road to finding it. Strange how things can be magical on the one hand, and heartbreaking on the other. We all begin with such enormous promise!

"I was invited to witness a psychic metal-bending experiment in September 1981, supervised by a professor in the physics department at London University. I saw the young people being tested bend thick strips of metal and then bend them back again over the course of an hour or so. And the people conducting the research were scientists, not mystics. At the time, witnessing those experiments was more exciting for me than rock and roll."

During a previous interview in Manhattan in 1984, Sting had made it clear that he was transfixed by the possible metaphysical import of those experiments and was quite immersed in inquiries into the occult. This afternoon, romping and reflecting on this secluded beach, he seems a far more sober presence. What's changed, or changed him?

"I have three children, plus another on the way from a woman dear to me," he says. "That kind of thing pulls you down from the clouds, I suppose. You know, all those kids in those experiments are losing their psychic powers as they conform to society's notions of normality, getting jobs, girlfriends, mortgages. I think that says something about society's innate power to discouarge specialties. I want to prevent that from happening to those I care about and want to see flourish."

He looks down the beach at Joe, who's constructing a sand castle with Trudie. "I would die for that little guy," he says after a long silence, "but I would much rather live for him."

It's just after sunset when we complete our circumnavigation of Montserrat and put in again at Old Road Bluff. Behind us, heat lightning is flashing through the roiled blue and purple clouds above Antigua, visible twenty-seven miles to the northeast. Everyone is smarting with healthy sunburns and professing a grateful weariness from the sail, vowing to head off for extended naps—except Sting. After returning to his rented villa across from the Vue Point Hotel (whose seaside cluster of impeccable cottages comprises one of only two worthy public lodgings on the island), he heads down the road to the AIR Studios complex to add guest vocals to "Money for Nothing," a track on Dire Straits' new *Brothers in Arms* LP.

Later that evening, everyone, including Sting and most of Dire Straits and its support staff, congregates at the Village Place, a secluded rum-bar-*cum*-eatery located in the hills above the tiny village of Salem. Beneath a sagging network of Christmas lights, the band members and assorted villagers are sipping Carib Lager while engrossed in one of several games of backgammon taking place on the patio or placing small bets on the solemn billiards match between two deadlocked locals in the adjacent shed. But the real action is at the long bar in the low-ceilinged main shack, where dread barkeep Danny Allen is cooking up batches of Mix-Up (a blend of Irish sea moss, brandy, and Guinness stout said to be an aphrodisiac) and the viciously potent Volcano (four kinds of rum, grenadine, pineapple juice, orange juice, and Montserrat lime juice). Jimmy Buffet has said that he named his 1979 *Volcano* album for Montserrat's active lava boiler, Galway's Soufrière, but the young bloods at the bar wink and assure you that it was named for the libation that Buffett and James Taylor downed endlessly on the premises and in the now-closed Agouti in Plymouth. Whatever the case, there is general agreement that it was Elton John who made the joint the nocturnal watering hole of choice for AIR denizens when he adopted it during the making of *Too Low for Zero.*

Midnight comes and goes, the place grows noisier and more raucous. Mark Knopfler arrives and wades into the genial fray. Steel Pulse pulsates from crisp, basso speakers hung overhead while the racially mixed clientele joke, jawbone, and flirt with each other, occasionally glancing over at the James Bond movie on the TV over the ancient refrigerator. But for slave rebellions like the legendary one staged on St. Patrick's Day, 1768, and the equally famed Fox Riot of 1889 in the neighboring village of Frith (wherein an angry mob held off police attempting to arrest the Fox family for illegal distillation of rum), the fun-loving citizenry of the island is surprisingly devoid of the racial friction that afflicts so much of the West Indies. When the sound system erupts with "Hot, Hot, Hot," a recent single by local soca star Arrow that was a huge hit in England, the crowd cheers in unison.

"I've got a theory about the Caribbean recording studios and why people come here," says Sting the next afternoon, barefoot in chic swim trunks and souvenir polo shirt, as he takes a poolside table at the Vue Point Hotel for a late lunch. "Wanna hear it?"

A coquettish teenage waitress arrives, encouraging him to try local delicacies like goatwater stew, spicy rice and peas (as kidney beans are known in the Indies), and mountain chicken (frog's legs). He opts instead for a club sandwich on rye toast and Lime Smash, the native soda pop, and offers his hypothesis.

"No European or American rock group comes to the Caribbean to record their *first* record," he begins, "because the costs are prohibitive and it'd be pretty silly, since it's really *urban* music that we all make. When you initially start touring, and you achieve any kind of popular grass roots response, you've primarily toured cities, industrial and depressive areas, in horrible clubs and halls with awful dressing rooms.

"Then you record the first album, which for the Police, of course, was the *Outlandos d'Amour* thing in 1978, and you do it in a cruddy, funky studio with egg cartons on the walls. You make your second album in more or less the same place on a shoestring budget [*Reggatta de Blanc* was cut in London's humble sixteen-track Surrey Sound Studios for a scant $6,000], after touring again on the same dreary trail. We kept costs down on our early American tour by loading our own equipment into vans and station wagons, because it usually takes two albums before you see any money.

"And then the bucks started coming in," he says with a wide grin as his food is set before him. "And we began to think about a state-of-the-technology studio in some smart locale. Then, more bucks came in, and we said," (here his dusky voice cracks in a yelp), "Hey, why don't we go and record in the *Caribbean!!*

"There are a variety of choices open to you: You can go to Nassau, to Barbados, to Jamaica, or come here. And it's a way of saying you've made it; it's a reward. You are ensconced in a tropical paradise, allowed to feel your new wealth and its attendant power. Following my awful separation from my wife [actress Frances Tomelty] in the early eighties, I went to Jamaica to escape, and I stayed at Golden Eye, the old Ian Fleming house in Oracabessa that Chris Blackwell of Island Records owns. While I was there, I sat at Fleming's old wooden desk overlooking the ocean, the one at which he wrote all his James Bond books, and I wrote "Every Breath You Take," "King of Pain," "Wrapped Around Your Finger," all these neat songs. And that was also the first time I tried sinsemilla. I brought those songs to Montserrat and we cut *Synchronicity*.

"I'm not much of a tourist; I've seen most of the world anyway, so I don't want to go out and find more new places. I bring my family here because I know what I can expect without any worries. I know I'm gonna be able to learn to windsurf, water-ski, all the middle-class stuff I never got the chance to do when I was a kid. For the time being, this kind of environment is also good for me creatively, but I think it would be a mistake for the Police to do another album in this kind of setting. I think it's best," he concludes, biting into his double-decker sandwich, "that we eventually get back to the squalor of our roots. Me, I'm also planting new ones."

Approximately one week later, a tanned and high-spirited Sting is roaming the wintry streets of New York City, searching for the right combination of musicians to help him bring his own work-in-progress to fruition. Booking time at the SIR rehearsal studios on Manhattan's West Side, he screens a host of the city's best axmen, and he is open and unabashed ("I couldn't have done it otherwise") in acknowledging the debt he owes to Vic Garbarini, former executive editor of *Musician* magazine, who played a key role in lining up the nation's top jazz-based instrumentalists.

"Sting knew I was in close touch with this network of players," says Garbarini, "and as far back as last October, when I was staying with Sting in his house in England, he had said to me, 'Maybe I should just give you a checkbook and let you hire me a band.' I thought he was kidding until he called me in December of '84 and said, 'Do you want a job? I want to work with highly skilled jazz musicians to ensure the quality of the project, and the rest will take care of itself.'

"I said to him, 'But you don't want the older jazzmen who grew up playing bebop. What you want are the young ones who were raised on jazz, fusion, and funk and are closet rock fans.' In other words, a more assimilated crew but still with a contemporary edge. I suggested he sign up Branford [Marsalis] sight unseen, because I knew Branford, and his sax has got that Wayne Shorter/Coltrane sensibility but also his own very contemporary funk-influenced sound. Sting agreed."

Next Garbarini drew up a laundry list of the cream-of-the-session crop, as well as the best and brightest new innovators. "Overnight, I put together workshop-type auditions with the full spectrum, from the avant-garde end of James Blood Ulmer sidemen to the neoclassical guys. By the second day, we had most of the group." Which was Marsalis, drummer Omar Hakim, late of

Weather Report, and Miles Davis alumnus Daryl Jones on bass. The latter two were pressed to set aside their own evolving career schedules to clear the decks for seven weeks of recording at Eddie Grant's Blue Wave Studios in Barbados, followed by a solid year of global concert chores. Keyboardist Kenny Kirkland came aboard at the end of the week and vocalists Dollette McDonald and Janice Pendarvis were added. Everybody scattered for a spell to wrap up any lingering commitments and then regrouped for a mere seven days of serious rehearsals before presenting a trio of sneak-preview shows on February 25, 26, and 27 at the jammed Ritz club in lower Manhattan.

"I set it up that way to create tension, create a galvanizing element," Sting explains. "It's no good saying, 'Well, let's do a rehearsal and then we'll have a gig in August.' That wouldn't have been right for me; I would have been bored. Having that gig to work for in a very short time meant we really had to work *hard.* I wanted to discipline them as far as learning the songs, and then let them play their asses off.

"Much black jazz music these days is played to white, middle-class audiences in a sort of conservatory environment. When you go to see Wynton Marsalis play, you might as well be going to hear chamber music. Many of them are not used to steamy, sweaty rock clubs where the stage is bouncing up and down and the kids are going berserk. So I looked 'round on the opening night at the Ritz and I was nervous, but they were all *frightened.*

"And most of them had never even seen me perform live! During rehearsals I'd been very low-key and matter-of-fact so they weren't prepared for the lunatic who arrived on Monday. The best music was played on Wednesday night, but most of the raw terror and joy was on Monday."

Decked out in baggy dark trousers and a bright red jacket over a white T-shirt, Sting bobbed and leapt around the stage, swinging his cream-colored Telecaster with a sure vengeance as he led the game ensemble through the anthemic "The Children's Crusade"; "Bourbon Street," about an immortal nightstalker inspired by novelist Anne Rice's *Interview with the Vampire*; and "Working the Black Seam," a foreboding parable that used the recent protracted coal miners strike in England as a metaphor for self-destructiveness; in that case, the pigheaded miners pitted against Margaret Thatcher's insensitive Tory resolve.

The immaculate harmonics of Andy Summers's deft chordings

and the reverberant, timbale-redolent grandeur of Stewart Copeland's reggae-rock percussion had been replaced by an interwoven tapestry of reflex virtuosity. The delicacy of Marsalis's affecting soprano and tenor sax solos offered an airy counterpoint to Jones's bold, deep-diving bass lines and Hakim's exultantly propulsive stick and cymbal flair. Kirkland's keyboard parried and thrusted in a seductive dance with the women's vivid, vivacious backup-singing, and lent the songs intoxicating color. When Sting did solo guitar-and-voice versions of "Roxanne" and "Message in a Bottle," the full house sang along with gusto. And when the band roared through rearranged versions of "Shadows in the Rain," "Driven to Tears," and "I Burn for You" from the *Brimstone and Treacle* soundtrack, the crowd seemed jolted by the fresh contours and fury in Sting's climbing vocals. Sting even inserted a couple of sassy Freddie King and Little Willie John blues standards for cocky good measure. With a deafening sendoff from the faithful, the man and his shock troops were well along on the road to Barbados.

"Look at this place!" urges Eddie Grant, his thick drape of dreadlocks reaching halfway down his broad back, as he treks through the converted stable in which are installed a spectacular forty-eight-track digital studio and a suite of business offices. Striding out into the bone-dry midday heat, the blazing sun making his nylon red-and-white tracksuit gleam fiercely, Grant moves past the bubbling fountain in the courtyard of his renovated plantation and onto the front porch of the main house. The long piazza, constructed, like the rest of the compound, of white marble, terra-cotta, and bleached coral brick, overlooks a swimming pool and terraced gardens, delineated by an elegant balustrade. Beyond this is a vast plain densely planted with sugarcane, a deep green and impenetrable sea of ripening stalks.

"Who could believe," he says evenly, his chest swelling, "that a boy named Edmond Montague Grant from Guyana, the son of a man who sold automobile parts, would one day possess Bayley's plantation?! In the 1880s, it was the virtual kingdom of a lordly white landowner and slave master—one of the biggest in the history of Barbados.

"In fact," notes the thirty-seven-year-old singer/songwriter/producer, "this plantation was the site of one of the bloodiest slave revolts in the Caribbean." He indicates the high ground on which we stand. "Right *here* is where the renegades set the fires that signaled the start of the rebellion."

In the warm glow of midday, the vista seems calm enough, too breathstealing in its elemental beauty to inspire anything but awed appreciation. But when the hazy dusk settles in, it isn't difficult to imagine the desperate drama unfolding on that Easter Sunday in April 1816, when the end of the Napoleonic Wars led to a slump in the sugar market and caused the brutal Bajan plantocracy to drive the slaves mercilessly to raise production. Promptly at 8:00 P.M. that Eastertide, when the slaves knew the governor would be off the island and most of the whites away in the capital city of Bridgetown, the plot was sprung. Bussa, the ranger (elite managerial slave) on the Bayley's grounds, gave the word to ignite the cornstalk and trash piles that would act as signal flares. Bussa broke into the stables that now house Grant's studio and made off with horses, arms, and ammunition. Within hours, the insurrection spread to seventy of the largest estates, and a season of depravity took hold. By the time the militia put down the revolt, one white civilian, one black soldier, and fifty slaves had perished in the fighting, with seventy more slaves being swiftly executed in the fields. After a cynical trial in Bridgetown, 132 surviving slaves were deported and 144 more put to death, their decapitated torsos hung from trees around the island, their heads placed on posts and railings around Bayley's and surrounding farms.

But the grisly displays of the carnage did not diminish the thralldom's hunger for freedom, and they won it in the 1830s. That in the month of April more than a century and a half later, the erstwhile Bayley's plantation should host the creation of a musical event by the once and future star of one of the planet's biggest rock bands is no less edifying to its current landlord.

"Sting called me on a Saturday afternoon, I believe, saying he wanted to see the place. He told me he'd considered and rejected other studios and wanted to fly down immediately. When he walked in, he said, 'Yup. This is it. I'll see you soon.' And he did. We've struck up a great friendship.

"I have to hand it to him, because it was a great step for him, a tremendous show of bravery to redefine himself outside of the institution that is the Police. He squeezed his balls and decided to go for broke, which is the kind of gamble I understand. 'Love Is the 7th Wave' is a song I particularly like, because it showed what a good listener he can be to the musical life around him. There's a belief in Barbados that the seventh wave is always the best and bluest wave for any swimmer, sailor, surfer. Hearing that song and the rest of the tracks in their various stages, I'm thinking he's going to see the album at No. 1.

"I was eager to directly participate in some way, so I played conga on 'Consider Me Gone,' and it was a treat. The man has courage, and a respectable game of tennis. Far as I am concerned, Sting is a regular Bajan now."

"Eddie is a motivated person who has brought about a lot without wasted effort," says Sting. "He's a rather retiring and reclusive fellow, and he only leaves the grounds to play squash with the Bajan champions at the Barbados Squash Club. Even when he's on the premises, he and his wife and family keep to themselves a great deal." He shrugs. "It's funny, really, how at ease he is holing up in his hideaway, because we were just the opposite, all catching a powerfully strong dose of island fever at the six-week mark, because there's only so much to do in Barbados when you're not working. We must have watched a video cassette of *Spinal Tap* at least fifteen times, until all of us had memorized every bloody line! Then we began to roll around on the ground, laughing hysterically at each other's remarks—whether they were jokes or not.

"Our demented state was further aggravated by the periodic power surges in the island's power supply, which would play havoc with the precision of the digital settings for each of the tracks, all of which must be perfectly preserved on floppy disks so they can be realigned later in a different studio for the remixing. We were driven batty by the tendency of the vocals to drop off at odd intervals until we discovered the power surges were the cause.

"There was genuine delight in the way we've all stretched ourselves in the studio, and I expect it to continue on the road. I want something more open-ended, flexible, and dangerous than a Springsteen or Prince show, although I like both. I'm working with musicians who are light-years ahead of me as players, and all they lack in this case is a unifying conceptual sense, which I provide. I've had to become more proficient as a musician, and they've had to deal with strict songs that have their own integrity. This album was written before they came together, so it'd be interesting to see what an album *for* the band would sound like. I'd like to try it.

"These guys are *not* sidemen, and when we start the tour we're going to sweep away all who've gone before us, devastating them.

No one can blow us off as musicians, performers, or anything else. We're gonna fucking wipe the table clean, and that's an open challenge."

At the end of the seventh week, it was time to put all such notions on the back burner and race to New York City to play the unmixed final tapes for the brass at A&M Records. Meeting with an enthusiastic response, Sting decided to linger in the city for a few days to unwind and collect his thoughts before taking the masters to Le Studio in the woods of Quebec for a final mix-down.

Having dinner at the *de rigueur* Cafe Luxembourg on West 70th Street, he devoured a lamb entrée, knocked back a few rounds of vodka and grapefruit juice, and ogled the waitresses—"There's something about girls in black uniforms and black stockings that drives me absolutely *cra-zy.*" His immediate desires sated, he ordered cappuccino and finally disclosed the title of the album: *The Dream of the Blue Turtles.*

Huh?

"Okay," he smirks. "Let me explain. During the week of rehearsals for the Ritz shows, I had a dream that I was back home in Hampshire, looking out the window into this big walled-in garden I have out back with its very neat flower bed and foliage. Suddenly, out of a hole in the wall came these large, macho, aggressive, and quite drunk blue turtles. They started doing backflips and other acrobatics, in the process utterly destroying my garden . . ."

He halts momentarily, noting the amazement on the face of his guests, and grins hugely, the thick smile-creases etched above the hollows of his deeply accentuated cheeks. In the past, Sting always seemed slightly forbidding up close, his high forehead, severe arching eyebrows, and long puggish nose creating an initial impression of parlous arrogance that a cruelly set mouth often confirmed.

With slight age lines in evidence on his smooth face, he appears much humbler and appealingly seasoned, the formerly taut lips markedly relaxed, the defiant glare of bygone days no longer in evidence. Once, his image was that of a pompous scamp guarding a venal secret. Now he strikes one as a serious artist, grateful for a genuine glimpse at personal satisfaction.

"You must give me a little space here," he pleads self-mockingly, and resumes his recollection. "So anyway, I'm somehow enjoying this curious spectacle, and the dream is so strong I remembered it perfectly when I woke up, to the point where it became part of my juggernaut to complete this record. Having undergone Jungian analysis, I've gotten proficient at interpreting my own dreams, Carl Jung having believed that they're doors into the innermost parts of your psyche. For me, the turtles are symbols of the subconscious, living under the sea, full of unrealized potential, very Jungian in their meaning."

The late Swiss psychologist, the man who theorized about the existence of a collective unconsciousness, and who coined the word "synchronicity" to describe the mystical roots of coincidence, did not regard dreams as random rehashes of the day's events and experiences. Jung wrote that dreams are psychic opportunities, "opening into that cosmic night which was psyche long before there was any ego consciousness. . . . Out of these all-uniting depths arises the dream, be it ever so childish, grotesque or immoral."

"I have dreams where I create the most unbelievable music, music like Mozart, that I don't consciously have the knowledge to write," says Sting. "It's there, I'm writing it, and it's real. So with the album I wanted to destroy a lot of preconceptions and expectations, and do something unsettlingly different. These blue turtles, these musicians, were gonna help me." He chuckles contentedly. "And they did."

And what of the Police? Few rock acts are so celebrated for their flamboyant infighting and contention. Almost since the group's establishment by American Stewart Copeland, the balance of power appeared tipped in the favor of the ultra-charismatic lead singer. Copeland would rail that Sting was not going to "push me around." Sting would lament that "our egos always get in the way because of our intense differences as people and because we're growing away from each other—me the fastest." Andy Summers, ever the diplomat, would chalk up the three-way tug-of-war to "creative sparks misfiring." I remind Sting that in 1984 he confided that, "the things that make us good together in the first place are still there, but they're more difficult to sustain." How long will the brittle alliance be sustained before it's disbanded?

"No one really knows," says Sting, with a quizzical expression. "And, in truth, no one is really concerned. We're all extremely busy. Stewart is immersed in a successful musical life that includes a solo album this summer. Andy's working on a solo record starting next month. We're pleasantly preoccupied, which is a good sign, rather than a bad one."

After dinner, Sting is in the mood for some musical diversion, so we head down to the Lone Star Cafe, a Greenwich Village gin mill renowned for its robust chili, terrible sightlines, fine sound system, and often-impeccable choice of bookings. Dr. John is holding forth this evening, with guitarist Hiram Bullock and bassist Will Lee of the David Letterman band sitting in, and Sting is so taken with Mac Rebbenack's incomparable gumbo of New Orleans rhumba-boogie and second-line finesse that we linger for two sets. Everyone is nicely snookered on Lone Star beer and more vodka when Sting begins bopping around the balcony, exclaiming, "Shit, this place is just like the music pubs I knew back in Newcastle!"

The select group of band members, record industry confidants, and friends are nearly as edgy as Sting on the evening of April 29. He has chosen this moment to unveil the completed record, introducing it in a private listening session in the conference room at A&M Records' Madison Avenue offices.

A sumptuous spread of fruits, cheeses, assorted pâtés, and other gourmet delicacies is laid out, and the Möet Chandon flows freely as the reel-to-reel deck on the room's costly sound system is carefully threaded with the precious master tape. The forward button is struck with a flourish, but the deck doesn't work.

A grumble is heard from the back of the room. It's Sting. He hasn't slept in nearly thirty-six hours. The sun sinks into the depths of the skyline, and Sting paces, cracking diffident jokes, as a solution is sought. The pacing continues.

Most of those present have already heard the rough mixes, marveling at the magnetism of the multitracked vocal harmonies on the first single, "Set Them Free." Murmured debates commence around the room; the majority seem to agree that the album is the equal of, if not superior to, any of the Police's LPs, but can't agree which song is the record's masterpiece. Perhaps the effervescent, Barbados-composed "Love Is the 7th Wave," with its chiming calypso brio and agile one-drop reggae drumming? Maybe "Fortress Around Your Heart," with its ebb-and-flow undertow and rising surges of thundersome rocking? Or "Russians," the moving hymn of parental anguish in a world that can no longer recognize itself in its military machinations, Sting intoning, "Believe me when I say to you / I hope the Russians love their children too."

The debate remains unresolved as a backup cassette of *The*

Dream of the Blue Turtles is located, slipped into the cartridge, and rewound. There is a low, rumbling hiss as the tape begins to roll . . . and Bruce Springsteen's "Born in the U.S.A." marches out of the monitors.

Stranded in the center of the conference room, Sting turns on his heel and strolls out to the bar in the hallway. He orders himself a brimming glass of champagne.

A quick sip. Then he lifts his Möet Chandon to no one in particular. "I guess I'm gonna have to find a totally, *totally* new sound for this solo thing," he announces. "I go all the way to the Caribbean with a group of the world's best jazz musicians, work my ass off, and I *still* wind up sounding a little too fuckin' much like the Boss!"

She shaved her head as penance. A darkly handsome young woman with regal cheekbones and easy poise, she rashly eradicated her innate dignity, razoring her lustrous mane right down to the scalp.

The act was in atonement for the affair she'd had with a friend of her husband's, shortly after conceiving their first child. "I think I was just stamping my foot for attention," she would later say of the 1973 infidelity.

Initially startled, her equally intense, impulsive spouse responded to her baldness by also undergoing tonsure.

"Now, I look back on it as a cheap, exhibitionist gimmick," says Peter Gabriel. "I wound up using it as a stage device. It was a desperate act to stand apart from others at a time when the competition in the rock and roll profession was so terribly intense."

Art rarely has an opportunity to imitate domestic life with such medieval severity, but then there have been few passages in the rock annals to match the grievous rise of Peter Gabriel. He was born into an upper-middle-class British family in the semirural county of Surrey and educated at Charterhouse, the famed seventeenth-century English "public school" named for the former Carthusian monastery in London in which it was

Peter Gabriel 1986

first installed. The Charterhouse monks, not to mention the *Tom Brown's School Days*–styled headmasters that came after them, were of notoriously stern mien. So it's not surprising that "thick, depressive, and pathetically unathletic" Peter Gabriel, as he remembers himself, was to burst straight from its gloomy "carrels" (private desk nooks) and Gothic dorms into the leadership of a stubbornly phantasmal band called Genesis.

Genesis was British pop's most intrepid purveyor of rock and roll dramaturgy, and Peter Gabriel was its principal vocalist and costumed Grand Guignol character. Gabriel would take the stage in fox-head masks, inverted-pyramid headdresses, giant daffodil casques, glowing-eyes and bat-wings getups, abstract Roman-helmet makeup, and silvery whiteface. Genesis's rambling compositions, with titles like "The Return of the Giant Hogweed" and "The Fountain of Salmacis," were brooding, mythical suites punctuated by Gabriel's tart oboe tenor. One either adored the dense, Lewis Carroll–like display or utterly disdained its unhurried sense of detachment.

Following the elaborate 1974–'75 tour supporting the release of *The Lamb Lies Down on Broadway,* Genesis's two-record rock opera of urban angst, Gabriel bowed out, murmuring that a series of personal and professional crises of confidence were overwhelming him. Drummer-singer Phil Collins took the helm in 1976, and he made it possible for the group to produce such commercial smashes as "Invisible Touch."

And Peter Gabriel, back from a year of creative solitude and domestic travail, is now the source of the adrenalizing "Sledgehammer" from *So,* a stunning collection of neoteric Brit rhythm and blues spiced with elements of Nigerian high life, Brazilian grooves, and Senegalese *griots.* Gabriel's solo presence has long since been stripped of all theatrical trappings and artifice, as was made apparent by his electrifying Amnesty International tour performance of "Biko" at the close of the "Conspiracy of Hope" caravan at Giants Stadium, in East Rutherford, New Jersey.

He stood sentinel-like in high-collared, drab-olive shirt and midnight slacks, sweating profusely as his singing cut the still night with the skin-tingling elegy to the slain South African poet-activist Steve Biko. "This is a song for a man of peace," Gabriel prefaced, as his new band pounded out a solemn cadence, "and it's dedicated to all the people of South Africa who've just been imprisoned in the last weekend."

The 55,000 in the stadium were left dumbstruck by the moving rendition.

"I feel empty and hollow now that this tour is done," Gabriel confided in a quiet moment after the show. "I'll miss the spirit we shared in the face of all the horrible pain the prisoners of conscience must face." One look at his elegantly lined features, the eyes fixed in a fiery stare, and it was plain that this was a fellow who understood suffering.

"Nice day to be a bird," assures Peter Gabriel, the man who composed the soundtrack to *Birdy,* director Alan Parker's stunning 1984 film adaptation of William Wharton's cult novel about a mentally and physically scarred Vietnam vet obsessed with birds and flight. As Gabriel offers the cheery comment, he shows a radiant but characteristically fleeting grin and gazes out over the rooftops of London's sedate Chelsea section.

"*Birdy* was about the struggle of the spirit," says Gabriel. "It was about the interplay between the traumatized Birdy, the wounded victim, and his best friend, who's ostensibly the tough one. But in the end, it's Birdy who's strong and his friend who's cracking. When I saw the rough cut of the film, I knew I had to do it. It haunted me."

Gabriel takes a seat at a small writing desk in a cozy upstairs quarter of his management office, tucked discreetly in the fashionable Walton Street shopping quarter where tony merchants like Saville-Edells and royal hatter John Boyd have their showrooms. It is a sunny day in May, and Gabriel looks as if it has arrived solely to gain his gratitude, as he speaks of the "eighteen months of torment" that overlapped with the start of recording for *So.*

"I was separated from my family," he says. A slight pause, and then he elects to go into detail. "This for me was a time of a lot of hurt, pain, and a lot of learning. I ended up in a couples therapy group, which was a powerful, humbling experience. Jill and I were wed in 1971, but we still have a lot to discover and resolve in each other. When you're looking at other couples who've made a similar mess of things, well, you see your problems much more easily on someone else's shoulders than you do on your own. You think, 'How can that guy do *that,* act like *this*—and then, 'Wait a moment! *I'm* doing that too?' "

The separation was haltingly healed with the help of marriage counselor Robin Skinner, coauthor, with Monty Python's John Cleese, of a recent book on relationships.

"I uncovered a lot," says Gabriel, "and it's in the songs on the new album, like 'In Your Eyes.' On two recent trips to Senegal, it was explained to me that many of their love songs are left ambiguous so that they could refer to the love between man and woman or the love between man and God. That interested me, because in our society it's a little like the sacred versus the profane—you know, church music, for instance, expresses a religious type of love, and romantic love belongs to the Devil, if you like.

"So I began playing in the lyric with a mixture of the two," he details, relating a stanza:

In your eyes
I see the doorway to a thousand churches
In your eyes
The resolution of all the fruitless searches
In your eyes
I see the light and the heat
In your eyes
Oh, I want to be that complete

"There was another song specifically about lust and spiritual love that didn't make it onto the album," he continues. "It was called 'This Is the Road.' I haven't finished it. A few others fell by the wayside, songs that will probably surface later. One is 'Sagrada,' a working title after the Church of the Sagrada Familia, which Gaudi, the visionary architect, began building in Barcelona in 1884 and was obsessed with until his death in 1926. The song was an interplay between his way of building and that of a lady named Sarah Winchester. She was the heir to the Winchester rifle fortune who, in San Jose, California, started building this enormous home because she was haunted by the ghosts of all the people who had been killed by the rifle. By her death in 1922, she'd added one hundred sixty rooms."

Gabriel's songs, both with Genesis and solo, are fraught with the themes of haunting, searching, and obsession; the potential solace and evil entrapments of religion; the desexualized attributes and sensual torments of love; and, most of all, the terrible yet exhilarating nearness of madness.

"Music has always been therapy for me," says Gabriel. "At one point after the repressive Charterhouse, I was offered a place at the London School of Film Technique, but the choice was between that and Genesis—I went for the relative release of Genesis. 'I Know What I Like (In Your Wardrobe),' a song from *Selling England by the Pound* [1973], gives a good idea of the kind of themes I was keen on investigating musically.

"In it I was picturing a formal English scene in which characters were really battling it out. I was influenced by D. H. Lawrence in the way that he has these territorial skirmishes going on beneath the plot. In this case, the blades of a lawn mower were an instrument of violence within the peacefulness of a summer garden." He grins strangely, a furtive wrinkle. "In the English way of life, beneath the restraint, calmness, and politeness, there's a seething *animal* waiting to get out."

Peter Gabriel was born at 4:30 P.M. on February 13, 1950, at Woking Hospital, Surrey, an Aquarian with his moon in Sagittarius. Weekend dairy farmer Ralph Gabriel, an electrical engineer who did critical World War II radar tests, met his wife, Irene, like him a scion of a large, well-off Victorian family, while on a skiing trip in the 1940s.

Peter and younger sister Anne were raised on the 100-acre Deep Pool Farm in Woking, a commuter town of approximately 77,000 on the ancient River Wey. "It was an extremely modest village that grew up around a railway stop built on the open heath in 1838," he says. "Although it was thirty miles from London, it was completely untainted by the city, a world apart from the land of the living."

When Ralph Gabriel was not delivering calves he was a technician in research and development for the Rediffusion Company in Hastings, where he designed the first fiber-optic cable-TV system. Called Dial-a-Program, a prototype was installed for experimental purposes in the medical department of Case Western Reserve in Ohio.

"Unfortunately, the patents only lasted for fifteen years," says Gabriel, "and the potential of cable TV was hardly recognized at the time. A lot of brilliant study was not made use of or capitalized on—extremely frustrating for my father."

The senior Gabriel, who retired to the remaining twenty acres of the farm five years ago, was determined that his son cultivate a shrewdness he lacked. And so, like his father and grandfather, Peter was pulled out of the local preparatory academy and sent to Charterhouse in nearby Godalming, in September 1963.

The traditional "fagging" (humiliation and enslavement tactics by upperclassmen) of freshmen, as well as the institution's almshouse-meager meal schedule, were virtually unaltered from the day in 1885 when British essayist and old Carthusian Max Beerbohm pointed out the headmaster's wife's fine necklace with the quip, "Every pearl represents a boy's empty stomach."

Somehow, the pimpled Peter Gabriel was still able to add pudginess to his other physical flaws, drawing more than his share of the hazing and physical harassment. He received his first headmaster-administered "caning" (beating) at sixteen for slipping off by train to nearby Guildford to meet his sweetheart and future wife, Jill Moore, the fourteen-year-old daughter of the Queen's Private Secretary, Sir Philip Moore. (Peter's own ancestors were titled aristocrats, Sir Thomas Gabriel serving as Lord Mayor of London in the 1860s.)

Back home in Woking, Gabriel's first acquaintance with rock and roll was a radio tape he made of Johnny Kidd and the Pirates' "Red River Rock." But it was during an autumn 1963 trip with his parents to various Kent coastal resorts that the diffident schoolboy, daydreaming in the back of the car, was struck by the thunderbolt that was the Beatles pealing "Please Please Me."

"I immediately bought a copy in a seaside shop," he says, still charged by the memory. "It triggered a tremendous personal awakening, a leap into a new realm. In no time I knew more than a hundred Beatles songs on piano, and classmate Tony Banks and I used to sneak off from Charterhouse to loiter around a shop called the Record Corner in Godalming. I also began playing the drums."

Gabriel and Banks started a "flower power" band called the Garden Wall. In the early summer of 1966 they formed a loose bond with guitarists Anthony Phillips and Mike Rutherford, members of another school combo called the Anon. Distracted from "hippie rock" by the sound of Stax-Volt soul, Peter moved on to drum in an R&B cover band called the Spoken Word. The shift in tastes had been occasioned by a taboo visit to the Ram Jam Club, the storied underground ska/R&B saloon in South London.

"I don't think there was a white face to be seen there but mine," says Gabriel, breaking into a beam, "and it was the best gig of my life as a spectator. Otis Redding was singing, with Wayne Jackson on trumpet, and that very night I found my heroes. Otis tore into 'Try a Little Tenderness,' and the rapport with the audience was extraordinary. I stood in the middle of the club, as close to the front as I could get without drawing attention to myself, and decided that I wanted to be a musician for life."

All consideration of higher education was shelved as the core of the defunct Garden Wall and the Anon combined in the winter of 1967 to become Genesis. The name was supplied by Jonathan King, another Charterhouse alumnus, who'd rocked the school in 1965 by writing and singing a worldwide Top 10 single on Decca called "Everyone's Gone to the Moon." Soon afterward, King got a job as assistant to the head of Decca Records, and in a rock variation on the old-boys network he began grooming Genesis for the label. A Bee Gees–derived song by Gabriel and Banks, "The Silent Sun," was the first Decca release in February 1968. An album, *From Genesis to Revelation,* was issued thirteen months later, but record buyers found the quasi-Biblical boast a bore and instead bought Cream's *Goodbye.*

In 1970, Genesis jumped to Charisma Records, the art-rock stable of the Nice and Lindisfarne. *Trespass* was recorded, and then lead guitarist Anthony Phillips quit. Ads in *Melody Maker* led to the hiring of guitarist Steve Hackett and drummer Phil Collins, who powered *Nursery Cryme* (1971) and *Foxtrot* (1972) to prosperous sales on the Continent. But the British music critics resented the largely privileged background of Genesis's lineup. These class distinctions had been somewhat magnified of late by the wedding of Jill and Peter on March 17, St. Patrick's Day, 1971, at St. James Chapel, with the lavish reception at St. James Palace.

"In England," Gabriel explains, "because rock and roll is pretty tied up, like football, with working-class mythology, there's quite a lot of press resentment to any ambitions in rock by middle-class people. That was definitely something to battle with in the first few years."

There were also mounting clashes within the group as Gabriel emerged as the sole identity of Genesis's convoluted compositions. Then in 1975, he unexpectedly resigned from the group. It was a jolt to its ultra-loyal devotees, but Peter had planned the departure since the difficult birth of his first daughter, Anna, in 1974. The womb-infected infant nearly died—"What came out was a green lump that was carried away to intensive care in silver foil, like chicken bones."

As the baby lingered on the critical list, Gabriel lost all interest in rock and roll stardom. His band was faced with a leader who now detested the lavish acclaim they'd resented him for. Gabriel pulled the plug on the star-making machine and moved his family to the rural anonymity of the lush Bath valley.

The change in Gabriel was so extreme that some feared for his sanity. "Peter spent the first six months making a vegetable garden and appeared to be going mad," says his wife, Jill. "He would come into the house and play the piano in a very alone world. But I could tell from the way he was playing that he *had* to go out on his own."

When Gabriel's solo LPs began to emerge, they revealed a flair for flinty introspection and doomsday conviction. Songs like "Solsbury Hill," an uplifting tale of the exhilarating loss of childhood innocence that was an allegory for the breakup of Genesis, were contrasted with apocalyptic keyboard soul-chillers like "Here Comes the Flood." Between 1977 and 1982 there were four separate solo offerings titled *Peter Gabriel*, each with artwork more sullen and unnerving than its predecessor. Happily, the records yielded hits, notably "Solsbury Hill," "D.I.Y.," "Games Without Frontiers," and "Shock the Monkey," but what in hell was transpiring behind the scenes?

A soothing copper glow is settling on central London as Gabriel fetches a hot spot of tea and gets comfortable in his Walton Street hideaway.

"I believe that you learn more from failing than from succeeding," he rules, intently regarding the wisps of steam swirling from his china cup. "Yet we have a built-in fear of failure, a *shame* of failure, which I think is pretty harmful. The thing with painful experiences is that you can handle them and bring them out, or you can *bury* them. In me there's a strong urge to bury them sometimes.

"For instance, looking back on my childhood, I always told myself it was a happy time, but it was actually a dreadful time, me hating and being frightened of school and my own loneliness, unable to ever sleep, feeling so isolated. What I'm interested in doing with my music is communicating relief from psychic pain, probably because I'm exploring it for myself. But there are those who argue that pain is also stored in the body.

"With mental pain there's the idea of catharsis, learnt in my realm of interest from the blues. When the blues singer sits there and pours out his heart, he's purging his soul a little bit, and he's doing so for all the audience, who can sympathize and maybe get a little emotion out, too. I know that when I *can* get emotion out, I suddenly feel more alive, just as if I was pulsing with new blood in a way I simply don't when I try to suppress things."

Gabriel's first attempt at shedding his physical and mental armor was est. In the course of the controversial assertiveness training, he confronted the isolation he'd lived with since childhood, particularly the seemingly insurmountable distance he felt from his father, for whom he harbored both an unspoken admiration and a smoldering resentment for his lack of physical or verbal warmth. Despite all its detractors, est at least enabled Peter to hug his dad for the first time in more than a decade.

"He was a bit put off, initially," says Peter with an almost imperceptible tremor. "But I think we like and are comfortable with it now."

While there may be those who deem the current dearth of theatrical disguises in Gabriel's concerts to be a sign of a healthier self-image, he is not so quick to discount the mask's powerful ability to reveal.

"Often in our culture we look at a mask as a device to hide behind. But in many cultures—African, Indian—it's a device through which you can *come out.* In the traditional masked ball situation you have people behaving a lot more bravely than usual. That's not an artificial part of their personality but rather an integral part of their persona that's been allowed a doorway through the mask."

This also implies that Gabriel may use makeup and costumes again.

"Oh sure," he says, nodding vigorously. "I'm also intrigued with projected images in performance, as I was in the Genesis days, and I'm looking into the possibilities of more of a visual show for the next time out. When I see someone like Laurie Anderson, with whom I cowrote 'This Is the Picture (Excellent Birds)' [a bonus track on the tape and CD of *So*], her effective use of media makes me itch a bit.

"I like some of the showmanship and gimmicks of rock and roll, whether it's Chuck Berry's duck walk, Pete Townshend's flailing arms, or the Sex Pistols' antipromotion. I've heard TV producer Jack Good telling how excited he was when Gene Vincent first came to this country to do his television show, and instead of this dark rock and roll monster, coming off the plane was a very polite southern gentleman with a very slight limp. Good then persuaded him to dress in leather and exaggerate the limp. It struck me as an early example of rock and roll myth-making, however contrived, but I like all that."

If personal and artistic emergence from his shell are Gabriel's primary goals, what was the intention behind the generic album titling—which was relinquished only in the States with the naming of the fourth solo album *Security*?

"First of all, it wasn't my intention to name the album *Security*, but rather that of the record company," he notes with enduring exasperation. "I originally thought I would avoid titles and make my records like magazines. When you look at home at a pile of magazines, you remember them usually by the picture on the cover; I wanted it to look like a body of work.

"However, in its wisdom, Geffen Records didn't appreciate this particular line of marketing and was concerned about possible loss of sales to label competitors—Atlantic and Mercury—which had also released records entitled *Peter Gabriel.* It was made plain to me that if I wanted the record released, they wanted a title. In 1982 I issued the helpfully named *Peter Gabriel Plays Live* album.

"Now, the new record has a universal title so that people won't end up buying the same record twice. I'm quite happy that that's happened, because there's a little change in style—I wanted the album to be elemental, alive, unselfconscious."

During this period of awakening and self-discovery, has Gabriel had any especially humbling professional experiences that made him confront his possible limitations as a communicator?

"As an artist there was a time, which any performer *dreads*, when I was booed offstage." He winces, then bursts into laugher. "This only happened to me *once,* but it was while opening for Frank Zappa in Berlin in 1980, and it was an audience older than my usual audience.

"I think they thought, 'Who is this arrogant little *shit* getting up and doing these stunts?' I was coming on strong, mind you, because when I get hostility I probably always come on stronger. But I made myself vulnerable, too, to see if there was any possibility that it would allow a change of mood. It didn't work.

"People were throwing stuff at me, wanted to *punch* me. There was a guy yelling, 'ENGLISH PIG, GO HOME!' I crawled back up onstage and started to do 'Here Comes the Flood,' which was literally the quietest number I had at that point, and that didn't work either. I walked off."

He sighs heavily. "It was my worst night ever as a performer.

Up until then I'd always been afraid of it happening. Now it had happened. Once the hurt and shock wore off, I began to adopt a different frame of mind. After a day's break, the next show was in Bremen with Zappa, and even though it wasn't going over again, I felt relaxed, intact. I began laughing and feeling at home, and the crowd responded. In the end, we did much better—it still wasn't fantastic—but I'd overcome my fear of being challenged, of being rejected by an audience."

Gabriel also let go of petty studio phobias about his work. On Phil Collins's *Hello, I Must Be Going!,* Collins helped himself to the groundbreaking gated drum sound Gabriel and engineer Hugh Padgham had perfected for Gabriel's third solo effort. Critics remarked that Collins had stolen Gabriel's new signature. And some were surprised to note that Peter sang backup on Collins's recent "Take Me Home" single.

"I respect Phil," Gabriel says tensely. "I think he's a natural musician who can sit down and play most things very well. There's respect between us, and we'll be happy to do odd pieces together."

Questions of undue borrowing and the sharing of creative credit inevitably lead to larger issues in the careers of Gabriel, Collins, and other white rockers blatantly influenced by modern funk and African pop.

"For *any* of us musicians who get ideas from other cultures, we get accused of cultural imperialism," says Gabriel. "There are things like the Bo Diddley rhythm that I've heard beat-for-beat in Congolese patterns. Part of what we consider our fundamental rock and roll heritage originated in Africa. Period. If you look at any school of music or art, it steals ruthlessly from anything that excites it. That's a pretty natural process.

"A, I think it's important to digest it a little rather than imitate it. B, I think if there is a lack of balance, people like me have a responsibility to provide it. At the 1982 World of Music, Arts, and Dance Festival I organized, it was exciting to have Burundi drummers playing with Echo and the Bunnymen, Indian dancers with the English Beat, Chinese opera with Simple Minds, and myself—a real mixture. Some of the rock and roll cynics at the time said there was no way audiences would take this, we'd get booed and have bottles thrown, but nothing of the sort occurred.

"I'm still seeking out African talent myself. I got Youssou

N'dour, the Senegalese singer who's a Bob Marley–type figure in his own country, into my Bath studios for 'In Your Eyes'; I think he deserves a much wider audience. And I'm pleased to see that in most record stores in England and the States you see an African section now, the way there was a reggae section ten years ago. Maybe in another decade there'll be a world-music section.

"Music is one of the ways that can combat racism and some of the other divisions between the First and Third Worlds, and rock has gotten richer for it.

"What we're seeing at the moment reminds me in some ways of the 1960s, but it is a lot more practical. The social engagement of rock musicians is positive, although I don't think we can change the world as directly as many people thought was once possible. What we *can* do is provide information and then let people make up their minds. It seems to me that the 'Sun City' project, which I think was very well done, helped—along with news broadcasts—to ignite an awareness in the States of the South African situation. It was a chain of influences. But I don't want to be preached at all the time by entertainers."

Nonetheless, there are urgent messages, subtle and unsubtle, on such *So* songs as "Don't Give Up," Gabriel's heart-tugging duet with Kate Bush, and "Mercy Street."

"True, true," says Gabriel, sipping the last of his tea. "The sensitive treatment Kate gave our give-and-take on that song was gratifying, because it's not just a song about a woman supporting a man in a demanding relationship. The chief thing dragging them down is unemployment, which is presently tearing the social fabric of Thatcher's England apart. The catalyst for 'Don't Give Up' was a photograph I saw by Dorothea Lange, inscribed 'In This Proud Land,' which showed the dust-bowl conditions during the Great Depression in America. Without a climate of self-esteem, it's impossible to function.

" 'Mercy Street' was inspired by the book of poetry and an unpublished play of the same name written by Anne Sexton, the troubled American housewife-turned-writer who, at around age twenty-eight, began writing what would become the collection *To Bedlam and Part Way Back.* A doctor in a mental hospital suggested that she write partly as therapy."

In 1974, Sexton committed suicide at age forty-six. It's been said that we have art in order that we not die from the truth. Certainly this was Anne Sexton's shattered gospel.

"When I discovered her work by chance in a bookstore," says Gabriel, "I was struck that, unlike most writers, who are conscious of their peers or their audience, she was writing entirely for herself. 'Mercy Street' is filled with the messages and imagery of dreams, and a constant search for a suitable father figure, whether it be a doctor, a priest, or God. That search kept her alive longer than many around her perhaps thought she could bear, gave her life meaning, and now her work gives hope to others. That's a kind of magic, I think. Creation as therapy, both the fact and the gentle endorsement of that, is a thread in the material on *So.*"

June 4, 1986, backstage at San Francisco's Cow Palace, 8:45 P.M. Peter Gabriel, dressed in a dark smock over a light-blue shirt and billowy black slacks, is a nervous wreck. Knitting his hands and stalking about as a concerned-looking Sting watches from a discreet distance, he seems to be in the throes of a severe anxiety attack. Sting steps over to put a hand on his shoulder, whispering a few cracks into his ear. Gabriel, his eyelids and brows accented with black greasepaint, chuckles lightly and stops pacing.

Veteran field marshal Bill Graham gives Gabriel and his band their cue, and they scamper up the narrow steps to the platform stage to deliver one of the most superb sets of the entire *Conspiracy of Hope* tour, cresting with a tumultuous version of "Shock the Monkey."

Earlier, Gabriel had stated that the song was not about shock therapy but rather "just a love song, although it's not really seen as that. It refers to jealousy as a trigger for an animal nature to surface."

Onstage, Gabriel imbues the song with a vivid dash of affirmation, testifying that humanity has the will to resist its baser urges, just as the jailer, torturer, and executioner can be dissuaded from their odious duties.

The throng loves the transporting warmth of the singer, and later that evening, as the assembled Amnesty troupe (Bryan Adams, Joan Baez, Jackson Browne, the Neville Brothers, Lou Reed, et al.) rushes before the footlights for the encore on "I Shall Be Released," Sting spies Gabriel ascending the stage steps.

"Come 'ere, mate," he calls out, hugging Peter with a hearty "well done" as they walk up together. Blooming on the old Carthusian's angular features is the fulfillment of finally belonging.

Several days after the Giants Stadium concert, Gabriel is in the Manhattan offices of Warner Bros. Records, taking stock of the whole hectic Amnesty tour and preparing to return to his family in Bath. Attired in his familiar dark clothing, he chats about the future, which may include a select schedule of dates to showcase songs from *So.* The talk turns to another song about psychic and physical torment that Gabriel decided to put on the new record. "We Do What We're Told (Milgram's 37)" is Gabriel's direct appeal for faith in life. The song refers to experiments conducted in New Haven, Connecticut, in the early 1960s by the late Stanley Milgram that tested obedience to authority versus allegiance to one's moral code.

"Various volunteers for the experiment were divided into two groups: 'students' and 'teachers.' The student was connected to electric terminals, and the teacher was put in the laboratory in front of a metal box with buttons that were said to be capable of generating electric shocks to the student. The teacher was then asked to give a memory test to the student and at each mistake was ordered by the scientist conducting the experiment to increase the voltage of electricity—so he thought he was participating in an experiment on punishment and learning.

"But actually," says Gabriel, "the 'student' was an actor, just *acting* the effects of electric shocks, and the test was to see how far the 'teacher' would go in obeying the order to administer the shocks before he would rebel against authority. In the main experiment, 63 percent of the participants were prepared to administer enough electricity to injure the person on the other end.

"At first this seems a very negative thing," says Gabriel, "but I was comforted that some had the strength to rebel, and in the *So* version of the song, which I've been performing in concert since around 1980, the emphasis is shifted to the positive side. I find it scary, particularly with the rise of the so-called Moral Majority, that there's such a readiness to judge other people. In Christ's words, 'Judge not, that ye not be judged.' "

In Peter Gabriel's words, this self-judgment: "There are three layers to me. The first is alert, amiable, and at ease with the world. Then there is the sad, small boy. Finally, there is this instinctive and at times aggressive character. I fluctuate between the three, but to strangers, the third layer only comes out in the music."

And it is the third layer of Gabriel that he himself knows the least. It is the mighty, adept, efficacious side of himself that he feels in performance but cannot relocate when the fury is spent.

He seeks clues to his nature in his father—"my introvert side"—and in the social, organizational, and musical skills of his mother—"my extrovert side"—but they are not accessible personalities. "They were compassionate, loving parents, but like so many from the English middle classes, they had difficulty in expressing emotions."

Anything felt or thought but left unexpressed becomes a secret, and as he came of age, Gabriel found that neither the education he was assaulted with at Charterhouse nor the compulsory chapel attendance intended to salve his bruised psyche offered any acknowledgment of the secrets of private experience. Only rock and roll provided this, and it demands total surrender.

Gabriel has become a confidant of psychotherapist R. D. Laing's and a disciple of John Lilly's sensory-deprivation tanks, where in the perfect darkness of saline-solution-filled confines he can float naked and dream without boundaries.

"I have a selfish life-style in a selfish world," Gabriel frets, and he senses the solution to his own dilemma will be more elusive than the one his wife, Jill, settled on in the wake of their marital reconciliation.

"I was brought up to be a wife and a mother," says Jill, whose second daughter, Melanie, was born in 1976, "but around me the roles of women were changing. It was OK to have a job. I felt very frustrated." And so she took one—counseling other married couples. "I used to watch Peter sing and think I'd like a bit of this person in real life. It worried me. And, of course, I resented his success. But I was attracted to it."

Is there no solution to the conflict between creative spark and personal desire? Carl Jung says in *Modern Man in Search of a Soul* that when a form of "art" is primarily personal it deserves to be treated as if it were a neurosis. The personal aspect is a limitation—and even a sin—in the realm of art. A great work of art is like a dream; for all its apparent obviousness, it does not explain itself and is never unequivocal.

So the search, the frustration, the longing for transcendence goes on.

Meantime, Peter Gabriel can be found in Bath, raising his daughters, wrestling with new songs like one about murdered Chilean folksinger Victor Jara, or arranging music for exhibits by avant-garde artists Stephen Rollov and Malcolm Poynter. He also wants a greater hand in film-scoring than was provided by his work on *Birdy* and the songs he contributed to *Against All Odds* ("Walk Through the Fire") and *Gremlins* ("Out Out"). After all, it was an invitation from director William Friedkin *(The Exorcist)* in 1974 to write an original script that spelled the last straw for Gabriel and the jealousy-strained Genesis; in the brittle denouement, Friedkin's offer was shelved.

Yet not forgotten. What was required, then as now, was a proper facility for brainstorming. To this end, Gabriel is devoting the winter to supervising the founding of a "future arts center" that will have two recording studios and much high-tech audio-visual hardware for the "experience designing" he wants to spend his forties doing.

"The idea of taking the funk on 'Sledgehammer' to a higher level is exhilarating, too," he says. "I used French-African drummer Manu Katche in conjunction with Wayne Jackson of the Memphis Horns on the track, and it was a commanding blend of parallel heritages. I love writing more about romantic sexuality, and I need to discover ways to let my attraction to African funk be mutually enhancing for the participants."

Surely there's a well-worn route to that worthy hybrid, one that Gabriel has already intuitively alighted upon. For the word "funk" is a combination of the Ki-Kongo *lu-fuki,* meaning "strong body odor," and *fumet,* the Creole term for "aroma of food and wine." As for any transcultural karmic rewards, well, in Kongo lore the smell of a hardworking person carries luck to all those it reaches.

Whenever Gabriel leaves his hearth in the west of England during the remainder of 1986, he'll be on tour, plus hustling other musicians ("I've already asked Phil Collins") into appearing at proposed simultaneous live concerts in East and West Berlin on September 16 to celebrate United Nations Peace Day. "We Do What We're Told (Milgram's 37)" may be one of the featured songs in his performance.

"I know why I took so long to record it," Gabriel mulls. "I think I had to wrestle with the subject matter until I could find an interpretation that identified the heartening side of the story, but that also had the ring of objective reality." The song's chorus, which he slowly recites, is simple and eloquent:

One doubt
One voice
One war
One truth
One dream

"I take dreams very seriously," he says softly. "I think everyone should."

Bono Vox 1987

Dublin is the city that cannot easily explain itself. Built in furtive spurts by Vikings, Englishmen, and Irish patriots, men whose emotions were too raw to pack into words, it remains an expanse of secrets. The kind that only face-to-face encounters can unlock.

Like Dublin, Bono is happy to talk, so long as you don't expect every facet of the full story in any of a half-dozen visits. He entered Dublin on May 10, 1960, a newborn in Rotunda Hospital soon baptized as Paul Hewson, second son of Robert and Iris Hewson. The Hewsons were "Dubs," products of the Oxmantown Road area in the center of Dublin, citizens known for their variable temperaments and worldly distrust of easy answers or fixed positions. In a country that has made totems of national identity and the Church, Dubs favor individuality over religion and cultural chauvinism. To a Dub, what's best about life and where it's lived are the new things that occur too quickly to be contained.

The Roman Catholic Robert Hewson earned his salary as a postal employee: a good safe job with a guaranteed pension. In August of 1950 he wed Iris Rankin, a Church of Ireland Protestant. A scandalous move even for a Dub. But Mr. Hewson held to his faith, deciding his wife should raise sons Norman and Paul as Protestants.

Paul was his "da" 's son, most comfortable with the awkward solution, quick to rage and slow to cool, but always leading with his heart. It was in the autumn of 1976 that Paul found a vocation equal to his temperament: rock and roll. Answering a note posted by a fellow student at Mount Temple Comprehensive School, Paul arrived at Larry Mullen, Jr.'s house to find Messrs. Adam Clayton, Dave and Dick Evans, Peter Martin, Ivan McCormick, and Larry himself eager to commence a directionless jam session. In subsequent rehearsals held in a Mount Temple classroom, singer Paul took the lead in organizing the collection of friends into players of recognizable songs (Deep Purple's "Smoke on the Water," Bay City Rollers' hits), while bassist Adam Clayton played the pragmatist in subtly paring down the participants.

The final foursome: Paul on vocals, Adam on bass, Larry on drums, and Dave Evans on lead guitar. It was Steve Rapid, vocalist with a local band called the Radiators, that would give U2 its name, telling Adam about the U2 spy plane, the U2 submarine, the U2 model of Everready battery. Paul, Larry, and Dave were ambivalent about the tag, but no one ever came up with a better one. (In time, the inviting ambiguity of its "You too" implication helped further the band's credo of youthful goodwill.)

Meantime, Paul's house at 10 Cedarwood Road on the Northside of the River Liffey was the hangout for his diverse collection of musical and nonmusical mates. They ultimately formed themselves into a club they called Lypton Village and doled out nicknames. Mate Derrick "Guggi" Watson rechristened Paul as Bono Vox, an alias Paul detested until he learned it was Latin for good voice. Bono renamed Dave Evans as the Edge, saying it captured the sharpness of his features and his mind, as well as his watchful, outsider's ways.

U2's first single was a "U2 Three" EP issued in September 1979 on the CBS Ireland label that contained three songs, "Out of Control," "Stories for Boys," and "Boy/Girl." The material sprang from droning, anthemic basement rock to pop and back, but was special for the wild longing in the vocals and the burred whine of the guitar.

Although it is often written that the band emerged from the British punk movement circa 1977, nothing could be further from the truth. U2's music never reflected any of the scabrous squall of punk, and the closest any of the members ever came to its nihilistic character was Bono's sly masquerade in the fall of 1977, when he caused a small furor in the corridors of Mount Temple by wearing a chain that dangled from earlobe to mouth, held at the lower lip by a safety pin. (The pin appeared to pierce his lip, causing a child at school to scurry from him in tears, but Bono had devised a way to simulate that effect. And he'd dropped the entire look by the next day.)

With the release of their debut *Boy* album in 1980, the distinctiveness of U2's music was fully manifest, the Edge's churring chords, Larry's detonating drums, and Adam's brash bass creating an almost mythological setting for Bono's stories of adolescent awakening. Over the course of a decade, U2 would issue another seven albums (*October*, 1981; *War*, 1983; *The Unforgettable Fire*, 1984; *Under a Blood Red Sky*, and *Wide Awake in America*, 1985; *The Joshua Tree*, 1987; *Rattle and Hum*, 1988) that would advance one of the most uniformly atmospheric sounds since the heyday of Hendrix.

The Edge's techniques, an ingenious exploitation of the overtones and reverberations of amplified guitar, grew out of his own limitations as a player. By utilizing sustain and vibrato pumped to the threshold of their palatability, and concocting piecemeal chord progressions that moved the songs by force of mood instead of melody, he furnished rock with a new sonic paintbox.

What gave U2 lift, however, were Bono's lyrics, a free-association oratory that linked the Dubliner in him with the conflicts of a world small enough to cry for help but large enough to ignore itself. With songs such as "Sunday Bloody Sunday," "Surrender," "The Unforgettable Fire," "Pride (in the Name of Love)," "I Still Haven't Found What I'm Looking For," and "Desire," dispatches of mortal distress, embattled brotherhood, and spiritual hunger were writ large across the imaginations of listeners. Critics sought to cast the band as civil rights activists, religious rockers, or distracted altruists. And while elements of each such perspective swirled through U2's records, close study reveals a purpose far less finite.

The music of U2 is intuitive in its humanism, harsh in its ideals, occurring where the conscience makes war on calculation. "The Unforgettable Fire" is less a song about Hiroshima than an attempt to evoke its meaning in the moment, summoning enlightenment to the consequences of evil, or horror at contemporary disinterest in what happened there. Or something else; it depends on what the song elicits when next it's played.

U2 believes the impulses of Everyman are moral, exploring what can cause them to misfire. So while "Pride (in the Name of Love)" is an elegy for the murdered Dr. Martin Luther King, it leaves open the question of who the real assassins may have been. So whenever the first chords ring forth, they never fail to prompt a fresh interlude of self-examination.

Yet in the midst of all this profundity and sapience, U2 drawns strength from its own naïveté. When the band released their two-record *Rattle and Hum*, they were attacked even in their own country for producing an unsolemn collection that celebrated doctrinaire rock historicism via Dylan ("All Along the Watchtower"), the Beatles ("Helter Skelter"), and Elvis (with three songs recorded at Memphis's Sun Studios, "Angel of Harlem," "Love Rescue Me," and "When Love Comes to Town," the last with B. B. King).

Perhaps the album was perceived as too much fun, and too unsophisticated by those who would chart a tight, logical course for U2. Yet rock and roll has no roadmap but its own instincts. Had U2 followed a route, it would either never have found any fragment of what it's looking for, or have lost interest in the trek a long time ago.

The following interview with Bono took place in San Francisco in the midst of the *Joshua Tree* tour of 1987. At the time, much was being written about the millennial symbolism of the Joshua tree depicted on the LP jacket, and the fact that it can flourish in the most arid climes. The band had encountered the tree while venturing into the California desert, and critics chided U2 for being so wide-eyed in its appropriations of all things American, just as they had earlier ribbed the group for its religious iconology. What, they seemed to ask, do these untutored Dublin lads really know of the world?

But such observers betray an ignorance of the cultural affinities a Dubliner will naturally seek out and amplify. The mesa- and desert-dwelling Joshua tree, so revered by native Indian tribes, is actually a spiritual cousin of the majestic fairy thorns found amid the stone dykes and bare hills of Ireland's ancient cairns and raths. Both are plants of prehistoric longevity and Biblical metaphor, sheltering creatures helpless against man while warning him of eternity.

Oh—and don't dare tell a Dubliner he doesn't understand the delicate use of religion in music. It so happens the first performance of Handel's *Messiah* was in Dublin, at the Charitable Musical Society's Hall off Fishamble Street. The year was 1742, and the concert was hailed as the rock of ages.

Do you think the pervasive rock star mentality of, as you've put it, "Getting satin jeans and a limo," has hurt the music industry in terms of artists building their careers and their voices?

I must say that I couldn't care less if it hurt the music industry, but what I do care about is whether it's hurt rock and roll, meaning the people who buy the records and go to the concerts, as well as the performers. I think it was in 1967 that John Lennon said, "The dream is over." And in 1977 I remember thinking the same thing. But it doesn't have to be over. There are those of us that are still dreaming, still trying to breathe life into the old forms of rock and roll. Rock and roll has given so much to me, and I want to give something back, but I don't want to be a part of what it's become, this ugly monster, this dinosaur. There's this story of St. George stabbing the dragon with his sword. Well, [*chuckles*] we need a few St. Georges around here.

You'd never think we would live long enough to see rock and roll take on a rubric and a costume.

I know. Rock's not about that. It's about pushing the frontiers further forward, in original ways. U2 has always tried to innovate a little bit, to find new sounds, and to try to write songs in a way other people weren't writing them. But rock and roll is also about spirit, and I think the true spirit of rock and roll is somewhere close to abandonment. Jerry Lee Lewis and "Great Balls of Fire," *that's* rock and roll. But it can also be Jimi Hendrix's "Star-Spangled Banner." Rock and roll can mean many things, but it must not stay in the same place.

Ralph Waldo Emerson once wrote that "A man is a God in ruins," yet in a song like "I Still Haven't Found What I'm Looking For" U2 seems to see a lot of potential in modern man.

First of all, I think that man has ruined God. [*laughter*] As for U2, we write songs on so many different levels: politically, sexually, spiritually. People sometimes ask me if there's a place for a spiritual sense in rock and roll music. I think if you dig deep into the rich history of American rock and roll, you find that all great early rock performers came out of old churches in the deep South, whether black or white, and they came out of gospel music. Whether it's Aretha Franklin or Elvis Presley.

Elvis, before he used to go onstage, he used to warm up doing gospel songs! That kind of spiritual confusion for a while knocked me off me feet. I felt very alone in that disorientation because rock and roll in the 1980s hasn't seemed to have that spiritual dimension or be that concerned with anything other than the material world. But now I realize that rock and roll has always encompassed both spirituality and sexuality.

Prince, James Brown, Jerry Lee Lewis, none of them seem to have noticed much difference between the sacred and the profane. It's all one to them as they run it through their psychic trombones. Their emotional investment isn't categorized. Their surrender is complete.

[*Grinning*] I take it that by psychic trombone you mean both their inner listening devices and their instruments. Now when I'm onstage and I'm doing "Bullet the Blue Sky," I'm gonna sing, "A man breathes into a psychic trombone / And through the walls we hear the city groan." [*laughter*]

I'm kind of caught up in this idea of the principle of surrender. As a pacifist, I would call myself an aggressive pacifist. I think you have to seek peace agressively; you can't just sit there with flowers in your hair and *wish* it. Peace doesn't exist of itself, it's *brought* into being; so that's one aspect of surrender. The turning of the other cheek—which is something I don't do very well—that's another aspect of surrender. Cooperation is another.

Edge's old man told me a story once that up in the Himalayas they have these little mountain goat trails around the highest peaks. Sometimes these goats will be going along these two-foot-wide trails, and they'll meet each other thousands of feet up. The way is so narrow, they have a choice of one either reversing course and following the other, or fighting it out. But what these smart mountain goats in the Himalayas have developed, according to Edge's old man, is a solution where one of them lies down, and the other climbs over him. *That* sounds like surrender to me.

And still another aspect of surrender is in the line from the Big Book that basically says, "Unless the seed shall die it cannot really live and grow." In our song "Surrender," which was inspired by the Martin Scorsese film *Taxi Driver,* I was trying to describe an ordinary situation that the movie brought back to me. It reminded me of a girl who got married, couldn't make it work, got into dire straits, and became a prostitute, and eventually she went to the tallest building to throw herself off. I don't agree with that aspect of surrender.

Surrender shouldn't be giving up. It's being open to *bending* your spirit in a wise way.

"A Celebration," the U2 single from 1982, was always most interest-

ing for its ambiguities. It implied that you can celebrate the wisdom that comes from a huge mistake, as easily as you can celebrate the elation that comes from a big success. It's always a very personal decision.

At that point, U2 was probably celebrating the fact that it could make it to the end of the song. [*laughter*] We were so awkward, musically speaking, when we got together as a band. We couldn't really play our instruments or anything. But that didn't *stop* us from playing them.

With "A Celebration" I was just trying to put my finger on a feeling I felt in Dublin at that time, which was that the tide was turning and people were standing up straight. The mood was shifting in the country. You know, the Irish people had 700 years of the British, and as soon as we got rid of them, we had the Church. I felt in that song that the climate was there for new possibilities, even if they were uncertain ones—meaning that it might be apolcalypse next week, but then again maybe it might *not* ever be.

You felt that in your own way you could influence the fates either way?

In a sense. Because we'd gotten somewhere ourselves by just feeling our way. For instance, Edge can't remember the chords to that song—or at least he couldn't the last time we asked him. It's incredible, because he doesn't play normal chords. He just makes them up, and it's almost a muscular memory, and he has to find his fingers on the fretboard before he can remember how to play things. So that if he hasn't played a song in a while, it's tricky.

So is the song itself. You sing in it that you "believe in an atomic bomb," meaning you believe in the potential of its dark power.

I believe it exists, yes. I threw that line in deliberately because I knew it would cause some confusion of a kind I like. I say, "I believe in a Third World War / I believe in an atomic bomb / I believe in the powers that be / But they won't overpower me." It was quite shocking at the time for people, but it's there to trigger an awareness.

Two of the emotions that shine through in the song "I Will Follow" are trust and daring, which are probably the two greatest avenues of human potential.

I like this idea of risk. I think that risk is important, and very important to rock and roll. Every time we make a record, we wonder if we're making a big mistake. It's like after we made the live *Under a Blood Red Sky*—which came after *Boy, October,* and *War*—everyone wanted us to be an all-out rock and roll band. They wanted us to be the new Who. We were good at making that kind of noise, but there would be no risk in making *War Part Two.* I like to think that we took a risk at turning right at Greenland and choosing instead to work with Brian Eno and Daniel Lanois on *The Unforgettable Fire* and *The Joshua Tree.*

You must take risks with your music—but also take risks at the microphone, where you have the choice either to reveal or conceal. As a writer and a singer, I wish to reveal rather than conceal because that's the essence of soul music—and I use that term in the widest way.

It's true that people did expect U2 to be the Who once its live sound had been shared on record, but U2 decided to reinstill subtlety, nuance, and tenderness with the next two LPs. It's nice to see a band interested in itself, rather than interested in what works in the marketplace. If rock is supposed to spring from youth and truth, why does it need these shrewd commercial rituals?

It doesn't. On "In God's Country" U2 says that we need "new dreams tonight." There are not enough dreams. U2 are dreamers, and our dreams have come true, a lot of them. When we first got together as a band to play music, people said we couldn't play, then people said we'd never make a living out of it, and so on.

With "In God's Country" I didn't know for a while if I was writing about Ireland or America. Eventually I dedicated the song to the Statue of Liberty, because I decided I wanted to write about the American Dream and how I fear for it turning into a nightmare as people stop asking questions because the answers are too difficult.

I was saying that this new era we're entering into is almost more traumatic than the Industrial Revolution was. We've got whole new technologies and computer chips that promise to set us free. I worry that they may enslave us. You see massive unemployment in the U.S. and America, and I wonder where the people are that will rise to the challenge. These ideas of being a Marxist-Leninist or Reaganite, these are *old* ideologies. Where are the new dreamers? Democrats and Republicans just seem to be reading the textbooks titled *How to Get Elected.*

Politicians are supposed to be leaders, but they're not allowed to lead, because they have to be backed by a complex party system that teaches them not to dream, and to be pragmatists and say, "Here's my card. Call me." These kinds of structures are suffocating, and they're applying tourniquets that stop the new blood from getting through.

In my country, the tragedy is that young people are being forced to leave it because there is no future for them there, and they are *our* new blood. I would love some of the new dreamers to be Irishmen and women, but we need them at home rather than in America.

U2 seems to be fascinated with the social experiment that America represents.

There's no such thing as an America, in one sense. It's a continent, not a country. And yet I love Americans because I find them still open-minded, with the ability to trust. But there's a danger in being so trusting—it can bring Reagan to power.

There was so much potential in the sixties, it's a shame it was diluted by drugs and so much abuse. But real changes did come about. The sixties got us to the eighties, but we had to get through the seventies with its flatulent rock and roll and full-of-shit attitudes. Musically, the best thing that came out of the seventies was the revolt, the reaction against corporate rock, as brought on by Patti Smith, Television, the Sex Pistols, and the Clash. At times the Clash became a cartoon, but nevertheless they made big music in the sense that it was *needed* music.

In 1976, a fifteen-year-old kid named Larry Mullen, Jr., put a note on a bulletin board at Mount Temple Comprehensive School in Dublin, looking for recruits for a rock band. Looking back on those auditions in Larry's kitchen, is U2 very different from what you thought it'd become?

It's funny. We met for the first time in 1976, I think it was September or October—nobody can *really* remember—in Larry's kitchen, which was about as big as the drum kit *in* the kitchen. We all wanted to be in a rock and roll band, and it didn't matter what kind of rock and roll band. I think Adam had one speaker and one amplifier, and we all plugged into it. I remember thinking—along the lines of so many others at the time—that rock and roll must go back to its roots. I remember getting out old Buddy Holly and Rolling Stones records and thinking, "We should make music like "Not Fade Away" and "Paint It Black"!

And we would try to play other people's songs, but we just couldn't play them. We played them so badly we decided to write our own songs. Eventually, we were called a punk band because we were a part of this punk era. The only thing was, we couldn't tell Larry that we were a punk band [*grinning*] because he didn't want to be in one. So I was getting my head shaved and listening to the Stooges and the MC5, and Larry was going, "We're not a punk band, now, are we?" And I'd say, "No, no, we're not a punk band. Just keep playing the drums there." [*laughter*] 'Cause he'd just turned fifteen years old and didn't respond to punk early on. He came in later. At age sixteen we got him to throw away his flared trousers and cut his hair.

The band's pre-U2 names were the Feedback and the Hype.

Ohhhh, the past has come back to haunt the future! Feedback, or *the* Feedback—or something like that—was a name given because of the sound we made when practicing. [*chuckles*] Ours was the sound of people tuning up. Then we called ourselves the Hype because of the lack of it. Also, I think Bowie had a band called the Hype years ago, and we were into Bowie at the time. Then we became U2 in '78.

Describe the session that produced the original demo version of "Out of Control."

Well, I wrote "Out of Control" on my eighteenth birthday. I'd just woken up, and the thought occurred to me that the two most important events in your life—birth and dying—are essentially out of your hands. You have no choice, it's out of your control. The song itself is juvenilia. I think we were trying to rip off a song by the Skids.

When we went to Japan recently, I found the most interesting interpretation of the words to "Out of Control" that I've ever heard in my life. I don't know where they got this, but they translated it as "Monday morning knitting ears of gold." [*laughter*] They're probably better lyrics than the ones I wrote!

The version on *Boy* ended up pretty good, but the demo version currently circulating, which was done at a four-track studio, that's pretty bad. I remember, after first hearing it, that I just wanted to stand on O'Connell Street on the bridge over the Liffey and jump off, because it was our best up to that point, but obviously just not good enough. Although I haven't changed a bit, because I think that about every record we record.

I always found it intriguing that the teachers at Mount Temple gave the band room to practice in, considering the fact that there's always been this historic tension between secondary school education and rock and roll.

Well, Adam got kicked out of high school for rock and roll, or at least he stopped doing anything else but rock. Edge handed in a few essays toward the end of his school days, but not much. However, Mount Temple has been turned into this Rock and Roll High

School in mythology, and the reality was that there were one or two teachers on the staff there that recognized us as something special and thought they shouldn't stop it. But there were also one or two who were after our blood.

But there was this unused music room, and I made a deal with this teacher that I wouldn't interrupt his classes—because I was a tearaway in those days and difficult to teach—if he let us use that room. So he let us use it. Eventually we just stopped doing our schoolwork, and our idea of homework was checking out old Velvet Underground records.

You and Edge had the same guitar teacher, right?

She was a classical guitar teacher who wasn't at the school but came in once in a while. Can you imagine me trying to learn classical or jazz guitar? That was funny. Edge and me had a *few* lessons with her.

Looking back, what was U2's initial 1980 tour of America like?

I loved being on a bus, coming across America, looking out the window, reading books, meeting people after the concerts. Going back to their places and sleeping on their floors, or them coming to sleep in our room. We used to have thirteen or fourteen sleeping in our hotel rooms every night.

I've very fond memories of that time, and I resent the fact that we're becoming cut off now from that experience. I go out the back doors of halls now and say hello to people, and I meet some great ones. But there are a lot of people who don't really see me anymore; they just see this idea they have of me, and they want a bit of it. Whether it's your shirt or whatever. But I know there's other people who are still into the music. And I still love being onstage in America. But the process of getting from one stage to another has become a less exciting one.

I've always felt that U2 has been effective at diffusing any adulatory frenzy in your shows, keeping fans focused on the concert rather than any movie in their heads.

I repeat myself here, but it's still the music that's special, not the musicians. We have to continue to get that across to ourselves as well as our audience.

Live, "Sunday Bloody Sunday" and "40" are two of U2's most potent antiwar anthems. The band appears to discover something new in them each time it plays them.

If you listen to the songs, *they'll* tell you how to perform them. With "Sunday Bloody Sunday," once Larry starts that beat and

Edge comes in with those opening chords, it seems to take on a life of its own. That song means so much to me because I'm not sure I got it right. I might have gotten it wrong.

I originally wanted to contrast the day of Bloody Sunday—when thirteen innocent people were shot dead in Derry in 1972 by the British Army—with Easter Sunday. I wanted to make that contrast because I thought it'd point out the awful irony that these two warring faiths share the same belief in the one God. It's so absurd, this Catholic and Protestant rivary.

In the end, I'm not sure I accomplished my aim successfully with the words, but I think we did do it with the music. The spirit of the song speaks louder than the flesh of it.

In 1916 James Joyce wrote, "The artist, like the God of the creation, remains within or behind or beyond or above his handiwork, invisible . . ."

[*Nodding*] I think that at U2 concerts it seems to me that the audience almost applaud themselves. I like that. When they hear songs from a few years ago, their own memories are woven into them.

As for the quote you've just read about disappearing behind the creativity, *that* can work against you as well. Around the time of "Sunday Bloody Sunday" I was reading the John Lennon handbook to songwriting, which says to take a statement, put a backbeat to it, and then go. But I stopped trying such broad strokes after "Sunday Bloody Sunday" because if you get them wrong, you can make complex situations into black and white ones when they ought to be gray.

Overall, how do you now regard The Unforgettable Fire *and* Joshua Tree *albums?*

Those last two records are documents of when they were made, and where we were as people. I love "4th of July" just as an instrumental sequence because it reminds me of some of Miles Davis's music. Adam and Edge were just improvising as the tape was turned on. The track often plays at shows as we take the stage, and it gives me a tingling reminder of the spontaneity and responsibility of those records' ideas. I loved the blurred colors of all *The Unforgettable Fire* because it arrived at a time when rock and roll felt slick and too precise.

Take a song like "Bullet the Blue Sky." How do you write about fear? I was trying to describe the fear I felt, based on a situation in which I found myself in El Salvador. I wanted to describe, in a very primitive way, these peasant farmers as they look up and see these helicopters and fighter planes from the corrupt government coming over their village to burn it out. What the government does is designate areas they call fire zones, which are basically areas sympathetic to the rebel guerrillas. Everyone is labeled a guerrilla, and they tell them to move or be burned out. They tell everyone to leave their village that they were born in and grew up in, because they can't seem to find which guy is the guerrilla.

But there's also an underlying image and theme in the song, which is that of a character who's sitting somewhere else far away, reflecting on the horror. He's a musician, and he won't go outside; he just won't. And if you ask him why he won't go out, he says, "Because outside is America." American foreign policy has led to a lot of hardship and deep bloodshed in Central America. And in the song it's as if the musician, with his intimate relationship to his instrument—his saxophone—can become a conscience, a vision apart from the world surrounding him.

People need to use music to make connections and links, not to insulate themselves. U2 are big admirers of Dr. Martin Luther King, dedicating "Pride (in the Name of Love)" to him. Dr. King once said that "nothing in the world is more dangerous than a sincere ignorance."

It's true. Many good people are comfortable with ignorance. And it's uncomfortable to know and feel you can't do something about a situation. As for me, I don't know more than a lot of people. I just read papers and watch the TV, and feel the same impotence so many others feel. But if you don't know what to do about something, you should find somebody else who does.

Unlike Dr. King, U2 make pathetic preachers. That's not our job. And we're not on a speaking tour or a lecture tour, we're on a rock and roll tour, hopefully making music that will inspire people to whatever they freely *want* to do, whether it's walk their girlfriend home or join Amnesty International. It's up to them. [*smiling*] I like to think that maybe they can do both.

You wrote your first blues song not long ago, after meeting Keith Richards.

I'd always envied people like Bob Dylan and the Rolling Stones because they have these traditional forms to plug into. We'd never written a conventional ballad or a proper blues! I recently spent some time with Keith Richards, whose music is still alive to all other forms of music, and seeing him hanging out and playing, I wanted to play along but I felt I had no suitable songs to offer.

So I went home and wrote a blues song in a few hours. It was set in a South African prison, and it was written about a man who is just about at the point of taking up violence. It goes: "And in the shithouse a shotgun / Praying hands hold me down / If only the hunter was hunted / In this tin can town. / Broken nose to the ceiling / Broken back to the floor / I scream at the silence / That crawls under the door. / The warden says / The exit is sold / If you want a way out / Silver and gold."

I wrote "Silver and Gold" down really quickly, and recorded it quickly. I'd never done anything completely on my own like that, separate from U2. I enjoyed it, and Edge, Adam, and Larry enjoyed it. It was something completely new for me.

We need new kinds of blues songs, and we also need to refresh our approach to love songs. "With or Without You" sounds like a new kind of love song.

Thank you. That's the way I feel about it. What I was interested in there was taking a love song out of the back seat of a Chevrolet and placing it down the road a few miles, where these two lovers got to later on in life. There's nothing more radical or revolutionary than two people loving each other. One, because it's so uncommon these days. Two, because it's so difficult to do.

I believe in the power of love, yet love is an elusive thing. I wanted to write a song that got into the mental violence of a real relationship. Because I've become interested in the violence of love, and how you see lovers together tearing at each other. The world that's described in most rock and roll love songs is all sweetie-pie, and I wanted to get to that place where people fight and spit and work it out along *real* lines.

"Trip Through Your Wires" is another kind of love song, a plea for connection, along with an acknowledgment that connections usually aren't easy to understand. They're often unexpected, and often accidental.

Yeah—"Angel or devil, I was thirsty and you wet my lips." The image of woman that runs through that song and all of *The Joshua Tree* has a real duality. You can't make your mind up whether this woman has come to rescue you from drowning, or if she's the siren who's drawing you onto the rocks. It's pure joy on one level, but with an unexpected sexual dilemma on another.

Sometimes I know what I'm writing about, but often I don't. There's a song called "Tomorrow" on *October* that I thought was about Northern Ireland and the violence of that situation, but it was really about the violence in my own life and a funeral I'd been to. I didn't know that until later.

"Gloria," for instance, was to document my own spiritual confusion at the time. I don't feel very well equipped for the job I've been given as a singer or songwriter. Maybe that's why I have the faith I do, because I'm very dependent on the idea that God has given me a gift. Therefore [*laughter*] it's His responsibility to get me through it!

Beastie Boys

1987

The suspicion nags: There is a latent message in the Beastie Boys' dense rap-rock. But how to discover it?

Well, hold the front of the Beastie Boys' *Licensed to Ill* album jacket up to a mirror, and the refracted image reveals a hidden affront—the tail-section serial number of the crashed plane on the cover reads: EAT ME.

Is this the covert communication in question? Nah, just a smidgen of frathouse smut.

To get to the bottom of this lingering minor mystery, one must plumb the psychic, acoustic, and personal bramble of the Beastie Boys' roots, the thicket of ambition that lifted this white, solidly middle-class burlesque of the ghetto's pariah rap and hip-hop culture to the top of the nation's record charts.

But first a word to the blissfully uninitiated. Late in 1986, the brattishly nicknamed trio known as the Beastie Boys (Adam "MCA" Yauch, Michael "Mike D" Diamond, Adam "King Ad-Rock" Horovitz) issued *Licensed to Ill,* an unprecedented album-length amalgam of hard-rock *Tilt,* tree-house poetry, and the appropriated defiances of underclass street rappers. It appeared on Def Jam, the aggressively peculiar new rap–speed metal–soul-and-vinegar subsidiary of Columbia Records, fabled stable of Bruce Springsteen, Billy Joel, and Barbra Streisand. Reactions ranged widely and wildly. For some, *Licensed to Ill* greeted the oracles like the braying din of indefatigably lousy neighbors. Others complained that the record rang out like a Little Rascals' Disco Night debate at the He-Man Woman-Haters Club. But a solid three million purchasers were impressed with what they heard as an inspired mixing-board bouillabaisse of hip-hop's torrid beatbox tick-tock and the tumultuous adrenalizations of early heavy metal. Moreover, the whole shrill lockstep was paced by back talk from baby-faced suburban nihilists weaned on *Star Wars,* the Iran-contra scam, and Gary Hart's stained underwear.

Licensed to Ill's first sublimely loutish single, "(You've Gotta) Fight for Your Right (to Party)," went Top 10 in a big hurry, and the LP itself not only swiftly notched the No. 1 slot in the U.S.A.'s sales surveys, but became the fastest-moving product in its record label's illustrious history. Two more hits, "Brass Monkey" and "She's Crafty," ensued.

Now the growing fear among detractors is that the Beasties' expanding following is as puerile, brash, and mutinous as its heroes' music.

The Beasties' comically cacophonous cant is a splenetic homage to beer shooters, suckerpunching, all-night fornication, angel-dust hors d'oeuvres, and horseplay with firearms. Interspersed with all the obnoxious raillery are lifted snippets of vintage Led Zeppelin, Steve Miller, and Aerosmith guitar riffs; muddy excerpts from the theme of the bygone "Mr. Ed" TV sitcom; guttural antigay rhetoric—plus other sonic snapshots of the scrap heap of civilization. Depending on the attitude of its devotees, *Licensed to Ill* is either a turntable parody of eighties teen rebellion, or a tape-deck checklist for a curbside Gomorrah.

In the larger world, the less def, i.e., hip, homemakers, and town fathers of America, shrug heavily and turn a deaf, i.e., disinterested, ear to the clamor—until they catch their kids repeating snatches of the doggerel soliloquies (of, in this case, "The New Style") that pass for lyrics:

"I got money and juice / Twin sisters in my bed / Their father had AIDS so I shot him in the head!"

Dismay has escalated as the Terrible Trio has begun to make stage appearances across the heartland, spraying Budweiser on spectators, scratching their crotches distractedly as a dumpy go-go dancer wriggles in an elevated cage beside them, and mumbling between-numbers repartee that gets quoted in "The Cribdeath, Iowa, Gazette": "How many songs have we done? . . . Only two? . . . Sorry, I smoked all this opium before. . . . If anybody wants to buy some, talk to the girl up there behind bars."

Once again, as P.T.A. groups howl and the music press winks, rock and roll has a lot of explaining to do. But how bad, in truth, can three pimply juveniles be if they could appear on "American Bandstand" and Joan Rivers's "Tonight Show" rip-off without shattering either program's scripted decorum? Hell, even Vanna White recently went backstage to meet them and lived to speak about it.

Every generation has its varieties of junk rock, purple pop, and raunch roll. In the fifties, there were the Doug Clark and the Hot Nuts, dark lords of the college-fraternity circuit. In the sixties, the Fugs and the Mothers of Invention took the wonderfully filthy Pigmeat Markham–pre-TV Redd Foxx approach to topical burlesque and ran it through an electronic biker-hippie encoder. Meanwhile, jive-speak monologuist Melvin Van Peebles kept the lunatic fringe of soul and rhythm and blues grandiloquently honest with the do-rag declamations of his brilliant *Brer Soul* LP.

Come the seventies, George Clinton's Parliament-Funkadelic crew had everybody babbling to a daffy downbeat. As the eighties arrived, Jamaican reggae toasters and dance-hall deejays helped trigger the inner-city Kool Herc–Kurtis Blow rapping that the Beasties are now bending to their own silly will.

Thing is, all of the aforementioned seminal influences were in it for the real deal, their brazen lives inseparable from the aberrant art. There wasn't a poseur, dilettante, or slumming moonlighter in the bunch.

The present mission, then, is to discover if the Beastie Boys are strictly jake, or simply an increasingly *Blade Runner*–styled society's answer to the Banana Splits (four live-action animal characters named Snorky, Bingo, Fleegle, and Drooper whose surreal-cute rock and roll band was a staple of Saturday-morning TV from 1968 to 1970—and they made albums, too).

This summer, the Beastie Boys barnstormed the States in two flamboyant phases (before dropping from sight to film their first star vehicle, tentatively titled *Scared Stupid*). The first leg of their road show included new Def Jam artists Public Enemy, the sinister two-man voice of the sub slums' ominously emerging denizens. The second strike, which was entitled the *Together Forever* tour, was shared by veteran colleagues Run-D.M.C., macho rappers of the black middle-class variety.

The European sprint of the *Together Forever* tour was marred by heated backstage fighting (Beasties' management depicted it as a "tiff") between the Boys and Run-D.M.C. at Switzerland's Montreaux Festival. Arriving in England, the Beasties were banned by the British Holiday Inns, and Adam "King Ad-Rock" Horovitz was arrested May 30 at a West London hotel for his alleged role in a bottle-and-beer-can-throwing incident before 3,000 fans at their concert earlier that evening. Four kids were reportedly injured and five collared by police in the show-canceling melee at the Royal Court Theater, at which the waggish audience chanted "We tamed the Beasties!" King Ad-Rock was ordered to return to London in midsummer for a court appearance (at which he was exonerated). All in all, the two joint international concert treks made for a disquieting spectacle.

Catching up with the Beasties cavalcade at its halfway mark, one finds the Boys themselves to be distinctly isolated from the mechanisms that ballyhooed their remarkable commercial beachhead. As such, the meeting proved an ideal opportunity to scrutinize the three supposed malcontents at close range, in order to determine precisely what they had to offer by way of content, offense, and pretense.

It's perfect weather for a hanging, or a hip-hop siege. An unrelenting assault of rain, flooding, and funereal gloom has moved New England officials to ask President Reagan to declare assorted states of emergency in the region, which would qualify afflicted areas for federal disaster relief. As a consequence, citizens of the traditional cradle of revolutionary democracy are in a tangibly edgy mood as the bad boys of rap invade their terrain.

Looming before a two-thirds-capacity crowd at the Providence Civic Center in Rhode Island, a supporting member of Public Enemy's act keeps a machine gun trained on the largely white teenage throng, while featured rappers Flavor-Flav and Chuck D spew boastful bile about gang violence ("My Uzi weighs a ton!") and the pleasure of misogyny (snidely admonishing the "Sophisticated Bitch" of the song title that she deserved to be beaten "till she almost died"). This is black rap at its grimmest, an invitation to stomp on tombstones and tenement corpses. A punk-thrash combo called Murphy's Law does a short set to clear the air, but they grate on already frayed nerves. By the time the headlining Beastie Boys are introduced, the faithful in the front rows look even paler than the acutely pasty-faced Boys themselves. It's Saturday night, but everybody's too bummed to boogie.

Several days onward, the Beasties troupe rolls into the Worcester, Massachusetts, Marriott at three in the afternoon for a 9:00 P.M. stand at the local arena. The three young stars, looking peaked from knit-together nights of postconcert partying, are roaming around the corridors of the bland motor hotel, desperate to elude a German rock writer, his wife, and the CBS International press agent who is squiring them around.

"She's such a bitch!" yowls MCA, twenty-two, an unshaven pug with broad shoulders and a hard stare, as he ducks into his room, slamming the door in the faces of the CBS flack and her party.

A booming, female "Fuck you!" is heard to resonate in the hallway. MCA collapses on his half-dismantled bed in laughter, as cohorts Mike D and King Ad-Rock take seats at either end of the suite, which looks as if it was redecorated with a hand grenade.

"Fuck *her*," says Mike D, twenty, the lanky, acne-caked Huntz Hall look-alike, who is best known for the sizable Volkswagen-bus ornament suspended on a gold chain around his bumpy neck. "We should get the keys to her room later and bust in."

"Yeah, it's room 504, isn't it?" rejoins MCA, who is clearly the ringleader and de facto theorist of the group.

"That room might be the German guy's and his wife's," warns nineteen-year-old King Ad-Rock, baby-faced wiseacre and ritual dissenter. "We'll kick the door down, and she'll have him tied up inside!"

The three grouse a bit more about what a "fucking snot" the CBS lady is, dish on various interviewers they've reduced to frustrated sobs, and then discuss luminaries they've encountered since their rise to notoriety.

"We get along all right with Johnny 'Rotten' Lydon," MCA offers. "He's a fucking nut job. We played on a bill with him once in Washington, D.C. Johnny is not like anybody you can actually carry on a conversation with. He just yells and screams and dances in the hallway—"

MCA's attention is suddenly drawn to the room's flickering TV, which displays the Nike running-shoe ad utilizing the Beatles "Revolution." Since the commercial licensing of "Revolution" and 250 other Beatles songs is controlled by Michael Jackson's publishing company, the talk turns to another marginally adjusted superstar. The Beastie Boys are openly annoyed at Jackson, who recently filed a cease and desist order against Los Angeles radio station KROQ for playing the Beasties' outré, unreleased rendition of the Fab Four's "I'm Down." Jackson had earlier refused to allow the Beasties to include that version on *Licensed to Ill.*

"Michael said something to [his producer] Quincy Jones to the effect of, 'I hate the record, and I hate them,' " explains Mike D with a smirk, "so it doesn't look too hopeful."

"I wonder," says MCA, picking a scrap of watermelon rind off a teetering pillar of room-service trays, "if Michael Jackson knows how to lick the pussy?"

"I dunno," says King Ad-Rock, his smooth brow abruptly furrowed, "but if Michael can bend down, he can do it, right?"

"It's bogus to use 'Revolution' to sell sneakers," MCA adds, "but TV is so fucking boring anyhow, I figure I can turn the picture to black and just listen to the Beatles on network television, which is pretty def."

Run-D.M.C. signed a deal with Adidas to pitch a line of basketball shoes. Has anybody approached the Beasties about product endorsements?

"All the time," MCA assures, nipping at the mangy melon rind and then putting it under his pillow. "We tell them to fuck off. A clothing company offered us a half-million dollars to stand there in their clothes for one minute."

"It seems," says Mike D, musing reflectively, "that every car commercial is just stealing a Motown song." And it also seems that every Mike D fan is stealing a VW hood ornament, or other brand, to wear, a national Mercedes-Benz spokesman reporting that dealers ordered 12,600 replacement ornaments this spring, nearly triple the amount sold last year.

"But on the other hand," says King Ad-Rock, "I'd rather watch a stupid car commercial rip off Motown than watch Bruce Willis do it. And I'd rather watch anything than Bruce Hornsby and the fucking Range. Actually, I used to work in a recording studio that did television commercials."

"Yo! We recorded 'Cookie Puss' at a studio that was a jingle house," MCA recalls. "A place called Celebration. Nobody in the music industry knows about the place because it's such a tight-ass, bullshit studio full of losers."

MCA is referring to the creation of the Beasties' most renowned underground effort, a twelve-inch independent single released in 1983. The A-side of the record documented an actual taped phone call to an unaware counter girl at a Manhattan Carvel outlet, the caller inquiring about the ice-cream company's nationally advertised children's "Cookie Puss" cake novelty. The B-side was "Beastie Revolution," a snide send-up of Rasta reggae and Jamaican deejay toasts, complete with jaundiced patois mimicry. *Creem* magazine recently described the single, with curious understatement, as "seemingly sexist and racist."

It's a toss-up as to which track is more contemptuous in tone, but the "Cookie Puss" tête-à-tête, a gleefully offensive aping of an insolent black youth harassing a female Carvel employee from a pay phone, probably wins out:

"Tom Carvel was gonna sue us," says MCA, "until his nephew Kevin talked him out of it. We're friends now with Tom Carvel's nephew."

"He put a good word in for us with his uncle," says Mike D. " 'Cookie Puss' is a big collector's item. I heard it now sells for between $75 and $100 in stores, but it never really sold all that much when we first put it out."

"I got like eight copies of that shit!" King Ad-Rock exclaims. "I could make a fortune!"

That's what obscure rocker Rick Rubin may have assumed when he first listened to "Cookie Puss." Regardless, he saw a perverse promise in the platter. Rubin, a graduate of Lido Beach High School, an integrated Long Island institution, had long been enamored of the G-string soul of Rick James and the Ohio Players, as well as the post–Led Zeppelin stridulations of such heavy-metal acts as AC/DC. His band, the Hose, combined these tastes into a rude blare that could have been termed "peep-show metal."

Rubin entered New York University in 1981, and began frequenting the downtown rap night spots. He ran around with rapper T LaRock and deejay Jazzy Jay, who made a rap record, "It's Yours," that featured an unconventionally conventional chorus break, just like a mainstream pop record would have.

It was a glimmer of a crossover ploy, and Rubin shrewdly sensed the winds of rap were shifting—in the direction of commerciality.

When "Cookie Puss," a hip-hop salvo from a white outfit, permeated the downtown scene, Rubin sprang into action. He started the Def Jam label in autumn 1984, headquartering it in his N.Y.U. dorm room.

At the time, Adam "MCA" Yauch was enrolled at the Elizabeth Seeger School on Franklin Street in Greenwich Village, and Michael "Mike D" Diamond was attending St. Ann's School in Brooklyn Heights. Fledgling bassist Yauch and guitarist-percussionist Diamond cofounded the original Beastie Boys in 1979 with guitarist John Berry (who named them) and drummer Kate Schellenbach. They were a marginally functional punk band when they encountered Adam "King Ad-Rock" Horovitz, a Brooklyn Tech dropout enrolled in New York's City As School (CAS) work-study program for problem pupils. Horovitz was also head of a punk group called The Young and the Useless. While hanging out together at Stimulators and Slits concerts at such clubs as Hurrah, Tier 3, and Rock Lounge, the chums elected to turn their two bands into a semipermanent double bill. Eventually, the three lads merged their ambitions under the Beasties banner, releasing *Polly Wog Stew,* a seven-inch EP, on the tiny Rat Cage label in 1982. When Rick Rubin appreciated "Cookie Puss," the sole track salvaged from an abortive studio session, the Beasties discarded their instruments in October 1983 and became rappers with Rubin (alias DJ Double R) as their stage deejay and studio Svengali.

Def Jam Records' inaugural release was LL Cool J's "I Need a Beat." The Beasties' "Rock Hard" came next. Rubin took a tape of "Rock Hard" to another collegiate New York entrepreneur, Russell Simmons. The son of a Queens school superintendent, Simmons was producing younger brother Run's rap group, Run-D.M.C., while at City College. Rubin worked out a distribution deal with Simmons's Rush Productions, and the Beasties' 1985 "Rock Hard"/ "Party's Gettin' Rough"/"Beastie Groove" EP became a sensation among the club cognoscenti, its invocation of "I'm a man who needs no introduction / Got a big tool of reproduction" a standard dance-floor chant.

When their single, "She's on It," was included in the shoddy Warner Bros. rap movie *Krush Groove,* the Beasties landed a six-week slot as the opening act on Madonna's *Virgin* tour—during which they were continually booed. They fared better on Run-D.M.C.'s *Raising Hell* concert sweep, but that hitch was denounced nationally for the violence that plagued its venues. The excursion to promote *Licensed to Ill* is therefore a crucial test of the Beastie Boys' viability as a draw.

As expected, the ticket-buyers seem to be predominantly white middle-class kids, with a healthy black representation on the fringes of the halls. However, judging from the New England dates, the black faces virtually vanish after Public Enemy's sets.

Canvassing the blacks as they leave, I am offered comments that dismiss the Beasties as "soft shit," "white clowns," or "corny." Yet all bestow lavish praise on Public Enemy, whose Def Jam debut LP, *Yo! Bum Rush the Show* (a reference to gate-crashing), is a stark replication of underclass rage, set to a bleakly nonmelodic power groove. Public Enemy's "Chuck D" Ridenhour and William "Flavor-Flav" Drayton began at Adelphi University's radio station on Long Island but are self-appointed spokesmen for an ultra-disenfranchised ghetto generation whose parents and grandparents have known only welfare. Regrettably, the Black Muslim–allied anger in their sound also has its own racist implications. Theirs is less a form of entertainment than a street-theater dress rehearsal for "The Fire This Time."

Which is why the Beastie Boys' performances are steeped in unnerving, wholly unintended ironies. As they bound before the footlights to deliver their raucous takeoffs and cartoon recastings of authentic inner-city rappers, the audience is dealt a plethora of current catch-phrases, crime colloquialisms, and drug nicknames—but no inkling of the painful realities they describe. Like the "Amos and Andy" radio show of a bygone era, the Beasties embody and parade fresh stereotypes of black-ghetto culture while flooding the country with a hip lexicon that whites can exploit to mocking or bigoted effect.

The Beasties themselves, although enmeshed in the colorful, bohemian side of eighties urban culture, are not exactly products of its mean streets. King Ad-Rock is the son of the late Doris Keefe Horovitz (to whom *Licensed to Ill* is dedicated) and distinguished forty-eight-year-old playwright-screenwriter Israel Horovitz, a Fulbright and Guggenheim fellow known for such stage and screen works as *The Indian Wants the Bronx, Author! Author!,* and the acclaimed new off-Broadway comedy-drama *North Shore Fish.* MCA's parents are accomplished architect Noel Yauch and New York City school-system administrator Frances Yauch. Mike D's mom is noted interior designer Hester Diamond. The Boys' credentials are plainly those of parental headaches from privileged households, and their decision to embrace rap was as casual as it was fashionable.

What became of the instruments the Beastie Boys once played?

"Some of it's in my parents' attic," says MCA, looking uncomfortable with the question. "We used to have stacks and stacks of amplifiers, because we bought these Univox amps that sounded like shit but looked really cool onstage. It was all bogus."

"But now it's really cool," Mike D ventures warily, "because we get a lot of free shit from guitar manufacturers. Adam [Horovitz] likes to say he was a guitar virtuoso, but when he joined the Beastie Boys, he only knew one chord!"

"Give me a guitar," King Ad-Rock protests, scanning the instrumentless room. "I'll show you!"

"I'd just like to say," Mike D continues, "that when we first met Adam Horovitz, hippy Adam was like, 'Look guys, there's nothing gay about talking to plants . . .' "

"Look, I had gerbils as pets," says King Ad-Rock, flushed. "That doesn't mean I walked around looking for butt hugs. I used to go to the same places, the same clubs, as these two guys, but I hung out with people who were a lot cooler and more intelligent than these guys. I went to better schools and had more advantages than these two. The friends I had back then, we're *all* friends with now. The friends *they* had back then, we don't even talk to."

"I stay in touch with *nobody,*" MCA retorts, King Ad-Rock's jibe having found its mark, " 'cause I don't need any of them. I knew they were bastards from the beginning.

"Anyhow," MCA continues, changing the subject, "we were getting good as a band around the time we played a show in Boston at the Rat."

"We sucked," says King Ad-Rock, testy. "We always sucked."

"We played a good show!" MCA insists, pressing the point, his dark eyes aflame. "There were times when I walked out feeling happy with the show we'd played. We never sounded like fucking Aerosmith, but we were fucking good. This was in 1984."

"It was the summer of '62," Mike D quips, "with the Strawberry Alarm Clock! You know—'Incense and Peppermints.' "

It's pointed out to Mike D that the Strawberry Alarm scored that hit in the psychedelic heydaze of 1967, not the Shirelles/Four Seasons pop equinox of 1962.

"I guess," Mike apologizes softly, "we don't know our rock history. It's true. We don't."

Such bantam bursts of vulnerability and vague embarrassment are in simmering conflict with the Beasties' impudent public pose, an image they lack the experience and stamina to sustain.

Collected within the blank walls of this shoebox-sized room, they are tangibly lonesome in each other's presence, starved for individual attention. Thanks to their fragile fury and its occupational focus, for perhaps the first time in their separate lives, they are not being ignored. It excites like restitution, and it tastes like revenge.

"Musically," King Ad-Rock cracks, deftly discrediting Mike D's confession, "we're pre–Al Green and post–Al Lewis, the actor who played Grandpa on 'The Munsters.' "

"It's just important right now, when we're going to Lincoln, Nebraska, and wherever, that we show our rap roots," Mike D mutters coldly, "because otherwise they stand a very good chance out there of never actually seeing a rap group."

How, by the way, did the Beastie Boys come to compose "(You've Gotta) Fight for Your Right (to Party)"?

"It was toward the end of the album," says MCA, growing surly. "That was one of the last things we recorded."

"It was summer 1986," says Mike D. "We wrote it in about five minutes. We were in the Palladium with Rick Rubin, drinking vodka and grapefruit juice, and 'Fight for Your Right' was written in the Michael Todd Room on napkins on top of those shitty lacy tables. I remember we made a point there of like, 'Look, we gotta get shit done,' and we sat at one table, really determined to accomplish something. It was just like it is now, trying to fit everything in. We have to fit our movie into this touring."

What's the plot of *Scared Stupid*?

"The plot," says King Ad-Rock, "is Yauch gets laid, loses his virginity."

"Yeah," MCA deadpans, "I get a hundred blow jobs a day, but I haven't gotten any girl to give up the pussy yet."

There is an oddly pregnant pause, and then MCA offers a personal vignette.

"I lost my virginity in a tent in Holland, and that's true. I was on the first day of a bike trip. It was one of those American youth-hostels trips where you're not allowed to have sex or do drugs. I was a little dude and she was nineteen, big, and real def. The leader of the trip found out that we were fucking after a while, and threw her off the trip because she was older and was supposed to know better than to fuck."

"I lost my virginity," King Ad-Rock volunteers, "when I was at camp."

"I lost mine," Mike D chimes in, "in my friend's basement. It was just one more thing I was trying to fit in."

His cohorts groan at what MCA decries as a "Doc-and-Johnny-type gag," and then they excuse themselves to prepare for the evening gig.

The assembled mob, nearly a sellout, are rowdier than previous recent houses, perhaps because it's a school night out. Public Enemy and Murphy's Law make no impression on the three-quarters Caucasian sea of restive adolescents, but when the lights go down for the main attraction, a forbidding spark is struck.

Actually, it's a can of hair spray, which a girl in the upper balcony has turned into a torch with her cigarette lighter. She hurtles the can toward the deejay's booth (which sits atop three towering cans of Jolt Cola), easily missing Hurricane, the six-foot, five-inch dreadlocked blood who also doubles as the Boys' bodyguard. Still, the effort has enough spontaneous verve to almost eclipse the onrush of the Beasties, who launch into a burping recitation of "Time to Get Ill."

The Boys are greeted with a mighty whoop, a sizable number of onlookers brandishing their heretofore hidden Budweiser in solidarity. The Beasties respond with shaken-and-sprayed suds of their own, their hand-held mikes becoming secondary props in the sodden melee. Deejay Hurricane moves from one music track of *Licensed to Ill* to the next, jumping his turntable needle and supplying scratchin' counterrhythms with a tad too much haste.

Thirty minutes into the contrived bacchanal, the crowd roar grows dull, the collective alcohol and sugar rush spent. Their jaws slack, their eyes glazed, they appear to be reeling with the last feeling they had anticipated—boredom.

The aisles suddenly clog with kids, but the traffic is flowing in the wrong direction—toward the exits. Ten minutes more, and the subtle trickle has turned into a torrent, spectators departing in packs of ten and twenty. Long before the obligatory encore, the hall is half-emptied.

Outside, the surprisingly subdued throng ambles or stumbles off into the darkness, some retrieving stashes of beer, others pointing in the direction of neighboring gin mills. Many are cold sober but clearly bemused. What's the problem?

"Aw, we saw enough," says one husky teenager from Charlestown, speaking for his huddled friends. "They weren't really playing the songs."

"There was no band," bitches a dungareed guy from Framingham, his arm around his disappointed date. "We expected live rock and roll, not some recorded stuff."

"Right. Check it out," says a skinny young man from Somerville, who's leading three blond ladies in leather and spandex. "We were up for some serious guitar and drums. Some good jamming on the raps. We couldn't believe it was just them and the damned sound system."

Didn't they realize that most rap music is merely syncopated monologues over prerecorded tracks?

"They had *one* real band there," the slim young man challenges, his narrow face stiffening with annoyance. "The Beastie Boys could've had their own musicians, too."

"Yeah," seconds one of his blondes, "we wanted to hear the music they played on the record. Not just some cheap tape recording of it."

Despite their miscomprehension, the disgruntled patrons have a point. Straight rap performances lack the musical dynamics to fully gratify an arena's worth of people, and there's certainly little in the essential, rote presentation to scrutinize, admire, or celebrate. Especially on this scale, the notion of live instrumental backing for hip-hop—the players primed to parry and thrust against the raps, building them into ballsy new configurations—is infinitely superior to what actually takes place. Besides, the Beasties were only going through the motions tonight, forgetting or disregarding the words to much of their material.

When confronted about the lack of genuine musical interest in their shows, the boys begin to get skittish in the extreme.

"Well, we play instruments in the studio," says Mike D apologetically. "We really do. We're not the Phony Boys."

But there are no such musical credits to be found on *Licensed to Ill*'s album sleeve.

"Listen," says MCA coolly, "most people don't know it, but we coproduce and write the songs for the records."

"We thought this whole Beastie thing up for ourselves about eight years ago," says King Ad-Rock, "and if we make albums that everybody *hates,* we'll still be happy."

Which raises a final question. Youth culture has been bluffed and gulled before by comfortable middle-class kids who were indulging a self-important passion or a convenient nihilism. Retracing the 1960s, the bulk of a privileged generation's political zealots disappeared into Wall Street boardrooms and "country chic" life-styles, leaving the working class to clean up the mess.

Are the Beastie Boys indeed in rock and roll for the long haul, or will they wind up as fat corporate executives or real estate magnates, their musical career a dimly recalled dalliance?

"As far as I'm concerned," says MCA, his voice exploding into a rattled bellow, "I'm just gonna fuck everybody! I wanna be an executive and a lawyer *and* a real estate magnate. Whattaya think, I'm naive and stupid?"

"Hey! Hey! Don't say that!" shouts Mike D, as he shoots King Ad-Rock a cautioning glance. "Be cool, man. Are you crazy or something? Don't tell 'em that!"

"Why the fuck not!" says MCA, on his feet, indignant. "Because it is—" He instantly reads the genuine alarm on his companions' faces, but his pompous ire has its own momentum. And though his voice drops to a skidding whisper, it's simply too late to stop those awful words:

"*—the truth.*"

Jon Bon Jovi

1987

Has somebody got a coat hanger? Quick! Hear me? Bon Jovi needs a coat hanger! This is an emergency! Lissun to me! This girl outside, she—I need a coat hanger for Mr. Jon Bon Jovi!"

The husky bruiser in black is barreling through the otherwise sedate corridors of WSHE-FM, a south Florida rock radio station, declaiming his distress.

Two startled young men poke their heads out of somewhere. "John!" yelps the willowy one to his puggish pal. "We can't have that guy running past a live microphone screaming that Bon Jovi needs a fucking coat hanger!" He tugs at the front of his frayed HEDONISM II T-shirt. "Think about it, man. Our image with parents of chicks in this state is bad enough without people getting *that* kinda announcement over the airwaves!"

"Outa my hands," says his lion-maned companion, Jon Bon Jovi, dressed in blue Adidas stretch pants and matching tank top and rubbing his cleft chin—the trademark punctuation of his Mediterranean good looks.

Bon Jovi picks up an issue of *Billboard* and begins thumbing through it, calmly thinking out loud.

"I tell you, I couldn't sleep last night. Too many girls outside the hotel screaming like crazy. Jeez! So I sat up listening to Hank Williams's *Greatest Hits Volume*

Two." The Williams song that finally took Jon's horny mind off his fortissimo female fans, he says, was "Mansion on the Hill," largely because it struck Jon that no less an artist than Bruce Springsteen may have gotten the idea for "that song on *Nebraska*, "Mansion on the Hill," directly from Hank—the concept, the title! People say I steal—hell, I borrow. I love Springsteen as much as anybody, but the next time somebody tries to tell me he's a complete original . . ."

It seems the insomniac Bon Jovi seeks a *Billboard*-like tally sheet to buttress his own humbler borrowings. Alas, art is not the business of keeping score.

Jon pauses, looks up at his jumpy friend as the hanger entreaty resounds in the background and shrugs. "Completely outa"—a small, growing grin—"my hands."

It's a sun-swept banner Saturday at WSHE-FM, 103.5, in Fort Lauderdale, Florida, on Saint Valentine's Weekend—traditional prelude to spring break in the edgy eighties. Heavy cruising along beaches and breakwaters from Miami Beach to Hollywood, Florida, is already bumper-to-bumper berserk, and every dashboard radio and ghetto blaster along the twenty-five-mile seaboard stretch has been synchronized for the just-concluded live chitchat with singer Jon Bon Jovi and guitarist/sidekick Richie Sambora. And now it's time to slip the concert-bound rockers back into their waiting limo. But, no, that's where one overwrought nymph, trying to seal herself up inside, has accidentally locked everybody, including herself, out. Hence, the frantic search for a wire hanger. Soon, a chauffeur springs the door, and these cowboys are on their way.

The brief interview was one more dash of genial hucksterism for a sold-out concert stand at the local sports arena by Bon Jovi, the biggest new American band since the advent of another coliseum-filling hard-metal act that carries its leader's last name: Van Halen.

Hard metal is a pop merger of hard-rock blare and heavy-metal bluster whose greatest identifiable traits are *any* identifiable traits at all—e.g., Eddie Van Halen's ferocious guitar virtuosity, Sammy Hagar's adenoidal howl, or Jon Bon Jovi's splendidly whooping good-time warble, served up on such likably loutish roadhouse fare as "Runaway," "In and Out of Love," "You Give Love a Bad Name," "Livin' on a Prayer," and "Wanted Dead or Alive."

Still, it's neither the petrous material nor Jon's pealing pipes that have enabled his band to notch several consecutive No. 1 singles from *Slippery When Wet*, the 10,000,000-selling album that knocked

Bruce Springsteen and the E Street Band Live/1975–85 out of the peak slot in the country's record surveys. Bon Jovi's massive acceptance isn't rooted in its musical prowess, though Sambora is a reasonably dextrous guitarist, Tico "Hit Man" Torres a flinty drummer, and Alec John Such and Dave Bryan more than facile on bass and keyboards, respectively. It isn't the recklessly choreographed stage show, either, in which John soars savagely on a Peter Pan wire, while the band weaves an elastic net of sportive stridor below.

No, the key elements in Bon Jovi's recent popularity ride are, in ascending order, the sloppy grin on Jon's mug, made ubiquitous nationwide by nonstop touring and numberless bedroom beefcake pinups; the fact—which he gleefully volunteers—that his group's handle "sounds like some sort of jeans or spaghetti sauce"; and, most of all, the corkscrew hair twisting across his rippling twenty-five-year-old chest. The bashful but game Jon Bon Jovi (baptized John Bongiovi) is strong evidence, both symbolic and actual, that rock and roll primacy—despite the majority of rock headliners who are a tad long in the tooth, stiff in the ligaments, and soft in the saddle—remains the province of newly exploding hormones amid the freedom with license to exploit them.

This mating dance between Bon Jovi, its baser urges, and its potential mass audience comes at a critical juncture in the rock epoch. After a period of standoffishness born of market sampling, focus groups, and a smattering of outside political pressure, MTV (and the record-industry trendmeisters it mirrors) is again dispensing hard metal in a big way—along with special programming that spotlights its chief practitioners, Bon Jovi and the Bon Jovi–discovered Cinderella. Not long ago, such acts were taboo to trumpet, because they upset parents and delivered only cult-sized sales for all the headaches they inspired. But now, with rock so accessible to twenty-to-forty-five-year-olds, teenaged kids absolutely demand something only they can love, and hard metal fits the high end of reflex rebellion at the record-store cash register.

The members of Cinderella, by the way, look exactly like their anti-Disney handle suggests: oily androgynists and reupholstered cross dressers, cranking out skull-splitting doses of cartoon despoliation. These pixilated dim bulbs can push an easy 3,000,000 albums a season to average kids with average sociosexual phobias. Catering to a mere developmental impulse in a generation weaned on a relentlessly recycled toy-rock rubric, Cinderella cannot hold a candle to Bon Jovi in terms of long-range commercial potential. That's because Bon Jovi appeals to those who have outgrown comic-book heroes and now want somebody who resembles them on their best night out.

Bon Jovi fans, particularly ones from borderline-rural suburbs like Jon's own Sayreville, New Jersey, fiercely identify with his apparent hormonal ferment and, in concert, cheer his every celebratory Muff Dive (a Bon Jovi–concocted quaff, equal parts vodka, peach schnapps, and cranberry juice, fast emerging as a juke-bar staple). While the guys in Bon Jovi's audience can easily if wishfully see themselves in Jon's good fortune, the girls, well, they envision him in a linen envelope.

Rock and roll is one livelihood without a heritage of rectitude. That the four horny instrumentalists who support the bandleader in Bon Jovi's eager enterprise are voluntarily becoming minor characters is owed largely to the fact that most are slightly older, more worldly-wise, and they're getting a flamboyantly undisguised charge out of showing the kid the ropes.

"When we met Jon," says Sambora, "we saw, for a change, an unjaded, professional young guy who knows and lives his business. We gave up wives, girlfriends, homes, you name it, to go 150 miles per hour with him toward the end zone."

Heard this speech before? *Uh-huh.* Except that when Howlin' Wolf, Muddy Waters, Jimi Hendrix, and Brian Wilson expressed the need to excel, their soliloquies had none of the language you hear in investment banking or the front offices of the NFL. True rock and roll demands purity of purpose in *some* visceral category or other.

"The song 'Wanted Dead or Alive' is about the way we live," Richie continues. "We are modern-day cowboys—we ride into town, put on a show, take the money, hit the bar, take the ladies, and we're gone. And we do the same thing the next night in another place." He winks. "The fans want to take a piece of you home, and their parents, they wanna throw us in jail, see us hung." He shrugs happily, nudging Jon. "So we're wanted: dead or alive."

"I don't mind," Jon says brightly. "No complaints here." Is this backhanded affirmation the trickle from an actual wellspring of creative passion? Where does Bon Jovi get its inspiration for such songs as "You Give Love a Bad Name" and the more pointed "Social Disease"?

"The gutter," Jon assures me straightfaced, even in this era of feckless sybarites and deflated debauchees. Bon Jovi's true quest, it seems, is for females who are professional cowgirls, who know and live *their* business.

"That," Jon smirks, "has a lot to do with why we named the album *Slippery When Wet.*"

"We gave Bon Jovi the best table in the house. They made this place their headquarters while they recorded *Slippery When Wet,*" says Eric Polson, twenty-three, manager of Vancouver, British Columbia's leading strip club, the No. 5 Orange Street Showroom Pub and Hotel on Main Street.

"In spring '86, the guys would come in every night, order hamburgers and a drink from our [insert commercial jingle here] thirty different kinds of Scotch and sixty imported beers," Polson elaborates, proudly gesturing around the oak-and-brass-appointed nightclub. "We made them feel at home. The No. 5 is not like the *unpleasant* strip clubs you usually see in the States. Our strippers are recruited from the finest dancers in Canada, and our clientele includes the best Vancouver business people and visiting foreign executives, as well as other dignitaries who are in town. The girls take the stage from an elevated area that leads directly to the dressing room, so there's a great view from everywhere in the room, but normally there is no mixing with the customers."

Normally?

"Well, see, the girls would come out before and after their acts to hang out with Jon and the band, help them unwind." Which is a polite way of saying that Norma Jean, Jessey, Cybelle, Laurie, Jamie, and Evelyn went out of their way, in every blood-rushing sense, to help these boys reach their avowed end zone with all pistons firing. Whenever they appeared on the raised strip platform to spotlight their attributes, the darlings put an extra half twist of zeal in their peel to please the randy rockers crawling over the front table. Afterward, they nuzzled with the lightheaded lads over cocktails, reacquainting them with a time-honored tenet of the rock life: What you don't see, ask for.

If Jon and his colleagues somehow lacked imagination when it came to informal applications of these girls' vocational verve, they were suitably galvanized, Eric Polson assures, "by Evelyn and Laurie, who do the shower act."

The shower act?

"You don't know about the shower routine? We have a special

performance every evening with Evelyn and Laurie. An illuminated glass ladder comes down from the ceiling, and they ascend as our custom-built light system goes into action. The girls dance for about ten to fifteen minutes and strip completely. Then our Plexiglas shower on stage is turned on. The girls hop in and soap up, get a nice lather going.

"Jon and the band were checking all this out, having a wonderful time, and they got the idea for the album from Evelyn and Laurie—*slippery when wet!*"

Back in Florida, as the 1987 Bon Jovi *Tour Without End* bumps and grinds onward, Bon Jovi confirms, "That's more or less how it was. We had done an old-West-style album-cover photo with this tough little five-year-old tomboy, who was dressed in dirty jeans and a cowboy hat. We put her in a corner with her punk-tomboy attitude and shot that for the cover, thinking we'd call the album *Wanted Dead or Alive.*

"We took the Polaroids of the cover back to the No. 5 Orange, and I was sitting there with my drink, looking at 'em, thinking they look too cold and stiff. And as I'm thinking, the shower routine starts and the two girls begin dancing to a Bon Jovi song, 'In and Out of Love.'

"I wasn't paying a lot of attention, just waiting for the girls to get off from work so we all could get out of there.

"So I'm looking over my shoulder at the girl, and I'm listening to Richie complaining about something, and then I'm watching the girl soaping herself up.

"We started talking nasty things, saying, 'I'll *bet* that's wet! Soap it up! Slippery when wet—just like the road sign!'

"Everybody thought it'd be a great album title, but we wondered, How do we take this shower act and get it onto record shelves in shops across Middle America? Big problem."

While Jon Bon Jovi wrestled with that marketing quandary—ultimately settling for a photo of a black-plastic trash bag splashed with water, the words written on it in his own fingertip script—the girls had dropped the soap, left the stage, and toweled off for a night in and/or out with the band. The after-show lineup would vary, Evelyn and Laurie sometimes going along for the ride, plus Norma Jean, the Marilyn Monroe look-alike; Jessey, a sandy blonde with a frizzy halo; Cybelle, a gorgeously ripe brunette; and Jamie, who's dark-haired and dramatically athletic; plus a few friends from the No. 5 Orange's sister strip spa, the Marble Arch.

The entire troupe would usually gravitate to the condominium Bon Jovi had rented for the more than two months it took for the band to complete its recording at Little Mountain Studios, Jon ushering the women into makeshift weight-training rooms to pump ironies until the sun came over the surrounding mountains.

"We'd put the girls into Jolly Jumpers," Jon says, referring to a spring-supported exercise harness devised to keep tots upright while providing happy bounceability. "They have amazing muscle tone. It certainly was an education," he summarizes.

More than likely. Does that mean that the lady heard moaning ("Ohhh, uuuhhhh, ohhhh, right there, ohhhh—you mean that's it?") in abruptly terminated ecstasy at the start of "*Social Disease*" was one of the No. 5 talent roster?

"Nah, that's Dirty Angie," says Bon Jovi. "She wasn't a stripper. She was one of Richie's other friends up there. We made a lot of friends, gave them nicknames. Richie, he calls me Captain Kidd. The King of Swing is Richie's nickname. His comes from two California women whose names have to be protected, but one of them is an L.A. rock star and she saw Richie one night, late. She called him the King of Swing, and I guess I should evade the rest, because he had a *lot* of fun with them."

Obviously, the band members and Jon share a certain code as well as a musical bond. Rock has traditionally been the world in which you can do as you please at any cost your conscience and physical constitution can stand. The life-style is predicated not so much on personal excess as on the will to pursue a curiosity about oneself to its limits.

When keyboardist Bryan says, "Before we sing harmony, we've got to get into the right frame of mind; we've got to drink a pint of beer and get some bare ass in our face," is he hinting at a behavioral pedigree by which the band is bound?

"Absolutely," says Jon. "Tico and Alec, they used to play in strip bars before we got together in 1983. The girls would turn around and flash the band nightly, because they couldn't show it all to the audience. That's why Tico wants to buy his own strip bar and call it Tico's Firehouse. He flew home during the making of the record to check out locations but hasn't found one yet.

"It's a dream for him, right? And every one of us has his own dream, something he's always wanted in the real world. When we got signed to Mercury Records—on July 1, 1983—there was a lot of tough stuff going on. Tico quit Frankie and the Knockouts; Alec quit Phantom's Opera to devote a life to being broke; people divorced and sold their houses; and me and Tico wound up living in this little apartment in Philadelphia, being pretty miserable a lot. The point of view in so many Bon Jovi songs, like 'Living on a Prayer,' is 'Whew, man, growing up is *tough.*' "

Jon was born on March 2, 1962, the son of hairdresser John Bongiovi, Sr., and his gift-shop-owner wife (and former Playboy Bunny), Carol, in Sayreville, New Jersey, a 110-year-old township tucked into the sprawling clay fields at the midsection of the Garden State. The Raritan River port's first important product was sun-baked brick from the gooey argil, and a good many stately edifices along the country's Eastern Seaboard were constructed at the turn of the century with Sayre & Fisher Brick Company's "reds." Today, the borough's chief baked exports are Hydrox cookies from the gigantic Sunshine Biscuits oven on Jernee Mill Road.

Jon, like his father, itched for something slacker than the factory life. His mother toted home his first guitar—acoustic—from a trade fair before he became a teenager. Jon distinctly recalls wrapping the instrument in a blanket and throwing it down the cellar stairs "to hear the weird *twong* of the strings as it crashed."

Al Parinello, a guitarist working in an area club band, gave fourteen-year-old Jon his first lessons.

"He asked me, 'Why do you want to learn to play?' I said, 'To get chicks, what else?' 'Good thinkin',' said Al, and the first song he taught me was 'House of the Rising Sun,' about the New Orleans whorehouse.

"That was the same year I lost my virginity—to an older girl. By fifteen, I was an old man. But I was never very good at picking up girls, and I'm still not." He seems embarrassed. "I had no lines, so music was my method."

To finance any additional ambitions, he toiled part time in the Sayreville 7-Eleven, commuting on his Suzuki 75 via the tracks of the Pennsylvania and Raritan River railroads to avoid being busted—he didn't have a driver's license. With some of his first paycheck, he purchased a copy of Bob Dylan's *Blood on the Tracks*—

no irony intended—the album that sparked his interest in music as a possible way to go.

"I began hanging out at the rock concerts at Kennedy Park or the block dances on the tennis courts behind the Borough Hall, getting an eighty-nine-cent pint of beer to oil me up. By this time, girls were easier to find, 'cause instead of going to Sayreville High basketball games, I was hitting the hippest Asbury Park nightclubs."

The leading one of the mid-to-late seventies was the Sunshine Inn, where the Bruce Springsteen–bossed Steel Mill gigged before crossing the street to the after-hours Upstage Club to watch the likes of B. B. King and Aretha Franklin bassist Chuck Rainey woodshed when they were in Asbury. Tico Torres and Alec Such were frequently among this slit-eyed crew, since they were musically active on the Jersey Shore's intersecting "Barbary Coast" circuit of strip joints—the Serenado, the Tropicana, et al.

When Rocky's Warehouse, a cantina catering to the younger crowd, became the Fast Lane, it joined the Stone Pony as one of the crucial see-and-be-seen teen spots.

"The first time I played the Fast Lane," says Jon, "was with the Fat Pet Clams from Outer Space. Later, I did better and jammed with Bruce and with the E Street Band. The clubs would close around 3:30 A.M., and I'd get to school at 8:00 A.M., be out of there at noon, go back to bed and then return to the clubs."

Jon was in a ten-piece rhythm and blues outfit called the Rest when it played the last dance permitted at Sayreville High. He and his girlfriend skipped the senior prom to spend the night sipping beer in Southside Johnny's dressing room during a concert at the Great Adventure amusement park. The next week, he and the Rest had their first 8,000-seat date at Freehold Raceway, on a bill with Hall and Oates.

Jon had other groups—the Wild Ones, Johnny and the Lechers, the Raze—the best being a Motown-minded combo, the Atlantic City Expressway. They opened for Springsteen, for Southside Johnny and the Asbury Jukes, for Squeeze, and then they broke up.

"I was a high school graduate, and in Sayreville that meant I was either gonna go to Middlesex County College, join the Service, get a job at the Sunshine plant or the Hercules chemical factory, or be a rock and roll star."

Jon wound up with a day job sweeping up in a New York City recording studio owned by his second cousin. "When no one was in the studio, I could go in with whoever was the working assistant engineer, and he would learn the board in the control room while I was learning to make records."

When "Runaway," a demo by Jon that included E Street keyboardist Roy Bittan, got chosen for a regional compilation LP of newcomers by WAAP deejay Chip Hobart, Bongiovi became Bon Jovi, enlisting Dave Bryan and the oversexed saloon stalwarts Jon had been bumping into: Tico, Alec, and their chum Richie, who had a combo called the Message.

If Jon had ever peeked in on the Sayreville High–Woodbridge High basketball games, he might have encountered Richie much earlier.

"I was in a bar band, like Jon, but I was committed to the team," recalls Sambora. "I brought my massive tape deck onto the court to play Mountain's "Mississippi Queen" for warm-ups. The coach kicked me off the varsity squad for partying too hard after we lost a game and mooning the cheerleaders' bus. For the time being, I get paid very well for similar behavior."

Since 1984, they've made three LPs together: *Bon Jovi, 7800° Fahrenheit* ("I thought," says Jon, "the title was the temperature where solid rock melted, but—aw, it's not important") and *Slippery When Wet.* Appropriately, Bon Jovi also put one song on the soundtrack to *Light of Day,* the Joan Jett–Michael J. Fox movie about a broken-down "van band" raging against life's bleak returns.

Weeks after Fort Lauderdale, Jon is stretched out in a Chicago hotel room, getting ready for another concert, ruminating about the forthcoming product.

"You know, during a layover in New York, we cut a few tracks with Cher, one of them called"—he chuckles—" 'We All Sleep Alone.' I'm coproducing her new album! Man, I can remember being a little jerk watching 'The Sonny and Cher Comedy Hour,' trying to convince my folks that Elton John, who was a guest, was John Lennon! Can you imagine? What a *stoopid* punk I was! Jeez!"

But he's gaining more deep background at each stop as Bon Jovi continues its *Tour Without End,* coming to your town sometime between now and Christmas. At each sports arena, Richie asks the management to set up the facility's pro basketball hoops so he can practice his dunk ("The other day, the Houston Rockets let me use their courts, gave me a uniform"); Tico mulls over the ifs and buts of Tico's Firehouse ("It would definitely be cool to do—maybe one room of dancin' girls, one room of dancin' guys; somethin' for everyone"); and Jon, sometimes wearing his souvenir No. 5 Orange staff shirt, fantasizes about the cowgirls in Canada ("We still keep in touch").

The hardest part for the members of Bon Jovi will be staying in sync with their outré appetites and ordinary aspirations as the record-company machinery lifts them toward a prime tax bracket and classier patronage. Bon Jovi's idea of a good time may be its sole link, however tenuous, to a voracious but vanishing rock-and-roll ethos in which you follow your flawed heart wherever it leads, never apologizing, never compromising, never needing to explain anything beyond the bare-wires candor of the music itself.

Whether it's Springsteen, The Who, or Joan Jett, they all have flourished in the past or the present because they became themselves, for better or worse. And Jimi Hendrix wasn't a victim of rock and roll; he died from being Jimi Hendrix. It's okay to be who you are in rock, as long as you're more comfortable with the fact than with the image. Otherwise, the truth is quickly airbrushed over, deleted from bios and press releases, and in the future is addressed, if at all, far beyond the purview of popular tastes and judgments.

If rock and roll means anything, it means that nobody should ever be afraid of his hopes and hungers, that you can get a special thrill out of the fact that there's only one you and you're never gonna come again, and that there's nothing more important than at least trying to get what you want in life, from the riveting woman across the room to the sold-out coliseum where you can re-create the big beat that pounds in your chest. It's all a matter of personal agenda. Someday, when these guys grow up, there will be more to this story.

The band is due for a sound check at greater Chicago's Rosemont Horizon entertainment complex. Bon Jovi has a lot of collective details to attend to before hitting the stage, including a stop to pick up a band friend, Seka.

Seka? The most prepossessingly seductive blond doxy in modern cinema porn? The supersiren who has headlined such classic cinema sex romps as *Between the Sheets*, *Lacy Affair Pts. I and II*, and the 1980 scorcher *Rockin' with Seka* (featuring, according to ads, "the hard pulse-pounding action that Seka fans have come to expect")—*that* Seka?

"Oh, sure," she confirms. "I'm a *very* big fan."

And so it goes: another town, another show, another canny, thoroughly professional cowgirl along for the ride.

As Eric Polson put it back at the strip pub's special good-bye bash, trying to characterize the *Slippery When Wet* band's last night in British Columbia, "Our club, our girls, are exactly like Bon Jovi—a high-energy party with a lot of friendliness and a *great* desire to please."

It is difficult to imagine. But the big brown morass that churns and eddies its way out of Lake Itasca, 446 miles up in the cloud country of northern Minnesota, is the beginning of the lazy Mississippi. By the time it sweeps past the port of Minneapolis, bending this way and that, shifting and twisting, slack and taut, forty-one dams have done their damnedest to moderate its onrush. And by the time it disgorges itself beneath the lusty delta country made notorious by Robert Johnson, the sense of relief it exudes is intoxicating.

Up around Duluth, the Mississippi is plenty bottled up. The parameters of its flowing passion are so narrow that you can't navigate it with anything bigger than a rowboat; looking down its curvaceous length, however, to where the headwaters surge into the Gulf of Mexico, it's wide enough to handle an aircraft carrier. It's not a pretty river by most standards, but there are those who find its changeability alluring, its protracted thrust a stimulating metaphor. Some iniquitous blues shouters of bygone days compared the wriggling Mississippi to a bedded woman in heat; others likened it to an amorous libertine at the peak of his powers. For a malefactor with an imagination, the snug font in the Northwest was high promise of the deep South finale.

Prince

1990

The year was 1973, the season was spring, and the swollen Mississippi had exploded its banks for the first time in half a century, inundating whole communities. All along the river, everything, to borrow a phrase from Prince's erotic first single, was soft and wet. Fourteen-year-old novice guitarist/keyboardist Prince Rogers Nelson, son of black bandleader John Nelson and second wife Mattie Shaw, left his home for good.

Prince was born on June 7, 1958, and grew up in a house on 5th Avenue South in Minneapolis. His father had bade his mother adieu when Prince was about ten. Mattie remarried, and Prince's stepfather, Hayward Baker, made it plain he didn't care for the boy's wanton ways—or the piano that he pounded with impunity. So Prince tried living with his Aunt Olivia for a while and then his father. John Nelson, in his moonlighting heyday, had led a snazzy jazz trio; but he had largely put his music career behind him, holding down a steady post at Honeywell Computers, and only occasionally adding keyboard accompaniment to downtown strip shows. His stage name, Prince Rogers, he'd bequeathed to his son.

John Nelson booted the boy out of his bachelor pad one morning upon discovering Prince had slipped a girl into the house as an overnight guest. Prince was ultimately befriended and sheltered by Bernadette Anderson, mother of his buddy Andre. By his sixteenth year, Prince had acquired a reputation as something of a freakish free spirit, remaining a good student at Central High School (albeit most attentive in music instructor Jimmy Hamilton's extracurricular "The Business of Music" course), while leading a band called Grand Central. The band included Andre Anderson on bass guitar, Andre's sister Linda on keyboards, and Morris Day on drums. In the summer of 1976, Grand Central was expanded and renamed Champagne; they began adding unusually lewd songs written by the olive-skinned front man with the feminine, "fuck-me" eyes. Practice sessions were held in Andre's basement, as were postpubescent orgies that—thanks to commemorative songs like "Soft and Wet"—are notorious to this day. Prince next tried living in New York for several months with his half sister Sharon, then returned to Minneapolis to form a touring band with Andre Cymone (as Anderson now prefers to be known) on bass.

Eventually, through the combined efforts of Minneapolis advertising agent Owen Husney, partner Gary Levinson, and Warner Bros. vice president of promotion Russ Thyret, Prince was signed to the label, and his first album, *For You,* appeared in April 1978.

Pitched as being barely eighteen (he was actually two months shy of twenty), Prince played all the instruments on the LP. Sales were spotty. When *Prince,* the second album, was issued in October 1979, the steamy "I Wanna Be Your Lover" secured a No. 1 berth in the black singles market, and "Why You Wanna Treat Me So Bad?" also did well. All of the singles had the funk-synth textures then popular in urban dance clubs, and the themes were suggestive, agitated, ribald, foretelling the perfect ending to a perfect evening on the town.

No one was quite prepared for the third album, *Dirty Mind,* a concept work about sexual discovery that many interpreted to be at least partly autobiographical. The songs were sung with the tremulous breathlessness of a newly aroused adolescent; and the story lines, though blatant in their delivery, somehow maintained an innocence that augmented their erotic appeal.

Live, Prince was far more than even his most rabid devotees had bargained for, initially performing naked but for a loose-fitting mackintosh, later opting for a studded purple greatcoat, black Lycra jockey shorts, legwarmers, and knee-length black boots. The explicit shows Prince unveiled were a wild ride in a category all their own. Sliding down a gleaming firepole, shedding clothing along the way, pouncing on a brass bed, and panting as he arched his bare back, he compared the seductive proceedings to the landing of a jumbo jet. "We are now making our final approach to satisfaction," he sighed in short-winded gulps. "Please bring your lips, your arms, your hips into the up and locked position—for landing!"

Prince kept the temperature rising with *Controversy.* Three of his four albums were gold, with sales of 500,000, when he released the two-record *1999* in 1982. This record yielded his first mainstream Top 10 success, "Little Red Corvette." This foggy-windows rock raver pared the Robert Johnson personification of woman as hot car down to a sleek, hair-curling homily to internal combustion. While in "Terraplane Blues" Johnson had leaned over the hood and assured his shapely conveyance that "I'm gonna get deep down in this connection / Keep on tangling with your wires," Prince was a driven man. His guarantee: "I'm gonna try to tame your / Little red love machine."

Prince no sooner gained fame than he shunned publicity, becoming a total recluse when not performing, shutting himself away in his lakeside mansion in northern Minnesota. But he could be reached, and he was pretty forthcoming on "not-so-private" topics, saying that as a twelve-year-old he used to sneak into his mother's bedroom to borrow her vibrator, and that when he's traveling he's afraid of using hotel bathtubs because "a maid could walk in."

In the summer of 1984, Prince starred in *Purple Rain,* a semi-autobiographical film released with a companion LP of coital doxology. The No. 1 album also contained Prince's first No. 1 singles, "When Doves Cry" and "Let's Go Crazy," plus another that fell one step short of the top spot, "Purple Rain." Production-wise, the record's most pioneering offering was the bewitchingly bare "When Doves Cry," whose bass track had been deleted by Prince just prior to completion of the LP. As a personal expression, "The Beautiful Ones" was especially beguiling, its thumping tone of petition stemming from Prince's love affair with Susannah Melvoin, sister of guitarist Wendy in his band, the Revolution. Many of *Purple Rain*'s songs were live cuts taken from an August 1983 concert at the First Avenue and 7th Street Entry, the famed Minneapolis rock club. (When these performances were re-created at the same venue for the film, portions of the numbers were lip-synched.)

The movie itself was a brace of broadly acted vignettes about sexual exploration and youthful star-gazing. Each was plugged into a patchy script about a broken home and a striving saloon band. What made the jump-edited pastiche shine were the MTV-friendly stage segments, ready-made videos whose cursive camera work and cutting rhythms revealed the most gifted live attraction in the history of rock. As an accompanying tour would confirm, Prince was a better bandleader than Sly Stone, a frenzied guitarist in the spirit of Hendrix, double the dancer that Michael Jackson aimed to be, a singer whose manic ingenuity jackknifed over James Brown and Billy Stewart, and a composer-arranger-producer who surpassed the herd of talented emulators pouring from his own stable (Morris Day, Terry Lewis and Jimmy Jam, Jesse Johnson, Alexander O'Neal, and so on).

Around the World in a Day arrived in spring 1985, Doug Henders's oblique cover painting depicting Prince, the band, and assorted partied-out personages gathered around what appeared to be a baptismal pool. A multicolored hillside in the background became, upon closer inspection, the torso of a reclining female. In the foreground, a golden ladder loomed in the pool, the many-runged symbol bisecting the landscape/nude at the navel as it pierced the clouds. The record was delivered to Warner Bros.' Burbank offices for a listening party in a company conference room bedecked with purple, lavender, and white helium balloons, the carpeted floor strewn with flowers. When the limo carrying Prince and his retainers arrived at the celebration, out stepped Wendy Melvoin dressed in gold pajamas and black wrap, followed by John Nelson in gray pjs and paisley robe, along with his son, who wore white silk sleepwear and matching high-heeled boots. As for the funky but dour music, it mixed Prince's current Joni Mitchell infatuation (circa *For the Roses* and *Court and Spark*) with *Sgt. Pepper's Lonely Hearts Club Band* psychedelicism and sprinklings of East Indian and Romany gypsy strains. "Raspberry Beret" and "Pop Life" were the prurient hits, but "The Ladder" provided the album's unifying theme. Cowritten by John Nelson and Prince, it described humankind's blind search for salvation in the land of "Sinaplenty." Redemption was cast as deliverance from loneliness in all its forms, the love of God's creation serving to "undress" the faithful and impart a "caress" of self-worth.

Prince's next project was *Under the Cherry Moon,* a movie filmed in the South of France. Mary Lambert, director of Madonna's splashy "Material Girl" video, was hired to direct, but she was quickly replaced by her employer. The vague plan for *Cherry Moon* envisioned a musical comedy–melodrama with the dingy black-and-white realism of *film noir.* What emerged was a $12 million dollar home movie-away-from-home. Prince played a flirtatious bistro pianist named Christopher Tracy, but mostly he played with himself. Plot was shelved in place of a series of fey pinups, swishy chats with sidekick Jerome Benton, and narcissistic love scenes in which the female was obscured by shadow, Greek columns, or both. The most curious segments include Christopher's fumbling climactic nuzzle with chilly English snob Mary Sharon (Kristin Scott Thomas), in which he looks as if he's never kissed a woman in his life. Shortly afterward, Christopher is gunned down by Mary's disapproving dad, and Prince's languid on-camera expiration delivers all the emotional wallop of a prig picking lint off his pants.

Under the Cherry Moon was so awful it shocked. A wildfire word-of-mouth response doomed the picture to earn a mere $3.2 million in over two hundred theaters in its first week of release. Within another two weeks, it mercifully disappeared.

Cherry Moon was a wholly unnecessary disaster, and nothing made this plainer than the video for "Kiss," the lead-off single from *Parade—Music from the Motion Picture "Under the Cherry Moon."* A brilliantly choreographed tryst between Prince and a veiled mystery woman, the mini-teleplay was so flawless, the physical interplay so effortlessly erotic that a video for once enhanced an already unforgettable piece of music. Not since "When Doves Cry" had a groove record been so fundamental in its components, the listener seduced into the experience of *learning* the rhythm's mechanism as it unfurled.

"Kiss" was a three-and-a-half minute miracle, triumphant in its No. 1 success. And the rest of *Parade* had enough exceptional moments ("New Position," "Girls and Boys," "Mountains," and the lovely "Anotherloverholenyohead") that it would have been considered stellar had it stood alone.

Faced with the challenge of restoring his persona to its former luster, Prince rebounded in March 1987 with *Sign o' the Times,* a great double LP (conceived as *Dream Factory* and then temporarily recast as the three-record *Crystal Ball*) that came complemented by a grand concert movie. Rock film buffs made wary by *Cherry Moon* missed out on a hugely entertaining experience—as Midnight Show attendees in hundreds of college towns can now attest. Sexy, witty, disturbing, the film is a delectable slice of beat-crazy bedlam, Prince pulling out all the eclectic stops with his best stage band—plus drummer-singer Sheila E., dancer-singer Cathy "Cat" Glover, and guest star Sheena Easton (who duets on "U Got the Look"). Not since the heyday of George Clinton's Parliament-Funkadelic sci-fi stage galas had any concert program been so panoramically engaging.

But Prince's material was far less abstract than Clinton's, his message unapologetically acute. *Sign o' the Times*'s title track was scalding, its harsh throb announcing the slow boil of underclass rage. The song was a denunciation of the stupidity of inner-city drug violence, but it also depicted the selfish, racist society that had precipitated it, asserting that governments more comfortable spending money on corrupt defense contracts rather than black and poor people would reap what they sow. A favorite on black *and* pop radio, the bleak "Sign o' the Times" hit No. 3 nationally, followed by the more lighthearted "U Got the Look," which reached No. 2.

Another Top 10 hit, "I Could Never Take the Place of Your Man," was the 'heads' side of a gender-and-jealousy coin Prince toyed with on *Sign o' the Times* ("tails" being the heatedly hypothetical "If I Was Your Girlfriend," which was directed at his ex, Susannah Melvoin). The latter song featured the narrative presence of Camille, a female alter ego of Prince's whose vocals were often speeded up and synthesized to surreal feminine effect. Camille also was the antagonist highlighted on "Housequake," "U Got the Look," and "Strange Relationship."

Overall, *Sign o' the Times* examined modern city life from the standpoint of its hedonistic hoi polloi. "Hot Thing," "Slow Love," "Starfish and Coffee," and "It's Gonna Be a Beautiful Night" traversed an emotional cycle from evening arousal and consummation, to daytime boredom and twilight optimism. Hovering behind this debauchery was "The Cross," another piece of ladder-related salvation rock, Prince's plangent guitar approximating the purgative joys of the afterlife.

In due course, Prince was suffering his own stations of the rugged cross, sister Tyka Nelson giving petty, deprecating interviews to the press in preparation for the release of her own (terrible) album, *Royal Blue.* And Lorna Nelson, a half sister on his father's side, sued him, claiming he'd cribbed "U Got the Look" from an earlier song of hers (she lost the case). Most punishing of all, the considerable virtues of his long-awaited 1988 *Lovesexy* album would be largely obscured—either by photographer Jean Baptiste Mondino's nude photo portrait of the star on *Lovesexy*'s cover, or by curiosity with the withdrawn record *Lovesexy* replaced, *The Black Album.*

The *Lovesexy* artwork—Prince wearing nothing but a crucifix—caused some record stores to ban the record, although the visual was as chaste as a Maxfield Parrish illustration (his previous albums had contained far more steamy inner-sleeve or poster visuals). As for content, Prince proclaimed in the record's opening moments that the strength to ignore drugs would separate the best of his contemporaries from the rest of the human wreckage: "Welcome to the new power generation. The reason my voice is so clear is there's no smack in my brain." The album's music was typically ahead of its time, "Alphabet Street" and "Dance On" stitching hip-hop polyrhythms and postrap percussion mixes into a more tailored and commercial form of house rock (neatly anticipating the last genre's mass acceptance at the start of 1990). "Eye No" and "Anna Stesia" urged fans to commit to a higher, libidinous power, reinforcing an oddball piety that made some critics compare *Lovesexy* to Bob Dylan's *Slow Train Running.*

If Prince's own essay in the *Lovesexy Tour Book* can be believed, his move to substitute the *Lovesexy* record for the completed *Black Album* was a moral and religious one. Describing the good and evil sides of himself in terms of the Camille character and its odious opposite—dubbed Spooky Electric—he explained that the decision to banish *The Black Album* involved nothing less than the struggle for his own soul. Embroidering the text with seven of *The Black Album*'s eight titles ("Le Grind," "Cindy C," "Dead on It," "Bob George," "Superfunkycalifragisexy," "2 Nigs United for West Compton," "Rock Hard in a Funky Place"), Prince wrote that the LP was created out of egotism, joking contempt for his current surroundings, and hatred for the competition. As such, he feared he'd become what he'd begot: " 'Tis Nobody funkier—let the *Black Album* fly.' Spooky Electric was talking, Camille started to cry. Tricked. A fool he had been. In the lowest utmostest. He had allowed the dark side of him 2 create something evil . . . Spooky Electric must die. Die in the hearts of all who want love. Die in the hearts of men who wants change. Die in the bodies of women who want babies that will grow up with a New Power Soul. Love Life Lovesexy—the feeling u get when u fall in love, not with a girl or a boy but with the heavens above. Lovesexy—endorphin. Camille figured out what 2 feel . . . God is alive! . . . Let Him touch you and your own Lovesexy will be born."

Translated, this means that Prince the record-maker chose the light (Camille) over the darkness (Spooky Electric) and thus pulled the plug on *The Black Album*—except for one track, "When 2 R in Love," which appeared on *Lovesexy.* The reference to "endorphin" is more recondite. Endorphins are groups of proteins produced by the pituitary gland, affecting mood and perception of pain, as well as learning and memory. While occurring naturally in the body, it was discovered in the 1970s that endorphins are chemically similar to opium-derived narcotics. (Acupuncture is thought to reduce pain by triggering the production of endorphins.) So Prince seemed to be saying that God created humans with the innate biochemical ability to enrapture—or envenom—themselves. This theory is akin to Arthur Koestler's thesis in his 1967 book, *The Ghost in the Machine.*

In real terms, Prince's dread of his own dark impulses meant the destruction in November 1987 of 500,000 copies of *The Black Album,* which had been manufactured at Warner's pressing plant in Aachen, West Germany, for initial European distribution. Assigned the catalog number of WX147, the album had been designated for official release ten days before Christmas, its packaging consisting of a jet black jacket *sans* identifying notations or corporate markings of any sort. But some forty copies of the canceled pressing survived the glue factory, along with a dozen prerelease cassettes that had been posted to London music critics. Bootlegs quickly sprang up in collectors' shops on both sides of the Atlantic, and *The Black Album* was widely reviewed in tandem with, or instead of, *Lovesexy.* Purchase of the contraband record, of course, constituted stealing from its creator.

Any unhurried listen to *The Black Album* showed that both its barkers and buyers were deceived by hyperbole. Compared to the dance highlights of *Sign o' the Times,* "Le Grind" was a dinky jam. "Cindy C" was a sketchy rocker reminiscent of Sly Stone's "Family Affair." "Superfunkycalifragisexy" proved a pleasant but protracted riff, tainted by lyric jests alluding to sadomasochism, sexual blackmaïl, and drinking blood. "Bob George" was a dimly reasoned monologue by a world-class ghetto misogynist who goads his woman at gunpoint. While these last two tracks might sound potentially titillating, they were really intriguing only when viewed as lampoons of the hateful cants of Oran "Juice" Jones, Ice T., or Public Enemy. And still they bored.

Not only was Prince wise to bury this debris, but a thorough examination of the bulk of his most notorious outtakes, remnants, and detritus reveals him to be a rather discerning editor of his own music. Take *The Chocolate Album,* an unreleased record of musically sequenced jam sessions reportedly done in Europe in 1987. At its swinging peak (in a portion that encompasses "Pretty Face," "Girl of My Dreams," "I Can't Stop," "We Can Fall," and "All Day, All Night") the music dips into influences as diverse as Fred Wesley and the Horny Horns, Cab Calloway, and Louis Jordan's jauntiest jump blues. Stylistically, *The Chocolate Album* could have worked as a third LP in the *Sign o' the Times* set, but no track here is half as good as the selections the public finally got. As for the withheld *Camille* album, which was supposed to have been a rough draft for *Sign o' the Times,* none of its highly trumpeted tracks ("Souly-A-Colia," "Export Lover," and "Let Me Feel You Up") can honestly be called memorable. In sum, Prince's much-touted bootleg catalog is a bust.

Those lusting after a revelatory unreleased Prince opus are advised to lobby for a compilation of his bonus B-sides from a decade's worth of singles: "How Come U Don't Call Me Anymore?" and "Gotta Stop (Messin' About)" (1982); "Irresistible Bitch" (1983); "17 Days," "Erotic City," "God," "Another Lonely Christmas" (all

1984); "She's Always in My Hair," "Hello," "Girl" (all 1985); "Love or Money," "Alexa de Paris (both 1986); "La La La He He Hee" and "Shockadelica" (1987); "Scarlet Pussy" and "Escape (Free Yo Mind from This Rat Race)" (both 1988); and "200 Balloons" (1989).

As a collaborator, producer, talent scout, and A&R man, Prince has nurtured, antagonized, and otherwise unleashed a surfeit of other artists and their albums. The majority are undistinguished, but a few are marvelous. The production team of Terry Lewis and Jimmy Jam deserve high praise for the construction of Janet Jackson's *Control* (1987) and *Rhythm Nation 1814* (1989) LPs, as does producer Andre Cymone for the Jody Watley solo albums. Other standout records from Prince's support crew include the Time's *What Time Is It?* (1982) and *Ice Cream Castle* (1984); Sheila E's *The Glamorous Life* (1984) and *Romance 1600* (1985); Madhouse's first and second LPS, *8* (1987) and *16* (1988); *Jill Jones* (1987), a slinky and jocose dance gem that contains the best version of "All Day, All Night"; and most especially the second album by Wendy and Lisa, *Fruit at the Bottom* (1989), every bit as fine in its fashion as Madonna's *Like a Prayer. The Cinderella Theory* (1989), George Clinton's debut on Prince's Paisley Park label, was also valuable but displayed little involvement with Prince beyond the loan of his horn section.

As for Prince himself, he rescued himself from creative depression and creeping cult status in 1989 with *Batman,* his nine-song soundtrack for the Jack Nicholson–Michael Keaton–Kim Basinger film phenomenon. Prince notched hits with "Batdance" (which deftly utilized sampled dialogue from the movie), "Partyman," "The Arms of Orion," and "Scandalous" (the last cowritten with John Nelson). But the wildest *Batman* by-product was the five-track, thirty-minute *Scandalous Sex Suite.* This CD maxi-single featured Kim Basinger, a reported paramour of Prince's, in an audibly explicit three-part ("The Crime," "The Passion," "The Rapture") simulation of a night of sexual congress. Also in the *Suite* were "When 2 R in Love" from *Lovesexy* and "Sex (The 80's Are Over and the Time Has Come 4 Monogamy and Trust)," another hair-curling homily on the spiritual gist of conjugation.

His next project, a musical film called *Graffiti Bridge,* promises pulsing intimacy on a supernatural plane. Yet much of the sex whispered and shrieked about in Prince's music is framed by frustration, insecurity, and disappointment. Nobody seeking nookie in his world ever gets enough, least of all the ringmaster, and when he comes close to fulfillment, a rash of chafing circumstances often intervene. "Peach" people suddenly prefer black partners, or vice versa, and would-be lovers of all persuasions scrimmage against more ravishing rivals. If childbearing is mentioned, the kids are frequently unwanted, inconvenient, or turn out to be boys when the procreators wanted girls.

Why the obsession with sex as damnable stumbling block? What kindled Prince's Dionysian overdrive in the first place?

Both his parents, John Nelson and Mattie Shaw, are devout Seventh Day Adventists. Likewise, Fred Anderson, husband of Bernadette Anderson, Prince's guardian after he left home. Anywhere authority resided during Prince's adolescence, Adventism held sway.

The modern Seventh Day Adventist denomination was born after an earlier sect's predictions of the Second Coming of Christ failed to materialize in 1844. Organized in Battle Creek, Michigan, in 1863, the Seventh Day Adventists drew much of their spiritual leadership from Ellen G. H. White, a young Maine woman whose visions and interpretations of Biblical prophesies dictated that the Second Coming and the Last Judgment were still impending, but the day and hour were unpredictable. Seventh Day Adventists view Saturday as the Sabbath, believe that man is mortal rather than immortal, and see death as a mystical sleep. During the Last Judgment, the righteous among the resurrected dead will be invited into heaven to spend the millennium in a sphere of exhaltation. The wicked will be destroyed by fire. Ultimately God will restore the burned and battered earth to its paradise state as the Garden of Eden.

Seventh Day Adventists view Christ alone as God, and take a fundamentalist, creationist approach to human history as recounted in Scripture. They are staunch advocates of good health through exercise and diet (two prominent Seventh Day Adventists, brothers J. H. and W. K. Kellogg, developed the international flaked cereal industry). And the medical profession is revered, the church's own Loma Linda University Medical Center helping to advance modern cancer treatment as well as organ transplant techniques.

Adventists shun pork, ham, shrimp, and other foods forbidden in the Old Testament, encourage vegetarianism, and strictly abstain from alcohol, tobacco, and all drugs and stimulants (including tea and coffee), unless prescribed by a physician. The church opposes participation in nonreligious worldly entertainment, whether movies, TV, theater, music, or dancing. Gambling and involvement in secret societies are also off-limits. Modesty of thought, word, and deed is emphasized, with the faithful being urged to avoid all cosmetics, "showiness" in clothing, and the wearing of jewelry.

The core creed of the Seventh Day Adventists is to spread the fearsome message of "the three angels" foretold in Revelation 14:6–12, wherein the first angel proclaimed the Day of Judgment, the second angel called for humanity to renounce decadence ("Fallen, fallen is Babylon the great, she who has made all nations drink the fierce wine of her fornication!"), and the third angel shouted that "if any man worship the beast and his image, and receive his mark in his forehead or in his hand, the same shall drink of the wine of the wrath of God . . . and shall be tormented with fire and brimstone."

Prince's music is rife with Adventist symbolism and dicta, the singer continually wrestling with his own belief that the flesh of mortal man cannot be sinful—even in the fever of fornication—if the act is intended to glorify God. Images of deathly sleep and spiritual delirium thread throughout his albums, along with the perpetual pursuit of sex and a morning-after awakening to Judgment Day. The title track to Prince's *1999* LP is a prime example of this rakish potpourri, as is the lewdly apocalyptic "Let's Go Crazy" from *Purple Rain.* But there isn't a moment in any of his songs when the war between his higher and lower impulses is completely resolved—including "God," in which he engages his Maker in an almost Job-like dialogue.

From the *Parade* album onward, Prince's more morbid unsaintly scenarios have multiplied, leading to a song on *Lovesexy* ("Postivity") in which personal damnation is described in terms of a .57 Magnum. The demonic Spooky Electric tempts the perspiring singer into pulling the trigger on himself, but Prince resists as he chants aloud, "Don't kiss the beast." The song is a grim test of wills, Prince insisting that we each have a "hang-up" or an inner "whirlwind" we must defeat in order to evade the demise of the soul.

Batman, however, was nothing less than the final faceoff, a literal dance marathon with the Devil. In "Electric Chair," Prince's dark side (The Joker) wondered if he could be damned for what goes on in his mind, while his better self (Batman) mused in "The Future" about the spiritual rewards the afterlife promised for the scrupulous.

The only truly happy track on *Batman* was "The Arms of Orion," which described the blissful death-as-sleep that all Adventists long for. Its theme revolved around the Greek myth of the sensual hunter Orion, a murder victim in a love triangle, whom the gods ennobled by placing him among the stars. The song's assumption was that a life informed by pure passion will find its reward, and yet the singer hedged, suspecting that any path remained an iffy gamble against eternity.

Obviously, little has changed at either end of the murky Mississippi since Robert Johnson went down to the crossroads at the midnight hour, shook hands with the Old Deceiver, agreed to an early grave, and was duly empowered to rock the blues in a ring of hellfire. It may not be everybody's idea of a square deal, but for those who feel the mighty tug of its torrid fringe benefits, there really is no choice. Voltaire said it best: "You must have the Devil in you to succeed in any of the arts."

Acknowledgments/ Bibliography

I would like to thank my various (music) editors over the years: Mary Campbell at the Associated Press; Peter Knobler, Greg Mitchell, Robert Smith, John Swenson, Mitchell Glazer, and Jon Pareles at *Crawdaddy*; Jann Wenner, Harriet Fier, Barbara Downey, Peter Herbst, Susan Murcko, Paul Nelson, Jim Henke, Terry McDonell, and Alan Weitz at *Rolling Stone*; Vic Garbarini, Jock Baird, Bill Flanagan, and Scott Isler at *Musician*; Kate Nolan at *Playboy*; Peter Bloch and Patrice Baldwin at *Penthouse*; Bob Guccione, Jr., Rudy Langlais, James Truman, Joe Levy, and Bob Keating at *Spin*; Roger Steffens and C. C. Smith at *The Reggae and African Beat*; Norm Pattiz, Thom Ferro, and Andy Denemark, my coproducer, at Westwood One Radio Networks; Bob LaBrasca at *L.A. Style*, and Ken Emerson and marvelous Margarett Loke at *The New York Times Magazine.*

Very special gratitude to my wife, Judy, for her unequaled love, advice, and encouragement. I'm also deeply thankful to Charles M. Young, my esteemed colleague, editorial critic, and incomparable cohort; to my dear pal and attorney Bruce C. Fishelman, Esq., and to Bob Merlis, whose twenty years of friendship, musical acumen, and support have been a delight.

At Henry Holt, my sincere appreciation to John Macrae III and Amy Hertz for their enthusiasm and expertise. And thanks to Nancy Finn for additional editorial assistance. Also, my fond gratitude to my agent, Jim Stein, for his tireless help and counsel.

Regarding photo source material utilized herein, the author would like to thank Wide World Photos, the Movie Star News archives, the publicity departments of Warner Bros. Records, Reprise Records, Capitol Records, RCA Records, Atlantic Records, Columbia Records, Big Records, Private Stock Records, Westwood One Radio Networks, Island Records, Deborah Feingold, Michael Smith (Professor Longhair), and the Stephen C. LaVere Collection.

General appreciation to Chris Blackwell, Peter Asher, Tommy Mottola, Lenny Waronker, Steven Baker, Jerry Wexler, John Sykes, Harry Sandler, Paul Wasserman, Jane Rose, Liz Beth Rosenberg, Donna Russo, Kathy Schenker, Susan Blond, Howard Kaufman, Eliot Hubbard, Jody Miller, Cheryl Ceretti, Ellen Darst, Ellen Zoe Golden, Chris Schuba, Howard Bloom, Andy Slater, Tony Dimitriades, David Leaf, and Maureen O'Connor.

Grateful acknowledgment is made for use of portions of the following song lyrics:

Most other lyrics printed herein are derived from direct quotation by their composers during interviews.

The original versions of essays in this book on Robert Johnson, Bob Wills, Chuck Berry, Ray Charles, Little Richard, Elvis Presley, Buddy Holly, Jerry Lee Lewis, Sam Cooke, Bill Haley, John Lennon, Mick Jagger, Aretha Frankin, Bob Dylan, Stevie Wonder, Jim Morrison, Jimi Hendrix, Sly Stone, Jimmy Page, Diana Ross, Bruce Springsteen, and Prince were written either during 1983 or 1984 and previously appeared in slightly or substantially different form in the book *Rock Stars,* published in 1984 by Stewart, Tabori & Chang (New York) and in 1985 by Crown/Outlet Books (New York). Most of them now reflect much additional research and interviewing done during 1989 and 1990, and are dated with regard to the time frame of this reporting.

As for the other articles collected herein, information regarding previous publication (in order of their appearance in the text) is as follows:

"The Professor Longhair Story: Lessons of a Rock and Roll Legend." *Rolling Stone,* March 20, 1980.

"James! The Power of Positive Badness." *Musician,* April 1986.

"Fear Strikes Home: The Silent Nights of Frankie Valli." *Crawdaddy*, February 1977.

"Back from the Bottom: Beach Boy Brian Wilson." *The New York Times Magazine*, June 26, 1988.

"Paul McCartney: Farewell to the First Solo Era." *Musician*, February 1988.

"George Harrison Reconsidered: After All Those Years of Mania and Moptops, Dark Suits and Deep Blues, Here Comes the Fun." *Musician*, November 1987.

"Keith Richards—'My Rock and Roll Life.' " "Timothy White's Rock Stars," Westwood One Radio Networks, week of January 23, 1989.

"Pete Townshend: The Iron Age," "Timothy White's Rock Stars," Westwood One Radio Networks, week of September 18, 1989.

"Steve Winwood, Rock's Gentle Aristocrat." *Musician*, October 1982; "Coming to America." *Musician*, November 1988.

"Dead on Arrival! The Grateful Dead." "Timothy White's Rock Stars," Westwood One Radio Networks, week of November 20, 1989.

"Eric Patrick Clapton." "Timothy White's Rock Stars," Westwood One Radio Networks, week of December 18, 1989; "Eric Clapton: Rollin' and Tumblin'," *Spin*, March 1990.

"Lightnin' Rod: Rod Stewart's Finest Rock." "Timothy White's Rock Stars," Westwood One Radio Networks, week of August 8, 1988.

Joni Mitchell—unpublished interview. March 17, 1988.

"Roots, Rastas and Reggae: Bob Marley's Jamaica." *Crawdaddy*, January 1976; entire transcript of original September 1975 Marley interview published as "(Part One) In This Oh Sweet Life." *The Reggae & African Beat*, June 1984; "(Part Two) Are You Picking Up Now?" *The Reggae & African Beat*, June 1985.

"Public Pitches & Stolen Moments with Pinin' Simon." *Crawdaddy*, February 1978.

"The David Bowie Interview: A Fifteen-Year Odyssey of Image and Imagination." *Musician*, May 1983.

"James Taylor Grins and Bears It." *Rolling Stone*, June 11, 1981.

"Bob Seger, Nobody's Fool." *Musician*, April 1983; "Bob Seger Forgives, but Doesn't Forget." *Musician*, June 1986.

"After Innocence: Ex-Eagle Don Henley and Comrade Danny

Kortchmar Aim for the Heart of the Matter." *L.A. Style,* February 1990.

"Bang the Heads Slowly: Ramones' Mook Rock." *Rolling Stone,* February 8, 1979.

"Michael Jackson: The Man in the Mirror." *Penthouse,* January 1988.

"Earthy Angels: How the Bee Gees Talk Dirty and Influence People." *Rolling Stone,* May 17, 1979.

"Pink Floyd: Roger Waters Exposes the Secrets of Rock and Roll's Most Self-Destructive Supergroup." *Penthouse,* September 1988.

"Fathers & Lovers: Carly Simon Learns to Say Goodbye." *Rolling Stone,* December 10, 1981.

"In Every Dream Home a Heartache: The Importance of Being Bryan Ferry." *Musician,* October 1985.

"Billy Joel—a Native Son Revealed." *Musician,* December 1982.

"Daryl Hall's Magic." *Penthouse,* March 1987.

"John Cougar Mellencamp: Rebel with a Cause." *The New York Times Magazine,* September 27, 1987.

"Last Tangos, New Beginnings: The Fleetwood Mac Nobody Knows." *Musician,* February 1989.

"Elvis Costello: A Man Out of Time Beats the Clock." *Musician,* October 1983.

"ZZ Top: How Three Bad Boys Became the Kingpins of Cactus Crunch." *Musician,* January 1986; "ZZ Top's Electric Mudd: An Historic Tribute to Muddy Waters, the Father of the Electric Blues." "Timothy White's Rock Stars," Westwood One Radio Networks, week of May 30, 1988.

"Rickie Lee Jones: A Walk on the Jazz Side of Life." *Rolling Stone,* August 9, 1979.

"Sting II." *Spin,* July 1985.

"Gabriel: After Flirting with Madness, Peter Gabriel Took Off All the Masks, and Found the Hardest Role to Play Was Himself." *Spin,* September 1986.

"U2: The Joshua Tree Tour." "Timothy White's Rock Stars," LBS Communications, week of May 18, 1987.

"Beastie Boys: Boys Just Wanna Have Fun." *Penthouse,* September 1987.

"The Dirty Little Secret That's Bon Jovi." *Playboy,* September 1987.

Index